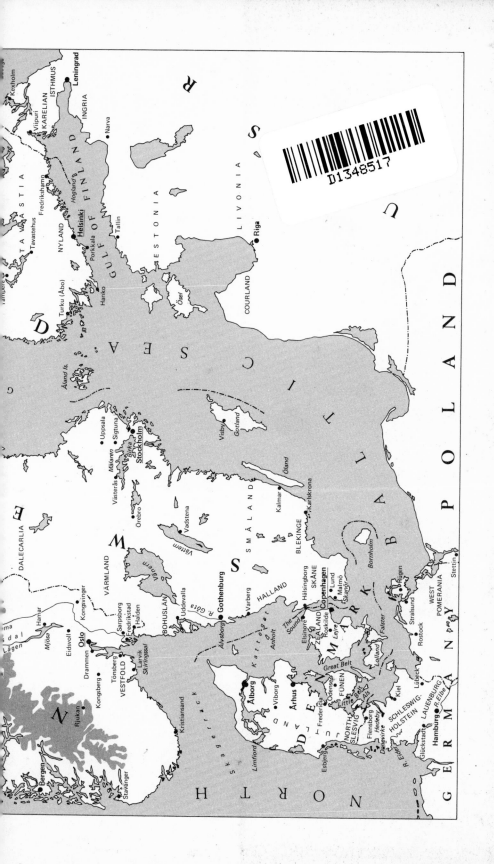

A HISTORY OF SCANDINAVIA

Denholm Christie
19, Silver Street,
Kincardine-on-Forth

1978.

A History of Scandinavia

Norway, Sweden, Denmark, Finland and Iceland

by
T. K. DERRY

London
GEORGE ALLEN & UNWIN
Boston   Sydney

First published in 1979

GEORGE ALLEN & UNWIN LTD
40 Museum Street, London WC1A 1LU

© T. K. Derry, 1979

British Library Cataloguing in Publication Data

Derry, Thomas Kingston
 A history of Scandinavia.
 1. Scandinavia – History
 I. Title
 948   DL46

 ISBN 0-04-948004-9

Published in the United States of America by the
University of Minnesota Press, 2037 University Avenue
Southeast, Minneapolis, Minnesota 55455.
Printed in Great Britain

Typeset in 11 on 12 point Imprint by Bedford Typesetters Ltd
and printed in Great Britain
by Unwin Brothers Limited, Old Woking, Surrey

Contents

Preface

This book traces the history of the Scandinavian countries from the earliest times to the present day, emphasising the common features in their inheritance from the past and in their contribution to the modern world. Scandinavian historians in general confine their attention to their own particular nation, and most writers from outside have likewise found in any one country a sufficiently complex subject of study. So it is: yet in these days of closer international relationships it seems worth while also to examine the development of these five small peoples in terms of the unity which underlies their surface divisions. They made their first impact on the outside world together as Vikings; in the later middle ages they joined to form the second-most extensive state in the Europe of that era; and, although the Union of Kalmar collapsed, the idea of re-creating unity was revived on various occasions as late as the 1860s. In our own time, indeed, each of these nations is known for the resolute assertion of its full political independence; but their social cohesion is strikingly attested by the institution and growth of the Nordic Council, which this year celebrates its silver jubilee.

The narrative is intended for readers who have little prior knowledge of Scandinavia and none of its languages. The Bibliography, which is in principle confined to works in English, therefore offers a fairly full list for further reading on Scandinavian subjects, accompanied by a short, purely introductory list for each of the component states. The Reference Notes, on the other hand, which are designed primarily for the use of students, cite special authorities, including the Scandinavian-language histories on which the present book is based. It is hoped that the Parallel Table of Events will make clear the common pattern of development. The endpaper map shows all significant placenames occurring in the text. Spelling has been simplified by substituting 'ö' for the less familiar Danish and Norwegian letter 'ø', and the reader may also like to know that 'å' is the equivalent of 'aa' (and is pronounced like 'au' in 'cause').

The author has been greatly encouraged by the generosity of the Nordic Cultural Council (*Nordisk Kulturfond*), which financed a tour of inquiry from Norway through Sweden and Denmark into Finland and in addition subsidised the preparation of the final manuscript for publication; it was expertly typed throughout by Mrs Maureen Canty. The author also owes a special debt to Professor S. H. Jungar, who acted as an invaluable guide for his visit to Turku. He was able, however, to assemble his materials in Oslo, thanks to the unfailing help and guidance of the staffs of the University Library and the respective libraries of the Nobel Institute, the Royal Norwegian Foreign Ministry, and the Storting. Lastly, his grateful thanks are due to the four Norwegian scholars who spared time to criticise successive portions of his draft, namely Dr Per Sveaas Andersen, Professor Gudmund Sandvik, Professor Per Fuglum, and Dr N. M. Udgaard. Remaining errors are of course the sole responsibility of the author.

Oslo, March 1977   T. K. DERRY

A HISTORY OF SCANDINAVIA

Chapter 1

The Unknown North

A DISTINCTIVE REGION OF EUROPE

Although Scandinavia today comprises five independent sovereign states, these peoples of the North (*Norden*) are still united by inherited ties of culture, political experience and social sympathy. Moreover, their way of life is conditioned by the distinctive region which they inhabit at the north-western extremity of the great Eurasian land-mass – seabound, northerly, and on the whole infertile – so that, with the important exception of the Danes, they have always been widely scattered. At the present time a population of 22 millions is spread over ten times the area of England, which has twice as many inhabitants, or three times that of California, which has about the same number of inhabitants. A brief general description may serve to emphasise a factor which underlies the entire historical development.

Both Finland and north Norway have a frontier towards Russia, whilst the Jutland peninsula provides a much shorter and more convenient land-bridge to continental Europe through the long-disputed territories of Slesvig-Holstein. With these exceptions, the region is wholly contained by the Atlantic Ocean and four of its tributaries – the Barents, Norwegian, North, and Baltic Seas. Although the Barents Sea was sailed by Norwegians as early as the tenth century AD (see p. 23), it first became of major political importance during the Second World War; and it is only since then that Arctic Scandinavia has obtained special consideration under the new name of *Nordkalotten* ('The Cap of the North'). But each of the other seas has had a continuous importance, due to the fact that, pending the development of air routes, long-distance communications throughout the Scandinavian region were easier by water than by land.

The Baltic Sea has played a big part in human affairs since prehistoric times. At its eastern end the Gulf of Finland offered easy access to the Russian rivers and the ancient overland routes from the Far East; for more than a millennium the centrally situated island of Gotland was a nodal point for north European commerce; and the entrance through the Skagerrak, Kattegat, and Sound or Belts, each of them bordered by Scandinavian territory, encouraged both Danes and Swedes to aspire to 'the dominion of the Baltic'. As for the North Sea, this has caused Norway and, in a less marked degree, Denmark and western Sweden to have a westward orientation, with a lively traffic passing to and from the coasts of Britain and nearby parts of the continent. Finally, the area of the Atlantic Ocean which lies between Norway and Greenland, known in the present century as the Norwegian Sea, gave ready access to the Faeroes and Iceland, which have become permanent components of Scandinavia, and on the shores of Greenland its culture has even obtained a precarious lodgement in the New World.

Denmark lies in the same latitudes as central Scotland. The other major components of the Scandinavian region, however, stretch so far towards the Arctic that much of the territory which looms so large on the map of Europe is sparsely inhabited or even uninhabitable. Deeply penetrating frost, long-continued snow-cover and complete winter darkness are handicaps for which the much advertised midnight sun of the summer is little compensation. Agriculture is further restricted by the poor average quality of the soils. Modern Denmark is, indeed, a farming country *par excellence*; but elsewhere the percentage of arable land made available by present-day techniques ranges from 9 in Finland and 8 in Sweden to 2·8 in Norway and 1 in Iceland.[1] In Iceland and along the Norwegian west coast the small farmer has always eked out his living from the harvest of the sea; in Sweden and Finland from the forest, which still clothes one-half of the former country and nearly three-quarters of the latter.

Comparison with other high-latitude regions of the world shows, indeed, that Man could have gained little more than a toe-hold in most of Scandinavia if it had not been for the westerly and south-westerly winds blowing across the Atlantic and the relatively warm waters of the Gulf Stream flowing beneath them. Man has nevertheless had to face heavy handicaps in his age-long struggle to impose civilisation on this region. Even today the typical Scandinavian is inured to the hardships of a bleak climate, serious obstacles to communication, and resources which are still in some respects severely restricted: how much harsher was his environment in the prehistoric times to be considered later in this chapter – and indeed at all times before the present era of unprecedentedly rapid technological advances.

Sweden, which is the largest of the Scandinavian countries, is spoken of by its present-day inhabitants as 'our long-drawn-out land'.[2] More than half of its total length of almost 1,000 miles is taken up by the ancient province of 'Norrland', which before the timber and mining developments of the nineteenth and twentieth centuries had very few resources to attract a settled population, whilst even today no less than 12 per cent of the whole country is classified as bare mountain or fell. The nucleus of the kingdom was 'Svealand', a region based on Lake Mälaren and its outlet to the Baltic in the vicinity of modern Stockholm. But until modern times this was separated by a belt of almost impenetrable forest from a second nucleus in Västergötland and Östergötland, lying on either side of Lake Vättern in the same latitude as the valuable island of Gotland. Both these nuclear areas contained good farmland to sustain a growing population, but they were separated by the stony highland of Småland from the great granary of Skåne at the tip of the Scandinavian peninsula, which from prehistoric times until the seventeenth century had its natural link with the adjacent Danish islands. Thus the Swedish kingdom's only outlet to the west was originally at the mouth of the river Göta, where Gothenburg now stands; so it has always depended primarily upon maritime communications along the Baltic Sea, where the inshore waters are liable to freeze for several months each year. Taken in conjunction with the fact that the land lies at an average height of about 1,000 feet, this goes far to explain the high cost of winter to the modern Swedish economy, estimated at 5 per cent of the entire national income.[3]

Finland's position being more remote from western climatic influences, it has even colder winters to contend with; but the average height of the land is only half that of Sweden – hence its even more extensive covering of pine, spruce and birch forest. The two countries are joined not only by the broad and desolate 'isthmus of Lapland' at the head of the long Bothnian Gulf but more effectively at its mouth, where the long chain of the Åland Islands has made movement easy between 'Svealand' and the fertile south-west corner of Finland. But the accessibility of the southern coastline from the far side of the Finnish Gulf and the length of the land frontier with Russia (already mentioned) give Finland as a whole the character of a border province between East and West. Conquest, however, is both difficult and unrewarding. One-tenth of the entire country is covered by lakes and, in the north, another considerable fraction by bogs and morasses, so that from the air the dry land is said to resemble an archipelago. To bring under the plough a higher proportion of this unpromising land-surface than is tilled in Sweden has cost the unremitting toil of many generations, who lived often in isolated homesteads and, until recently, commonly bore the marks of overwork and undernourishment.

Norway, separated from Sweden by the long mountain-ridge or 'keel' which forms the backbone of the Peninsula – the only effective natural land frontier within northern Europe – is still more 'long-drawn-out'. It has, indeed, the great advantage that the long west coast is not only warmed by the Gulf Stream but also traversed by the sheltered waterway of the Leads. But the Finnmark plateau facing the Barents Sea is a barren area of greater dimensions than any of the Swedish fell districts, and along most of the west coast the mountains descend to sea level so precipitously as to present a major obstacle even to the road and railway engineers of today.* Again, the mildness of the west-coast climate is

---

* The railway route between Oslo and Bergen, the principal west-coast city, was not completed until 1909 and involves a climb of more than 4,000 ft; in 1976 the road route was still interrupted by a ferry crossing.

more than counterbalanced by the scarcity of the big, easily worked corn-growing districts which have enabled the Swedes at most periods to feed themselves: since the thirteenth century the Norwegians have always depended partly upon imported corn. Moreover, with an average altitude exceeding 1,500 ft and the long fiords penetrating into the heart of the country, physical conditions in Norway have done even more than in Sweden to encourage local particularism. The isolated small farms and fishing hamlets of the west, perched precariously on the sides of narrow fiords or on the rocky coastal islands, still breed a different outlook from the relatively fertile valleys which debouch upon the Oslofiord, or from the second large farming area of the Tröndelag on both sides of Trondheim – to say nothing of the very thinly populated coastal strip of the county of Nordland, which leads past the Lofoten Islands towards the North Cape and the wastes of Finnmark.

Denmark, as already indicated, was less handicapped by Nature and was from very early times more fully inhabited than her Scandinavian neighbours. Furthermore, her location made her the way by which new impulses commonly reached them from the continent. Although western Jutland with its sandy soil and long lines of dunes is barren and devoid of natural harbours, the north-south land route along the peninsula is of great antiquity. As for the Danish islands, of which about 100 are inhabited, they share with east Jutland a generally fertile soil and ease of access; and from Zealand – which is larger than the other main islands (Fünen, the stepping-stone to Jutland; Lolland and Falster, projecting southwards towards Germany) – the farmlands of the Danes formerly stretched on, as already noted, across the narrow Sound into Skåne. In climate and much else Denmark bears a resemblance to East Anglia which must have made settlement in the Danelaw congenial to its conquerors.

Iceland bears the opposite character of a 'land of ice and fire',* where Man still finds himself to an unusual degree at the mercy of the elements. Nearly every type of volcano occurs on the island, which also contains the biggest glacier to be found anywhere outside the polar regions and Greenland; out of a total area less than three times that of Denmark, 10 per cent is covered by lava and 11·5 by glaciers. With its wind-swept coast, wet climate and torrential rivers, Iceland had little to attract settlers except patches of good grazing for their cattle, a little forest (which was soon destroyed), and its teeming fish and bird life. Although lying entirely south of the Arctic Circle, the island was left uninhabited until the dawn of the historic period; even then, it was seen to present an abnormally severe challenge, as the choice of name implies. Much the same may be said of the Faeroes or *Insulae Ovium*, so small and infertile that sheep-

---

* *The thousand years struggle against ice and fire* is the title chosen by the geographer Sigurdur Thorarinsson for an account published at Reykjavik in 1956. The conjunction of the two forces even produces such a phenomenon as the formation of huge cauldrons of sulphurous warm water under the glaciers, which from time to time break through the ice to destroy all vegetation and even the fish, as their contents pass out to sea.

grazing quickly became and long remained the principal resource of its inhabitants, scattered over seventeen islands. As for Greenland, the tiny settlements along its western coast lay on the very rim of the medieval world, which makes it understandable that the first Scandinavian enterprise there ended in failure, whilst the second did not gather much momentum until our own day.

IN THE AGES OF STONE AND BRONZE

In the case of Scandinavia the prehistoric period, known to us only through the often uncertain interpretation of sporadic archaeological finds, was of longer duration than in more genial lands to the south. Far into the first millennium of the Christian era, when events in other parts of Europe had been brought to some extent into focus by the labours of annalists and the first historians, the north remained a *terra incognita* to whose existence the civilised world was almost indifferent. We have no source at our disposal comparable to Caesar's factual account of his enemies in Gaul or Tacitus's romantic picture of the Germans, and as late as AD 731, the date of the completion of Bede's *Ecclesiastical History of the English Nation*, the zeal of Christian missionaries – who are often the earliest sources of reliable information – had barely touched the southern border of Denmark. This hidden past will here be treated very briefly, although it is a striking fact that, except for the Finns, the peoples of Scandinavia today inhabit territory which was in the possession of their direct ancestors long before the Greeks and Romans gave shape to the classical civilisation of the Mediterranean lands.

In Denmark the earliest evidence of man's handiwork is a find of deer bones which had been split to extract the marrow at a period antedating the last Ice Age – in other words, the delicacy had been conveyed to some human mouth not less than 50,000 years ago. But it is not until *c.* 10,000 BC, during the long, intermittent retreat of the ice, that we can trace the presence of flint-using reindeer hunters on what is now Danish soil; a little later on there were also seal hunters, who maintained themselves with their harpoons at the edge of the Arctic ice, as the Greenlanders have done in modern times. In both cases they entered Denmark from the south.

The first men may have come to northern Norway by a slow migration up the west coast, where a rather similar type of hunting is certainly in evidence by *c.* 8,000 BC; alternatively, they may have arrived after long roamings across the tundra from the east, though direct evidence for this has not yet been unearthed. The entry into Sweden and Finland was made later. Indeed, there was at first little or no Sweden to be entered, since the melting of the edges of the ice-cap, which had made a lodgement possible on the coast of Norway, did not take effect there until the eighth millennium. The level of the land thereupon rose gradually – a process which still continues at the rate of 1–2 ft per century – as the overlying ice relaxed its gigantic pressure, whilst the Baltic basin into which the water poured became for a time a huge freshwater lake. Settlement can be traced in Sweden from about 6,000 BC, but Finland still remained for a long time very sparsely inhabited; in neither case have we any positive indication as yet of the route by which the first men came.

Before the period of increasing warmth about the beginning of the fifth millennium, when the melting of the ice caused the present sea channels to replace the great rivers which once debouched from the Baltic lake, a migratory people had already left some traces on the land mass which was to become the Danish islands. Their implements were chiefly of bone; their only domesticated animal was the dog. Soon after the re-formation of the Baltic Sea, however, the so-called 'kitchen middens' provide plentiful evidence of habitation along the coasts, where a flint-using population enjoyed an animal dietary ranging from shellfish to game birds. Similar remains are to be found along the coast of Norway and at the receding edge of the water in south Sweden; in Norway especially, naturalistic carvings and drawings on smooth rock-faces also give us the first fleeting glimpses of modes of thought. So much care could hardly have been lavished upon lifelike representations of beasts, birds, and fishes unless they were believed to be in some mysterious way propitious for human efforts to compass their death: does not the elaborately equipped modern hunter still talk about sportsman's luck?

In northern Scandinavia this way of life continued without noticeable change throughout the third millennium BC, whilst farther south the first agriculturists made their entry upon the Scandinavian scene, with 'slash-and-burn' farming in patches of the forest, semi-nomadic stock-keeping, and eventually the building of more or less permanent settlements in wood or wattle and daub. Successive improvements in pottery and toolmaking mark the arrival of several waves of immigrants from the south – or, in the case of Finland, from the east. One such group must have brought to Denmark from overseas the cult of the megalith, impelling men to bury their dead at a prodigious labour cost. Both dolmens and passage-graves are found in greater concentration here than anywhere else in western Europe, and a single passage-grave may contain as many as a hundred skeletons. Before its abandonment about the year 2,000 BC, the institution spread to Swedish coastal districts, though it did not reach Norway. Then came the northward advance into Jutland of new peoples, who were content to bury their dead in single graves, with stones beneath and a shallow earth mound above the recumbent body.

This event, of which we do not know the inward significance, marks what seems to have been a major turning-point in the early history of the north. For these people carried with them the improved tool-cum-weapon known from its shape as the 'boat-axe', and were also the first horse-riders on Scandinavian soil, having brought that art of the steppes from some earlier home, perhaps in the neighbourhood of the Black Sea. If so, it is easy to picture them as a rather limited number of nomads, forming an aristocracy with which the existing population eventually intermingled – and from which it perhaps adopted an Indo-European language.

Be that as it may, a long period of climatic improvement, during which the glaciers retreated to the highest mountain tops, now encouraged the spread of settlement. Inland the forests began to fall to the axe; along the coast the amber of Jutland and the Baltic shoreline stimulated trade with regions as far away as the Iberian Peninsula. Nevertheless, except in their most southern latitudes these lands were too inaccessible and relatively too infertile to attract much further immigration, so the extensive land-winning of this Late Neolithic period was in all probability achieved by the peoples who are known to us as Scandinavians. Like all other European populations, they are essentially mongrels, but it is likely that they already displayed that noticeably large element of tall, dolichocephalic blonds which racial fanatics in the early twentieth century were to acclaim as the pure Nordic type.

Remarkable progress was made in the Bronze Age (*c.* 1,500–500 BC), when Denmark and southern Sweden excelled in working an alloy for which both the copper and the tin had to be imported from distant sources of supply in central Europe. Furs and slaves were sent south, as well as the much-prized amber; not only did raw materials come in return, but also finished products, such as the first bronze swords, which would provoke both wonder and imitation. The central importance of trade stimulated the growth of a ruling class made up of successful traders, whose members were laid pompously to rest with their new weapons under great mounds of earth or stone. Indeed, until cremation came into vogue in the Late Bronze Age, the tannin of their oak coffins in some cases preserved the actual clothes in which they were buried – the oldest woollen textiles still extant. The way of life at this period is also brought closer to us by the survival of a characteristic long, curved horn of bronze, the *lur*, often found in pairs and still capable of producing its trombone-like sounds. They perhaps played some part in sun-worship, as did almost certainly Denmark's most remarkable treasure from this era – a gilded disk, mounted on six wheels and drawn by a gilded horse, which is constructed on such a small scale that the whole model could easily have been carried through the fields, where it perhaps served to invoke the sun-god's blessing on the crops.

The prevalence of fertility rites of one sort or another is also suggested by the stylised rock-carvings with which Bronze Age men embellished suitable smooth surfaces all across southern Norway and Sweden and in the islands of the Baltic. The subjects of the carvings remind us that this rich northern culture, which derived its artistic motifs from as far away as Mycenean Greece – and not infrequently improved upon its borrowings – rested upon the basis of the farmer's toil. We are shown men ploughing with oxen, driving both two- and four-wheeled vehicles, riding horses, and bearing arms to defend their soil. Boats with high-raised prows, propelled by as many as fifty paddles and presented sometimes in whole fleets, emphasise the water passages in which Nature had made these lands so rich. But among the stylistically drawn human figures some are of giant size: were these the divinities they sought to propitiate, or priest-kings who mediated between Man and the unknown?

CONTACTS WITH CLASSICAL CIVILISATION

Bog-iron, precipitated in small lumps below the peat in marshy pools, is a readily accessible raw material in many parts of Scandinavia. Yet the last half-millennium before Christ, when iron making became known there, yields so few archaeological remains – Tröndelag, for instance, would appear to have made virtually no use of iron – as to suggest the hypothesis that the population declined. Certainly the climate, which had for about 2,000 years been drier than it is nowadays, became both wetter and colder, so that towards the north deciduous trees began to disappear and on the high ground the glaciers began to re-form. Clearly the semi-nomadic population of northern hunters found its means of livelihood painfully restricted, whilst throughout Scandinavia more effort was required to provide adequate clothing and shelter. People resorted to the use of trousers and underwear, and built themselves long-houses, in which the cattle wintering at one end constituted unhygienic but warmth-giving company for the human occupants.

Whether or not they were fewer than before cannot be determined, but they were undoubtedly poorer, as their trade relations with the higher civilisation of the Mediterranean area were interrupted by the advance across Europe of the Celts. Their impact causes this to be known in Scandinavia as the Celtic Iron Age; the two major treasures from this period found in Jutland are both of Celtic provenance. One is a silver bowl with highly realistic embellishments in relief, including a representation of a human sacrifice; its suggested use was for catching a victim's blood. The other, believed to have been a votive offering, is a pair of ceremonial vehicles, exhibiting the special skill of the Celts as wheelwrights. A still more interesting find, from the island of Als off south-east Jutland, is a war canoe which carried 22–24 paddlers and is the oldest surviving specimen of a boat in Scandinavia. It contained deliberately damaged war equipment, including some single-edged iron swords, which was evidently offered as booty to a god of war. Thus Denmark in the early third century BC practised a rite which Caesar observed as a feature of Celtic culture during his conquest of Gaul.

The first direct contacts with the civilised world likewise belong to this period. The Greek geographer Pytheas of Marseilles, whose vanished writings are cited by later scholars, penetrated far enough into the north to record such characteristic phenomena as the short summer nights, the few varieties of grain, and the frequent rain which caused it to be threshed under cover. He probably visited south Norway – though his Thule or farthest north has also been identified with the Shetlands or even with Iceland – as well as Jutland, in whose vicinity he places the people called the Teutones. Yet, at a time when Alexander the Great had newly opened up vast regions of the east for study, news of the north roused little interest. Two centuries later, the Cimbri and the Teutones were to emerge from that Jutland area to threaten much of the Mediterranean world before they were overwhelmed by the Consul Marius in the valleys of the Rhône and Po. Even then, the expansion of the Roman power continued for another century without any substantial increase in Rome's knowledge of the northern barbarians.

In AD 5 the Emperor Augustus sent his Rhine fleet as far as the 'Cimbrian promontory', which caused the Jutland tribes to dispatch propitiatory embassies to the Romans. Nevertheless, in Northern history the prime event of the next four hundred years was a non-event: the frontier of the great Empire, which set a lasting imprint on so much of western and central Europe, did not advance permanently across the Rhine. For Pliny the Elder, Tacitus, and even Ptolemy, what lay beyond Jutland was the unexplored island or islands of 'Scatinavia', which a misreading of the manuscript of Pliny turned into 'Scandinavia' alias 'Skandia'.

Some tribes or peoples of the north were known by name. Tacitus in particular describes the *civitates Suionum*, who have 'not merely arms and men but powerful fleets',[4] who pay respect to wealth, and who yield absolute obedience to one supreme ruler. Making allowance for the author's rhetoric, we have here a clear reference to the Svear, who were to provide the original nucleus of the Swedish kingdom. For Norway no names of peoples are recorded, but Pliny uses 'Saevo' for the mass of mountains believed to lie north of the entrance to the Kattegat and 'Nerigon' for the great island south of Thule. The Romans appear to have known nothing of the people we call the Finns, who may at this very time have been making their way to the northern shore of the Gulf of Finland, by water from Estonia and by land at the Karelian Isthmus, whence they very slowly penetrated the hinterland. Tacitus does, however, employ the name 'Fenni' for a nomadic people, using primitive bone weapons, who live east of the Svear. These may be identified as the Lapps,* about whose origins and arrival in Scandinavia nothing is

---

* The people who call themselves *Samek* are distinguished at the present day by their Mongol appearance and still semi-nomadic way of life. The evidence of place-names and still more their adoption of a Finno-Ugrian language point to an early concentration in Finland, but nearly two-thirds now live in the Norwegian county of Finnmark; 'Fin' is an old Norwegian name for this people. 'Lapp', a designation common to all the Scandinavian languages, probably originated as a term of contempt, though it has also been more agreeably derived from *löper* ('runner') in allusion to their speed on skis, much used in their herding of reindeer.

definitely established: they may well have been its earliest inhabitants, thrust back into an isolated existence farther north by the slowly advancing frontier of settlement.

Rome's interest in this world of barbarians was almost entirely economic, for trade across Europe developed almost automatically once the barrier of Celtic power had been removed by Roman arms. Exports from or through Jutland included the established commodities of amber, furs and slaves, the last of which would be in greater demand when the Empire ceased to supply itself by fresh conquests. In addition, cattle on the hoof, hides and skins, and dairy produce could all be marketed farther south. As for what was sent in return, better-quality arms would never lack customers, whilst other semi-luxuries and luxuries would soon create their own market among chieftains and prosperous farmers. By the reign of Hadrian the imperial coinage had penetrated to Finland; Scandinavians drank from mass-produced bronze vessels, identical with the types used in Pompeii before the eruption; and coloured glasses, engraved in the factories of Gaul and the Rhineland, could be admired in homes as far north as the Tröndelag. The fine arts, too, are well represented, as on the Danish island of Lolland, where two silver beakers have come to light which are exquisitely decorated with scenes from the *Iliad*.

At first these wares were mainly brought by road from Italy itself to the great frontier mart at the legionary post of Carnuntum, which guarded the middle Danube. From there the traffic passed through the territory of the Marcomanni and along the valleys of the Elbe, Oder, and Vistula. But after the Marcomannic Wars in the second century AD the trade was based for the most part on provincial products, which were shipped down the Rhine. At the same time a new artistic trend becomes evident, in the gold and silver work which originated among the Goths. This great Germanic people certainly maintained close contacts with Scandinavia, from which they may have drawn some of their ruling families, though the long-held belief that their general place of origin was the island of Gotland and the adjacent territories of the Swedish mainland has never been substantiated. In Tacitus's time they were located near the mouth of the Vistula, and it was the destruction of the Marcomanni which enabled them to migrate eastwards along the Roman frontier. The kingdom which they then established on the north shores of the Black Sea enjoyed such fame in far-off Scandinavia that the overthrow of its king, Ermanaric, by the Huns in AD 375 is the earliest historical event to be clearly described in Scandinavian lays.

Since the Goths were certainly among the early users of the runic alphabet, it is tempting to include this together with the art-forms which they transmitted to the northern peoples. Modern investigators, however, who find the origin of this alphabet in contacts made with a North Italic model during the second century BC, surmise that its unrecorded spread into the north may have been the work of the retreating remnants of the

Cimbri and the Teutones from Jutland. An important part in its later diffusion may have been played by the Heruli, who often figure as rune-masters: this mysterious people, a part of whom were conquered by Ermanaric, perhaps set out on their long wanderings from Denmark. In any case, Denmark and southern Norway are the lands where the earliest decipherable runic inscriptions have been found, dating from the third century of the Christian era, and for many hundreds of years runic writing was much more widely used in Scandinavia than anywhere else.

Archaeology reveals that in Denmark and elsewhere in southern Scandinavia the so-called 'Roman Iron Age' was marked by the growth of new settlements with rectangular fields, as the introduction of a stronger, iron-shod plough enabled heavier soils to be planted with a variety of crops, especially rye. The wide availability of bog-iron meant that home-made iron tools now became plentiful, as the grave-finds show. But the weapons which likewise accompanied the farmer to his final resting-place are a reminder that the possession of land and goods might be contested. The clinker-built, iron-riveted boat, propelled by fifteen pairs of oars, which was excavated at Nydam is evidence that by the fourth century the men of Jutland at least were dangerously mobile. The Danish islands, too, yield accumulations of weapons and armour of a Roman type, though we have no means of telling whether they represent booty won in raids or equipment which had been legitimately acquired by service in Roman auxiliary forces, for which barbarians were increasingly recruited.

It is tempting, however, to connect some of these military hoards with what may well have been a major event in Danish history, though recorded exclusively by the sixth-century Gothic historian, Jordanes. He states that the Heruli, who in his time were in conflict with the Lombards in central Europe, had formerly been expelled from their homes by the Danes, when the latter first came to Denmark from Sweden. This suggests that the Danish kingdom was founded originally among the islands, perhaps centring on Lejre in Zealand, which according to tradition was the ancient capital. Such a beginning would account for the separate status long retained by Jutland, which may have been more or less peace-fully annexed by the islanders after the departure of the Angles and Jutes in search of the new homes which they eventually found on the other side of the North Sea. It will be remembered that Bede preserves the tradition of 'a country called Anglia, which is said to remain desert to this day'.[5]

THE GREAT MIGRATIONS AND THE HEROIC AGE

Writing in the period of the Great Migrations, Jordanes described Scandinavia in two memorable phrases as 'a hive of races or a womb of nations':[6] for he believed that Goths, Burgundians and Lombards had all originated there. But, although he recites the names of more than twenty tribes, neither he nor Cassiodorus (the Roman author whose work he condensed) appears to have had any direct knowledge of events inside the region. Indeed, we owe to the Byzantine historian Procopius, who actually contemplated journeying to 'Thule', our only definite piece of information about Scandinavia in this period, namely that a remnant of the Heruli had made its way back. But the archaeological remains indicate that for nearly two centuries the break-up of the Roman Empire in the west yielded rich spoil for Scandinavia from many parts of the Mediterranean world. Gold in particular came north in such profusion that the period from *c.* 450 to *c.* 550 has been called 'a veritable age of gold for the northern barbarians'.[7] If the Gallehus horns from Slesvig – melted down by a thief in modern times – contained the largest weight of gold of any such object of Scandinavian design, the hundreds of gold amulets known as bracteates, which originated as barbarian imitations of the coinage of Constantine the Great, show that some gold reached many hands.

Nevertheless, the prevalence of hoards, whose rich contents may be contrasted with the modest grave-finds from earlier periods, is evidence above all that this was a Time of Troubles, when men buried their treasures for safety – and might not live to retrieve them. Some Scandinavian warriors, indeed, took service in the Mediterranean lands, where they earned the freshly minted Italian *solidi* which are found in quantity on the Baltic islands. But the remains of hill-forts of this period, scattered all over southern Scandinavia, testify to warfare in the homelands.

These wars, though much less famous than that in which Ermanaric had fallen, likewise provided the subject-matter for heroic lays. Although none survive, something of their contents can be gleaned from the Anglo-Saxon epic of *Beowulf*. For its unknown author, whilst composing in a later age and for an English court, assumes that his hearers will readily appreciate allusions to stories that had been borne across the North Sea by their ancestors. The opening lines are explicit on this point: 'We have indeed heard tell of the splendour of warrior Danes in days gone by, of the kings of that nation, and of how their high-born men achieved deeds of valour.'[8] Accordingly, the tale of Beowulf's semi-magical encounters with the monsters of the moor and lake, and with the treasure-guarding dragon by which he is eventually slain, has its place in a kind of historical setting.

Thus the palace of Hrothgar, to whose rescue Beowulf was come, the 'mighty mead-hall greater than any children of men had ever heard tell of . . . that lofty towering hall with its broad horns', may perhaps be identified as Lejre, the first Danish capital, whilst the death of King Hygelac, whom 'Fate carried off, after he had courted misfortune by his proud courage, seeking a feud with the Frisians', is a genuine historical event of about the year 520, as recorded by the Frankish chronicler, Gregory of Tours. The numerous references to the wars between the Svear and the Geats are, indeed, more puzzling. Their maritime character makes it possible to conclude that *geatas* refers, in some cases at least, to the Jutes. Yet the older view, that we have here the echo of a long struggle, in which the Svear at last gained the ascendancy over the people of Västergötland, seems to be supported by the conclusion of the poem. For when the funeral pyre was kindled under the body of Beowulf their king, 'A Geatish woman . . . sang again and again a funeral chant, saying that she sorely dreaded that she would know days of mourning, and a time of great slaughter and terror among the host, with humiliation and captivity.'

The uncertainties regarding the interpretation of *Beowulf* are a reminder that, in the period immediately following the Great Migrations – when it was presumably composed – the outside world still had no very coherent picture of events inside Scandinavia. Investigation of the archaeological remains, however, has disclosed the occurrence of a revolutionary change. The region known to us as Denmark ceased, perhaps for the first time, to be culturally in the van. In Norway the west coast apparently received fewer impulses than before from across the North Sea; instead, the main finds are located in the east region and in the Tröndelag – the districts which had the easiest access to Sweden. It was the land of the Svear, centring on the north side of the Baltic inlet which is now Lake Mälaren, that had now become the richest part of the north. A notable increase of cattle pasture through the continued rise of the Baltic coastline may help to account for this, as does certainly the establishment of close trade relations with the island of Gotland. This pre-eminence, attested above all by the tombs of the kings at Old Uppsala and the splendidly adorned weapons and harness of the chieftains in the near-by boat graves at Vendel, received dramatic confirmation only a generation ago, when the Sutton Hoo excavations revealed a hitherto unsuspected link between this Swedish culture and the East Anglian kingdom in the time of the Heptarchy.

Although the ship-burial at Sutton Hoo has no known parallel in the seventh century except among the Svear, the foreign dynasty whose presence in East Anglia would best account for the finds is judged – on the strength of a list of East Anglian royal names – to have been not Svear but Geat. This would not, however, alter the general significance of the fact that so much of this treasure, which has transformed our idea of the cultural level reached by pagan English society, is of Swedish provenance. Whether it is a case of direct importation or of Swedish craftsmen at work in England or of English craftsmen inspired by Swedish art-forms, 'The Swedish element appears as powerful leaven in . . . the East Anglian court.'[9] It has even been suggested that this leaven, at first dynastic, was reinforced by 'a second influx of important Geat exiles with Danish connections . . . after the final overthrow of the Geat kingdom . . . The literary sequel to this is Beowulf.'[10]

In view of the doubts already mentioned about the identity of the

'Geats', all that can be claimed with any certainty is the general pre-eminence of the Svear, in accordance with the traditions of their kings, as later recorded in the *Ynglingatal*.* It may well be that their maritime strength enabled them to establish some form of suzerainty over the island of Gotland whilst the inland realm of the Geats was still independent. At all events, by the eighth century the Svear joined with the islanders in the conduct of trade settlements on the far side of the Baltic at Grobin and Apuole, and they may even have seized the coast of Courland. This was also a period of rapid expansion from central Sweden into the Åland islands, but beyond this there was as yet no more than a slow spreading-out of the Finns from the coast into the almost empty hinterland of Tavastia in the south-west and Karelia in the vicinity of Lake Ladoga. In both cases only a loose tribal organisation existed, under chieftains whose boat graves are found along the coast.

Eighth-century Norway was still a land of very small rulerships, some of which are recalled in the names of existing districts with such terminations as -*rike* and -*land*. Only in the south-east, where communications were comparatively easy, can we trace a more important dynasty, whose Swedish connections secured it a place in the *Ynglingatal*, whilst Romerike (north of modern Oslo) boasts a gigantic mound, which was built for some unknown purpose by a ruler who disposed of the equivalent of an entire season's labour from 500 men. Meanwhile, Denmark's progress towards unity received more encouragement than Norway's from the lie of the land, but the course of events remains obscure. Uncertainty envelops, for example, the statecraft of King Harald Wartooth, who is supposed to have united all Denmark and conquered much of Sweden before he was killed at Bravellir in Östergötland in a battle celebrated in the legends of all Scandinavia – but which may lie anywhere between AD 100 and 750. The only hard facts available concern Danish raids on Frisia, which are recorded by the Franks. It is reasonable to infer that these were intended to wrest a share in the new trade which the Franks were establishing with the Arab world, when the older trade of Jutland with the Baltic lands had been impaired by the westward advance of the Slav peoples.

The evidence of place-names, however, shows that in all the more habitable parts of Scandinavia the clearance of forest, the draining of marsh and the following of valley or fiord into the hinterland continued steadily, generation by generation. The erection of hill-forts for defence has already been mentioned. The assembly of the freemen of each locality in the *thing* was equally born of necessity: besides the settlement of

---

* 'The List of the Ynglings', composed in the late eighth century by the Norwegian skald Tjodolv and cited almost in full by Snorri (see p. 62). The thirty generations of Ynglings whom he supposes to have reigned in the vicinity of Uppsala are largely legendary, but archaeological evidence supports his claim that this area of Sweden had links with the early kingships in eastern Norway; some of the Swedish royal names occur independently in *Beowulf*.

disputes between neighbours about land boundaries and the sharing of
rights and obligations in the use of forest and waste, each community had
a direct interest in agreeing upon a tariff of payments for manslaughter
(*wergild*) as a less wasteful alternative to the traditional blood feud among
the families concerned. In addition, each chieftain or large farmer maintained his *hov*, where the gods, the local nature-spirits and the ancestors
who watched jealously over their former home were all to be placated
by an appropriate ritual. These were three sources from which larger
forms of social organisation were gradually being developed, but apart
from the uncertain interpretation of laconic runic inscriptions the process
is hidden from us.

To sum up, in the late eighth century, when the tide of Muslim conquest
had been turned back from western Europe and Charlemagne was building
his Frankish empire on Christian foundations, the north remained almost
entirely outside the sphere of interest of civilised man. In the 720s,
indeed, the archbishop of Utrecht, the English-born Willibrord, briefly
extended his mission as 'the apostle of the Frisians' to reach the Danes,
but with no lasting results. Whilst trade passed overland through Jutland,
and Frisian vessels also plied the North Sea to Norway, the primary
products brought out of Scandinavia were not apparently valuable enough
in quality or quantity to induce the Franks or any other major people to
press forward into the north.

But what if the impulse should arise to drive men in the opposite
direction? The design of a twenty-oared boat, found in western Norway,
shows that during these centuries of seclusion rapid advances were being
made in the construction of vessels fit to face the open sea. The means of
taking their neighbours to the southward by surprise would lie ready to
the hands of Scandinavians, whenever the motives for so doing became
sufficiently strong.

Chapter 2

Homelands of the Vikings

THE IMPACT OF THE VIKINGS

The Vikings delivered the last of the great pagan assaults which threatened to overthrow western Christendom in the dark centuries between the fall of the Roman Empire of the West and the proclamation of the First Crusade. Whilst 'man of the creeks' is perhaps the least unsatisfactory of many explanations for the original sense of the word 'viking', there is no doubt that in the world of the ninth and tenth centuries it denoted a 'pirate' or 'sea-robber' who emerged from the north. The monastic chroniclers who provided the principal contemporary records of this period often knew from first-hand experience that plunder, and especially the plunder of rich coastal abbeys which had no defence except their sacrosanctity, had provided the prime attraction, and that the raids then spread like wildfire. The chroniclers also reveal how completely Christendom was taken by surprise, how inept were its countermeasures (at least until the time of Alfred), and how hard it was for Churchmen to find any explanation of their sufferings except the Wrath of God – a viewpoint which encouraged the natural human tendency to exaggerate.

The Church had indeed good reason to petition for 'deliverance from the fury of the Northmen'.* The religious beliefs of the Vikings encouraged brutality towards the followers of the White Christ at the same time as their practical interests led them to cow resistance by acts of deliberate cruelty, because they normally operated with small numbers in the midst of a hostile population. Nevertheless, the Viking expeditions – a term which is stretched to cover every Scandinavian activity abroad in the late pagan period – amounted to much more than a series of murderous raids which ransacked Christendom for plunder. Where they found land which was virtually unoccupied, they organised settlement; and when piracy did not pay the Vikings were eager to trade. Indeed, the Swedish

---

* P. H. Sawyer, *The Age of the Vikings* (2nd ed., 1971) p. 138, cites Léopold Delisle for the absence of this petition from surviving French Carolingian litanies. But Delisle had found an antiphonary from this period, with the prayer: *De gente fera Normannica nos libera, quae nostra vastat, Deus, regna. Senum jugulat et juvenum ac virginum puerorum quoque catervam.*[1] The reference to indiscriminate throat-cutting seems sufficiently explicit.

ventures in the east were commercially motivated from the outset, and they provided the wherewithal for competition with the Frisian traders, which was one aspect of the ventures of their fellow Vikings in the west.

The underlying causes of the events of these two centuries, in which the Scandinavian peoples made their biggest impact on the world, have never been clearly established. Contemporaries supposed that over-population, which it was tempting to connect with the well attested Scandinavian practice of polygamy (at least among the chieftains), was an important incentive. The study of place-names, however, suggests that, except in the coastal districts of western Norway, there was no serious scarcity of land for internal colonisation. On the other hand, the writers of the sagas (see p. 62), who lived when the events of the Viking era were still a treasured folk memory, take the view that the common human passion for adventure and renown had exercised an especially compelling influence among the peoples of the north. The runic texts on individual memorials, which become much more numerous in this period of great activity, to some extent confirm this and often emphasise the pursuit of riches. Since the wealth acquired by raiding gave enhanced social status, it is clear that each successful early raid will have had a snowball effect, leading to more fully organised activities affecting larger numbers.

From the Baltic to the Irish Sea, all the main Viking routes had previously been used to some extent for peaceful commerce. But the peoples of Scandinavia seem to have been slow to adopt the sail, as employed by the Frisians and other seafarers of western Europe, so that it was not until about the end of the eighth century that their large seagoing vessels were regularly propelled by sails as well as oars. The Norwegians in particular then evolved masterpieces of design, such as the light, clinker-built Gokstad ship, with its oaken keel, well-stepped mast, and the rudder hung on the starboard side, projecting below the keel and yet easily raised for beaching. A modern replica took only four weeks to sail across the Atlantic, when it achieved a maximum speed of 10–11 knots. In ships like this a short sea-passage at the right time of year was both rapid and easy; on arrival at the other side they could readily be hauled up the beach or else rowed far inland from a river mouth. Later on, however, a broader and deeper-hulled vessel was developed, more suitable for bulky cargo or long-distance migration. With only the most primitive aids to navigation, Norse mariners were among the very first who willingly sailed out of sight of land; having reached the roughly calculated latitude of their destination, they struck out fearlessly even across the western ocean. This expertise in the arts of the sea, which stimulated every Viking activity, even left a mark on language, for both Ireland and Normandy retain words of Scandinavian origin embedded in their modern maritime vocabulary.

It was on 8 January 793 that 'The harrowing inroads of heathen men made lamentable havoc in the church of God in Holy-island', as the Anglo-Saxon Chronicle records[2] – a disaster which astonished so well informed and travelled a scholar as Alcuin. Yet neither this precisely dated raid on Lindisfarne nor the killing of the sheriff of Dorset, when he accosted 'three ships of the Northmen from the land of robbers', which may have occurred half a dozen years earlier, marks the true beginning of Scandinavian seaborne operations. The Swedes, as we have seen, had already reached across the Baltic in search of trade. When the Danes in 776-7 had harboured a Saxon chieftain fleeing from Charlemagne's armies, the failure of the latter to take punitive action is plausibly attributed to his awareness of Danish strength at sea. As for the Norwegians, it seems likely that their take-over of Shetland and Orkney from the Picts, about which history is silent, had begun early enough to provide staging-points in the islands for such exploratory attacks as that on Lindisfarne.

During the opening decades of the ninth century expeditions originating chiefly in west Norway descended on the Hebrides and the Scottish mainland, on western Ireland, and on every coast bordering the Irish Sea. The Hebrides were quickly overrun, and they were eventually linked with the Isle of Man in a Norse kingdom with a mixed Norse-Celtic civilisation. But the great prize was Ireland, where the Norsemen founded Dublin in 836 and established other trade centres round the coast. Although the interior never passed completely into their possession, it was from Ireland that they later entered, and moved eastwards across, north-west England. They also made their way during this burst of astonishing energy into open Atlantic waters, to colonise both the Faeroes and Iceland.

The Danes, as we know from Erse chronicles, made an unsuccessful attempt to oust the Norwegians from Ireland, but their natural line of advance was towards England and France. Moreover, their expeditions had at the outset important political objectives, since their rulers had good cause to mount a counter-offensive against the frontiers of the empire of Charlemagne, who by 800 had succeeded in diverting profitable trade routes to run south of Danish territory. The weakening and sub-division of the Frankish Empire after his death soon gave the Danes their chance. In 845 they sacked Hamburg, and although they never penetrated far into Germany they overran the Low Countries and much of northern France, advancing up the Seine to Paris. On the other side of the Channel sporadic raiding gave place in 865 to the operations of a more considerable force, whose well organised units became established in the Danelaw. Half a century later, the Danes – led, according to the saga story, by a Norwegian chieftain – carved out a second and more enduring realm for themselves in the duchy of Normandy.

Farther south the Norwegians and, to a lesser extent, the Danes challenged the power of the Muslims, whose records show that as early as 844 the 'idolaters' sent eighty ships up the Guadalquivir against Seville, of which fifty made good their escape back to Aquitaine. But, although some of the parties which entered the Mediterranean raided Morocco, they found it easier to make a further lodgement among the Franks at the mouth of the Rhône than in the heavily defended territories of the Muslim world; this was more successfully approached from a different direction and with different methods by the Swedes.

Very little is known about the beginnings of the lucrative Swedish commerce with the east, of which there are traces as early as the seventh century. In 839, however, a Frankish chronicler reported the passage down the Rhine of an embassy which was on its way back by a roundabout route from Byzantium to the 'Khaganate of Rus', being unable to travel by the Dnieper valley on account of unrest among the Slav tribes; its members said they were of Swedish origin. Arabic sources based on information from about the same period likewise refer to the 'Khakan of the Russes', whose island headquarters is described on a site corresponding to that of Novgorod, where the river Volkhov issues from lake Ilmen. Lastly, there is the evidence of the *Russian Primary Chronicle*, written more than two hundred years after the event, which finds the starting-point of Russian history in a ninth-century invitation to 'Rus' princes to rule over Novgorod and two other cities.

Although the word 'Rus' is nearly identical with the modern Finnish and Estonian name for the Swedes, the Swedish impact on Russia was not comparable, say, to the Danish impact on eastern England. The fact that the Scandinavian peoples called Russia *Gardarike* ('land of cities') seems to imply that they found the cities already in existence, a supposition that is abundantly confirmed by the absence of clear archaeological evidence for a large Swedish population having lived at any time in the great Russian river towns; the only possible exception is Old Ladoga, close to the debouchment of the Volkhov into the great lake – and this was quickly eclipsed by Novgorod, which lies 100 miles up-river. But small bands of Swedes, being better armed and disciplined than the Finno-Ugrian and Slav tribes of western Russia, would be able to extract a very profitable tribute of slaves and furs.

When the profits of their long-distance trade were insufficient, the Swedes did indeed display their military prowess in raids across the Black Sea against Byzantium or across the Caspian into north-east Iran; from 860 onwards these figure in Greek and Muslim records. Their chief interest, however, was the great trade route. This passed first along the Gulf of Finland, where it benefited in some degree the coastal population: 800 Anglo-Saxon coins, for instance, have been found on Finnish soil. From the river Neva and lake Ladoga the vessels of the Swedes bore them on upstream until they reached easy portages to the Volga, which carried them down to Bolgar. Arab travellers knew them as regular visitors to the big eastern trade mart conducted there, who sometimes also went on south-east to the river-mouth. Later, the Swedes turned their attention to the valley of the Dnieper, to which they gained access either from Novgorod or by passing up the river Dvina from Courland. About the year 950 a Byzantine emperor noted that most of the Dnieper cataracts had 'Rus' as well as Slavic names,* which points clearly to the role of the Swedish merchants as pioneers of the trade with Byzantium. Moreover, at Kiev (which had now eclipsed Novgorod) the river was crossed by the great caravan route from the Far East to Central Europe, which provided further commercial opportunities.

The profits gained by participation in all these rich trades – or, when chance offered, by plundering them – reveal themselves in the predominance of Arabic coins in the silver hoards of Viking Scandinavia. For a century and a half they derived mainly from the eastern provinces of the Caliphate, whilst from about 970 those of its western provinces occur more frequently, intermingled with the products of Byzantine mints. At the close of the tenth century, however, the contents of the coin hoards are for the first time chiefly Anglo-Saxon and German, a highly significant change which corresponds to a new departure in Viking activities.

The middle decades had been marked by a lull, during which the only major ventures were launched from the new settlements overseas, such as the Irish ports; in the original homelands the Viking impulse appeared to have subsided. But in the 980s a second wave of expeditions begins, which is characterised by the employment of a more disciplined army, the selection of alternative objectives in France and England, and concentration on the systematic exaction of tribute. A clear motive for the change is to be seen in a dearth of Arabic silver; this was due partly to the exhaustion of the silver mines in several regions of the Muslim world and partly to the closing of the trade route from the Volga, which may be attributed to the princes of Kiev, who no longer recognised any close link with the land of their forebears. Since a new, more westerly trade route, which reached the Baltic from Mesopotamia and Syria via Poland, spread much less treasure among the Scandinavian lands, danegeld was a form of compensation which figured very prominently in the last Viking campaigns.

The England of Ethelred the Redeless was the principal victim of extortions and reprisals which culminated in Sweyn Forkbeard's conquest, completed shortly before his death at Gainsborough in the late autumn of 1014, and in the two further years of convulsive struggle which ended in the acceptance of his son Cnut as undisputed king of all England. Cnut was a Christian; the Vikings were ceasing to be a pagan force operating from outside the boundaries of Christendom.

* The 'Rus' name for the Fourth Cataract, $Αειφόρ$, occurs as *Aifur* on a runic inscription in Gotland.[3]

CONTEMPORARY DEVELOPMENTS IN SCANDINAVIAN SOCIETY

The two centuries in which the Scandinavian peoples had this enormous impact upon Europe left deep marks on their own internal development as well. The place-names show that in Denmark many new villages were being established as offshoots of older ones, whilst in Sweden much new soil came under the plough on the lower ground in both the central and southern regions. Where villages existed, the distribution of strips in the open fields according to the sequence in which the farmhouses lay – *solskifte* or 'allotment sunwise' – came in at this time, perhaps by imitation of an English practice adopted in the Danelaw. In Norway the picture is more variegated, as marginal soil in the poorer districts of the west coast fell out of cultivation when opportunities opened up overseas. Yet this was the period in which seasonal grazing on the Norwegian mountains was commonly organised by means of the *seter* or summer dairy; both cereal and dairy farming expanded into new areas in the east; and the fishing/hunting economy was likewise expanding in the far north. Agriculture too profited from the advanced technical skills which built the Viking ships: with the increased use of iron better ploughs were constructed, and the improved tools certainly included a superior quality of axe, apt for felling the forest as well as the foeman.

A special stimulus to development was the plentiful supply of slave labour, of which there is little evidence in earlier centuries. A poem in the *Elder Edda* (see p. 27) indicates the place of the thrall at the base of the rural pyramid:

> With bast he bound, and burdens carried . . .
> Home bore faggots the whole day long . . .
> Ground they dunged, and swine they guarded,
> Goats they tended, and turf they dug.[4]

The total numbers are unknown, but human booty was easy to collect, transport and dispose of in slave markets all across Europe from Dublin to Bolgar. An internal Scandinavian market was also established, on the islands at the mouth of the Göta, where the three nascent kingdoms met. Craftsmen we may suppose were often brought home by their captors, as were certainly many younger women, by whom slave numbers were to some extent replenished; although a female slave might be of noble birth, it was only in Sweden that the master's child by her was born free. The labour force of a substantial freeman's farm seems normally to have included some half-dozen slaves; and they might even be left to conduct the dull routine of agriculture whilst the farmer-trader – a type which flourished particularly on Gotland – roamed the seas in search of more adventurous gains. But the employment of slave labour was most advantageous in the heavy and exacting work of clearing and tilling new land, since customary law regarded the thrall as a chattel and the owner was not accountable for his death, whether by exhaustion or direct ill-usage.

While new land was won for cultivation by pressures at which we can only guess, the growth of a homogeneous trading area throughout the northern seas led naturally to the growth of the earliest Scandinavian towns. Hedeby was the first to achieve renown; as early as 808 it appears to be referred to in a Frankish chronicle, which says that a Danish king had compelled the merchants of a Slav settlement in the Baltic to transfer themselves to a site under his control – a practice apparently copied from Charlemagne. Hedeby's position, at the foot of a fiord leading into the Baltic and within 10½ miles of a river debouching into the North Sea, made it an ideal centre for east–west traffic, which at the cost of some river-rowing and a single portage could avoid the arduous passage round the Skaw. Hedeby was also served by the ancient land route from north Jutland and had connections with the main tracks running south across Germany. The fortified area was about sixty acres, which would provide space for a large open-air market as well as for the operations of local industries, such as bronze casting, glass making, and the carving of objects of bronze, horn, and doubtless wood. Finds of material from all over western Europe suggest that the chief activity of the town was its long-distance commerce.

An Arab merchant from Cordoba has left an unflattering account of the dirt and noise of Hedeby, whose inhabitants are said to make a sound in their throats when singing like the barking of a dog, only worse – perhaps the very first allusion to the Danish glottal stop? Towards the year 900 its wealth made it the object of a successful attack by a Swedish chieftain, but the yoke was shaken off after about forty years and the town remained prosperous until the early eleventh century. It was then eclipsed by nearby Slesvig, which was accessible to vessels of deeper draught. Before 1050 Hedeby was burnt down, perhaps on the occasion of its capture by the Norwegian king, Harald Hardrada.

Birka on lake Mälaren, west of modern Stockholm, is in the vicinity of a large farm (Helgö), where recent finds show that, a century or more before the Viking Age proper, a farmer-trader might already possess two such strangely assorted valuables as an Irish crozier and a small image of Buddha. The town itself was indeed ideally situated as an entrepôt both for the trade which came out of Russia and for furs and other northern products, easily conveyed from the hinterland in winter over the snow and ice. In addition, Birka had easy sea communication with Hedeby and, like Hedeby, its own local industries, including some of considerable refinement: filigree wire was drawn here and an oriental pendant could be copied by means of moulds. The fortified area comprises only 29 acres, but there were two natural harbours outside the town and an artificial harbour with a basin 80 metres long. The 1,200 graves which have been excavated yielded a total of 131 Arabic coins; 40 of them also contained fragments of oriental silk. Since the burials date from *c*. 800 to *c*. 960, after which this once busy port fell silent, the last years of the tenth century may be presumed to have seen a new generation of merchants transfer their activities to Sigtuna (p. 43) and across to Gotland, where the less professional farmer-traders already conducted a very profitable trade. Although the town of Visby had not yet arisen, the Baltic island provides 700 out of about 1,000 finds of silver from the Sweden of the Viking Age.

Skiringssal in Norway, on the west side of the Oslofiord, though a market centre of modest dimensions, is of special interest as a port which was made known to king Alfred by Othere, a Norwegian chieftain who had sailed beyond the North Cape far into the Barents Sea and south to Hedeby. His account of his home on the border of Finnmark, where he kept tame reindeer and exacted tribute in kind from the neighbouring Lapps, likewise sheds light upon Skiringssal's distant sources of supply. Its exports include the walrus ivory and ropes, sealskins, furs, and eider-down brought down from the north; furs, etc., from its own hinterland; and perhaps some products of the local metal and soapstone industries. Since no fortification has been traced, this is believed to have been chiefly a seasonal market; the graves yield Frisian cloth, a Carolingian sword blade, and ornaments of English and Irish origin. This partly westward orientation was shared by the trade centres of north Jutland, such as Århus and the recently rediscovered port of Vendila, near modern Ålborg.

Each of the three Scandinavian homelands now possessed the nucleus of a merchant class, whose growth was stimulated by the coming into existence of communities of Scandinavian traders abroad – at the early establishments along the great Russian rivers; at key points seized in the campaigns on the continent, such as the island of Noirmoutier at the mouth of the Loire; in York, whose area doubled under its Danish kings, and the five boroughs of the Danelaw; and in the Irish ports, where the Vikings were eventually transformed into peaceful 'hostmen'. Craftsmen, too, became more numerous; they made some wares for export, as we have seen, and were encouraged to imitate for the domestic market the most highly prized imports, such as the pattern-welded and other fine-quality swords from continental weapon-smiths or the costly ecclesiastical ornaments which were being put to secular uses. Nevertheless, Scandinavian society continued to consist mainly of the earls, the free men, and the thralls (whose case we have already examined).

The status of a free man varied to some extent in accordance with the size of his farm, the number of his slaves or other workforce, and especially the presence or absence of any form of rent or other obligation due, for example, to some previous holder of the land. The farm very often accommodated an 'enlarged family', comprising members of two or three generations, notably in the case of the udal farmer (*odelsbonde*), whose land was retained in the family by strict rights of inheritance. In western Norway at least, the ancient germanic system of *wergild* exacted compensation for the slaying of a man at five different rates: the value of a freed slave was half that of any ordinary peasant or a quarter that of the possessor of udal land, whilst the *wergild* of a chieftain was twice or four times, and that of a king eight times, that of an *odelsbonde*. Nevertheless, every free man was theoretically entitled to attend his local *thing*, which in turn was represented by its more prominent members at the *lagthing*, where laws were made and major disputes settled for a self-contained region or *land*. Accordingly, the relationship between the free man and the earl or king, who was his only fully recognised superior, was markedly different from that which obtained under the feudal practices which were growing up on the continent.

Jarl ('earl') was originally a title given – perhaps by a king – to a local leader or chieftain; indeed, the word has even been boldly derived from 'Heruli'. By the start of the Viking Age the office was generally hereditary. Except in Denmark, where the monarchy (as we have seen) had political objects in view, earls were more likely than kings to place themselves at the head of Viking expeditions: the founder of the Viking earldom of Orkney, for example, was the son and brother of successive earls of Möre in west Norway. But the two centuries of Viking activities abroad were marked by a consolidation of authority at home, a change which prompted unruly elements to go 'a-viking' and discouraged them from returning. The earldom in the original sense tended to become merged with the title of king, to reappear later as a rank conceded to a leading subject of the crown.

Konung ('king') means 'person of noble origin'. The earliest Scandinavian kings of whom we have any definite knowledge, the Swedish Ynglings with their offshoot in south-east Norway, traced their descent through a long line of traditionally named ancestors back to the gods. Even a purely local dynasty similarly sought to bolster up its position by means of a record of past achievements, historical or mythical, which it would be the business of the court poet or *skald* to celebrate. This did not, however, mean that monarchy was hereditary in the modern sense; a king might be succeeded by any son, oldest or youngest, legitimate or the fruit of any chance liaison, or even by a brother or other near relation preferred for some reason by the *thing*. Where several provinces had united, the approval of each of their *things* might at first be required to confirm the choice of the most important; in Sweden each new king for many centuries continued to make a formal tour (*Eriksgata*) to receive the homage of each ancient province. In early days the royal court was in any case a peripatetic organisation, since the king travelled round the royal farms, where he collected and consumed whatever each district contributed to his support.

As for his functions, the Scandinavian king had no absolute authority as judge or lawgiver, though it was natural for him to take the lead in decision making and the execution of judgements. In time of peace he was deemed to be responsible for the general welfare of his people. It was he who conducted the principal sacrifices by which the gods were propitiated to ensure good harvests. His mystical significance is well illustrated by the story of a Norwegian king, the father of Harald Fairhair (p. 30), whose corpse was supposed to have been quartered in order that each part of the kingdom might enjoy prosperity through his continued presence. The king would likewise be expected to deal satisfactorily with any new phenomenon which might affect a slowly moving rural society. Such was the development of the first towns: at Birka there was already a royal bailiff in the middle of the ninth century.

But in the Viking Age the king was first and foremost a leader of warriors, who caroused with him in his timbered hall and received rich gifts of booty from the royal hand. A successful leader of Viking forays had a ready-made nucleus of armed followers to establish him as a king, whether overseas or on returning home. At the same time, the menace of Viking chiefs returning in this way to terrorise their fellow countrymen encouraged kings already in possession to build up new institutions to protect their subjects. The name of *hird* for the royal retinue came to Scandinavia from the Danelaw about the end of the pagan period, but a body of royal retainers seems to have existed earlier, at all events in Norway. An elaborate system of rules was gradually evolved for its management; the essential tie, however, was that of personal loyalty to the king, whose first regular officials, such as the marshal and the standard-bearer, were drawn from the *hirdmenn*. The naval levy or *leidang* may likewise have owed something to practices observed abroad, but as a form of general military organisation it was appropriate only to maritime peoples such as the Scandinavian. Each district provided men, equipment and supplies for one or more warships of a given size: thus in Sweden an area designated as a *hundari* is believed to have furnished 100 men as crew for four 24-oared vessels.

The *Leidang* does not figure in what we know of the original Viking expeditions, but it seems likely that it began with the power which Viking chiefs exercised over the coastal population in their own neighbourhoods. Later on, it was the king who called it out, though in Norway at least he was not entitled to muster more than half its strength for purposes which he could not represent as defensive. Certainly, at the close of the heathen period central authority was on the increase. This is demonstrably true in the case of Denmark, where four permanent military camps have been traced, whose meticulous construction argues for the view that they housed more disciplined armies than any seen in the west since the fall of Rome. Their precisely circular shape suggests a possible connection with the 'gyros', which the Rus-people are said by a Byzantine source[5] to have used as winter quarters. At all events, these camps accommodated

about 5,000 men, who must surely have been mercenaries in the employment of Danish kings about the end of the tenth century, when (as already
noted) Viking expeditions aimed at the exaction of tribute. In the same
period, too, Scandinavian kings provided themselves with another source
of power – regular mints, where English moneyers struck coins in imitation
of the danegeld money brought back from the unhappy realm of Ethelred
the Redeless.

THE PAGAN CULTURE AT ITS ZENITH

The triumphs of the Scandinavian peoples in this age as warriors, traders
and discoverers are almost matched by their achievements in the arts. By
the middle of the ninth century the contents of a royal ship-burial,
marvellously preserved in blue clay near one of the outer reaches of the
Oslofiord, show an expertise in carving which was scarcely excelled in
any part of Europe. Ten artists are believed to have been employed in
connection with the Oseberg ship, their work marking the transition
from the Swedish Vendel graves to the first of four Viking styles; the
second is represented in the Gokstad ship, where a similar form of burial
took place near the end of the century. All four are based on a form of
ornamentation which uses animals in a wholly abstract way; this had
been widespread in Europe during the Great Migrations, but it was the
Vikings who carried these new elaborations to many lands, including
Anglo-Saxon England. The skill of the Viking craftsmen is revealed in
the often overwhelming profusion of detailed ornament, and most of all
in their ability to suggest a haunting menace in the heads of men and
beasts. But, although the styles enable the archaeologist to place many
of his finds in their chronological sequence, even the experts confess:
'The meaning and emotional content of the art are at best obscure.'[6]

This is all the more unfortunate because the growth of a Scandinavian
literature awaited the introduction of the Latin alphabet by the Church.
Runic inscriptions, which are numerous in this period, consist almost
exclusively of laconically worded memorials to the dead or notices of
benefactions, such as the building of some causeway. Otherwise, the only
strictly contemporary source is the skaldic poetry, which was being
developed from about the middle of the ninth century, perhaps under
the stimulus of contacts with the Irish court bards. These short lays,
which often survive embedded in the historical sagas, such as Snorri's
Heimskringla (see p. 62), were transmitted orally without alteration
because of the admiration which their original hearers felt for their
most artificial features; these included elaborate and complex rhythms,
carefully contrived alliterations, and the constant resort to 'kennings', of
which 'whale bath' for ocean and 'swan of the sea-god' for a ship are
among the simplest specimens. The subject-matter was usually war or
some other form of hazardous adventure, recalled for the entertainment

primarily of the poet's lord. But the audience in the great man's hall would be qualified to check the main facts and resentful of over-gross exaggerations, where the deeds of individuals were concerned. The skaldic poems are therefore a reliable source for the general course of events, and for the attitude to life – and death – of the men by whom those events were shaped.

Information is relatively plentiful regarding the religion of the Vikings. Pioneer missionaries recorded what they learnt of the pagan faith which they believed to have been the main inspiration of the Viking invasions. A good many runes have a religious significance, though the precise interpretation may be uncertain, and the Icelandic sagas described the milieu of a pagan society of which the islanders retained a vivid tradition. Moreover, the collection of early Nordic poems known as the *Elder Edda** contains a masterpiece of religious verse, 'The Sibyl's Prophecy' (*Voluspå*), where the myths are reviewed by a pagan Icelander who must have lived when the triumph of Christianity already impended. This religion still claims our attention, because (except for differences of emphasis) the same pantheon was familiar to all the peoples of Scandinavia; it coloured their way of thinking for several centuries after the conversion, and as late as the nineteenth century provided picturesque trappings for the literary cult of Scandinavianism.

In view of the common origins of the Germanic peoples, it is natural to look for parallels to the deities whom the English worshipped before the landing of St Augustine and whose names are enshrined in the four middle days of the week. Our 'Tiw' corresponds, indeed, with the Scandinavian 'Tyr', but in Viking times this great war god figures very seldom either in place-names or in legends as compared with Woden or Thor. The former perhaps received additional publicity because he was deemed to be the god of poetry as well as war; as 'lord of the spear' he inspired the frenzy of the warrior who ran berserk through the battle. But in western Scandinavia the most popular divinity was 'Thor the Thunderer', who defended Heaven from the giants, mankind from monsters, and Viking communities from retaliation or reconquest by the followers of the White Christ. Numerous amulets have been found in circumstances which suggest that, when threatened by conversion, Vikings believed that Thor's hammer, worked in silver or even rough iron, could countervail the magic sign of the cross.

In Sweden the 'God of the World' was Freyr, whose idol emphasised his physical potency as god of fertility and whose progeny was supposed

---

* So called because it was erroneously believed to be the work on which Snorri founded his treatise on the art of skaldic poetry, which is known as the Prose Edda. The Elder or Poetic Edda, of which a single manuscript was discovered in 1643, comprises 34 poems of the 8th–12th centuries, committed to writing at the end of that period. Their Norse and Icelandic authors are unknown, and it is conjectured that some poems were composed in the British Isles, perhaps under Celtic influence. How *Edda*, the Old Norse word for 'great-grandmother', came to mean 'poetry' is likewise the subject of conjecture.

to include the ancestor of the Ynglings. He and his voluptuous sister, Freyja, belonged mysteriously to a special tribe of divinities, the *Vanir*, who at the world's beginning had waged war against the generality of gods or *Aesir* – a story which may have been designed to place fertility alongside conflict as a governing principle in the affairs of men. Yet Aesir and Vanir alike are doomed to perish along with mankind in the 'wolf-time' of Ragnarok, before this 'twilight of the gods' in turn leads on to a new Golden Age. It is tempting to conjecture that the poet here places in the Sibyl's mouth some dimly caught echo of the fears and hopes regarding the Millennium, which gripped much of Christendom as the Year of Our Lord 1000 drew near. But modern man cannot judge of this, any more than he can judge of the true inward meaning of the many lesser divinities whose adventures provided congenial subject-matter for generations of artists and craftsmen, from the makers of the Gotland picture-stones in the ninth century to the designers of Norwegian church portals in the twelfth – or even of that most homely type of supernatural being, the dwarfs and elves of mountain and stream.

How was such a religion practised? It seems to have had few temples and fewer priests. The only clear description of any temple building is that which the chronicler Adam of Bremen recorded from an eyewitness of the great shrine at Uppsala, 'entirely decked out in gold' and adjoined by a sacred grove, where 'each and every tree is believed divine because of the death and putrefaction of the victims hanging there'.[7] As for the priesthood, the class of *godar*, who served the gods in Iceland, seems to have had no regular counterpart elsewhere. Family cults which paid due respect to ancestors and the spirits of the locality probably loomed larger in men's lives, with the householder himself as priest. Thus in the 1020s a Christian Norwegian skald, who had journeyed through half-converted western Sweden, described more than one unwelcoming reception at a lonely farm, where the doors were shut while its inmates worshipped the old gods.[8]

Nevertheless, major religious festivals, presided over by king or chieftain, were occasions on which men entered into a kind of communion with the gods of war and fertility and with ancestral spirits. Mead and beer were drunk in honour of the god; the feasters consumed horse flesh, which had a special sanctity; and their persons were liberally sprinkled with the blood of sacrifice. The victims were usually animals, but the sagas tell of Thor's stone, 'upon which the bones of men sentenced to be sacrificed were broken',[9] and a conquered enemy was said to be 'given to Woden' when the hideous blood-eagle was carved through the living back. The Swedes regularly offered up nine human beings at the great celebrations held every ninth year at Uppsala, and in the remoter past they had been known to encourage the crops by sacrificing the king in person.

Life was cheap, and the only consolation the poet found was to 'know one thing that never dies, the verdict on each man dead'.[10] What paganism taught about death and the afterworld is suggested by the ship burials, which derive much of their value for posterity from the desire to equip the traveller into the unknown with both necessities and luxuries from the present life. The concept of the journey seems to have been hazy, for the ship was not made ready for sailing and in some cases was burnt together with the corpse. But the accepted picture of the future life required that the dead man should be accompanied voluntarily or involuntarily by a wife or concubine: the ritual slaughter of a half-stupefied slave-girl is described in horrifying detail by an Arab who witnessed the obsequies of a Swedish 'Rus' merchant in 922. The typical Viking warrior, however, must have been buried unceremoniously where he fell. Most probably, he had been content to picture his entry unaccompanied into Valhall, 'the hall of the slain', where the brave were said to do daily battle with one another in the great courtyard – and to be reconciled each night in readiness for more bloodshed on the morrow.

EMERGENCE OF THE THREE KINGDOMS AND TWO ATLANTIC OUTPOSTS

The religious beliefs of the Vikings, like their common use of the 'Danish tongue',* encouraged a degree of co-operation which causes a modern French scholar to declare, 'Cosmopolitanism is one of the most original features of the Viking world.'[11] Any raid leader of proved skill and resourcefulness might attract a personal following from outside his homeland, and runic inscriptions confirm the saga tradition that major enterprises normally enlisted support from regions that were politically quite disconnected; this was facilitated by the Danish practice of adopting a temporary 'law of the army', under which members of a given expedition might contract to obey a 'king of the sea'.[12] As traders and settlers, too, Danes and Norwegians intermingled in the kingdom of York, in some districts of Normandy, and in the Irish ports. Even in eastern Europe, which was fully accessible to the Swedes alone, an Icelander is to be found fighting in Courland and a future Norwegian king in Finland, whilst by the close of the tenth century the Byzantine emperor made no distinction between the Swedes and other Scandinavians whom he recruited for his 'Varangian Guard'.

At the same time, however, the wars waged by Scandinavians, both externally and amongst themselves, in this period of superabundant energy were causing the three kingdoms to take shape. The unification of Denmark was encouraged by the existence of hostile neighbours. Godfred, who ruled among the Danes in the time of Charlemagne, may have

---

* The expression *dansk tunga*, which is thought to have originated outside Scandinavia, was used in the early Middle Ages to designate the closely related languages of all the Scandinavian countries; it occurs, for example, in Greygoose (p. 418, ref. note 3/14) and the works of Saxo and Snorri.

exercised suzerainty rather than kingship over the Danish islands and Skåne. Yet he was strong enough to secure the basis of his royal authority in Jutland by digging the Danevirke across the peninsula; reconstructed later, this is still the only large-scale permanent fortification ever built on Scandinavian soil. *Annales Regni Francorum* also records Godfred's attack on Charlemagne's Slav allies, the Abodrites, as well as the initial naval ventures directed against the Frankish empire. But in the rest of the ninth century history tells of only one strong Danish ruler, Horik, the author of the attack on Hamburg already mentioned, and in the first third of the following century – the period in which Alfred's descendants reconquered the Danelaw – the trade centre at Hedeby had fallen into Swedish hands.

Then came three generations of powerful Danish kings, the earliest we have adequate records of; they are known to posterity as Gorm the Old, Harald Gormsson or Bluetooth, and Sweyn Forkbeard. The first of them (who died before 950) restored the unity of Denmark, which thus became a kingdom identifiable with that of today shortly before Edgar was crowned as the first king of all England. Harald lost part of Jutland to the German emperor, but his authority extended directly or indirectly over most of Norway. Sweyn, who may well have stationed his mercenaries in the circular camps described above, reconquered south Jutland and directed three major attacks against the shores of England. In the end, no tribute could buy him off; by the time of his sudden death, at Gainsborough in February 1014, the king of Denmark was also king of England in place of Ethelred. Thus Denmark had become a European power.

Norway was harder to unite. Not only was the territory much less compact, but the configuration of the long west coast encouraged the proliferation of petty rulers, whilst the eastern seaboard tended from very early times to fall within the Danish orbit. However, towards the end of the ninth century an important initiative was undertaken by Harald Fairhair, who as a child had inherited the little kingdom of Vestfold, on the coast south-west of modern Oslo. In alliance with the ruler of the powerful Tröndelag earldom of Lade, he began to suppress their small rivals, who often preyed on trade passing down the coast, and shortly before the year 900 a famous victory at Hafrsfiord (near Stavanger) made him master of the coastal districts up to the border of the Tröndelag. Both Harald and his son Eric married Danish princesses, but the earls of Lade were far from acknowledging any superiority: their hostility – rather than the fratricidal habits which earned him the surname 'Bloodaxe' – explains the fact that in 945, only five years after his father's death, Eric fled to Northumbria, where he had a second brief reign in the Viking kingdom of York.

Eric's place in Norway was taken by his youngest brother Haakon, who had been brought up at the court of King Athelstan of Wessex, and who made a premature attempt to impose the faith he had acquired there upon his native land. The fifteen years of his reign were taken up largely with a struggle against the heirs of Eric, backed by their Danish mother, who eventually took his place. They in their turn enjoyed a notable triumph over the Lade earldom, which was trying to expand southwards beyond the Tröndelag, and secured for themselves the tribute in kind paid to the earls from the far north. But within a decade Harald Gormsson, king of Denmark, finding his nephews' rule in Norway too independent, drove them out, and reinstated an earl of Lade to rule the country under his suzerainty. This earl Haakon, however, was a doughty warrior and champion of paganism, who long before his death in 995 had virtually shaken off the Danish yoke, so that only the petty kings of the south-eastern districts nearest to Denmark remained indisputably under Danish control.

The kingdom of the Svear, as we have seen, played a dominant role in the opening up of the rich eastern trades, a venture which by the close of the tenth century had passed its climax. But in the meanwhile little progress was made towards unification with the mainland territories stretching south to the Danish border. St Ansgar (see p. 34) believed the realm of the Svear to be based chiefly on islands, a view which is confirmed by the account given to king Alfred by a visitor who had sailed along the Baltic to the mouth of the Vistula: he assigned to their rule the islands of Öland and Gotland and the small coastal province of Blekinge. Thus in all probability Olof Skötkonung, who became king a little before AD 1000, was the first Svear ruler who was also 'King of the Goths' – that is to say, of the two major provinces of Östergötland and Västergötland.

Whilst Denmark, Norway, and Sweden slowly and successively took shape as kingdoms of the pattern made familiar by contact with less loosely organised peoples in other parts of Europe, out in the Atlantic the Scandinavians formed two wholly new societies, which have formed a permanent part of their cultural sphere. The archipelago of the Faeroes has, indeed, developed a distinctive way of life whilst remaining the dependency of a kingdom, though not always of the same kingdom. Iceland, on the other hand, derives its parliamentary republic from origins far older than those of any other similarly constituted European state of today. Not only so, but the Icelanders brought Greenland within the Scandinavian sphere of influence and made the first brief European incursion on to the North American mainland.

Lying half-way along the submarine ridge running northwards from Scotland to Iceland, the Faeroes were readily found by adventurous sailors on passage between western Norway and the Scottish islands. The Irish geographer Dicuil, writing in 825, knew that Celtic monks had abandoned their habitations there about the turn of the century on account of the Vikings – a statement which seems to imply that the latter came as unwelcome settlers rather than as sporadic raiders. 'Thor's harbour' or Torshavn, the present-day capital, became the assembly-place of the new inhabitants, and finds of Norwegian soapstone vessels attest their dependence on west Norway for necessary imports. It is likely that sheep grazing had been introduced by the monks, in which case wool and rough woollen cloth may have been exported from a very early date as well as down and seabirds' feathers. Otherwise, the history of this tiny, outlying population during the pagan period is untraced, and probably untraceable.

In contrast, the settlement of Iceland is more fully recorded than any other of the early medieval migrations of peoples. A find of Roman copper coins suggests that the island had chance visitors before the Irish 'fathers', whose presence is indicated by half a dozen *papa* place-names; these monks were virtually hermits, who withdrew or at all events disappeared soon after the first Scandinavians arrived, leaving behind books and other paraphernalia of their religion. A Swede from Denmark is said to have sighted it first and a settler in the Faeroes, likewise blown off course, to have called the unknown land 'Iceland'; but it was certainly from west Norway that the first permanent settlers came in or about the year 874. The twelfth-century 'Book of the Land-taking' (*Landnámabók*) gives about 400 names of individuals, showing that many turbulent characters were glad to leave west Norway, at all events after the petty Viking chiefs had been defeated at Hafrsfiord, whilst Norsemen from the Scottish islands, Ireland and Man also took part in the venture. Besides their families, cattle and household possessions, the colonists brought with them many slaves and more or less servile dependants, so that the total Celtic element in the Icelandic population may have been nearer one-half than the one-seventh who figure among the land-takers. Many of the properties recorded in the Book were of great size, to allow full scope for fishing and fowling alongside the herding of sheep and cattle.

Although a few settlers from outside Norway were Christians, the ancient gods had accompanied the exodus, and their worship was the concern of the chief man in each locality, called its *godi* – a word derived from 'god'. No place of sacrifice has been certainly identified, possibly because they were built of timber, but there was much killing of animals in honour of Thor (as in west Norway), and in time of emergency human offerings as well. At least two factors tended, however, to loosen the grip of the old faith. The people were too widely dispersed for ready attendance at any ceremonial, whilst their remoteness from any foreign enemy and the small part which cereal crops played in the island's economy (even at that early period) made it a less pressing duty to placate the divinities of war and fertility.

The thirty-six (later thirty-nine) *godar* also exercised as chieftains whatever secular authority these scattered communities at first found necessary; only two district *things* are known to have been set up in accordance with Norwegian practice. But after the passage of half a century, which had brought the population up to about 20,000 souls, it was thought desirable to organise a *thing* for the whole commonwealth and at the same time to regularise the use of Norwegian customary law by reference to the decisions taken at the *lagthing* of western Norway, from where so many of them had come. An emissary was accordingly sent over, on whose return the *Althing* was established as an annual assembly which every free man on the island was entitled to attend. From the outset (*c.* 930) this ancient parliament, whose history is almost continuous down to our own day, had a 'lawman' as president, who recited a portion of the law at each session, the assembly being regarded as a judicial body which added to the laws when necessary. In addition, the period of its meeting every summer had a great influence in promoting the growth of a distinctive culture among a widely scattered people. After the first generation the island was divided into Quarters, each having its own court, where better knowledge of the facts in any local dispute made it easier to arrive at a decision. But both the judicial and the legislative work were regularly entrusted to select groups of members, who were in effect nominees of the *godar*. Litigation abounded, but when his rights had been determined it was left to the individual to obtain redress. As early as the 960s a *godi* might gather as many as 1,500 men to support him in a feud; the Icelander whose family was not powerful therefore put his land and claims under the protection of one that was.

In a society riddled by family feuds which resemble Sicilian vendettas, it is scarcely surprising that the greatest historical achievement recorded in the saga literature should start with a banishment for murder. Greenland was indeed discovered in the early years of the Icelandic settlement, when their ships were storm-driven far away to the westward. But the true pioneer was Eric the Red, who had been exiled from Norway to Iceland on account of a murder and banished from Iceland for three years on account of more murders. He spent this period in exploring the less inaccessible west coast of the huge and barren tract of country to which he gave a propagandist name. Then in 985 or 986 he set out a second time, in charge of twenty-five ships loaded with settler families, cattle, and equipment, of which fourteen duly completed the hazardous voyage.

The venture grew into two main communities, eastern and western, the former situated not far beyond Cape Farewell, the latter just below the Arctic Circle and the entrance to Davis Strait, in the vicinity of the modern capital of Godthaab. Pasture land in the inner reaches of the fiords enabled the so-called eastern settlement to grow to 190 farms, the western had only 90; the total population may have reached 3,000. They were linked with Iceland and Norway mainly by ties of trade, exchanging furs and walrus products for corn and other luxuries. In the summer months seal-hunting took them far up the Davis Strait, which they crossed to explore the other side; their need of timber would be a strong incentive, and the American shore had been sighted by vessels blown off course on their way from Norway to the Greenland settlement. Accordingly, about the year 1000 Eric's son, Leif, sailed to 'Markland', which may be identified as some wooded region on the coast of Labrador and was probably visited from time to time down to the fourteenth century. Leif continued south to 'Vinland', where grapes and corn were found growing wild, but attempts to settle were defeated after several years by hostile natives. Although the existence of 'Vinland' was known to Adam of Bremen in the 1070s and later to the writers of the sagas, the first satisfactory identification was made as recently as 1960 (see p. 395) – and it remains possible that a landfall by Norsemen in New England (about which there has been much speculation) may eventually be substantiated.*

THE FIRST CHRISTIAN MISSIONS

When the second century of Viking activity drew to its close, neither the crystallisation of the homelands into three kingdoms nor the creation of the distant Atlantic settlements had yet occasioned any decisive advance of Christian civilisation into Scandinavia. Peaceful contacts had, indeed, brought about many individual conversions, especially among traders, who often found it convenient to take the first step towards baptism, the *prima signatio*, as an assurance of their trustworthiness. Wherever Vikings became settlers, as in many parts of the British Isles, the higher religion soon prevailed. But it was not until the 980s that the new series of Viking expeditions, referred to previously (see p. 20), appears to have given a direct stimulus to missionary work as a form of self-protection.

Denmark is to some extent an exception. Encouraged perhaps by the knowledge that it had for a short time accepted a Christian ruler at the beginning of the century, Louis the Pious and the Papacy set up a Danish mission from Holstein in 822. Ansgar, a monk from the famous Benedictine house at Corbie in Picardy, built the first church in Slesvig, twice visited Birka to preach among the Swedes, and was made archbishop of Hamburg, the see being transferred to Bremen after the Viking onslaught in 845. His death followed twenty years later, but a Scandinavian mission on a very modest scale survived until 888 in the hands of Ansgar's successor and biographer, Rimbert. The ultimate failure of the venture seems to be attributable mainly to the weakening of the Frankish power. Three-quarters of a century elapsed before the revival of the Empire under the first German emperors gave Harald Gormsson cause to fear

---

* Excavations on the site of a Greenland farm, which belonged to the leader of one of the 'Vinland' expeditions, have yielded a piece of anthracite coal: Rhode Island, where it could have been picked up on the surface and close to the shore, is suggested as the likely place of origin of a lustrous material unobtainable in Greenland.[13]

that his paganism might be made a pretext for foreign intervention. A priest who endured the ordeal by fire then provided the occasion for his conversion, and a famous runic inscription records that he 'made the Danes Christian'. This event in *c.* 965 did not, however, completely settle the issue, since within twenty years the throne was usurped by his son, Sweyn Forkbeard, who was himself a pagan; but Sweyn tolerated missionary bishops, so long as their activities were based on England rather than the Hamburg-Bremen archbishopric, which he suspected of interfering in secular affairs.

In Norway the early events are less well known, but in all probability the outright failure of the missionaries who accompanied the youthful King Haakon on his return from Wessex was followed by some unrecorded penetration of Christianity into the eastern districts, where Danish influence was strongest. The sequel in any case was a revival of the pagan cults under Earl Haakon (see p. 38), who in the last quarter of the tenth century based his rule upon the staunchly heathen Tröndelag. The skalds rejoiced accordingly:

> Now as afore earth burgeoneth,
> Since once again a generous lord
> Lets shield-bearing men wend their way
> With glad hearts to holy places.[14]

If Norway, in spite of much intercourse with the Danelaw and other areas in which their kinsmen had gradually adopted the religion of their neighbours, remained a predominantly heathen country, it is safe to conclude that the infiltration of Christianity into Sweden had been even slower. For Swedish interests were still directed mainly towards the east, where until far-off Byzantium was reached the contacts were with heathen societies. In 988 a Danish chieftain, who had helped to convert his fellow countrymen of the islands, was consecrated by Bremen as a missionary bishop for the Swedes. No Swedish king, however, was converted until 1008, whereupon the reign of Olof Skötkonung marked the beginning of a conflict over religion which was not finally settled among the Swedes for another hundred years – and lasted still longer among their Finnish neighbours. Nevertheless, the year 1016, when (as already related) the Danish prince Cnut ascended the throne of England, can be seen in retrospect to mark the beginning of the transformation of Viking Scandinavia into an outpost of the Christendom it had so long assailed.

Chapter 3

Outpost of Christendom

INTRODUCTION: THE DYNASTIES, 1016–1319

A new era in the history of the north was now to be inaugurated by Denmark, which supplied 'the first viking leader to be admitted into the civilised fraternity of Christian kings'.[1] The Scandinavian empire of Cnut the Great proved, however, to be no more than a brief prelude to a period of three centuries during which the most obvious feature of Scandinavian history is the establishment of three Christian but wholly separate and often mutually hostile kingdoms. That process followed a common pattern. Once the conversion was completed, the institutions of monarchy grew up in a constant interplay with the power of the church; each state enjoyed a period or periods of expansion beyond its original frontiers; and all came to possess social and cultural characteristics which to some extent distinguished them as a group from the rest of medieval Christendom. But this common pattern of events may be easier to trace with the help of a bare résumé of the dynastic history, which is most sedulously recorded by contemporary chroniclers.

In Denmark the first independent king after Cnut was his nephew, Sweyn Estridsen, who was succeeded by five of his sons in turn, including another Cnut ('the Saint'). But in 1131 family rivalries provoked the murder of a possible claimant to the throne in the next generation, by name Cnut Lavard; this led to nearly thirty years of civil war, in the course of which weak kings paid homage to German Emperors and German knights were brought in to fight Danish battles. Valdemar the Great and his two sons, Cnut VI and Valdemar II, then presided over the most memorable period of Danish expansion along the Baltic. This was followed by a marked decline during the short reigns of the three sons of the second Valdemar and that of his grandson, Eric Klipping, who in 1282 conceded a Great Charter to the barons. His murder was followed, however, by the banishment of some baronial leaders and an attempt to return to an expansionist policy under his son, Eric Menved, whose long reign (1286–1319) ended in failure.

In Norway Cnut's death and the dissolution of his empire was followed by a revival of unity and strength under Magnus I and Harald

Hardrada, the son and half-brother of Cnut's defeated opponent, Olav the Saint. After Harald's death at Stamfordbridge in 1066, his descendants ruled Norway until 1130, when the death of Sigurd the Crusader in-augurated a period of almost a century during which civil war was a dominant feature of Norwegian life, even under so brilliant a ruler as Sverre. But an 'age of greatness' was ushered in by his grandson, Haakon IV, whose long reign (1217–63) was marked by the annexation of Iceland and Greenland. Haakon's son Magnus was an eminent legislator, on whom the name of 'Lawmender' (*Lagaböter*) was posthumously bestowed; and although the elder of Haakon's two grandsons, named Eric, was forced by the nobles into a quarrel with the church, the younger (Haakon V, 1299–1319) restored the authority of the Norwegian crown in every respect – but failed to provide a male heir of full age to wear it after him.

In Sweden, where Olof Skötkonung was the first known 'king of Swedes *and* Goths', the eleventh century was a further age of internal conflict. After the extinction of the Svear line in the 1060s a dynasty from Västergötland held sway for some sixty years, and when this too became extinct a king named Sverker transferred the centre of power to his native province of Östergötland. About the year 1156 his murder brought an Eric, later 'the Saint', briefly to the throne and gave rise to a century-long feud, during which the kingship was grasped by Sverkers and Erics in alternation. A more important event, however, was the rise of the great earls, which culminated in the marriage of Earl Birger to a sister of the last of the Eric line and the accession of his son Valdemar in 1250 as the first of the so-called 'Folkung' kings. During much of his elder son's reign Earl Birger was a powerful figure behind the throne, which within a few years of his death in 1266 was usurped by the Earl's younger son Magnus. He figured as a strong organiser both of the monarchy and of the privileged classes which served it, albeit that his surname of Ladulås ('Barnlock') suggests that he was also the protector of the peasants against unjust food levies by their lords. Magnus died in 1290, and, during the minority of his ten-year-old son Birger, the Marshal, Torgils Knutsson, continued the policy of expansion into Finnish ter-ritory which had been established by the great earl. But in 1306 his younger brothers persuaded King Birger to make away with the Marshal as an 'over-mighty subject' – the very position to which they themselves aspired. By 1319 they too had been made away with, in the course of a bitter fraternal struggle which cost Birger his throne.

THE ERA OF CONVERSION

Cnut the Great became king of England in 1016, succeeded his elder brother as king of Denmark in 1018, and soon afterwards began his ultimately victorious conflict with Olaf of Norway, later the Saint, and his Swedish allies. But the most spectacular indication that a new era had dawned in Scandinavian affairs was the scene at the coronation of Conrad IV as Holy Roman Emperor on Easter Day 1027, when the former Viking chief walked in procession at his side. The motives for Cnut's famous pilgrimage to Rome included, indeed, his need to expiate the murder of a brother-in-law before the cathedral altar at Roskilde, yet it was as a loyal son of the Church that Cnut built up the second-largest European power bloc of the time.

At its fullest extent Cnut's North Sea realm included England, Denmark, and Norway. He also held a number of outposts on the south shore of the Baltic, where he engaged his English subjects in battle against the Wends, and his letters and coins asserted a claim to be 'King of part of Sweden' or 'King of the Svear'.[2] If he had not died when he was barely forty years of age, so puissant a monarch would almost certainly have left a lasting imprint on Scandinavia as a whole, instead of completing no more than the conversion of his Danish subjects. Once his English kingdom was reduced to order, Cnut ceased to tolerate any survival of pagan practices among the housecarls he had brought from Denmark, and the Church in England, to which he gave generous endowments, sent clergy to complete the missionary work still needed in Denmark itself, though for political reasons the bishops continued to be consecrated by the see of Bremen. At Cnut's death heathenism survived only in obscurity and chiefly in Skåne, across which the mission front was advancing into Sweden.

In the meantime Norway too had become a Christian land under a Christian ruler, but the result was achieved by a complicated process which owed nothing to King Cnut. The king who set it in motion was Olav Tryggvesson, a formidable Viking chief and sometime ally of Cnut's pagan father, who was confirmed in England shortly before he sailed for Norway in 995 to challenge the position of the heathen Earl Haakon of Lade. The earl had lost his popularity with his subjects and was opportunely murdered by a slave, whereupon Olav's descent from Harald Fairhair helped to secure his acceptance as king, except in the Danish-controlled south-eastern districts. He founded Nidaros (more familiar under its modern name of Trondheim) as his base, and sailed along the coast, exacting submission and conversion from chieftains and *lagthings*. Since the penalties for refusal included mutilation or death, the mission conducted by a handful of clergy must have enjoyed considerable success as far as the king's arm and time reached. But after a reign of only five years Olav Tryggvesson was killed in battle at Svolder, somewhere south of the Sound, by an alliance in which the prime movers were the sons of the dead Earl Haakon; they then ruled Norway under a restored Danish suzerainty – a weak position, which would discourage them from interfering with their subjects in matters of religion.

In the summer of 1015, when Cnut was too busy with the reconquest of England after his father's death to defend the position of his subordinate earls in Norway, a second Olav set sail from England. He had only two shiploads of fighting men, but the future saint had fought an average of two battles a year since the age of twelve (as the Skalds admiringly relate), and as a descendant of Harald Fairhair he quickly won recognition in the eastern valley district where he was born. The Lade earls were decisively defeated in a battle at the mouth of the Oslofiord, after which Olav reigned for ten years as the first king of all Norway, east, west, and north. When every allowance is made for the accretion of pious legend he remains a less ungentle figure than his namesake, and this Olav had a deeper knowledge of Christian society, having fought latterly on the side of King Ethelred, whom he had accompanied into exile in Normandy, where he was himself baptised. In 1024 Olav induced a *lagthing* on the west coast to make the first formal adoption of a system of church law, which he had drawn up in agreement with his English adviser, Bishop Grimkell, and which must greatly have strengthened the hands of his missionaries, who are thought to have come chiefly from the Danelaw.

Cnut, however, was biding his time, whilst he maintained at his court in England not only a young Earl Haakon of Lade but an increasing number of malcontents from Norway, to whom his superior power and wealth would be a natural attraction. At first the Swedish king helped Olav to stave off attack by carrying the war into Skåne, but he was eventually driven back into Norway, and in 1028 a combination between Cnut's fleet in the south and a landing by the earl in the Tröndelag compelled Olav to flee overland to Sweden and to Russia, where his Swedish wife had a half-sister married to the Grand Duke Jaroslav. But he was soon tempted to return because the drowning of Cnut's viceroy, Earl Haakon, in the Pentland Firth created a kind of interregnum in Norway before the arrival of Cnut's ten-year-old son Sweyn to act as king under the guidance of his English mother, Aelfgifu of Northampton. Olav brought with him a nucleus of Swedes and such Norwegians as he could gather on his passage through the mountains into the Tröndelag; some more men joined him, together with his half-brother Harald, from his native region in the east; and since the battle was fought inland, which was highly unusual in this land of ship-borne forces, the king's experience of warfare abroad gave him some advantage. Perhaps the royal army was greatly inferior in numbers to the peasantry of the Tröndelag and the men whom disaffected chieftains had brought from some other areas; all that is certain is that the battle of Stiklestad (29 July 1030) ended in the death of King Olav and the rout of his supporters.

The participants on both sides included Christians and heathen, though the sagas claim that Olav's battle-cry was 'Christ's men': be that as it may, what he had lost in life he won in death. Aelfgifu and her son made themselves hated by imposing new taxes in a time of widespread dearth, and the presence of the English queen perhaps caused the people to be more keenly aware that Sweyn too was a foreigner. It is also conceivable that as fellow Christians some of them found it difficult to offer opposition to the sanctification of their defeated enemy. Whatever the full explanation in terms of mass psychology, only twelve months after the battle Grimkell was able to have the king's battered remains ceremoniously reinterred at Trondheim, where they wrought the miracles appropriate to sainthood. Within five years Olav's young son Magnus was brought back from Russia to replace Sweyn, and although it was the collapse of Cnut's empire after his death later in the same year (1035) which prevented an immediate Danish challenge, the memory of Saint Olav was by now completing the conversion of Norway.

Much less is known about the impact of the Swedish kings. Olof Skötkonung or 'tax king', who (as we have seen) is believed to have been the first monarch to rule both Svear and Götar, had been baptised in Västergötland, which was within easy reach of Denmark, and the first bishop's see was established in that province. But the monarchy remained weak, and as late as 1081–5 the Svear temporarily drove out a king who repeated Olof's refusal to take part in the nine-yearly celebrations at the great pagan sanctuary in Uppsala. By the end of the century the temple had been finally destroyed, but the obstinacy of the struggle against heathenism among the Svear was such that, out of a total of six missionary dioceses known to have existed about 1120, no fewer than four were concentrated in Svealand. Only thirty-seven years later the Swedish Church is supposed to have become so firmly established that a crusade was launched for the conversion of Finland. King Eric, who led the crusade, and the English-born bishop Henry of Uppsala who helped him, have achieved later renown as the patron saints of Sweden and Finland respectively; but in the absence of any contemporary report it seems more likely that what took place in 1157 was primarily a punitive expedition.

Our complete ignorance as to when and how Christianity achieved its first tentative lodgements among the widely scattered Finns is a reminder that, in the case of all the Scandinavian peoples, the new faith spread through many channels. Whilst the attitude of royalty attracts most attention, the conversion of a particular chieftain or *thing* by some forceful missionary might influence a whole district, irrespective of the view held by a king in the distance. Certainly the mission churches owed their greatest debt to individual clergy who faced the hardships and risks of what was often an unknown land – the travelling bishops (*episcopi vagantes*), the priests who attached themselves initially to royal courts, and the brethren from far-off monasteries, such as Westphalian Herford or Evesham in the heart of England. Some individual names are indeed preserved, especially if they bore upon the rivalry between the Anglo-Saxon church province and that of Hamburg-Bremen, which had charge of the mission to the north and also possessed an indefatigable champion and chronicler in Adam of Bremen, who visited the Danish court during the reign of Sweyn Estridsen. But in general the work of the pioneers sank into oblivion as the missionary church gave place to the folk church – a transition which is most clearly visible in Iceland.

The first missionary entered the island in company with a native convert he had made in Germany, and was followed about ten years later by others sent by Olav Tryggvesson, who was then imposing the new faith by violent methods in Norway. As many of the Icelanders proved obdurate, the Norwegian king sent another missionary in the summer of the year 1000 whilst retaining four hostages in Norway, one for each Quarter. The Althing was then prompted by its Lawman – who was himself a heathen – to avoid the prospect of civil war and/or Norwegian intervention by formally adopting Christianity as the religion of their island, subject to the right of any individual to offer heathen sacrifice in private and to continue the exposure of unwanted children. Churches were then erected sporadically as the *godar* saw fit, but about twenty years passed before the influence of Olav the Saint, who sent one of his English bishops, Bernard 'the Book-wise', and materials for a public church near the Althing's place of assembly, caused heathen practices to be finally abolished. The Church then became fully integrated in the Icelandic social system, with the *godar* as patrons of livings and the choice of bishops ratified by the Althing. In 1056 Isleifr Gizurarson, who had been sent for theological training to the monastic school in Herford by his father, a chieftain who 'did everything in his power to strengthen Christianity',[3] reached the episcopate, which thereafter was held commonly by scions of the bigger landowning families. This partly explains the fact that Iceland in 1097 was the first Scandinavian country to introduce tithes – half of which went to the landowner who maintained the church – and the last to pay heed to papal demands for the celibacy of the clergy.

In general, the folk churches of the Scandinavians were slow to bring private life into conformity with the new ideas, as the church sections of their earliest provincial lawbooks clearly show. Some types of Nature and ancestor worship lingered on until the Reformation and even beyond; the nomadic Lapps, whose conversion was not seriously attempted before the sixteenth century, are only the extreme illustration of the tendency for physical remoteness to mean spiritual isolation. In Iceland, where building material of any kind was hard to come by, the chieftains were encouraged to erect churches on their estates by the belief that the number of persons they could contain was the number that would enter the kingdom of heaven. Elsewhere the timber churches rose quickly in the forest clearings, and in Norway (where, even in the eleventh century, the wood was prudently laid on a stone foundation) a score of the more elaborate specimens of *Stavkirke* still survive. Their intricately beautiful construction astonishes the beholder, but the resemblance to an upturned keel, the lavish display of dragon heads and, above all, the portals carved with scenes from heathen mythology remind us forcibly that in distant places the traditions of the old pagan world were slow to disappear. By 1100, however, austere churches of stone had begun to figure in the Scandinavian landscape, especially in Denmark, and the first permanent cathedrals arose – at Lund in sandstone, at Ribe (south-west Jutland) in tufa imported from the valley of the Rhône. These bore silent witness to an increasing conformity with the ecclesiastical practices of lands nearer Rome.

CHURCH AND KING

The Church proved to be a great organising and unifying force in medieval Scandinavia, imposing a system derived from the usages of the Roman Empire upon peoples who had never borne its yoke. Even the struggle between the Hildebrandine papacy and the German emperors, which wrought such havoc elsewhere, served to strengthen the ecclesiastical framework in northern Europe. In 1103, when Bremen had taken sides with an antipope, the Danish see of Lund was given metropolitan status in relation to all the northern countries and, although Norway and Sweden were restored to Bremen for one decade, Lund's supremacy was not permanently reduced for half a century. When Nicholas Breakspear (later Pope Hadrian IV) was sent north as papal legate in 1152 to rid the Norwegian and Swedish churches of lay interference, the result was the creation of a geographically much larger archbishopric of Trondheim, comprising Norway, Iceland and other territories colonised by Norwegians overseas; these included two dioceses (Orkney, and Sodor and Man) previously placed under the English primate at York. Breakspear judged the Swedish church to be still too weak to dispense with Danish control, but only twelve years later, when the Danish monarchy was in disfavour at Rome because of support given to an antipope, the Swedish Crown obtained a practically independent status for the new archdiocese of Uppsala. The loyalty of the archbishop of Lund was, however, rewarded by continuing his formal position as the primate by whom the Swedish archbishop was to be consecrated. Finally, in 1216 the pope placed under Uppsala the Finnish missionary bishopric, to which the Danes at that time laid claim, and the visit of a papal legate, William of Sabina, in 1247–8 resulted in the full establishment of a Swedish church province, with cathedral chapters to elect its bishops.

Since northern Europe contained no pattern of ancient Roman cities – and indeed few cities of any kind – the early sees were variously located. Denmark possessed nine by about 1060, of which three had been set up in trade centres, three on royal domains, two at the meeting-places of provincial *things*, and one at a spot marked only by the hermitage of a local saint. One of the earliest Norwegian bishoprics was founded on an island, where certain sacred remains – allegedly including those of an Irish princess (St Sunniva) – had been brought to light while the redoubtable Olav Tryggvesson was evangelising in the district. Eventually, however, they were all located in trade centres – four at ports, the fifth and last (Hamar, 1152) on the site of an important inland fair. Of the six early Swedish bishoprics one was at Sigtuna, the trade centre which had replaced Birka, another at Eskilstuna, the burial-place of a martyred English bishop Eskil. These and other sees were soon moved – from Sigtuna for example, to the neighbourhood of Uppsala, where in the later Middle Ages the great cathedral built over the bones of the national saint Eric proclaimed the wealth and magnificence of the largest northern see. Meanwhile, the Bishop for Finland had settled at Åbo,* which was then its only town.

The original Icelandic bishopric at Skálholt and that at Hólar, which was set up in 1106 to serve the most populous northern Quarter, were located on farm estates which provided part of the episcopal revenues. This was also the case with two of the other four outlying dioceses under Trondheim, namely the Faeroes, where the population was never rich enough to complete its cathedral, and Greenland, where a very modest cathedral was built in the eastern settlement, to which Leif had originally brought the new faith at Olav Tryggvesson's behest. The Orkneys and Man had their respective cathedrals in the two small ports of Kirkwall and Peel, the former dignified by its dedication to St Magnus, an Orkney earl whose pious death is extolled in the sagas.

In Scandinavia, as in England, the growth of parishes is less easily traced than that of dioceses. In Denmark it was certainly rapid, for figures given by Adam of Bremen suggest that by the 1070s half as many churches had already been established as existed at the time of the Reformation. In Iceland, on the other hand, the official introduction of Christianity was followed, as we have seen, by a period of uncertain length during which the supply of churches depended entirely on the readiness of chieftains to provide a building and employ a priest – whose status was often little better than a thrall's. In Norway, where the Anglo-Saxon influence was strongest, it is possible to discern a threefold pattern – a head church for the *fylke* or shire, a district church or minster, and a little privately owned church which became the cult centre of its immediate neighbourhood; each of these had had some counterpart in the pagan system of worship. Still less is known about the origin of the Swedish or Finnish parish, but it seems likely that the sacred grove of the heathen religion was often the basis, whilst in other cases the geographical position of a church automatically created its circle of parishioners.

However it was formed, the parish was the organisation which brought the new cult into the life of the individual. He was most keenly aware of the outward forms, such as the receiving of the sacraments and the observance of holy days, in which were incorporated the ancient communal beer-feasts: the beer was now to be blessed, and the first cup drunk 'in

* Generally known in recent times by its Finnish name of Turku.

honour of Christ and the Blessed Virgin for good years and peace'.[4] At the same time the teachings of the Church slowly eroded the Viking way of life in such matters as polygamy, the blood feud, the exposure of unwanted infants, and the holding of slaves. The parishioner also found the Church a drain upon his economic resources, especially through the introduction of tithe upon both crops and livestock and the collection at midsummer of the small cash payment known as Peter's Pence. All this was more stringently administered as the priest was brought more fully under the supervision of the bishop. He was normally a peasant singled out from among his fellow peasants, but his training and ordination were under episcopal control, which meant that the ideas of Church reformers seeped through eventually to all levels of lay society.

History has more to say about the relations between bishops, especially archbishops, and kings. In northern Europe as a whole, the papal policy was to support monarchy as the secular institution through which Rome's influence could be most effectively exercised, whilst in the case of Denmark the wish to offset the power of the Holy Roman Emperors provided an additional incentive. The frequent civil wars gave special opportunities of intervention against a system of royal elections, which paid little heed to primogeniture and none to legitimate birth, and in favour of any measure to enhance the dignity of the royal office.

When the Norwegian king Olav after his death at Stiklestad became a saint by popular acclaim and was revered throughout the north, it was natural that the papacy should favour canonisation to strengthen the Scandinavian monarchies. In 1101 Denmark was accorded a royal saint in the person of Cnut II, a grand-nephew of Cnut the Great. The English monks installed at Odense made much of the fact that he had been killed before the high altar of the church they tended; public opinion, however, remembered this Cnut as an oppressive ruler, who had provoked the rebellion in which he met his end, and refused to make a nationally honoured saint of him. In 1170 Denmark acquired a second royal saint in the person of Cnut Lavard (see p. 36), the father of the reigning king Valdemar I, the translation of whose remains was attended by the Swedish archbishop and the bishop of Oslo. Eric of Sweden (see p. 40) was allegedly slain while attending mass by a Danish pretender to his throne, but a century elapsed before he was recognised as a patron saint at Uppsala, the supposed scene of his death. St Henry, who had accompanied St Eric to Finland, is a more real figure: his martyrdom, which according to one version was the work of a convert who resented the material burdens imposed by the new religion, might plausibly have followed upon the royal expedition, and his position as the Apostle of Finland was accepted within a generation by the Church at Åbo.

A more definite landmark in the growth of ecclesiastical support for monarchy was the introduction of a coronation rite presided over by the archbishop, which conferred a new sanctity upon the crown in return for concessions by its wearer. The ceremony was brought to the north in 1164, when a child king of Norway, Magnus V, was crowned in Bergen by Archbishop Eystein, the price being a solemn recognition of St Olav as 'Eternal King' of a realm which at the end of each reign was in theory to revert to ecclesiastical custody. The earliest Danish coronation followed only seven years later, when Valdemar the Great had his son crowned during his own lifetime in order to render the kingship less clearly elective. The result was a series of revolts among the nobility, which continued until the king's friend Absalon (see p. 51) became archbishop in 1177.

In the meantime an inveterate struggle had commenced in Norway under Sverre, a claimant who emerged from obscurity in the Faeroes to usurp the throne and drive Eystein into exile in England. Returning in 1187 under a kind of truce, Eystein was able to devote his last years to the introduction in his own cathedral of the gothic style he had learnt to admire at Canterbury. But his successor refused to crown Sverre and fled to Denmark, where he received papal support, and Innocent III eventually laid Sverre and his followers under an interdict. In the meantime, however, the king had exacted his coronation by the archbishop's suffragans, whilst his rights were skilfully defended in 'a discourse against the bishops'; as a former candidate for the priesthood and a political tactician of the first order, Sverre may well have been the actual author. Yet civil strife did not end with his death in 1202 or even with the opening of the reign of his grandson, Haakon IV, in 1217. An illegitimate child aged thirteen, he was at first overshadowed by his ambitious guardian and rival for the throne, Earl Skule, and thirty years passed before he was crowned with great pomp by William of Sabina, the legate who also acted as a special representative of the pope in Sweden. But when King Haakon, like the Danish Valdemar, later arranged for his son to be crowned while he was still alive, he consolidated the position of the Norwegian monarchy by first inducing the regional *things* in 1260 to approve a fixed order of succession.

The earliest recorded coronation in Sweden took place in 1210, but neither the Danish nor the Swedish kings were able to introduce the hereditary principle as in Norway, so the system of royal elections long continued to weaken the monarchy and strengthen the magnates, both lay and ecclesiastical. In the course of the thirteenth century the growth of feudal influences brought the position of the bishops closer to that of the secular lords; arguing that the spiritual was inherently superior to the temporal sword, they increased their claims as regards rights of jurisdiction, patronage, and especially freedom from taxation. In Denmark the struggle continued at intervals for fifty years; two archbishops were flung into prison, and the realm was twice placed under interdict; but the final result was a compromise, the Church agreeing to pay taxes but retaining all its other privileges. In Norway King Magnus 'Lawmender' signed a concordat at Tönsberg in 1277, which was interpreted by the churchmen as giving them all they claimed, even in matters of taxation. But during the minority of his son, Eric the so-called 'Priest-hater', the barons insisted on a narrower interpretation of the financial clauses of the concordat, which in other respects governed the relations of Church and King for the rest of the middle ages. In Sweden the alliance of Church and King was very briefly interrupted, when Torgils Knutsson (see p. 37) reduced ecclesiastical privileges in accordance with the wishes of the secular lords. But after he had been executed in 1306, nominally as an enemy of the Church, its position was much the same as in the other two kingdoms.

The general status of the clergy in Scandinavian society was based, as elsewhere, on revenues derived from the extensive ownership of land and many accompanying privileges. But in return they were the class that contributed most to the civilised arts, through which that society slowly emerged from its primitive condition. The replacement of runic writing by the Latin script stimulated the keeping of records of all kinds as well as the growth of literature. Monastic granges began the slow process of adapting southern improvements in agriculture, such as the three-field system of tillage, to the harsher conditions of the north. More generally, a kind of internationalism was fostered among these isolated peoples by the Benedictine and Cistercian monks and Augustinian canons, who set up their houses in many parts of Scandinavia: for they retained an obligatory contact with their mother house and the headquarters of their order, however distant. There were even two monasteries established in Greenland. In the thirteenth century, too, the arrival of the friars was specially important for the lower classes, whom they influenced directly both in the towns, where their convents were originally established in the poorer quarters, and in the surrounding country districts, where they came to preach and beg. In Denmark, for example, the Dominicans arrived in 1223 and set up their first house in Lund, the ecclesiastical capital; the Franciscans, who entered the country a decade later, spread to eleven towns in nine years. In Finland the Dominican friary at Åbo did much to consolidate the conversion, and everywhere the friars formed a link with the rising universities, especially Paris.

EXPANSIONIST POLICIES

The intention that lay behind Cnut the Great's empire-building is much disputed: perhaps the saga writer was justified in his comment, 'He was a man of great luck in everything connected with power.'[5] Two things are certain. One is that the empire did not outlast its founder: within seven years all his three sons were dead, and the English sent overseas for Ethelred's son, the future Edward the Confessor, whilst the body of Harthacnut, the last Danish king of England, still lay in London awaiting burial. The other is that the example of Cnut's empire was not forgotten.

As late as the time of the Hundred Years War there was talk of reviving the claim of his descendants to the English throne; more seriously, Cnut's achievement stimulated expansionist policies in the Scandinavian states and the eventual revival of the thought of unity.

In 1042–7 the thrones of Denmark and Norway were temporarily reunited when Magnus succeeded Harthacnut in accordance with an agreement that the last survivor should be king of both realms, which the Danes had made in order to secure help against the Wends. Magnus drove the latter back to their homes on the south shore of the Baltic by a great victory at Lyrskog Heath in Slesvig (1043); but the Swedes, who did not want too strong a kingdom as their neighbour, encouraged the Danes to resist Norwegian rule. Magnus died young, and Harald Hardrada, the uncle who inherited his claims, was forced in the end to yield Denmark to the son of Cnut's sister, Sweyn Estridsen. He came to terms with the Swedes regarding the frontier of his provinces on the Scandinavian mainland, and in 1101 the Swedish-Norwegian frontier at the mouth of the river Göta was likewise fixed by a royal agreement, in which the Danish king may also have participated.

Thus the way was cleared for each of the three kingdoms to develop as an independent sovereignty. The three royal families intermarried, and from the outbreak of the civil wars, which in the twelfth century afflicted each country in turn, members of all three dynasties fished eagerly in troubled waters. Nevertheless it was not until the regrouping of powerful interests through the rise of a quasi-feudal nobility, which was mainly a fourteenth-century phenomenon, that the reunion of the north became a serious political objective.

In the meantime external ambitions were directed towards new enterprises which, though much less comprehensive than those of the immediate past, made some impact on the rest of Europe. At first, the claim to the English throne was naturally to the fore. Harald Hardrada, who had a formidable reputation as a soldier on account of his youthful exploits in the Byzantine emperor's Varangian Guard, nevertheless failed in two attempts; in 1058 an expedition under his elder son obtained help from the Welsh and the Norsemen of Dublin, but was somehow repelled,* and in 1066 the king himself received the surrender of York before he met his death at Stamfordbridge. Two Danish attempts followed under Cnut, later the Saint. In 1075 he crossed the North Sea with 200 ships of war, but the only definite result was a raid on York Minster. Ten years later he made an agreement with the king of Norway and the count of Flanders, news of which caused William the Conqueror to fetch French mercenaries to England and strip the coast of supplies. In the end, however, disputes with his own subjects kept Cnut's fleet in the

---

* An Irish chronicle describes a major naval project, frustrated only by the will of God.[6] The Anglo-Saxon Chronicle, less interested in the ways of Providence, says curtly: 'A naval armament came from Norway. It is tedious to tell how it all fell out.'[7]

Limfiord, where one of the great circular Viking camps had probably been for the last time brought into use.

By the end of the century the attention of the kings of Norway was turned in a more northerly direction, where Scotland offered an easier opponent than England and where in general the outward expansion of their people in the Viking Age encouraged them to claim if not an empire then at least an effective sphere of influence. Magnus Bareleg conducted a series of campaigns round the north coast of Scotland – where he presumably learnt to wear the kilt – and in Man, Dublin, and even Anglesey, where in 1098 he put to flight its Norman invaders. A modern English historian's description of this last event claims airily that Magnus 'happened to be cruising with his pirate fleet in the Irish Sea',[8] but Norway had in fact solid interests to assert in western waters. The ties of kinship and trade were strong, and the rulers of Viking kingdoms and earldoms, whose territory might lie closer to other states than to Norway, could nevertheless be brought into a condition of loose dependence by suitable demonstrations of Norwegian naval power, based on the *leidang*. Magnus died in 1103 whilst campaigning in northern Ireland, after which divided and disputed successions discouraged further action, although (as we have seen) the Norwegian archbishopric of Trondheim included all the regions settled by Norsemen outside England and Ireland. But when Sverre emerged temporarily victorious from the civil wars, he increased the royal powers and lands in both Orkney and Shetland as their punishment for having sided with his opponents; he also rounded off Norway's mainland territory by the inclusion of Jämtland,* which had formed part of the Swedish church province.

Sverre's grandson, Haakon IV, who reigned for nearly half a century, brought the Norwegian maritime empire likewise to its zenith. The importance of Bergen as a trade centre, which impressed the legate on his coronation visit in 1247,† strengthened the Norwegian hold on Shetland and the Faeroes: west Norway being their natural source of supply, the population of these island groups paid tax and accepted a royal governor or *sysselmann*. The Orkneys, Outer and Inner Hebrides, and Man, on the other hand, had a natural contact with the rulers of the Scottish mainland, who had already asserted their sovereignty over Norse settlers in Caithness and Sutherland; but at this time the petty kings and earls of the islands, whose affairs are known chiefly through the *Orkneyinga Saga*, still gravitated towards the Norwegian crown. For Haakon IV was seen to be strong enough to execute justice in Norway against the murderers of an Orkney earl, to protect the Hebrides against

* Though lying east of the watershed or Keel, Jämtland had its principal trade connections with the Tröndelag; Härjedal, a smaller, very mountainous district which adjoins it on the south, had passed under Norwegian control about a century earlier.

† The St Albans chronicler Matthew Paris, who visited Bergen one year after William of Sabina and was a great admirer of King Haakon, professed to have seen more than 200 vessels lying in the harbour.

the incursions of the Anglo-Norman lords of Galloway, and to send his archbishop to consecrate Peel cathedral on the Isle of Man – 16 miles from the Scottish and 30 from the English mainland.

The reign ended, however, with a measuring of forces, as a result of which the Norwegian empire gave up its weakest members. In order to protect the Hebrides from attack by the Scottish king, Alexander III, Haakon called out the *leidang* in Norway; no help came from the earl of Orkney, but he was able to muster a total of at least 120 ships, from which he organised forays on the Kintyre peninsula and at the mouth of the Clyde. Alexander, however, skilfully avoided any major conflict until the October weather made further amphibious operations impracticable, whereupon the losses incurred by a landing-party, which the Scots surprised at Largs, induced the aged king to break off the campaign. He died at Kirkwall before the Christmas of 1263, and three years later his successor prudently sold the Hebrides and Man to the Scottish crown at the treaty of Perth for a lump sum and a small annual payment. But the anticlimax at the close of the long reign must not be allowed to obscure the fact that across more distant seas Haakon IV had gained two major accessions of sovereignty for Norway, which went far to justify the description of the thirteenth century as its 'age of greatness'.[9]

The Icelandic commonwealth owed its independent status to geographical isolation rather than to any direct acknowledgement of its independence by Norwegian kings, whose subjects had led the settlement of the island. According to tradition, Harald Fairhair had planned to set up his earl there and the Danish king, Harald Gormsson, who was Norway's suzerain, intended at one time to send a punitive expedition. Moreover, the only treaty between the commonwealth and any foreign power, made with Olav the Saint *c.* 1022, gave his subjects full rights of citizenship on the island in return for rather smaller privileges accorded to Icelanders resident in Norway. Yet in practice the republic was left in peace for many generations; its primitive institutions of self-government proved sufficiently adaptable, as in the crisis over the introduction of Christianity, and the kings of Norway were in any case not strong enough to intervene effectively in its affairs.

But in the course of the twelfth century conditions on the island deteriorated. The bishops, supported by the see of Trondheim, became wealthier and more contentious, whilst the secular authority of the *godar* came to mean the activities of half a dozen clans which quarrelled persistently, bitterly and bloodily with each other. The economic situation also became more precarious. The profits of stock-keeping diminished, perhaps because the natural grazing-grounds were exhausted, and the Icelanders had no timber for shipbuilding, so they were increasingly dependent on the readiness of Norwegian merchants to undertake a voyage which usually involved wintering on the island. There they collected animal products, especially skins and rough woollen cloth,

Icelandic horses and the much-prized falcons, and even sulphur, which was in demand in western Europe by 1200 for the manufacture of Greek fire. In return they supplied meal, timber, honey, malt and other necessaries – in many cases on the basis of a triangular trade, involving the Norwegian ship in a passage to England or some other country outside Scandinavia. To safeguard this traffic from interruption, the Icelanders needed the king of Norway's help.

Haakon for his part seized upon the chieftains' feuds as an opportunity for intervention. When members of the leading families visited Norway, they were encouraged to further their private ambitions by joining the royal *hird*, but the pledge they then took enabled the king to put pressure on them to further his ambitions as well. The great saga writer Snorri (see p. 62), who belonged to the rising family of the Sturlungs and was several times lawman on the island, was one of those who entered into close relations with the royal court; on returning home, however, he opposed the royal policy and was murdered with the king's connivance. Six years later, matters came to a head on the occasion of King Haakon's coronation (1247), when the papal legate is said by the saga to have supported the subjection of the Icelanders on the ground that 'It was unreasonable that their country did not serve a king like every other country in the world.'[10] Bishops of Norwegian birth pressed the royal claims, as did certain lay emissaries of King Haakon, including the organiser of Snorri's death, Gizurr Thorvaldsson,* who after a long stay in Norway returned to the island in 1258 as Haakon's earl. Four years later the intrigues between the Sturlungs and their rivals, which since the third decade of the century had erupted in more frequent scenes of violence, ended in an exhausted submission to the Norwegian Crown. An agreement, commonly known as the Ancient Covenant (*Gamli Sátt-máli*), was approved at an incomplete gathering of the Althing and endorsed subsequently by other representative Icelanders. A tribute of 40 ells of wadmal (the native woollen cloth) was to be rendered annually by every taxpayer in token of allegiance. In return, the king undertook to maintain peace and the laws of Iceland, and to send from Norway six ships in each of the next two summers and thereafter as many as 'the king and our best men shall deem most serviceable for the country'.[11]

Royal officials replaced the *godar*, the legal functions of the Althing were remodelled on the pattern of the Norwegian judiciary, and a small poll-tax was exacted by the crown. But an attempt to call out the *leidang* in Iceland in 1286, when Norway needed support, proved a failure, as did a later attempt to increase taxation. On the other hand, by 1303 the Althing was complaining that exports were not matched by imports and

* 1209–68. The descendant of a long line of chieftains, including the first native-born bishop (see p. 41). He had 70 men on his side when Snorri was done to death in a cellar, but was not always so well protected. His daughter's wedding, planned to reconcile rival clans, was marred by the intervention of his enemies, who killed off 25 of the guests whilst the resourceful host lay hidden in a tub of whey.

that Norway was breaking a specific promise to make the necessary provision.

In Greenland, too, a bishop appointed from Norway was instructed in 1247 to act as intermediary for King Haakon. Nevertheless, fourteen years elapsed before he heard from Norwegians who had spent several winters there that its people offered submission in the form of a small payment to the crown for every homicide. Apart from the honour of owning so distant a possession, the king knew that the exchange of iron and timber for walrus tusks was highly profitable for his Norwegian subjects. Although by the end of the century elephant ivory was ousting the Greenland commodity from the European market, it seems clear that the monarchy still felt an obligation to send an annual ship to Greenland; probably one of the two ships which since 1273 had been promised as an annual provision for the Faeroes sailed on to the north-west.

In view of the seafaring interests of the Scandinavian peoples, the Crusades might be expected to figure largely in their history during these central medieval centuries. In 1110 a Norwegian king, Sigurd the Crusader, was indeed the first foreign potentate to visit the new Kingdom of Jerusalem, where his sixty ships took part in the siege of Sidon. Even earlier, a Danish king had died in Cyprus on his way to the Holy Land as a pilgrim, and many other individual Scandinavians made the same journey either on crusade or on pilgrimage; in 1148, for instance, an Orkney earl set out, who found time to sample the new Provençal love poetry on his way. But for Danes and Swedes at least, it was easier and far more profitable to go a-crusading across the Baltic Sea.

The heathen Wends from the Slav lands between the Elbe and the Oder soon recovered from their defeat at Lyrskog Heath in 1043; they again invaded south Jutland and their fleets dominated the southern Baltic. As late as 1157 they attacked Århus, north of the Belts, but in that year the Danish civil wars ended, so King Valdemar 'the Great' and Bishop Absalon* were free to launch a counter-attack. Unfortunately for Danish interests, their expansionist ventures had to compete with those of rival 'crusaders', for Saxon and other German settlers had long been advancing eastwards into Wendish territory. Valdemar's first operations against the Wends were perforce made in alliance with Henry the Lion, duke of Saxony – and ended in a quarrel over the booty. Nevertheless, the most important of Valdemar's twenty-two campaigns resulted in the destruction in 1169 of a great heathen temple at Arkona on the island of Rügen, the conversion of the islanders, and its subjection as a Danish fief.

Since Valdemar I also strengthened the Danevirke and otherwise

* 1128–1201. A childhood companion of the future King Valdemar, who became bishop of Roskilde (1158) and archbishop of Lund (1177); in 1167 he built a castle in the Sound, overlooking the haven which became Copenhagen. He is eulogised by Saxo (p. 61) to an extent which is nowadays held extravagant, but there is no doubt that he was an outstanding figure as a smiter of the heathen, a champion of the claims of the Church, and an adviser of kings in a period of substantial Danish achievements.

increased the fortifications of Denmark, his two sons had a strong base for further advances. Moreover, their position *vis-à-vis* the German princes was temporarily improved, first by the bringing of Henry the Lion under the control of the Empire, and then by the diversion of imperial attention to Italy; one clear sign of the improvement was the abandonment after half a century of the homage which Danish kings had begun to pay to the emperor in 1134, when they were weakened by the civil war. In 1184 Absalon, acting on behalf of the young king Cnut VI, defeated the prince of Pomerania in a naval battle off Stralsund and reduced to subjection the two Slav states of Pomerania and Mecklenburg.

In 1202, a year after Absalon's death, Cnut was succeeded by his more enterprising brother, Valdemar II, whom a later generation styled 'the Victorious'. He aimed at nothing less than the domination of the Baltic Sea, where trade was now rapidly expanding. While duke of Slesvig during his brother's reign, he had reacted against interference by the German count of Holstein by crossing the Eider to occupy his county, and had obtained the submission of Hamburg and the rising commercial centre of Lübeck. In 1215 his conquest of the entire coastline between Elbe and Oder was recognised by the emperor Frederick II, who was deeply embroiled in the affairs of Italy. Valdemar then turned his attention to the eastern shores of the Baltic, where German settlers in the vicinity of Riga had asked for help against the heathen Estonians who lay beyond. In June 1219 he made an unopposed landing on the south side of the Gulf of Finland and defeated the Estonians in a pitched battle at Lydanis – a crusading exploit to which tradition assigns the first use of a white cross on a red banner as the *Dannebrog* or national flag. The city of Tallinn or 'Danes' Town' was duly founded, but it is probable that lasting control of the rich trade route from Novgorod was never within reach. For the centuries-long German advance across the Slav lands was too firmly based upon surplus population, surplus capital (accumulating in the Hanse towns), and the natural resources of a much bigger hinterland than the Danes commanded.

A chance event precipitated the collapse of their Baltic empire. Whilst hunting on one of the smaller Danish islands, Valdemar and his eldest son were kidnapped by one of the dependent German princes, who then joined together to defeat an attempt to rescue the king by force. After two years in captivity (1223–5), Valdemar obtained his freedom by agreeing to sacrifice every conquest except Rügen and Estonia. The pope released him from his forced promise, but in 1227 his hopes of regaining a part of what he had lost were crushed by the German princes at Bornhöved in Holstein, when the people of Ditmarsh – one of his conquests in the west of that province – regained their liberty by deserting to the winning side. In the following decade the mediation of the pope enabled Denmark to rescue the districts of Tallinn and Narva from the Germans, who had overrun most of Estonia under the leadership of the Knights of the

Sword. Its Church therefore remained under the see of Lund, but the feudal masters of the Estonian countryside were Germans, as were the merchants of Tallinn.

Danes and Swedes were to some extent rivals in the struggle for territory along the Baltic trade routes. The Danes invaded Finland at least twice (1191, 1202) and with sufficient success for the pope to authorise their archbishop to give episcopal rank to a Danish cleric who was preaching among the Finns. A few years later the Swedes replied by an expedition to northern Estonia, where a heavy defeat did not prevent them from establishing some settlers on Ösel and other islands. Their attention was, however, concentrated mainly on Finland, to which their situation gave them an easier approach than either their Danish or their German rivals.

The conquest of Finland was the most notable Swedish achievement during the high Middle Ages; its political effects lasted until 1809, whilst its social and cultural effects have set a partly Scandinavian stamp upon the Finnish people down to the present day. The sequence of events is, however, extremely difficult to trace. The so-called crusade of St Eric in 1157 was certainly not the starting-point, for place-names show that Swedish colonists had been moving along the coast from the Åland Islands for at least a century before this, and heathen burial methods had fallen into disuse. Moreover, the fact that key religious words came into the Finnish language from Slav sources suggests that the conversion of the Russians around the year 1000 was followed quite rapidly by the dispatch of Orthodox missionaries into Finland from the Grand Duchy of Novgorod. Since Russian sources refer to early friction with the Swedes regarding the trade route, it is likely that several politico-religious attempts to stake out a Swedish claim in Finland have passed unrecorded.

Bishop Henry, as we have seen, is a less shadowy figure than St Eric, and it has been plausibly suggested that he had accompanied Nicholas Breakspear, a fellow Englishman, to Sweden, in which case his attempt to evangelise Finland may have been prompted by the legate. Its success cannot have been very great, for a papal bull dated 1171 or 1172 (which is the earliest documentary source for the conversion) characterises the Finns as converts who renounce the faith as soon as their enemies – presumably the Novgorodians – have withdrawn, and recommends the Swedes to treat them as subjects, not allies. This was easier said than done. In 1227 most of Tavastia was overrun by the forces of Novgorod, and nearly a decade later its people rebelled fiercely against the regime imposed by a second English bishop, Thomas, who was working under special letters of apostolic protection for the Church in Finland. The papacy then sought to take advantage of the weakening of Novgorod by the Tatar invasion of Russia: a crusade along both shores of the Baltic might win for Rome peoples who were in process of conversion from heathendom to the Orthodox faith – such as the Karelians or eastern Finns, whom a Grand Duke of Novgorod had recently attempted to baptise *en masse*. The result was a failure. In 1240 the Swedish *leidang*, its Tavastian supporters, and whatever other elements had rallied to the crusading cause were defeated by Alexander Prince of Novgorod at the Neva. Two years later the Germans were likewise defeated by him at Lake Peipus and, when Bishop Thomas left the scene in 1245, the Karelians were becoming reconciled to the Orthodox faith of the victors, on whose side they had fought, and the situation in Tavastia was still uncertain.

Hence the importance of the so-called second crusade of 1249, when Earl Birger's expedition completed the subjugation of Tavastia, where he established the castle of Tavastehus (Hameenlinna). He also planted a Swedish colony in Nyland, the coastal district east of Turku, and the growth of Swedish power on the southern coast may have stimulated the movement of Swedes along the coast of Ostrobothnia farther north. Karelia, however, remained in dispute, since Novgorod was so far weakened by the Tatar ascendancy that the German rivals of the Swedes staked out their claim by appointing a bishop for the Karelians at the same time as the Swedish influence was slowly extended eastwards along the coast.

In 1293 a thirty-year struggle for Karelia was opened by Marshal Torgils Knutsson, who made his base at Viipuri, which he strongly fortified. By the turn of the century Swedish armies had reached the shores of Lake Ladoga and they held a fort near the site of modern Leningrad. But the Novgorodians soon rallied, and in 1318 they even carried the war westwards as far as Turku. Five years later, peace was made at Nöteborg (Pähkinäsaari) through the mediation of the Germans, whose primary interest was to prevent a Swedish domination of the trade route from Russia to the west. The Swedes kept the westernmost Karelian districts, which they controlled already from Viipuri, but Ladoga Karelia with its easily accessible natural resources remained in Russian hands. The agreed boundary, which was not formally modified for more than two and a half centuries, ran in a north-westerly direction from the head of the Finnish Gulf through a very thinly inhabited hinterland to reach the Bothnian Gulf south of modern Oulu, leaving a part of the shore-line there to the Karelian salmon-fishers. Whilst a free passage to the Neva was placed under a special guarantee, Lapland and the far north in general were of such little interest to the negotiators that the Russo-Swedish border was left completely undefined.

Finland was now a province of Sweden with the same governmental and class structures, though the former was tempered by Finnish custom and the latter by the fact that the continued influx of colonists from Sweden did not as yet bring with it the creation of a higher nobility. Much authority was vested in the castellans of the three fortresses, but in 1362 the equal status of the province was confirmed by its participation in the election to the throne. The Finnish church was securely established under the see of Turku, which in 1291 was placed for the first time in the hands of a native Finn and in the next century sent more students to Paris than did any other Scandinavian diocese.

THE SCANDINAVIAN COMMUNITY

All these expansionist programmes were handicapped by the smallness of the Scandinavian populations. They were still small in comparison with other west European countries, in spite of a period of rapid internal development, revealed chiefly by the place-names; this began in the eleventh century and by the thirteenth had affected even Sweden, which had hitherto lagged behind. At the latter period Denmark is believed to have had a population of about 1 million (including Skåne), Sweden rather more than half that figure, and Norway less than half.[12] The Icelanders, who numbered about 50,000 on the basis of a tax calculation made in 1096, are not likely to have increased substantially in the next two centuries, and the extent of the inhabited area in Finland suggests a population between that of Iceland and Norway. An attempted estimate of comparative strength, assigning a notional 10 to Denmark, allots 6 to Sweden with Finland, 4 to Norway, and 1 to Iceland together with Greenland and the Faeroes.[13] It was a population living mainly by self-sufficient agriculture, with cattle farming predominant on the higher ground and the poorer soils elsewhere. Hunting and fishing still provided a rather meagre livelihood on the fringe of the settled areas, whilst in two districts (Lofoten and Skåne) seasonal fisheries already provided a staple trade. Methods of tillage continued to be primitive and the farms widely scattered except in Denmark, where the fertile plains had encouraged the early growth of village communities. In the twelfth century the more advanced three-field rotation of crops reached Denmark, from where it continued slowly northwards.

In such a society, old forms of organisation lingered long. Although monarchy, as we have seen, acquired a higher status through its alliance with the Church, it continued to lean for support upon the *hird* and the *leidang*. In Norway the various gradations of *hirdmann* were still important in the thirteenth century, by which time its upper ranks swore allegiance in the manner of feudal knights, whilst the *leidang* in each country fell eventually into disuse as a levy but continued as a tax, like the English ship-money. Although the limited supply of arable land caused an increasing proportion of free men to become tenants, the *thing* only slowly lost its function as the main organ of local and provincial administration. In purely local affairs the assembly of all free men was left in full control, except for the royal claim to the ownership of at least a part of the common or waste. At the level of the province the free men's representatives who formed the *landsthing* more readily attracted a king's attention and his desire to control both litigation and lawmaking. One instrument for the purpose resulted from the introduction to Jutland in the eleventh century of an area of government known as the *syssel*, derived from the English county; both Denmark and Norway eventually instituted the *sysselmann* as a kind of regional governor. Still more important was a new practice of royal nominations to the ancient office of Lawman – originally, as in Iceland, a president chosen by the members of the *thing* because his familiarity with laws not yet formulated in writing was essential for the conduct of its proceedings.

The jurisprudence of all the Scandinavian countries retains many features which distinguish it from the legal principles developed elsewhere in western Europe, a result which is partly attributable to a gradual transition from customary law to provincial codes and thence to a law promulgated by the sovereign for the whole realm. The earliest surviving texts date from the thirteenth century, but we know that the Althing ordered the Icelandic laws to be written down in the winter of 1117–18 in 'the scroll which Haflidi caused to be made'[14] – and that this action imitated what had already been done in western Norway. By then the primitive germanic law processes, involving *wergild* and compurgation, were disappearing under the influence of the Church, which was prompt to record ecclesiastical law in writing. The fifteen or more regional codes now tended to become fewer, losing much of their prestige as kings gradually succeeded in treating the approval of new legislation by the *thing* as no more than a traditional formality.

The final step was first taken in Norway, where King Magnus Law-mender instituted a national code in 1275; he also defied the terms of the union with Iceland by substituting a code based largely upon Norwegian law for the existing Icelandic laws. A code applicable to the whole of Sweden was first completed about 1350, but it had an influential antecedent in a modernisation of the laws of the Uppland province (which included both Stockholm and Uppsala), made at the close of the previous century. This code of King Magnus Ericsson applied to Finland as well, though there local custom continued to prevail in many spheres. In 1241 Valdemar II promulgated a code for Jutland, which began with the canon law maxim, 'Law shall build the land', but down to the sixteenth century separate legal systems were in operation in Jutland, Skåne, and the Danish islands.

In at least two important respects this growth of royal power was accompanied by an increase in the liberty of the subject. Slavery, which in the Viking period had its established place in Scandinavian agriculture, presents a grim picture in the provincial laws, even after the introduction of Christianity. Icelandic law requires owners to refrain from killing slaves on legally prescribed holy days and throughout Lent; a west Norway code allows the children of a dead slave to be exposed in a grave in the churchyard, provided that the last survivor is kept alive. The system was indeed ameliorated by such practices as the assigning of plots of land to slave households and the giving of freedom as a reward for faithful service; but its final disappearance awaited the time when rural society came to possess what Marxists later styled a reserve army of labour. Slavery will therefore have lingered longest in outlying areas. The only known date of abolition is in Sweden, where a law of 1335 forbids the last relics of slavery in two provinces. In Norway, where royal slaves are named about 1150, the silence of the records suggests that the institution had lost all significance by the close of the twelfth century, as it did soon afterwards in Denmark. In Iceland, where Celtic Irish slaves certainly figured in the original settlement, it is thought that economic considerations may have brought the institution spontaneously to an end when church law eventually forbade the exposure of unwanted children, who are assumed to have included especially the offspring of slaves.

The other increase of liberty came through the growth of towns and trade. The rural community satisfied such needs as it could not itself supply – salt, for example, and in some areas iron – by resort to small-scale markets and annual fairs; the latter, held usually when the winter ice and snow made long-distance transport practicable, had existed in Viking times. But dried and salted fish, hewn timber, cattle and dairy products, and (by 1200) copper and iron, which German miners had begun to extract from Swedish mountains, were exports for which Europe now offered a ready sale. Bergen early became the entrepôt for the dried cod brought down the Norwegian west coast from Lofoten, and in the later twelfth century replaced Trondheim as the principal royal seat; its economy was, however, increasingly dominated by German traders, who by 1260 were taking up permanent residence in the port where their deep-bottomed 'cogs' had found such profitable cargoes. Copenhagen, the name of which means 'merchants' harbour', was well situated in relation to the herring fisheries which created the huge seasonal market at Skanör on the south-west tip of the mainland opposite; it was Denmark's largest town long before the fifteenth century, when it replaced nearby Roskilde as the capital. Stockholm, too, owed its rise to trade, eclipsing Sigtuna in the later thirteenth century, when prosperity depended upon the closest possible proximity to the flourishing commerce of the Baltic Sea. Visby, on the island of Gotland, grew up at the same period and for the same reason; founded by German merchants on Swedish soil, it was for a time the most important of all the Baltic towns.

By about 1300, indeed, the ubiquitous and well-organised German traders were becoming a serious threat to the independence of each of the Scandinavian kingdoms, a factor which was to drive them towards unity. But in the meantime the proliferation of towns had a great social influence. They were most numerous in Denmark, where the dozen known to Adam of Bremen expanded to about eighty, including nearly all those which exist today. The Norwegian and Swedish towns together were about half as many as the Danish, whilst Finland had only Turku and Iceland no town at all. In Denmark the formation of gilds – which had an earlier history in many parts of Scandinavia as religious associations, both Christian and (probably) pagan – made it easier for merchants and craftsmen to claim the right to conduct their own affairs; by 1200 Slesvig at least had its own municipal law. In Norway trading places had long possessed a traditional form of law, the *Bjarköyrett*, but Magnus Law-mender set up a special municipal code, based on institutions already existing in Bergen; this divided authority between a town council and the royal representative. His Swedish namesake and contemporary, Magnus Barnlock, issued monopolistic royal charters, of which the prime beneficiaries were often German traders. But the town councils and craft gilds which these foreigners brought from their native land also spelt out additional powers of self-government for Swedish citizens, who were glad to take up residence inside the walls which the Germans promptly erected. In Swedish, the very word for town (*stad*) is German.

The freedom of the ancient Scandinavian community was, however, being steadily reduced by the growing power of the magnates, in relation both to the general mass of free men and to the monarchy which leaned on them for support. In 1134 a claimant to the throne of Denmark routed the royal levies at Fotevig in Skåne with great slaughter by the impact of 300 German cavalrymen. This battle may be linked with the castle building, first undertaken by Danish nobles in the reign of Valdemar the Great, as the events which mark the arrival on Scandinavian soil of the military methods of the feudal age.

Feudal political relationships never became fully established except in Denmark, and the Norwegian terrain in particular discouraged the dependence upon bodies of armoured knights, able to strike where they pleased, which formed the military basis of the system. Moreover, in Scandinavia the fiefs seldom became family property, which could be handed on without royal intervention from one generation to another, whilst the privileges of the lord were commonly intertwined with duties as the king's representative. In many cases the peasant might at first feel that he would pay less and receive better protection when his obligations to the crown were transferred to the fief-holder. But in the light of later history it was an ominous feature of the Danish royal estate records that as early as 1231 less than half the farmers on the large island of Falster still owned their land. Still more ominous was an event of 1253, when the duchy of Slesvig was granted through the solemn form of investiture 'by standard' to a junior branch of the Danish royal house, allied by marriage to the German counts of Holstein. Only eight years later, when the regent of Denmark tried to reduce the status of the fief, the royal forces were crushed by the Holsteiners at the battle of Lohede, so that in this instance the fief became hereditary. Though the change in the other kingdoms was more gradual and less dramatic, Iceland was the only part of Scandinavia in which a category of peasant chieftains held their own as the recognised leaders of the community.

In all three kingdoms the nobility originated partly among new categories of higher crown officials. *Jarl* or earl reached a new zenith before the title of duke was introduced, mainly in the thirteenth century, from the continent; thus the position of Birger Jarl, when his son became king of Sweden, has been likened to that of the Frankish mayors of the palace. Other court appointments, such as the office of chancellor, marshal, or justiciar (the Swedish *drots*), likewise set apart the individual and to some extent his family. At a slightly lower level Norway had its *lendmenn*, who received the revenue from crown land; they are mentioned by skalds as early as the eleventh century, and by the thirteenth they rank above other members of the royal *hird*, with the continental name of baron marking their status as the king's vassals or 'men'. Sverre's *sysselmenn* or governors and their subordinate *årmenn* were at first placed in closer dependence on the Norwegian crown. In Denmark the *ombudsmand* began as a mere bailiff who administered a royal estate, but the law of Jutland (1241) introduced *len* from Germany – a term for the bailiff's restricted functions which expanded into an equivalent for 'fief'. In Sweden, too, the ancient offices of lawman and district governor acquired a definitely feudal character, when the occupants received lands on a life tenure and took a fief-holder's oath of loyalty.

The nobility of medieval Scandinavia was never a very numerous class: by the fourteenth century it comprised about 350 Danish and about 100 Swedish families, whilst the Norwegian element was so small that its members commonly sought to consolidate their position by inter-marriage with their peers in the other two lands. In Sweden the term *frälse* or 'free' was used for many centuries with reference to the exemption of noble and ecclesiastical land from the payment of taxes and other dues to the crown, granted by the statute of Alsnö (*c.* 1280); the same kind of grant had been made in Denmark in the 1240s and in Norway in the 1270s. In 1282 the rights of the Danish nobility were defined in a document closely resembling the English Magna Carta, one clause of which obliged the crown to summon the magnates annually to a general legis-lative and judicial assembly known as the *Danehof*. This institution, which endured for one and a half centuries, had a parallel in more oc-casional assemblies held in the other kingdoms, but the Scandinavian nobles influenced government more effectively through the small Council or *Råd*. As the provinces with their *things* gave place to a centralised royal administration, the king naturally sought advice and support from owners of big estates and holders of high office; and it was equally natural that during a royal minority – such as each kingdom experienced at least once during the thirteenth century – the advisers became a power behind the throne.

A strong king might recover lost ground, as did Haakon V of Norway, when he succeeded his crippled brother Eric, who had come to the throne at the age of twelve. During his reign of twenty years he reduced his Council both in numbers and status; he also set up new castles – Akershus in Oslo (which now became the capital), Vardöhus in East Finnmark, and Bohus in the extreme south – with royal castellans and garrisons. But at his death in 1319 Haakon had no male heir, so the Norwegian crown passed by agreement to the three-year-old son of his daughter, Princess Ingebjorg, and the effective power to the nobility.

In Sweden the nobles triumphed at the same juncture, at the end of an insensate struggle between the young King Birger and his two brothers, one of whom, Duke Eric, had acquired Norwegian fiefs as Ingebjorg's husband and wrested adjacent lands in western Sweden from King Birger. In 1317, the king captured his younger brothers by guile, but after they had died mysteriously in prison their followers among the nobility drove him from the realm, murdered his son, and presented Ingebjorg's child, who had just inherited Norway, for election to a second throne.

The situation of the Danish monarchy at this juncture was more parlous. In 1286 the murder of King Eric Klipping had occasioned the banishment of eight constitutionalist nobles, who for nearly two decades raided Danish territory with the physical support of Haakon V of Norway, where they had their base, and the spiritual support of the archbishop of Lund. In his later years, indeed, the new king, Eric Menved, tried to restore the prestige of the monarchy by military interventions in Sweden (where he backed King Birger against his brothers) and in north Germany. But the only tangible result was an enormous bill for the hire of German mercenaries, which he met by mortgaging the royal estates, including the whole island of Fünen, and increasing the taxation on the remaining freehold peasants. In 1313 he was confronted by a big peasant revolt in Jutland, which had the support of some nobles and could only be suppressed by additional military expenditure. Furthermore, the weakening of the Danish monarchy had encouraged the banished nobles and, later, the Swedish Duke Eric to establish themselves on the Kattegat coastline, where the three kingdoms met in the vicinity of modern Gothenburg, to the south of which Eric secured the Danish fief of North Halland* with the fortress of Varberg.

Thus, when King Eric Menved died in the same year as King Haakon, three weak monarchies were confronted by partly feudalised nobilities. In many cases nobles held fiefs in more than one country; the Kattegat area provided them with the nucleus of a cohesive Scandinavia; and more generally the noble class had a common economic interest in the privileged exploitation of their estates and a common social basis in the ideas of chivalry imported from the south. From 1319 onwards the unification

* Halland and Blekinge, the coastal districts adjoining the two sides of the Scanian peninsula, were grouped with Skåne under the sovereignty of Denmark.

of the north was again a possibility, as in the reign of Cnut the Great, but before examining the chequered course and ultimate failure of the attempt some brief reference must be made to the cultural achievements of the period now ending.

THE SAGA HERITAGE

As an outpost of medieval Christendom, Scandinavia received its main cultural influences from the more advanced societies of the continent and Norman England. Latin writing and stone or brick churches were introduced by clergy and craftsmen of Anglo-Saxon or German origins; cathedrals and monasteries reproduced some of the glories of Romanesque and Gothic architecture in a harsher climate; and new intellectual currents entered the life of the north from Rome, from Paris (where Scandinavian students formed their own 'nation'), and even from the canonists of Bologna. But apart from the Norwegian stave churches already referred to, the ecclesiastical and secular buildings which survive from these centuries, and all that remains of their furnishings, are of historical rather than artistic interest. The crucifixes, altar frontals, and painted figures of the saints, no less than the tapestries and carved wooden implements which were once the pride of manor houses and timbered farms, are broadly speaking unremarkable in comparison with contemporary achievement elsewhere – a very different situation from that which obtained in the era of the Viking ship-burials.

The Viking skalds, however, had stimulated an interest in historical narrative which still bore important fruit. Ari Thorgilsson the Learned (*Fródi*) wrote his *Islendingabók* in the 'Danish tongue', giving a concise factual account of the settlement of the island down to 1120; later in the same century two Latin chronicles were compiled in Norwegian monasteries; and by about 1320 the culturally backward Swedes had produced a history of their recent past in the *Chronicle of Eric*, a vernacular imitation of the French in rhyming verse. These works are valuable chiefly as records of events which might otherwise have passed into oblivion. But the Danish historian Saxo Grammaticus ('the Latinist') reaches the artistic level of the major medieval chroniclers. The first half of his *Gesta Danorum*, which begins with a Trojan warrior named Dan and provides Gorm the Old with sixty royal predecessors (including Hamlet), is a tissue of patriotic legends, comparable to Geoffrey of Monmouth's account of King Arthur of the Round Table. But the second half, which carries the story down to the year 1185 – perhaps two decades before the time of its composition – brings to life a century and a half of the nation's history as seen through the eyes of one who gloried in the co-operation of Church and State.

The interest in history is also the starting-point of a much greater literary achievement, namely the saga-writing which, though based primarily on Iceland, has always been treated as part of the common cultural inheritance of the Scandinavian peoples. Here the whole world stands in debt to them for what is really a special form of tale-telling: the name 'saga' reappears in the English noun 'saw' – a saying which deserves to be repeated. The saga began as a form of recitation, employed at the banquets of the Icelanders in the days before the introduction of the Latin script made it possible for a more or less lengthy composition to be recorded in writing. Those early colonists did not lack material for tales of heroic realism in their own grim island, in the Norway they had left, and in other parts of the Viking world with which they kept in contact. The long winter evenings provided plenty of opportunities for appreciative listening in the warmth of the firelit hall; and it is at least possible that the infusion of Celtic blood heightened the Icelander's sense of drama and imaginative grasp of language. At all events the result was the creation of a form of prose epic which, once it had been safely committed to parchment, was as sure of immortality as the *Iliad* itself.

The saga-writers may be said to begin with Ari Fródi, the pioneer of Icelandic historiography, and they close with Sturla Thórdarson (1214–84), who wrote both about the termination of Icelandic independence and about the Norwegian kings by whom this was accomplished. But the historical sagas have made their biggest impact through Snorri's *Heimskringla*, which Carlyle numbered 'among the great history books of the world'.[15] It is partly an original compilation and partly a recension of older royal sagas from which Snorri's consummate artistry creates a convincing picture of the long succession of Norway's kings. Modern scholars have pointed out, however, that he had access to no primary materials except the work of the skalds, from which he made valuable quotations; otherwise his chief importance is as a repository of tradition – though he also sheds light upon conditions within his own experience, which covered Norway and to some extent Sweden as well as his native island.

There are, however, contemporary sagas, such as that which an Icelandic abbot wrote 'when King Sverre sat over him and settled what he should write',[16] and the sagas of the Icelandic bishops depend partly on well kept monastic records, whilst historical facts handed down from generation to generation also provide a reliable background for many of the so-called family sagas. *Egil's Saga*, for instance, carries the reader to York during the little-known reign of Eric Blood-axe, and cites the rhyming eulogy by which the skald mollified the king, whom he had formerly insulted. The *Orkneyinga Saga* and those of Eric the Red and his son Leif are still more valuable, for against a background of individual achievement they give the history of whole regions which would otherwise be almost blank.

Nevertheless, the genius of the saga-writers is shown above all in the great fiction sagas, of which twelve were composed in the final half-century of the art. These deal with men and women who lived and died about two hundred years earlier. Thus the imagination could play freely upon events handed down by tradition in a small, unchanging society, producing results which have been acclaimed as putting the entire literary achievement of medieval Europe before the time of Dante completely in the shade. Character is conveyed by what men say and do, making explanation superfluous; extreme economy of language heightens the effect; and a remorseless Fate is felt to brood over the scene in the eruption-twisted, barren island. *Njáls Saga* is justly the most famous of all, with its two heroes precipitated into an undying feud by a scheming woman; touching episodes like that of the dog, which calls to mind the faithful hound of Ulysses in far-off Ithaca; and the final burning of Njal, his wife, and the little grandson lying between them in bed, after his enemies have offered the woman the chance of escape. ' "Young was I when I was given to Njal" (she replies), "and we have promised that one fate should befall us both" . . . Then they signed themselves and the boy with the cross, and gave over their souls into God's hand, and that was the last word that men heard them utter.'[17]

Chapter 4

The Union of Three Crowns

LATE-MEDIEVAL SCANDINAVIA: SOME ECONOMIC AND SOCIAL
FEATURES

In the Scandinavian countries the period known to present-day historians
as the late Middle Ages continued until one-third of the way through
the sixteenth century: for it was the Reformation, not the Renaissance,
which spread the most decisive changes among the peoples of northern
Europe. The period is one in which special interest attaches to international politics, because of the great experiment in political unity which
was then attempted. But it is desirable first to notice the general setting
in which these political developments took place and by which they were
to a large extent moulded.

All over Europe the fourteenth century was an era of economic decline,
which it is tempting to connect with a worsening of the climate, such as is
indeed reported in the annals of Iceland, where heavy winter snowfalls
and excessive spring rains are said to have increased the havoc from
volcanic eruptions and earthquakes. However initiated, this decline was
greatly intensified by the ravages of the Black Death,* which entered
Europe along the trade routes from the Far East, galley-borne to Sicily
in October 1347. Since the nature of bubonic plague (not to speak of its
pneumonic and septicaemic variants) was an impenetrable mystery, its
spread was unhindered, so that in the course of about three years something
like one-third of the European population perished in what must still
be reckoned to have been the supreme catastrophe of their history. The
disease was carried to Norway in August 1349 in the hold of an English
ship, spreading from Bergen along the coast and up the valleys; thence
it was passed to Sweden, Finland and Denmark (which was also infected
from Germany); and spared only Iceland, which however suffered heavily
during a later resuscitation in the years 1402–4.

In formerly well-populated corn-growing districts the immediate
effect of the Black Death, in Scandinavia as elsewhere, was to reduce

---

* The name is not contemporary and is first found in Scandinavia, as *svarta döden*
(Sweden 1555) and *sorte död* (Denmark, c. 1600), allegedly through a mistranslation of
atra mors 'the terrible death'.[1]

rents and raise wages, since big landowners – such as the Crown, the Church, and the nobility – would perforce accept small profits to secure continued cultivation; at worst they might be impelled by labour shortage to replace tillage to some extent by sheep-grazing. But in the small-scale cattle-keeping economy which prevailed in the less fertile parts of Scandinavia recovery on any terms was often impossible: once the stock had perished, the enclave of farmland reverted to the waste. The results imposed a particularly heavy burden on Norway, where one farm in seven lay desolate for many generations – in some cases for ever – and capital resources are believed to have shrunk by two-thirds. Most of the native nobility therefore disappeared into the ranks of the peasantry, so that in the late fourteenth century only 60 knights remained in place of 270 at its beginning. In the long run this fostered a characteristic sense of dignity and independence in the peasant class but, in an age when the nobles were becoming the dominant force in the political life of the north, the direct result was that Norway played a rapidly diminishing part in its counsels. For similar reasons, fifteenth-century Iceland contained too few substantial proprietors to offer any opposition to the encroachments of Danes and other foreigners.

In Sweden the category of independent, tax-paying peasants retained its importance and soon resumed the task of carving out new farms in the northern forests, as also happened in the Finnish hinterland. But the poverty of the Crown in a period of general depression caused many estates to pass into noble hands, whereupon the peasants on the estate paid rent and services to the landowner in lieu of taxes to the government. In Denmark, where there was much less unoccupied land in reserve and the exactions of Crown and Church were very heavy, the position of the independent peasant deteriorated faster. There was a rapid increase in medium-sized farms rented from the nobility, and by the middle of the fifteenth century the east Danish islands had adopted a system known as *vornedskab*, under which a tenant's son could be forced to take over the tenancy, whilst restrictions on the movement of labourers made it easier to compel the performance of increasingly onerous work-rents.

At the close of the Middle Ages the proportion of land in peasant ownership was about one-half in Sweden, one-quarter in Norway, and one-eighth in Denmark. The proportion of Crown land had in all cases sunk to a low level, whereas there were significant differences in Church estates, which in Norway amounted to nearly one-half, in Denmark one-third, and in Sweden one-fifth. But the most significant difference was the nobles' share: in Norway only 13, in Sweden 21·8, and in Denmark 33 per cent.[2]

The growth of class barriers in Denmark, to which these figures point, is partly attributable to the easy access from Germany: immigrants who came northwards as estate managers or captains of mercenaries introduced the German social structure when they themselves became landowners. In trade and industry this German influence was still more pervasive, for the period of depression in the fourteenth and fifteenth centuries caused the north German cities to intensify the pressure which their merchants had long exercised in neighbouring lands by developing the rather loose interurban organisation known as the Hanseatic League. By 1400 it had a membership of about seventy towns, with its headquarters in Lübeck, four 'Counters' or privileged settlements for its merchants, and a special interest in Baltic trade, as was evidenced by the location of one Counter at Novgorod.

Though it nearly always aroused resentment, the German influence was in many respects beneficial. In Sweden the early exploitation of the iron ore of Dalecarlia and its famous Kopparberg or 'copper mountain' – which boasts a miners' charter from 1347 – was indebted to Germans for capital, technical knowledge, and methods of organisation. Even before the blast furnace came into use in the fifteenth century, *osmund* iron was a Swedish manufacture which sold all over western Europe and commanded a 50 per cent higher price than the native German product.[3] Hanse merchants were the driving-force in the export not only of metals but also of the animal products which at this time made the southern provinces the wealthiest. Town life was so largely of German provenance that both Stockholm and Kalmar found it necessary to stipulate that at least half the members of the town council must be Swedes. In Denmark the towns were for the most part older and therefore less strongly influenced by the German immigrants. There the chief Hanse interest was in the great international market resulting from the herring fishery off Skanör. In the end the League went to war to bring it under their direct control (see p. 71), but when the herring shoals first provided their harvest in those waters Lübeck at once acquired a strong position in the trade, both as a purveyor of the salt for preserving the catch and because much of it was shipped to western markets via the overland passage from Lübeck to Hamburg, the route round the Skaw being shunned as hazardous.

German traders, as we have seen, were eager to develop the market for the dried cod of north Norway, based on Bergen, which in the mid-fourteenth century became the fourth of the Hanseatic Counters. German organising skill encouraged a fishing population for supplying their trade to grow up wherever boats and nets could find shelter along the inhospitable northern coastline. Bergen, Oslo, and Tönsberg were also stimulated to export the timber and animal products of the hinterland; and the Baltic corn which they received in return was soon indispensable for the provisioning of many districts. On the other hand, Norway's weakness encouraged exorbitant demands, fulfilment of which made the country still weaker. Hanseatic economic privileges extended from a monopoly of imports to control over inland trade and handicrafts; in Bergen, and to a smaller extent in the other two ports, the Hanse merchant community and its dependents, including artisans, claimed an extra-territorial position; and when they were thwarted Lübeck led the way in resorting to the weapon of a commercial blockade. This was effective because the Norwegians were no longer a shipping nation. The English interlopers, for example – east-coast fishermen, followed by Bristol traders – who by 1412 had begun to visit Iceland with welcome imports, found their presence in those distant waters challenged by Hanseatic rather than Norwegian vessels.[4]

If the Scandinavian peoples were driven together by the impulse to resist alien influences upon their economic life, they were also to some extent drawn together by a common cultural heritage, of which the saga literature had laid the foundation. Although the fourteenth and fifteenth centuries produced no work of comparable distinction, it was the period in which balladry was greatly in vogue throughout the north. Since this art form had entered Denmark first (together with all the paraphernalia of southern chivalry) many of the tales and legends, which circulated through Scandinavia in ballad form by word of mouth, were of Danish origin. Their influence on the popular imagination was enhanced by their use as an accompaniment to round dances (*folkevisedanser*), which in the isolation of the Faeroes survived into the present century. Much of the common literature, however, was religious, the Church being still the chief custodian of the written word. One of its treasures is 'The Lily', a highly original poem in a comparatively modern form of versification, the work of an Icelandic monk who almost certainly composed it whilst relegated to perform a heavy penance at Trondheim. The most famous and extensive prose writing which survives from Scandinavian sources of this period is also religious, namely the work of the Swedish saint, Birgitta; it is significant that she pleaded for the retention of a common Scandinavian language.

As the founder of a religious order which is still active in more than one continent, Birgitta is the individual Scandinavian whose fame is most widespread among that great majority of mankind to whom the personages of history as such make no appeal. As the daughter, wife and mother of Swedish Lawmen, her life story is in some ways typical of that age of noble privilege. Birgitta was married at a very early age, to become the mistress of a large household; was often in attendance on the queen consort, Blanche of Namur; and received the lands on which she founded her monastery at Vadstena as a gift from King Magnus. Never-theless, she did not hesitate to criticise what she found amiss in the marital relations of the royal couple, and when the king tried to restrict the financial privileges of the nobles she denounced him bitterly. Yet she is deservedly remembered best for her impact on the affairs of Europe, when in her widowhood she believed that God had called her to be *sponsa mea et canale meum*.

Travelling across a plague-stricken continent, Birgitta arrived in Rome for the year of jubilee (1350), to press for the acceptance of two special 'revelations' – the name which she gave to her ecstasies and visionary meditations. These called upon the pope to return from Avignon to the Apostolic City, and on his return to authorise a new order on lines which had been revealed to her; Pope Urban V came back to Rome, but for no more than two years, and authorised the Birgittines, but only as a branch of the existing Augustinian Order. Birgitta's voluminous revelations, recorded by her in her native language and turned into the surviving Latin version by her confessor, concerned themselves with many purely religious themes, such as the adoration of the Virgin Mary. Yet few secular matters lay outside the interests of this remarkable woman, who could (and did) offer advice on such topics as how to end the Hundred Years War and the need to cultivate the proper crusading spirit for a Swedish attack on Novgorod (see p. 70). In addition, her long residence in Rome, where she died after an exhausting pilgrimage to Jerusalem in 1373, provided a Scandinavian presence – far more memorable than that of Cnut the Great – which influenced Italians, Spaniards, and the devout of many nations.

Birgitta's remains were brought home to Vadstena, of which one of her daughters became the first abbess. Another daughter had been sent to Norway as mistress of the household to the child queen, Margaret of Denmark. One of Birgitta's devoted followers was Hemming, bishop of Turku, whom the Finns came to venerate as a saint. In due course the new order, with its distinctive double foundations of monks and nuns under the rule of an abbess, began to spread through pre-Reformation Europe (where it came to number about eighty houses) along with the cult of its canonised originator, known to the English as Saint Bridget. The mother house at Vadstena became the finest flower of northern Christianity and, in the phrase of the eminent Norwegian historian who first examined the Vatican archives, 'a kind of miniature Scandinavia *per se*'.[5]

In the world of the arts Scandinavia, as has already been indicated, produced nothing to compare with the glories of Renaissance Italy. But, in some regions at least, its society showed qualities which the fellow countrymen of Boccaccio or Machiavelli could not but admire. In the winter of 1431–2 a Venetian merchant, blown badly off course on a voyage to Flanders, made his landfall in one of the outermost islands of the Lofotens. For three months the fisherfolk shared their one-room huts and scanty winter supplies with the strangers, who marvelled to see piety, chastity, honesty, and even cleanliness flourish in such poor surroundings: 'We can in truth say that we were in the first circle of paradise.'[6] When spring came, they rowed south with their hosts as far as Trondheim, where the governor entertained them with Latin conversation and clerical company at a well furnished table. But the 53-day journey across the mountains into central Sweden, for which he provided horses, money and a guide, confirmed the Italians in their impression of a country handicapped by severe natural conditions – they learnt about the making of bark-bread, for example – yet in essentials civilised and astonishingly hospitable. It was also a united Scandinavia through which they travelled, though they chose the route across Sweden rather than the direct way south via Denmark because Eric, the king of the united realm, was then at war with the Hanseatics.

THE MAKING OF THE UNION

The union of the three Scandinavian kingdoms, consummated at Kalmar in 1397, has a twofold historical significance. In its own day, it constituted the second largest accumulation of European territories under a single sovereign, and in retrospect it stands out as an achievement which the Scandinavian peoples proved unable to perpetuate and unwilling to repeat – in spite of its varying but always considerable advantages. The union of Kalmar grew to some extent out of a general trend towards the creation of larger political entities in the era of the formation of Poland-Lithuania, the growth of the Burgundian dominions, and the expansion of the Principality of Moscow. But it also had its roots in social tendencies already noticed and in a rather tortuous course of dynastic developments to which attention must now be directed.

In May 1319 Magnus Ericsson, the child of the Norwegian Princess Ingebjorg and the deceased Swedish Duke Eric, duly inherited the crown of Norway and in July he was elected king of Sweden; the tax-paying peasants took part for the first time in the Swedish election, but councillors from both countries had already arranged with Ingebjorg for each to be ruled separately by its Council throughout the prospective minority. In November of the same eventful year the death of King Eric Menved likewise enhanced the power of the Danish nobility, who imposed an accession charter upon his younger brother, Christopher II, giving the Council such rights as a veto on any declaration of war. When this was defied by the new king and further ruinous expenditure incurred by an active foreign policy, Denmark became the scene of civil war, from which Count Gert of Holstein and his cousin emerged in possession of so many fiefs that Christopher's death in 1332 was followed by an interregnum under their arbitrary rule and that of their German followers.

The Princess Ingebjorg, who at first shared in the regency of both Norway and Sweden, tried to secure additional territory from a weakened and distracted Denmark, so as to expand her late husband's duchy into a mid-Scandinavian realm centred upon Varberg, where she resided. However, she was discredited by her intrigues with a Danish nobleman of that region (whom she eventually married), and the additions went to her son instead. When Magnus came of age in 1332, he was already in possession of Danish Halland; soon afterwards a popular revolt enabled him to purchase the rich Danish province of Skåne (together with Blekinge), and for a time he even held parts of Zealand.

But in the long run the nobles were too strong for him. The financial resources of the Crown were impaired by the Black Death, which may also account for Magnus's abandonment of the crusade into Karelia promoted by Birgitta. When his younger son Haakon came of age in 1355, he handed Norway over to him to be ruled separately according to an agreement with the Norwegian Council; thereupon members of the Swedish Council fomented a separatist claim in Sweden on behalf of his elder son Eric. After the death of the latter in 1359, Magnus and Haakon joined forces to hold Sweden and Norway together as one realm, but they lost Skåne to the reviving power of the king of Denmark – a loss which was not compensated in Swedish eyes by Haakon's marriage in 1363 to the ten-year-old Danish princess Margaret. The nobility rose against Magnus and transferred the crown of Sweden to his nephew Albrecht, whose father was the ruler of Mecklenburg, which with its Hanse towns of Rostock and Wismar was at that time the most powerful German duchy on the Baltic coast. Other Germans followed in the new king's train, whom the Vadstena chronicle likened to 'birds of prey alighting on the mountain tops'.[7] In 1371 Haakon organised a rising on his father's behalf; this failed, but it caused Albrecht to transfer many fiefs back into Swedish hands, especially those of the justiciar Bo Jonsson Grip,* who at his death in 1386 held all three of the royal castles in Finland and half a dozen other fiefs – about 1,500 properties spread over 340 parishes. The possession of these then became the object of a further contest between king and nobles.

The vanished union was, however, destined to be restored and extended from a different direction. When the fortunes of Denmark, as already related, had reached their nadir, the assassination of Count Gert of Holstein in 1340 – in a *coup* contrived by a Jutland squire, Niels Ebbesen, at the head of only fifty men – made it possible to restore the native line of kings in the person of Valdemar III Atterdag.† Having started with only a part of north Jutland in his possession, he bought back the estates which had been alienated to the Holsteiners, selling the Danish claims in Estonia for the purpose and also applying military pressure. After recovering the mainland provinces from Sweden (as already mentioned) he attacked Gotland, where his pitiless massacre of an ill equipped army of

---

* The surname 'Grip' was taken from the griffin on his coat of arms, a practice followed by other Swedish families on their ennoblement – 'Vasa' from their vase, Oxenstierna from their emblem of an ox's forehead (*stirn*). Albrecht himself replaced the lion emblem of the Folkung kings by the Three Crowns; the origin is unknown, but its retention became a matter of great significance to his successors.

† 1321–75. He was Christopher II's youngest son and had been brought up partly at the court of his foster-father, the emperor Lewis IV, where he would imbibe the high ideas of the secular ruler's authority taught by Marsilius of Padua. The soubriquet *Atterdag* may have been given in allusion to the 'new day' which certainly dawned for Denmark under his rule.

peasants under the walls of Visby is amply attested by modern excavations. Valdemar succeeded in having the Hanse port transferred to Danish sovereignty along with the rest of the island, but the Hanseatic League under the traders of Lübeck and in alliance with Sweden took up the challenge and for a time compelled him to leave Denmark. Before his return the Council was forced to accept the treaty of Stralsund (1370), under which a fifteen-year lease of three coastal forts gave the Hanse merchants full control of the Skänor fisheries and their League even obtained a formal veto on the choice of king. But Valdemar III was duly restored, and when he died five years after the treaty he still had the upper hand of the Holsteiners and was planning to recover Slesvig, whose duke had left no heir. Moreover, in each recovered territory he had strengthened the central power by granting the fortresses and their surrounding fiefs to castellans of proved loyalty.

Upon this basis his daughter Margaret proceeded to build up the greatest personal position ever achieved in Scandinavia. Her inner nature is as little known to us as her outward appearance – which the alabaster effigy on her splendid tomb in Roskilde cathedral depicts as eternally young. If she was first and foremost the child of a mighty father, her mother was the sister of a duke of Slesvig – which gave her a direct connection with the problem of Denmark's southern frontier. In addition, as the young bride of King Haakon she had experienced life in Norway in straitened circumstances: a letter survives in which she begs her husband to arrange credit with a Hanse merchant in Oslo, as otherwise her attendants must leave her. And, as we have already seen, in this impressionable early period of her life she had a Swedish mistress of her household, who no doubt introduced her to the problems of the third Scandinavian kingdom.

At the time of the treaty of Stralsund King Valdemar had agreed with the Duke of Mecklenburg that the Danish throne should pass to the son of Margaret's elder sister Ingeborg, who had married the heir to the dukedom. However, on her father's death in 1375, Margaret scored her first great diplomatic success by inducing the Danish Council to elect her own five-year-old son Olav instead. The price was an accession charter imposing many limitations on the Crown, but she displayed as regent a capacity for the management of men which caused a Hanse representative to describe the turbulent nobility of Denmark as being seized with 'respect for that lady's wisdom and authority, so that they offered her their services'.[8] Only five years later Olav inherited Norway from his father, King Haakon VI, whereupon Margaret's second regency marked the beginning of a Dano-Norwegian Union which was to last for more than four centuries. As Olav also inherited the claims of the dispossessed Folkung dynasty in Sweden, the death of Bo Jonsson Grip offered an opportunity for ousting King Albrecht; but in the very next year (1387) Olav died suddenly at seventeen, before he had any chance of prosecuting his claim as 'true heir to Sweden'[9] – which his mother was not.

Margaret reacted with astonishing promptitude and resource. Within a week she had been hailed at the Skåne *landsthing* as Denmark's 'sovereign lady, master, and guardian', and in February 1388 a meeting of Norwegian lords accepted her as their 'mighty lady and master' in defiance of the law of succession. Fortified by these testimonies to her skill as a ruler of two kingdoms, she made a treaty in March with the Swedish nobles who had Bo Jonsson Grip's estates at their disposal. They recognised her as Sweden's 'sovereign lady and rightful master', to whom they undertook to transfer all Grip's fortresses and most of his lands in return for a general confirmation of noble privileges.

The settlement in Sweden was of course contingent upon the final overthrow of King Albrecht, who had been recruiting his forces in Germany. In February 1389 his army of mercenaries was defeated by Swedes and Danes at Falköping in Västergötland, and he himself was led from the battlefield in fetters. Stockholm, however, held out for nine more years, as the German merchants intimidated its Swedish inhabitants by a series of murders and the city was kept supplied by the so-called 'Victualling Brothers' (*Vitaliebröder*). These were actually Baltic pirates, who ranged as far afield as Bergen from the Mecklenburg ports of Rostock and Wismar, damaging trade to such an extent that eventually the Hanseatics, in return for the renewal of all their privileges, negotiated Albrecht's release from captivity on terms which gave Margaret possession of the Swedish capital. The Victualling Brothers were not evicted from Finland (where Bo Jonsson's son was also helping the Germans) until 1399, and Gotland, which Albrecht had sold to the Teutonic Knights, was not recovered until 1408.

Meanwhile, however, the union had been given a more formal basis by a solemn coronation, of which the scene was the Swedish town of Kalmar, close to the then border with Denmark, and the appropriate day Trinity Sunday, 1397. Although the burgesses of Lübeck addressed Margaret not unreasonably as 'Lady King', her intention from the first was to provide the union with a suitable male head. Her choice had fallen on her grand-nephew, Eric of Pomerania,* who had been accepted by the Norwegian Council in 1389 as hereditary sovereign. Seven years later his acceptance by the other two kingdoms as sovereign elect prepared the way for the crowning, which was performed by the Danish and Swedish archbishops. The Norwegian episcopate was represented only by the bishop of Orkney, who happened to be an Englishman, but the parchment attestation of the ceremony included twelve Norwegians among its sixty-seven signatories.

Special interest attaches, however, to a second document, whose

---

* 1382–1459. He was the eldest child of the daughter of her sister Ingeborg, who had married the ruler of the coastal duchy of Pomerania; this included the island of Rügen, where Eric eventually died in exile.

ambiguous character is mainly responsible for making this occasion 'the most intensively discussed single event in Nordic history'.[10] It is now generally agreed that this document, which is written on paper and has the seals imprinted instead of their being attached in the regular way, is not a constitution, although attested by representatives of all three kingdoms. Viewed as a draft which never received formal approval, it remains a puzzle, since no contemporary evidence is forthcoming as to why a project of such far-reaching significance was allowed to pass into oblivion. Its terms provided that the three realms should be for ever united under one king, that they should have a common defence policy and diplomacy, and that they should promote mutual harmony by making any sentence of banishment from one kingdom applicable to the other two; they were, however, to be kept expressly separate from each other in all matters of law and administration. So far, so good: but Margaret may well have deprecated the proposed succession arrangements, allowing the three realms a free choice among Eric's direct descendants or, if his line failed, elsewhere. For the coronation document, formally attested on parchment, had given the sovereign such full rights of disposal over the royal fiefs and castles that he could ensure the transfer of the crown to whatever successor he might prefer.

THE UNION IN OPERATION, 1397–1448

Although Eric came of age in 1401, Margaret continued for the remaining eleven years of her life to be sole ruler in all but name. She took little part in the affairs of Europe, for (as the Holsteiners observed) 'This very cunning woman would not light several fires together'.[11] Before her death on board ship in Flensborg harbour, she had recovered Finland and Gotland, as already mentioned, and was in process of winning the natural southern limit for her realms by the recovery of Slesvig. At the same time she strove to provide the union monarchy with a sound economic basis. Crown lands which had passed into the hands of the nobility or Church were 'resumed' – in Sweden if they had been alienated under Albrecht, in Denmark under her own father. New taxes were imposed, and old ones more strictly exacted: this affected also Norway, where there had been few rich estates for resumption by the crown. Finally, in 1405 a new coinage was struck, in which the same weight of silver provided one-third more currency than before.

Each of Queen Margaret's measures hurt the interests of powerful classes, but she made little use of the separate Councils of her three kingdoms or their traditional posts of dignity, where discontent might find leadership. Instead, she chose with great skill a body of civil and ecclesiastical officials to carry out her system of government. With the co-operation of the pope, she placed Danes in Swedish and Norwegian bishoprics, whilst many of the royal castles and estates were administered by castellans and bailiffs (*fogder*) of foreign extraction. This has often been criticised by posterity as a deliberate policy of promoting Danes at the expense of the rest of her subjects; but the fact that she employed more Germans in Denmark than elsewhere suggests that the queen was mainly interested in securing a loyal and efficient administration.

The dignity and allure of this first 'Semiramis of the North' can only be imagined, and we know almost nothing of her plans for creating a lasting loyalty to the Union. She travelled much, and in her later years is said to have spent more time in Sweden than in her native Denmark. She encouraged intermarriages among the nobility of her three realms. Her piety was noted by contemporaries, and it is reasonable to see a Scandinavian motive in the strong backing she gave to the canonisation of Saint Birgitta, which was obtained in 1391 – after the Swedish people had contributed heavily to the cost of the promotion. Certainly the frequent visits which the queen paid to Vadstena helped to make it a great cultural centre. She also patronised the Birgittine houses in Denmark; and, although the big Birgittine monastery in Bergen was a much later foundation, the queen's interest in the order no doubt encouraged the spread of a 'Birgittine language', which brought many Swedish expressions into use among Norwegians as well as Danes.

The building up of the Union by extension of the royal power was an aim which Queen Margaret pursued with far-sighted tact and caution; her successor pursued the same aim less skilfully. King Eric had the advantages of a kingly appearance and personal charm. He had undergone a long period of careful tutelage by his grand-aunt, and the secure status of the new triple monarchy had been marked by his marriage to a daughter of Henry IV of England. Although Philippa unfortunately failed to provide the Union with an heir, she proved a popular queen and continued the royal interest in the Birgittines of Vadstena, among whom she lies buried. Nevertheless, Eric's independent reign ended after more than a quarter of a century in his dethronement.

He was faced in all his realms with the perennial problem of how to maintain an adequate central authority, based on sufficient financial resources, in a society where the nobility claimed possession of royal fiefs and powers of control over royal policies. When he used loyalty and efficiency as the criteria by which to judge candidates for appointments, the result was the introduction of Danes and Germans to many posts where they could be denounced as foreigners. In the Church, for example, a Dane was translated from the Norwegian see of Bergen to the Swedish archbishopric of Uppsala, whereupon a rival candidate who had the chapter's support carried the dispute to the Council of Basle. Whilst bishops were an important factor in the control of the king's council in each kingdom, military power rested with the castellans or bailiffs of the royal castles. Eric therefore denied these posts to members of the higher nobility and confided them to persons of lower rank, who often came from outside the country in question – members of immigrant families from another part of Scandinavia or fellow Pomeranians or, in one case, an Italian who had been his interpreter when he visited the Pope. He took particular interest in Finland, where he set up a supreme court to control the administration and considerably increased the lower nobility. Moreover, the three Finnish castles were left in Swedish hands, presumably on account of the threat from Russia.

Since a Union must have a capital, the central administration was based upon Copenhagen, where members summoned from the three Councils also met in company with representatives of the towns – a Nordic parliament in embryo, begun by Queen Margaret. The entire organisation of the Union, indeed, was still very rudimentary, but the nobility of all three states had a mounting territorial interest in its continuance, as being helpful for the exploitation of their scattered properties and the furtherance of family interests. But political unity is a plant of delicate growth; in this case, at least three favourable conditions were needed, none of which proved to be available.

The first was a clear line of succession: but Eric had to make do with a plan to provide for his decease by an automatic transfer of the royal castles in that event to his Pomeranian cousin, Duke Bogislaw IX. The second obvious requirement was a period of internal harmony, during which the Union might cease to be questioned as a breach with old tradition and a substitution of autocracy for the oligarchies of the past. No such period was provided, because Eric was soon in financial difficulties. Extra taxes reduced his initial popularity; and when the need for ready money caused him to lease out fiefs for fixed sums, leaving the fief-holder to exact what he could, the dislike of foreign bailiffs turned to hatred. But the financial measure which aroused most resentment was almost certainly a heavy depreciation of the currency when the king introduced a copper coinage; this was given the same nominal value as the silver, while allowing only silver to be accepted in tax payments.

All this, however, might eventually have been forgiven him if King Eric had satisfied the third need, namely prestige for the Union abroad. His Pomeranian possessions made him keenly alive to the tempting situation which had arisen on the south shore of the Baltic after the defeat of the Teutonic knights by the Poles at Tannenberg in 1410. On the sea, too, his wife's fellow countrymen, and still more the Dutch, were challenging the Hanseatic trade monopoly, a challenge in which many Scandinavian traders would be glad to see him join. It therefore seemed natural for the Union, which controlled the entrance to the Baltic with all its northern coasts to the head of the Gulf of Finland, to aspire to the dominion of that sea. But it was also natural for Eric to continue Queen Margaret's work for the recovery of Slesvig – and the double effort was quite beyond his means.

In the year after his accession he induced the *Danehof* to assert his

claim to the whole of Slesvig, and he later obtained a decision from the
Emperor Sigismund (who was his cousin) to the effect that Slesvig could
not have been alienated from Denmark as a hereditary fief. The result,
however, was an exhausting twenty-year war against its Germanised
nobles, who received strong support from Holstein. On what we may term
the other front, Eric began by encouraging the Danish towns, especially
Copenhagen and Malmö, through the grant of trade privileges which
overrode the interests of the Hanse merchants. When the League resorted
to war, its forces were defeated in the Sound and again in an attack on
Copenhagen, which was defended by 200 of the new cannon, and in
1429 the king erected a fort, Krogen near Elsinore, to enable him to
exact tolls on all foreign vessels passing through the Sound. Since the
middle of the previous century this more expeditious route to the Baltic,
formerly deemed too dangerous, had been coming into vogue with Dutch
and other mariners, who for more than four centuries provided a major
source of income to the Danish crown. Nevertheless, the Hanseatic
League exerted such heavy pressure by a trade blockade of the three
kingdoms that the king could not persevere to the end with either of his
projects. In 1432 he came to terms with the Holsteiners, who by the close
of the decade established a single, almost independent state of Slesvig-
Holstein under Count Adolf VIII of Schaumburg; and in 1435 Eric
restored the privileges of the Hanse towns, at the same time exempting
them from the new Sound tolls.

Danish as well as Swedish nobles were prompt to resent the high
cost of an unsuccessful foreign policy which they had not been asked to
approve. But the operative cause of rebellion was the hardship which the
Hanse blockade imposed on the compact and relatively well organised
Swedish mining interests. The iron and copper of Dalecarlia, worked
by small mine owners and skilled artisans who were mainly of German
origin, provided Sweden with its most valuable export, which depended
entirely upon Hanse merchants for its conveyance to foreign markets. The
blockade was therefore acutely felt in a region where the presence of
foreign bailiffs exacting heavy taxes was already bitterly resented. This
explosive situation gave scope to a highly talented leader, whose attacks
upon the mismanagement of the Union made him a national hero, though
he entertained no designs against the Union itself.

Engelbrekt Engelbrektsson belonged to a prosperous mine-owning
family, whose founder had probably come over from Germany before
1300. He ranked as a small squire and is first heard of in 1432, when he
headed a peasant outbreak against a particularly oppressive bailiff. Two
years later this was followed by a large-scale revolt, in which his initial
body of supporters from the mining district was swelled by townspeople,
bishops resentful of foreign Churchmen, and eventually by lords of the
Council. By January 1435 he had been appointed chief military commander at a meeting of the Council (reinforced by additional members) at

Arboga, and in October a compromise settlement was negotiated with the king; in transferring posts of authority to native Swedes, Eric gave an important fief to Engelbrektsson but revived the office of Marshal for a magnate, Karl Knutsson Bonde. Next January, however, the quarrel with the king was formally reopened at a second great Council meeting at Arboga, this time with support promised from a similar rising in Norway. Engelbrekt was made joint ruler with Karl, and again took the field at the head of an army of peasants. But in April (1436) his meteoric career ended in his murder by the son of a Lawman, a personal enemy to whom Karl and other magnates subsequently afforded protection – though they never hesitated to invoke the memory of Engelbrektsson as a champion of the national liberties.

In September of the same year Eric conceded the control of Swedish fiefs and other demands made by the Swedish nobility; the Danish Council, having rather similar grievances against the king, supported their action on the understanding that the possessions of Danish nobles in Sweden would be left undisturbed. But the king had not in reality abandoned his absolutist aims, including provision for a Pomeranian successor to his thrones, so Karl – who had already taken the lead in executing Engelbrektsson's principal lieutenant and suppressing further disturbances among the peasantry – was elevated by his fellow nobles in 1438 to the position of Guardian of the Realm (*Riksförestånдare*). A year later the Swedish Council followed the example of the Danish in formally deposing King Eric, who maintained himself as a kind of royal pirate in the island of Gotland whilst negotiating for his restoration. He was still supported by one faction in the Swedish nobility, and the kingdom of Norway (where the rising had quickly ebbed away) remained for three years on offer to him.*

In 1441 the Swedish again followed the example of the Danish Council in conferring the throne upon Christopher of Bavaria, who was the son of Eric's sister and a Wittelsbach duke. He conciliated Karl Knutsson with large fiefs in Finland, where he took up residence at Viipuri. In Denmark the only trouble which the new sovereign encountered was a peasant rising in Jutland, quickly suppressed with the help of the military skills he had acquired in the wars of the Empire against the Hussites. His acceptance by the Norwegian Council was, indeed, belated, but its members were allowed unwonted power during his reign, the only cause of disharmony being his new concessions to the Hanse merchants, whom he could not afford to disoblige. In general King Christopher's policy was to ally himself with the towns and the Church without deviating from the promise to respect the rights of the Councils which he had made

---

* The attitude of the Icelanders, for whom 1400–1540 was a period in which 'economic conditions were generally good',[12] may be inferred from their resentment of King Eric's attempts to stop the trade with English vessels, which now exported their stockfish and fish-oil. These attempts, made by ordinance and treaty, were renewed in 1449.

in his accession charters. Even the failure to wrest Gotland from Eric, which aroused some resentment, may be regarded as a further illustration of a slow-moving prudence which might in time have enabled his realms to find common interests promoted by a common loyalty. But time was denied him: in 1448 Christopher died suddenly at the age of thirty-two, leaving a young wife, Dorothea of Brandenburg, but no heir.

THE FIRST OLDENBURG SOVEREIGNS

The Danish nobles offered the vacant throne to the most strongly placed member of their order, namely the Count Adolf who (as we have seen) held sway in Slesvig-Holstein; but he was unwilling to put his possessions under their control and instead proposed his 22-year-old nephew, Christian of Oldenburg, whom they accepted. Thus the ruler of an obscure German county, having married his predecessor's widow, became the founder of a dynasty which continued in the direct male line for more than four centuries. Christian was prompt to sign accession charters confirming the rights of the nobility, but one section of Swedish magnates had already brought back Karl Knutsson from Finland: in 1449 he was crowned king in Sweden and also in Norway, where the archbishop exacted the fullest privileges for the Church. The sequel, however, was a meeting of councillors at Halmstad in Halland, at which the general desire to preserve the Union found expression in an agreement that the realms should be reunited under the king who lived longest or at all events through the choice of his successor.

Gotland had already been surrendered into quasi-Danish hands* by ex-king Eric, and in Norway the death of the archbishop made it easier for its crown to revert to Christian. But the latter was soon at war with King Karl, who ravaged Skåne and was never subjugated by the Danish armies, although they ranged far into Sweden and had the help of the Hanseatics. His rule was felt to be arbitrary, however, not only by the heavily taxed peasants but also by a party of nobles, and in 1457 he was driven out by an insurrection under the great family of the Oxenstiernas. Christian then reigned in his stead. Karl subsequently recovered the throne for two shorter periods, in 1464–5 and from 1467 until his death in 1470; but the interminable conflicts between rival groups of magnates†

---

* The hands were those of Oluf Axelsson Tott, one of the seven sons born to a Halland nobleman in his two Swedish marriages; four had their principal interests in Denmark and three in Sweden, but all put the family first. The fiefs in their possession ranged from Halland to the Russian border.

† The confused struggle in Sweden at this time bears a striking resemblance to the contemporary Wars of the Roses; but Karl put a gloss of disinterestedness upon his actions by skilful propaganda, such as the 'Chronicle of Charles' (*Karlskronikan*), a rhyming account of events from 1397 to 1452, produced by members of his chancery when his power was at its height. The appeal to Swedish nationalism, of which Karl professed to be the devoted champion, is seasoned with popular jests at the expense of both the Danish and Norwegian peoples.

left King Christian with a reasonable prospect of imposing the Union as a less troublesome alternative for Sweden.

In the meantime the death of his uncle Count Adolf had enabled him to extend his power south of the Danish Jutland frontier. By the treaty of Ribe (1460) the nobles of the county of Holstein and the duchy of Slesvig elected the House of Oldenburg as their sovereign, on condition that county and duchy – which were fiefs respectively of the Empire and the Crown of Denmark – should remain indissolubly connected with each other; this arrangement was made to suit the territorial interest of noble landowners, whose privileges were explicitly guaranteed. Christian had also to spend large sums in buying out the claims of other members of his family, which raised his already high level of expenditure. The Swedes, finding his taxation heavier than King Karl's, decried him as 'King Leaky-Purse', and his need for loans weakened his resistance to the Hanse demands for privileges.

The steady decline of the Norwegian kingdom was clearly shown in this connection, when the murder of the king's castellan by the German residents in Bergen was atoned for by a payment of only 700 marks, which was less than one-tenth of the sum exacted by the Church for the murder of the bishop in the same riot. Norway also suffered a more permanent loss on account of Christian's straitened finances, when a dowry was needed for marrying his daughter Margaret to the heir to the Scottish throne. In addition to the cancellation of the small annual pay-ment for the Hebrides and Man, which was already thirty-four years in arrears, Christian· was due to produce 60,000 guilders in cash. The Orkneys were mortgaged to Scotland for 50,000 of these, and when the time came for the wedding (1469) the king had only 2,000 guilders available and mortgaged Shetland for the balance. The Orkneys were already predominantly Scottish in outlook, and the bishopric had recently been placed under the see of St Andrews. But close trade relations with western Norway were to keep the Norwegian language and culture alive in Shetland for several centuries. It was a bitter reflection for Norwegians that the islands had been mortgaged for so paltry a sum as 8,000 guilders, especially for any of them who may have learnt that, only five years after the royal wedding, the king borrowed more than three times that amount from the Hanseatics for a journey to Rome. According to a contemporary Scottish chronicler, the Scots gained a good queen into the bargain: 'She deemed it a greater thing to be queen in Scotland than daughter of a king who wears three crowns.'[13]

In 1470 the death of Karl gave Christian a fresh chance to assert his right to the third of those crowns, a right which was still upheld by the Oxenstiernas, Vasas, and others of the great Swedish families, who were supported by the agrarian classes of the central provinces. The position of Guardian of the Realm, which Karl had held before he aspired to the throne, was immediately claimed by his nephew, Sten Sture, who was linked by marriage with the Axelsson Totts, whose special Swedish interests centred on cattle and butter exports sent southwards. Sture also enjoyed the support of the miners and of the Stockholm merchant class. In October 1471 he attacked a powerful Danish army, which was encamped with its Swedish allies on the Brunkeberg hill outside Stockholm. After a bitter struggle the Danes were defeated and the citizens of Stockholm increased their losses by cutting down the bridge by which the invaders sought to regain their ships.

For the remaining ten years of the long reign of Christian I Sten Sture's position as Guardian in Sweden was not directly challenged. The alleged national character of his famous victory, which Swedish historians compare to Agincourt, was emphasised by the splendid effigy of St George slaying the dragon set up by Sture in the Great Church at Stockholm, in allusion to the battle song which had been on the lips of his men at Brunkeberg. But his power rested to a great extent upon the Axelssons, whose territorial possessions (as we have seen) were partly Danish, and negotiations for the recognition of the Oldenburg monarchy were never completely broken off.

Christian had strengthened his position in Denmark, where the towns as a whole were more important than in the other northern countries, by including five burgesses from each town – together with two peasants from every district – in the first meeting of the Estates, which was held in 1468; he also helped them by renewing the ban on German inland trade. He gained more of a metropolitan status for Copenhagen by maintaining a splendid if expensive court and by securing papal authority for a university there, though this was one year junior to Sten Sture's foundation at Uppsala in 1477. The resemblance to the 'new monarchies' now making their appearance in other parts of Europe was still more evident under Christian I's son Hans (John), who came to the throne in 1481. Although the nobles imposed restrictions in the charter, he placed his reliance on commoners and backed the towns against the encroachments of German traders at the cost of a war against Lübeck, which was won with the help of the first effective Danish fleet since the Viking era.

The contest for the third crown continued with little interruption throughout the reign of Hans, albeit that the three Councils in 1483 approved a new constitution (the Kalmar Recess) under which the Swedish nobles would have received full control of fiefs and taxation. Sten Sture strengthened his position by taking away their Swedish and Finnish fiefs from his former allies in the Axelsson family, who withdrew to Denmark. They failed, however, to hand over Gotland to the Swedes, which involved a breach of the terms agreed at Kalmar, whilst the Danes for their part were encouraged to renew the conflict by the situation in Finland. Possession of the fortress of Olofsborg (built by one of the Axelssons) on the ill-defined Russian frontier was now disputed by Ivan

III, who had recently added Novgorod to the Grand Duchy of Moscow. In 1495 the Russians made the first of their many alliances with Denmark against Sweden, and although their invasion of Finland was eventually repelled – chiefly by the efforts of one of Sture's younger rivals, named Svante Nilsson – Sture's Dalecarlian supporters were soon afterwards defeated by Hans, who in 1497 was crowned king in Stockholm.

The result was no more than a four years' truce, during which Sten Sture held the Finnish fiefs, where he plotted with Svante Nilsson and an able clerical go-between, named Hemming Gadh.* News of a reverse suffered by Hans in far-off Ditmarsh then encouraged a new rising, which had regained nearly all Sweden for Sture by the time of his death in 1503. A group of Councillors gave the Guardianship to Svante, who received notable assistance from Gadh in the conduct of siege warfare, diplomacy, and public relations. But Hans's claim to the throne was formally endorsed by the Emperor Maximilian and enforced by practical measures of blockade and warfare, so that the Swedish people wearied of the blood-letting and expense, whilst the nobles were intimidated by his confiscation of their Danish inheritances and also began to fear a peasant rising. Accordingly, when Svante Nilsson died in 1512 – one year before King Hans – the Swedish Council engaged itself to pay tribute if it failed to accept him in due course as king, whilst its immediate choice for a new Guardian, Eric Trolle, belonged to a family which had many of its estates in Denmark.

The Union was beset with other difficulties in Hans's time. One was created by his mother, Queen Dorothea, who induced him to assign one-half of Slesvig-Holstein to his younger brother, Frederick. A second was his embroilment in the affairs of Ditmarsh in Holstein, which he and his brother invaded in 1500, anticipating an easy conquest of the peasant republic, which had been virtually independent since the battle of Bornhöved; but king and duke were routed on a narrow causeway through the marshes, with heavy losses in men and prestige. A third was the dangerous situation which arose in 1501–2 in Norway.

When Sten Sture had re-emerged from Finland and was besieging Hans's supporters in Stockholm, a Swedish-Norwegian nobleman, Knut Alvsson, crossed the border and overran south-eastern Norway with such sweeping success that the rising spread as far as Bergen. However, the 21-year-old heir to the throne, Prince Christian, came to the rescue in the sensitive area near modern Gothenburg, where the three kingdoms joined, and the Danish castellan eventually decoyed Knut

* *c.* 1450–1520. He had been for nearly twenty years Sten Sture's envoy to the Papal Curia, where he found time to study Italian military tactics as well as the art of negotiation. His ability to swear in three languages perhaps contributed more than his doctorate in canon law to his effective haranguing of the common people, which set an example for the Vasa kings. After entering the service of the younger Sture, he was taken as a hostage by Christian II, to whom he transferred his services; but this did not save him from execution in Finland in December 1520.

Alvsson from Akershus Castle, which he had occupied. The perfidious blow which did him to death in Oslo harbour is termed by Ibsen a blow to Norway's heart – a true verdict, for although Alvsson's ambitions were selfish and personal many of his supporters would have seized upon his continued success as a chance to improve Norway's declining national status. As it was, the election of the third Oldenburg sovereign was held at a joint meeting of the Danish and Norwegian Councils where half the representatives of Norway were Danes or Swedes; and in the subsequent events which brought the union of three crowns finally to an end, the Norwegian role was almost that of an onlooker.

CHRISTIAN II

Although his reign lasted only ten years (1513–23), Christian II presents us with the spectacle of a strong if unbalanced personality which left an enduring imprint upon the history of northern Europe. His policy was in many ways enlightened, seeking to introduce to Scandinavia modern developments from the Renaissance era in lands farther south. To carry out such a policy required a high level of monarchical authority, which might gain the support of the other classes but not that of the nobles. It also required self-control, an equable judgement, and consistency – qualities in which Christian was not necessarily more deficient than his great English contemporary, Henry VIII, but which he needed in larger measure because his realms were less unified. At the major crises of his career he seemed to take drastic action without sufficient regard for its long-term consequences, but may have acted deliberately. When Erasmus once deprecated the violence of Luther to him, the king replied significantly: 'Gentle medicines produce no results; the best and most effective remedies are those which shake up the entire body.'[14]

Hans had caused his son to be brought up for a time in a middle-class Copenhagen family, and Christian already showed bourgeois sympathies before he was sent to Norway for the second time in 1506 to serve as his father's viceroy. He put down a trifling rebellion with disproportionate severity; extracted evidence by torture against the bishop of Hamar, who was suspect on account of his Swedish connections; and secured full control over the Church by arranging for his chancellor to be preferred to the see of Trondheim. But he also helped the burgesses of Oslo and Tönsberg by taking away the privileges of the German Rostock merchants; and when his father quarrelled with the Hanseatics, Christian reduced their position in Bergen to the benefit of native merchants and those from England and Scotland. Moreover, bourgeois Bergen had a lasting influence on his career, because the daughter of a Dutch market-woman became his 'little dove' (*Dyveke*), who returned with him in 1511 to Copenhagen in company with her mother, Sigbrit Willums.

Although Christian's lack of sympathy with the privileged classes caused some Jutland nobles to propose Hans's brother, Duke Frederick, as his successor, Christian was duly accepted as king except in Sweden, where the conciliatory Eric Trolle had been quickly deprived of the control of affairs. Indeed, his position received a higher European recognition than was accorded to any other of his line through his marriage to Elisabeth of Hapsburg, younger sister of the future emperor Charles V. This resulted in strong pressure for the abandonment of Dyveke, which would in any case have been welcomed by the nobility, who bitterly resented the authority exercised by her shrewd mother over financial and other public business. Dyveke died in mysterious circumstances in the fourth year of the reign. One consequence was the worsening of the king's relations with the nobles, one of whom was executed for the supposed murder without any evidence of his guilt; another, a challenging increase in the influence of Sigbrit, who remained permanently at the centre of an inner council of royal advisers, which also included the mayor of Malmö and other commoners.

In foreign policy, Christian relied on Dutch support against Lübeck, which Charles V even declared to be lawfully subject to Danish suzerainty; sought financial support from the Fuggers for a triangular trade between Russia, Scandinavia, and western Europe; and planned to use the Sound tolls to build up a position for Copenhagen as the great entrepôt for all the Baltic trades. His domestic policies were equally far-reaching. Christian reorganised the Chancery in Copenhagen, which he staffed with officials from the enlightened middle class. Their determination to safeguard the royal revenues was felt as far afield as Norway, and in nine years the number of districts in Denmark which rendered direct accounts of what was due from them to the crown (*regnskabslen*) rose from forty-three to more than sixty.[15] Then in 1521, after prolonged negotiation with the Council, new legal codes based largely on Dutch models were approved for country and town respectively. The former included a ban on 'the wicked, unchristian custom of selling peasants as creatures without soul',[16] which was found to exist in Zealand and others of the east Danish islands.

But the king's ability to overawe the Danish nobles depended in the long run upon a solution being found for the situation in Sweden, where Trolle's supporters on the Council had been outwitted by Svante Nilsson's twenty-year-old son, who for propaganda reasons styled himself 'Sten Sture the Younger'. Seizing possession of his father's castles and fiefs, he had been helped by Hemming Gadh to become Guardian of the Realm, and hoped to play upon the national feelings of the masses to make himself king. His chief opponent on the Council was Gustav Trolle, a son of the former Guardian and the newly appointed archbishop of Uppsala, with whom a trial of strength quickly developed over the episcopal castle and fief of Stäket, which Sture claimed for himself and besieged. In 1517 he summoned an 'assembly of the realm' (*riksmöte*), where the policy of his supporters in the Council and nobility was endorsed by mine owners, men of Dalecarlia, the town council of Stockholm, and 'ordinary peasants'; and in spite of excommunication the next year he captured the castle, imprisoned the archbishop, and broke some of his supporters on the wheel.

The Danish fleet had intervened twice without effect in these proceedings, though on the second occasion Christian by a ruse secured hostages who included Hemming Gadh and a youthful member of the Vasa family named Gustav. In 1519, however, he rebuilt the key fortress of Älvsborg to deprive the Swedish rebels of any support from the west, and next year advanced north from Denmark with a large force of German, French, and Scottish mercenaries. Two victories opened the way into the heart of Sweden. Sten Sture died of his wounds while retreating to Stockholm; and soon its castle, held by his widow Christina Gyllenstierna, was the only centre of resistance. She capitulated in September, and on 4 November 1520 Christian II was crowned in Stockholm as hereditary king of Sweden.

In legal theory his position was now stronger than that of any of his five predecessors on the Union throne. In practice, too, it was strengthened by the discrediting of the defeated noble opposition in the eyes of the Stockholm merchants, the mining community and those elements among the peasantry to whom Sture had directed his powerful demagogic appeals. But in concert with the archbishop – or possibly prompted by him – Christian II proceeded to make his position doubly secure by a stroke of truly machiavellian ruthlessness. When the traditional three days' coronation festivities were completed, the king's enemies were rounded up in Stockholm castle and tried by archbishop Trolle and other clerics for heresy, as shown in their disregard of his ecclesiastical rights and authority. Christina produced a signed document to show that what had been done was approved by the Assembly, but this was treated as evidence against all concerned. They were duly found guilty and handed over to the king, who because the crime was heresy was no longer bound by the full amnesty which he had granted when Stockholm surrendered.

The royal executioner set to work immediately, his eighty-two victims including two bishops, noblemen from many of the great families, such as the Vasas and Gyllenstiernas, some Stockholm burgesses, and other minor figures who in some cases were not implicated as heretics. The market-place ran with blood and resounded with the lamentations of onlookers; when the bodies were eventually burnt on a huge pyre, the exhumed remains of Sten Sture and a child of his were added to crown the horrifying scene. That the Bloodbath was not attributable to a sudden fit of rage is shown by the fact that the executions spread as far as Finland and were continued during the king's return journey across southern Sweden, the total number of victims being estimated at 600.

Political crimes do not always fail in their purpose, at any rate in the short run; Christian's action might well have cowed the Swedish people into submission long enough for the advantages of his plans for the future of the Union to win their support. But at this juncture the scattered remnants of the national resistance movement found a youthful leader, richly endowed with courage, eloquence and personal magnetism. For Gustav Vasa had escaped from Danish custody to Lübeck and was vainly trying to rouse the southern provinces of Sweden at the time of the Bloodbath, in which his father and other relations perished. As the nephew of Christina, he was well entitled to take up the Sture-cause, but met at first with so little support that he contemplated fleeing in desperation across the Norwegian frontier. However, in January 1521, when there were rumours of a further punitive campaign from Denmark, the peasants of Dalecarlia responded to his appeal. The miners joined them to form an army of rebellion, to which the nobles one by one adhered, and next year Gustav received help from Lübeck in men, ships and money. Archbishop Trolle, whom Christian had left in charge of the country, was driven out, and in June 1523 an Assembly of the Realm unanimously elected Gustav king of Sweden.

Meanwhile, the Danish nobility had plucked up courage to resist Christian, whose plans for a new-type Renaissance monarchy they had always regarded as 'tyranny'. The king's uncle, Frederick, was now ready to take the lead, as he felt his own position to be threatened when Christian was directly invested with the duchy of Holstein by his brother-in-law, now Emperor. Heavy taxes, due partly to the costs of the campaign in Sweden, created general discontent, and in some districts the peasants had special grievances against extortionate royal bailiffs. Furthermore, the hostility of the nobles towards the king was no longer counterbalanced by the united support of the Church. During the troubles in Sweden he had become embroiled with a papal legate who was selling indulgences, and whose profits the king confiscated because he sided with Sten Sture. The pope was placated over this, as also over the execution of two bishops in the Bloodbath; the latter offence was expiated by throwing the blame upon a royal secretary, who was burnt at the stake as a heretic two months after the king had approved his appointment as archbishop of Lund. But it is probable that the clergy as a whole were even more alarmed by the favour which their Renaissance prince showed to German humanist scholars, whom he welcomed to Copenhagen university, and more tentatively to Lutheran preachers.

In December 1522 a rebellion was launched by eighteen Jutland nobles, of whom four were bishops. Copenhagen and Malmö remained loyal to the king, but when the Estates of Jutland paid homage to Frederick, who had enlisted the support of Lübeck, the king's nerve failed him, and in April 1523 he sailed for the Netherlands, accompanied by his wife and children and the much-hated Sigbrit. Christian hoped to be restored by the powerful help of the Emperor Charles V; in fact, however, the union of three crowns came to a final end with the sudden eclipse of this highly gifted, but despotic and unstable ruler.

Chapter 5

The Lutheran Kingdoms

THE FRAMING OF A NEW ERA

The central events in Scandinavian history during the second quarter of the sixteenth century have their counterpart in the growth of other national monarchies. Gustavus of Sweden was not the only 'mighty lord that brake the bonds of Rome'. Christian III of Denmark reduced the ancient kingdom of Norway to the status of a province in the very same year in which the principality of Wales was incorporated into the parliamentary constitution of England, though Norway's submergence in the larger unit was less complete and less durable. The rapid rise in population and the higher level of prices, too, were general European phenomena which stimulated a trend towards more centralised and less inefficient forms of government, as exemplified also in Scandinavia.

In these countries, Gustavus Vasa claims pride of place. Like our own Henry VIII, he was fortunate in his length of days – no later Swedish king before the twentieth century matches his reign of thirty-seven years – and in leaving three children who in various degrees carried on their father's work. He was a man of imposing presence; ruthless when crossed, charming when pleased; and a demagogic orator, who knew how to play upon the feelings of his subjects. Above all, Gustavus was a tremendous worker, who watched over every aspect of his country's affairs as if it had been a private estate, the end-product which was achieved by mid-century being a stronger rule exercised over a more prosperous people.

His position was initially very weak. In 1524, indeed, the sequel to his capture of Stockholm was that his powerful allies in Lübeck negotiated his recognition as king of Sweden by the Danes; but he had to give up the Norwegian border district which he had occupied as far as Oslo. Only one year later the peasants and miners of Dalecarlia rose against the master they had so recently brought to power, and they were no sooner put down than they rose again, this time in support of a pretender who gave himself out to be Sten Sture's young son, who was actually resident at court. To avoid relying upon feudal levies under nobles whose loyalty was dubious, the king had to hire German mercenaries at a cost that he could ill afford. In 1527, however, a Riksdag at Västerås, to which he addressed high-pitched threats of abdication, agreed that he might take possession of the wealth of the Church, the nobles being conciliated by fiefs of monastic lands and the right to reclaim recent gifts. The royal authority then began to grow: in 1533, when the Dalecarlians had refused to surrender church bells for melting down, they were finally crushed by executions, confiscation of mining property, and division of the dales into two smaller units. Even so, the poor southern province of Småland rose in 1542 under a peasant leader in a kind of Pilgrimage of Grace, with which the king found it necessary to temporise for a whole winter before making an end of resistance by a two-pronged advance across the province, followed by further executions, heavy fines, and deportations to Finland.

The king was now indeed master of his realm, which in the latter part of the reign enjoyed a tranquillity unknown since the rising under Engelbrektsson. So much Church land had been retained in the royal hands that the total percentage of Crown holdings rose from 5·5 to 28·2, whilst those of the nobility and the independent peasants were left almost unchanged at 22·4 and 49·4 per cent respectively.[1] A part of the king's resources went to maintain a standing army of native recruits from each province; these cost less than German mercenaries, and a war-chest was accumulated, which Gustavus passed on intact to his heir. The Riksdag entailed the throne upon his eldest son, whose mother was a German princess, and authorised him to allocate duchies for the support of the sons by his second wife, a scion of the Swedish nobility. Most important of all, Gustavus built up a central administration, so that the historic provinces ceased to be virtually autonomous – a task in which he for a time employed a German chancellor who had been in the service of the Emperor. By the end of the reign more than two-thirds of the country was under the direct financial control of the king's treasury, major fiefs being entrusted only to such nobles as were related to the royal house.

Since dues of every description were paid mainly in kind, Crown goods made up the bulk of Sweden's exports. The king took a keen interest in internal communications, because he had foodstuffs to sell in the best market; he watched over the growth of the ports and over the foreign merchants who frequented them; and promoted both the copper and iron industries. It was in Gustavus's reign that German immigrants introduced the first hammers for making the bar iron which later replaced *osmund* iron as Sweden's most profitable manufacture. Best of all, he enabled the farmed area to expand by assuring the peasant of peace in which to 'till his blood-sprayed lands'.[2]

The two kings of Denmark whose reigns covered the same period were less dynamic figures. Frederick I, who was fifty-two years of age when he succeeded his nephew Christian II, pursued a cautious policy in Church and State, recognising that he was the nobles' nominee and residing for preference at Gottorp in his original duchy. In November

1531 he had to face a long-awaited attack from the man he had ousted, who landed in eastern Norway with a small army which the Emperor had allowed him to raise in the Netherlands. Christian was supported by the archbishop of Trondheim and recognised as king by most Norwegians, but failed to take the fortresses at Bohus (against which he marched) or Oslo before the break-up of the ice allowed relief to reach the latter from Denmark. With a lack of resolution which had not been characteristic of his earlier career, he then let himself be talked into accepting a safe conduct for a parley with his uncle at Copenhagen. Instead of meeting Frederick, he was carried off to a distant castle for lifelong captivity – a deed of infamy in which the representatives of Sweden and Lübeck concurred with the Danish king and Council. Frederick might now have become less hesitant in his Church policy, which was tolerant of Lutheranism but had proceeded no further than to forbid bishops to seek confirmation of appointment from, or make payments to, the Curia. However, he died only eight months after ex-king Christian II had ceased to be a constant threat.

The sequel was the last civil war in the history of Denmark. The majority in the Council wished to elect as their new king the twelve-year-old younger son, Prince Hans, who was being brought up in the Catholic faith, rather than the elder son, the later King Christian III, who had been present when Luther testified at the Diet of Worms and had welcomed fellow Lutherans to the part of Slesvig entrusted to him by his father. The election was postponed for a year – partly to enable the Norwegian Council to be represented – during which time an open conflict was precipitated by the intervention of a third party. This was Count Christopher of Oldenburg, a grand-nephew of King Christian I, who landed in Zealand with an expedition furnished by the mayor of Lübeck, demanding the restoration of the imprisoned ex-king Christian II. As the townsmen of Copenhagen and Malmö and the great mass of the peasantry still honoured the ex-king as their champion against noble privilege, the count won control over both Skåne and the islands, and the peasants of north Jutland also rose in his support. But Johan Rantzau, a Holstein nobleman of long military experience who had accompanied his master on the memorable visit to Worms, brought a force of German mercenaries northwards. After crushing the Jutland peasant army at Ålborg, he crossed to the islands, exacting fearful retribution on behalf of the scared and plundered nobility. A Danish naval victory, in which some Swedish ships assisted, completed the discomfiture of Lübeck, which had hoped in vain to reassert its ancient ascendancy in the Baltic. The so-called Count's War ended when, more than two years after the outbreak of this bitter struggle, the citizens of Copenhagen were starved into surrender.

In August 1536, six days after his entry into his capital, Christian III ordered the arrest of the bishops, who were saddled with the responsibility for the civil war and deposed from their office. The lay members of the Council, who were themselves in danger of arrest, agreed to the confiscation of the Church lands (which enabled the king to meet his huge military expenses) and to the establishment of Lutheranism. The religious settlement was approved at a full meeting of Estates in October, when the new king also issued an accession charter, which confirmed the existing privileges of the Danish nobility.

The same document settled the fate of Norway, where the Council in the south under strong Danish influence had been quick to recognise Christian III. Archbishop Olav Englebrektsson, on the other hand, had hoped against hope for the intervention of the Emperor on behalf of ex-king Christian's son-in-law, Frederick Count Palatine. For Norway this represented the national as well as the Catholic cause, so at a further meeting of the Norwegian Council in Trondheim in January 1536 the archbishop was able to have his opponents arrested and their leader murdered – only to fail completely in an attempt to capture the fortresses of Bergen and Oslo. It was now too late for him to change sides, as he had done on previous occasions. When Danish troops advanced north next spring, Norway's last Catholic archbishop fled into exile without a blow being struck on his behalf.

In anticipation of this dénouement the charter declared as follows:

> Norway shall henceforth be and remain under the Crown of Denmark, the same as any of the other provinces, Jutland, Fünen, Zealand, or Skåne, and it shall henceforth neither be nor be called a kingdom in itself.[3]

Although a kingdom with strong historic memories could not be totally abolished by a form of words, the flame of national feeling for a time burnt low. As there was no longer a Norwegian Council, in foreign eyes Norway was part of Denmark; and what mattered more, in Danish eyes it was 'the same as any of the other provinces' in the sense of being fully available for noble fiefs and other forms of exploitation. In return, the charter bound the Danish Council and people to defend the king's right to Norway against any challenge.

Christian III's reign of twenty-three years resembled that of Gustavus of Sweden as a period of economic recovery from the ravages of civil war and of a great increase in the centralised authority of the Crown. A further inroad was made into the power of the nobility by securing the full recognition of Christian's young son Frederick in each province as heir to the throne under the charter. The king strengthened his hold upon the principal fiefs: in 1533 two-thirds of these had been mortgaged, in almost half the cases pledged for life; by 1545 only two-fifths were mortgaged, and the pledges for life had been reduced from twenty-one to five.[4] Christian III's advisers were mostly Germans from the Duchies, but he made employment in the Rent Chamber or the Chancery the route by which young nobles might expect to make their way up to a fief and eventual membership of the Council. Whereas the Rent Chamber functioned as a kind of finance ministry, the 'German Chancery' which he brought with him from the Duchies took charge of foreign affairs as well as those of Slesvig-Holstein, leaving the Danish Chancery as a virtual Ministry of the Interior. As for the economy, agricultural exports flourished to the profit of king and nobles, but the condition of the peasants was depressed, the freeholders of Jutland in particular having been deprived of their property as rebels. The influence of the urban middle class was likewise reduced as a result of its having backed the losing side in the struggle for the throne.

The convulsions which had attended the break-up of the Scandinavian Union might have been expected to range Danes and Swedes on opposite sides in any later conflict. This was not so, however, because ex-King Christian II and his family were a threat to the new rulers in both countries. Swedish forces had served by land and sea against Count Christopher, Gustavus being as anxious as the future Christian III to render Lübeck less powerful to intervene in their affairs. Later on, when it seemed possible that Charles V might seriously press the claim of Frederick Count Palatine to both the Scandinavian thrones, their occupants signed the Alliance of Brömsebro; this bound them to refuse any unilateral settlement with any such claimant, and included a mutual territorial guarantee valid for fifty years. As an alliance this is not to be regarded too seriously, for soon afterwards the Danish king made his own peace with the Emperor at Speyer (1544). Nevertheless, it is a significant fact that no serious breach took place between the northern kingdoms during the period in which an enduring spiritual and moral link between their peoples was being created by the Lutheran Reformation.

THE IMPACT OF THE REFORMATION

The teachings of Luther entered the Scandinavian countries through three main channels – German preachers moving north, native enthusiasts who had caught fire as students in Wittenberg and other centres of Reformation thought and action in Germany, and Hanse merchants spreading the new faith in foreign communities where they had long been established. Yet to a greater extent than in most other parts of Europe the course of events was directly determined by the kings, which helps to explain the fact that in each case the final result was the setting up of a monolithic State Church whose position was scarcely challenged for three centuries.

Christian II in the heyday of his power asked the Elector of Saxony to send him a preacher: this was in 1519, only two years after the nailing up of the 95 theses at Wittenberg. Martin Reinhardt then came and preached before the court and in one of the Copenhagen churches, making some converts among the upper classes, where his language was understood. But the king's views were still at the stage of pre-Lutheran humanism when he was driven out by his uncle Frederick, who had strong support from the bishops. The ex-king then for a time became a Lutheran, which may partly account for the cautious attitude adopted by his successor in face of the rapid advance of the new doctrine from Slesvig-Holstein into Denmark itself. It was not until 1527 that Frederick followed his separation of the Danish episcopacy from the Curia (see p. 88) by announcing to the Council his intention of tolerating both the rival beliefs: 'For His Grace is king and judge over life and property for his realm, not over the souls of men.'[5] In 1529, indeed, he sent to Copenhagen the eloquent ex-monk, Hans Tausen, who had already made Viborg in Jutland a great centre of Reformed teaching, whilst trade connections with north Germany had brought it to Malmö, where it had the support of a printing-press. Yet no final decision was taken at a full meeting of the Council in Copenhagen next year, when twenty-one preachers presented a Danish version of their faith, quite independent of the Confession of Augsburg, which dates from the same summer.

Since Duke Christian had established Lutheranism in his duchy of North Slesvig during his father's lifetime, his victory in the civil war was followed by the sweeping away of the Catholic bishops, as already related, and by the introduction of a fully Lutheran Church Ordinance. In its Latin form this was proclaimed in September 1537, when Bugenhagen (who spent two years as Luther's representative in Copenhagen) consecrated seven new bishops. Known at first as 'superintendents', they had no link with the apostolic succession; what was of more practical importance was that, having been stripped of the episcopal estates, they could never again aspire to the status of the lay nobility. The lower clergy too, now that they could become fathers of families, were likely to be more dependent upon noble patronage, whilst the whole ethos of Lutheranism emphasised respect for the powers that be. The Ordinance, as formally approved in a Danish version in 1539, fixed the order of service and made Luther's Catechism the standard of doctrine. The University of Copenhagen, where Tausen for a time taught Hebrew, encouraged evangelical preaching based on the closer study of the Bible, so long at least as it feared a Catholic revival.

The course of events in Sweden ran roughly parallel. Gustavus almost from the outset of his reign was denounced by rebels for his hostility to the papacy, which was occasioned by its support for his vanquished enemy, Archbishop Trolle. In 1524 he appointed Olaus Petri, the elder of two brothers who had studied under Luther at Wittenberg, as preacher at the Great Church in Stockholm, and he soon afterwards chose another reformer (Laurentius Andreae) as chancellor. But when he made his great attack on Church property at the Vasterås Riksdag in 1527 (see p. 87), the king's attitude in matters of doctrine eas expressed only in a vague formula which required that the Word of God be 'purely preached'.[6] Moreover, when new bishops were needed in connection with his coronation, he had them consecrated by a bishop whose appointment had received papal approval before the quarrel over archbishop Trolle became a definite breach, thus preserving the apostolic succession.

In 1536, however, which was the year of decisive change in Denmark, Gustavus allowed a Church synod to adopt a Swedish version of the Mass and other Reformation measures, including clerical marriage, as desired by Laurentius Petri (the younger brother of Olaus), whom he had chosen for the archbishopric of Uppsala five years before. But Olaus Petri, who provided the service books and much other propaganda for the movement, soon aroused the king's suspicions as aiming at a popular church which would be only loosely dependent on the crown; together with Chancellor Laurentius, he was condemned to death for treason, and although they were duly reprieved Gustavus transferred control to a kind of minister of ecclesiastical affairs. This was Georg Norman, a German noble and an intimate of Luther, who had come to Sweden as tutor to his heir, Prince Eric, and who now tuned the pulpits to emphasise obedience to the earthly sovereign and supported the royal confiscation of silver and other 'unnecessary' valuables from the churches, which was one cause of the great rebellion of 1542. Norman's policy was then moderated, but Laurentius Petri had to wait more than forty years for acceptance of the Church Ordinance he had planned at the start of his archiepiscopate. In comparison with Denmark, the result was a Lutheranism which established itself more gradually and broke less completely with medieval tradition.

In Finland the wealth of the Church was too small to attract much of Gustavus's attention, but in 1528 he appointed to the see of Turku a Dominican friar who made such concessions to Protestantism as the king insisted on. The students whom the new bishop sent to Wittenberg included Mikael Agricola, who returned in 1539 to produce Lutheran manuals in Finnish and instruct the ordinands in the cathedral school. Because the king found him too nationalist in his outlook, he was not made bishop until 1554 and his see was reduced by the creation of a separate bishopric of Viipuri. Nevertheless, in the remaining three years of Agricola's life Lutheranism was firmly established on a conservative basis, Catholic forms and ceremonies being retained with the exception of such as he found 'downright blasphemous'.[7]

Meanwhile, Danish rulers had imposed Lutheranism on Norway and Iceland. The new doctrines had been preached by a German monk to his fellow countrymen in Bergen in 1526, and three years later they reached Stavanger as well. Danish fief-holders were prompt to plunder the monasteries, but Archbishop Olav Engelbrektsson was able to base his appeal for a national resistance on the general acceptance of Catholic institutions by a conservative rural population. After he had fled the country in the spring of 1537, a leaderless people submitted sullenly to a small Danish force, even when the pious and well-loved bishop of Hamar was arrested in his own cathedral city. The new Lutheran 'superintendents' included at least one bishop who turned his coat in time,* but the ranks of the lower clergy could only gradually be reinforced by genuine Lutherans trained in Copenhagen. The confiscation of lands and valuables on the same footing as in the Danish Reformation did not make the new order more popular; but what chiefly deadened the life of the Church in Norway for many generations to come was the use of the Danish language as the medium of all worship and religious instruction. The Norwegians had even to wait seventy years before the Church Ordinance, designed primarily for Denmark, was adapted to the earlier Norwegian ecclesiastical law and custom.

In Iceland both bishops sided with Olav Engelbrektsson, whose suffragans they were, and combated the first infiltration of Lutheran teaching through books which Hanse merchants brought from Hamburg. In 1541, however, King Christian III sent a governor with two warships to enforce conformity with the rest of his dominions, whereupon the diocese of Skálholt submitted and was given a new bishop, but Hólar in the north of the island remained obdurate. This northern bishop, Jón Arason, was more of a chieftain than a churchman, with armed retinues under his own command and that of his two sons by a concubine. He eventually took the Lutheran bishop of Skálholt prisoner, drove out the king's representative, and restored the monasteries, which in Iceland had retained much of their earlier importance. But he and his sons were soon afterwards captured by a rival chieftain, and in November 1550 all three were beheaded by Danish orders, thus providing the Catholic cause during the Scandinavian Reformation with its first and last martyrs. The Crown became the biggest landowner on the island, but its remoteness caused other changes. Whilst Jón Arason was revered as a national hero and near-saint, the Danish officials (who now became more numerous) found it necessary to make heresy a capital offence and punish persistent absence from Lutheran church service by flogging.

By mid-century the institutions of the Reformed Church were established throughout the Scandinavian lands; it remains to consider its cultural impact. The transfer of ecclesiastical wealth, which benefited chiefly the Crown, was acceptable to the many, insofar as the monastic orders and other features of the old order were felt to be alien and corrupt. But the extent to which the life of the parish underwent a spiritual and moral revival depended largely at the outset upon the visitations carried out by earnest bishops, such as Peder Palladius in Zealand, or by the German superintendent Norman in several of the Swedish provinces. It

---

* Hans Rev, bishop of Oslo, who had sided with Christian II as late as 1531–2; when he returned in 1541 from a four-year sojourn in Copenhagen as Superintendent of his former diocese plus that of Hamar, it seemed a felicitous chance that his name meant 'fox'.

would be unrealistic to suppose that Lutheran teaching on justification by faith or even on the nature of the Sacrament meant very much to the average layman, at any rate until Luther's catechism was impressed upon the minds of successive generations. But the new forms of service made an immediate impact, because they – like the accompanying sermon – were now rendered as a rule in the vernacular; and even Norway, where the country people (as we have seen) resented the use of Danish, appears to have welcomed the congregational hymn-singing, which began with the use of translations from the work of Luther himself and other German divines. Soon each Scandinavian country had its own cherished hymn-writers, whose genius surmounted every handicap, such as the poverty-stricken Icelandic parson, Hallgrimur Pétursson, who died a leper but whose *Hymns of the Passion* have been reprinted more than sixty times.[8]

As in other Protestant countries, an enduring influence was exerted by translations of the Bible. Denmark owed its first version of the New Testament to the changing impulses of ex-king Christian II, who visited Luther in the year following the first publication of his German Bible and sent the first copies of the translation he had ordered to Denmark from Antwerp in 1524 – seven years before he recrossed the North Sea as an avowed champion of the old faith. Hans Tausen rendered the first five books of the Old Testament from the Hebrew, but the Danish Bible of 1550 was a collaborative translation from the German, presided over by Palladius. In Sweden the New Testament was published in 1526 under the auspices of Chancellor Laurentius, Gustav Vasa's complete Bible in 1541 under those of the archbishop, whose brother, Olaus Petri, played a part in both these renderings from Luther's German. No Bible was printed in Norway, which had no press, but an Icelandic version was printed in 1584 at Hólar, where the only press was located, with the bishop of that see as the main translator.

In Denmark, and still more in Sweden, the publication of the Bible in the vernacular was a capital event, not only in the religious life of home and church and school but also in the development of the language, for which it supplied a standard form. As for Finland, where the native language had not previously appeared in print, Agricola's translations of the Scriptures and other religious writings are virtually the starting-point, for they established the dialect of Turku and the south-western districts as the norm. He published the New Testament in 1548, to which he added such books of the Old Testament as he had leisure to translate in the remaining nine years of his life. The first complete Finnish Bible was published in Stockholm in 1642.

Whilst the Reformation stimulated nationalist influences in each of the Scandinavian lands, though at varying paces, it also bound them together by strong cultural ties established with north Germany. This was especially true of the crucial early years, when Scandinavian theological students flocked to Wittenberg and other centres of Lutheran teaching and discussion. The universities of Copenhagen and Uppsala and their dependent cathedral schools in due course became self-sufficient for theological studies, but the clergy continued to look to Martin Luther as the earthly founder of their faith, whose writings, from his Bible to his hymns, from his polemical treatises to his Shorter Catechism, had a unique authority. In Sweden, as we shall see, the Counter-Reformation was to present a serious challenge, but by 1600 the *Confessio Augustana* was accepted by all. After the passage of three and three-quarter centuries, the view of religion which was shaped in Germany still receives an ampler recognition in Scandinavia than in its homeland.

THE SEVEN YEARS WAR OF THE NORTH, 1563–70

The deaths of Christian III and Gustavus Vasa in 1559 and 1560 respectively put the fortunes of the two kingdoms in the hands of young men, to whom a bold policy was inherently attractive. Frederick II of Denmark began his reign auspiciously with a campaign under the aged Johan Rantzau, which reconquered Ditmarsh for the benefit of himself and his two uncles, who held the duchies of Slesvig-Holstein. Encouraged by this, he took no step to renew the alliance of Brömsebro and outraged Swedish opinion by flaunting the three crowns in his coat of arms, on the specious grounds that what the Swedes regarded as their national emblem was a symbol of the Union, freely available to either of its former members. As for Eric XIV of Sweden, whose education had given him the outlook of a typical Renaissance prince, he was not the man to ignore a challenge, especially one which connected with a real clash of interests.

The advance of Lutheranism in the German trading towns on the other side of the Baltic Sea had brought about the final collapse of the once powerful German military orders. Courland in the south passed into Polish hands, whilst in the north-east Ivan the Terrible in 1558 staked out the Russian claim by his capture of the port of Narva. In between lay a region which both Denmark and Sweden aspired to dominate, as through it passed increasingly valuable trade routes between Russia and the west. The Danes bought the island of Ösel, from which King Frederick's younger brother tried without success to advance to the mainland of Estonia. In 1561 the Swedes took possession of the port of Tallinn, from which they moved forward across Estonia into Livonia, where their ambitions crossed with those of the Poles – and of King Eric's brother, Duke John.

Gustavus had allotted dukedoms to each of his three younger sons, but at the time of Eric's accession the youngest, Duke Charles, was only ten years of age and the middle one already showed signs of insanity, so John alone was in a position to claim independent powers. He had been invested with the whole of Finland as a separate administrative unit, and was not deterred by restrictions of his alleged rights, imposed by the

Riksdag at Eric's request; by marrying the sister of the last Jagellon king of Poland, he marked out his intention to pursue a foreign policy of his own. The Finns, who naturally welcomed the improved formal status of their country as a duchy with a resident duke, backed John's attempt to acquire fiefs in Livonia as pledges for his wife's unpaid dowry. Since this conflicted with the Polish policy pursued by the Crown, the Riksdag declared him guilty of high treason; a brief siege of Turku castle ended in the imprisonment of himself and his duchess in Sweden and the execution of thirty Finnish nobles.

These events encouraged Frederick to declare war in August 1563, the month of Duke John's overthrow. He had Poland for an ally as well as Lübeck, where hopes were still cherished of regaining control of Sweden's trade. Eric had no ally, albeit that he was a most indefatigable suitor for the hand of Elizabeth of England; but his subjects were ready to offer a stubborn resistance against the Danish challenge to their independence, so painfully established in the previous generation. Moreover, the nervous instability which incapacitated King Eric for a long conflict must not be allowed to obscure the enthusiasm for the art of war which he derived from his classical studies. The small regular army inherited from his father was trained to adopt a novel linear formation, with the bearers of firearms interspersed between the blocks of pikemen. The navy likewise was expanded and improved, some warships being constructed with a double hull which enclosed a ballast of iron ore at the waterline.

On land the Swedes were outmatched by Denmark's German mercenaries and their German commander, Daniel Rantzau, a member of the well-known Holstein family. They lost Älvsborg, their only outlet to the west, in the first month of the war, and in 1565 were decisively beaten by Rantzau at Axtorna in Halland. Two years later he penetrated far enough into Sweden to threaten Stockholm itself in a winter campaign, though this failed eventually through supply difficulties and in 1569 Rantzau died of wounds. The Swedish armies for their part proved strong enough to ravage from time to time the Danish mainland provinces of Halland, Skåne, and Blekinge; to occupy Jämtland and Härjedalen in Norway, from where they briefly gained possession of Trondheim; and to sweep through the Norwegian provinces of the south-east to Oslo and even beyond. But when the war ended not a single Danish-owned fortress was in Swedish hands.

At sea, however, the Swedes completely defeated the blockade, albeit that Stockholm was at first reduced to eking out its salt supply, usually obtained from Danzig, from a reserve which Gustavus had accumulated in the aisles of the Great Church. In 1565-6 Klas Horn, who (like Blake a century later) was a general turned admiral, won two major victories over the fleets of Denmark and Lübeck, the Danes losing a further 15 ships and about 4,000 men through bad seamanship off the coast of Gotland.

Swedish trade across the Baltic was no longer seriously molested, and for a time the Danes even lost control of the traffic through the Sound. It was not until the summer of 1569 – nearly three years after Horn's death from plague – that Danish maritime power was to some extent reasserted by a profitable raid on Swedish trade at Tallinn.

Before the war ended in 1570 at the Peace of Stettin, Sweden had passed through a revolution, which makes the continuance of her military efforts truly remarkable. As early as 1567 Eric became obsessed by nervous suspicions. After he had stabbed a member of the Sture family to death with his own hands and required other nobles who were held on treason charges to be butchered by prison warders, the realm had to be left in the charge of the Council whilst the king slowly regained his sanity. During that period Duke John was released from captivity, ready to side with disaffected noblemen. Next year the coronation of Eric's mistress, whom he had married privately, provided a pretext for rebellion, the underlying reason being the power exercised by the king's secretary Jöran Persson, the ambitious son of a poor parson, whose career had begun under Gustavus. The young Duke Charles captured Stockholm for the rebels, who made John king; in January 1569 this was ratified by a Riksdag, and after nine years in confinement Eric died of arsenic poisoning, for which John was probably responsible.

No territory changed hands at the peace-making, though the Swedes had to pay heavily to recover Älvsborg, their frontier post at the mouth of the Göta. The treaty sought, indeed, to prevent the recurrence of such wasteful strife by providing for future disputes to be settled by delegations from the Councils of the two kingdoms, whose members would be temporarily released from their ties of allegiance; if this method failed, foreign princes were to be requested to arbitrate. But the war had left many bitter and angry memories on both sides, both because of its unusual length and because of the savagery with which it had been waged. King Eric himself recorded his storming of Rönneby in Blekinge in these terms:

> Then there was a tremendous killing inside. The water in the river was coloured red as blood. And the enemy were so demoralised that we had little trouble with them but stuck into them like a herd of wild boars, sparing none; we slaughtered all that could bear arms, so that more than 2,000 men in the town were done away with, besides some women and children who were slaughtered by the Finns.[9]

Such acts as this were usually excused as reprisals, but more often the whole countryside was laid waste deliberately in order to deprive the enemy of a base for a later advance. In the year when Rönneby was stormed, the Danish armies had destroyed 1,400 farms in two districts of Sweden, to which Rantzau added another 683 during his later advance towards Stockholm. Other examples could be given from the experience of Norway, where the Swedes burnt the town of Sarpsborg and the cathedral at Hamar, whilst also ravaging an unrecorded number of farms and slaughtering the cattle.

As a subject people, however, the attitude of the Norwegians to the war was ambivalent. Trondheim, for example, which surrendered to the Swedes without any serious defence, was recovered after only two months by an expedition mounted by the Danish governor of Bergen with peasants from that region: but in the meantime the local officials in Trondheim had pledged allegiance to the Swedish crown. More generally, the peasantry in border districts made a private peace with the Swedish peasantry across the frontier, whilst in some parts of west Norway there was a point-blank refusal to bear arms or pay taxes for the war. The unwillingness of the Norwegian people to fight for a restoration of the Scandinavian Union or indeed for any Danish cause may help to explain the fact that the Danish nobility, many of whom held fiefs in Norway, were the staunchest supporters of the peace policy which prevailed in Scandinavia for the next forty years.

THE REFORMATION CONSOLIDATED

For a quarter of a century after the Peace of Stettin, Denmark and Sweden followed divergent paths. The remainder of Frederick II's reign was a period of tranquillity, in which king and nobles prospered: if its foremost architectural memorial is the royal castle of Kronborg at Elsinore, intended to give the entrance to the Sound a more effective protection than Eric of Pomerania's fort, some seventy comfortable manor houses also survive, built from rising rent-rolls. The cost of the war was recovered chiefly from higher taxation on both Danish and Norwegian farm properties; but even before it ended, the basis for a wealthy monarchy had been laid by levying the Sound dues on value of cargo instead of size of vessel, which tripled the yield. Frederick was a pleasure-loving monarch, though not without interest in the arts and sciences (see p. 109), and he left much power in the hands of the nobility and his chancellor, Niels Kaas, who remained in office until his death in 1594 – six years after his royal master had been succeeded by his son, Christian IV, at the age of eleven.

As a student at Wittenberg, Kaas had sat at the feet of Philip Melanchthon, who taught a doctrine of the Sacrament which was more directly opposed to the Catholic than that of Luther. This view was proclaimed at Copenhagen by Niels Hemmingsen, a professor of theology with a European reputation, who was denounced as a crypto-Calvinist by the king's brother-in-law, the Elector of Saxony. He was removed from his Chair but consoled with a canonry; he also continued to advise Kaas in Church matters. In these circumstances the attempts of the Jesuits to work secretly in Copenhagen for the Counter-Reformation had no effect;

they had made one valuable convert in Norway, who entered the order at Louvain in 1564, but he did not venture into Denmark until 1606, when he was promptly expelled.

The situation in Sweden presents a contrast, especially in matters of religion. The way in which John III had been brought to the throne obliged him, indeed, to conciliate the nobles, to whom he accorded the valuable privilege of exemption from military service for such of their peasants as resided within one Swedish mile (10·7 km) of a manor house. But he had no intention of accepting the constitutional oligarchy which they claimed to be the traditional form of government in Sweden, sub-verted by his father – a claim that was propounded by Erik Sparre, an eloquent and learned champion of noble pretensions, in *Pro lege, rege, et grege*. Neither did he intend to allow his brother, Duke Charles, to play the sort of role he himself had played under King Eric. And he had his own strongly held views on the nature of the Church, which were very much closer to the Catholic tradition than most Lutherans could possibly approve. He is said to have admired the Anglican version of Protestantism, with which he came in contact when sent to England to plead his brother's suit with Queen Elizabeth; but his interest in theology was kindled mainly by the Early Fathers, whose works he had studied during his imprison-ment.

In 1571 Archbishop Laurentius Petri produced his long-delayed Church Ordinance. This was vague as to doctrine, taking no stand about Melanchthon's adaptation of Lutheranism, and permissive about the retention of Catholic ceremonial, but firm about organisation, which was to be based on an elected episcopate: for Sweden, unlike Denmark and Norway, had preserved its cathedral chapters. Two years later the arch-bishop's death was followed by further regulations from the king, who claimed that their oath of obedience to the Ordinance bound the clergy to accept such supplementary articles. In 1577 these culminated in a new liturgy, familiarly known from its binding as the Red Book, which the clergy accepted only under protest; its ritual for the Mass marked a return to many Roman usages and employed language which could be construed as conveying the Roman doctrine that the Mass is a sacrifice.

Even if John was not a crypto-Catholic, it was certainly his doing that the Counter-Reformation gained a temporary foothold in his dominions, using Poland – where the movement was making steady progress – as a springboard. Two confessors had been allowed to accompany his Catholic wife from Poland, and when her husband became king other emissaries followed. The most remarkable of these was the Norwegian Jesuit, Laurits Nilssön or *Klosterlasse*, whose recruitment has been mentioned. Although well aware of his identity, King John set him up in a secularised priory at Stockholm as head of a royal college for the training of Lutheran divines. In the first session (1576–7) he converted thirty of his students, six of whom were sent secretly to Rome at the king's expense, and after another three years the Roman Catholic community in Sweden mustered 237 members. *Klosterlasse*'s activities were then exposed through a blunder on his part and his mission came abruptly to an end, though the Jesuits continued to attract some Swedish students to two other colleges in Polish territory. As for King John, he had received a Jesuit confessor and the Catholic Sacrament; but in policy he had gone no further than to propose conditions for reconciliation which the Pope found unacceptable.

However, a Catholic restoration remained a possibility for Sweden, since John had allowed his son Sigismund to be brought up in his mother's faith, believing that he would later choose otherwise. This he did not do, and his Catholicism was an important factor in the negotiations, ably conducted by Eric Sparre, which brought about his election in 1587 to the throne of Poland. Five years later his father's death left him the titular head of two kingdoms, the result being a bitter struggle in which Duke Charles made himself the champion of the Swedish Lutheran cause; he had never admitted the Red Book to his duchy, and his personal leanings were probably towards Calvinism. Before the new king arrived from Poland in the autumn of 1593, Charles joined with the Council in summoning an assembly of clergy at Uppsala, where the Red Book was condemned and one of its foremost opponents elected archbishop, and where – in spite of the duke's leanings – the Augsburg Confession was belatedly but unanimously adopted. Thereupon the president of the assembly is said to have pronounced the memorable words: 'Now is Sweden become as one man, and we have all one Lord and God.'[10] The final resolutions were afterwards sent out for signature by representatives of all classes in the same way as the Scottish National Covenant on a later day of decision.

Sigismund was duly crowned king of Sweden, yet no rights of public worship were conceded to his Catholic followers. When he therefore returned in some indignation to Poland, Duke Charles induced the three lower Estates of the Riksdag to declare him regent; but this arrangement proved increasingly unwelcome to the nobles on the Council, when they saw that Charles would do much more than Sigismund to reduce their authority. Matters first came to a head in Finland, where the nobility strongly favoured the new link with Poland and Charles tried to weaken their hold on the country by supporting a peasant rising known as the Club War. The club-wielders were mercilessly put down by their lords, who in the following year (1598) sent their army to intervene on Sigismund's side in Sweden. He had landed at Kalmar with a number of councillors who had fled from Duke Charles, but after his forces had been defeated at Stångebro in September he handed over the councillors and returned to Poland. Although Stockholm, Kalmar, and the Finnish fortresses were still held for a time on his behalf, his plans for a naval blockade came to nothing and he never revisited Sweden.

The unexpected ease of the dénouement left Duke Charles cautious but not generous. For four years after Sigismund's deposition by the Riksdag in 1599, he was content to be styled 'administrator of the realm': his vanquished rival had both a half-brother and a son, and to break the line of succession for the second time in less than half a century might prove dangerous to the Vasa dynasty. But the surrender of the fortresses into his hands was followed by merciless reprisals. In Finland the nobility never again figured as a kind of corporate leadership; in Sweden aristocratic families long recalled with horror 'the slaughter-bench of Linköping'.[11] In spite of a pledge that they should be tried by impartial foreign princes, Erik Sparre and four other high nobles who had been surrendered to Charles after Stångebro were beheaded in the market-place in 1600, after a so-called trial by his nominees in which he himself acted as prosecutor.

In 1604, a year after Charles had been proclaimed king, a new Pact of Succession secured the crown to his heirs, including on certain conditions the female line. The Reformation settlement was now firmly re-established, except for the continuing threat from the Vasa kings of Poland, where some Swedish Catholic sympathisers had taken refuge. This Polish hostility was one factor in the problems of the Baltic, in which Christian IV of Denmark, whose minority terminated in 1596, likewise took a strong interest.

CHRISTIAN IV AND THE KALMAR WAR

After the treaty of Stettin Frederick II had taken little interest in the struggle for the Baltic coastlands, considering that Denmark profited sufficiently from the toll which he levied on the traffic through the Sound – increasing amounts of corn, timber, naval stores, and Swedish metals, in exchange for the textiles, wine, and colonial products from lands farther west. Whilst he was content to assert his position by means of a predominant navy, the Swedes had become involved in a 25-year struggle against the Russians, whose incursions across the border cause this period to be known in Finnish history as 'The Long Wrath'.[12] However, King John had quickly allied himself with the Poles; together they won the battle of Wenden in 1578, which prepared the way for the storming of Narva by a French-born commander of the Swedish army, Pontus de la Gardie, who put 6,000 of its inhabitants to the sword. Estonia was claimed in vain by the Poles as the price of Sigismund's election to their throne; in 1595 it passed in its entirety to Sweden at the Peace of Teusina. By this treaty the Russians also agreed that Tallinn and Viipuri should become the two staple towns for their trade with the outside world.

A more valuable gain than the unkept promise was a revision and extension of boundaries, which added new territory to Finland beyond Olofsborg and in theory partitioned the Arctic wilderness all the way to the Barents

Sea, which it reached a little east of Varangerfiord; Russian claims west of this unmarked line were transferred to the Swedes. The persons most directly affected were the Lapps, whose way of life had recently been described to the world by Olaus Magnus (see p. 108). They were not only reindeer-herders but fishermen and fur-trappers, whose nomadic habits and virtual defencelessness had resulted in the levying of taxes in kind over large, undefined areas by Norway, Russia, and Sweden, the representatives of the third power being the *Birkaler* – the Finnish traders of the far north. Gustavus Vasa had begun the appointment of bailiffs to control relations with the Lapps, and his youngest son now proposed to assert a territorial claim wherever the Birkaler had penetrated to the Lapp settlements in the Norwegian fiords between Lofoten and the North Cape. Thus the Swedes aimed at an overland approach to the sea route passing round that cape to the new Russian port of Archangel, the use of which was clearly detrimental to their attempted control of Russian trade – and still more to the Danish Sound tolls.

Frederick II of Denmark had claimed naval supremacy in 'the king's stream', as he called this passage and, indeed, the whole expanse of waters lying between his Norwegian and Icelandic possessions. In 1583 he secured an agreement by which England made an annual payment for permission to sail there, and France later followed suit. He also tried to bring the Icelandic trade and fisheries into the hands of his own subjects instead of Englishmen and Germans and encouraged adventurers such as Mogens Heinesen,* to whom he gave a monopoly of trade with the Faeroes, a half-share in ships captured on unlawful passage to the White Sea, and backing for a bold but unsuccessful attempt to reach east Greenland. It was therefore natural that Frederick's heir on coming of age should take up the challenge presented by the Swedish claim to rights of sovereignty which the Norwegians had exercised since the time of Othere.

Christian IV was a man of action rather than reflection, brave, artistic, and interested in all kinds of practical concerns; he is the one sovereign of the long Oldenburg line who not only became a popular hero in his lifetime but has been widely and on the whole gratefully remembered by posterity. This is partly due to his passionate interest in architecture and town-planning, to which Copenhagen is indebted for many of its finest buildings and a score of towns in Denmark, Norway, and the Duchies for their originally rectangular ground-plan or even for the selection of their site. He likewise commanded his subjects' attention through his full-blooded family life. After the death of his queen, a Brandenburg princess who bore him three sons, Christian incurred a morganatic marriage with a young noblewoman (Kirsten Munk), by whom he had a son and six

* 1545–89. The son of a Norwegian clergyman and his Faeroese wife, and born in the islands, where his half-brother became *lagmann*; as a trader, he exploited the islanders shamelessly, but is still regarded as a heroic champion of their independent rights; he was beheaded for piracy against an English ship in 1585, when he had temporarily become a privateer in Dutch service, the sentence being afterwards annulled.

daughters; she eventually proved unfaithful, whereupon he consoled himself elsewhere. In addition, he cut a considerable figure in Europe in his earlier years, when Denmark was still unquestionably the leading power of the north; on a state visit to his brother-in-law, James I of Great Britain, he presented his host with a warship believed to be superior to any of his own.

In 1599, accordingly, one of the earliest of more than thirty visits to Norway took the young king to the fortress of Vardöhus, in the area threatened by the Swedish claims, after which he sailed his eight warships along the Murman coast beyond, intercepting English and Dutch vessels which had ignored his sovereign rights over the seas. There followed a series of disputes, as the Swedes built blockhouses and churches to stake out their claims and pressed the unhappy Lapps for taxes, all of which led to retaliation by Danes and Norwegians. Resort was made to the conciliation procedure provided by the treaty of Stettin, and in 1603 a court of arbitration was set up; but to Christian's chagrin these frontier meetings served chiefly to betray to the Swedish king the fact that the Danish nobles were far more reluctant than his own subjects to allow the two countries to drift into another war. At his coronation in 1607 Charles IX styled himself 'king of the Lapps in Nordland';[13] on founding the new west-coast port of Gothenburg, he gave its Dutch settlers fishing rights in the far north; and he planned to build up a position in the Arctic from which he might be able eventually to close the Archangel route to Russia.

However, as early as 1600 Charles had carried the struggle against Sigismund across the Baltic by launching a sudden attack from Estonia upon the Polish province of Livonia, which now included the great Hanse port of Riga. Once the advantage of surprise had been lost, the Swedish army, which had abandoned the improved formations designed by King Eric, was unable to face the renowned Polish cavalry. In 1605 the Poles advanced to relieve the siege of Riga with a force which the Swedes outnumbered by three to one; but it was the latter who fled from the field of Kirkholm after losing at least half their men. A rebellion in Poland nevertheless enabled Charles to continue the war, and he regained some of his lost prestige by intervening in the internal struggles of Russia's 'Time of Troubles' to oppose a pro-Polish candidate for the throne. In 1610 Jakob de la Gardie, son of the conqueror of Narva, entered Moscow; for a short time it seemed possible that one of Charles's two sons might be made Tsar or that northern Russia as far as Archangel and the White Sea, much of which was held by him, might fall permanently into Swedish hands.

But Charles's entanglement in the east presented Christian IV with an opportunity, not merely to settle the dispute in the Arctic regions but also to restore the Union – and by so doing to rid himself of the tutelage of the Danish nobility. In preparation for this he had doubled the navy, established an arsenal at Copenhagen, and built or extended a number of fortresses in his mainland provinces. When the Council persistently opposed a declaration of war, pointing out that on the last occasion Sweden had proved impossible to occupy, he forced their hand by declaring that he would if necessary commence hostilities in his independent capacity as duke of Slesvig-Holstein. The fiercest struggle was for Kalmar, the fortress just inside the Swedish frontier, of which the Danes finally gained full control in spite of an initially successful counter-attack headed by the Swedish king's sixteen-year-old son, Gustav Adolf. In 1612, the second year's fighting gained the key position of Älvsborg for the Danes; but their overland advance on Stockholm was stopped by 'scorched earth' tactics, an epidemic on the eastern flank, and an open mutiny when Norwegian soldiers on the western flank were ordered to cross the frontier into Sweden. Their patriotism was too local to be roused by the renewed Swedish occupation of Jämtland and Härjedalen, though for propaganda purposes much was made of an exploit by the peasantry of Gudbrandsdal, who successfully waylaid the smaller of two parties of Scottish mercenaries on their marauding march from the west coast of Norway to join their employers in Sweden.

In the late summer Christian's fleet sailed unopposed into the immediate vicinity of Stockholm, but had no soldiers with it to force a decision. Since it was too expensive to retain his German and other mercenary troops for another campaign, he made peace at Knäred in January 1613 on terms which were generally to his advantage. Both sides returned their conquests and accepted the principle of freedom of trade between the two kingdoms – which meant that the Swedes were for the first time expressly exempted from the Sound tolls. But the Swedes gave up their claims in the far north, both those based on the treaty of Teusina and the right to tax the Lapps on the Atlantic coast farther west. They also had to pay seven times as heavily as before to ransom Älvsborg – with which Gothenburg was included – and complete the payment within six years. The sum was equivalent to the entire value of four normal harvests, but was raised in time with the help of increased sales of copper on the Amsterdam market and the obtaining of a loan, which likewise came significantly from Dutch sources. For the trading powers of Europe did not wish either Danes or Swedes to achieve a final preponderance over their rivals.

The kingdom of the Vasas had now for the second time escaped reunion with the Danish crown. When the same issue was joined a third time, the prospect would be that of Sweden enforcing its will upon the kingdom of the Oldenburgs. Charles IX, who had been partly disabled by a stroke in 1609, had died in the first autumn of the war, leaving his imperilled country to a regency. But the young heir was Gustavus Adolphus, whose meteoric career brought Sweden so far towards preponderance that it more than justified his father's prophetic words: *Ille faciet.*[14]

SOCIAL DEVELOPMENT

In Scandinavia as in most other parts of Europe, the social and economic decline which characterised the late middle ages had been followed by a period of relatively steady advance, reaching to the closing years of the sixteenth century. In population,[15] so far as we can judge, the Scandinavian lands were still completely eclipsed by their neighbours – by Russia as well as Germany, by Poland-Lithuania even more than by England and Wales. If the English and Welsh mustered about 4,500,000 souls in 1600, the Scandinavians were probably about one-third as numerous. The margin of error is, however, enormous: in Sweden, for instance, the tax raised in 1571 for the ransoming of Älvsborg has given rise to population estimates that range between 430,000 and 830,000. By European standards Scandinavia certainly contained no large towns – and very few which a Dutchman, for example, would have classed as towns at all. On the other hand, it had considerable undeveloped areas available for the expansion of self-supporting agriculture, whilst some developed areas produced foodstuffs and industrial raw materials for a foreign market, so that their inhabitants shared fully in the general stimulus of the price rise which culminated at the end of the century.

The new Danish manor houses of Frederick II's reign represented the wealth which the nobles gained from exporting their grain – this commanded a sale among expanding populations abroad in spite of its rather low quality – and especially their stall-fed cattle. They had a virtual monopoly of this trade, which fetched high prices in both Germany and the Netherlands. South Sweden, as we have seen, also sold foodstuffs, but copper and iron were the great Swedish staples. The former derived a special stimulus from the adoption of a copper currency, notably in Spain; the latter from the conversion of the principal works to the production of bar iron instead of *osmund*, with the result that by 1600 iron already made up one-half of all Swedish exports, measured by value. This, like so many technical advances throughout western Europe, was promoted mainly by a Dutchman, whom John III placed in control.

In Norway the economic recovery at this time is even more significant, because in it lay the seeds for an eventual recovery of the national identity as well. In the later part of the century the traditional exports of dried cod were supplemented from the herring shoals, which moved from Skåne into the north. But the biggest development had begun a little earlier, through the introduction of the water-driven saw, which enabled Norway to provide building materials for the Netherlands and other deforested regions of western Europe. At first, every peasant had his own little mill. Later, when woodland near the coast was exhausted, they floated their logs down the rivers to larger mills; even then, a part of the profits spread far into the hinterland. In the same way, Finnish peasants derived some modest profit by the export of tar from their native forests.

Swedish iron and Norwegian timber were carried abroad in Dutch, German and other foreign vessels, which also brought in salt, cloth, wine and other imports. Denmark alone had a considerable mercantile marine of its own, trading into the Baltic, to Amsterdam, and to some extent to Iceland, where the king owned the sulphur mines and tried to get Danish merchants to oust the Hanseatics. But in Royal Copenhagen, as it was increasingly called, the biggest source of wealth was the toll on foreign vessels passing the Sound, which by the end of the century yielded the crown an income equal to two-thirds of its receipts from all Danish and Norwegian fiefs. Every corporate town now had a jealously guarded monopoly of trade in its own hinterland, and improvement of handicrafts in some cases attracted foreign immigrants with new skills and capital. But neither Copenhagen nor Stockholm nor Bergen,* to say nothing of the smaller ports, such as the three Danish provincial centres of Malmö, Elsinore, and Ålborg, contained any merchant class with sufficient wealth and standing to rival the nobility.

The economic interests of king and nobles were closely identified. The former had acquired large quantities of land which had been Church property, but it easily slipped through the royal fingers in rewards for services rendered; during the last fifteen years of his life Charles IX recovered no fewer than 373 farms which had been alienated by the Crown since the death of his father. And kings were no less interested than nobles in sales and exchanges of smaller properties, in order to form the large manorial domains which yielded the biggest direct profit; though Frederick II of Denmark, who bought up at least 1,000 farms in two areas, was not alone in his special concern with hunting rights. But for royal and noble landowners alike, profitability depended above all on the status of other elements in the rural population, which varied considerably from country to country.

Conditions were hardest for the peasant in Denmark, where most of the remaining freeholds had been confiscated after the Count's War and where the lord was often empowered to act as a local magistrate; moreover, German lords and bailiffs tended to introduce more stringent practices from Holstein and the lands beyond. In particular, he was weighed down by two obligations – the week-work which must be performed if he lived on or near a noble's manorial demesne; and the rent which was usually exacted from tenant farmers in kind, so that the lord might reap the full benefit from rising prices. In Sweden the nobles had similar privileges in relation to peasants living on their estates, who rendered services which (in theory) were compensated by the exemption of such estate land from

* With an estimated population of 6,000–7,000, it was the largest town in Norway and increasingly cosmopolitan. In 1559 the Danish governor compelled German craftsmen to become citizens or leave the country, but the German traders were still important, with Bremen now predominant in their Counter. Many other foreigners lived in the town without acquiring Norwegian citizenship, whilst 200–300 of the 1,450 names entered on the burgess roll in the second half of the century point to foreign origins.[16]

regular taxation. But one-half of all Swedish farms were held by independent, tax-paying peasants. In Finland, where the cultivated area was
more than doubled in this century, freeholders predominated, whilst the
peasants of Norway also retained most of their freedom, since conditions
of tenancy there did not include labour services on a manorial estate and
noble estate-owners were virtually extinct. But each Scandinavian country
possessed a considerable class of landless labourers and cottars, increasing
with the growth of population, who competed for work and tiny holdings
on any conditions offered. Although history is almost silent about their
position, something can be inferred from the frequent outcries against
the prevalence of beggars.

After the downfall of the Catholic prelates, the power of the king was
tempered only by that of the nobility, comprising by 1600 rather fewer
than 250 Danish and about 400 Swedish families,[17] the latter of whom
included a number permanently established in Finland. They constituted
the first estate in the Estates General, where they met representatives of the
clergy, burgesses, and peasants, chosen in various ways, on occasions when
the Crown desired a demonstration of popular support. A new sovereign
or heir to the throne, new taxation, or new legislation might receive
approval in this form of meeting, which in sixteenth-century Sweden
was becoming crystallised into the Riksdag. Nevertheless, the only
regular check upon the monarch's freedom of action was provided by the
Council, composed of leading nobles, some of whom held the chief offices
of state. In Denmark its position was secured by the bargain struck with
each king in his accession charter, whilst in Sweden the higher nobility
struggled constantly to make the king exercise his powers 'with the counsel
of his council' and not through 'low-born secretaries'[18] such as Persson,
whom they had tortured to death in the reign of Eric XIV.

The social structure helps to explain the fact that the Renaissance in
Scandinavia followed so tardily upon the heels of the Reformation,
which elsewhere it had to some extent preceded. During what has been
called elsewhere the Age of the Grammar Schools the Scandinavian
middle class was in no position to replace the Catholic foundations from
new wealth. Rural children seldom received any instruction beyond their
compulsory training in the catechism by the new Lutheran clergy. In
the towns, Sweden under Charles IX had a few schools which offered a
secular training, but ambitious families looked abroad for their education;
a Danish reform of 1606 designated the Latin Schools expressly for the
preparation of future ordinands. As for the universities, Copenhagen
was closed down at the time of the Count's War, and it was not until
1569 that it was put on a more satisfactory basis by the institution of a
college (*Kommunitetet*) to maintain 100 students; the emphasis, however,
was still laid almost entirely upon theological studies. This was likewise
the case at Uppsala when, after being closed throughout the reign of
Gustavus, it sprang fully to life again under the auspices of a group

of divines who had taken the lead at the Uppsala Assembly in 1593.

The nobility prepared their sons for public service by sending them abroad. This is even true of the greatest Scandinavian luminary of this age, Tycho Brahe, whose father – a member of the Danish Council – had sent him to Leipzig to study law. Returning after ten years in foreign lands, he made an international reputation by his discovery of the 'new star' in Cassiopeia (*De nova stella*, 1573) and was equipped by a grateful sovereign with an observatory and ancillary workshops on the island of Hven (the modern Ven) in the Sound.* For more than two decades this was the most important centre of astronomical study in the western world, until Brahe's arrogance provoked a quarrel with the youthful Christian IV. In 1599 he moved to Prague, where he was joined by Kepler as his assistant, and where he died in 1601.

Their travels abroad made young nobles increasingly familiar with Renaissance architecture and other arts, which began to show themselves in the external design and internal furnishings of their homes, at least in Denmark, where money was most plentiful. But this was still mainly a question of enlisting foreign talent. In literature, on the other hand, some valuable work was achieved in the vernacular, particularly in the fields of religion – the new Lutheran hymns have already been mentioned – and history. Saxo was translated into Danish by one of the earliest modern historians of Denmark, and a tiny group of Norwegian humanists completed several nostalgic writings about Norway's past greatness and a translation of Snorri, though very little of their work was printed until a later generation. Since the Scandinavian languages, then as now, were unknown to the world at large, the most influential history was the *Historia de gentibus septentrionalibus*, published by a Swedish Catholic priest at Rome in 1555. This was Olaus Magnus, incumbent of a Stockholm parish at the time of the Bloodbath, who had accompanied his brother Johannes, the last Catholic archbishop, into lifelong exile. His object was to show how significant a province his Church had lost, for which reason he began with the separate publication of the first plausibly shaped map of the northern seas (*carta marina*, Venice, 1539). With the help of some hundreds of Italian woodcuts, which are still frequently reproduced, his book presented a vivid if fanciful picture of the whole way of life of the northern peoples. It was translated almost immediately into Italian, German, and French, to which Dutch and English versions were added in the next century.

The north was so remote from the rest of Europe, however, that the culture of the Renaissance made its way there chiefly through its appeal

---

* 1546–1601. He substituted observation for speculation, equipping his island residence of Uraniborg ('Castle of the Heavens') with twenty-eight major instruments of his own invention, many of which were installed underground to escape the wind; distinguished visitors included James VI of Scotland. But Brahe's systematic neglect of his duties as a fief-holder, which incensed Christian IV, extended even to the withholding of fuel for a beacon to guide shipping in the Sound.

to powerful sovereigns. Eric of Sweden, whose passion for the classics was accompanied by musical ability, a fondness for rich embellishments, and the desire to patronise all the arts, would have had a great impact, had he reigned longer. His half-brothers, too, were men of intellectual accomplishments far ahead of most of their subjects. But Denmark's greater wealth at this time gave greater opportunities to her kings. Frederick II, the patron of Tycho Brahe, had English musicians to play for him in his magnificent Renaissance palace at Elsinore, a generation before Shakespeare made it the scene for the most widely known of Renaissance dramas. And in his son, Christian IV, whose restless nature dominated the life of his realm for better and worse during more than half a century, we encounter a Renaissance prince whose sense of beauty found expression in buildings which have long outlived the collapse of his political ambitions.

Chapter 6

The Dominion of the Baltic I, 1613-1660

THE RISE OF GUSTAVUS ADOLPHUS

Gustavus II Adolphus was called *il re d'oro* ('the golden king') by Italians because of his fair hair and ruddy complexion and 'the Dragon King' by an English nobleman reporting to Charles I on his prowess in the battle-field, but he has gone down in European annals above all as 'the lion of the north',[1] the apocalyptic source of deliverance for the stricken Protes-tants of Germany. For Scandinavia, however, his military impact on the Thirty Years War is only a small part of the whole: he raised Sweden to the status of a great power, eclipsed the ablest of modern Danish rulers, and made the dominion of the Baltic a natural goal for his successors.

Charles IX's heir was endowed by Nature with a robust physique, so that he shared readily in the hardships of the soldiers' life; the Vasa gift of oratory – he was equally eloquent in Swedish and German and fluent in six other languages; and a keen intellect, which enabled him to penetrate deeply into the problems of domestic and foreign politics. But it was his character and temperament which endeared him to all classes of his subjects, even the turbulent nobility. His anger was quickly aroused but easily placated; he knew how to combine royal dignity with comradely affability; and, whilst remaining a devout Lutheran, he learnt to see the merits of religious toleration. A leader of his quality is seldom born on the steps of a throne, and it is seldom indeed that such an heir receives his crown at a time when a great transformation can be rapidly accomp-lished. When Gustavus's father died in October 1611, Sweden, as we have seen, lay almost at the mercy of the Danes; when he himself fell at Lützen in November 1632, the Swedes were the strongest single force in the whole of northern and central Europe.

Gustavus had attended Council meetings since he was ten, and had been given an independent military command from the outbreak of the war with Denmark. It was therefore not surprising that the regency for which provision had been made lasted less than three months, during which an accession charter, designed to restore the power which the nobles had lost in his father's reign, was negotiated as the price for the recognition of the new king by the Riksdag. This provided that all seats in the Council and the key posts in the administration were to be reserved for the nobility, and that the legislative and financial powers of the Crown were to be exercised in collaboration with the Council and, more loosely, with the Riksdag. But the course of the domestic policy of the new reign clearly depended upon its success in handling the acute foreign problems of the Danish war and the Swedish involvement with Russia and Poland.

In 1613 the Peace of Knäred enabled Gustavus to face eastwards. An armistice with the Poles, which his father had made in 1610, was renewed from year to year, whilst he sought to win as much land as possible from the first Romanov, now precariously established on the Russian throne. De la Gardie had been hard pressed during the Danish war, but he retained possession of Novgorod and the king himself conducted an elaborate siege of Pskov, the key position at the south end of Lake Peipus, whilst an attempt was also made to advance north from Kexholm on Lake Ladoga, with the White Sea coastline as the ultimate Swedish objective. Pskov, however, held out stubbornly, and the Russians received diplomatic support from England and the Netherlands, whose merchants had no desire to see the whole of Russia's trade with the west placed under Swedish control. Accordingly, Novgorod was returned at the Peace of Stolbova (1617) and there was no further gain of territory in the far north. But the treaty gave Sweden both Ingria on the south shore of the Gulf of Finland and Kexholm on the north shore, with the frontier to the east drawn in such a way that only the far side of Lake Ladoga was in Russia. Gustavus's exultant comment to the Riksdag – 'I hope to God it shall now be hard for the Russians to hop over that stream'[2] – was justified by Russia's exclusion from the Baltic throughout the remainder of a momentous century.

These gains were the fruits in large part of Russia's Time of Troubles, but for success in the renewal of the Polish war, which now followed, Gustavus depended in part upon the growth of his navy, which henceforth secured the transport of his troops across the Baltic, but chiefly upon his accomplishments as a maker and leader of armies. Though he derived something from his early classical studies, from two months intensive training by de la Gardie (given when he was fourteen), and from a general knowledge of the Dutch methods of warfare, as improved by Maurice of Nassau, he seems to have learnt most by reflecting upon his own early experiences in the field.

The nucleus of a new type of army was found by an extension of the system initiated by his grandfather; nine provinces provided an infantry regiment apiece, one man in ten being called out on each occasion. The cavalry on the other hand included a few 'heavies', reluctantly provided by the nobles, as well as a number of regiments of volunteer light horsemen. Some German, Scottish, or English mercenaries were also employed from the outset, a proportion which increased in the king's last years, when Germany could be made to pay for the upkeep of forces whose casualties did not disturb Swedish public opinion. Whatever the source from which they were drawn, Gustavus's troops were to an increasing extent superior to their opponents in drill, discipline, and armament. On the chequer-board of the seventeenth-century battlefield he had the advantage of better artillery, composed of 24-pounders, made light enough to be moved by road as well as river, and 3-pounders manhandled by each regiment for its own protection. The pikes of his infantry had strengthened heads and their muskets were comparatively light. The musketeers, who were carefully trained to fire rapidly, rank by rank, were placed on the flanks of the brigade units, and were also interspersed between the cavalry squadrons; the pikemen were required to take the offensive during the period of reloading. But it was the cavalry whose intervention was usually decisive; they were taught to charge home, relying more on the sword than the pistol; in spite of their undersized horses, the Finns in particular earned the nickname of *Hakkapeliitta* ('choppers').

In 1618 the outbreak of the Thirty Years War strengthened the religious argument for turning against Gustavus's cousin and rival, Sigismund of Poland, 'who allows himself to be governed by that Devil's party the Jesuits',[3] as the king had already informed the Riksdag. In 1621 he attacked Livonia, which had been a Polish province for sixty years, and in less than two months his artillery captured Riga, the great trading city and fortress through which passed one-third of Polish exports. Though partly attributable to Poland's preoccupation with a Turkish war, it was this rapid success which revealed Gustavus to Europe at large as a force to be reckoned with. Five years later he won the decisive battle for the province at Wallhof, where the famous Polish cavalry were routed without serious loss to his own forces, and he was then able to transfer the main weight of his attack to Poland's Prussian possessions farther south. In 1629 the Poles were driven to accept the six-year truce of Altmark, whereby they surrendered Livonia and conceded an immensely valuable licence for levying tolls at every Baltic port between Estonia and Danzig – and even there the Swedes were to receive a share of nearly two-thirds.

Since Sigismund had received help from the Emperor, and since the Imperial general, Wallenstein, had now carried his victorious contest with the German Protestants as far as the Baltic shores, the time had come for Gustavus to take the great decision whether he should intervene directly in that war. In resolving to do so, he was in no way deterred by the disaster (see p. 117) which had overtaken the other Lutheran king, Christian IV of Denmark, as the result of his attempted intervention. For the king of Sweden now enjoyed the enthusiastic support of a united people; this was brought about by domestic policies as skilful as his conduct of the wars.

Gustavus Adolphus was peculiarly fortunate in his close and lasting association with Axel Oxenstierna, a noble of high lineage who had become the leading figure in the Council before the death of Charles IX. Though only 28 years of age, he stepped almost automatically into the chancellorship, where he showed a cool sagacity which was the ideal counterpart to his master's fiery spirit. Two other important advisers were men of middle-class origin, namely the king's former tutor, Johan Skytte, who became the first governor-general of Livonia, and his chaplain, Johannes Rudbeck,* who accompanied him on the Russian campaign and was an ecclesiastical and educational reformer.

In 1617 the Riksdag was for the first time formally organised as an assembly of four Estates, though the tax-paying peasants were not always summoned and the town representatives commonly left the defence of the middle class to the clergy, who had the archbishop and bishops at their head. Its legislative and financial powers were not often invoked by the king, but its meetings, with a maximum attendance of more than 500, served to obtain and demonstrate widespread support for the royal policies. The position of the nobles as the predominant Estate was clarified by an ordinance of 1626, which divided them into three classes: counts and barons; descendants of former Councillors; and other possessors of patents of nobility. Each noble family had one vote, cast by its chosen spokesman and head, but the final decision was by a majority of classes, so that the views of the higher nobility who constituted the first two, very select classes, would always prevail. But this systematisation of the government did not alter the fact that the king was the mainspring of the whole. His personal magnetism and his military successes had drawn the nobility to his side, and they were now fully content to serve him in the Council, in the command of armies and conquered provinces, in a newly established Supreme Court (where they were allotted the majority of seats), and in the chief posts of a system of collegial administration. This was introduced gradually on the Dutch model, and by 1630 included a Court Martial under Jakob de la Gardie, which was concerned with recruitment and logistics as much as the laws of war.

National unity and self-confidence were strengthened, not only by military success, but also by a new zeal for the Church and for education. In the Estonian and Livonian provinces Rudbeck and other ecclesiastics conducted a successful mission against the effects of the Counter-Reformation and in Kexholm a Lutheran peasantry replaced the Orthodox Karelians, who fled across the new frontier to Russia. The first three *gymnasia*, designed to provide the preliminary grounding for civil officials as much as for ordinands, were established in the 1620s, and Uppsala University entered upon its first golden age, with Gustavus as virtually a

* Both Skytte (1577–1645) and Rudbeck (1581–1646) completed their education at German universities; the former was ennobled by Charles IX in 1604, the latter from 1619 onwards was bishop of Västerås.

second founder; before the king's death, both a *gymnasium* and a university had been established as far away as Skytte's seat of government at Dorpat.

Finally, we must notice the skill with which Gustavus and Oxenstierna developed the Swedish economy, so that it could bear the strain of constant war. A new system of staple towns was set up, to which an export monopoly was granted for their own shipping; roads and waterways were improved; and the taxes were modernised so as to raise a much larger cash revenue than ever before. The most striking development, however, was the increased encouragement given to foreign capital and foreign immigrants; including mercenary soldiers, these became so numerous in this century and so successful that immigrant families eventually constituted two-fifths of the House of Nobles. The best known is Louis De Geer,* who became a Swedish citizen in 1627 and for a quarter of a century exercised a dominant influence on heavy industry, commerce, and finance. Dutchmen administered the Prussian tolls on Sweden's behalf; Scots and English merchants swelled the predominantly foreign population of Gothenburg, refounded on a new site after its destruction in the Kalmar War; and Germans and Walloons brought in the liquation process and improved methods of minting for copper, new types of forge and the masonry blast-furnace for the iron industry.

The Swedish copper output was now approaching its peak and, as it had no serious rival nearer than Japan, the profits were enormous. Gustavus helped to keep the metal in short supply by his use of copper coins negotiable in the same way as silver, albeit that his two-dollar piece had a diameter of $9\frac{1}{2}$ inches and weighed more than 8 pounds. The greatest days of the bar-iron industry still lay ahead; it was a cheaper product and therefore less profitable, but gave Sweden a further advantage over other states in that she was now self-sufficient as regards all armaments and even had an export of cannon. As for her own artillery, a Scotsman who served under Gustavus Adolphus in Germany noted with pride that it 'had the reputation to be the most exactly composed of any in Christendom'.[4]

THE EXPANSIVE POLICIES OF CHRISTIAN IV

For Denmark the war of Kalmar had been no more than a brief interruption in a period of peace and prosperity which had lasted for more than half a century. Since its result seemed to have vindicated Christian IV's position as the leading sovereign in northern Europe, he returned with zest to his many-sided activities as the 'father of his peoples', of which his many architectural triumphs are the visible memorial. The Italian

* 1587–1652. Born in Liège; settled in Amsterdam in 1615 as a merchant, shipowner, and banker with international interests; and moved finally to Sweden in 1641, when he was ennobled. Three years later he engaged a Dutch fleet for Swedish service at a critical moment by his personal credit, but his biggest achievements were as an armaments manufacturer.

Renaissance style made its entrance chiefly through the Netherlands, though there is a tradition of uncertain value that Inigo Jones came to Denmark at the king's invitation on his return from Italy. At Frederiksborg, which took more than twenty years to build, Christian raised on an island site the most splendid palace of his day, and he spent even longer in reconstructing Rosenborg at Copenhagen, the house of his studies and pleasures, where he eventually died. Other new buildings, such as the stock exchange and the observatory, were likewise intended to give the city the grandeur appropriate to the capital of a far-reaching monarchy, but clearly served practical objects as well. So did the low earthworks and angular bastions of the new fortifications, which were to play their part in the historic defence of Copenhagen in 1658-9.

Christian IV's new towns, which so often preserve their founder's name, were similarly designed for purposes of war as well as peace. Christianopel had been founded in 1599 as a counterweight to Kalmar – which lay just across the border from Blekinge; Christianstad was added for the protection of Skåne, and Christianshavn on the north side of Copenhagen to strengthen the defences of the Sound. Another interesting venture was Glückstadt, located on the east bank of the Elbe in 1616 to rival Hamburg, where the usual rectangles gave place to a hexagonal design, with massive bastions at the corners and streets radiating from a central square. Before the close of the Thirty Years War the half which was completed had already withstood two sieges. When medieval Oslo was burnt to the ground in August 1624, the king arrived on the scene within a few weeks with plans for locating his new Norwegian capital of Christiania* close under the guns of the Akershus fortress. Lastly, in his old age he laid out Christiansand as a trade centre for the south coast of Norway, in a position where he had previously improved an island fortification to strengthen his control of the Skagerrak.

Christian IV's superabundant energy and love of detail attracted him to the schemes for close regulation of the economy as an infallible source of national wealth and power, which were becoming current in his time and were much later identified by the term mercantilism. Privileges were offered to foreign artisans at the expense of the craft gilds, which for a few years were formally abolished, and a number of monopolistic 'manufactures', such as silk and clothing companies, were set up; although provided with a cheap supply of labour from the Copenhagen House of Correction and a kind of foundling hospital, their contribution to the balance of trade was negligible and they were soon abandoned. The king's personal interest and introduction of foreign workmen had a more lasting effect in the impetus given to the Norwegian mining industries. When silver was found in 1623, he visited the district in person while the

* The name of Oslo, which was officially re-adopted in 1925, will be used for convenience throughout the book. The reader may also like to notice that in modern Norwegian usage Christiansand, etc., are spelt with an initial 'K'.

snow was still on the ground, to establish the mining town of Kongsberg ('King's Mountain') and to order the construction of Norway's first high-road to link it with the coast. Silver, copper, and iron mining were all placed for a time under companies, and although the results were in many cases disappointing some twenty-three mines remained in operation after the king's death.

Since Christian was pre-eminently a sailor king, he made special efforts to improve the trade balance by means of Danish ventures overseas, which might intercept the profits earned by Dutch and other foreign merchants at Danish expense. In 1602 the trade with Iceland had been made a monopoly for the merchants of Copenhagen, Malmö, and Elsinore, which in 1619 was converted into a joint stock company subscribed almost entirely in the first-named city. Glückstadt proved an excellent market for the sale of Icelandic produce, such as dried fish, down, and friezes; the monopoly was extended to cover the Faeroes and north Norway; and the company's ships also hunted whale and seal. Although King Christian tried to regulate prices, both in this and still more in later reigns the system imposed great hardship upon the Icelanders, who were forced to sell cheap and buy dear. He did, however, send warships to deal with the pirates and buccaneers who often raided the island,* and sent a large sum to ransom captives who were carried off to the Barbary States. Christian's ships were active even farther west, in attempts to reach the long-lost Greenland colony and to find the North-West Passage; two crews wintered in 63°N., but only the Norwegian captain and two men returned alive. More ambitious ventures were those of the Danish East and West India Companies, founded in 1616 and 1625 respectively under the influence of Dutch immigrants, of which the main tangible result was the acquisition of a trading post at Tranquebar on the Coromandel Coast, south of Madras.

In order to maintain his very profitable control of the entrance to the Baltic, Christian employed an able Scottish shipwright for his many new warships, even designing some special features with his own hand. The arsenal at Copenhagen continued to grow; Norway was required to produce its own small vessels to do duty in the skerries; and an attempt was made by special privileges to induce merchants in both Denmark and Norway to build dual-purpose ships (*defensionsskibe*) – 250-tonners which could mount adequate guns for war. Much less was accomplished for the army, where Christian, like most European sovereigns of the day, placed his faith in a force of mercenaries: the peasantry had been used to some extent in the Kalmar War, where he found them to be 'worse than brute cattle'.[5] But in 1614 a National Militia was set up, a force of 4,000 men

---

* Two warships were sent in 1618, carrying commissioners who also delivered judgements at the Althing; the Algerian pirates returned, however, nine years later, when they took several hundred prisoners, of whom only thirty-seven were ransomed and made their way home from slavery in 1632.

raised from freehold and crown properties in return for exemption from taxes; this suited the Council, because it gave little additional power to the king and imposed no burden on the estates of the nobility. Moreover, the nobles as a class seem to have been more interested by this time in the arts of peace than of war, though the king included military training in the curriculum of an Academy for their sons, which he established in 1623 in a former monastery at Sorö in south Zealand; this numbered the future king Charles X of Sweden among its foreign pupils.

Like his predecessors in the twelfth century, Christian was tempted to seek aggrandisement in north Germany, where his younger brother Ulrich had already obtained the secularised bishopric of Schwerin. If the sees of Bremen and Verden could be secured for his own second son (later King Frederick III), Danish power would be extended from Holstein to the whole of the Elbe and Weser estuaries. The disasters which the Protestant cause suffered in the opening phase of the Thirty Years War offered a favourable opportunity: both Holland and England solicited Christian's intervention, and Elizabeth of Bohemia – wife of the 'Winter King' whom the Catholic armies had ousted from Prague – was his niece. He assembled troops in Holstein, secured the episcopal elections as desired for his son, and then rashly accepted command of the forces of the states of the Lower Saxon Circle. The rashness consisted not only in the failure to await a guarantee of Dutch or English help but even more in his readiness to accept the breakdown of negotiations which might have brought Gustavus Adolphus into the field at this juncture to share the burden and the credit of championing the Protestant cause.

Since Christian intervened in his capacity as duke of Holstein, the Danish Council was unable to stop him, although his army of German mercenaries (paid from the Sound dues) had to be reinforced increasingly from Danish sources. As his allies of the Lower Saxon Circle proved ineffective and even treacherous, the king did well to keep the field in the Elbe-Weser region for more than twelve months against a possible conjunction of his two veteran opponents, Tilly and Wallenstein. In August 1626 he seized a chance of confronting the former when the latter had turned towards Silesia, only to find that Wallenstein had left some supporting troops; the Danish king therefore tried to retire north again, but was forced to make a stand in front of the small fortified town of Lutter am Barenberge, near Hamelin.

The armies were about equal in size, and Tilly's initial attack was repelled by a thrust which brought Christian's infantry right inside the enemy position. But the League's cavalry did great execution among them, and when their line eventually broke Christian's horsemen joined in the flight, the king himself being among the last to quit the field. Having lost more than half his men and all his artillery, he had no option but to retreat to the Elbe estuary, where he raised fresh troops and held out against Tilly until the following summer. But, when Wallenstein returned in triumph from his Silesian campaign, he swept almost un-opposed into Holstein, whilst Christian had to escape from Glücksburg by sea, deserted by every German ally except Mecklenburg.

The consequences for Denmark were catastrophic. The king's Danish and German cavalry fled north in panic before the enemy, plundering as they went, so that the two duchies and then the whole of Jutland passed rapidly into the hands of Wallenstein's cosmopolitan host. Whilst the well-to-do, including even the clergy, followed the example of the nobles in making good their escape to the islands, where they were safe under the protection of the fleet, the bulk of the Jutland population remained for one and a half years at the mercy of an army of occupation which lived off the country and despoiled the farms of recalcitrant Protestants. Social cleavages became a source of weakness to the whole state, when the unprivileged saw that the nobles did not justify their privileges by setting any example of courage and self-sacrifice in the hour of need. On the contrary, falling profits increased their reluctance to pay taxes. When the war left the country saddled with a huge debt, so that twice as much had to be raised in direct taxation as in the first years of the century, two-thirds was exacted from the peasants and the nobility still tried to escape any payment.

Christian himself had shown exemplary courage, but had lost much of his prestige through the disastrous results of a policy against which his Council had warned him in vain, and his impetuous nature could not stomach the lesson that his ends must be limited by the means at his disposal. The last two decades of the long reign therefore present a bleak contrast to its earlier successes, and they were also clouded by family troubles. The heir to the throne, Prince Christian, had shown none of his father's martial qualities, though sharing his weakness for drink and women. The ageing king was now deserted by Kirsten Munk; her place in his affections was taken by a low-born mistress, but he arranged important marriages for his many daughters by Kirsten, thus providing himself with sons-in-law to help in his struggle against the mounting opposition of the Council and the nobility in general.

For Scandinavia as a whole, Christian's 'war with the Emperor' spelt the end of any possibility that the two kings might join forces to champion the Protestant cause in the Empire and perhaps forget old disputes in sharing the profits of their intervention. Though pressed by other powers to enter the war at the same time as Christian, Gustavus Adolphus had preferred to turn his arms against Poland rather than accept the king of Denmark as leader of a joint enterprise. In 1628, indeed, the Scandinavian sovereigns for a brief space recognised their common interest in thwarting Wallenstein, who with the resounding new title of 'general over the oceanic and Baltic seas'[6] threatened to establish a Catholic fleet in northern waters, which might imperil both Sweden's recent conquests and the Danes' last refuge in their own islands. Accordingly, they joined to put men and supplies into Stralsund, which Wallenstein was determined to capture for a naval base, and they succeeded in relieving the siege, although Danish troops which landed in Pomerania were crushed by Wallenstein soon afterwards.

The sequel was a meeting between the two kings in February 1629, at which Gustavus offered to supply three-quarters of the men and money for joint operations in Germany under his direction. But Christian, bitterly resentful of the turn of events which made Sweden inevitably the predominant partner in any such enterprise, was interested only in a show of Scandinavian solidarity to help him in the peace negotiations on which he had already embarked with the Empire. He gained some extra bargaining power for the peace which he signed at Lübeck in June, his territories being left intact, though he had to surrender his claims in north Germany and agree to his formal exclusion from all German affairs. He had, however, thrown away his last chance of conciliating the rising power of Sweden.

THE LION OF THE NORTH

The Imperial Edict of Restitution, published in the month after the abortive meeting between the Lutheran kings, was the culminating point of twelve years of war, in which the armies of the Emperor and the Catholic League had reduced the German Protestant states to a condition of almost complete defencelessness. Whilst the larger still sought safety in neutrality, the smaller fell under Catholic control along with the bishoprics, such as Bremen and Verden, and other restituted Church property. In August 1629, 8,000 Protestants went into exile from Augsburg, where the religion of the Augsburg Confession could no longer be practised, and a similar fate threatened even Magdeburg, whose position on the Elbe made it the key to north Germany. The help of the king of Sweden, whose record of military successes was now crowned by the Truce of Altmark (see p. 112), was therefore implored by his German co-religionists, many of whom saw in him the Lion who was to come out of the North in accordance with Old Testament prophecy to compass the overthrow of a modern Babylon.* His coming would also be welcomed by the Dutch and English supporters of the Protestant cause, whilst Cardinal Richelieu hailed him as 'the rising sun' whose rays might dispel the chill of the Habsburg shadow over Europe.

Religion was far from being the sole reason for Gustavus's response to the appeal: as Oxenstierna subsequently acknowledged, 'His late Majesty had other large causes of war'.[7] One of these may well have been the danger to his own throne, if the triumphant forces of the Counter-Reformation should champion the claims of the Polish Vasas; another,

---

* One version of the prophecy, attributed to the sixteenth-century alchemist and physician Paracelsus, ran through twenty-one printings in Germany in 1631–2.

the desire to raise the prestige of Swedish arms still higher in comparison with the Danes, so recently discomfited in the same field of war. To what extent Gustavus's imagination was also attracted by the idea of building up authority over the German states is unknown, but some form of union for the north German Protestants may already have been in the mind of this great organiser. Almost certainly he intended to make such annexations along the coastline as would complete his 'dominion of the Baltic', to which he laid claim in his official proclamation of war.[8] Was he not the heir of the long line of great 'gothic' conquerors (see p. 129), in which he and his people fondly believed? Yet it would be doing 'the Protestant hero' less than justice to deny the driving-force of his religious beliefs, which turned invaders of Germany into crusaders and which helped to bind his subjects to him in life and in death.

Before he set sail from Stockholm on 30 May 1630 for his momentous undertaking, Gustavus took solemn leave of the first three Estates, and commended four-year-old Christina, the only surviving child by his Brandenburg queen, to the care of the Council. He landed at Peenemünde, east of Stralsund, whose garrison – which had become wholly Swedish – helped to raise his force to a strength of 26,000 men. After consolidating his base area on the Baltic coast, he moved up the valley of the Oder to Bärwalde, where early in the New Year he signed a treaty which brought him French subsidies without seriously hampering his future actions.

The dismissal of Wallenstein from the Emperor's service in the previous autumn had brought about a lull in the general war, but in May 1631 the army of the Catholic League under Tilly and his brilliant lieutenant, Pappenheim, succeeded in capturing Magdeburg, 20,000 lives being lost in the ensuing holocaust. The king of Sweden was blamed by Protestant opinion at the time, as well as by many later historians, for failing to march to the rescue of the citizens, whose resistance he had certainly encouraged. He was, however, engaged in protracted negotiations for support from the two remaining Protestant Electors: his Brandenburg brother-in-law refused the modest role of a non-combatant ally until June, when Swedish artillery was trained on his palace in Berlin, whilst John George of Saxony waited to become a temporary combatant at the side of the Swedes until a triumphant Tilly had already entered his territories.

Advancing from the Oder to the Elbe – which he crossed at Wittenberg – on 7 September 1631 Gustavus joined battle on level ground at Breitenfeld six miles north of Leipzig, from which Tilly had advanced with 23,000 foot and 12,000 horse. The king had on his side about 42,000 men in all, but their numerical advantage was outweighed by the fact that his 18,000 Saxon allies operated as a separate force; they were put to flight by Tilly's Croatian cavalry in the third hour of the fighting, which began in early afternoon. The Swedes, however, stood their ground, with their small squares of infantry and cavalry supporting each other and changing front as the situation required, whilst the musketeers maintained a rate of fire which was three times that of their opponents. When evening fell, the resourcefulness of the Swedish cavalry under Oxenstierna's son-in-law, Gustav Horn, the superior manoeuvrability of their infantry, and the greater strength of their artillery combined to take in flank and rear the close-packed formations of the enemy. Tilly's long-invincible army of veterans was routed, having suffered nearly ten times as many casualties as the Swedes and abandoned all their guns. At a single stroke Gustavus Adolphus appeared to be the Heaven-ordained deliverer of half Europe. The triumphant German Protestants added a new verse to Luther's *Ein' feste Burg*, which had been sung before the battle; the Emperor, too, paid tribute to the result by contemplating flight from Vienna to Graz or even across the Alps.

Perhaps the king should have made straight for the Habsburg capital, as Horn and Oxenstierna desired – and this is the strategy which so eminent an authority as Clausewitz approves in retrospect. But Gustavus preferred to see his unreliable Saxon allies head south towards the heartlands of the Empire, while he himself turned along the so-called Priests' Alley into western Germany. In November the Swedish was the first foreign army to enter Frankfurt-am-Main since the earliest days of the Holy Roman Empire, and after keeping Christmas at Mainz its master engaged in negotiations which showed his determination to continue the war, irrespective of the wishes of allies and satellites, until Sweden had received indemnification (*satisfactio*) for its past efforts and insurance (*assecuratio*) for its future safety. Sometimes he pictured himself becoming Emperor, but his final intention (formulated after his arrival at Nuremburg in June) seems to have been to form the Protestant German states, including as he hoped the chief Imperial Cities, into a permanent alliance or *corpus evangelicorum*, which would maintain a standing army under his command. As for Swedish territorial claims, these in the king's opinion need not be defined at the moment, since his reading of Grotius – whose treatise accompanied him on every campaign – convinced him that by the law of nations every state which was either conquered or liberated from conquest by Swedish arms was lawfully at his disposal.

When Gustavus took the field again in 1632, his first objective was the great Catholic state of Bavaria. In April he forced a passage over the Lech, though it was swollen with melting Alpine snows and closely guarded by Tilly – who was fatally wounded in the struggle – and in the next month he entered both Augsburg and Munich. Though the direct route down the Danube valley remained blocked at Ingolstadt, he had now brought his army within striking distance of Vienna – only to find that his Saxon allies could not be relied upon to face Wallenstein, who had resumed the Emperor's service. When Wallenstein entered Prague the Saxons retreated from Bohemia, with the result that Gustavus was soon heavily outnumbered.

At the beginning of this year's campaigning, he had altogether 120,000 men at his disposal – of whom only 13,000 were native Swedes[9] – but the need to maintain garrisons in many parts of Germany and to protect his line of communications back to the Baltic coast against the incursions of Pappenheim drained away troops from the main theatre. Two summer months were spent in skirmishing round Nuremberg, until Oxenstierna had brought enough men from elsewhere in Germany to equalise the numbers. Gustavus then attacked Wallenstein, under the mistaken impression that he was abandoning his strongly held position near Alte Feste ('the old fortress'); instead the king was repulsed there with heavy losses, which included the capture of one of his chief subordinates (Torstensson) and the wounding of another (Banér).

Gustavus's first tactical failure since he landed in Germany was followed by a strategic error. He marched away to the south-west to secure Swabia as a well-found base for next year's campaign, when he would raise new levies; but he was forced to turn back, because Wallenstein's movement north into Saxony brought an anguished appeal for help from the Elector and constituted in any case a direct threat to his own line of communications back to the coast. Battle was joined at Lützen, south-west of Leipzig, on a misty November morning, when Gustavus had the advantage in numbers, pending the arrival of Pappenheim's cavalry, on whose absence from the scene he had originally counted. An impenetrable mist having delayed his attack until 11 a.m., the king's first advance on the right wing under his personal command was checked by Pappenheim's arrival, until the latter sustained a fatal wound. Gustavus was then victorious on right and centre, but the return of the mist heightened his anxiety for the left wing, where one of his staunchest German supporters, Duke Bernhard of Saxe-Weimar, was in fact hard pressed by Wallenstein's Croats. Leading a cavalry regiment to the rescue, the king was wounded, separated from his escort, and killed as he lay on the ground. The tide of battle continued to ebb and flow over the battered body of their fallen hero; but Bernhard was able to rally his men, so that when the light failed they held the field. Wallenstein had lost all his artillery and more men than his opponents, and he no longer barred their line of communications to the sea.

A blood-stained silken shirt may still be seen in Stockholm, in which the heart of the great king was wrapped for its long journey home. In a sense the heart had also gone out of the war, which lost the element of idealism that he had imparted to the middle phase of the long struggle. For Sweden too, this untimely death meant the end of an era of creative activity, in which the national life had borne a special stamp of unity and high endeavour. But this, like the romance of Elizabethan England or the grandeurs of the France of Louis XIV, has had an imponderable influence upon later generations of the Swedish people. And throughout the western world men's imaginations are still kindled by a dazzling military achievement, which in two decades of war raised an obscure, small nation to the rank of a great European power. Looking back in after-years, a Scottish colonel, one of the many mercenaries who served in the armies of Gustavus Adolphus, still hailed him as 'the Captain of Kings and the King of Captains'.[10]

SWEDEN AND DENMARK, 1632–1648

The German policy of Gustavus Adolphus was continued by his eminent chancellor, Axel Oxenstierna, throughout the confused struggles which constitute the last phase of the Thirty Years War. A few months after the battle of Lützen he succeeded in grouping together the Protestant states of Germany in the League of Heilbronn, with the Swedish general Horn and Duke Bernhard of Saxe-Weimar exercising virtually independent commands. But after Wallenstein's intrigues had ended in his murder by the Emperor's order, the imperialists under new leadership brought forward a strong body of well trained Spanish infantry, which led to the defeat of both Protestant generals at Nördlingen in Swabia, where the Swedes lost more than half their men and Horn himself was taken prisoner. A hurried retreat to the Rhine and the dissolution of the new League seemed to mark the definitive collapse of Gustavus's plans, especially as Sweden in 1635 was able to renew her truce with Poland only at the price of relinquishing the Prussian tolls, which had hitherto supplied in large measure the sinews of war.

Nevertheless, Sweden remained a participant in the European conflict to the bitter end. Financially, this was made possible by increased subsidies from France and by the ruthless exploitation of occupied territory to feed and help pay for the armies. Politically, it was mainly the achievement of Oxenstierna, who remained on the continent to direct affairs there until 1636 and then used his authority at home as an elder statesman. His influence was not easily shaken off, even after the termination in 1644 of the regency, in which he was the central figure, exercising powers conferred by the Council and the Riksdag upon the Chancellor and four other high officials, of whom two were members of his own family. Moreover, when a regular constitution was set up for the first time in 1634, it had been based on proposals which Axel Oxenstierna presented as the intentions of his late master.

The 'Form of Government' is a document of sixty-five clauses, which begins with religion and ends with detailed prescriptions for a regency. The Riksdag was formally accorded rights of legislation but not of regular assembly; instead, provision was made on grounds of convenience and security for recourse to a committee, in which the Riksdag would be represented by a nobleman from every district of Sweden and Finland, by the bishops, and by one burgess from each of six principal towns. The Council was given a regular membership of twenty-five nobles, including an inner ring of five which effectively controlled policy. These five were the heads of administrative colleges, namely the Chancery, High Court, War Department, Admiralty, and Treasury, which were linked with each of the thirty-seven provinces of the expanded Swedish dominions through a resident governor (*landshövding*); this office, with a scope resembling that of the French *intendant*, was reserved for noblemen. Oxenstierna claimed that the proposed system preserved 'the dignity of the Crown, the authority of the Council, and the due rights and liberties of the Estates'.[11] Though it received the approval of the Riksdag, the result was the continuance of a regime in which not only power but also – as we shall see later (p. 130) – great wealth accrued to the Oxenstiernas and their fellow nobles.

The armies which the Chancellor maintained in Germany now comprised 85 per cent of mercenaries, native Swedish and Finnish troops being reserved for strategic garrisons and spearheads of attack. The commanders, however, were Swedes trained in the school of Gustavus Adolphus, who enhanced the prestige of their country as a military power, albeit that they now figured as foreign conquerors rather than crusaders for a cause. Horn's place as commander-in-chief was taken by Johan Banér, who punished the Saxons for seceding to the Imperialists by his victory at Wittstock (1636), in which two of his Scottish generals played a leading part. Nine years later his successor, Lennart Torstensson, after destroying the Bavarian cavalry at Jankau, came within 30 miles of Vienna. In 1646–8 Karl Gustav Wrangel, promoted commander-in-chief at thirty-two after distinguished service at sea (see p. 126), shared with the great French Marshal Turenne in the conduct of the campaign which reduced Bavaria to despair. Indeed, the very last month of the war saw a Swedish army fighting its way into the hapless city of Prague, from which it returned with loot of enormous value, including the famous Silver Bible of the Goths.

The position of Denmark during the years which followed the Peace of Lübeck stood in stark contrast to that of Sweden. The unsuccessful war left the embittered king to face a heavy public debt, a hostile Council, and a nobility resentful of the pressure which obliged them at last to contribute a modest share of the taxes. The burgesses protested twice against noble privileges and even pleaded to some extent the cause of the peasants, who were no longer summoned to the Estates and therefore had no means of pleading for themselves. The results were negligible, except for the support the burgesses were able to give to the Council's proposal to reduce expenditure by substituting the national militia for the costly standing army of mercenaries. The nobles now agreed to a limited conscription of peasants from their estates, provided the arrangements were left under their management, and by 1643 the militia could muster about 18,000 men. But the king still insisted that the vulnerable Holstein frontier could only be defended by professional soldiers. Although the fleet was a smaller drain on the finances, being manned by crews levied in the Norwegian and other coastal districts, and drawing three-fifths of its officers from the middle class, defence continued to be the main item in a budget which was all the more burdensome because of falling prices for Denmark's staple exports.

Clearly this was a country which could not afford another war; yet King Christian's policies seemed recklessly to ignore the risk, and from 1636 onwards they were abetted by an ambitious son-in-law, Corfits Ulfeldt. The king's economic policy challenged the Dutch, whose fleet could at any time imperil his control of Baltic waters. He increased the Sound tolls nine times in ten years; raised the export duties on Norwegian timber; and in 1640–1 sent another (future) son-in-law, Hannibal Sehested,* on a mission to Madrid, which did a further disservice to Dutch trade by trying to arrange direct commercial connections with Spain through Glückstadt. At the same time the Danish king continued to dabble in German affairs, inducing the Emperor to grant the Elbe tolls for five years to Glückstadt and again acquiring the bishopric of Bremen for Prince Frederick. This policy in turn led on to attempts to counteract the successes of the Swedes, of which Christian was extremely jealous.

As early as the winter of 1630–1 he had tried to establish a link with the ever-hesitant Elector of Saxony, and followed this up by intriguing with both Tilly and Wallenstein and by making a new bid for command of the Lower Saxon Circle. These moves caused considerable alarm to Gustavus Adolphus, after whose death they gave place to Danish offers of mediation; Oxenstierna foiled the first by his creation of the League of Heilbronn, but they were renewed in 1638, when King Christian tried to turn to his own advantage the abortive peace preliminaries of Hamburg. Oxenstierna was not the man to turn a blind eye to such activities; still less to ignore the direct loss to Sweden's hard-won Baltic empire from the imposition of the Sound tolls upon all items of trade coming from Swedish-controlled ports overseas. By 1643 he judged the time to be ripe for striking against Denmark from positions on the continent – a route which her navy could not close.

In September Torstensson received the Council's orders to march north from the borders of Moravia. Crossing the frontier into Holstein in December without declaration of war, he overran both duchies before the month ended, the duke of Holstein-Gottorp (see footnote p. 131) being conspicuous as offering no opposition. By the end of January Torstensson also held all Jutland, though most of its small garrison was able to join King Christian in Fünen, as ordered. Gustav Horn then occupied all Skåne except Malmö, and although the small Norwegian army established by Sehested made some sallies across the frontier into Sweden it was only the disparity between the navies which held up a converging movement by the Swedish forces across the Danish islands. At sea Christian was for a

---

* 1609–66. A more statesmanlike figure than Corfits Ulfeldt (1606–64), as appeared when they both went into exile in Sweden. Hannibal was made Stattholder of Norway in 1642, the year of his marriage, and by 1651 he had centralised the finances (not without benefit to himself), stimulated trade, and restored self-confidence; this found expression in a new military organisation, which survived his downfall.

time successful, blockading the Swedish fleet in the fiord at Kiel after a drawn battle off Kolberg Heath, where he retained command in spite of the loss of an eye and thirteen other wounds. But Dutch intervention was decisive. The squadron hired by De Geer joined forces with the Swedes soon after their escape from Kiel (as the result of a failure for which the Danish admiral paid with his head), and in October 1644 Wrangel had in consequence a marked superiority of numbers when he encountered and virtually annihilated the Danish fleet off Femern. In the following summer the hopelessness of the Danish position was further emphasised by the passage of 400 Dutch merchantmen through the Sound under naval protection, all Sound payments being withheld as a form of sanctions.

However, Corfits Ulfeldt was able to negotiate some modifications of the Swedish demands in the treaty concluded at Brömsebro in August, thanks to the desire of the French and Dutch (who acted as mediators) to avoid making Sweden so powerful that she no longer served their interests either in the Baltic or in the German war. Yet the cession of the Baltic islands of Gotland and Ösel and the liberation of all Swedish possessions from the Sound tolls showed clearly that the dominion of the Baltic had slipped from Christian's hands; this was confirmed by the reduction of the tolls for Dutch vessels to the level of 1628. The loss of Jämtland and Härje-dalen, which lie east of the watershed or 'keel', was a blow felt chiefly by the Norwegians; but the retention of Halland by the Swedes on a temporary basis, to ensure fulfilment of the new arrangement regarding the tolls, must have caused widespread misgivings that the last had not been heard of Swedish demands for permanent possession of all three of the Scanian provinces.

The decision to make peace with Denmark, and still more the long-drawn-out negotiations with the Empire at Osnabrück, were influenced by the pacific inclinations of Queen Christina, who came of age in September 1644. The European peace settlement of Westphalia did not, indeed, realise every Swedish aim: nothing came of the projected *corpus evangeli-corum*, and in the Habsburg territories the Emperor made no concessions to his persecuted Protestant subjects. Moreover, Sweden reluctantly handed over one-half of Pomerania to Brandenburg; and the war indemnity which she accepted for paying off her armies was one-quarter the size of her original demand. On the other hand, the cession of Western Pomerania, including Stettin and the mouths of the Oder, and of the two Mecklenburg ports of Wismar and Warnemünde gave Sweden rather more than a foothold on the south shore of the Baltic. Farther west, the bishoprics of Bremen and Verden, occupied during the Danish war, were likewise assigned as fiefs to Sweden – valuable both for the Elbe-Weser trade and as a base from which the attack on Denmark could be renewed at any time across the Holstein frontier. No less important for the future was the involvement in German affairs which followed from Sweden's new position as a holder of Imperial fiefs and a guarantor of the settlement.

Christian IV of Denmark died in February 1648, a few months before the signature of the great European peace treaties, in which his country had no part. His last years were darkened by disagreements with Corfits Ulfeldt, who now ruled in agreement with the Council rather than with his father-in-law, and by the death of his eldest son, Prince Christian. His own death followed before there had been time to arrange the formal election of Prince Frederick as heir to the throne. Financially, Denmark had now sunk so low that, when the most splendid of her kings was finally laid to rest, his crown was in pawn and even the silken cloth which covered his coffin had to be bought on credit. But the eyes of Europe were turned upon Sweden, where a youthful queen reigned in brilliance over the youngest of great powers.

SWEDEN IN THE ASCENDANT

The peace of Westphalia provided no more than a short breathing-space in the contest for the Baltic Sea and its shores. The end of their long struggle against Spain enabled the Dutch to give closer attention to the political interests arising out of their huge trade in Baltic grain, timber, and naval stores; two-thirds of the traffic through the Sound passed under their flag. Dutch shipping now faced a growing rivalry from England, emerging from its civil wars as a militant republic ready to employ Blake's fleet if need be to promote its commerce. French trade interests in the area were smaller, but Cardinal Mazarin followed Richelieu in steadily wooing the friendship of Sweden, which he regarded as his strongest potential ally against Spain. But the Baltic area itself furnished the Swedes with two prospective enemies: Brandenburg resented the partitioning of Pomerania, whilst Poland under Sigismund's younger son, John Casimir, still asserted a claim to the throne of Sweden. Denmark would add a third enemy, as soon as any occasion might offer for redressing the damage done to her by the peace of Brömsebro.

Nevertheless, Frederick III made little effective use of the breathing-space. In contrast to his father's popularity with the broad masses of his subjects, which had survived every national calamity – even those that were clearly of his own making – Frederick was a man of great reserve who seldom revealed the motives for his actions. He had been trained in theological and other academic studies for his secularised German bishoprics, and when these did not eventuate he had been made stattholder of Slesvig-Holstein, where he acquired German advisers; his queen, too, was a German. The most significant internal development in the early years of his reign was that the Duchies adopted the principles of hereditary succession. In Denmark, on the contrary, the nobles seized their chance to impose an onerous accession charter as the price of Frederick's election to the throne: when one of his twenty-three councillors died, he must fill the vacancy from a list supplied by the nobles of the same county; and when his councillors disagreed with him over the interpretation of any of the many far-reaching provisions of the charter, their decision should 'be in force'.[12]

There were two interrelated problems of great urgency – the burden of debt and the expenditure needed for the strengthening of the defences which had proved so inadequate in 1643–5. The resources of the peasantry as tax-subjects were already squeezed dry, whilst a big increase in indirect taxation bore heavily on the middle classes, which became more and more restive; yet the Council accepted the refusal of the nobility to add to their contribution. As for defence, a new fortress was constructed at Fredericia in Jutland, near the narrowest part of the Little Belt, and some 40-gun ships were added to the navy. But lack of money made it necessary to reduce the number of professional soldiers and expand the national militia to fill their place. After long negotiations, the nobility agreed in April 1652 to a more effective recruitment of infantry companies from the peasants on their estates, whilst additional cavalrymen were to be provided by parishes, clergy, and local officials. Training, however, was badly neglected in the militia and even in the navy.

In 1649 Ulfeldt had been sent on an embassy to the Netherlands, where he negotiated a defence pact together with a treaty for redeeming the Dutch toll payments. The short-term result was to involve Denmark to some extent in the Anglo-Dutch war of 1652–4, when an English merchant fleet was held for a time under embargo in the Sound, but the Danes were excused from overt participation because the effect might be to bring the Swedes in against their Dutch allies; the redemption treaty was then given up, in order to satisfy English and Swedish objections that the Dutch were gaining an advantage over their trade. But the defence pact, which provided for support by 4,000 men against attack by a third party, was to prove its worth in Denmark's hour of greatest need. Ulfeldt nevertheless shared in the downfall of the late king's sons-in-law, all five of whom were attacked by their enemies on the Council for peculation in various forms. He and his wife, Leonora Christina, fled to Sweden, where his weak character and strong intelligence gained new prominence for him in the service of his country's enemies. Sehested, on the other hand, who was in receipt of one-sixteenth of all the farm rents in Norway, received a pardon in exchange for the surrender of his gains. But he too went abroad in disgrace, depriving his country for the time being of a talented administrator.

Meanwhile Sweden dazzled the eyes of contemporary observers, from the French Catholic envoy, Hector Pierre Chanut, to Bulstrode Whitelocke, the representative of Puritan England. The extravagant entertainments of the court were indeed a novelty in a country where, on so recent an occasion as the funeral of Gustavus Adolphus, the Council had wished to keep foreign visitors away, 'lest they witness our poverty'.[13] But what chiefly attracted attention was the riddle of the young queen's personality. Christina had been educated on her father's instructions like a boy, was extremely hardy, and long recalled her pleasure as a child of six at the sight of great men on their knees before her. In her girlhood she combined precocious intellectual interests with an appetite for romantic intrigue. As a ruler she could get her own way with the 'public Councils', of which Whitelocke remarks: 'They seldom differ or dissent from what the Queen proposes, so great is her influence over them.'[14] Yet at twenty-four this lifelong lover of power was to astonish the world by the almost unique spectacle of a purely voluntary abdication.

This brilliant court life marked the emergence of the Swedish upper classes from cultural barbarism. Gustavus's great work for education was continued by the Church through such leaders as Bishop Matthiae, Christina's tutor and a personal friend of the Czech pedagogue Comenius; the influence of the latter is traceable in the school law of 1649, which greatly strengthened the *gymnasia*. Uppsala university, the established training-ground for the officials of the expanding State, enjoyed the first of its many triumphs in the field of natural science in Christina's reign when Olof Rudbeck, son of the bishop, supplemented the work of Harvey by discovering the lymphatics. In 1640 Finland had been given its own university (Åbo Academy), which gradually attracted a student body of about 400 or one-third that of Uppsala. Historical and philological studies were encouraged by the cult of 'gothicism' – the belief that the Swedes were direct descendants not merely of the conquerors of Rome but of the most eminent people of all antiquity, who had made their home in Sweden shortly after the Flood. This claim, which had been asserted at the Council of Basle and in a propaganda work by Archbishop Johannes Magnus,* now served to explain and dignify Sweden's military triumphs and even to give a new importance to its native language. Sweden also for the first time produced a major poet in Georg Stiernhielm, whose *Hercules*, an allegory composed in felicitous hexameters, directed the mind of noble youth to the choice between pleasure and the life of heroic endeavour; the author had himself served as an official under Skytte in Livonia.

Of the many foreigners who were drawn to the Swedish court the most illustrious was Descartes, who died there under the stress of a regime which required him to attend the queen for philosophical discussion at five o'clock on winter mornings. Her interest in Cartesianism was quite genuine, but other foreign practitioners were invited to feed the new taste for luxury, from the painting of portraits to the production of ballets. Stiernhielm, for instance, had to provide texts which Christina's French dancing-masters set to music. The most enduring impact, however, was that of the architects, such as the Frenchman Jean de la Vallée and the

---

* *Historia de omnibus gothorum sveonumque regibus*, published after his death by his brother Olaus at Rome in 1554; this popular work also embellished the dynastic record with Magog, son of Japhet, six unidentifiable early kings named Eric, and six named Charles.

German Nicodemus Tessin, who erected new public buildings in the capital and mansions for the higher nobility both there and in the country-side. The best of the furnishings too were of foreign design, whether spoils of war from central Europe, such as are said to have aroused Christina's interest in Italian art, or the Silver Throne which her early favourite Magnus Gabriel de la Gardie (a son of Jakob) had made for her in Augsburg.

But the financial basis of all this was very insecure. The expansion of Sweden had certainly brought some profit. Generals and civil officials had received large grants of land in conquered territory and, until the armies in Germany were paid off, officers drawn largely from the lower nobility could earn cash salaries whilst living in garrison areas at foreign expense. Moreover, in 1651 Oxenstierna established a College of Commerce to direct trade: more ships now passed westwards through the Sound from ports under Swedish control than from those under Poland; Swedish copper production reached a peak of 3,000 tons (1650)[15] and, although the native mercantile marine grew rather slowly, the Swedish flag had been planted at Delaware in the New World (see p. 135) and on the Gold Coast. Throughout the war years, however, the Crown had paid for services rendered by sales or direct donations both of its own estates and of the right to levy the taxes on other estates, where the peasants were freeholders but would be forced into a kind of subjection to the lord who received their taxes. This policy was continued recklessly by Christina, to meet.the expenses of an extravagant court and to endow many of her new nobles; in ten years the number of counts and barons rose from thirteen to about eighty and the two lower grades of nobility were doubled.[16]

Matters came to a head at the Riksdag which preceded her coronation in 1650. By that time it was evident that the new provinces could not pay the full cost of their administration and that an army had to be maintained if the fruits of victory were to be preserved. The three lower Estates therefore demanded the restitution (*reduktion*) of alienated lands and rights, so that the Crown might be able to meet its necessary expenses. The clergy and burgesses felt that the nobles had benefited disproportionately from the national efforts, and they did not wish to see an increase in indirect taxes. The peasants feared that a process under which two-thirds of the soil of Sweden and Finland was now brought in one way or another under the control of noble estate-owners might end in the introduction of serfdom, as practised in Livonia and other trans-Baltic lands. The queen at first encouraged these complaints in order to isolate the nobles and force them to comply with her wishes in another issue; this done, she continued with land alienations which left an even worse situation for her successor.

The issue in question was the succession, which arose out of Christina's decision not to marry her cousin Charles, son of the Count Palatine of

Zweibrücken by his marriage to the daughter of Charles IX; he had been brought up in Sweden and stood for the authority of the royal family against the encroachments of the Oxenstiernas and other high nobles. In spite of their opposition, Queen Christina had him made generalissimo of the Swedish forces in Germany; then provisional heir to the throne in the event of her death without issue; and finally – through the help of the lower Estates in 1650, as indicated above – hereditary prince with full rights of succession. Next year she informed the Council of her intention to abdicate, which she carried out in June 1654, whereupon Charles was crowned king the following day. On her departure into well-endowed exile, Christina was publicly received into the Church of Rome – a faith which was proscribed in Sweden but which had been presented to her in its most attractive form by both Chanut and Descartes. Other motives may also have entered in, such as a physical repugnance to matrimony, impatience with the routine work of monarchy, and the belief that as an ex-queen she might play a dramatic part on the wider European stage.* But the primary importance of a decision which still engages the attention of historical novelists lay in its direct political consequences: in the opinion of Ulfeldt, who studied her policy at close quarters, 'The Queen desired peace among all her neighbours, and although she was very courageous, yet she loved not the wars.'[17]

DENMARK IN ECLIPSE

The half-German nephew of Gustavus Adolphus, who now became king of Sweden as Charles X Gustav, had served with marked success under Torstensson and was a soldier to his fingertips. On his accession he married a daughter of the duke of Holstein-Gottorp, thus cementing an alliance with the king of Denmark's rival for the control of the duchies,† and he used the imminence of war to carry through a small-scale restitution of estates to the Crown at a Riksdag held in 1655. An offensive campaign would provide support for his armies, and Poland offered a plausible objective: the coastline south of Livonia might pass at any time from Polish into Russian hands, and a chance to forestall the Russians now offered itself whilst the Poles were engaged in repressing a Cossack rebellion farther south. In July 1655 Charles X launched a three-pronged attack,

* When she died in Rome in 1689 she was best known as a patron of the arts and champion of the Catholic faith. In 1657, however, she created a European sensation by arranging the murder – at Fontainebleau and almost in her presence – of her Italian equerry, accused of betraying her plans to obtain the throne of Naples; and ten years later, when she revisited Sweden for the second and last time, she was planning to succeed her second cousin, John Casimir, on the throne of Poland.

† In spite of the union of 1460, lands in both duchies had been apportioned on a permanent basis in 1544, so that some were held by the king of Denmark as duke of Slesvig-Holstein, whilst others were the hereditary property of the dukes of Holstein-Gottorp. Gustavus Adolphus had allied himself with the duchy in the year of his death, as a means of 'putting a bridle upon the Jute'.[18]

which resulted in the occupation of both Warsaw and Cracow and the expulsion of the Vasa king of Poland from his country. The war blazed up again the following year, when Charles forced the Elector of Brandenburg to become his ally, and with his support won the three-day battle of Warsaw whilst outnumbered five to one; but Swedish resources were insufficient to suppress the national risings in widely separated areas of Poland. By 1657 Russia, the Netherlands, Brandenburg and the Emperor had each in turn taken steps to hold Swedish ambitions in check, whereupon Frederick III of Denmark decided that the moment was favourable for righting the wrongs inflicted by the peace of Brömsebro.

Although both the Estates and the Council supported the king's decision, the Danish armies mustered hardly more than one-third of the 90,000 men at the disposal of Charles Gustav: since Denmark's inferiority in population and total economic resources at this time was approximately in the order of two to three, the small muster of troops suggests a lack of enthusiasm as well as organisation. Charles, who had already transferred part of his strength in case defensive operations should be needed against Denmark, was glad to break off his unprofitable campaign in Poland and march his veterans across to Holstein – from which point he had the company and advice of Corfits Ulfeldt. The Swedes recovered Bremen, which had been occupied by the Danes, and with some support from their king's father-in-law in Gottorp overran the whole of Jutland. A substantial force had, however, been able to withdraw into the new fortress of Fredericia, whose defences surprised the Swedes by their strength. The besiegers were twice as numerous as the garrison, but it was a heavy further shock to Danish morale when Wrangel in late October took only an hour and a half to storm the position, the Danish losses being 1,100 killed and 2,000 taken prisoner; the Swedish, 74 men killed and 195 wounded. Nevertheless, time might still be on the side of King Frederick. The Norwegian army had regained both Jämtland and Härjedalen, and had even raided a Swedish silver mine in Norrland. The offer of North Jutland had failed to tempt Cromwell to supply an English fleet, and without outside help the Swedes were not strong enough at sea to transport their troops to the Danish islands. Meanwhile, Sweden's enemies farther south were preparing to intervene.

But on 30 January 1658, the very day on which the Emperor, the King of Poland and the Elector of Brandenburg signed an alliance against Charles X, the unusually intense cold induced him to venture over the ice of the Little Belt and so occupy Fünen. A week later the King continued this unprecedented march over the Great Belt, with the infantry trudging behind the cavalry and some sledge-borne guns. The cold was now much less severe and a strong wind increased the risk that the ice might break; a French envoy who accompanied the march claimed that, in the path made by the horses, as much as two feet of melted snow-water lay on top of the ice. Lolland, the largest of the three islands on the route chosen for the crossing, contained a fortress garrisoned by more than 1,000 men, but Ulfeldt negotiated its surrender to the advancing Swedes, whose first cavalry regiment landed on Zealand on 8 February. Although the 7,000 men who had crossed the ice possessed no line of communications and were outnumbered by the Danish troops in Zealand – including reinforcements which had defended Skåne with success during the autumn – the surprise completed the demoralisation of the Danes, who capitulated within a week of the landing.

The terms of the treaty of Roskilde required Denmark to cede all three provinces east of the Sound (Skåne, Blekinge, and the already mortgaged Halland); these had been Danish territory from time immemorial, were wholly Danish in sympathy, and constituted the most fertile corn-growing area of the kingdom. Norway was deprived of Bohuslen in the south-east and Tröndelag in the north: thus the far north was cut off from the rest of the country, and what remained of the more populous provinces was open to Swedish attack from all sides. Denmark had also to sacrifice the Baltic island of Bornholm, and to accept a reduced status for its sovereign in the Duchies, where the duke of Holstein-Gottorp ceased to be his vassal. But the term which was of most interest to other maritime powers was that which bound the Danes 'so far as possible'[19] to close the Sound and the Belts to foreign ships of war that were hostile to themselves or to the Swedes. This presupposed that Denmark would now accept the status of a subordinate ally of the victorious king of Sweden, who even before the war began had suggested the possibility of an agreement with the Danes for converting the Baltic Sea into a *mare clausum*, such as Selden had propounded round the coast of Britain.[20]

Having signed the treaty at the end of February, King Frederick procrastinated regarding the details of the alliance, knowing that his resistance to its obligations would have Dutch support; Charles X, on the other hand, was impatient to turn his army, now based on Kiel, against the Emperor and his other continental enemies. He therefore abandoned the idea of a Scandinavian alliance and reverted to plans for an outright conquest of Denmark, which would be consolidated by the deportation of the nobility to Livonia, the transfer of the university to Gothenburg, and the placing of Norway under a separate governor; the later history of Skåne shows that the bonds of nationality were not at that time indissoluble.

In August 1658 the warrior king launched from Kiel a kind of blitzkrieg without any declaration of war or even a plausible pretext. Although his fleet immediately closed the sea approaches to Copenhagen, the burning of the suburbs by their inhabitants showed that the citizens were rallying to the support of their king, who said, 'I shall die in my nest.'[21] In September the abject surrender of Kronborg provided Charles with the artillery he lacked for an attack on the capital, but at the end of the following month a powerful Dutch fleet defeated Wrangel in the Sound and reached Copenhagen with supplies and 2,200 Dutch soldiers to supplement the small garrison and the citizen reserve. Having lost the advantage of surprise, the Swedes resorted in February 1659 to a night attack, which was repulsed with heavy losses, King Frederick fighting in person on the ramparts. This proved to be the turning-point. Resistance to the Swedish forces of occupation had mounted rapidly in Skåne and on Bornholm, which was completely restored to Danish hands. The Norwegians captured Trondheim from a tiny garrison which eventually ran out of ammunition, and held on stubbornly to their own newly erected fortress of Fredriksten, on a crag outside Halden. And in November 1659 a second Dutch fleet – which at first operated together with the British navy – enabled Charles X's continental enemies to reconquer Fünen for King Frederick.

In the course of the year Britain and Holland, with the partial support of France, had formed the Concert of The Hague for imposing such a settlement upon the Scandinavian powers as would safeguard their own interests in Baltic trade – a development which was not wholly welcome to Frederick and extremely unpalatable to Charles. He summoned a Riksdag at Gothenburg, where he called for further efforts: if the Dutch could not be bought off by an offer to partition Denmark with them, it might still be possible to render the Danes more amenable to Swedish control by a successful winter campaign in Norway. But in February 1660, before news of a second failure at Halden reached Gothenburg, Charles X Gustav had succumbed to a sudden illness at the age of thirty-seven. The sword, on which he had relied to settle every problem, might have gained additional advantages for Sweden in a rapidly changing international situation. But as the throne passed to a child of four, only a second Axel Oxenstierna could have continued the war with its widespread ramifications.

The Peace of Oliva brought the Polish war to an end without any further accession of territory to Sweden along the disputed Baltic shore, though Poland at long last renounced the claim of its Vasa kings to the Swedish throne and accepted the loss of Livonia. The same treaty made peace with the Emperor and the Elector of Brandenburg, East Prussia passing finally into the possession of the latter; and soon afterwards a truce with Russia (made in the spring of 1658) in turn became the Peace of Kardis, leaving frontiers unchanged. In the meantime, Denmark's negotiations with Sweden had been finally completed by Sehested, who re-entered King Frederick's service at this juncture after observing the war from the Swedish camp. The treaty of Copenhagen, signed on 27 May 1660, modified that of Roskilde in three important respects. The Danish Crown recovered the Tröndelag outright; Bornholm was bartered for financial compensation in the form of properties in Skåne, which King Frederick had to buy for the purpose from their noble owners; and the removal of the servitude regarding the passage of the Sound by warships hostile to Sweden ended the threat of an implied Swedish suzerainty over Denmark.

The peace settlement of 1658–60 is a great landmark in Scandinavian history, aggrandising Sweden at the expense of both Denmark and Norway and giving the last-named a brief experience of a partition which might have prevented the revival that impended. It was also a cardinal event in the struggle for the dominion of the Baltic, where both Sweden and Denmark had lost their best chances and would soon be faced by stronger rivals. In the New World they were already outfaced: Fort Christina at Wilmington on the Delaware, established in 1638, had been captured by the Dutch in September 1655, when Charles X was already at war in Poland.* But in the next generation the most important change in the fortunes of both the Scandinavian monarchies was to be internal – the decline of the nobility as a political force and the acceptance of a royal autocracy.

* At the time of its transfer to the English in the Second Dutch War, the settlement contained about 110 'boweries' or farm properties, belonging mainly to Swedes or Finns; but no result followed the instruction given to the Swedish envoy at the court of St James's 'to try in a polite way to prevail upon England to restore New Sweden'.[22] The Swedish language and direct affiliation to the Church of Sweden survived, however, down to the late eighteenth century.

Chapter 7

The Dominion of the Baltic II, 1660-1721

ABSOLUTE MONARCHY ESTABLISHED IN DENMARK

The tomb of King Frederick III in Roskilde cathedral bears the in-scription: 'Here he rests, to whom Denmark owes its existence.'[1] The courage which he showed in the desperate crisis of 1658-60 had indeed played a large part in securing the survival of his country; but Frederick III was to an even greater extent responsible for the kind of existence on which it entered during the last ten years of his life, through the construc-tion of a new constitutional framework destined to endure for nearly two centuries. The opportunity for this arose directly out of the war, when the king decided to throw in his lot with the citizens of Copenhagen rather than with the nobility, whom public opinion accused of running 'like hares'[2] before the enemy. In that momentous August of 1658, two days before the Swedish invaders came in sight of the city, he had made them a far-reaching grant of privileges: control of their own taxation, access to offices hitherto reserved to the nobility, and rights of land purchase on an equal footing with them. The citizen reserve having played its part manfully throughout the siege, the return of peace in May 1660 found the Estate of burgesses in possession of a prestige which the king could use against their common enemy, the nobles. They had a well established leader in the mayor of Copenhagen, Hans Nansen, and were allied with the clergy through Hans Svane, bishop of Zealand, who had found use for a spear as well as a crozier.*

In September the three Estates were called to Copenhagen in order to provide the new taxes which were urgently needed in a country ravaged by war, shorn of several of its richest provinces, and faced with bankruptcy. The nobles reluctantly agreed that a new excise should be imposed equally on all classes, but they resisted a scheme for the reorganisation of fiefs

---

* Nansen (1598–1667) was an enterprising merchant, who had traded with Russia and spent eighteen summers in Iceland; an ancestor of the Norwegian explorer. Svane (1606–68) was likewise of middle-class origins; his spear (which is in the Danish National Museum) was bought in 1651, four years before he was advanced to the episcopacy from a professorship of theology.

so as to render them more profitable to the Crown, claiming that it involved infringement of the accession charter of 1648. The two lower Estates were then prompted by the king's principal German adviser, Christopher Gabel, to propose that the monarchy should be made hereditary. When this proposal was rejected by the Council as representing the interest of the nobility, the king after some apparent hesitation agreed to force the issue. The gates of the capital were closed to stop the nobles from leaving, and the whole country was placed under military control to prevent possible interference by their supporters – or by the Swedes. In this way the Estate of nobles was induced to make a formal concession to King Frederick III of a throne which should henceforth pass to his heirs as of right, the only reservations being for the unity of the realm and the preservation of the privileges of the Estates.

Although this action did not in itself invalidate the accession charter for the reign then in progress, the Estates decided that, there being no agreed alternative, the charter should be returned to the king and replaced by a law formulated at his discretion. They were then reinforced by some peasants from the environs of Copenhagen for the purpose of taking an oath of allegiance, ceremoniously administered in front of the palace; and before the end of November the members of the Estates departed for their homes, without any inkling (so far as posterity can judge) that their discussions would not be resumed for one and three-quarter centuries. In practice, power was now concentrated in the hands of King Frederick and his chosen advisers, among whom Hannibal Sehested was increasingly prominent alongside Gabel and the German queen; Nansen became President of Copenhagen and Svane Denmark's only post-Reformation archbishop. The legal basis quickly followed, when in January 1661 the nobility, clergy and representative burgesses were invited to sign the 'Act of Autocratic Hereditary Government', implying that autocracy was a necessary concomitant of heredity in a monarchical constitution. The document was signed without overt protest in every province, so that the king acquired a kind of plebiscitary right to fix at his own discretion the terms on which the autocracy should be based. He was not even obliged to publish those terms. They were formulated in 1665 as the *lex regia*, which was sealed by the king in 1669 and read to the Privy Council next year on the occasion of the accession of Frederick's eldest son; but only an extract was included in the legal code of 1683, and it was not until 1709 that subjects were finally permitted to know the exact details of their subjection.

The first draft of this remarkable document was made by two Danish jurists on the basis of advice from Germans in Glückstadt, and seems to have represented the views of Gabel rather than Sehested. The final version was penned by Peder Schumacher (later Count Griffenfeld),* who

---

* 1635–99. The brilliant son of a Copenhagen wine merchant of German origins, he studied at Leyden and Queen's College, Oxford – where Hobbes's *Leviathan* would be a common topic of discussion – and returned home in 1662 after visiting the Paris of Louis XIV.

had recently been appointed librarian and private secretary to the king; he continued to rise rapidly in the royal favour under Frederick III and his successor, Christian V, by whom he was eventually appointed Chancellor of the Realm – a post which foreign diplomats equated with chief minister. We may perhaps attribute to his influence the fact that the most purely absolutist of European constitutions seems to be based less upon the divine right of kings than upon the Hobbesian idea of a contract, reference being made in the preamble to the voluntary and permanent surrender of power made to the Crown of Denmark by its Council and Estates.

> 'The King shall hereafter be regarded by all his subjects as being above all human laws and knowing no other superior or judge over him in matters spiritual or temporal save God alone.'[3]

An explicit exception was made for three national interests: the maintenance of the Lutheran religion, the king being described as leader rather than head of the Church; the integrity of the kingdom, no part of which must be ceded or used for apanages for younger sons; and a strict line of succession. Inheritance through a female was to be permitted if there was no heir in the male line of Frederick III's descendants – a contingency which did not arise until 1863 – and periods of regency were to be curtailed by declaring the absolute monarch to be of age on his thirteenth birthday. In all other respects the legislative, judicial and administrative authority of the king was henceforth to be unlimited and unchangeable, for any restriction which a particular sovereign might impose upon himself was automatically cancelled at his death and whoever had participated in the 'usurpation' was declared guilty of *lèse-majesté*.

In practice, none of the later Oldenburg sovereigns was tempted to use his powers to the full in the manner of a modern dictator; in no case was their influence on the national life as great as that which Christian IV had exercised for many years in spite of the restraints which could legally be imposed in his time by the Council. For the mass of their subjects the effect of the *lex regia*, as it filtered through to them in the teachings of the clergy and other officials, can only have been to place the king as 'father of his people' on a rather loftier pedestal than he had stood on in earlier centuries. But, for the small minority who had political ambitions and came into direct contact with the court, the need to acquire and retain the favour of the king, the queen, or a royal mistress was a factor which often influenced their policies to the detriment of the public interest. Their personal situation was also precarious. The fate which befell Griffenfeld was soon to show this (see p. 146), and even earlier the monarchy displayed its arbitrary power in the case of Corfits Ulfeldt's wife, who was held in prison without trial for twenty-two years under inhuman conditions, chiefly to satisfy Frederick III's queen, who had long envied her beauty and talent.*

---

* Leonora Christina was kidnapped at Dover in 1663 with the connivance of King

In general, however, the standard of legislation and administration improved. The chief glory of the next reign was the *Danish Code of Christian V* (1683), drawn up by a committee of experts, who based it on equality before the law, employed language that was generally comprehensible, and – except where treason was concerned – were more humane than most contemporary penologists. A critical English observer wrote of these laws: 'For justice, brevity and perspicuity they exceed all that I know in the world.'[4] The administration had already been remodelled on the collegial system, as observed by Sehested during his years in exile. A supreme court was instituted, in which the king sometimes presided in person, and there were separate colleges for war, navy, and commerce, as well as the Rent Chamber which continued to run the finances. But the heart of the system was the Danish Chancery, which shared the responsibility for external relations with the still influential German Chancery, whilst in domestic affairs its authority became paramount. Fiefs were now replaced by counties (*amter*), whose governors were salaried officials. Each county had a county clerk, with independent authority over tax collection and the administration of conscription laws, and (in theory) a watching brief for the interests of the peasants; the towns, too, had mayors and councils nominated by the Crown, though their elected representatives apportioned the taxes. In 1670 the edifice was crowned by the formation of a Privy Council (*Gehejmeråd*) of leading ministers on the French model, as proposed by Griffenfeld, who became its first secretary.

Distinction of classes was reinforced in 1671 by the introduction of a new nobility of counts and barons, based on service rendered to the Crown and recruited largely from Holsteiners and other foreigners; its members received large land grants, to which were attached exemptions from taxation. An official table of precedence underlined the fact that upstart bureaucrats might rank higher than inactive nobles of ancient lineage, a policy which was also served by the distribution of the Orders of the Elephant and the Dannebrog. But the burgesses were able to strengthen their social position by extensive land purchases, as Crown estates came into the market to pay off part of the public debt, which in 1660 was estimated at one-fifth of the value of all landed property in the country. The clergy too were better placed than before, since tithe payments had been adjusted in their favour and private patronage of livings abolished, so that the choice of incumbent passed eventually to the Crown.

In close imitation of Colbert's France, the Danish autocracy sought to improve the financial situation by further extension of the state direction of commerce and industry, already practised by Christian IV. The East

Charles II; she had returned to Denmark with her husband in 1660, after which he committed fresh treason in Germany, was sentenced to death *in absentia*, and died as a mentally deranged fugitive (1664). Her long years in captivity are movingly recorded in *Jammersminde*, translated into English as *The Memoirs of Leonora Christina*.

India Company based on Tranquebar was re-formed in 1670, and a West India Company was founded on the possession of St Thomas in the Virgin Islands, first occupied in 1666. In addition there was a Guinea Company; a trade and fisheries monopoly for Greenland, held (but not seriously exploited) by a consortium of three admirals; and a project for trade with Russia. The last of these in particular would serve the object stated by Griffenfeld when he set up the College of Commerce in 1666: 'To get back into the traffic of which we have been dispossessed by ᵁ ˜rounding neighbours who are not nearly so conveniently placed.'[5] Thus Copenhagen still aspired to a dominant position in Baltic trade, and tax concessions were given to the new companies on cargoes stored in its harbour for re-export. New industries were attempted, such as tobacco-spinning, the making of Dutch tiles, cutlery and other metal-working crafts, and various clothing manufactures. In spite of the hostility of the gilds, these activities helped to swell the population of the capital, which doubled in forty years, so that by 1700 it was about 70,000. The small towns, however, remained sunk in poverty, and even Copenhagen failed to make the most of the great migration of Huguenot industrialists from France in the 1680s. A number of French silk weavers were then encouraged to settle by banning all importation of manufactured silk: but the clergy resented the grant of religious freedom to the newcomers and native tradesmen complained that their wares were too dear, with the result that they moved on to Brandenburg and Sweden. It was only in the closing years of the century that the Danish textile industries as a whole became prosperous, thanks to the long wars which hampered their continental competitors.

For the peasant majority of the population the autocratic regime brought little change, except that in 1682 a full land survey was completed, which at least gave a fairer basis for the imposition of land taxes; it remained in use for one and a half centuries. Out of a total of about 59,000 peasant farms placed on record in 1682, no more than 1,700 belonged to peasant freeholders – considerably fewer than the number recorded as derelict (*ödegaard*). Nobles owned about one-half; the Crown, in spite of the post-war sales, still owned one-quarter; and middle-class proprietors owned about 15 per cent, the remaining farms being in the hands of institutions.[6] It would be unrealistic to suppose that the new middle-class landowners were less ruthless than others; the great variations in the peasant's lot, which make it rash to generalise, depended rather on the region in which he lived and the character or circumstances of the individual master or his bailiff. But the low level of agricultural prices in Europe at this time made it very difficult for the farmer to save, so that a single poor harvest – such as that of 1661, the very first after the wartime devastations – brought him close to starvation. At such times the position of the cottars (*husmaend*) and farm servants was even worse. In Zealand the number of cottar holdings increased in 1660–1700 from 60 to 75 per 100 farms,[7] whilst evidence from Jutland suggests that in prosperous years young men emigrated southwards into the Duchies and the Hanse towns in search of freer conditions.

NORWAY AND ICELAND IN THE NEW ERA

The Norwegian people had never lost sight of the fact that their throne passed by heredity and not by election like the Danish – a distinction which its Danish kings had naturally regarded with approval – but they had no power to assert a special position in relation to the revolution made in Copenhagen in 1660. Not until August of the following year were Norwegian representatives called upon to play any part; and then it was the king's fifteen-year-old heir, Prince Christian, who came to Oslo in order that the nobles, the clergy, and a third Estate made up of burgesses, craftsmen, and peasants might formally pledge their allegiance to the new autocratic monarchy. Nevertheless, a revolution which was accepted seemingly with indifference was to give Norway a greatly improved status, since Danes and Norwegians without respect to classes or persons stood in theory on the same humble level as equal subjects of an all-powerful sovereign. Denmark was still predominant in population, wealth and cultural activity, but Norway's economic advances were preparing the way for the 'twin kingdoms' of the Age of Holberg.

The administration continued to be based upon the office of Stattholder, which from 1664 to 1699 was held by U. F. Gyldenlöve, an illegitimate son of Frederick III, who had been brought up by the queen and became very influential. He obtained a separate High Court for Norway, improved the defences, and won widespread popularity by cutting the costs of government and simplifying the taxes. But Copenhagen, where Gyldenlöve resided for much more of his time than at Akershus Castle or in his Norwegian countship at Larvik, retained the management of Norwegian affairs in its bureaucratic Colleges, which operated through county governors and an array of civil, ecclesiastical, and military officials. These normally received their training in the university, departmental offices, or military and naval headquarters, all of which were concentrated in the capital; and only there was it possible to establish contact with the court, which was more than ever the best avenue to promotion. Yet to an increasing extent the decay of the old Norwegian nobility – which mustered only eighteen members to receive Prince Christian in 1661 – was compensated by the growth of a new bureaucracy strongly rooted in the native soil. This phenomenon showed itself first in the Church, where many cures of souls were served for several generations by members of the same family: whilst remaining part of a Danish ecclesiastical hierarchy, their general interests became localised in Norway. The growth of the Norwegian army provided scope for native commanders alongside the foreign professionals, and by 1700 even a county governorship was sometimes given to a Norwegian.

Special importance attaches to the *Norwegian Code of Christian V*, promulgated four years after the Danish, since it is still valid as the starting-point of the modern statute-book. The first draft was made by a Norwegian commission, whose members were nominated by Gyldenlöve; this was revised by Danes, to secure closer conformity with Danish practice, and finalised by a second commission in Norway, including judicial members who had Danish sympathies. The main lines followed those of the Danish code, penalties being in many cases more severe than under earlier Norwegian law, which had for example allowed some forms of murder to be met by a fine. But Norway preserved its udal land law, traditional practices for the regulation of farming and fisheries, and a procedure in property cases which required the professional magistrate to take account of the views of the village moot (*bygdething*) regarding local conditions and customs. Furthermore, the code incorporated in a somewhat milder form an ordinance in sixteen paragraphs, drawn up by Gyldenlöve a year or two earlier, protecting the peasantry against excessive claims for payments and services by landowners, clergy and other officials.

In Norway as in Denmark, much Crown land had been sold after 1660 to pay the costs of the war – and the new middle-class owners were equally ready to exploit their tenants. But about 1680 the number of peasant freeholders in Norway began to increase again, because the industrial situation there attracted middle-class money to other forms of investment than land, whilst at the same time it provided many peasants (as we shall shortly see) with subsidiary earnings which they could use to buy up land. Protected also by Gyldenlöve's ordinance and the new Code, the Norwegian peasantry as a whole kept their traditional liberties – with the significant exception of those who lived on specially privileged estates, such as Gyldenlöve's countship of Larvik, where compulsory deliveries of charcoal for the ironworks were rigorously exacted.

The mining of iron ore, copper and silver all helped to create a more expansive industrial situation than in Denmark, but what benefited the peasant most was the increasing demand for his timber. The part that it played in the rebuilding of London after the Great Fire of 1666 is often referred to in this connection; for a very much longer period Norwegian pine was the cheap material from which the Dutch made their ubiquitous 'fly-ships'. The larger farmers derived a steady profit from the stands of timber on their property, and the smaller in many cases derived a supplementary income from felling, haulage and flotation. These remained big factors in Norwegian rural life, even after the institution of 'quantum saws' by an ordinance of 1688: these were the mills which had been established for at least thirty years and were therefore allotted an export quota, others being restricted to sawing for purely local requirements.

The quantum saws are by no means the earliest example of the interest which the absolutist monarchy took in the economic development of its second kingdom, through which both Christian V and Frederick IV made a toilsome official progress. In 1662 a new charter of privileges was granted after investigation to eight towns, each of which was designated as the trade centre for a large surrounding district and had a monopoly of the more important handicrafts. Smaller ports (*ladesteder*) were placed in subordination to the nearest privileged town, which had its principal officials appointed by the Crown with responsibility for the payment of all dues. The towns drew many foreign immigrants, including some who could provide the capital which Norway had always lacked. The south coast was readily accessible to Danes from Jutland and Germans from the Duchies; Bergen and other west-coast ports attracted the Dutch, Scots and English, who knew of possible openings through the shipping connection. The Crown encouraged the newcomers, whose descendants in due course provided Norway with its first firmly established native-born bourgeoisie. In 1689 a Holsteiner, who had traded in Bergen for some years with marked success, was even appointed director of commerce for Norway. He provided the city with a kind of industrial estate based on seven different manufactures; but all that survived the bankruptcy of the director was one papermill and one oil-mill.

The ironworks were more enduringly successful. These multiplied near the coast of southern Norway, wherever water power for the hammers and charcoal for the furnaces were readily available, the latter commodity weighing twice as heavily in the running costs as the ore, which was often brought from a distance. They had a flourishing export of stoves, firebacks, and cast-iron utensils of all kinds to Denmark, Germany and other markets; the larger establishments also supplied all the needs of the Crown in cannon and shot, with something left over for Denmark's allies. The ironworks, like the mining enterprises, attracted capitalist entrepreneurs and skilled artisans from abroad.

In addition to the growth of these relatively new exports, Norway retained its traditional markets for dried cod and salted herring. It was therefore a natural nursery of seamen, but they found employment chiefly in Dutch and English ships (including even warships), as Norwegian commodities were nearly always fetched from the wharves by foreign vessels. A sizeable mercantile marine dates, however, from the European war of 1689–97, when both the English and the Dutch were engaged against Louis XIV of France, which gave a small neutral people its chance. In eight years Bergen doubled its tonnage, and shipping based on Oslo rose from an almost negligible quantity to about half the amount owned in Bergen.

During the long period when Norway had no mercantile marine, contacts with Iceland dwindled to the purely cultural.* The Icelanders accepted the constitutional revolution in Copenhagen a year later than the Norwe-

* *Historia rerum Norvegicarum* (4 vols, 1711), written by the eminent Icelandic historian Thormod Torfaeus, who held an official post in Norway, was the first survey of Norwegian history in a language which could be read by scholars outside Scandinavia.

gians, at a somewhat informal meeting held on the arrival of a new governor, who found that the Althing had dispersed and both Lawmen had resigned office. The governor, who was a Norwegian by birth, did not visit the island again, and it was not until after his death in 1683 that provision was made for a resident *amtmand* and for a separate official in charge of taxation and other financial matters, including the trade regulations. The trade monopoly, which after 1662 controlled the fisheries and Crown estates as well as imports and exports, was indeed the central feature of the administrative system. In the time of Christian IV the Danish merchants concerned had paid dues of 16 dollars a year for each harbour visited; this was later changed to 20 dollars for each ship, and by 1706 their annual payment had risen to more than 20,000 dollars.[8]

In theory, the needs of the islanders were well catered for by a division into commercial districts, so that the absence of internal communications should not prevent the necessary supplies from reaching the coastal fishing hamlets and isolated farmsteads in any part of the island; each area would export its own products in return, and there were scheduled prices for both imports and exports. In practice, the monopoly enabled the merchants to import low-quality goods and to refuse to export anything which was not of the highest quality, thus amply recouping themselves for the dues they paid. Moreover, when the Icelanders tried to get better bargains by dealing with foreign fishermen or trading outside their commercial district, the *amtmand* punished infringements of the rules by floggings, by forfeiture of property, and even by penal servitude in Denmark. The first decade of the new century brought some amelioration as regards both prices and penalties, but in 1707–9 a smallpox epidemic which killed one-third of the population left the remaining 35,000 more defenceless than ever.

From 1620 to 1662 the Faeroes formed a minor part of the Icelandic trade monopoly, but in the latter year the archipelago was granted as a fief to Christopher Gabel, who controlled the trade as well as the Crown lands, which were more than half of all farm properties. He and his son after him proved ruthless masters, but in 1709 the State took over the whole administration, including the trade monopoly, which then proved highly beneficial. The close resemblance between the Faeroese language and the West Norway dialects perhaps accounts for the fact that after the Reformation the churches were for a time attached to the diocese of Bergen; they were transferred in about 1620 to the see of Zealand, but two generations later the introduction of the *Norwegian Code of Christian V* reaffirmed the status of the islands as a territory (*land*) of the ancient kingdom of Norway.

INTER-SCANDINAVIAN RELATIONS

In the years when the Danish monarchy was adopting the forms of absolutism, the Swedish was being adapted to the requirements of a long regency, which the higher nobility were determined to bend to their purposes. Charles X's will, to which the lower Estates attached more weight than to the Form of Government, would have given much authority to his widow and his brother, but after the Council had increased its prestige by negotiating peace it succeeded in concentrating authority in the hands of a small group of its own members. So far from continuing with Charles X's *reduktion*, they made further alienations of Crown lands, and under the flamboyant leadership of the Chancellor, Magnus de la Gardie, attempted with little success to solve the administrative problems involved in the return to conditions of peace. De la Gardie is best remembered for his wealth – his income at one time equalled one-twentieth of the entire Swedish revenue – his lavish patronage of the arts, and his many magnificent country seats, to one or other of which he would retire for long periods when the political situation became too difficult for him. His French descent, however, also deserves to be borne in mind, for it may have lessened his ability to control his peers and certainly influenced his views on foreign policy.

In the 1660s both Sweden and Denmark were pacifically inclined, each desiring to form such alliances as would strengthen its position *vis-à-vis* the other without risking serious involvement in any European conflict. The consequence was a series of rapid changes, of which the most striking occurred in the Anglo-Dutch war of 1664–7, when Frederick III of Denmark-Norway made a secret pact with England, which was to be allowed to capture a fleet of Dutch East Indiamen sheltering in the neutral port of Bergen, in return for half the booty. However, the commander of the Bergen fortress was not privy to the plot and helped to repel the English attack, after which Frederick figured briefly in the war as an ally of the Netherlanders. The most important result of the episode, however, was that it discredited Hannibal Sehested, who died in 1666 in Paris: his conversations with a French priest – the so-called 'Political Testament' – present the case for a *rapprochement* with Sweden, which he had worked for and might eventually have achieved.

Sweden's policy was for a time almost as tortuous as Denmark's: in 1668 its long-standing orientation towards France was even abandoned for membership of an anti-French triple alliance with England and the Netherlands. But by 1672 the power of Louis XIV had become so preponderant in Europe that de la Gardie judged it prudent to undertake, in return for much-needed French subsidies, to build up forces in the German provinces. A peaceful demonstration of strength so near its borders would deter Brandenburg from supporting Louis's Dutch enemies, whilst the help given to Louis would dimish his interest in a close relationship with Denmark, which Sehested had fostered through a commercial treaty with secret articles appended. The sequel was not what de la Gardie expected. Prolonged Dutch resistance to Louis led to an alliance of German states against him, to which Denmark offered conditional support. Their agreement with Louis then required the Swedes to advance into Brandenburg, where the Elector's forces defeated them in June 1675 at Fehrbellin. The immediate losses were only about 600 men, but many others deserted during the retreat through Mecklenburg back to Pomerania; the news gave the first serious shock to Sweden's military reputation since the battle of Nördlingen more than forty years before.

Earlier in the same month the young king of Denmark, Christian V, had arranged a meeting with the duke of Holstein-Gottorp, who was his brother-in-law; this was now made into an opportunity for forcing the duke into submission, and with their rear thus safeguarded Danish armies advanced south in support of the German alliance. During the winter of 1675-6 the Danes helped the Brandenburgers to overrun Swedish Pomerania and themselves captured Wismar, albeit that Griffenfeld by devious means kept alive his own policy, which was at all costs to retain the friendship of France. The events of the next three years were to show that his appreciation of Danish interests was almost certainly correct; but in March 1676 the all-powerful minister's many enemies induced the king to assert his authority by ordering his arrest for high treason.*

Although the regency in Sweden had terminated officially in 1672, Charles XI was a late developer, who did not bring to an end the mismanagement of his realm by the high nobility until the courage and resource which he showed in face of disaster gave him the necessary prestige and self-confidence. The Danes now seized their opportunity. In April 1676 their greatest admiral, Niels Juel, won his first victory in the capture of Gotland; in June the Dutch and Danish fleets together obtained command of the sea; Gyldenlöve with the Norwegian army moved south to threaten Gothenburg; and before the end of the month the king himself landed at the head of his troops to reconquer Skåne. When the Swedish forces temporarily withdrew from the province, the peasants considered themselves to be released from their oath of allegiance to their new masters and gave every assistance to Christian V. For a time the Swedes lost possession of every town in Skåne except Malmö, but they defeated a detachment advancing through Halland to join hands with Gyldenlöve in August, and in December won a hard-fought battle against superior numbers at Lund: Charles XI in person rallied the Swedish cavalry for the decisive onslaught, and both armies are believed to have left more than half their men dead or dying on the field.

Christian V continued to prosecute the war with considerable success, sharing with his allies in the conquest of all the Swedish possessions in Germany, securing full command in Baltic waters by Juel's big naval victory in Köge Bay, laying siege to Bohus with a greater weight of artillery than had ever been seen in the north before, and driving Magnus de la

---

* Griffenfeld was tried by a special commission, which condemned him to death by a majority of 10 to 1, although the evidence proved nothing beyond the acceptance of bribes and such indiscretions as the diary note, 'The King answered the ambassador like a child.'⁹ A reprieve was staged at the exact moment when the axe was due to fall, leaving him as a state prisoner for the remaining twenty-three years of his life.

Gardie out of Uddevalla, which remained in Norwegian hands until the return of peace in 1679. But he had to relax his grip on Skåne, which was gradually reconquered by Charles XI's closest associate, Johan Gyllenstierna, who was appointed governor-general. In the forests of north Skåne resistance was prolonged by sharpshooters (*snaphaner*), first organised as guerrillas in 1658, whose leaders the Swedes impaled on stakes by the roadside.

In August 1679 Louis XIV forced the Danes to make peace with him by threatening to invade Oldenburg; his only concession was a verbal promise to withdraw his support from the claims advanced by Gottorp. Next month he also required them to come to terms with the Swedes without any gains at their expense, though Brandenburg and other German states had been allowed small acquisitions from the Swedish overseas possessions. Yet the result was the growth of a common interest between Danes and Swedes. The Swedes resented their position as a French satellite under the Sun King's patronage, and therefore made the most of his failure to secure customs advantages which he had promised them in his negotiations with the Dutch; the Danes for their part would have been glad to see a loss inflicted on their Dutch allies, who had made peace with France without in any way consulting Danish interests. Accordingly, the peace treaty signed at Lund was accompanied by a defensive alliance, to which were attached a number of secret articles. These provided for mutual consultation before making any alliance with a third party and before entering upon any war of aggression, for co-operation in all dealings with the Empire, and for joint measures against the Netherlands, which might be military as well as fiscal. Gyllenstierna was sent on an imposing mission to Copenhagen, whence he returned with Christian V's sister as his sovereign's long-pledged bride.

The idea that the two Scandinavian powers by standing together would be able to wrest control of the Baltic trades from the hands of the Dutch had been mooted for many years, most notably by Sehested. This time its advocate was Gyllenstierna, and his unexpected death in 1680 at the age of forty-five is one obvious reason why this proved to be one of the turning-points at which Scandinavian history failed to turn. Whether he would have succeeded in his ultimate aim, which was to use Danish friendship for winning fresh territories for Sweden in Germany, cannot be known; as it was, there was no common front against the Dutch and the Swedes showed no readiness to abandon their support for the dukes of Holstein-Gottorp, which had for so many years disturbed relations with the Danish monarchy. By 1683 a Dutch fleet sailed the Baltic in support of Swedish interests, whilst the Danes were encouraged by a French naval demonstration and regular French subsidies to deprive the Gottorp dukedom of its lands in Slesvig. However, in 1687–9 the Emperor acted as mediator at the conference of Altona, when Britain and the Netherlands eventually guaranteed the duke his lands and rights, including the *jus armorum* –

the right to the army and fortresses which were his protection against the Danes. The situation in Slesvig having been restored without Sweden being involved in war, the two maritime powers hoped in return to receive Swedish support in their own war against Louis XIV. But Charles XI was no less determined than the king of Denmark-Norway to seek the profits of neutrality.

Having obtained no lasting advantage from their French alliance, the Danish government made a direct gain from the European war by hiring out 20,000 mercenaries to serve the Protestant cause on the battlefields of Ireland and the continent. Meanwhile, the two Scandinavian powers expanded their mercantile marines, both with new vessels and with Dutch ships masquerading under a neutral flag; and in 1691 they even established a league of armed neutrality, which had been vainly proposed as far back as the first Anglo-Dutch war. In the course of the decade Sweden came to have at least eighty-five large vessels of more than 250 tons. The growth of Norwegian shipping caused an English pamphleteer to remark with surprise in 1694 that 'most sea-towns in Norway now send yearly to England, France, and Holland twenty, thirty, or forty large fly-boats, and ships of other building'.[10] The Norwegians also possessed 58 big armed merchantmen at the outbreak of the war, as compared with Denmark's 49; but the wartime prosperity of Danish commerce can be clearly traced in the mounting profits of the East India Company. Nevertheless, this first league of armed neutrality petered out during the later war years, when Sweden and, later, Denmark-Norway found it more advantageous to come to terms separately with the maritime powers.

When Christian V died in 1699, his will urged his successors to right the wrongs done to the Danish crown both by the Gottorp pretensions in Slesvig – where he had just razed the duke's new fortresses – and by the Swedish usurpation of Skåne. But after their second conquest of the province in 1679, the Swedes had followed up the severities practised by Gyllenstierna with a systematic attempt to change the national outlook of the inhabitants. Although their rights were guaranteed by the peace treaty, in 1681 the Estates of clergy and burgesses found it prudent to accept Swedish law and church organisation, and two years later the nobility – whose privileges were at stake – was induced by economic concessions to add its consent. Lund university, which had been founded in 1668 to keep Scanian students away from Copenhagen, now began to live up to its official title as *Academia Carolina Conciliatrix* by making Swedish culture acceptable to the upper classes, whilst the children of the peasantry imbibed the Swedish catechism and were taught to sing Swedish versions of their Danish Lutheran hymns. The eventual total success of this enforced change of nationality, to which the history of modern Europe has hitherto provided few complete parallels, constitutes an impressive illustration of the unity which underlies the surface differences in the civilisations of the Scandinavian peoples. But the change was at least helped by the increased administrative efficiency which Sweden developed at this time, as it too became an autocracy.

ABSOLUTISM IN SWEDEN

In Sweden, as in Denmark-Norway, the introduction of absolutism followed a lost war, and in both cases it was brought about because the events of the war had raised the king's reputation and encouraged him to take advantage of the accumulated ill-will of the lower Estates towards the nobility. But, the Swedish situation in 1679 being far less catastrophic than the Danish in 1660, the constitutional changes were introduced piecemeal and over a longer period. As on the earlier occasion, the most urgent problem was a huge financial deficit due primarily to war expenditure, but in Sweden a remedy lay closer to hand than in Denmark, through the *reduktion* or resumption of lands by the Crown; this had been initiated by Charles X in 1655, but was virtually abandoned by the great nobles who dominated the Council during the regency and at the start of the new war. In 1674 – less than two years before he led the decisive charge at Lund – the young king was described by an Italian observer[11] as 'a person who seems bashful, timid, and unable to look anyone in the face', though he added prophetically, 'he fences well and rides well'.

At the Riksdag of 1680 the king combined with the lower Estates and the lesser nobility to crush the great Council families by instituting a severe investigation of the lax administration of the regency; this was already under examination, but the intention now was to make its members pay dearly for the military failures which public opinion would be glad to lay at their door. The next step was a demand for a further Reduction. This was sponsored in the first instance by the peasant Estate, but was finally accepted even by the House of Nobles under tumultuous pressure from its lesser members, whose intention was that only the largest properties should suffer and who in many cases held military or civil posts of which the salaries were withheld pending approval for new sources of revenue. Finally, the discomfiture of the Council was completed by the answers which the Estates gave to certain questions posed by the king after the formal closing of the session. The Form of Government was declared to have no authority over the king, and the Council of the Realm to be a merely consultative body; for the king, though pledged to rule in accordance with the law, was to be deemed responsible for the keeping of his pledge to God alone.

In the course of the decade then opening, Charles XI consolidated his position in relation both to the Council and the Riksdag. The former was renamed the Royal Council, and its lordly dignitaries were replaced by officials whose primary concern was to execute the king's instructions. In 1689 they even requested the deletion from the minutes of the old Council of the Realm of all 'offensive passages'[12] impugning the royal prerogative.

This request was backed by the Riksdag, which had earlier been induced to declare that legislation was the concern of the Crown, though they hoped that in major matters the Estates might still be consulted. Even vague appeals to the favourable construction which the king might be pleased to place upon the medieval law of Sweden, as restricting the practice of autocratic government, were silenced by a growing belief in the Divine Right of Kings. In the Declaration of Sovereignty of 1693 the Riksdag left no restriction whatever upon the rights of the monarch, 'being responsible to no person on earth for his actions but having power and might to govern and rule his realm according to his pleasure as a Christian king'.[13]

The practical effects of autocratic rule were felt first and foremost in the public finances. In 1682 eight of the fifteen surviving members of the Council which had been accused of misgovernment during the regency were sentenced to very heavy fines: de la Gardie had to pay 350,000 dollars and lost all but one of his estates. At the same time a much wider circle of the higher nobility were the principal losers by the Reductions, which began in earnest in 1680. The resolution of that year restored to the Crown properties which it had alienated as fiefs and, in certain 'inalienable areas' of the land, those which it had given away or sold outright; an exception was, however, made for small fiefs yielding a revenue of less than 600 dollars, which were of interest to the lesser nobles only. In 1682 these were swept into the net, and the limitation to 'inalienable areas' was also gradually abolished. The consequent inquiries, which involved most parts of Sweden, Finland, and the Swedish empire, were not completed before the turn of the century – nor has modern scholarship as yet been able to penetrate the mass of surviving records far enough to state the total results in terms of acreage or rentals. But it is probable that the Crown regained altogether about three-quarters of the farms alienated to the nobles, which would mean that in Sweden proper their share of the cultivated land fell from two-thirds to one-third,[14] and it is certain that by 1693 the national debt had been liquidated and the public accounts brought into balance.

This over-all result was achieved mainly at the expense of the class which was best able to bear it, and the most important social result of the Reductions was that the peasants no longer risked the infiltration into Sweden of continental ideas of landownership, which would have placed their political rights in jeopardy. Nevertheless, the nobles as a class suffered less than might be expected. On the one hand, they were usually able to retain the privileged part of their estates which lay in proximity to their manor houses, and the very oldest noble properties were in any case unaffected. On the other hand, they made good some part of their heavy economic losses by continued participation in public life. In 1700 one noble in ten held a commission in the army, where ranks above a captaincy were virtually reserved for their class. Moreover, the older families became intermixed with those of new counts and barons: the majority of Charles XI's peerages were given to commoners who had risen in his service, as officials in charge of government departments or as members of the Royal Council, which still played a considerable part in the conduct of foreign affairs.

In Sweden, as in Denmark-Norway, the Crown pursued mercantilist policies which increased the importance of the middle class. By 1685 more than half the exports were made up of iron and steel; copper and brass now constituted less than a quarter and the only other export of much value was pitch and tar. Privileges were granted to trading companies of various kinds, and by 1686 manufactures were sufficiently advanced to warrant the introduction of a protective tariff. But, although Stockholm by the end of the century may have had upwards of 55,000 inhabitants, many of these were connected with the court and the administration rather than with trade or industry, whilst Gothenburg and other trading communities were not more than a tenth the size of the capital. The status of the merchant class was still impaired by the extent to which exports were fetched from Sweden by foreign shippers, but it continued to attract foreigners from the Swedish empire and outside. The great inventive genius, Christopher Polhem,* was a Pomeranian immigrant's son to whom the College of Mines gave facilities for his novel applications of water power to mining. In 1699 he founded a great metal-working establishment in Dalecarlia, and his advanced ideas for canals and other improvements won a ready hearing from the new king, Charles XII.

The autocratic monarchy gave firm leadership to the Estate of clergy, in which the bishops ceased to have any independent authority. The Church Ordinance was revised in accordance with royal instructions in 1686, when an ecclesiastical system was set up which has lasted to the present day; at the outset uniformity of practice was exacted even in sermon making – where Latin was to be used more sparingly. The Reduction placed many livings in the gift of the Crown, and others were appropriated: in Finland, for instance, 178 out of 199 parishes were in the royal hands by 1693. In that year a new School Ordinance promoted loyalty as well as godliness. There was also a new version of the catechism to be studied by every confirmand, with a penalty for absenteeism to be imposed upon the offender's parents. And, whereas in the past it had been enough for the constable to accompany the bishop on his visitations, it was now the express concern of the provincial governor to see that 'no delusive heretical doctrines be disseminated, openly or secretly, among our subjects'.[15] Among gentler measures mention must be made of the new hymn book prescribed in 1695, which influenced both religion and popular culture for more than a century to come. The clergy were also assigned an important part in the Swedish empire: in Ingria and Kexholm they replaced the

---

* 1661–1751. 'The Father of Swedish Engineering', many of whose intricate models have survived to adorn the Museum of Technology in Stockholm; he anticipated Henry Cort's rolling-mill by nearly forty years, for instance, and adapted water power to new purposes. But his ideas for large-scale manufactures based on labour-saving machinery had limited scope in a country which lacked capital rather than workers.

Orthodox by the Lutheran liturgy, and in both Estonia and Livonia Finnish rather than German priests were chosen for preferment.

In general, the autocracy sought to impose a Swedish culture upon the empire. In the German provinces, indeed, its rights were restricted to the setting up of a Supreme Court, as Imperial fiefs retained German law and custom. But in Livonia, which was the largest province of all, public office was open only to persons who attended the university of Dorpat, where the professors were Swedes, and everywhere the Reduction brought in Crown functionaries to look after the lands which had formerly been allotted to victorious generals. However, the Swedish empire was so short-lived that its effects may be summarised very briefly. Financially, the Swedes did all they could to develop trade, especially the transit trade from Russia through Riga and other Baltic ports in their possession and that of the German Empire flowing through their German provinces. By 1700, 21·1 per cent of the total ordinary revenue was derived from the Baltic provinces and 15·5 per cent from those in North Germany.[16] Socially, the Swedish rendered the same service as better known empires in providing wide opportunities for ambitious men to carve out careers. Militarily, the overseas garrisons had a special importance, because they enabled Sweden to maintain forces at little or no cost to herself in positions from which they could easily take the offensive, if need be. Finally, the Swedish empire may be viewed as a national enterprise which aroused relatively little antagonism among the politically less developed peoples upon whom it was imposed. The exception, however, was provided by the German nobles of Livonia, who used the provincial Diet to defend their privileges against assimilation to Swedish practice and claimed in particular that the Reduction was inapplicable to lands which had been granted to them by earlier sovereigns before the Swedish conquest. In 1694 their leader, Johan Patkul, escaped into exile from Stockholm, where his protests resulted in a death sentence *in absentia* for high treason.

Though Charles XI was temperamentally cautious and pacific, he never doubted that adequate means of defence were essential to the pre-servation of Sweden's position as a great power, which had so nearly been forfeited in the wars of 1674–9. Immediately on the return of peace, he authorised his naval adviser, Hans Wachtmeister (who had served with the English fleet in the second Anglo-Dutch war), to construct a new naval base at Karlskrona in the re-annexed Danish territory. Here he built up a more powerful fleet, in a position which allowed quick access both to the Sound and to the south shore of the Baltic; by the end of the reign his thirty-seven ships of the line formed the largest war fleet in Europe after those of Britain, Holland, and France.

But the most far-reaching contribution which the autocracy made to the armed forces was Charles XI's great expansion of the *indelningsverk* ('allotment system'), tentatively introduced by Gustavus Adolphus and elaborated in 1682, when it was given a framework which stood for two centuries. By agreement with the Estate of peasants conscription was henceforth based upon the duty of an average-sized province to provide an infantry regiment of 1,200 men; each pair of farms recruited as a rule one landless labourer for the purpose, and must also take its turn in finding a replacement for wartime casualties. The recruit received wages, a cottage or other quarters, and allowances for time spent in military training, in return for which he worked on the farm where he was accommodated. Besides the twenty-three infantry regiments raised in this way, about 11,000 cavalrymen were provided by large farmers and other property-holders, who were exempted from taxation on their property if they furnished the man, the horse, and the prescribed equipment. The moral strength of the system resulted from its local basis, which was made more effective by placing the officers in the local milieu, with a Crown farm as their residence and part of their emoluments. Since the garrisons abroad, as well as the corps of artillery and engineers, were manned by mercenaries, the main practical difficulty of the *indelningsverk* was the long distances to be travelled on mobilisation; but by the death of Charles XI in 1697 every regiment had been trained in marching to a central assembly point as part of its regular manoeuvres, and detailed arrangements existed for bringing it forward to a scheduled place of embarkation or position on the frontier.

Throughout the European war then ending, Charles had hoped that his country's status might be recognised by his being chosen as mediator at its close – a distinction of which death robbed him. If a good chance had occurred for some more directly profitable action, he would certainly have seized it, but his basic view of Sweden's situation probably differed very little from that which Molesworth had derived from his visit to the Danish court:

> The Swedes . . . have still their eye upon Denmark, and long to be sole Monarchs of the North and Masters of the Baltic Sea . . . The interest of almost all the other princes of Europe concurs in preservation of the Danes . . . by obstructing any further accession of power and territories to the Swedes.[17]

'THE NAME AT WHICH THE WORLD GREW PALE'

Charles XII of Sweden* is the warrior king *par excellence*. He shot his first bear at the age of 11 years 7 months, as recorded in his admiring father's diary; from shortly after his eighteenth birthday, he planned, conducted, and shared every hardship of a continuous series of campaigns, which for almost a decade enjoyed a run of success without parallel in the history of modern Europe; and even after the turn of his fortunes at Poltava, war

---

* 1682–1718. He succeeded his father in April 1697; in November the Riksdag decided that the regency provided in Charles XI's will was superfluous; and in December the 15½-year-old sovereign placed the crown upon his own head.

remained his profession down to the hour of his death in the trenches before Fredriksten. Because his efforts ended in failure, Charles's ability as a statesman is often called in question. His inscrutable nature adds to the difficulty of determining the precise political scope of his 'grand design', and it is impossible to judge how much of it might have been saved from eventual ruin, if the designer had not died childless at the age of thirty-five. It is, however, important in any case to bear in mind that in the affairs of Scandinavia this dazzling figure was matched against a rival whose resolution and diplomatic resourcefulness increased with the years. Frederick IV, who succeeded to the Danish-Norwegian throne in 1699, was ten years older than his Swedish cousin, but his father had made no attempt to prepare him for kingship as Charles XI had done, and he also lacked the hardy physique of the Swedish prince. But Frederick IV possessed a cool head, a strong sense of justice and a powerful will; these were largely responsible for the fact that the long period of war from 1709 to 1720 – for the first and last time in Denmark's later history – brought benefits to Denmark which were more than commensurate with the nation's sufferings.

The two new reigns began, however, with a serious reverse inflicted on Denmark in its attempt to break the bond of encirclement created by the traditional alliance between Sweden and Holstein-Gottorp, which was reaffirmed by the marriage of the reigning duke to the elder of Charles XII's two sisters, Hedvig Sophia. A counter-encirclement had been planned before this by Christian V, whose overtures to the rulers of Saxony and Russia – zealously promoted behind the scenes by Patkul – bore fruit in the year of his son's accession. Accordingly, in March 1700 a Saxon invasion of Livonia, made without any declaration of war, gave the signal for a Danish attack on Tönning, a fortress erected under Swedish protection on the ducal territory in Holstein. Swedish and Gottorpian troops available for the defence were heavily outnumbered, but the maritime powers intervened promptly as guarantors of the Altona agreement. An Anglo-Dutch squadron appeared in the Sound and helped to bottle up the Danish fleet in Copenhagen whilst a Swedish force landed on the coast of Zealand, an operation in which Charles XII underwent his baptism of fire. However, only a fortnight later peace was restored at Travendal: the Danes did not relish the prospect of another Swedish siege of Copenhagen, whilst the maritime powers wished to free their hands for the impending final struggle against Louis XIV – in which they again entertained vain hopes of Swedish support. The Travendal agreement confirmed the duke of Holstein-Gottorp's entitlement to his own army and fortresses; it also safeguarded the Swedes against any hostilities by Denmark in support of Saxony.

For the next nine years Frederick IV's subjects continued to enjoy the profits of a long period of peace, which had been only briefly interrupted. But in 1701 the king reorganised the national militia so as to reduce the dependence of the country upon its mercenary forces, which had proved insufficient in the emergency of the previous year. About 15,000 men were to be provided by groups of farms and about one-ninth that number of dragoons by Crown estates. Landowners were responsible for seeing that the men were available; they served for six years and were mustered regularly for training in the churchyard on Sundays after divine service. The result was a great improvement on the smaller militia of the preceding century (which had fallen almost into disuse after 1679), but there were two unfortunate consequences. One was that the king felt justified in hiring out his remaining mercenaries for the war against Louis XIV, which meant that they were not returned for his own use until their service ended in 1713 – four years after his reinvolvement in the Great Northern War. The other was the opportunity given to landowners to use the military requirements as a reason for refusing the pass which authorised movement off the estate. King Frederick, nevertheless, made himself one of the most popular of his line by an ordinance of 1702, which freed subjects born since his accession from the form of serfdom (*vornedskab*) still recognised by law in Zealand and other islands of eastern Denmark.

Meanwhile Charles XII, who in the Zealand landing had been under the tutelage of his military instructor, in person led his armies deep into Europe against Augustus, elector of Saxony (who was also the newly chosen king of Poland), and Tsar Peter of Russia, not yet 'the Great'. The Carolines, as they are fondly called by their admiring descendants, were well trained, well organised, and well equipped. The flintlock musket, the grenade and the cavalryman's pistol all played an important part in battle, but Charles XII's general combat order was 'to get into them' (*at gå på*) – the infantry companies advancing in steady formation, two-thirds with bayonet, one-third with push of pike, whilst the squadrons of horse made a shock impact, having been trained to ride the last 100–150 yards at a full gallop, 'man by man and knee against knee'.[18] In most respects the battlefield presented the same chequerboard appearance as under Charles's predecessors, with similar manoeuvrings, but the famous Swedish artillery played a smaller part than before, which eventually proved a weakness. One reason was the difficulty of moving heavy guns and their ammunition supply to support armies which – unlike those of the other supreme strategist of that age, the duke of Marlborough – seldom followed the valleys of navigable rivers.

In the late autumn of 1700 the troops which had been mustered for the abruptly terminated campaign against the Danes were transported to the coast of Livonia, where they found that the Saxons (who received little support from the Livonian nobility) had already been repelled from Riga. However, the third member of the coalition, namely the Russian Tsar, had now declared war and was besieging Narva in Estonia with a force of about 35,000 men. With an experienced general, C. G. Rehnskiöld, as his second-in-command, Charles headed a week-long march through the November mire, terminating in an immediate attack on the enemy's fortified camp against odds of three to one. Helped by a snowstorm blowing in the faces of the Russians, the Swedes carried the ditch and wall, which were defended by 140 cannon, in the first quarter of an hour and eventually drove the Russians from the entire position with heavy losses; the Swedes took so many prisoners that all except high-ranking officers were allowed to make their way home. This tremendous victory, which gave Charles a European reputation, proved the young king as well as the troops whose hardships and battle risks he had shared. It may also have caused him to underestimate his most dangerous opponent, for the Tsar had left his raw levies to fight under a foreign commander whilst he went in search of reinforcements elsewhere.

In July 1701 the Saxons were driven back by a second feat of arms at the crossing of the Dvina, after which the Polish duchy of Courland was overrun and the Polish Commonwealth urged to disown its Saxon king. If Poland could be converted into a satellite, the Swedish dominion of the Baltic would be further extended and the ground prepared for coming to grips with the Russians; in the previous winter a small but significant expedition had vainly tried to capture Archangel by surprise. On the first anniversary of the Dvina crossing Charles defeated a superior number of Saxons at Klissow, where the young duke of Gottorp was among only 300 killed on the Swedish side; Warsaw had been occupied before the battle and the occupation of Cracow followed, but Charles found it much easier to march through the vast plains of Poland than to bend its people to his will. In 1704 the Polish Diet were induced to elect one of their own nobles (Stanislas Leszczynski) as a rival king under Swedish protection. This time, however, King Augustus had the support of Russian troops, so two more years elapsed before the battle of Fraustadt, in which Rehnskiöld defeated twice his own numbers in two hours, thus destroying the last vestiges of Saxon power in Poland. In the autumn of 1706 Charles marched across Silesian territory into Saxony itself, and when he had entered Leipzig the Elector promptly came to terms with him at the nearby castle of Altranstädt. He formally gave up the Polish throne, deserted his Russian allies, and surrendered Patkul to Charles, who had him broken on the wheel.

Whilst he wintered in Saxony, the Swedish king received a flattering visit from Marlborough, who feared that he might now intervene in the Spanish Succession war as an unwelcome mediator or even as an outright supporter of Louis XIV, the ancient ally of his house. But Charles was content with using the opportunity to exact toleration for the Silesian Protestants from the Emperor, as Gustavus Adolphus had intended to do; his own 'grand design', so far as we can fathom it, was still centred upon the dominion of the Baltic, which might now at last be within the Swedish grasp. He had already used his position in Poland to make a number of trade agreements, under which Riga was to handle both the exports of its Polish hinterland and the transit trade passing through Polish territory on its way between Russia and western Europe. Although he had guaranteed the possessions of the new king Stanislas, he hoped to acquire Courland, perhaps Polish

Livonia (in the upper valley of the Dvina), and possibly even the West Prussian ports, for which the Poles might be compensated elsewhere. These, however, were idle dreams, unless he could inflict such a shattering defeat upon the Russians that they would shrink back eastwards. For during the six years in which his attention had been engrossed by the affairs of Poland the Russians had secured the whole course of the Neva, at the mouth of which Peter had laid the foundations of St Petersburg; they had occupied Narva and Dorpat; and they had ravaged much of his own Livonian province.

Accordingly, King Charles made good his losses with new recruits, German as well as Swedish, and in the late summer of 1707 moved north-eastwards out of Saxony at the head of about 44,000 men. The Russians supposed that this was the preliminary stage in a Swedish attempt to rectify the position on the shores of the Baltic. Charles, however, had in mind the much bolder exploit of a direct advance on Moscow, which might bring about the collapse of Peter's very unpopular regime; and as the direct route lay through infertile districts of Russia, which the Tsar might be expected to lay waste completely as a means of defence, he instructed General A. D. Lewenhaupt, who commanded in Riga, to meet him before the frontier with a large supply-train and 16,000 reinforcements. The Swedes conducted a successful winter campaign in Poland, and consolidated King Stanislas's position as they fought their way across the country, outmanoeuvring the Russians at a series of river crossings. In July 1708, when they finally barred his way with a force twice as big as his own at Holovzin, the Swedish king waded through the river at the head of his infantry to attack a fortified position on the far side, and was again victorious. But it was noted that this time the Russians fought tenaciously throughout the day and that they made good their escape.

At this point fortune, which had hitherto favoured the bold, turned against Charles XII. The battle had cleared for him the way to the Dnieper, but he dare not risk a direct advance on Moscow by the road through Smolensk until Lewenhaupt caught up with him. He was due on 15 August, but his advance was held up by abnormal summer rains – and to judge by later events, concerning which more information is available, he was not the man to rise to an emergency. After a month's waiting, Charles decided to take a more southerly route through the Russian province of Severia, where supplies should be available and the detour involved not too serious. The Russians, however, moved on inner lines to bar his way, and also inflicted heavy losses on Lewenhaupt, who had been given farther to go in order to reach the main force. Charles therefore turned still farther south to secure winter quarters in the Ukraine, where he also hoped to get support from the Cossacks, who were in rebellion against the Tsar. The Cossacks were not ready, and the discomfiture of Charles and his army was completed by a winter of record severity. Whilst Marlborough's army in the Low Countries shivered in their winter quarters during three months of severe cold and heavy snow, many of the Swedes had no quarters at all until after Christmas – and they were serving under a sky so cold that birds fell dead out of the air and more limbs were lost from frostbite than from enemy action.

In the spring of 1709 Charles's dwindling forces could not hope to resume the march on Moscow from the Ukraine until substantial help could be obtained from Cossacks, Turks and Tatars near at hand, or from Polish and Swedish resources in the distance. In the meantime, a victory would restore the morale of the dispirited army and by raising Swedish prestige make help more likely to materialise. Even so, it is difficult to understand the decision to launch an attack on 28 June, when Charles himself was for the first time incapacitated by a wound in the foot. The objective was a fortified Russian position which hindered the prosecution of the siege of Poltava, a town on a tributary of the Dnieper. Rehnskiöld in supreme command was not effectively supported by his rival Lewenhaupt, who commanded the infantry; but in the main this was a surprise attack at dawn, which failed because it lost the element of surprise when the Swedes came up against additional redoubts which the Russians had constructed overnight. They were then quickly defeated by superior numbers and fire-power, the Russians being strong in artillery and the Swedes having left theirs behind for the sake of the intended surprise. They had lost 6,900 men killed and 2,760 taken prisoner,[19] the latter total including Rehnskiöld and the head of the king's field chancery, Count Piper.

Three days later, the costly failure was turned into irrevocable disaster. Having led the retreat to the Dnieper, which was reached at Perevolotjna, Charles agreed that he should be ferried across the river on a stretcher, with a view to making a rendezvous at Ochakov on the Black Sea for a march back to Poland, for which Turkish assistance would be needed. Lewenhaupt had with him at least 6,000 men who were ready to fight, a number about equal to that of the Russians who overtook his army at the river, though the enemy could also muster about 2,000 Cossacks in support. But he and other senior officers had lost their nerve, and after twice sending the colonels to invite the opinion of the troops sided with an alleged majority in favour of surrender. Thus the Caroline army, still more than 14,000 strong, passed into Russian captivity, and the dominion of the Baltic slipped for ever from Sweden's outstretched hand.

SWEDEN AND DENMARK-NORWAY BROUGHT INTO BALANCE

Bereft of his army, Charles XII of Sweden spent more than five years on Turkish soil before he returned to the theatre of war in northern Europe. The flooding of Russian soldiers across Poland after Poltava was one obstacle; the closing of the frontier between Turkey and the Empire on account of plague was another; and the alternative of a return by sea involved the risk of interception by the Danes. But the king also had a positive reason for staying where he was, namely his assiduous negotiations with his Turkish hosts. In each of three successive years he induced them to declare war on Russia, but they always allowed themselves to be bought off; finally in 1713 they took their troublesome guest prisoner after an eight-hours siege of his quarters at Bender, in which the king himself kept the fight going against enormous odds. What was most important, however, was Charles's ability to maintain his autocratic authority over Sweden, in which he had not set foot since the autumn of 1700. His younger sister, Ulrika Eleonora, the Royal Council under Count Arvid Horn, the Secret Committee of the Estates, and finally the Riksdag itself expressed their independent opinions in favour of a compromise peace, but the king's instructions – which sometimes took a year to reach them across Europe – were concerned only to put the prosecution of the war on to a more efficient basis.

In the meantime Sweden's enemies seized their chance. Frederick IV of Denmark and Augustus of Saxony made treaties with the Tsar, on the general basis that each party should retain whatever conquests he could achieve. In 1710 the Russians besieged and captured Riga, Tallinn, and Viipuri, and Augustus ousted his rival from the throne of Poland. The Danes, who had landed in Skåne in November of the previous year, received less help than before from the inhabitants, who may have found their slogan of 'Now or never' a dubious incentive. They overran the open country, but failed to take Malmö or the naval base of Karlskrona. Early in the New Year the governor, Magnus Stenbock – who, together with Horn, had been promoted major-general on the field of Narva – re-entered the province with an army hastily assembled in Småland, and manoeuvred the Danes back along their long lines of communication to Hälsingborg, their port of entry. There he defeated them so decisively that the half which survived were glad to make good their escape to Zealand. The skill and self-sacrifice of a Norwegian captain* prevented Wachtmeister from securing command of the Sound in October 1710; but throughout the next year the Danes were quiescent because the plague had spread to Scandinavia and was most lethal in Copenhagen, which lost one-third of its inhabitants.

When the three allies turned their attention to the Swedish possessions in north Germany, Stenbock again went to the rescue. His landing in Pomerania was hampered by the Danish fleet, which intercepted its supplies, but in December 1712 he managed to isolate the Danish army, on which he inflicted a second crushing defeat at Gadebusch in Mecklenburg; the Swedes were outnumbered in foot and horse, but their field artillery had novel advantages.† However, instead of challenging the allies in

* Ivar Huitfeldt (1665–1710), who had served in the Dutch navy and was present at the battles of Beachy Head and La Hogue, sacrificed ship and crew to hold up the Swedish advance into Köge Bay.

† These included a screw-setting to control the fall of shot, invented by Polhem, who corresponded with Charles throughout the war.

Poland, as King Charles intended, Stenbock turned north into Holstein with a view to seizing possession of Jutland. This time the well-established Swedish strategy miscarried. The Russians and Saxons followed him north, so in fear of being surrounded Stenbock negotiated a secret agreement with Baron Görtz – minister for the nominally neutral regency in Holstein-Gottorp – so as to take refuge in Tönning. But there his army was starved into surrender; Stenbock died a prisoner of war in Copenhagen, and discovery of the clandestine agreement warranted King Frederick in occupying all the Gottorp lands in both Holstein and Slesvig.

In November 1714 Charles XII at long last arrived at Stralsund* to face a truly desperate situation. In the preceding year the peace of Utrecht had freed both Prussia and Hanover – whose Elector in August 1714 became King George I of Great Britain – to intervene actively in the north; the Hanoverians had already occupied Verden, and Prussian forces were soon to enter part of Pomerania. When a Danish fleet with a modicum of British assistance again interrupted supplies from across the Baltic, Charles was forced to leave Stralsund to its fate; the Danes, who already held Bremen, overran all that remained of Swedish Pomerania. But the situation farther east was even darker for the Swedes, since Peter the Great had wrested from their grasp not only the Baltic provinces but also Finland, which had been for so many centuries an integral part of the realm.

The fall of Viipuri in 1710 had been the prelude to a large-scale invasion of a country whose resources were already gravely depleted. In 1696–7 a series of three severe winters and late springs had brought starvation to a nation of widely scattered, self-sufficient farm households with no reserves to fall back on. The government in Stockholm – like that of the United Kingdom when faced with the Irish potato famine a century and a half later – failed lamentably in coping with the situation, which resulted in the death of about one-third of the Finnish population from malnutrition and its attendant diseases. Moreover the warlike Finns had made a disproportionately large contribution to the armies in the ensuing war: at Narva they were almost as numerous as the Swedes, and all in all they supplied one-seventh of their people for military service. Accordingly, in 1713 the Russians were able to advance overland from Viipuri, whilst the Swedish fleet arrived too late to prevent a further landing in the vicinity of Helsinki, after which the Russian galley squadrons controlled the passage through the Leads. An able Swedish general, C. G. Armfelt, now replaced an incompetent predecessor, but in spite of a brave stand at an isthmus between two lakes south of modern Tampere he was driven back into Ostrobothnia. There the final battle of Storkyro was fought in the February cold; the Finnish infantry were eventually outflanked by Cossacks and virtually annihilated, in a struggle which the commander of the Russians described

---

* He travelled incognito to avoid any commitment to the Emperor, by whose permission he made the journey; the distance from Pitesci on the Turkish frontier was about 1,500 miles, which he covered in fourteen days, nearly two-thirds of it on horseback.

as the hardest since Poltava. Armfelt withdrew with some cavalry into Sweden, and in July (1714) a further naval success extended Russian control as far as the Åland Islands.

The seven-year occupation which followed lives on in Finnish tradition as 'The Great Wrath'.[20] The population, indeed, expanded again after the fearful casualties of the long years of war, but this is attributable to the hardihood of the native peasantry. Whilst the upper classes, including the bishop of Viipuri and many clergy, fled to Sweden in advance of the Russian invaders, farms were kept going by women who harnessed themselves to the plough. The Russians devastated those areas where they wished to deny supplies to the enemy forces if they returned, but in general the rule of the soldiers was preferred to the Russian civil administration, which began to take over in 1717. Two factors, however, weighed heavily throughout – the hardships imposed by the cessation of all trade connections with the west, and the severities, including deportation of whole families, by which the Russians tried to stamp out Finnish partisan activities; in Ingria these had begun as soon as the Tsar laid the foundations of St Petersburg.

Charles XII demanded that guerrilla warfare should continue in Finland, whatever the cost in human suffering. This is fairly representative of the policies he pursued after his last-minute escape from Stralsund in December 1715; having landed in Skåne, he never revisited Stockholm, which was too remote from the main theatre of war. In the previous year, however, he had reorganised the administrative colleges under six heads, who were intended to meet with him as a kind of Cabinet, and had taken some measures to help the financial difficulties, which became acute when the Swedish armies ceased to be supported by enemy territory or their conquered provinces. Heavier taxes were imposed upon the upper classes; Polhem and others were given every encouragement to expand iron and other exports; and systematic privateering was arranged off all those Baltic ports which had passed under enemy control. Meanwhile, the execution of the royal foreign policy was transferred from Count Horn to Görtz, the adroit negotiator from Holstein-Gottorp; its young duke, Charles Frederick, who was the Swedish king's nephew and possible heir, had already taken refuge in Sweden. When new armies had been raised, Charles XII expected that new victories would enable him to restore the situation by playing upon the mutual rivalries of his opponents. The first objective was Norway, the second north Germany, from where Peter's strong position in the Baltic provinces might eventually be taken in the rear. As late as 1718 Charles cited the Thirty Years War as a precedent in reaching the conclusion: 'It would be possible to carry on one that lasted forty years, as long as we made peace with one enemy after the other and got a tolerable and secure peace in the end.'[21]

Within three months of his arrival in Sweden the king had collected enough troops for a winter campaign in Norway; the Norwegian army had contributed little to the operations against Skåne, mainly for want of leadership, but since then it had sent about half its strength to serve the needs of the monarchy in Denmark and farther south. Charles's immediate object, however, was not an outright conquest but the creation of a diversion to stave off a second enemy landing in Skåne; he also hoped that his arrival in Norway would deter the Elector-King in England from sending British ships to Baltic waters, for fear the Swedes might be intending to stir up the embers of the 'Fifteen rebellion in Scotland. Oslo was occupied in early March, but not the Akershus fortress, against which Charles needed to employ heavy artillery from Gothenburg. The Danish-Norwegian fleet prevented this by its control of the coastal waters, so in the spring the Swedes were pressed back as far as the frontier fortress outside Halden. At midsummer a night attack gained him the town – which was set on fire by the Norwegians – but not Fredriksten. He had lost 500 men, including three major-generals, and only a few days later a convoy of food and ammunition was destroyed in the Leads by a young and highly enterprising Norwegian commander, Tordenskiold,* whereupon the campaign was abandoned.

The Allied landing in Skåne, however, did not materialise, although 40,000 Russians were available to operate alongside 30,000 Danes. Time was lost in awaiting the return of the ships which had been serving against Charles XII in Norway. But the main factor was the growing reluctance of the Tsar to run any risk on behalf of associates who were so jealous of his aggrandisement; a vivid example had been provided at the fall of Wismar in April, when the defenders of Sweden's last outpost south of the Baltic had been allowed to couple their surrender to the Danes, Brandenburgers, and Hanoverians with the condition that no Russians should share in the occupation of the city. In September 1716 Peter cancelled the Skåne operation for that year, and throughout the next Charles XII was able to fend it off by his efforts to widen the rift among his opponents, negotiating with representatives of both sides and also with pretenders to both the English and the Russian thrones. His chief emissary, Görtz, was held prisoner for a while by the Dutch at British request, but by May 1718 he was actively engaged in a congress with the Russians in the Åland Islands, where the acquisition of Norway by Sweden was under consideration as a fair return for acceptance of the loss of the Baltic provinces.

In that year Charles mustered the largest of all his armies, with a strength of 65,000 men contributed mainly by the *indelningsverk*, and re-entered southeastern Norway. This time he sent a smaller force under Armfelt against Trondheim, and the main body was equipped with siege artillery; although

---

* 1690–1720. Peter Wessel, son of a Trondheim merchant, had run away from home at fourteen to accompany Frederick IV's entourage on his return to Copenhagen. Ennobled as 'Lord Thundershield' after capturing a Swedish admiral and a thirty-gun frigate in 1715; he reached the rank of vice-admiral before he was killed in a duel at the age of thirty. An English historian ranks him after Charles XII as 'certainly the most heroic figure of the Great Northern War'.[22]

he intended to use Norway as a springboard for a leap into Denmark, whence he would eventually reach Germany, its permanent retention might well have formed part of any compromise peace. The advance in the south began with the investment of Fredriksten; but when the parallels were nearing the fortress and its fall was almost certainly imminent, the king – who had survived so many more hazardous situations in battle and on the march – was shot dead, as he leant over the trench parapet in the late November evening. It is possible that the bullet was Swedish, not Norwegian; certainly Frederick of Hesse, who in 1715 had become the husband of Charles's younger sister, Ulrika Eleonora, showed considerable forethought in his arrangements for securing her the succession, which the dead king (who never married) had left unsettled. Baron Görtz represented the rival Gottorp interest in the person of the young duke, Charles Frederick, the son of Charles XII's elder sister; but Görtz was immediately arrested, and his execution on trumped-up charges marked the end of the autocratic regime, though the Holstein Party continued to vex Swedish politics.

The war, however, was not wound up as rapidly as the autocracy by which it had been waged. Danish, and more particularly Norwegian, prestige rose with the disaster which befell Armfelt's army, more than 2,000 of its men being frozen to death as they retreated across the mountains into Sweden, and the success of an advance from Norway into Bohuslen, to which Tordenskiold contributed brilliantly at Dynekilen. In the same summer (1719) the Russian galley fleet systematically devastated the coastline north and south of Stockholm, so that scarcely a house was left standing all along the Leads. The hopes of the Swedes were sustained for a time by ultimately unsuccessful proposals for British naval intervention in their favour; but when the Russians renewed their pressure on a smaller scale in the two following summers, they had to recognise the failure of their 21-year struggle by signing the decisive Peace of Nystad (30 August 1721).

The terms available from less obdurate enemies had been accepted earlier. In the winter of 1719–20 two treaties were negotiated in Stockholm by George I's ambassador and future secretary of state, Lord Carteret; by the first Sweden surrendered Bremen-Verden to Hanover, and by the second Stettin and the neighbouring parts of Pomerania to Brandenburg-Prussia. In June 1720 the treaty of Frederiksborg with the Danes was made more palatable by the return of territory then under Danish occupation, not only in Bohuslen but also in Pomerania, where the French were anxious for the Swedish presence to be maintained. But its two main provisions clearly marked Sweden's decline. She bound herself to give no more support to the dukes of Holstein-Gottorp, whose lands in Slesvig were guaranteed to Denmark by both Britain and her temporary ally, France; this removed what had been called the cornerstone of Swedish foreign policy. Sweden also agreed to the ending of the exemption from the Sound tolls which she had enjoyed for three-quarters of a century, a change which clearly benefited Denmark whilst it also met the British desire that there should be no 'most favoured nation' in the Baltic trades.

The treaty of Nystad transferred to Russian sovereignty the three Baltic provinces of Ingria, Estonia, and Livonia – the entire coastline from the Neva to the Dvina together with its hinterland, the zone of Swedish imperialism. A clause which entitled the Swedes to import a given quantity of duty-free corn from Riga underlined chiefly the seriousness of the economic loss. But the cession in addition of eastern Karelia, including Viipuri and the smaller fortress of Kexholm, showed more clearly the fundamental shift in the balance of power: the Swedes must henceforth live in the shadow of a colossus whose strength they could not match. From a geopolitical standpoint Sweden was now no stronger than Denmark-Norway, and neither power could any longer aspire to the dominion of the Baltic.

Chapter 8

Monarchies in Equipoise, 1721-1792

When the Great Northern War ended, Sweden had lost a part of Finland and the whole of her more recent acquisitions, excepting the island of Rügen, the port of Stralsund and the Pomeranian hinterland west of the river Peene. Her briefly held status as a great power was clearly lost. The situation was not altogether better for victorious Denmark, since the gains from Gottorp did not balance the final renunciation of Skåne and Sweden's Sound toll payments were no compensation for twelve years' war expenditure. Henceforth the Twin Kingdoms, too, abandoned the hopes of acting as a great power, which Christian IV had cherished and which had reawakened in the mind of his great-grandson after the catastrophe to Swedish arms in 1709. Accordingly, during the last two generations of the *ancien régime* these two powers of the second rank figure in the general history of Europe chiefly as a favourite object for the diplomacy of their stronger neighbours, who sought to employ them, either together or (more often) in rivalry, as an element in the rapidly changing combinations of international politics. Their internal history, however, has an independent interest, which justifies its being taken as our starting-point.

In Sweden the 'Age of Freedom' begins with the reaction against autocratic monarchy after the death of Charles XII in 1718 and ends with its partial reinstatement by the *coup d'état* of Gustavus III in 1772. In Denmark-Norway the autocratic system of government was left unchallenged, but there too 1770–72 marks a turning-point, when the autocracy was diverted to new purposes by Struensee. The Swedish Age of Freedom may be described first, both because it interested contemporaries as presenting a kind of parallel to British parliamentary institutions and because historians still disagree about its merits and demerits.

Whoever fired the fatal shot at Fredriksten, the result was not only a favourable opportunity for Ulrika Eleonora and her husband to secure possession of the throne for her, but also a chance for the nobility to regain its political predominance by making a 'free' Riksdag its chosen instrument. So far as relations with the monarchy were concerned, this was a feasible policy, since Ulrika's recognition as Queen by the Council was confirmed by the Riksdag through election and not on the basis of hereditary right. The lower nobility proceeded at once to reform the voting system of their Estate: henceforth each noble family had one vote of equal weight in all decisions. The Estates then framed a new constitution, which the Queen found so uncongenial that in March 1720 she abdicated in favour of her husband, Prince Frederick of Hesse, who was accepted at the price of further concessions. For the next half-century the powers of the crown were almost nominal, consisting chiefly of the presidency of the renamed Council of State, where the king had a double vote and a casting vote when necessary, and a closely limited control of appointments; in the case of Councillors, for example, he must choose among three candidates put forward by the three upper Estates of the Riksdag.

The real power lay at first with the Council of twenty-four nobles, headed by Count Arvid Horn.* His policy of peace abroad and moderate reform at home was generally acceptable to the Riksdag; the nobles retained the monopoly of high office and their exemptions from taxation, but these were partly compensated by the opening of all lower offices to clergy and burgesses and their retention of demesne lands already sold to them by nobles. At the same time the position of the peasantry was improved by regularising the sale of crown farms to their occupants, so that the proportion of farm properties held by tax-paying peasants – those whose representatives constituted the fourth Estate of the Riksdag – rose between 1700 and 1772 from 31·5 to 46·9 per cent.[1] Nevertheless, when the prosperity which the Horn regime brought to the country had eroded the memory of war's sufferings, he was overthrown by the chauvinists among the nobles and richer merchants, who derided the men of peace as 'nightcaps' (*nattmössor*); the latter in return dubbed their opponents the 'hats' (*hattar*), in allusion to the tricorn headgear of the military. Count C. G. Tessin, son of the palace architect, was elected to the key office of *Lantmarskalk* or president of the House of Nobles, and for a whole generation Sweden became the scene of unbridled party conflict.

The Riksdag now began to exercise the sovereignty which it had possessed in theory since 1719, using its triennial sessions not only for legislation and financial control but also to examine the work of the Council, whose members lay under a perpetual threat of impeachment and trial by a committee of the Estates. Although the Council bore some resemblance to the English Cabinet, the structure of the Riksdag was very different from that of the Houses of Parliament. The House of Nobles, indeed, was not unlike the English House of Lords, but its very much

* 1664–1742. Having served Charles XII as soldier and diplomat, he was made president of the Royal Council in 1709 but opposed the continuation of the war; after securing the election of Frederick to the throne, he held the chancellorship from 1720 to 1738. He resembled his contemporary, Walpole, in his sense of the possible and ability to manage men, but w as more adventurous in youth and more austere in his later years.

larger membership of about 2,000 necessarily included many heads oɟ families who but for their privileges of rank resembled small country squires. Each of the other three Estates, however, had a definite class basis. The clergy included the bishop and representatives for each diocese; the burgesses, whose representation was roughly proportionate to the size of the town, returned mainly municipal officials and merchants; whereas the peasant representatives, elected from among their own kind, formed a democratic body without parallel in eighteenth-century Europe – albeit that a secretary was chosen for it by the other Estates. All decisions were taken by a majority of the Estates voting separately – even those of the numerous committees, in which the nobility always had double representation. Special importance attached to the Secret Committee of 100 members under the chairmanship of the *Lantmarskalk*, from which the peasants were normally excluded, on the ground that they could not be trusted with confidential matters of foreign policy and defence; another objection to their presence, however, was their disposition to champion the royal interests on a body which during Riksdag sessions usurped most of the functions of the executive.

As for the results of this system of government, Sweden certainly enjoyed a large measure of political liberty as compared with the situation under the regimes that preceded and followed. The activities of party clubs, the scrutiny of voting lists by whips, the publication in 1732–4 of *Then Swänska Argus*, a periodical in which Olof von Dalin (see p. 176) followed the path marked out by Addison and Steele, and the pamphlet warfare over questions of politics and economics – all this has a very modern ring. But both the long period of Hat rule from 1739 to 1764 and the following eight years, during which the Caps intermittently took their place, were marked also by extremes of political corruption, with open and large-scale purchase of votes and proxies in each Estate by Russian, French, British, and Danish ministers.

This stimulated the growth of a spirit of violence, which at times threatened even the stability of the monarchy. Both Frederick I, and his successor, Adolphus Frederick (see p. 178), were weak kings handicapped by their foreign birth, but the latter had a highly intelligent and ambitious consort in Louisa Ulrica, a sister of Frederick the Great of Prussia. In 1756 she encouraged him to challenge the decision of a Riksdag committee that, if he refused his signature to an appointment, it should be affixed in facsimile. The King and Queen were assured of some military support for a planned monarchist *coup d'état*, but the plans were discovered by the use of torture and eight ringleaders sent to the scaffold. Twelve years later, when Adolphus Frederick wished to press the Council – then dominated by the Caps – to summon the Riksdag, he was able to carry the day only by means of a formal abdication, thus entitling Hat officials to declare that, so long as there was no king, government could not be carried on. Nevertheless, when he died in 1771 the court was at loggerheads with both parties and Hat noblemen were fulminating against their party opponents: 'In the last resort we shall go forth sword in hand to defend the rights of our absent fellows.'[2]

At first sight the Twin Kingdoms present a complete contrast to conditions in Sweden, since their form of government was as conspicuous for the absence of serious friction as for the want of liberty. In the last ten years of his reign Frederick IV succeeded in paying off more than one-half of the debt which had accumulated during the long war, largely through the sale of crown lands, and the public respected the image he created of himself: 'If we ever have a day off, we must make up time by taking it from our night's rest, because the work has to be done.'[3] In his earlier years he had indulged himself in a bigamous morganatic marriage, but in his old age Pietism appealed to him, as it did more effectively to his son, Christian VI, whose reign of sixteen years (1730–46) was marked by a wave of Pietist measures. However, what best illustrates the paradox of absolutism was the fact that this shy, austere sovereign felt impelled to build Christiansborg, the largest and most expensive of Copenhagen's many palaces, and to surround it by iron chains to keep his subjects at a distance of 120 feet from the walls.

Frederick V removed his father's chains from the palace together with the restraints of Pietism and even of ordinary sobriety; it was perhaps characteristic of his easygoing nature that, whereas his physically feeble father had travelled as far as Trondheim overland and given four months in all to his Norwegian journey, Frederick got no farther north than Oslo and brought a company of French actors with him for diversion. His popularity was enhanced by his marriage to Louisa, the surprisingly charming daughter of George II of Britain and Hanover, after whose early death he married a German princess, Juliane. Frederick himself died relatively young in 1766, whereupon the autocratic system which had worked smoothly for more than a century headed quickly, as we shall see later, towards a breakdown. In Denmark-Norway, as in Sweden, the 1770s belong to a different era; but it would be wrong to infer from the contrasting forms of government that the previous era was one of contrast pure and simple.

The bitter internal conflicts which marked the Swedish Age of Freedom were concerned above all with the spoils of office, distributed by the predominant political party among its henchmen. In 1730 the families represented in the House of Nobles held two-fifths of all the posts in the civil administration and nearly every regimental commission, whilst the Estate of clergy were office-holders to a man and a large proportion of town representatives had local government appointments. A generation later, when the party strife reached its climax, the 'Younger Caps' were engaged primarily in an assault on the privileges of office-bearers, which were stubbornly defended by the Hat nobles and other groups in possession.

In the Twin Kingdoms, on the other hand, the struggle for office was more muted, because the road to power lay through the favour of the sovereign and his entourage and not through adherence to a party, which might smack of treason. Whilst in Denmark the kings still distrusted the old nobility, the new nobility of service ran the administration through the colleges, much as in Sweden. In Norway the dominant influence in a slowly reviving national life was provided quite clearly by the aspiring families of civil, ecclesiastical and military officials, trained in Copenhagen but often native-born. By mid-century, however, the highest posts in the service of the Oldenburg monarchy were held to a great extent, not by Danes or even Norwegians, but by Germans from the Duchies or from the smaller states of north Germany. Frederick V's chief confidant was Count A. G. Moltke, a scion of the Mecklenburg family which was later to produce the great Prussian field-marshal. Under his influence the king relied increasingly upon his foreign minister, J. H. E. Bernstorff, who was a Hanoverian. So began the 'rule of Their Excellencies', in which a nephew, A. P. Bernstorff, was to play a still more distinguished part.

SOCIAL AND ECONOMIC TRENDS

One valuable by-product of this system of rule by officials was the achievement of the Scandinavian clergy in compiling the first reliable census returns in Europe. In 1721–49 the population of Sweden rose from 1·5 to 1·8 millions, and that of Finland as defined by the treaty of Åbo (see p. 178) from 300,000 to 400,000. The first totals for the Twin Kingdoms date from 1769, when Denmark had about 800,000, Norway 728,000, and Iceland 46,000 inhabitants; the inclusion of the Duchies of Slesvig-Holstein would raise the figure to 2 millions – about 25 per cent less than for Sweden-Finland. The Scandinavian towns continued throughout the century to be small and few. Copenhagen, which rose from 75,000 to 100,000, was by far the most considerable. Stockholm's population grew from 43,000 to 73,000 in 1720–60, but then remained almost stationary until after 1800; Bergen, which had 14,000 inhabitants in 1770, was not merely the largest town in Norway but had only Gothenburg and Stralsund as serious rivals among the remaining provincial trade centres under the rule of either monarchy.

The structure of society was uniform throughout Scandinavia, except for the fact that Norway (and Iceland) had few large estates, no aristocracy on the land, and comparatively little exploitation of the peasants as tenants, even under middle-class landowners. Throughout the richer farm lands of Denmark and Sweden nobles and wealthy bourgeois owned numerous estates, which were worked by tenants whose condition was in many respects unfree. Their situation was most severely depressed in Denmark, after Christian VI had been induced to rescind his initial decision to abolish the militia and at the same time compensated the nobles for his father's abolition of *vornedskab*. Accordingly, a decree of 1733 bound the

Danish peasant to the soil, so that landlords should have no difficulty in providing one man – usually a labourer rather than a farmer – per hundred acres to serve in the militia, and also in retaining all the manpower they needed on the land at a time when agricultural depression encouraged migration in search of better conditions elsewhere. Subsequent measures, dating from 1735 to 1764, elaborated this system of *stavnsbånd* or *adscriptio glebae* to cover all males between four and forty years of age and to make acceptance of a tenancy compulsory, even when the completion of his military service would have left the peasant otherwise free to leave the estate.

By mid-century Norway had about twice as many farm owners as farm tenants, thanks to the sale of crown and parish-church lands,* and in Sweden the Age of Freedom saw a great increase in landowning peasants, both through the sale of crown estates and through an arrangement by which nobles transferred land on payment of a fixed rent. But the growth of population brought an increase in two easily forgotten categories of country people, whose lot was inferior to that of tenants as well as owners of tax-assessed farm properties. On the one hand, there was the cottar (*husmann, torpare*), whose cottage usually stood on a diminutive smallholding, which he was only free to cultivate when his services were not required by the farmer from whom he received it. On the other hand, there was the labourer who had at best a mere patch of land and – unless he picked up a handicraft – no certain means of livelihood. In Sweden these categories had been subject to severe discipline since the reign of Charles XI. In Denmark they were often forced into the militia; and even in less closely controlled Norway an ordinance of 1754 demanded that, with the exception of one son and one daughter in each cottar family, all above sixteen years of age should take employment by the year at fixed low wages and preferably in the parish where they were born.

During the first years of recovery after the Great Northern War, when the Scandinavian governments were grappling with the burden of debt, agriculture attracted rather less official attention than industry. But from the 1730s onwards the emergence of Europe from a long-continued agricultural depression and the accompanying rise in corn prices encouraged a new interest in farming techniques. At the same time governments became concerned to foster rural life for the sake of an increasing population, which was now regarded as the supreme source of national wealth. In Denmark, for example, corn production was encouraged at the expense of the traditional cattle exports, and in 1735 its exporters were granted a monopoly of the corn trade to southern Norway.

The Danish tenant farmer, compelled to render customary labour

* In the 1720s Frederick IV used his autocratic powers to sell the lands and tithes belonging to parish churches, the purchaser becoming legally responsible for the upkeep of the fabric. Many of the 600 parish churches disposed of in this way disappeared, including some of the ancient *stavkirker*.

services to his lord, was not attracted by new techniques; it is difficult to picture Holberg's *Jeppe på Bjerget* – a classic Danish Hodge – using Tull's seeding-machine. But improvements began in Holstein and were carried northwards by German proprietors, who were attracted by cheap land and sought to introduce a better rotation of crops and other changes. This drew the attention of Count Moltke, who persuaded his royal master to encourage new ideas by giving them publicity in an 'Economic Magazine for Denmark and Norway', which made its appearance in 1757 under the editorship of Erik Pontoppidan, a former bishop of Bergen. Crop experiments were diligently reported, as well as advances in the consolidation of arable strips and commutation of labour services, which were the essential preliminaries to any widespread technical progress. In 1765 an important example was set on the Bernstorff family's estates near Copenhagen as regards enclosure, commutation, and the stimulation of improved practices of all kinds by making the farms inheritable. In Norway lack of communications hampered the spread of new methods introduced by middle-class proprietors and by clergy farming their glebe. More land was, indeed, brought under cultivation, especially by the labours of cottars, and a law of 1769 enabled one-half of a udal farm to be shared out among younger sons, who would be likely to cultivate more intensively; but the Scotch-model plough and the potato are the clearest examples of the modest improvements which at mid-century were just beginning to spread from valley to valley.

The higher political status of the class of tax-paying peasants, who in Sweden and Finland constituted the fourth Estate of the Riksdag, probably made a difference. At all events, in 1734–62 a series of laws encouraged enclosure, and Linnaeus (see p. 176) lent his great authority to the introduction of improved techniques, which Scottish Jacobite immigrants were particularly quick to bring into use on their newly acquired properties. It has been claimed that by 1772 one-third of the farms already had their arable strips wholly or partly consolidated. C. G. Tessin wrote ironically of 'agronomy, the epidemic disease of our time',[4] and in J. G. Wallerius Uppsala had already produced one of the founders of agricultural chemistry.

Although industrial undertakings, such as mines and ironworks, were often situated in purely rural surroundings, the fact that only about one-tenth of the Scandinavian population lived in towns is a pointer to the relatively small part played by industry and commerce. This was not for want of trying, as the governments of this era intensified their efforts to improve the trade balance by stimulating manufactures, which might replace imports, and native shipping, which might deprive the foreigner of freight earnings. The Hat Party in Sweden was strongly mercantilist, and sought to foster the European pre-eminence of the ironmasters – who were among its most loyal supporters. In 1747 it established the Iron Office (*Jernkontoret*), where officials elected by the ironmasters ran an export monopoly, production quotas, and a cheap credit system for mines and smelting works – whose expenses included much buying-up of land in order to exact charcoal supplies from the tenants. The most profitable market was still in Britain, but some bar-iron also went through Swedish Pomerania into Germany and some to southern Europe, where Swedish hoops were in particular demand for fish-barrels. In addition, the Iron Office employed distinguished technologists, following to some extent in the footsteps of Polhem, who had recorded iron-working techniques in his 'Political Testament', compiled a few years before his death in 1751.

Sweden-Finland had a second valuable export commodity in tar, of which the Finnish forests were the principal source for the shipbuilders of western Europe. But the Office for Manufactures, established in 1739, had much less success in its efforts to promote large-scale production of textiles and other consumption goods for the home market. Imports were forbidden; foreign workers were encouraged, including non-Lutherans; and the infant industries were nourished by tax exemptions and direct subsidies. However, in the 1760s the Younger Caps tried to grapple with a trade depression and a rapid depreciation of the paper currency used by the Hats to finance an aggressive foreign policy, including their mercantilist ambitions. A new finance policy abandoned parts of the existing economic programme, though the Caps gave little positive support to the free-trade doctrines which were presented to the Riksdag of 1765–6 by the progressive Finnish thinker, Anders Chydenius.*

The autocratic sovereigns of Denmark-Norway pursued broadly similar economic aims, inspired by the paternalist sentiments which one of them expressed as follows: 'I seek only the happiness of my subjects; for if they prosper, I prosper; and there can be no prosperity for them, unless commerce and manufactures flourish.'[5] The Twin Kingdoms had no industrial export to match the Swedish iron, but the Norwegians contributed very heavily to the balance of trade with their primary products, pre-eminently fish and timber but also including some valuable copper and a little silver. The ironware which was the chief Norwegian industrial product went very largely to Denmark, where it was granted a monopoly in 1730. The previously mentioned Danish corn monopoly which was established five years later might be regarded as a fair equivalent, had not Swedish iron goods of superior quality continued to find their way across the Danish frontiers. In general, the College of Commerce at Copenhagen never succeeded in organising textile or other manufactures on a scale which could make the many bans on importation fully effective.

---

* 1729–1803. A clergyman's son, educated at Åbo Academy and ordained in 1753; a pioneer of smallpox inoculation in Scandinavia and of various improvements to agriculture, but best known as the author of *Den nationale winsten* ('The Nation's Profit'), which anticipates some of the ideas of Adam Smith. He opposed the class policy of the Hats, championed the freedom of the press, and made himself the first spokesman of the much oppressed farm labourers.

The Danish East India Company was wound up soon after the end of the Great Northern War, and in 1740 Copenhagen's shipping tonnage was still 20 per cent below its pre-war level. But a new monopoly was granted to an Asiatic Company, which lasted for more than a century (1732–1839), whilst the trade of the Danish West Indies increased greatly after the purchase of St Croix from the French in 1733; here sugar was produced for the Copenhagen refineries by slave labour, fetched from the much older Danish outpost at Christiansborg on the Guinea coast in modern Ghana. Another ambitious venture was the General Trading Company, which operated from Copenhagen in 1747–74. Its prime object was to capture the Baltic entrepôt trade, but in 1750 it took over the contact with Greenland, which had been re-established by a Norwegian missionary (see p. 175), and in 1764 it was also given the monopoly of the trade with Iceland and with the isolated Norwegian county of Finnmark. Both Danish and Norwegian shipping, however, received their biggest stimulus from the European wars; in 1756–63, for example, vessels under the Danish flag had a virtual monopoly of the Mediterranean trades.

The position of Swedish iron on the European market was so strong that the Swedes were able to emulate the English Navigation Acts by their Products Edict of 1724, refusing access to foreign ships unless they carried the products of their own country. This encouraged native shipping in such trades as the importation of salt from the Mediterranean, but the price proved to be higher than when the Dutch were the importers; there was also a general rise in freight costs, because foreign vessels had often to sail in ballast when they came to Swedish ports to fetch the iron. However, in 1731 the native shipping received a further stimulus through the establishment of a Swedish East India Company, whose founders included English and Dutch merchants who had been excluded from participation in similar monopolies in their own countries. The headquarters were in Gothenburg, which became a centre for re-exportation, but the huge East Indiamen were built chiefly in Stockholm, where finance was readily available from the 'nobility of the quays' (*skeppsbroadeln*).

A state-directed economy tended always to favour the capital city from which the direction was organised. In Sweden and Finland, for example, the ports north of Stockholm and Åbo respectively were expected to pass their products to the world through Stockholm. Copenhagen in 1726 added to its many advantages over the smaller Danish ports a monopoly for the importation of 'the four species' – salt (with an exception for the fishing port of Ålborg), wine, tobacco, and grape brandy – modified after a six-year outcry to a tax remission of two-thirds when these commodities were supplied to the provinces via the capital. The Norwegian ports, especially Bergen, were even more bitterly aware of the advantages enjoyed by Copenhagen merchants in the far north of Norway and in the former Norwegian empire: hence a slowly growing desire for financial, administrative, and even cultural institutions of their own. When the

Swedish-Norwegian frontier was clearly demarcated along the northern part of the Keel or watershed in 1751, the resulting treaty was the sole document bearing an international relation to be lodged in the Norwegian archives throughout the period of the Twin Kingdoms.

CULTURAL ADVANCES

The Scandinavian clergy, who had been stripped of so many economic and social advantages at the Reformation, had nevertheless retained a very strong intellectual ascendancy. Whilst the reading public remained small, the pulpit commanded wide attention – and its occupant played a key role in society by teaching his flock the paramount obligation to 'render unto Caesar the things which are Caesar's'. Schools and universities were very much under clerical control, and they paid great attention to the provision and preparation of candidates for ordination. The best known poets were the hymn-writers, such as the Icelander who meditated on the Passion and a Danish bishop of Scottish descent, Thomas Kingo; and it is significant that, when another cleric with Scots blood in his veins, Peter Dass of Nordland, gave Norway its first modern poet, his catechism verses (though published posthumously) were in print a quarter of a century before his secular masterpiece, *Nordland's Trumpet*. Yet by the dawn of the eighteenth century, the overall result was a reign of orthodoxy which had become as stifling to the free life of the spirit as to that of the intellect.

A spiritual revival came through the spread of Pietism from Germany. Its influence was strongly felt among Charles XII's Carolines during the years of heart-breaking captivity after Poltava. In Denmark-Norway an important landmark was the foundation in 1714 of a College of Missions, after two German Pietists had already been at work in Tranquebar. One result was a mission to the Lapps, which was initiated by a West Norway Pietist in 1716 and led on to the foundation of a *Seminarium Lapponicum* at Trondheim, where a clergyman of the next generation developed the study of the Lapp language and culture. The Swedes had been active in this field throughout the previous century, building churches (which also advanced their own secular concerns) and maintaining an important school for Lapps, founded in 1632 by Johan Skytte. In 1755 Sweden provided its Lapp subjects with a New Testament in their own language, by which date conversion was nominally complete on both sides of the Swedish-Norwegian border. But for yet another century their own form of Nature worship continued in remote places under the *shamans*, whose drums produced strange ecstasies* – the Lapp magic which had been proverbial in the world of Shakespeare. Another west Norway clergyman, Hans

---

* As late as 1693 a *shaman* was burnt alive by sentence of a Swedish court, together with his drums – the decorated artefacts from which the modern anthropologist derives 'a picture of the entire Lapp world'.[6]

Egede,* had long cherished the dream he fulfilled in 1721, when he sailed from Bergen to west Greenland to bring the gospel and the benefits of trade to whatever inhabitants he might find there. Egede toiled for fifteen years to convert and civilise the native Greenlanders, and the monarchy remained a supporter both of the mission and of the resulting trading station after his return. Christian VI, as already noted, was himself a Pietist, and though the ideas of the German Count Zinzendorf and the Herrnhutian revivalists were too extreme for his taste, he issued a strict ordinance on Sabbath observance in preparation for the Confirmation Ordinance with which he celebrated the bicentenary of the Reformation in Denmark. Although these measures were followed by the Conventicle Ordinance to prevent the formation of dissenting congregations and discourage religious exercises under lay leadership (such as were favoured by the Herrnhutians), Pietism nevertheless did much to enable the individual to seek out a way of salvation for himself and his fellows. The Schools Ordinance of 1739 was unfortunately sabotaged by landowners and farmers in both kingdoms to save expense, but its basis in the idea that reading was the proper concomitant of confirmation likewise had a long-term influence.

In the life of the intellect, a new outlook began to appear through the advance of the Enlightenment, the great European trend of thought which was later to motivate in part the work of the so-called 'enlightened despots'. In Denmark-Norway it makes its entry in the person of Ludvig Holberg, a Norwegian from a modest bourgeois milieu, who left his native Bergen for ever at the age of twenty-one and imbibed on his travels the freer ideas already current in Queen Anne's Oxford and other intellectual centres abroad. He eventually settled down in Copenhagen as that almost unique figure, a university professor whose influence penetrated the life and literature of a whole nation. Holberg is best known for a series of twenty-six comedies in the style of Molière which he wrote for the newly founded Copenhagen theatre in 1722–7. But he was also a historian, whose Norwegian origins did not prevent him from concluding that the union of the Twin Kingdoms had been beneficial to them both; the author of a Latin satire (*Nils Klim*), which rivals *Gulliver's Travels* in interest – witness the existence of 27 distinct translations distributed among eight languages; and a common-sense philosopher after the fashion of Samuel Johnson. Holberg's plays are still staple fare in the theatres of Scandinavia, but Europe as a whole has strangely neglected a writer who in his own generation had no obvious superior in range of intellect except Voltaire. Nevertheless, his purely literary achievement was the most important part, since he gave the Danish language a status which saved it from being

---

* 1686–1758. The Apostle of Greenland expected to work among its long-lost Norse inhabitants, but instead conducted an immensely laborious mission among their successors, the Greenlanders of today. By his exploration of the coast from 60° to 66°, his book on the natural history, and above all by his efforts to organise colonisation (which he continued after he settled in 1736 in Denmark), Egede ensured that Greenland – off whose shores the Dutch and English hunted whales – remained a Scandinavian sphere of interest.

engulfed by the German tongue which predominated at court, among the Germanised nobility, and in official circles.

In Sweden Dalin included among his many-sided literary activities as poet and publicist a comedy in the manner of Holberg, and the arts in general had influential patrons in Count C. G. Tessin and in Queen Louisa Ulrica; the first small-scale Academy of Letters, founded in 1753, was so much her creation that its work was suspended between her attempted *coup d'état* in 1756 and her son's triumph over the opposition to the court in 1772. Whilst French and English influences competed for control in the arts, Swedish science had an independent base. The study of mineralogy and technical devices of all kinds was fostered (as we have seen) by the iron industry, and Polhem's contribution to the art of war was paralleled by that of another great savant, Emanuel Swedenborg, who invented machinery to convey Charles XII's supply vessels overland for the siege of Fredriksten. But after Swedenborg's pioneering work in many branches of science and technology had culminated in the three volumes of his *Opera philosophica et mineralia* (1734), he made his way via physiology to religious speculation. This lesser Newton is therefore remembered chiefly as the founder of the New Church, which came into existence in London twelve years after his death there in 1772.

Meanwhile, in 1739 the Academy of Science (*Vetenskapsakademien*) had begun its distinguished career. One of its first members was Anders Celsius, the astronomer, whose name is commonly associated with the centigrade thermometer but who also worked with French scientists in Swedish Lapland to establish the flattening of the earth at the Poles. The early publications of the Academy included the pioneer population tables, which P. W. Wargentin (who was also distinguished in astronomy) introduced in connection with the first census of Sweden and Finland in 1749. By the end of the Age of Freedom two of the most illustrious Swedish chemists were also at work, namely T. O. Bergman, the creator of affinity tables, and C. W. Scheele, who discovered oxygen in 1773 – a year before Priestley. Both men died young, in 1784 and 1786 respectively, but Scheele's career has a special interest: his place of birth was Stralsund, in the only surviving fragment of Sweden's trans-Baltic empire, and he came to Uppsala as an assistant apothecary – a social handicap which delayed his election to the Academy until 1775.

Yet the best known name of all from that first Golden Age of Swedish science is that of Carl Linnaeus, ennobled in 1761. He was a clergyman's son, whose early studies were partly financed by Celsius, and had a highly successful medical practice in rivalry with Rosén von Rosenstein, the author of the first treatise in Europe on the ailments of children. But his lifelong interest was in botany, which he first studied in the parsonage garden, and for which he devised his binomial system of nomenclature; this was later extended to the animal kingdom and widely publicised through his many Latin works, such as the *Systema Naturae*, of which twelve editions appeared in the author's lifetime. In Sweden itself Linnaeus had an important influence on agricultural practices, created a new interest in Lapland, and as professor of botany at Uppsala inspired many generations of pupils with his own semireligious appreciation of the wonders of Nature. One result was the participation of a number of Swedish students in the recording of the flora and fauna of what were then little-known lands, as for example in the first two voyages of Captain Cook. According to a modern French historian,[7] Linnaeus 'revealed the North to the world'; perhaps it would be truer to say that he showed it in a more favourable light than that in which it appeared on the diplomatic chessboard, to which we must now turn.

A DIMINISHED ROLE IN INTERNATIONAL RELATIONS

In the first years of peace, Swedish eyes were turned mainly eastwards: optimists hoped that the situation in Europe might one day present a chance of recovering lost provinces in the Baltic, including south-eastern Finland, whilst pessimists watched in alarm lest Russia might plan some further encroachment by its support for the Holstein-Gottorp claimant to the throne. In 1727 Duke Charles Frederick married Anna, daughter of Peter the Great, so after his death in 1739 the claimant was one-half Russian. Danish eyes were similarly fixed on the southern border: optimists hoped to get rid of this same Gottorp family's claims in Holstein, whilst pessimists feared a revival of its recently abandoned claims in Slesvig. But, since neither of the Scandinavian powers was now strong enough to take any positive action without outside support, each of them entered into a bewildering series of relationships with states of greater magnitude, expressed in terms of treaties, marriage alliances, subsidies, and bribes received by political groups or individual politicians. The three main foreign influences were the following: the Russian, which often played upon the traditional Danish hostility towards Sweden; the French, which aimed at an active alliance with the Swedes, but for two decades subsidised Denmark as well, so as to strengthen the position of the Swedish ally; and the British, which from 1731 onwards sought in general to counterwork the policies of France but which also had a particular concern with trade. Thus the growth of the British market for Norwegian timber helped to make the British firm friends of Denmark-Norway, so long at least as the Danes did not revive Baltic ambitions which might hamper Britain's importation of iron and naval stores from Sweden and Finland.

In these circumstances the Scandinavian states displayed considerable skill in avoiding direct involvement in any of the principal campaigns of the four major European conflicts which punctuate the period between the treaty of Nystad in 1721 and the outbreak of the French Revolution. Both of them played, indeed, a minor part in the Seven Years War of 1756–63; otherwise, it was only Sweden which resorted to arms and this was done by way of renewing her traditional conflict with Russia, which came to a head in 1741 and again in 1788. On the latter occasion, as we shall see, Denmark too was briefly involved.

The war of 1741 had several causes, including subsidies from France, which desired a Swedish intervention to deter the Russians from joining in the War of the Austrian Succession, and the intrigues of Elizabeth, granddaughter of Peter the Great, who was expected to welcome and reward a Swedish distraction while she was arranging to supplant the infant Tsar Ivan VI. Essentially, however, it was an ill prepared Hat Party war of revenge, which ended in a complete fiasco. In the first month the Swedes suffered a heavy defeat from superior numbers at Villmanstrand, on their side of the Russo-Finnish border, and Elizabeth, after seizing the throne without Swedish help, took the opportunity to offer Finland the position of an independent buffer state. The only immediate consequence of this historically significant proposal was to add to the demoralisation of the Swedish-Finnish army, many of whose officers took leave to attend the Riksdag. When active hostilities were resumed in the following summer, Helsinki was surrendered without a fight to a Russian force no more numerous than its intended defenders, and the whole of Finland passed under the control of a Scottish general in the Russian service (James Keith), whose comparatively mild sway became known to Finns as 'the Lesser Wrath'.[8] But under the treaty of Åbo, which ended the war after negotiations which extended from February to August (1743), only a section of south-eastern Finland containing about one-tenth of its remaining population was transferred to Russian sovereignty, on condition that a candidate sponsored by Russia was accepted as heir to the Swedish throne.

This question had come to the fore with the death in 1741 of Queen Ulrika Eleonora, the successor-designate to her childless husband, King Frederick I; whereupon all four Estates of the Riksdag nominated Charles Peter Ulrik, the thirteen-year-old duke of Holstein-Gottorp, in her place. But the Empress Elizabeth, who had at first favoured this choice, decided to adopt him as heir to her own throne instead. She then demanded that the Swedes should accept his second-cousin, Adolphus Frederick,* and at the end of a conflict involving Danish interests as well (see p. 179), the Tsarina had her way.

Having failed in the more ambitious project of recovering the provinces which had been lost to Russia, the Hat Party saw in the outbreak of the Seven Years War the chance to secure more modest gains – a rectification of the Pomeranian frontier beyond the Peene at the expense of Frederick II of Prussia, who was already facing overwhelming odds. French subsidies were again available, so military advances were made each summer,

---

* 1710–71. This scion of the house of Gottorp was well known to the Empress as Peter's guardian, whilst on his mother's side he was descended from Charles XI of Sweden. He married Louisa Ulrica of Prussia in 1743; in 1747 he was appointed commander-in-chief – an office in which he showed considerable ability; and he reigned from 1751 to 1771.

followed by retirements every winter; and noble officers, as before, did not hesitate to quit the field for the council chamber. In 1762, however, the death of Elizabeth brought Peter to the Russian throne; he made peace with Frederick, of whom he was a fanatical admirer, and the Prussian king was then free to turn his attention to events in Pomerania. In the same month the Swedes were helped by his relationship with their queen to make good their escape from war; but they had gained no territory, incurred heavy expenditure, and suffered heavy loss of life – from disease and disorganisation as much as the sword of the enemy. Thus the long Hat regime ended with a wartime inflation which was evident to all, for prices had doubled between 1755 and 1764. A small minority may also have surmised the astonishing fact that the casualties of the Pomeranian or 'Potato' War* were of the same order as – if not actually greater than – the Swedish military losses in all the illustrious campaigns of Charles XII.†

In the absence of any overt party conflicts, Denmark-Norway steered a more resolutely pacific course. In 1734 Horn obtained a defence pact, enlisting the support of the Twin Kingdoms against the claims of the Gottorp family to the Swedish throne, a rather shadowy Scandinavian alliance which remained nominally in force for nearly thirty years. But there was no involvement in the Russo-Swedish conflict of 1741–3 until the still unsettled question of the inheritance of the throne of Sweden arose, as already related, whereupon Danish money was employed on behalf of their own Crown Prince Frederick. As soon as it was discovered that Charles Peter Ulrik was no longer available, the peasants rallied to the side of the Dane, who could at least be trusted to bring back autocracy in place of a discredited parliamentary regime. Feeling in his favour was strongest in Skåne, but the lead was taken by the Dalecarlians, who found customs duties on the Dano-Norwegian frontier particularly irksome at a time of trade depression and whose regiment had incurred the heaviest losses at Villmanstrand. A majority of the Secret Committee decided in favour of Prince Frederick – but then came news that the Russians were willing to give back most of Finland if their candidate was accepted. A body of 4,500 Dalecarlians, who had arrived to carry the day in Stockholm, was then suppressed by force, and Adolphus Frederick elected by all four Estates, the peasants of Skåne still dissenting.

Although the project for a dynastic union of Scandinavia was not formally revived until the opening years of the next century, the accession of

---

* The potato had been introduced experimentally to Sweden in 1724, but its adoption became commoner with the return home of soldiers who had seen its widespread cultivation in Prussian Pomerania.

† Strictly comparable figures would be difficult to establish: Nordmann gives 'about 40,000 men' as the losses in the war of 1757–62, and Professor R. Hatton says that the loss of men in the wars of Charles XII was 'certainly less than 30,000',[9] of whom about 8,000 eventually returned from imprisonment in Russia. The last figure includes some Finnish civilians, but may be balanced by the number of military personnel recovered from the hands of the Danes.

Adolphus Frederick to the Swedish throne in 1751 was immediately followed by the betrothal of his five-year-old son Gustavus to a daughter of his former rival, now Frederick V of Denmark-Norway, which would have produced an eventual claim to Frederick's throne if his two sons had had no issue. But the betrothal – which led on in 1766 to an unhappy marriage – also formed part of a general project for Scandinavian co-operation, cherished by the then Danish foreign minister, J. H. E. Bernstorff, whose cosmopolitan background encouraged him to envisage a 'nordic system'[10] linked with greater powers. His fine-spun diplomacy aimed at the elimination of the Gottorp claims in Holstein, to which the Swedes but not the Russians were now amenable, so that Russia and Scandinavia might stand together to secure peace 'from the Elbe to the borders of China'.[11] A limited success was achieved in the early part of the Seven Years War, when economic and not dynastic interests brought the two Scandinavian monarchies together in a policy of armed neutrality to protect their merchant shipping from the warring powers, particularly Britain. In September 1756 a joint squadron cruised between the Norwegian coast and Jutland, but did not venture into the English Channel. Next year the Swedes proposed the closing of the Sound and Belts to safeguard Scandinavian commerce in the Baltic, and, when Bernstorff judged this step to be dangerously bellicose, made their own arrangements to enlist the support of Russia for making armed neutrality effective in the Baltic region. In 1760 Bernstorff belatedly adhered to the Russo-Swedish agreement.

In 1762, however, the accession of Peter III of Russia, which (as we have seen) led the Swedes to make a hasty withdrawal from their campaign in Pomerania, had the opposite effect on Denmark's position: for Charles Peter Ulrik intended to maintain the claims of the House of Gottorp in Holstein and revive its claims in Slesvig. The Danes had three advantages at this juncture – a strong neutrality guard already posted in Holstein, a French general (C. L. de St Germain) who had been brought in the previous year as commander-in-chief, and a superior fleet. But, since their French allies were not disposed to help them, their military prospects were at best uncertain, until Peter was deposed at his wife's instigation on the very day when he intended to leave for the battle-front.

Whereas Peter had offered Norway to the Swedes if they would help in his projected campaign against the Danes, the new Empress Catherine preferred to consolidate a special relationship with Denmark, which lasted for almost a century. She made peace at once, and in 1767 an exchange (*mageskifte*) already contemplated by Bernstorff was at last agreed upon, so that at the coming of age of her son Paul in 1773 all Gottorp claims in the Duchies would be renounced in return for Oldenburg and another minor possession of the Danish monarchy. As for Sweden, Catherine's able minister Panin, who had spent twelve years as Russian representative in Stockholm, worked hard to establish a comprehensive grouping of northern powers, in which Sweden as well as Denmark-Norway would be among those to be ranged on the Empress's side against the Bourbon monarchies of France and Spain. With this in view, the Russo-Danish alliance was strengthened to provide for joint action in case of any threat to the parliamentary institutions which made Sweden amenable to outside influence; if she proved quite unmanageable, both allies should be entitled to territorial gains at her expense. Bernstorff signed the amplified treaty in 1769, but in the following year the outlook for the Scandinavian countries began to be affected by internal changes; these must be considered before tracing their relations with Europe any further.

ENLIGHTENED DESPOTISM IN SCANDINAVIA

The accession of Christian VII in 1766 revealed a fatal flaw in the Danish *lex regia*, which had made no provision for the physical incapacity of the autocrat. Mental aberrations which can now be identified as incipient *dementia praecox* were already apparent at the time of the young king's marriage to his English cousin, Caroline Matilda, but in 1768 he proved capable of undertaking an eight-month foreign tour, during which he was enthusiastically received in London and Paris and accepted honorary degrees from both Oxford and Cambridge. He was accompanied on his journey by a German physician from Holstein, Dr Friedrich Struensee, whose considerable medical talents soon established a complete ascendancy over the king; indeed, he seems to have been much less resentful than his subjects of the fact that soon after their return to Denmark the court doctor also became the queen's lover. After securing the dismissal of Bernstorff and the replacement of the Privy Council by a Cabinet under his direct control, Struensee was in a position to gratify his love of power and progressive ideology by reconstructing the entire administration of the Twin Kingdoms; as an uninhibited supporter of the Enlightenment, he attempted in sixteen months as much as more prudent despots in sixteen years.

His 1,880 decrees set up a new civil court in Copenhagen, which survived his downfall, and a ban on torture, which did not. Complete freedom of the press was proclaimed, a measure which brought him the congratulations of Voltaire but also stimulated the growth of opposition. The Norwegians benefited by the abolition of the Danish corn monopoly and by a modification of the udal law to the advantage of farm purchasers: Norwegian sailors and soldiers were nevertheless among the first elements in Copenhagen to demonstrate against the new regime. Minorities of all kinds, from Herrnhuters to illegitimate children, were accorded better treatment; officials were reduced in number, but paid in salaries instead of perquisites; and the public finances might be expected to profit in the long run by the abolition of subsidies and the stimulus of free trade. But there was no long run: Struensee spoke no Danish, had no idea of appealing to public opinion, and was faced with the implacable enmity of the dowager queen,

Juliane, who hoped that her own son, Prince Frederick, as heir-presumptive might soon replace his imbecile half-brother on the throne.

Struensee's overthrow by a palace conspiracy, his trial for treason, and subsequent execution – whose barbarities Juliane observed with pleasure through an opera glass – interested all Europe. So did the fate of Caroline Matilda, whom her brother, King George III, deemed largely responsible for her own misfortunes and sent to spend the rest of her short life as a disgraced divorcee in Hanover. For the history of Scandinavia it is more important to note the brevity of the reaction, in which Juliane, her son, and his former tutor, O. H. Guldberg, who presided over a strengthened form of Privy Council, swept aside even such innocent reforms as a balanced budget. Moreover, that short period was marked by two features which boded well for Denmark's future – in the first seven years a foreign policy brilliantly conducted by A. P. Bernstorff, a nephew of the earlier minister, and the steadfast opposition of Guldberg to the German influence which had predominated for more than a century in the upper levels of society. Then in April 1784 despotism again became enlightened, when the sixteen-year-old Crown Prince Frederick overthrew the cabal at a Council meeting, by securing his father's signature and the magic word *approberet* ('approved') to a list of new ministers before the old ones knew what he was about.

The Crown Prince, who from this resolute beginning acted as regent until his unhappy father's death in 1808, was no intellectual and interested himself chiefly in the more showy aspects of military exercises and ceremonial; but he had sagacity enough to empower a group of abler men to carry through the reforms which he saw his kingdoms needed. Their leader was Bernstorff, whose second period in office lasted from 1784 to his death in 1797. H. E. Schimmelmann, whose father had come to Denmark from Hamburg at the instigation of the elder Bernstorff, inherited control of the finances and, although his plans were wrecked by the Napoleonic wars, held office for a total period of forty years. The third dominant figure was C. D. F. Reventlow, who belonged to the older Danish nobility; he had spent some time in England, studying at Oxford but learning more from his observation of the prosperity of English tenant farmers. He was the moving spirit and chairman of the Great Land Commission of 1786, whose secretary was a lawyer, Christian Colbjörnsen, accustomed to the freer land system of his native Norway and a firm believer in the duty of the autocratic monarchy to make its subjects equal in practice as well as in theory.

The primacy accorded to agriculture in the teaching of the French physiocrats, together with the scope for experiment provided by rising corn prices, had already induced the Reventlows and Bernstorffs to alleviate the condition of the peasantry on their own estates: the intention now was to provide a legal framework for a universal change, to be brought gradually into effect. How degraded the condition of the peasants was is shown by the very first measure, which in 1786–7 forbade landlords and their bailiffs to inflict physical punishment upon their tenants by the use of the long whip or fetters, by making them ride the wooden horse, or requiring them to go about encased in a barrel known familiarly as 'the Spanish mantle'. The second stage was to encourage the tenant to improve his holding by the institution of independent tribunals to award compensation for disturbance. But the most important change of all was the abolition of the *stavnsbånd*, which was initiated in 1788 but involved such far-reaching consequences that it did not apply to all age-groups until 1800. Ten years before this, however, the law had given the tenant a further protection – one which was not usual in England – by setting the minimum duration for a lease at the lifetime of the tenant and his wife; and by 1799 all work-rents had to be clearly defined, with the result that they quickly ceased to be a common feature of farm tenancies.

After about two decades three-fifths of the land worked by peasant farmers was peasant-owned, and there were fewer farm tenants than cottars. Economically, the result was that about the same proportion of the land as was peasant-owned had been enclosed – rather more on the islands and less in more backward Jutland – and that improved methods of agriculture had doubled the average yield. Thus the peasant had a surplus for market during the period of war in Europe, when corn, butter and bacon all fetched higher prices. As for the social results, it was in 1792 – the year of the downfall of the French monarchy – that Copenhagen raised its Monument to the Freedom of the Peasant, 'the liberty of the subject which its beloved king established for the honourable class, the labours of whose hands maintain and defend the State'.[12] A Danish historian of today still looks back upon this period as 'perhaps the happiest time that Denmark has ever known.'[13] This may be so, but at the turn of the century owners and tenants of farms were slightly outnumbered by the cottar class, half of whom had no land and all of whom paid rent in labour, to which their masters now attached the maximum importance.

Industry and commerce were likewise freed from restriction by commissions acting on the principles most clearly advocated in Adam Smith's *Wealth of Nations*, of which a Danish translation had appeared within three years of the original publication in 1776. The growth of prosperity was certainly stimulated by technological advances, such as the opening of the Eider Canal to carry small ships across Holstein, the introduction of the first steam engine in 1790 and of the more effective Watt engine in 1804, and the building or rebuilding by the latter date of at least thirty-three Danish harbours. But the main factor was the liberation of trade from monopolies and other restrictions. In 1787, for example, all subjects of the crown were empowered to trade with Iceland and in 1788 the importation of corn to southern Norway was thrown open to all comers on payment of a moderate tariff. Next year dealings with Finnmark were made completely free, the Tromsö district being added to the county as a further inducement to traders; the result was a wholly new prosperity. In Denmark itself the freeing of the cattle export business was followed by the trebling of exports in six years, and in 1793 the Danish entrepôt trade was stimulated by allowing facilities for every port to hold uncustomed goods for re-export. The process culminated in the tariff of 1797, which ranged between 5 per cent on raw materials and 24 per cent on fully manufactured articles; trade then proved so resilient that these drastic reductions in rates did not lead to any reduction in income from customs. Total revenue doubled between 1786 and 1806, but growing military expenditure made it impossible for Schimmelmann to balance the national accounts. A new monetary unit, the *spesidaler* or specie-dollar, which he had set up in 1791, was already seriously depreciated by the end of the century – except in the Duchies, where alone it retained its full basis in silver, a circumstance which promoted dealings with Hamburg rather than Copenhagen.

But the Enlightenment had broad social effects, which the financial disasters of later years could not efface. Struensee's work for law reform and better organised poor relief was taken up and amplified; a visit which John Howard had paid to Denmark in 1781 led to some eventual improvement of the prisoner's lot; and in 1795 a system of conciliation courts was introduced, which still operates in both Denmark and Norway as an informal method of reducing litigation. A series of laws gave the Jews a freer position than in most parts of the Continent, and in 1792 Denmark led the world in the abolition of the slave trade, albeit that a ten-year delay was conceded, during which slaveholders were entitled to borrow public money in order to increase their holdings. Lastly, the Great School Commission was set up in 1789 under the inspiration of German educational advances; within two years it had founded a training college for teachers; and by the turn of the century it was ready with a plan for village schools, to be based on compulsory attendance from five to the age of confirmation. The fact that the Commission was not able to enact a comprehensive school-law until 1814 does not reduce the honour due to the two Reventlow brothers and other noblemen, who strove to spread to a whole nation the benefits which they had provided for the children on their own estates long before the war years intervened to hinder the completion of their public work.

In Sweden enlightened despotism achieved no single result which was commensurate with the liberation of the peasantry in Denmark; but Gustavus III, whom the poet of the next age looked back upon as 'the enchanter on the throne',[14] attracts attention through the drama of his rise and fall as well as by some of his positive achievements. Frederick the Great's sister had reared her son in the spirit of the Enlightenment, with C. G. Tessin and Olof von Dalin as his early tutors, and in 1771 the news of his father's death found him in Paris, where the prince was in contact with the Encyclopedists and other advanced thinkers of the day. In returning home to face the unresolved conflict between the Hats, still strongly entrenched in the House of Nobles, and the Younger Caps predominant in the lower Estates, he was encouraged to take drastic action by a subsidy treaty which he signed before leaving France.

The summer of 1772 appeared propitious for an attempt to regain what the Swedish monarchy had lost under its two foreign kings, because the Russians were preoccupied with war against the Turks as well as with their arrangements for initiating the partition of Poland – the latter a clear pointer to the pretexts for foreign intervention which Sweden's free constitution likewise provided. Smarting under a recent defeat by the Caps, a number of nobles under a Finnish colonel, Jakob Sprengtporten (who had the support of his much younger half-brother Göran), arranged for military revolts in the king's name in Finland and also in Skåne. The Scanian rising broke out prematurely, and news of it quickly reached the Council in Stockholm,* which prepared to arrest the king. Meanwhile, Sprengtporten got control of Helsinki with its rising fortress of Sveaborg (p. 188), but was prevented by unfavourable winds from launching the intended expedition against the capital. However, the young king, taking the risk of acting on his own, won Stockholm by a bold appeal to the Guards regiments and to the unprivileged populace. The Councillors were arrested without a drop of blood being spilt in their defence, and two days later a new Form of Government was unanimously approved by the Riksdag after listening to an eloquent harangue from the king, which was backed by cannon pointed at their place of assembly.

The constitution of 1772 was a compromise, designed to end party faction without making too great inroads into the privileges of the nobility, from whose ranks the original promoters of the royalist *coup d'état* had been drawn. The Council was reduced to a body of advisers, composed mainly of high officials; some members possessing legal qualifications acted with the king as a final court of appeal. The Riksdag, which was to meet only when required by the king (who also chose the presiding officer of each Estate), still had joint control with the Crown over legislation and finance; but its only independent powers were that its sanction was needed for any war of aggression and that it could restrict the duration of any new tax. During the remaining twenty years of the reign, the Riksdag was summoned only four times, and each session was short. As for the bureaucracy, a vaguely worded clause in the constitution laid down that appointments should be made without regard to birth or favour, 'unless found in combination with ability'.[15] But, although the very names of Hats and Caps were proscribed, Gustavus necessarily leant for support upon those families of the Hat nobility which had assisted his climb to power; the fact that the chief committees of the Riksdag still contained twice as many nobles as clergy or burgesses and no representatives of the tax-paying

* The British secret service, at that time in league with the Russians, had already informed the Council of a report about an impending *coup*, contained in a letter from the French minister in Stockholm, which had been intercepted in Hanover.

peasants shows that the conflict of classes had merely been driven into the background.

Prompt measures were taken to deal with the financial crisis, which had been rendered more acute by a series of poor harvests. Internal barriers to the circulation of grain were removed and its importation was made easier. Inflation was checked by the introduction of a new currency, based on the silver *riksdaler*, the old money being redeemed at half value. The tariff was reduced; the major ports lost their privileges over other ports, and it was made easier for newcomers to gain admission to the urban craft gilds. All these innovations in some degree benefited the peasants, and in 1783 a land-survey ordinance encouraged the villager to consolidate his strips – though in practice enclosure derived more stimulus from the example set from that year onwards by Rutger Maclean (p. 197). But the most ambitious scheme to promote the growing of more food for a rapidly increasing population was a crown monopoly of distilling, which was designed to stop farmers from diverting their grain to this more profitable object; in this case, however, enlightenment had to give way to outraged interests.

Enlightened measures of more general import included the abolition of torture in the first week after the *coup d'état* and the removal of many death penalties by a king who admired the writings of Beccaria. The operation of the law courts was investigated as part of a general purge and reform of the whole bureaucratic system; Finland, for example, to which Gustavus paid many visits, was given a second appeal court, and its four counties were extended to six. Like his Prussian uncle, Gustavus was a freemason* and he granted a wide degree of religious toleration, not only to foreign immigrants, including the Jews, but also to the Pietist groups (at which the Lutheran clergy as a whole looked askance) and the Swedenborgians. There were, however, other sides to the complex character of the king, who saw fit to protect his own position by a return to censorship and the institution of a police force (including secret police) on the French model. In 1778, indeed, his talents as an orator and the celebration of the birth of an heir combined to produce strong expressions of loyalty to the throne from every Estate; but when the Riksdag was summoned a second time in 1786, bad harvests had again caused discontent, which encouraged the nobles to take the lead in denouncing the rule of royal favourites.

In the last six years of his reign Gustavus III sought to alleviate discontent by the distractions of a glorious foreign policy. But before turning to the international relationships which had grown up since 1770–2, mention must be made of the cultural achievements associated with a king whose personality was perhaps more akin to that of the great actor than the great statesman. The longstanding French influence on Swedish society culmina-

---

* Both Gustavus and his brother Charles became members in 1771; it has been suggested that the former hoped to succeed Charles Edward Stuart as Grand Master of the Scottish rite, a possible step towards his eventual election to the throne of Poland.[16]

ted in Gustavus's court, which became a kind of northern Versailles, much influenced by the king's several visits to the artistic capitals of Europe. A Royal Opera House was opened in 1782, and the king established private theatres at Gripsholm and other palaces. In 1786 the Swedish Academy in its modern form was founded on the model of the French for the encouragement of poetry, scholarship, and rhetoric. At its opening the king emphasised – perhaps with an eye to the dangers which threatened the *ancien régime* in France – that it should also serve as a bulwark of traditional values. He bestowed only a modest pension and post upon Carl Michael Bellman, the convivial Swedish counterpart of Burns. But he himself collaborated with a second poet, J. H. Kellgren, in the authorship of historical plays and operas, some of them recalling the splendours of earlier Swedish monarchs, of whom Gustavus III could claim to be the enlightened heir.

SCANDINAVIA AND EUROPE, 1770–1792

The Struensee regime in Denmark had been treated with contempt by Catherine II of Russia, but his fall was quickly followed by the completion of the settlement regarding Gottorp and the renewal of the Russo-Danish alliance. Meanwhile Gustavus III, who knew that he had been lucky to escape the intervention of the two allies in support of the parliamentary constitution in Sweden, safeguarded his position by employing French subsidies to improve the defences.

A new situation was created during the American War of Independence, when the intervention of France and Spain on behalf of the colonists caused neutral trade to suffer heavy losses at the hands of both sides. A. P. Bernstorff then demanded that the combatants should accept three propositions, which had been formulated in 1759 by a Copenhagen professor, Martin Hübner, whom the elder Bernstorff had sent to England as an intermediary on prize cases. Except for contraband of war, neutral goods should be immune from capture while conveyed on enemy ships; likewise, enemy goods on neutral ships; and neutral shipping should be entitled to trade with enemy ports, unless they were blockaded in practice and not by a mere proclamation of blockade. These principles, which did not receive full international recognition until 1856, formed the basis of a Russo-Danish convention of 9 June 1780; two months later this became the Armed Neutrality of the North, with Sweden, Prussia and (temporarily) Holland as additional adherents. The Russians were offended and the agreement was to some extent weakened by Bernstorff's action in making a private arrangement with England for the exemption of the foodstuffs and timber (other than shipbuilding materials) of the Twin Kingdoms from seizure as contraband. How far the Armed Neutrality was effective in reducing searches and seizures by the British Navy is uncertain, but for the Norwegian mercantile marine at least this seems to have been a period of steady growth; although particularly exposed to the activities of British patrol vessels, it ended the war with its tonnage almost doubled and more than twice as many ships which had been built abroad.

Although the war revealed a common interest and profit in the organisation of neutral trade, Gustavus III did not regard neutrality as a sufficiently glorious objective for his policy. Regular manoeuvres were held from the beginning of his reign, and the ships of the line were doubled. An 'army fleet' of oared galleys to operate inside the skerries, first planned after the fiasco of the Russian war of 1741–3, was now fully developed; and on an island in Helsinki harbour the massive fortress of Sveaborg, which had been under construction for a quarter of a century, at last became fully available to protect the Finnish frontier from being bypassed by Russian movements along the Gulf. Since the settlement of the Gottorp claims gave the House of Oldenburg security on its southern frontier, Gustavus would have liked to make his own western frontier more secure by the transfer of Norway to the Swedish crown. With this in view, he planned a sudden, unprovoked attack on Copenhagen; but this required the connivance of Catherine the Great, who refused to desert her Danish ally. The domestic difficulties already mentioned then prompted the king to engage in the much bigger and, in the eyes of many of his subjects, more appealing adventure of an attack on Russia itself, when that power was preoccupied by a new war against the Turks.

Accordingly, in June 1788 Swedes disguised as Cossacks were used to create a border incident, after which a part of the Swedish-Finnish army moved across the Russian frontier towards Fredrikshamn (Hamina); but the main body was to be shipped across for an all-out attack on St Petersburg. This bold amphibious operation was brought to a standstill in the second week of the war, when a drawn battle off Hogland in the Gulf of Finland failed to wrest command of the sea from the Russians, who thus obtained a breathing-space in which to collect their forces. In August the king also withdrew his troops from the siege of Fredrikshamn to Finland, which became the scene of a grave mutiny known as the League of Anjala (to be examined separately), and before the end of the month Denmark-Norway entered the war under Russian pressure as an 'auxiliary power'. Crown Prince Frederick, who had recently paid Norway the honour of the first royal visit for half a century and had also made Danish rule more popular by ending the corn monopoly, accompanied the advance of 15,000 Norwegian soldiers against Gothenburg. The Swedes were heavily outnumbered, but the campaign lasted only a few autumn weeks, as Britain and Prussia intervened to negotiate an armistice; both powers wished to check the growth of Russian influence in the north, and the British had important commercial interests in Gothenburg. Thus the equipoise within Scandinavia was quickly restored.

The Russo-Swedish war continued, however, through two more campaigning seasons, with minor forays across the frontier from either side and naval operations involving both types of fleet. These culminated in July 1790, when the Swedes lost one-third of their ships of the line in breaking their way out of the Gulf of Viipuri, but a week later faced the Russians again with their galley fleet at Svensksund (west of Fredrikshamn), where it had been defeated a year before. This time the Swedes won their greatest galley victory, destroying fifty-two enemy vessels for a loss of six of their own. The Peace of Värälä, signed in the following month, involved no territorial changes, but it registered the formal abandonment of any Russian claim to intervene in Sweden's internal affairs; and in the autumn of 1791 their common hostility towards the French Revolution caused Catherine and Gustavus to make a defence pact, valid for eight years.

The domestic crisis, precipitated by the reverses in the opening phase of the war, had more far-reaching consequences. After the retirement across the frontier from Fredrikshamn, no fewer than 112 officers in the camp at Anjala entered secretly into communication with the Russian Empress to stop the war. They included a handful of Finnish separatists, led by the younger Sprengtporten, who had fled to Russia in 1786, feeling that his services to Gustavus in the *coup d'état* had been insufficiently rewarded (see p. 185). But their action was based primarily on the king's patent disregard for the constitution, which required the consent of the Riksdag for any war of aggression. Gustavus, however, though he had been brought by his failure as a military strategist to contemplate abdication, again showed his skill in political strategy by the use he made of the Danish declaration of war. Leaving his brother Charles in charge in Finland – where he temporised with the mutineers – he himself hurried to Dalecarlia, scene of the earliest Vasa triumphs, where his oratory rallied the populace to his support against two traditional enemies – the Danes and the nobility. He was thus able to continue the war; the leading 'Anjala-men' were arrested, though only one of them was eventually executed for high treason; and in February 1789 the Estates were summoned for a final reckoning.

Having changed the constitution once in alliance with the nobles, Gustavus now changed it again with the lower Estates as his allies. When the nobility proved recalcitrant, they were bitterly reproached in a speech from the throne and a score of their leaders placed under house arrest – a *coup* which was easily carried out, as the secret police had the support both of the Stockholm burgesses and volunteers from Dalecarlia. An Act of Union and Security was then adopted by the three lower Estates, although the modification of privileges which ensured their support for other changes was legally invalid because the nobles still rejected it. Henceforth the monarch was entitled to dispense with the Council, which had served the state for five centuries, had fuller control of the bureaucracy, and was able to declare war as and when he pleased; the only important remaining check upon his freedom of action was the right of his subjects to vote the taxes. In return for their compliance with the royal demands the three lower Estates were given the right to occupy most public offices, including one-half of the seats in a new Supreme Court, and to buy all types of land except that in the immediate vicinity of a nobleman's manor house. Thus the Swedish peasant had almost complete access to the ownership of Swedish soil; by 1809 about 15 per cent of all outlying noble property was his, and by 1815 he had acquired the major part of a further 3,500 farms from the Crown.[17] Though motivated largely by political expediency, these were impressive concessions for an enlightened despot to have introduced three months before the meeting of the French Estates-General at Versailles heralded the downfall of the *ancien régime*.

Events in France at first aroused little revolutionary feeling in Scandinavia, where a complacent public opinion thought of the French as engaged in claiming social rights which were already recognised in the north. But the people of the towns – especially those with close trade connections with France, such as Bergen and Trondheim – followed the unfolding drama with sympathetic interest in the pages of the press, which had struggled into existence after the relaxation of the censorship, and drank to the new French principles of Liberty, Equality, and Fraternity. As for government policy, A. P. Bernstorff was a resolute non-interventionist, but Gustavus III in the course of 1790 came to fear the influence that the developments in France might have upon his own subjects and forbade any further mention of them in the newspapers. In 1791 he encouraged Count Axel von Fersen* in his attempt to rescue the French royal family, and he was one of the first rulers to demand European intervention. He did not live to see its consequences for Louis XVI, but the radical element in the conspiracy which ended his own life in March 1792 seems to have been influenced less by current happenings in France than by the teachings of Rousseau and their exemplification in the United States of America.

Gustavus III was shot by a former captain of the royal guards during a masked ball at the Opera House; only two months previously his financial measures had been approved by the Riksdag with scarcely a murmur, but the hatred felt by nobles and army officers was inveterate. The king died a lingering death of gangrene, which gave time for him to prevent the intended *coup d'état* and also added to the romantic lustre which still surrounds his name. Less than a month later, the long wars of the French Revolution and Empire ushered in a new period, in which the relationship between sovereign and subject began to be seen in terms of nationality rather than dynastic allegiance. Europe was to make a more incisive impact upon Scandinavian affairs than in any previous quarter-century; but it

* 1755–1810. The son of a leading Hat noble, a confidant of Gustavus III, and Marshal of the Realm under Gustavus IV, but best known as the organiser of the attempted Flight to Varennes, the 'Glass-coachman of a thousand, driving through the ambrosial night' in one of Carlyle's most dramatic passages.[18] He had been in the French service at the siege of Yorktown, became colonel of the Royal-Suédois regiment, and was allegedly a lover of Queen Marie-Antoinette. He returned to Paris in February 1792 in a second attempt to help the royal family, and was henceforth regarded as one of the staunchest champions of the *ancien régime*.

acted upon a Scandinavia in which nationalism was already preparing the way for structural change.

THE GROWTH OF SEPARATIST TENDENCIES

Since the second quarter of the sixteenth century, the European chanceries had been accustomed to deal with two Scandinavian monarchies, whose realms stretched from Iceland to the Finnish-Russian frontier and had as attached possessions to the Duchies of Slesvig-Holstein and less well established claims on the far side of the Baltic Sea. Except for traders and the occasional adventurous traveller, foreigners were content to have a cursory knowledge of Denmark and Sweden, the other territories – apart from a natural German interest in the nearby Duchies – being as unfamiliar as Scotland and Wales were to continental visitors to the court of the early Georges. For a time, indeed, a division into two and not more than two definite entities seemed to be accepted by the Scandinavian peoples themselves, for after the long period of fruitless internecine conflicts the upper classes shared Holberg's view that existing arrangements were the most rational, whilst the masses were more concerned to win their daily bread than to assert claims of nationality. Yet the two generations of peace can be seen in retrospect to have helped the growth of attitudes which were to give the Scandinavia of the nineteenth and twentieth centuries a very different aspect.

Sweden's loss of empire, followed by the party struggles of the Age of Freedom, might have been expected to weaken its hold on the loyalty of the Finns, especially after the further sacrifice of Finnish territory in 1743. But the position of a buffer-state called into existence by Russian favour, as offered by the Empress Elizabeth, made little appeal to the population at large, so long as there was any prospect that allegiance to the Swedish Crown might bring adequate protection. Although Sprengtporten after his flight to Russia became the Empress Catherine's adviser on Finnish questions, his supporters at first amounted to no more than a little group of landowning officers in the border districts which were most exposed to Russian threats. It was, indeed, the officers of six Finnish regiments who subsequently brought about the League of Anjala; but, although one of the preliminary documents urged Catherine to negotiate with 'the nation's representatives'[19] and a so-called Diet of border gentry elected Sprengtporten as its leader, the main object of the League was to end an unprofitable war – an object which was forgotten as soon as the campaign of 1789 brought a few successes on the frontier.

These political activities would almost certainly have developed much faster if Finland had not formed an equal part of a composite realm; its inhabitants enjoyed the same rights of representation in the Riksdag and were subject to the same laws as those of Sweden. In the years of peace the population in fact grew faster: in Gustavus's reign 3,000 new farms were carved out through the assignment of crown property when commons were enclosed; some areas were opened up by new military roads; and the product known in the west as 'Stockholm tar' began to arrive there in Finnish ships from Finnish ports. Culturally, however, Finland remained a Swedish province, where upper-class families treasured their Swedish origins and aspiring native Finns were prone to adopt Swedish surnames, and where the Finnish language was relegated to its use in church and other dealings of the official class with the masses. Åbo Academy nurtured such luminaries as Chydenius and Kellgren, but the most significant figure was the university librarian and later professor, H. G. Porthan,* who organised Finland's first learned society and periodical; he also began the systematic collection of Finnish folk poetry, much of it passed down by word of mouth from the pre-Christian era, out of which the national epic *Kalevala* was eventually to take shape.

In contrast to the Swedish ascendancy which – with the minor exception of Pomerania – prevailed throughout the dominions of the Swedish monarchy, the House of Oldenburg was hemmed in on two sides by alien cultures strong enough to support political discontent. In spite of Holberg's work on behalf of the Danish language and literature, Denmark itself was permeated for more than a hundred years by German influences at court, in society and throughout the government. As we have seen, these culminated with Struensee and were reversed after his fall; but in the last decades of the eighteenth century two out of three leading ministers were of German origin and the German Chancery was still one of the main instruments of administration. Such was the vigour of the German culture, which generation by generation had entrenched itself more securely in the borderlands between the Kingdom of Denmark and Germany proper. In 1773 Slesvig-Holstein, as we have seen, became attached to Denmark by firmer political ties than at any time since the close of the middle ages. But only sixteen years later, when the first attempt was made to impose new taxes in the Duchies without the voluntary co-operation of the nobility, the dynasty's desire to establish a unitary state (*helstat*) met with an opposition in which German nationalist feelings began to play a part.

Norwegian protests against the actions of the unitary state had a different basis. Although each of the main regions of Norway possessed distinctive dialects, which the more reflective inhabitants knew to be derived from the older Norwegian usages of the middle ages, language as the basis of a separate culture was not yet a powerful divisive force.† On the two main occasions when the peasants rose against the authorities, their hostility was directed against the officials on the spot and not against the

---

* 1739–1804. His *De poesi fennica*, published in 1766–78, was preceded in 1745 by a Finnish-Latin-Swedish dictionary of 16,000 words, which held the field for *c.* 80 years, compiled by his grand-uncle, Daniel Juslenius (1676–1752). Both these pioneers of Finnish studies were of Swedish family and intensely loyal to the Swedish connection.

† In 1771 a dialogue to illustrate peasant grievances was for the first time published in dialect; but its anonymous author[20] was a clergyman and he appended a Danish translation.

Father of his peoples in royal Copenhagen, sitting at the apex of their little world. In 1765, when Bergen was the scene of a demonstration against a widely resented poll-tax, the mob which poured into the town from its impoverished hinterland assaulted the regional governor – a Norwegian by birth – and a bailiff, as being personally responsible for the unfair imposition. A large part of the tax was eventually remitted, and a commission of three Danish officials which conducted a full inquiry was critical of both governor and bailiff, but in the end sentences of life imprisonment were passed on two of the popular leaders. Two decades later a disgruntled farmer on the south coast conducted a more formidable agitation against the malpractices of officials and the misuse of town privileges which they abetted; he was supported for a while by 800 men in arms. A commission was again appointed, composed this time of Norwegian officials, and many grievances were redressed – as it had been expected would happen when the petitions of the peasantry became properly known to the king or crown prince in Copenhagen. But although Christian Lofthuus was a leader of wide repute among his fellow peasants, so that his arrest in March 1787 had to be contrived by stealth, the movement which he led soon ebbed away; he died ten years later still a prisoner in Akershus castle, waiting for his case to be heard on appeal, and twelve of his supporters were not set free until 1800.

A wedge was nevertheless being driven between the peoples of the Twin Kingdoms by a section of the Norwegian middle class, which had long envied and resented the commercial privileges of the Copenhagen merchants. This feeling became stronger as Norway drew closer to Denmark in population and came to exceed it in wealth per head: why should Norwegians be denied a bank to help their commerce, a university to train officials for their special needs, a supreme court and a treasury of their own? The need for a bank, for example, was being mooted in Oslo within a decade or so of the establishment of Copenhagen's first bank in 1736. These practical demands were accompanied by other expressions of a separate national identity, such as the Trondheim Scientific Academy, set up in 1760 to promote learned studies of advantage to Norway, and the Norwegian Society in Copenhagen. Organised in 1772 to combat German cultural influences in the capital, it inspired J. H. Wessel's still amusing comedy, 'Love Without Stockings', but was chiefly significant as a rallying-point for Norwegian students, where future officials sang 'Norway, Nursery of Giants!' with appropriate libations. But the most influential support for national claims came from a small but very wealthy group which owned the timber yards and ironworks of the south-eastern ports together with many of the forests of their hinterland.

This patrician class, as it was termed, had close contacts with Sweden because of flotation agreements for timber where rivers crossed the border, whilst Gustavus III kept himself informed of unrest in Norway through spies and, in the last few years of his reign, through a consul-general, who was the only foreign representative posted to eighteenth-century Oslo. From 1772 onwards some Norwegian patricians had secret dealings with the king of Sweden, in the belief that Norway was too weak to stand alone but would be granted a much freer position in a union under the Swedish crown than it possessed under the House of Oldenburg. As Gustavus's plans for expansion were eventually diverted from Denmark to the attack on Russia, any attempted assessment of how the Norwegians might have fared in practice under his sovereignty would be meaningless, but the idea of liberty through union with Sweden remained to influence the nationalist thinking of the following generation.

Whereas Norway, Finland, and the Duchies all had important elements in their population which were stimulated to envisage political change by the self-assurance generated by prosperity, Iceland received no such encouragement. In the middle of the century the autocratic monarchy did, indeed, for the first time give internal control of the economy to a native Icelandic *fogd* or bailiff, Skúli Magnússon; he made great efforts to raise the condition of the people by bringing over Danish and Norwegian farmers to improve the agriculture, by introducing better boats and tackle for the fisheries, and by setting up a woollen manufactory at Reykjavik with skilled German weavers. But he was bitterly opposed by the Copenhagen company which had long held the trade monopoly, and by the General Trading Company which replaced it after an interval of direct control by the Crown. The government in Copenhagen, which assisted Skúli's plans for the welfare of its Icelandic subjects, eventually resumed this control of the trade until it was finally thrown open in 1787.

By that time, however, it was almost too late for private enterprise to revive the economy of an island whose inhabitants suffered almost incessant harassment at the hands of Nature. Its eighteenth-century annals recorded no fewer than forty-three years which were marked by earthquakes, eruptions, abnormally prolonged winters, epidemics, or failure of the fisheries, culminating in the volcanic outbreak of 1783; this caused such devastation that a Danish government commission contemplated the resettlement of the Icelandic population in Jutland. By 1786 it had fallen to 38,400 – about three-quarters its size at the outset of what was for other European peoples a century of rapid growth. In 1800 the Althing, whose legislative powers had been in abeyance since the Reformation, was formally abolished; the new law court which took over its political functions and the surviving bishopric were concentrated in Reykjavik, which mustered 300 inhabitants.

Yet in these discouraging circumstances the Icelanders found in their isolation a source of strength, preserving their national identity through the literature of the sagas, which had been written in the language they still spoke and treated of places and lineages still familiar to them. The surviving manuscripts had been collected in the early years of the century by a native scholar, Arni Magnusson, who bequeathed them to the university in

Copenhagen, thus promoting an interest which spread from Scandinavia to other lands – and which in the long run did much to help the 'saga island' to emerge from its existing status as a rather minor dependency. When a native poet who was in Danish official employment (Eggert Ólafsson) in company with Iceland's first state physician[21] wrote *Reise igiennom Island*, this earliest modern account of the island did not find a publisher in Copenhagen until 1772, which was four years after its main author's death. An English translation appeared, however, in 1805 – the very year in which the battle of Trafalgar presaged great changes in all the Scandinavian countries through the interaction of land and sea power, the latter being of special importance for the remote Atlantic island.

Chapter 9

The Impact of European War, 1792-1815

Except for the short-lived peace of Amiens in 1802–3, Europe was destined to remain at war for more than twenty-two years, during which the ideas generated by the French Revolution marched with the French armies as far afield as Moscow. But for two-thirds of this momentous period Scandinavia remained under the old order, comparatively little affected by new ideas and only twice involved in brief hostilities – when the British fleet descended on Copenhagen in 1801 and when a Swedish force was sent to support the Third Coalition in Germany in 1805.

In Sweden the assassination of Gustavus III was followed by a regency under his younger brother, Duke Charles, ruling on behalf of his thirteen-year-old nephew, Gustavus IV. The Regent ignored the last wishes of the dying king by driving from office his favourite, G. M. Armfelt, and allowed the nobles who had backed the assassin to escape punishment. His own interests being in freemasonry and occultism rather than government, he left the country largely in the hands of a fellow mason, G. A. Reuterholm, the son of a former leader of the Cap Party, who tried to get rid of Gustavian influences upon the young king by unmasking an alleged conspiracy; this resulted in Armfelt's fleeing for a time to Russia. Reuterholm also tried to improve the financial situation by negotiating for subsidies from revolutionary France, but after quarrelling with the Directory had to turn to Russia instead. The Empress Catherine encouraged negotiations for a marriage between her granddaughter and the new king of Sweden, but these broke down over the demand that she should continue to practise the Orthodox religion, to which her intended husband refused his consent, much to Reuterholm's discomfiture; when Gustavus came of age in 1796, he retired abroad.

Like his father before him, Gustavus IV inherited a very difficult situation, but he was much less able to cope with it. Though religious, dutiful, and not unintelligent, he was too narrow-minded and introspective to make a popular leader in a crisis. For nearly a decade, however, the

SCOTS INDEPENDENT SCHEDULE 2020

ISSUE NO	2020 EDITION	FINAL COPY TO ALLOA	1ST PROOFS	EMERGY, p1 COPY & FINAL PROOFS	FREE PRESS PRINT	DESPATCH
1	Jan. SI	Tues 18th Dec 2019	Wed 19th Dec 2019	Sun 23rd Dec 2019	Mon. 24th Dec 2019	Friday 28th Dec '19
2	Feb. SI	Tues Jan 21 2020	Wed Jan 22 2020	Sun Jan 26 2020	Mon Jan 27 2020	w/c Jan 27th 2020
3	Mar. SI	Tues Feb 18 2020	Wed Feb 19 2020	Sun Feb 23 2020	Mon Feb 24 2020	w/c Feb 24th 2020
4	Apr. SI	Tues 24th Mar 2020	Wed 25th Mar 2020	Sun 29th Mar 2020	Mon 30th Mar 2020	w/c 30th Mar 2020
5	May SI	Tues 21st April 2020	Wed 22nd April 2020	Sun 26th April 2020	Mon 27th april 2020	w/c 27th Apr 2020
6	June SI	Tues 26th May 2020	Wed 27th May 2020	Sun 31st May 2020	Mon 1st June 2020	w/c 1st June 2020
7	July SI	Tues 23rd June 2020	Wed 24th June 2020	Sun 28th June 2020	Mon 29th June 2020	w/c 29th June 2020
8	Aug SI	Tues 21st July 2020	Wed 22nd July 2020	Sun 26th July 2020	Mon 27th July 2020	w/c 27th July 2020
9	Sept. SI	Tues 25th Aug 2020	Wed 26th Aug 2020	Sun 30th Aug 2020	Mon 31st Aug 2020	w/c 31st Aug 2020
10	Oct. SI	Tues 22nd Sept 2020	Wed 23rd Sept 2020	Sun 27th Sept 2020	Mon 28th Sept 2020	w/c 28th Sept 2020
11	Nov. SI	Tues 20th Oct 2020	Wed 21st Oct 2020	Sun 25th Oct 2020	Mon 26th Oct 2020	w/c 26th Oct 2020
12	Dec. SI	Tues 24th Nov 2020	Wed 25th Nov 2020	Sun 29th Nov 2020	Mon 30th Nov 2020	w/c 30th Nov 2020
1	Jan. 2021 SI	Tues 15th Dec 2020	Wed 16th Dec 2020	Sun 20th Dec 2020	Mon 21st Dec 2020	w/c 21st Dec 2020

young king ruled with success. He made Axel von Fersen marshal of the realm, and restored Armfelt to favour, but relied mainly upon officials chosen from the newer noble families. Opposition showed itself most clearly when the Riksdag was summoned in 1800 to deal with the financial emergency caused by the cost of the Russian war, which was more than five times the annual budget and was rendered insupportable by two bad harvests. A group of young nobles, headed by Hans Järta,* demonstrated their 'Jacobin' sympathies by demanding that the necessary new taxes should be given a time limit, and when this was refused sought to renounce their peerages. However, all four Estates agreed to a revaluation of the currency, which was successfully completed with the help of a supply of silver obtained by pawning the Mecklenburg port of Wismar.

The king also interested himself in agriculture. An important pioneering work had been done by a Skåne landowner of Scottish descent named Rutger Maclean, who enclosed his land, resited his farms, abolished work rents and payments in kind, and proved able to secure a bigger income from a more prosperous tenantry. But in spite of earlier legislation, technical progress was held up by the general reluctance to abandon the time-hallowed tenure of scattered strips, and the example set by the Danes since the 1780s even caused the more enterprising among the Skåne farmers to emigrate across the Sound. In 1803, therefore, a General Enclosure Act was made for Skåne, which after four years was extended to all regions except Dalecarlia, Norrland, and Finland, where land won from the forest did not lend itself to reorganisation. With the help of local agricultural societies and – in 1811 – a Royal Agricultural Academy, Sweden was on the way to becoming a corn-exporting country. In Pomerania the royal interests ranged even wider, for in 1806 enclosure was introduced there as part of a project to attach the province more closely to Sweden by abolishing serfdom, the Diet based on class privilege, and the separate organisation of the Church.

In the Twin Kingdoms the personal authority of the Crown Prince Regent increased after the death in 1797 of A. P. Bernstorff, whose son Christian took his place as foreign minister; Prince Frederick's instructions came to be executed mainly by young adjutants, known to the public from their plumed headgear as 'the red feathers'. This tendency was accentuated in 1805, when the Prince placed himself at army headquarters in Holstein; but he was a conscientious administrator of the reforms made in his youth, which continued to work smoothly. His lack of judgement showed, however, in the Patent of September 1806, which took advantage of the formal dissolution of the Holy Roman Empire to proclaim the incorporation of Holstein as a crown possession, thus exacerbating relations with its German population. As regards his Scandinavian subjects, too, the shortcomings

---

* 1774–1847: originally Baron Hierta. He played a large part in the drafting of the constitution of 1809, in which he advocated the incorporation of traditional elements, and ended up as the closest Swedish counterpart to Edmund Burke.

of the old order were clearly shown in the mishandling of a novel problem that arose at this juncture in Norway.

In 1796 a popular religious movement, broadly similar to the Methodism which had recently aroused so many parts of England and Wales, began under the leadership of a 25-year-old peasant, Hans Nielsen Hauge, who had experienced a sudden conversion, singing a German Pietist hymn as he followed the plough. Like John Wesley, he combined the gifts of the magnetic preacher and winner of souls with those of the practical organiser. On his evangelistic journeys into almost every region of Norway he created groups of 'friends', as he called them, for purposes of religious edification and economic improvement. His message being directed chiefly to his fellow peasants, he came into contact with some who were eager to plant new settlements in the wilds and with a larger number who had moved into the towns, where they needed guidance as to how they might better themselves in face of the hostility of the established inhabitants. Many of Hauge's plans for agricultural, commercial, and industrial activities succeeded, not only on account of his own shrewdness but because his followers had the moral strength and mutual confidence which make for prosperity.

Haugeanism aroused immediate suspicion among the authorities in Church and State, accustomed to rule over a generally compliant and wholly unorganised peasant population. Its leader's work was frequently impeded by charges of vagabondism or breach of the Conventicle Act of 1741, and in 1804 he was confined in Akershus Castle pending a full investigation of his activities. The rigours of his imprisonment and his disillusionment on finding, like other peasant leaders before him, that he looked in vain to the king as the father of his people broke Hauge's health, albeit that he was let out on licence when war came, in order to organise emergency salt works. He was finally discharged at Christmas 1814 on payment of a heavy fine; by then Haugeans had already figured in the first parliament of an independent Norway. In politics, the movement was marked by the same hostility to officialdom – in this case the rationalist clergy – as had been shown by the Norwegian peasantry on other occasions, but this time the peasants had been able to channel their strength into something approaching a nation-wide organisation. In the Church, too, Haugeanism had lasting consequences: although its supporters made no attempt to form a dissenting body, for which the penalties were severe, they provided the nucleus for a laymen's movement, fundamentalist in theology and puritan in its ethics, which is still a force to be reckoned with in many parts of western and south-western Norway.

Hauge's teachings were spread to a great extent by tracts, and his secular undertakings included both paper mills and printing works. But in the period when French revolutionary ideas were advancing across Europe, political discussion was restricted throughout Scandinavia by the revival and strengthening of the censorship. In Sweden, indeed, Reuterholm began the reaction against Gustavianism by relaxing the curb on the press, but quickly found it necessary to check the vigour of debate by returning to the system of penalties imposed in 1774; he even closed down the Swedish Academy. Gustavus IV restored the privileges of the Academy, but detected the presence of a nest of Jacobins in Uppsala University, from which he withdrew his patronage; in 1798 all periodicals were placed under supervision, and six years later French newspapers and books were denied admission to the realm. In Denmark-Norway, where the freedom of the press had been perhaps the most valuable result of the short-lived regime of Struensee, liberty of discussion produced no overt act more serious than a strike among the Copenhagen carpenters, but it proved prejudicial to negotiations with Russia for a new league of armed neutrality. Accordingly, in September 1799 a draconian law required all newspapers, periodicals and pamphlets to be submitted to police scrutiny before sale. Two revolutionary writers were banished, and spent the rest of their lives in Paris.*

Two other factors, however, helped to maintain a generally conservative climate of opinion. The first was the strength of the economic ties with Britain, which tended to turn the attention of the dominant classes away from France. For the Swedish ironmasters Britain was still their most important export market, where high prices were obtainable from the armament industries in spite of Russian competition and the growth of the native output of puddled iron. For the Danish agriculturists it was likewise a market of increasing importance, since a low-grade quality of foreign corn was a welcome import for feeding the rapidly growing industrial population. For the Norwegian timber exporters, too, the needs of wartime Britain spelt high prices and quick sales. The second factor was the lesson which the Scandinavian countries had learnt from previous wars, namely that their remoteness from the main theatres of a European conflict made neutrality possible for them, and that as neutrals they could enjoy the profits both of the carrying trade and of other trades diverted from their peacetime channels.

'The subdued murmuring of the idle, the unfortunate, and the imprudent went unnoticed amidst the gaiety and contentment which were generally prevalent among the business classes.'[1] This was the picture drawn, indeed, in retrospect by a rich Norwegian ironmaster, timber exporter and shipowner. But it represents a state of public opinion which was widespread throughout Scandinavia during a veritable Golden Age. Even in far-off Iceland the importation in 1806 of sugar was twenty-five times and that of tobacco ten times as great as it had been a generation earlier.[2]

REWARDS OF NEUTRALITY

'What power on earth can endanger confederate Scandinavia?' inquired a Danish historian[3] on a visit to London in 1792. Britain had begun its war

* P. A. Heiberg (1758–1841) became a translator in the French foreign ministry; M. C. Bruun (1775–1826) achieved a new career as a founder of the Paris Geographical Society and author of the classic *Précis de la géographie universelle*.

against France by seizing nearly 200 Norwegian and Danish vessels bound for French ports, but in 1794 the Scandinavian monarchies were to combine in an agreement which exacted some regard for neutral rights. Each signatory provided eight ships of the line to protect their trade, operating first in the approaches to the Baltic and later in the North Sea as well. The regular export trades, the re-exportation of imports from the colonial empires, and the carrying trade each enjoyed boom conditions; and in 1796–8, when the Royal Navy temporarily lost control of the Mediterranean, the British government actively encouraged neutrals to traffic in those waters. The sequel, however, was a short but bitter struggle over the rights of convoys, which the Scandinavian powers first introduced as a protection against the French, the Danish East Indiamen being escorted home from as far afield as St Helena.

After Nelson's victory in Aboukir Bay (August 1798) had eliminated the French fleet from the Mediterranean, the British navy sought to hinder all traffic with French-controlled ports by subjecting convoys to strict visitation and eventual seizure. In the summer of 1800 a Danish frigate offered resistance in the English Channel and was captured together with its convoy, whereupon a British envoy was sent to Copenhagen with an escort of seven warships, which cruised in the Sound until the Danes promised to abandon convoying. But the new Danish foreign minister, Christian Bernstorff, had already urged the Russian Tsar Paul to re-form the Armed Neutrality of the North; this was accomplished in November, when the King of Sweden signed an agreement in St Petersburg, to which both Denmark-Norway and Prussia also adhered. However, when the winter ice closed the ports of the inner Baltic, Denmark was effectively isolated from the other Armed Neutrals, so, in January 1801, 149 Danish and Norwegian merchant vessels were seized in British harbours. At the end of March a Danish army corps marched in consequence on Hamburg, where it secured possession of British property to the value of £15 million, but the main trial of strength took place in the roadstead off Copenhagen on 2 April. Seventeen British ships of the line had passed the heavily fortified entrance to the Sound in safety by skirting the Swedish shore, where the intervention of the Swedish artillery had been deprecated by the Danes – for fear their allies might afterwards claim exemption from the Sound tolls.

The Danish fleet had not been made ready for sea; this required six weeks for fitting out the ships and mustering their crews, a decisive step which had been postponed in the hope of avoiding a direct confrontation with the British navy. But public opinion supported the government's decision to resist: in the words of the poet Oehlenschläger (see p. 286), then serving as a volunteer with his fellow students, 'Feeling for the old, heroic naval tradition had taken possession of the entire nation and especially the capital.'[4] Favoured by the wind, two-thirds of the British force sailed in from the south; this enabled Nelson to avoid the main defences of the port but not a line of blockships, whose crews were reinforced from the shore whilst they put up a strong and spirited resistance. After six hours fighting the issue was still uncertain, as five British ships of the line were aground, though the Commander-in-Chief (Sir Hyde Parker) had seven more in reserve to the northward. At this juncture Nelson urged the Crown Prince Regent to break off the engagement, on the plea that otherwise he 'will be obliged to set on fire all the Floating-batteries he has taken, without having the power to save the brave Danes who have defended them'.[5] The Prince capitulated without consulting his naval commander, which made it all the easier for his subjects to feel that their navy – manned as much by Norwegians as by Danes – had distinguished itself greatly in this encounter.

The British fleet sailed on to Karlskrona, but action against the Swedes was suspended when news arrived of the murder of Tsar Paul, which had taken place a week before the battle of Copenhagen. His son, Alexander I, came to terms with the British, so the League of Armed Neutrality was brought to an end, and it was not renewed after the brief intermission in the European war in 1802–3. Neutral commerce nevertheless flourished more than ever. An Anglo-Swedish trade treaty gave liberal concessions over the interpretation of contraband; Copenhagen reached the zenith of its prosperity as an entrepôt market in these years, especially as Hamburg (from which the Danish forces were quickly withdrawn) came eventually under French control; and Norwegian timber, of which the British market absorbed 60 per cent and attracted the more expensive grades, was exported in record quantities.

In the light of later events the government of Denmark-Norway appears to have been unwise in allowing the carrying trade, by which its subjects were now earning very large profits, to occasion many legalistic claims against Britain: for the British resented any lack of sympathy among the smaller powers for their struggle against French control of the continent. Yet the Swedes, who had rather similar interests to protect, did not fare very much better in spite of Gustavus's decision to take the side of Britain in the war of the Third Coalition.

In 1803–5 the king of Sweden made a long visit to the court of his father-in-law, the Grand Duke of Baden, when he learnt to sympathise with the many minor German sovereigns whom Napoleon had dispossessed and was horrified by the murder of the Duc d'Enghien, whom he had kidnapped from Baden territory. Gustavus therefore ignored his ministers' appeals to him to conserve the profits of neutrality, declared war on France (October 1805), and took command himself in Swedish Pomerania, where he had the support of Russian troops and British subsidies. But he showed no aptitude as a commander; within twelve months he had lost his only conquest, the small province of Lauenburg, and he owed it chiefly to his Russian allies that an armistice with the French left his Pomeranian possessions intact. Nevertheless, when the coalition in whose support he had originally been enlisted reached the last stage of its collapse at the peace of Tilsit and

Russia became the ally of France, he denounced the armistice. By this time his passionate devotion to legitimism had inspired a mystical identification of Napoleon with the Great Beast of the Apocalypse; but he was also influenced by Canning's promises of fresh subsidies and 10,000 men from the King's Hanoverian Legion to help him maintain the Pomeranian bridgehead. Within a month the Legion was withdrawn from the island of Rügen for operations against Denmark, and, although a veteran Swedish general contrived to extricate the Swedish forces from what was now a hopeless position in Pomerania, Gustavus returned to Stockholm a broken man. His subjects still had the British alliance, which gave naval protection for Swedish trade, but fearful possibilities lay in the fact that Alexander of Russia now shared with Napoleon the mastery of the whole European mainland.

In 1805 Prince Frederick and his foreign minister had placed themselves with the Danish army in Holstein, hoping to safeguard the neutrality of his possessions against both sides. In the light of the experience gained in 1801 some improvements had been made to the forts protecting Copenhagen, but the fleet was left immobile: Danish neutrality might be imperilled by any step which drew attention to an asset whose prospective value to either side in the European war had been enormously increased by Nelson's destruction of the Franco-Spanish fleet at Trafalgar. This situation continued until July 1807, when Canning was apprised of the rumours of the negotiations between Napoleon and Alexander at Tilsit, which reached London at almost the same time as two mistaken reports from British diplomats. One of these alleged that the Danish fleet was being made ready for action in the yards at Copenhagen, the other, that in Holstein the Danes were preparing to close the ports to British trade and accept occupation by the French. It is easy to condemn Canning, who had been brought to the foreign office as protagonist of a vigorous policy only four months before, for acting over-hastily; but – like Churchill in a still greater emergency at the time of the battle of Oran in July 1940 – his prime concern was at all costs to secure the island against the risk of invasion by a force which had already overwhelmed western and central Europe.

When Canning learnt that he had been misinformed about the Danish intentions, battleships and transports were already on their way to the Sound, accompanied by a 37-year-old diplomat, Francis Jackson, who was given a week in which to obtain the transfer of the Danish fleet to British hands for the duration of the war. A refusal was followed by the landing of about 30,000 men (including the troops from Rügen, already mentioned) north of the Danish capital, which they gradually invested. The Danes offered very little resistance to these ominous preparations, being reluctant to provoke an attack and having in any case only half as many men on the spot to resist one. Prince Frederick, who had brought his father and the rest of the royal family south to his headquarters at Kiel, took the strangely optimistic view that his loyal subjects in Copenhagen could hold out for a couple of months; the longer nights would then enable him to ferry the main army across from Holstein without interference by the British fleet.

The Commander-in-Chief, Lord Cathcart, would have preferred to starve the city into surrender, but he was reminded by Jackson and others that the possession of the Danish fleet was required immediately. After the loyal but militarily incompetent commandant had rejected three demands for surrender, Cathcart ordered a bombardment which continued for three successive nights. Estimates of the loss of life range as high as 2,000;[6] certainly the 14,000 projectiles, which included many of the new Congreve rockets, succeeded in setting on fire the central districts of the city, which were not completely rebuilt for a generation. Capitulation in defiance of Prince Frederick's wishes was followed by a six-week occupation of Copenhagen, after which the British expedition returned home with the Danish fleet and £2 million worth of naval stores. One consequence of this brutal attack upon an unoffending neutral was to damage Britain's reputation as an upholder of morality in international relations; another, of immediate practical significance, was to drive the Crown Prince Regent – who was now powerless to prevent the French from overrunning the Danish islands as well as Jutland – into the arms of Napoleon. In October he signed an alliance which bound him not only to enforce the Continental System but also to join in an attack on Sweden.

Thus the two halves of Scandinavia were pulled in opposite directions by the opposing forces of the supreme land power, uneasily shared between France and Russia, and the supreme sea power, whose frontier was now the European coastline.

THE FATEFUL YEARS, 1808–1810

So long as Napoleon's alliance with Alexander remained even nominally in force, his Continental System might in the long run bring about the defeat of Britain. For the time being, therefore, Scandinavia was second only to the Iberian Peninsula in its importance to both sides – Britain using it as a trade route to the continent to replace those which were more effectively closed by Napoleon's commands, whilst the French (and in principle also the Russians) demanded its strict adherence to the embargo on British trade. One immediate consequence was that for nearly two years (from February 1808 to December 1809) the two halves of Scandinavia were once more at war with each other; bearing this in mind, we may consider Denmark-Norway first.

Frederick VI's long-delayed accession to the throne at this moment*

---

* Although Christian VII continued to attend Cabinet meetings, he had been king only in name since April 1784, when a rescript declared that his personal orders had no authority unless countersigned by the Crown Prince; the classic Danish historian of the period terms this 'a very clear breach of the Lex Regia'.[7] His death in March 1808 was due to the shock of seeing Spanish troops (see p. 206) enter Rendsborg in Slesvig, where he had resided since the siege of Copenhagen.

rendered the position of the Twin Kingdoms still more hazardous, for he formally abolished the Cabinet (*statsråd*) and issued his instructions directly to the Colleges, thus making the will of the monarch more directly felt than before. And what he willed was the maintenance of the French alliance at all costs as the only hope of exacting due retribution for Britain's wanton disregard for his rights as a neutral. The campaign against Sweden, as we shall see (p. 206), proved a disappointment. As for the war at sea, the loss of his last ship of the line in March 1808 left him with no recourse except privateering and the fitting out of numerous small gunboats; these were rowed out to cut off British merchantmen when the frigates protecting a convoy were becalmed. These activities sustained the morale of the Norwegian coastal population; but they were not economically very significant, except to individual captors of prizes.

The Danish colonies passed into British hands; the lucrative carrying trade in colonial wares likewise came abruptly to an end; some 1,400 ships were confiscated; and about 7,000 Norwegian and Danish seamen were confined in the hulks at Chatham and other British ports. Denmark's swift transition from wealth to poverty was marked by rapidly mounting inflation; military expenditure vastly exceeded the tax revenue; and by 1811 capital payments on foreign loans had to be suspended. The situation for the State was all the more ominous because the duchies of Slesvig-Holstein proved able to maintain the value of their currency, which was based on a separate bank at Altona.

The Danes nevertheless derived some advantage from their close links with the continent. Corn prices were high, so the farmers profited greatly from their recently won economic independence. Although industry had now to accept the competition of French manufactures, quick fortunes were made by trade under licence and by smuggling. Highly profitable under-cover contacts were maintained with the British, who had seized Heligoland in 1807 for commercial access to the mainland and two years later safe-guarded their shipping routes by occupying the little island of Anholt in the middle of the Kattegat.

The Norwegian economy, on the other hand, was completely vulnerable, both because its overseas trade was oriented predominantly towards the British market and because its southern provinces depended on corn imports from Jutland, which could be entirely cut off by the British navy. In the middle years of the long war the king for a time mitigated the distress of his subjects in Norway by issuing licences for timber export which waived his obligations under the Continental System; the British, being very short of timber, not only sent manufactures in return but also relaxed the block-ade of Danish corn ships. In general, however, the interruption of all exports brought widespread unemployment. In spite of liberal expenditure by the Danish authorities and the bringing of Russian corn from Archangel right down the west coast, south-east Norway received only one-sixth of its regular corn imports. The poor often depended on bark bread for bare survival, and in some districts the census of 1815 was to show that since the beginning of the century the population had actually diminished.

King Frederick seems to have appreciated the dangers of the political situation, in which Norway was being forced apart from Denmark by the severance of sea communications at a time when Sweden as the ally of Britain might be judged to be a more attractive partner. As soon as the British expedition was mounted against Copenhagen, he had sought to rally Norwegian opinion by appointing a commission of government (*Regjeringskommisjon*) under Prince Christian August, a distant connection of the royal family who had already made a name in Norway as a comradely commander-in-chief. Business interests were conciliated to some extent by new credit facilities, though requests for a bank of issue were still rejected; a separate court of appeal was set up for Norway as well as a prize court; and the distribution of foodstuffs was entrusted to a provisioning commission.

The moving spirit in this last-named institution was Count Herman Wedel Jarlsberg, the heir to extensive properties on the south coast of Norway, who had gained financial experience under Schimmelmann. In December 1809 he canalised the nationalist sentiments of the upper classes into a society to promote their country's welfare, *Selskabet for Norges Vel*. By that time the king had decided to replace government through commission by sending a royal vice-stattholder, but his two realms continued to be driven apart by the naval situation.

Although the long blockade of the coasts of Denmark-Norway undoubtedly promoted the eventual separation of the two countries, the treatment accorded to Iceland indicates that this was not the deliberate aim of British policy. For the fate of the Icelanders, as we have already suggested, depended upon the wishes of the power which was now the undisputed mistress of the seas and as such had a free choice of insular possessions. Yet when the Danish governor and the chief justice* were captured on the high seas in an attempt to run the blockade, they were after some delay allowed to complete their journey to Copenhagen. Icelandic prisoners in Britain were also released, and freedom of trade with British ports was granted in accordance with the justice's request. By 1809 British traders were well established on the island, to which both Danish and American vessels were also given access. There followed a remarkable interlude, when a Danish privateer captain, named Jörgen

---

* Magnus Stephensen (1762–1833), who had imbibed the principles of the Enlightenment during his legal studies in Copenhagen, provided his native island with its first periodical and a vigorous society (1794) for the promotion of arts and sciences. The displacement of the Governor in 1809–10 was believed to be due to his machinations, but he retained his judicial office for the rest of his life, in which capacity he gave new scope to Icelandic jurisprudence.

Jürgensen,* broke his parole as a prisoner of war by absconding from England as interpreter for the principal British merchant engaged in the new Icelandic trade. English merchants abetted him when he effected a *coup d'état* – with a force of twelve sailors; he arrested the Danish governor, issued a proclamation of independence for the island, and even commenced the construction of a primitive fort. But within two months a British man-of-war reversed the situation by arresting Jürgensen, dismantling the fortification and giving the governor a passage to England in search of an indemnity. This was refused him, but the final result of the episode was that the Icelanders enjoyed full self-government until the end of the war.

Meanwhile, in 1808–10 the position of Sweden and Finland had become no less hazardous than that of the Twin Kingdoms and even more complex. Their only friend was Britain, whose navy dominated Baltic waters, whose trade made Gothenburg the most prosperous entrepôt market in Europe, and whose subsidies to some extent supplied the sinews of war. But Britain's military interests were increasingly directed to the war in the Peninsula. Sweden's potential enemies, on the other hand, included France and every upholder of the Continental System, such as Prussia and more particularly Russia, who was not likely to neglect the opportunity for strengthening her frontier in the north-west. Accordingly, on 21 February 1808 the Russians invaded Finland, whilst the French offered their help for an attack from the opposite quarter by Denmark-Norway.

In this graver national emergency Gustavus IV's leadership proved no more effective than in the Pomeranian campaign. He succeeded in setting up a militia (*lantvärn*) as a reserve force, but it was not properly equipped or quartered and its decimation by disease became a byword. Moreover, he decided that the western front was the more important, a fateful decision which was not justified either by the pressure which 10,000 Norwegians under Prince Christian August were likely to exercise inside Swedish territory or by the threat of invasion from across the Sound. Bernadotte, as governor of the Hanse towns, was instructed by Napoleon to engage only his Spanish allies in support of the latter operation, which in any case faced the hazard of British naval control of Danish waters. The effectiveness of that control was to be convincingly demonstrated later in the year, when the Spaniards were shipped away from the Danish islands to Sweden, with a view to their eventual engagement in the rising against the French which had begun in their native land in May. In addition, Gustavus showed

---

* 1780–1844. This singular adventurer, whose father was clockmaker to the Danish court, had been apprentice on an English collier and rose to be an officer in the British Navy before the privateering episode, whilst after his return in disgrace from Iceland he was employed for four years as a Foreign Office agent on the Continent. Reduced to theft by his passion for gambling, he was transported to Tasmania, where he quickly became a district constable. W. J. Hooker, the distinguished British botanist, who was in Iceland at the same time as Jürgensen, considered that his intervention there was well received by the general population of the island.[8]

himself at his most intransigent when a British force under Sir John Moore arrived off Gothenburg; he summoned its commander to Stockholm and tried to place him under arrest for refusing to set aside the orders of his own government, whereupon the expedition sailed back home.

In June the king went to Åland, but by then it was too late for him to build up his forces in the east, where the real danger lay. At the outbreak of hostilities his army in Finland had been almost as numerous as the Russian invaders, but orders had been issued to the commander-in-chief, General W. M. Klingspor, that in the event of a winter campaign he was to retire northwards into Ostrobothnia so as to husband his resources. He did so, and much of the lost ground was recovered in the spring, especially through the efforts of his second-in-command, C. J. Adlercreutz, whose victory at Lapua in July is still celebrated by a holiday in southern Ostrobothnia. But the coastline along the Gulf of Finland remained in enemy hands, owing to the inexplicable surrender in May of the key fortress of Sveaborg.* The British and Swedish navies having bottled up the Russian fleet on the other side of the Gulf of Finland, the king directed reinforcements to land along the Bothnian coast, so as to link up with Klingspor. Their failure caused him to deprive three Guards regiments of their precedence and, after Adlercreutz too had been defeated in September on the coast at Oravainen, north-west of Lapua, with a loss of 750 lives, there was a second retreat into the north. This time Klingspor's men were completely outnumbered by the Russians, who followed them round the head of the Gulf of Bothnia. In November they agreed to abandon Finland, the last remnants of the Finnish army being demobilised under a further agreement of 25 March 1809, whilst for Sweden itself hostilities continued until the following September.

In the meantime the annexation of Finland, proclaimed by the Russian commander-in-chief when the war began, had been ratified on 29 March by the Diet of Borgå, at which his new subjects pledged their loyalty to Alexander, who in return promised to govern them as Grand Duke in accordance with their existing laws and liberties. His generosity was partly due to the influence of his principal Finnish adviser, Göran Sprengtporten, who had been at his side during the war, whilst its ready acceptance points to the diffusion since the days of the League of Anjala of the belief that Russian suzerainty in some form was becoming inevitable. This in turn goes far to explain the events which constitute the greatest disaster in Swedish history. Although a later writer of genius, J. L. Runeberg (see p. 233), made scapegoats of Klingspor and Cronstedt, a spirit of defeatism seems from the outset to have pervaded the upper classes in general. The peasants in the ranks of the Finnish army often fought more resolutely

---

*Admiral Cronstedt, who had been mainly responsible for the great naval victory at Svenskund in 1790, had 2,000 pieces of artillery and superior numbers of men for defending the position which he gave up without a fight. It has been claimed that his action was instigated by Duke Charles or other conspirators against the king; all that is certain is that the morale of his officers was very low.

than their officers, and peasant guerrillas offered noteworthy resistance to the invaders from behind the lines. But when the summer campaign of 1808 ended in failure, even the most nationally-minded Finns accepted the inevitability of submission to a Russian empire which had been growing in strength for a hundred years and was now the ally of the great Napoleon.

Earlier in the month in which Finland passed irrevocably from their grasp, the Swedes cut their losses by overthrowing the Gustavian monarchy and system of government. Plans to murder or depose Gustavus IV had been in existence since the fiasco of the Pomeranian campaign, and his disciplinary action against the Guards officers (already mentioned) had further antagonised the noble class, which had procured his father's assassination only sixteen years before. The main factor, however, was the king's refusal to accept the loss of territory as inevitable, even after it became known that Napoleon had expressly approved Alexander's war of conquest at their Erfurt meeting in October 1808. Instead, Gustavus planned to reoccupy Finland and also to effect a landing on Zealand as a counterstroke against the Danes. Unable to obtain British subsidies for these objects, he ordered a special war levy, to which his civil advisers offered as much opposition as they dare, but the decisive intervention was by the military.

After coming to an understanding with its Norwegian opponents under Christian August, a part of the western army marched against Stockholm with Georg Adlersparre, one of the 'Jacobin' nobles of the Riksdag of 1800, in command. The king's intention was to take refuge with his loyal forces in Skåne, who might have quelled the rising, but on 13 March he was made prisoner in the palace at Stockholm by a party of half a dozen officers organised by General Adlercreutz, whose performance in the Finnish war had brought him to the fore. The subsequent arrival of the troops from the west completed the *coup*, Duke Charles – who had long been out of favour with his nephew – becoming regent for the second time and presiding over a ministry drawn from existing officials.

When the Estates met on 1 May, the clergy and the peasants were still disposed to support Gustavus, but he had already renounced the throne for himself, though not for his nine-year-old son, Prince Gustav. In December the royal family exchanged imprisonment for exile. The triumph of the anti-Gustavians also required the setting up of a new constitution, which was prepared by a constitutional committee – the first in Swedish history – with Hans Järta as secretary and twice as many members from the nobility as from each of the other Estates. A system which limited the monarchy and strengthened the bureaucracy (see p. 216) was adopted by the Riksdag in early June, whereupon Duke Charles was acclaimed as king; but he and Adlersparre had to combine to browbeat the peasant leaders before their Estate reluctantly agreed to the continuance of a formal guarantee for class privileges.

After failing in an attempted *rapprochement* with Napoleon, the new government had no option but to continue the war. Although they for a time recovered the territory which the Russians had occupied at the head of the Gulf of Bothnia, they were unable to dislodge them from the Åland Islands, invaded in March. When peace was made at Fredrikshamn in September, Sweden lost the archipelago and a coastal strip at the head of the Gulf of Bothnia as well as Finland, in all about one-third of the territory which had been under the Swedish Crown since the central middle ages. In the west, however, their enemies engaged in no further operations of any significance. Danish plans for a winter attack on Skåne came to nothing because the ice failed them in the Sound, whilst the Norwegian army preferred a waiting policy in the hope of some political advantage from the revolution across the border. In December (1809) Charles XIII made peace on the basis of the *status quo*.

The main issue in Scandinavia was now the succession to the Swedish throne, for King Charles lacked an heir and was already ageing. The choice of King Frederick might have been attractive, as it would have given a fully united Scandinavia some ability to withstand the pressure of the great powers. This possibility could not, however, be seriously entertained by the Swedes, unless the Danish king were willing to become a constitutional monarch on the lines of the constitution they had just adopted; but he was too honourable and too short-sighted to sacrifice principle to expediency, either in 1809 or when the question arose for a second time in 1810. But the anti-Gustavians found a suitable candidate to keep out the child Prince Gustav in Prince Christian August. He had deserved well of them by helping Adlersparre at the time of the *coup*, and his popularity with the Norwegian army and people encouraged the hope that he might bring about the transfer of Norway to the crown of Sweden; this idea had already been mooted by Count Wedel Jarlsberg and other influential Norwegians.

Elected heir by the Riksdag in July 1809, Christian August did not arrive in Sweden until the New Year, by which time peace had been restored between his two fatherlands. In the following May his sudden death from a stroke was attributed by the masses, whose favour he had immediately won, to the machinations of the Gustavians, the sequel being a singular outrage which illuminates the deep cleavages below the surface of Swedish society. When Axel von Fersen, the friend of Gustavus III and now the champion of his little grandson, in his capacity as Marshal of the Realm conducted Christian August's funeral procession through the streets of the capital, he was mobbed and brutally murdered before the impassive gaze of the regiments lining the route. The choice of another heir to the throne was clearly momentous for Sweden's future, and this time it was complicated by the need to consider what might be the wishes of Napoleon, with whom peace had been made in January.

The full intentions of the French Emperor in this matter were not made clear to contemporaries and have been the subject of surmise by many later historians; but his first preference seems to have been his Danish ally, King Frederick, and failing him he was willing to accept an elder brother of Christian August, who was proposed by Adlersparre. This was indicated to a coureir whom the Swedish government sent to Paris, but a duplicate courier had arrived there first in the person of an army lieutenant, Baron C. E. Mörner, who hoped to find a French marshal for the vacancy. Bernadotte, who had made more friends than enemies when he served against Swedish forces in Germany, was the natural choice, and although he was out of favour with Napoleon he received his unofficial encouragement to seize an opportunity which might enhance French prestige. Accordingly, when the Riksdag met to consider the matter at Örebro – out of reach of pressure from the Stockholm mob – Bernadotte's candidature was strongly supported by the French vice-consul from Gothenburg, whilst the King of Denmark withheld his support from Adlersparre's candidate, although he was his brother-in-law. Bernadotte's election was followed by his arrival in Sweden in October 1810; as Crown Prince Charles John, he immediately acquired a complete ascendancy over his adoptive father, Charles XIII, whereupon Sweden entered upon a new era of purposeful government, soon to be marked by the acquisition of the Norwegian crown.

AN INDEPENDENT NORWAY?

One month after Charles John's arrival in Sweden, Napoleon exacted a declaration of war against Britain, but the Swedes did not allow this formality to interfere with a very profitable smuggling trade. Accordingly, in January 1812 the French Emperor marked his displeasure by the sudden seizure of Swedish Pomerania, which was one of the most obvious loopholes in his blockade of the continent against British goods, already seriously weakened by the refusal of further co-operation by the Russians. Charles John's first attempt to increase the army had provoked resistance by the pea antry in Skåne, which was forcibly repressed. But the Riksdag now agreed to conscription of the younger age-groups (though the conscript was entitled to hire a substitute) and helped the Crown Prince to execute his policy by authorising the confiscation of newspapers and periodicals for the nebulous offence of 'imperilling the public safety'.[9] In April 1812 he linked Sweden's fortunes with those of Russia in the treaty of St Petersburg, and in the course of the summer made peace with Britain.

Tsar Alexander rejected, however, a tentative proposal for the return of Finland or at least the Åland Islands: on the contrary, this was the year in which he greatly strengthened his hold on his new subjects by incorporating in the Grand Duchy the Finnish territories annexed in 1721 and 1743 and giving it a new capital at Helsinki, much nearer than Turku to the Russian border. Instead, he would reward Swedish help in his forthcoming struggle with France by supporting the annexation of Norway. The tsar planned, indeed, to compensate the Danish monarch by gains in Germany, conditional upon his adherence to the Russo-Swedish alliance; but King Frederick showed no inclination to change sides at this fateful moment, both because of his genuine paternal affection for his Norwegian subjects and more particularly because of his belief that Napoleon's military genius would continue to get the better of any hostile combination.

In fact, the Danish hold on Norway was already weakening. In 1811, indeed, Frederick reluctantly met Norwegian wishes, as voiced by Wedel Jarlsberg, through the granting of a charter for the long-desired university, which two years later came formally into existence with the help of funds collected by the Welfare Society. But discontent received a fresh stimulus from a decline in the profits of the licence trade, as Russia's breach with Napoleon meant that its timber competed in the English market, where the Norwegian product was already disadvantaged by a doubling of the tariff in order to encourage Canadian interests. In the spring of 1812 a Norwegian entrepreneur, Carsten Anker,* wrote urgently to Prince Christian Frederick,† the heir to the throne of the Twin Kingdoms: 'Denmark cannot save us, neither can Napoleon . . . So Norway is lost to Denmark and thrown upon its own resources.'[10] The fisheries did badly that year and the harvest was exceptionally poor, whilst the whole Norwegian economy was imperilled by the continuing decline of the Danish currency, on which it was still dependent. Finally, in January 1813 a National Bank was set up in Copenhagen to replace the Currency Bank, established forty years before; new notes were then issued with a nominal silver value of one-tenth that of the existing notes, which were called in for compulsory replacement – an arrangement difficult to distinguish from a national bankruptcy.

Charles John, as might perhaps be expected, played his part in the drama of Napoleon's downfall with a skill which King Frederick could not match. When the French Emperor entered Moscow, he made his offer of help to Alexander – whose position then seemed at best precarious – conditional upon the surrender of Finland to him as a pledge; but when the retreat from Moscow was followed by the rising of the Germans in the wake of the retreating French, he promptly strengthened the original Russo-Swedish agreement over Norway by an Anglo-Swedish treaty, signed at Stockholm in March 1813, entitling him to British diplomatic or naval support for its acquisition. He was then given command of the Fourth Coalition's northern army of 158,000 men, which defeated two of the

* 1747–1824. He had lived for many years in Denmark, where he became a director of the Asiatic Company, which sent him to London for three years as its contact with the East India Company's representatives; he returned in 1811 to his residence at Eidsvoll in Norway, which later served as the meeting-place of the constitutional assembly.

† Prince Christian Frederick (1786–1848) was receiving political advice from Carsten Anker as early as 1801 – four years before the death of his father, the Prince Frederick who had been so long eclipsed by his namesake (see p. 182), brought the young prince close to the succession. He became King of Denmark, 1839–48.

French marshals who had once been his fellows and took part in the decisive Battle of the Nations at Leipzig in October 1813. But the Swedish component suffered no more than 0·3 per cent of the Allied casualties on that historic field, so that the loyalty of the Swedish Crown Prince to the coalition was already suspect when he turned aside from the main campaign to exact his claim upon the Danes.

In the meantime King Frederick's conduct had made things easier for Charles John. In May he rejected an offer from the latter to be content with an outright surrender of the Tröndelag, leaving the fate of the rest of Norway to the general peace settlement; in the summer he sent troops to assist Napoleon at the time when even the Austrians under Metternich had decided that it paid to join the other side; and these still formed part of the left flank of the French armies as they retreated west from Leipzig. The sequel was a short campaign and a rapidly negotiated treaty. In December Charles John fought two engagements with the Danes, who were driven back across Holstein to Rendsborg on the border of Slesvig, and then conceded a temporary armistice. Having Russians as well as Swedes under his command, he was now in full possession of Frederick's most valuable province, and the latter then bowed to the inevitable, the terms of surrender being less stringent than they might otherwise have been, because the Allies were pressing for Charles John's participation in their advance across the Netherlands.

By the treaty of Kiel, signed on 14/15 January 1814, Frederick surrendered Norway to the king of Sweden to 'constitute a kingdom united with the kingdom of Sweden'. But the former Norse colonies of Iceland, Greenland and the Faeroes were tacitly excluded from the cession, whilst Swedish Pomerania, Rügen, and a million dollars were to compensate for what was ceded – a noteworthy contrast to the absence of any compensation from Britain for the loss of Heligoland or for the seizure of the fleet in 1807. Another clause provided that a due proportion of the national debt of the Twin Kingdoms should follow the Norwegian crown. This laid up trouble for the future, but Charles John was freed for the advance on Paris. He had secured his main objective, namely the strategic unity of the Scandinavian peninsula, and in any case he cherished hopes at this juncture that he might be able to exchange the position he had won for himself in northern Europe for the rule in one form or another of post-Napoleonic France.

The handing over of Norway, to which King Frederick had bound himself, required the co-operation of his heir, Christian Frederick, whom he had sent there as Stattholder in the previous May; at that time it was already possible to foresee a situation in which resistance by the prince might save the situation for them both by facilitating the later reunion of the two halves of a divided monarchy. But when Christian Frederick proceeded at this juncture to sound the leaders of opinion in Norway, he found that the American and French revolutions had imbued them with the idea of the sovereignty of the people, so instead of claiming the Norwegian throne as his inheritance, of which he could not be rightfully deprived by the action of King Frederick, the prince decided to summon a representative assembly to frame a constitution and elect a monarch. In the meantime he acted as regent, in which capacity he sent Carsten Anker to plead Norway's cause in London and in every way fostered the belief that independence was attainable.

When choosing delegates for the election, the people of each parish took an oath to defend their country's freedom, and it was in an atmosphere charged with patriotic emotion that the representatives of counties and towns met at Eidsvoll in April. Out of 112 members present – those from Finnmark and Nordland could not get through in time – 57 were civil, ecclesiastical, or military officials, 37 peasants, and 18 merchants or men of property,[11] and as we might expect, the official element took the lead. Using the French constitution of 1791 as their principal model, the 'Eidsvoll men', as they are reverently called, aimed at a separation of powers, and the king was to have no more than a suspensive veto over the legislation of an elected Storting or 'great *Thing*'. The constitution was solemnly adopted on 17 May, which is still celebrated for the achievement of its makers, but not for their accompanying choice of Christian Frederick as king.

Wedel Jarlsberg headed a group among the constitution makers, who believed all along that a surrender to Swedish demands was probably desirable and in any case inevitable, whereas the newly chosen sovereign hoped against hope that the powers might respect a *fait accompli*. Whilst the Allied leaders were settling the future of France in Paris, they cold-shouldered Charles John's French ambitions, but Tsar Alexander firmly supported his treaty claims to Norway. In London Carsten Anker found the Whig opposition outspokenly sympathetic but Lord Liverpool's Cabinet determined to carry out its treaty obligations; the Tory ministers did not, however, wish to give Charles John too strong a position in northern Europe and therefore endorsed the Norwegian claim to self-government. A Foreign Office official, who was sent to explain this, arrived after the end of the assembly at Eidsvoll, but the tightening of the British naval blockade made it clear that the four Allied powers were in any case united in the demands for treaty fulfilment which were put forward by their commissioners in Copenhagen and Oslo. Nevertheless, Charles John was not disposed to rely on their continued good will; at the end of July he took command in person of the Swedish army which had long been waiting on the frontier, superior in numbers, training and equipment.

A campaign of less that a fortnight's duration, which brought the Swedes steadily nearer Oslo, ended in the Convention of Moss, whereby the Norwegians agreed that Christian Frederick should vanish from the scene and that a union with the Swedish crown should be established. The further negotiations, however, were to be conducted by a Storting elected under the new Norwegian constitution, which Charles John accepted as a basis of government. Under the presidency of Wilhelm Christie, an able civil servant of Scottish ancestry, the Storting effected the union with the minimum of disturbance to the institutions set up on 17 May, though provisions were added to exclude foreigners from office and to restrict the power of the crown in using the armed forces of Norway outside its own frontiers. On 4 November the Storting recorded its agreement that the throne had passed from Christian Frederick – who had retired unobtrusively to Denmark – to Charles XIII. Charles John, waiting at Halden with an army which the Norwegians no longer had any means of resisting, was duly informed that the king of Sweden was now 'unanimously elected and recognised'[12] as king of Norway. The word 'recognised' paid lip-service at least to the Swedish view that their rights in Norway were derived from the Treaty of Kiel, but 'elected' implied Charles John's tacit acceptance of the Norwegian view that those rights derived from the will of the people as expressed through the Storting. Thus the rift was already present which in three generations was to break the union, but what mattered to Charles John at the moment was to prevent his position from being impugned at the congress of Vienna, where the claims of legitimate sovereigns were once more in the ascendant.

The king of Denmark, who attended in person though uninvited, was warmly received by his Austrian hosts and by every representative of legitimist principles except the Tsar, who saw in Frederick only the last ally of Napoleon. Yet Charles John's relations with Alexander also seemed at this time less secure, since the latter interested himself in the idea of territorial compensation for Prince Gustav, of whom he had become the guardian. The United Kingdoms of Sweden and Norway were, indeed, represented at the congress by a leading Swedish diplomat, Carl Löwenhielm,* who demanded the cancellation of the compensation due to the Danish crown under the treaty of Kiel, on the ground that Norway had not been surrendered according to promise but acquired later by Swedish arms. Nevertheless, during Napoleon's Hundred Days Charles John is known once more to have toyed with the thought of a new career in his native France.

The Final Act of the Vienna congress, signed a few days before the battle of Waterloo, included a compromise settlement for Scandinavia. Denmark had to reconcile itself to the transfer of Swedish Pomerania and Rügen to Prussia, but acquired the little duchy of Lauenburg on the Holstein frontier and a much-needed sum of money; this represented some compensation for territory not received and the payment due from Sweden under the treaty of Kiel. King Frederick was also relieved of the presence of a Russian garrison in Holstein, maintained there until the formal completion of peace with Alexander, but had to agree to the inclusion of the

---

* 1772–1861. An illegitimate son of King Charles XIII, who since 1812 had served with great success as ambassador in St Petersburg; in 1822–39, a staunchly conservative member of Charles John's Cabinet.

Duchy as a member state of the new German Confederation. Sweden lost in Pomerania its last remaining bridgehead in Germany, but the Prussians made a substantial payment, of which a large share went to Prince Charles John in person.* And although the restored Bourbon monarchy would have liked him to be ousted like his fellow marshal, Joachim Murat, king of Naples, the congress ended without any legitimist challenge to his position as sole survivor of all the Napoleonic interlopers, a crown prince who had enriched his new fatherland with a second crown.

THE REMODELLING OF SCANDINAVIA COMPLETED

In the eyes of the rest of Europe, the principal change which had been brought about in Scandinavia was the change in sovereignty – the transfer of the crown of Norway and the acquisition of Finland as a grand duchy by the tsardom. The obvious result was a twofold modification of the balance of power in the north: Russia altogether overshadowed Sweden-Norway, even when due allowance is made for the strategic unification of the peninsula, whilst Sweden-Norway nevertheless was too strong in comparison with the reduced kingdom of Denmark for an equipoise to be re-established inside Scandinavia. In retrospect, however, the change which attracts most attention is the introduction into both Sweden and Norway of political institutions which have lasted to the present day, and the fact that Finland too succeeded in preserving a special form of self-government after its inclusion among the vast possessions of the House of Romanov.

A brief survey of the new situation may begin with Denmark, which for better and worse had the closest connection with Europe at large. When King Frederick returned home from the congress, he was received with loyal enthusiasm by his people, who were relieved at the departure of the Russians and supposed that his journey to Vienna had saved them from further losses. In April 1814 he had revived the Cabinet; otherwise no change was made in the organisation of the autocracy. In Holstein Frederick delayed the revival of the Estates, to which he was pledged by the constitution of the German Confederation. In Iceland the pre-war political control was re-established, the English traders being ordered to leave the island and a free-trade petition from Magnus Stephensen in principle rejected. In general the old regime remained in full force wherever the Danish flag still flew – including the little colonies in the West Indies, the Gold Coast and India, which were duly restored by Britain. But the fact that autocracy was compatible with social amelioration was shown by the completion in 1814 of the work of the Great School Commission through the extension to Jutland of the primary schools established on the islands

* His private fortune, which became an important political instrument, also benefited from compensation paid by Britain because Guadeloupe – not far from St Barthélemy, which Gustavus III had obtained on a visit to Louis XVI in 1784 – though promised to Sweden at the treaty of Stockholm, had been restored to the French monarchy.

SCOTLAND —— SEE ACTS OF Scottish Parliament 1564

eight years before. Although the introduction of the 'monitorial system' from England made the instruction for a time very mechanical, Denmark was one of the first countries in Europe where every child had a right to the three Rs. And Hans Andersen, the washerwoman's son from Odense, could find royal and other patrons to bring his genius to fruition (see p. 287).

Although the transfer of the Norwegian crown could not fully compensate the Swedes for the loss of Finland, which had been an integral part of the realm for so many centuries, Charles John's position as the virtual head of state was now well established. He never learnt to speak either Swedish or Norwegian and was given to alarming fits of rage, but he possessed the advantages of charm, military prestige, and the long experience in the handling of men and affairs which had brought him to the top. Strong government reconciled many Gustavians to the new dynastic prospect, but Charles John never lost his fear that sympathisers with legitimacy abroad might incite his subjects to rise on behalf of Prince Gustav. He was therefore disposed to identify all political opposition with treason, albeit that his countermeasures were based on the payment of private pensions from his personal funds and an apparatus of secret agents on the French model rather than on any overt move against the constitution set up in 1809.

At the time of its replacement in 1975 (see p. 360) this was the oldest written constitution still in force in Europe, and as recently as the period of the two world wars it left the monarchy in a considerably more powerful position than, say, in Britain. But when first formulated it marked chiefly a strengthening of the legislature, to be achieved without detriment to the generally accepted principle of a separation of powers. The four Estates must be summoned at intervals of not more than five years for the purpose of making laws and provision for the public finances. They were entitled to control the king's ministers by examining the records of their decisions, as a result of which they might demand dismissal or launch an impeachment. They also elected an *ombudsman* to protect the interests of the private citizen against bureaucratic encroachments.

However, it was laid down in principle: 'The king is entitled alone to govern the realm in the manner that this constitution provides',[13] which gave him an unfettered choice of advisers and officials, the control of the armed forces and foreign relations, and a veto on legislation. His council of nine members had the right to tender their advice, which was to be recorded, but the royal decisions required only the countersignature of the head of the department concerned; except in the case of the departments of justice, foreign affairs, and the court chancery, this might be an official who was not one of the nine councillors who formed the Cabinet. Lower grades of official were irremovable except by legal process, but the king's control of appointments was strengthened by the fact that his choice was no longer restricted to members of the nobility except in the case of the supreme court, where they were still entitled to one-half of the seats. Lastly, it must be noted that the crown could govern by administrative ordinances so long as the Riksdag was not in session, and that the press law of 1812 did not allow any appeal against the government's view of what was 'perilous to the public safety'.

In Norway the position of the new monarchy was in many respects less assured than in Sweden. The international situation having caused the French marshal to use the minimum of force in asserting his claims, it was only natural for the uninstructed majority of the Norwegian population to look back to the brief months of complete independence as a national dream which had been needlessly shattered. Among the better informed upper classes, on the other hand, the pro-Swedish element though wealthy was completely outnumbered by those clergy and civil and military officials who had only with reluctance renounced their cultural and family ties with Denmark. But the biggest obstacle to an effective welding together of Norway and Sweden was the Norwegian constitution. For the resourceful bureaucrats who drafted it intended that Norway should continue to be ruled by their class, irrespective of any change of sovereign; and when they altered its provisions to meet the inescapable necessity of a union with Sweden, they ensured that the control to be exercised over their institutions from Stockholm should be minimal.

The Norwegian bore a broad resemblance to the Swedish constitution, which was indeed known to the 'Eidsvoll men', though they chose to give closer attention to the American and French constitutions of 1786 and 1791 and even to the practices of the parliament at Westminster. The separation of powers was aimed at in both countries, and they were similarly distributed between an elected legislature, an independent judiciary, and an executive appointed by the crown. There were, however, important differences, related to the much more pronounced class structure of Swedish society and to the active personal role of Swedish kings.

The members of the Norwegian Storting were, indeed, to be chosen through a system of indirect election, but the primary voters included the entire property-holding class and the representatives themselves must be resident in the constituencies, two-thirds of which were to be allotted to rural areas. Moreover, the Storting was designed as a single-chamber parliament, whose members divided themselves for their legislative work into an *Odelsting* and a *Lagting* of three-quarters and one-quarter; this was to secure double consideration for every measure, but if the Lagting refused to pass what the Odelsting had introduced it could always be overruled by a two-thirds majority of the whole house. Thus there was no legal obstacle to the domination of the Norwegian legislature by the peasantry, whereas their fellows in Sweden still constituted only one of the four Estates. Not only so, but the Storting functioned more freely than the Riksdag, since it was entitled to meet at intervals of three as compared with five years and, what was more important, it was able to override the wishes of the sovereign, whose veto could only suspend the enactment of a measure until it was passed by three Stortings in succession.

The king's council for Norway was also less subject to his personal authority than were his Swedish ministers. Since the court normally resided in Stockholm, the constitution provided for the king to be represented in Oslo by a viceroy, who must be of the royal family, or a *stattholder*, who was at the outset a Swedish nobleman. But the main link was an arrangement by which the leading Norwegian minister (*statsminister*) and two others serving in rotation were allocated to Stockholm, where they presented Norwegian business for the king's approval. This business was, however, prepared by their colleagues in Oslo, who formed the effective Cabinet under the nominal presidency of the Stattholder. Although matters which concerned both kingdoms were treated at a joint council, where the king presided over the three Norwegian and nine Swedish ministers, the system did not facilitate the progress towards amalgamation which Charles John would have favoured. On the other hand, no immediate difficulty arose regarding the conduct of the international relations of the United Kingdoms, which the Norwegians regarded as the direct concern of the sovereign, employing the Swedish foreign minister to carry out his personal instructions.

Whereas Norway was placed in readiness to play an increasingly active part in all Scandinavian combinations, Finland had fallen into a different political orbit. Yet its future was to be shaped by institutions derived from its long association with Sweden. For the promise which Alexander had made at the Diet of Borgå meant that his rule as grand duke was to be based upon the powers which its last two sovereigns had exercised under the Form of Government of 1772, as modified to the advantage of the crown in 1789. Legislative authority therefore rested nominally with a Diet of four Estates, corresponding to the former representation of Finland in the Riksdag at Stockholm. But since the Swedish kings had been under no obligation to summon the Riksdag, the Grand Duke could allow the Diet to fall into abeyance; his ordinances had the force of law, whilst financial needs were covered by the land tax and customs dues, neither of which required legislative approval for their collection. Executive authority, however, was distributed among three institutions. A resident governor-general was responsible for maintaining law and order and controlled the Russian garrison. A committee for Finnish affairs in St Petersburg, headed by a special secretary of state, transacted business with the Grand Duke in person. Thirdly, a Senate was instituted as in Russia, where it had been set up by Peter the Great a century before. The senators were to be Finnish citizens, nominated by the Grand Duke for fixed periods, of whom one section dealt with native domestic affairs, whilst another formed the Supreme Court; as the proceedings were in Swedish, the governor-general normally left them in the charge of the vice-chairman, whose position was that of a prime minister in embryo. Sprengtporten was the first governor-general and Armfelt – who was expelled from Sweden in 1811 under suspicion of being an adherent of Prince Gustav – the first secretary of state in a smoothly running system. A full generation was to elapse before changes in international politics combined with internal cultural developments to bring Finland once more within the sphere of Scandinavian interests.

Chapter 10

Nationalism and Scandinavianism, 1815-1864

THE POLITICAL SCENE

Despite the drastic remodelling of institutions, the Scandinavian countries still bore a strong family resemblance to one another. Each of them was governed in its day-to-day affairs by a strong bureaucracy. Each of them emerged impoverished from the war period, and had to struggle for about two decades to restore the value of its currency. All except Sweden were involved in internal conflicts which were rooted in the nationalist sentiments then gathering force in Europe, and all were to a greater or less extent influenced by the wider nationalist concept of Scandinavianism, intended to be a counterpart of pan-Germanism or pan-Slavism. The result was the discomfiture of the kingdom of Denmark and, to a great extent, of Sweden-Norway in the war over Slesvig-Holstein, with which this chapter ends. Its result emphasised the basic weakness of their position in international relations. But their internal affairs, to which attention will first be directed, were likewise determined more clearly than before by the trend of events among more powerful peoples in the world outside the frontiers of Scandinavia.

In 1815–30, whilst the shadow of the so-called Holy Alliance stretched far across Europe, the Danish king and people resigned themselves to the loss of Norway as a common misfortune which drew them together in a desire to avoid all further changes. The paternalist rule of the ageing King Frederick enjoyed wide popularity, but when 'dangerous thoughts' nevertheless occurred they were repressed in a manner characteristic of the age of Metternich. In 1821 an obscure cleric who agitated for a reformed constitution was sentenced to death under the censorship law of 1799, and he was actually imprisoned for more than twenty years. In 1826 a less obscure colleague, N. F. S. Grundtvig (see p. 230), was fined for criticising the rationalist theology then in vogue and ordered to submit any further writings for police censorship before publication.

In Sweden, where the name of 'liberal' had been in use since the constitutional discussions of 1809, opposition continued to manifest itself in the Riksdag under the leadership of C. H. Anckarsvärd, a noble who had taken part in Adlersparre's action against Gustavus IV. But after his accession to the throne in 1818 Charles John showed himself more than ever to be an adroit, if often imperious, manager of men; his instruments included his private fortune and a favourite, Magnus Brahe,* who helped to control both the Riksdag and the army. Accordingly, little was achieved by the three Riksdags elected in 1815–30, beyond the voicing of demands for the reduction of civil and military expenditure.

The Norwegian Storting with its more frequent meetings gave Charles John more trouble – in spite of the fact that, in the autumn of his accession year, 270 peasants were arrested after a demonstration in favour of a return to a royal autocracy, which they equated with lower taxes. Sheer poverty was, indeed, one reason for an attempt to repudiate any share in the national debt of the former Twin Kingdoms, which produced a remonstrance from the great powers at the Congress of Aix-la-Chapelle and was not finally abandoned until 1821, when the Storting reluctantly agreed to assume about one-eighth of the burden. However, the representatives of the official class, who dominated the Storting, were able to get the full support of the peasant members in resisting the new king's many attempts to increase the powers of the monarchy, whether by a constitutional amendment which would make his veto on legislation permanent (as in Sweden) or by a measure to reintroduce nobility, abolished over his veto in 1821. High symbolic significance therefore attached itself to a petty demonstration in Oslo in 1829, when a by no means tumultuous assembly was dispersed without casualties in the 'Battle of the Marketplace': for the king's Norwegian subjects were asserting the right to celebrate the anniversary of their free constitution of 17 May in preference to 4 November, the date of the inauguration of the Union.

In Scandinavia as elsewhere, a change of atmosphere and some modification of institutions followed the French Revolution of July 1830. In Norway Charles John met the rising demand for some share in the control of foreign policy† by agreeing in 1835 that one Norwegian minister should attend for business affecting his country at the 'Ministerial Council', the form of meeting in which the King transacted foreign business with two members of his Swedish Cabinet. Moreover, in the following year a Norwegian subject was for the first time appointed to the office of Stattholder in Oslo, where four high-ranking Swedes had been successively cold-shouldered. In Sweden the Liberals began to increase their influence as early as December 1830, when *Aftonbladet* was established to publicise

---

* 1790–1844. The son of one of the nobles who opposed Gustavus III, he early became a devoted admirer of Charles John; active in the Riksdag from 1828, Chief of General Staff, 1828–40, and Marshal of the Realm, 1834–44.

† Lasting resentment had been aroused by the Swedish foreign minister's mishandling of the Bodö Case: in 1821 British smugglers, who had been duly arrested in the new north Norway port of Bodö, secured an indemnity of £18,000 on the strength of forged documents; the full truth came to light twelve years later, by which time the forger was police inspector for Glasgow.[1]

their views under L. J. Hierta,* whose 44-year membership of the Riksdag had begun in 1828. By 1840 the opposition had brought about a remodelling of the Cabinet, so that the majority of members were actual heads of government departments, a change of system which brought into power some officials who shared the views of the Liberals regarding economic reform (see p. 227). A further impetus in this direction resulted from the accession of Charles John's only son as Oscar I in 1844, for the new sovereign had philanthropic interests, which had been strengthened by a prolonged stay in Germany on account of his health. He also began his reign by conciliating the Norwegian Storting over such matters as his title, which in all Norwegian references was henceforth to name Norway before Sweden, and a union flag design, in which the Norwegian colours were given exactly the same prominence as the Swedish.

Representative government likewise made some advances in both the United Kingdoms. In Norway the Storting of 1833 numbered 45 peasants among its 96 members, but owing to their lack of political experience power soon slipped from their hands. In 1837, however, the introduction of elected local councils in every rural district as well as in the few towns began an educational process which within a generation equipped the peasants to challenge the ascendancy of the official class. In Sweden the landowning farmers had never lost control of local affairs, but a law of 1843 broadened the local franchise to include many other middle-class elements. This was in keeping with a series of minor changes in the organisation of the four Estates, which granted representation to the universities, proprietors of industrial undertakings, and additional categories of farm owners.

On Denmark the effect of the July Revolution in France was more direct and at the same time more complex, since a constitutional change, which was obviously overdue, involved a confrontation with German separatist claims. Thus before the close of the year 1830 Holstein was one of a number of members of the German Confederation where the setting up of Estates was being demanded on the basis of the Vienna settlement; and a Holstein official (who was imprisoned for his pains) had even proposed a constitution on the Norwegian model for a united Slesvig-Holstein, to be linked with Denmark by the monarchy alone. The policy of that monarchy, on the contrary, was at all costs to preserve the Unified State (*Helstat*) all the way to the Elbe, so the situation was met by the establishment in 1834 of purely consultative Estates for each of four regions, namely the Danish islands, including Iceland and the Faeroes; Jutland; Slesvig; and Holstein with Lauenburg. A substantial property qualification was required for electors, which was doubled for candidates, and as a fur-

---

* 1801–72; editor until 1852, after which he figured chiefly as a highly successful publisher and industrial entrepreneur. Freedom of the press was not established until 1844, but *Aftonbladet* evaded repeated orders for its suppression by successive modifications of name, ending up as 'Aftonbladet the 23rd'.

ther precaution against lower-class influence the Estates for the islands were not to meet at Copenhagen but in the little cathedral city of Roskilde.

Although their functions were merely advisory, the biennial meetings of the Estates had some important effects. In Slesvig as well as Holstein their outlook was German, because most of the Slesvig Danes were too poor to qualify for the franchise; attempts to prevent any use of the Danish language at the Estates generated great ill will among all nationally-minded Danes throughout the Monarchy. At the same time the meetings built up a new habit of political activity among a large section of the middle class, especially when further measures of 1837 and 1841 introduced local self-government – though on the same narrow class basis – in town and country. Moreover, liberalism acquired an organ in the Copenhagen newspaper *Fædrelandet* (first founded as a periodical in 1834) and a leader in a young lawyer, Orla Lehmann, who used the Estates to champion the Danish cause in Slesvig, so that this became merged with the demand for further constitutional reform in a 'national liberal' movement.

The accession of Christian VIII in 1839 proved, indeed, a disappointment to all those who pinned their faith to the romantic liberalism which had characterised his rule of Norway in his youth. In May 1846 the liberals demonstrated their support for the cause of reform in conditions on the land – the voicing of which had already cost Lehmann three months in prison – by forming a society of 'Friends of the Farmer' (*Bondevennerne*). But later in the same year the problem of the succession caused Christian to issue a Patent or 'open letter' which, as we shall see in a later context (p. 237), was immediately contested in the Duchies. Accordingly, in the last months of his life he decided to superimpose upon the advisory Estates a joint Estates of the Realm with legislative and financial authority, a decision which his son and successor, Frederick VII, was prompt to implement. One of those present has recorded the scene when, on 29 January 1848, 'in a silence so profound that the stroke of the pen could be plainly heard, the king signed the order with a firm hand, thereby abolishing absolutism'.[2]

It was not until the first week in March that the news of the downfall of King Louis Philippe, spreading across Europe from Paris, inaugurated the main series of events in the Year of Revolutions. In the lands of the Danish monarchy it had two closely interrelated results: the separatists in Slesvig-Holstein demanded their freedom, and the national liberals, who became the predominant force in Copenhagen, demanded a fully constitutional regime, with its basis not in the projected Joint Estates – where the two Duchies were to have had as many representatives as the Kingdom – but in the incorporation of Slesvig with Denmark. The first phases of a three-year war for the Duchies (see p. 239) therefore provided a disturbing background for the epoch-making institutional changes which took place in Copenhagen. In March demonstrations organised by Lehmann caused Frederick to form a new government of ministers whom he declared to be responsible to him as a constitutional king; though headed by a moderate conservative, Count A. W. Moltke, it included the liberal cleric D. C. Monrad* and Lehmann. Freedom of the press was conceded; cottars were freed from compulsory labour services and all adult land workers from the infliction of corporal punishment by their masters; and the principle of equality was marked by the extension of conscription to all classes. These changes prepared the way for the election in October of a constituent assembly; the franchise was democratic, but the military situation prevented the inclusion of Slesvig in the voting.

After the addition of royal nominees, who had one-quarter of the seats, the assembly was about equally divided among Conservatives, National Liberals, and Friends of the Farmer. On 5 June in the following year – still celebrated as Constitution Day – the royal assent was given to a system devised chiefly by Lehmann and Monrad. The basis was the democratic electorate already set up in October: a vote allowed to all men over 30 years of age who lived independently 'with their own cloth and table' (*med egen dug og disk*). The resulting legislature was to consist of two houses, whose powers were equal; the *Folketing* was to be elected triennially in single-member constituencies, the *Landsting* at different intervals in an electoral college chosen by the primary voters in each county. Members of the Landsting were also required to be of a minimum age of 40 instead of 25 and were quite clearly distinguished from the Folketing by an income qualification of 1,200 dollars a year, which acted as a constitutional safe-guard for the rights of property. The executive powers remained vested in the Crown: its ministers were not made explicitly responsible to either house in the Rigsdag, and they retained the right to issue provisional laws between sessions. Yet with all its limitations the Danish constitution of 1849, which also specified freedom of religion, of the press and of public assembly, was a remarkable triumph for liberal principles in a year when reaction was already spreading across Europe.

The Year of Revolutions had produced no such fundamental changes in the other Scandinavian countries. Franchise reform and even a republic were among the demands made by street rioters in Stockholm in March; they were put down with a loss of about thirty lives. A more lasting conse-quence of the news from Paris was that King Oscar ceased to sympathise with any liberal causes, whilst effective franchise reform was delayed until the 1860s; the heir to the throne, Prince Charles, became for a time involved with a reactionary 'junker party' in the House of Nobles. As for Norway, its south-eastern counties were the centre of an extensive movement on the

---

* 1811–87. In July 1848 he brought forward the first draft – using Belgium as his model – for the constitution, enacted under a more conservative government in 1849. Bishop, 1849–55; director of Copenhagen elementary schools, 1855–9; Cabinet minister and finally premier, 1859–64; emigrated to New Zealand, returned after four years, and was restored to his bishopric.

lines of English Chartism, in which Marcus Thrane* employed a periodical (written largely by himself), a society with numerous local branches, petitions, and an assembly of delegates in the capital to voice demands for manhood suffrage and social reform. This evoked no response from the Storting, and the authorities eventually sent 117 persons to prison for revolutionary activities. Although one by-product of the movement was the start of the parliamentary career of Johan Sverdrup (see p. 261), the future organiser of a Liberal-Radical Party (Venstre), the Norwegian franchise was not widened until 1885.

A SLOWLY CHANGING SOCIETY

Marcus Thrane was a man before his time, who tried to alleviate the condition of the masses in a land where the proletariat was still widely scattered and very largely rural. The only direct result of his campaign was to hasten the enactment of a government measure to increase the contractual rights of the cottar class, who were very much at the mercy of the farmers from whom they rented their cottages and scraps of land. But his failure in politics does not diminish his importance in social history – a pre-Marxian socialist calling attention to bitter problems of rural poverty in a region of Europe where outside opinion supposed that contentment reigned supreme.

By the middle of the nineteenth century Scandinavia had experienced rather more than a generation of rapidly increasing populations. Sweden, which had $2\frac{1}{3}$ million inhabitants in 1810, now had almost $3\frac{1}{2}$ million. The Kingdom of Denmark in the same period had risen from one to nearly $1\frac{1}{2}$ millions; Norway from 880,000 (in 1801) to 1,400,000; Finland from 830,000 in the Swedish province to 1,600,000 in the larger area of the Grand Duchy, and Iceland from 47,000 to 59,000.[3] In contrast to countries like Britain, which were then in the throes of the great industrial changes, the town population in Scandinavia was almost stationary; the exports consisted mainly of primary products, such as timber, bar iron, low-grade corn, and fish, for which the foreign demand was in many cases restricted by high tariffs; and in many areas the typical farming family lived very largely on what they could produce for their own consumption. Most farms would include fishing, hunting, timber, and pasture rights which might be very extensive, whilst the product of the tilled ground was newly increased by the spread of the potato, a foodstuff which also supplied brandy. But what of those who had no established farm property to feed them?

The population figures point to the making of clearances on many exist-

* 1817–90. The son of a dismissed director of the Bank of Norway, he had previously made a poor living as a schoolmaster but had managed to spend two impressionable months in Paris. His agitation cost him four years imprisonment, after which he emigrated to the United States, where his socialist propaganda was varied but unsuccessful; one of his last ventures was a play based on the trial of the Haymarket anarchists of 1886.

ing farms, which in some cases provided for a category of tenant whose holding and ancillary rights were normally inferior to those of the existing owners and leaseholders. A much more precarious position was that of the cottars, who bargained with a farmer for the chance to set up homes of their own, with or without some scrap of land belonging to the farm, in return for a rent payable in farm labour or by handicraft earnings; in old age they were often liable to eviction. Lastly, the household on the larger farms included, together with the family, a mass of labourers and dairy maids, all of whom worked long hours for little more than board and lodging. This proletarian or near-proletarian element in society was not new, but its rapid growth made it more significant than in earlier times. In Sweden it is believed to have constituted 20 per cent of the population in 1750 and nearly 40 per cent in 1850, with the main increase occurring in the last forty years of the period.[4] In Norway the single category of *husmenn* was reported as numbering 40,000 in 1801 and 65,000 in 1855.[5] Denmark at the beginning of the century already had rather more *husmenn* than farmers, and the continuing effect of the great land reforms was to increase the demand for their labour. Returns from one Zealand county in the 1840s show that eleven estates then employed more than 100 *husmenn* apiece, who occupied on an average the equivalent of one-fortieth of a medium-sized farm; their rent normally included about twenty-five days' free labour, other labour on demand at fixed wages, and some payment in money.[6]

Whilst the cottar and labourer remained in the background, the *bonde* was achieving a social prominence which makes the standard translation of 'peasant' often misleading. His legal position still varied enormously. In Denmark about half the manors remained in the hands of nobles, but many of these were improving landlords who did not care to rely upon the labour services (*hoveri*) which their tenants were reluctant to render. In Sweden, where the percentage of nobles in the population shrank in a hundred years from 0·5 to 0·3, one-half of their privileged land had passed by 1850 to other owners, of whom about one in two were peasants.[7] In Norway, after the Storting in 1821 had ordered the sale of the remaining church lands, three in four of the landholders were owners and they included only a very small category of proprietors who did not work on their land.[8] Economically, the position of the Scandinavian *bonde* was still more variable. Apart from differences in rent (if any) and land tax assessments, fertility ranged from the rich soils of Skåne and the Danish islands to the marginal lands of the Norwegian west coast and the far north of the peninsula.* Everywhere, however, he was becoming more sure of himself, as is shown by his emergence into political life. The high proportion of peasants

* A traveller who visited northern Sweden in 1838 made a distinction between new settlers, who had a regular diet of bark bread, and older settlers, who mixed the bark with an equal proportion of rye to bake a loaf which he found to be 'far from uneatable', though 'tasting strongly of timber'.[9]

in the Norwegian Storting of 1833 has already been mentioned; the peasants of western Sweden were likewise an important factor in the opposition at the Riksdag of 1840–1; and the Friends of the Farmer formed a solid phalanx in the Danish constitutional assembly of 1849.

Nevertheless, the dominant role was now played by the middle class, a term which did not as yet include the yeoman farmer. Its members staffed the bureaucracy: even in Sweden by mid-century two-thirds of the civil service posts and almost half the army commissions were no longer in the possession of the nobility, whilst in Norway the last relics of aristocratic influence were in the Stattholdership, which was held from 1836 to 1856 by members of the two principal ex-noble families of Wedel Jarlsberg and Lövenskiold. Posts in the Church and the university, likewise included under government, were virtually a middle-class preserve. To this must be added the non-proletarian element in the population of the towns and other centres of trade and industry, which constituted only a small fraction of each country's inhabitants – in Sweden, for example, from 1750 to 1850 one in fifty belonged to the Estate of burgesses[10] – but made a disproportionately large contribution to the liberal/radical element which fostered social change.

The liberal influence was felt most strongly in the attempt to modernise the economic structure of each country, so that private enterprise might flourish. As elsewhere on the continent, the abolition of gild restrictions – for which the main Norwegian legislation was passed in 1839, the Swedish in 1846, and the Danish in 1857 – and of the commercial monopolies of the chartered towns, which disappeared by stages between 1842 and 1864, prepared the way for the great industrial changes of the following era. So did the relaxation of controls over particular industries, as in the case of Swedish iron, which began to recover ground lost to Britain through the enterprise of a new class of independent ironmasters.

These measures were accompanied by a gradual relaxation of tariffs. As between Sweden and Norway, the inter-state treaty of 1827 accorded free passage overland and half-duty on seaborne goods. Swedish manufactures went in exchange for Norway's abundant supply of fish, and the Norwegians also benefited by a reciprocal agreement for free access for shipping. In Denmark uniform lower duties were introduced in 1838 for the kingdom and the duchies, intended to bind them closer together and to counter the influence of the German Zollverein. Six years later a wholesale reduction of import and export duties was brought about in Norway, in spite of opposition from the peasants, who feared that direct taxes would be increased instead. In Sweden a move in the same direction was held up in 1848, when outside events caused King Oscar to react against all liberal tendencies, so that the main reductions were not made until 1857. Eight years later, however, Gripenstedt's tariff treaty with France marked the general acceptance by all three Scandinavian kingdoms of the free-trade trend then prevalent throughout Europe.

The Scandinavian economies were too poor for these liberal impulses to produce big results without direct assistance from the State, especially for the all-important expansion of communications. New high roads, planned in many cases by military engineers, slowly opened up narrow valleys and steep mountain passes to such wheeled traffic as could face the gradients. Sweden led the way in building its own paddle-steamers, thanks to Samuel Owen,* and in 1832 Charles John completed the Göta Canal, linking the Baltic with the North Sea via the great central lakes, which had been planned a generation earlier by Telford. Each Scandinavian government was prompt in organising a system of packet-boats, which were the first public means of transport from point to point all along the coast. But partly for this reason, the railway was a latecomer to Scandinavian soil.

In 1844 trade interests induced the Danish authorities to join Altona with Kiel, and three years later a very short stretch of rail was laid in the Kingdom itself, from Copenhagen to Roskilde. The first Norwegian railway, designed by Robert Stephenson and intended primarily to carry timber from Eidsvoll to Oslo, was opened in 1854; the first short line in Sweden, in 1856. However, in the previous year King Oscar had secured full powers of direction for Nils Ericson,† who by 1862 had completed the Swedish western main line from Stockholm to Gothenburg and brought the southern main line to Malmö under construction. Both the railways and the telegraphs of Scandinavia, which date from the same period, were predominantly State undertakings and the State raised most of the capital required. It was not until 1856–7 that the first large commercial banks were established – *Enskilda Bank* in Stockholm, which A. O. Wallenberg based on the American pattern; *Creditbanken* in Oslo, which held its own in the London commercial crisis of October–December, 1857; and *Privatbanken* in Copenhagen under the direction of C. F. Tietgen (see p. 251).

By that time the economies were more strongly based than they had been since the first decade of the century. In 1850–65 the Swedish output of pig-iron rose by nearly one-half, whilst the introduction of the steam-powered sawmill made timber a more important export than bar-iron. The same period saw a rapid rise in the flow of trade through Copenhagen, which again outshone Hamburg, especially after the abolition of the Sound Dues in 1857. For Norway a new era began with the repeal of the British Navigation Acts in 1849, which enabled a greatly expanded mercantile marine to earn high profits with its cheaply built and cheaply manned

* 1774–1854. An English mechanic who first visited Sweden to install a steam engine, settled there in 1806, and established a machine workshop and foundry in Stockholm, where he built more than thirty ship's engines and (1843) the first Swedish railway engine. As a Methodist and temperance worker, he was also an associate of George Scott (see n 231).

† 1802–1870. Brother of the great inventor, John Ericsson (1803–89), who left Sweden for England in 1826 and became an American citizen in 1848. Both brothers received their early training on the Göta Canal works, and Nils's many canal designs included the Saimaa canal in Finland. He planned his railways on the basis that economically backward districts should be served first.

wooden sailing ships. And each country, Finland included, developed textile factories (though most of them were still water-powered) and small engineering workshops, which showed that they were no longer altogether beyond the periphery of the great industrial changes.

Many of the outstanding achievements of Scandinavian liberalism, however, had humanitarian rather than purely economic objects. Oscar I, for example, encouraged his subjects in both kingdoms in the reform of the criminal law, of prison conditions, and of the poor relief system or lack of system. In Sweden public health became the concern of parish councils as early as 1843, whilst Norway in 1848 was ahead of the rest of the civilised world in its law for the better treatment of the mentally afflicted. In matters of religion the Danish autocracy in 1814 was one of the first European governments to give civil rights to the Jews, which in 1834 were extended to the franchise for the consultative Estates of the Kingdom, though Jews could not stand for election. The Danish constitution of 1849, already described, was the first Scandinavian law to enshrine the principle of religious liberty, which was conceded in practice in Norway in 1844, in Sweden not until 1860. Mention must also be made of the movement for the emancipation of women, which began in the economic sphere with the concession of equal rights of inheritance, enacted in all three kingdoms by 1857, and of access to all forms of employment, which in that year was granted to the unmarried women of Denmark. Further progress was stimulated by novelists, who highlighted the miseries inflicted upon the daughters of the middle classes by the social necessity of making a 'suitable' marriage; Camilla Collett's *The County Governor's Daughters*, published in 1855, was an influential Norwegian anticipation of the realist school of writing.

Universal elementary education, which had been introduced in Denmark in 1814, reached Sweden in 1844 and Norway in 1860; by 1865 state-subsidised elementary schools were being introduced on a less comprehensive basis in Finland too. Although peasant children in many areas received only the most rudimentary instruction from teachers who visited the larger farms for a few weeks at a time, and secondary education was to be had only in the towns, some of them managed nevertheless to reach the university, which opened the way for them into the Church and the civil administration. In the first half of the nineteenth century peasants already formed 15 per cent of the Swedish student body, 8 of the Finnish, 5 of the Norwegian, and 2 per cent of the Danish.[11] Denmark, however, was also developing an alternative form of higher education, better adapted to the needs of the sons (and daughters) of farmers and cottars.

The first Folk High School was founded in 1844 to promote Danish national feeling in North Slesvig, but by 1863 the Rigsdag was subsidising fifteen schools with about 500 pupils all over rural Denmark. Their courses were residential, lasting normally for the five winter months when young people could be spared from the land. The essential feature was the replacement of the traditional book learning by what Grundtvig, the prophet and chief propagandist of the movement, called 'the living word'; this was to be imparted by the discourses of emotionally engaged teachers, discussion carried far beyond the walls of the classroom, and such relaxations as community singing. Such methods were well calculated to emancipate the spirit of a rustic people: pupils returned home with an enhanced pride in their nation's past, a wider approach to its present problems, and a touch of idealism which would make them better citizens and more progressive agriculturists. In 1865 the movement reached Norway and three years later Sweden, where it appealed especially to the farmers of Skåne.

Another movement of a broadly educational character which spread throughout Scandinavia was the work for temperance, an international social crusade which had a special importance in northern Europe, where the cold winter and generally monotonous diet maximised the appeal of cheap potato brandy. Legislation against private distilling and the introduction of heavy liquor taxes were therefore stubbornly opposed by the farmer class. South Sweden provided an important temperance advocate in one of its parish priests, Per Wieselgren, active from the 1830s, and Norway in a layman, K. N. G. Andresen, whose *Temperance Catechism* of 1844 was translated into many languages. In 1847 a Scandinavian temperance congress was held in Copenhagen, but little progress was made among the Danes until the next generation; household stills were forbidden in 1845 in Norway and ten years later in Sweden. The problem was also studied in a wider context by a Norwegian pioneer in the social sciences, Eilert Sundt, who reported in 1859 that a third of the adult male population were 'unreliable' where drink was concerned, though little more than a thirtieth were habitual drunkards. More generally, Sundt's various studies of the moral, social, and cultural environment of the peasantry, based largely upon statistics collected from his fellow clergymen, offered a rational explanation of the light and dark features of a way of life which neither the romantic writers nor the dogmatic urban reformers had properly appreciated.

The prominence of the clergy in the social movements described above is a reminder that the Church was still a force which moulded society. In Denmark the long life, abundant gifts, and strong popular appeal of Bishop Grundtvig* gave a special warmth and unconventionality to worship, which influenced the other Scandinavian churches and has left an enduring mark upon the ecclesiastical practices of modern Denmark. In Norway the clergy of the High Church sought in vain to combat the Haugean influences, which gave a strongly Puritanical atmosphere to the religion of the west and south-west coastal districts. Finland had its own Hauge at this time in the person of Paavo Ruotsalainen, a peasant preacher

* 1783–1872. He made a name in archaeology, history and literature, but his ideas on church organisation were too close to Congregationalism for the authorities; for some years he was forbidden to preach, and although appointed a bishop (1861) he received no diocese. But his influence is still felt all over Scandinavia through his hymns and through the Grundtvigian tradition surviving in many folk high schools.

who never learnt to write but who, five years before his death in 1852, dictated *Some Words to the Converted*; its publication was a major event in the history of the Finnish-language movement. There were also remarkable developments in Sweden. The university of Lund and much of the surrounding region were given a leaning towards a strictly interpreted Lutheranism by Henrik Schartau, whose teachings were still in print a century after his death in 1825. A very different type of church leader was C. O. Rosenius; his evangelical appeal – 'Come as thou art' – created a revivalist movement which was organised on a permanent basis in Sweden and also influenced both Norway and Denmark. The far north, too, had its evangelist in L. L. Læstadius, who established a dangerously ecstatic type of revivalism among the Lapps; this soon subsided, but the puritan outlook of the Læstadians spread from Sweden both to north Norway and to Finland.

From the social angle an important feature of nearly all these movements was the emphasis they laid on lay activity. This was strengthened at mid-century, when Home Missions (*Indremisjonen*) spread to Scandinavia from Germany; though led by clergy, the movement relied mainly on laymen to carry out its work of social as well as spiritual reclamation in town and country. Foreign missions, which also date from this period (see p. 300), likewise relied upon lay men and women to raise the funds through local branches and to provide recruits for work in the field, who were in some cases refused ordination. Lastly, we must note the impetus given in this direction by the nonconformist bodies which now entered Scandinavia from outside. Quakers came to Stavanger in pursuit of the evangelical work they had done among Norwegian prisoners of war in Britain. The presence of English workers in Stockholm in 1830 brought the Methodist minister, George Scott, to that city, where he preached for twelve years to crowded congregations. He was then deported on a charge of defaming the spiritual condition of Sweden during a lecture tour in the United States; but his Swedish disciples included Rosenius and one of the future leaders of the Swedish Baptists, whilst Methodism soon re-entered Scandinavia from America. In 1839 the Baptist faith arrived in Copenhagen, from where it spread rapidly to Norway and Sweden; strong clerical opposition to the doctrine of adult baptism gave the Baptists, who in Sweden formed the biggest nonconformist connexion in Scandinavia, a special place in the assertion of the rights of the laity.

Religion played a considerable part in the early stages of the emigration to North America, which began in 1825 with a party of Quakers and Haugeans from Stavanger who received the help of American Quakers in making the first settlement in Upper New York State. In Sweden the movement began twenty years later with the wholesale migration of a native religious sect under its founder, and the second main party was composed of Baptists. Danish emigration, which did not start until the 1850s, was strongly influenced at first by Mormon missionaries who were busy proselytising in Scandinavia; in that decade, nearly 2,000 Danes arrived in Utah. However, in the early 1860s the annual average of emigrants amounted to no more than 4,710 from Norway, 2,509 from Sweden, and 1,049 from Denmark, which as a proportion of population was significant only in the case of the Norwegians, who were leaving for the New World at the rate of 2·86 per thousand inhabitants. The social and economic causes, which operated much more powerfully in the later years of the century, will therefore be left for examination in a later chapter (see p. 300).

RISING INFLUENCE OF NATIONALISM

The concept of nationality – 'the something in virtue of which a nation continues to exist even when it has lost its autonomy'[12] – made at this time a much wider appeal than liberalism to the variously situated but in every case predominantly rural peoples of Scandinavia. Thus the Swedes found consolation for the loss of Finland in the patriotism of the Gothic Society, whose members extolled a Nordic past in which their own 'Gothic' ancestors loomed larger than life-size. Besides the poet Tegnèr (see p. 286) and E. G. Geijer, later famous as a historian, its members included P. H. Ling, whose desire to strengthen his nation, as Napoleonic Germany had found strength in the *Turnverein*, took shape in the pioneer Gymnastics Institute which he conducted in Stockholm from 1813 to 1839. The Norwegians, whose nationality had received so large a measure of recognition in 1814, whilst emphasising their constitutional separateness from Sweden, were also concerned to separate their national language from that of Denmark. The Icelanders, too, experienced a fresh national stimulus through the medium of lyrical poetry: in 1805 the earliest contact with Steffens and the dawn of Romanticism in Copenhagen (see p. 238) had resulted in the writing of *Eldgamla Isafold*, 'which became so popular that it has since remained the national song of Iceland'.[13]

The Danes alone were fated to be losers through this rising influence. In the long run it would vitiate all their belated efforts to establish an equitable relationship with the Icelanders, and in the short run it faced them with the intractable problem of Slesvig-Holstein; this was to cost them two wars and the eventual loss of both the Duchies, one of them containing a Danish minority which was no less nationally-minded than its German majority. But since the events in Denmark are more complex, it will be convenient to start with a brief reference to the stirrings of nationalism among the Finns.

Though shut off at this time from the main current of events in western Europe (including Scandinavia proper), Finland under its first three grand dukes experienced a half-century of outwardly harmonious development. In 1812 Alexander had moved the capital from Turku to Helsinki, and the university followed as the result of a disastrous fire in 1827. But he directed the construction of dignified public buildings for the new capital, and also conciliated the Lutheran clergy by raising Turku to an archbishopric. Nicholas I, known elsewhere as the Iron Tsar, appreciated the help of the 'Guards of Finland' in crushing the Polish rebellion and infringed their constitution only once, when he required the admission to public office of Finnish subjects belonging to the Orthodox Church, of which their Grand Duke was the head. The reign of Alexander II began auspiciously with the opening in 1856 of the Saimaa Canal, which linked eastern Finland more closely with St Petersburg but also opened up its forests for the timber trade to western Europe. Seven years later, when Finland remained quiet during the second great rebellion of the Poles, he marked his satisfaction by summoning the Diet, which had last met at Borgå in 1809.

During this period Swedish remained the language of administration and culture, having been brought to Finland originally by a ruling class which still held much of the land and by a Swedish peasantry who predominated in many south-western coastal districts. It was also the language which was necessarily used by the student population, and it was common practice for families with social aspirations to conceal a Finnish origin behind an adopted Swedish surname. This was accordingly the language in which J. L. Runeberg published from 1848 onwards his *Tales of Ensign Stål*, re-creating the war of 1809 as a saga of Finnish heroism; its dedicatory poem, 'Our Land', has been translated to provide the Finnish national anthem of today. But although the Swedish language was the obvious link with the freer societies of the west, as instanced in the attendance of some students from Finland at a student meeting at Uppsala in 1843 (see p. 239), the Crimean War did not bring to the surface any desire for reunion with Sweden on the part of Swedish-speaking Finns.

On the contrary, the nationalist awakening came among the Finnish-speaking peasantry, under the guidance of enthusiasts born on the other side of the language barrier who were nevertheless imbued with the Romantic view that the native language somehow embodied the nation's true identity. The movement began in Åbo/Turku as early as 1823 with a history teacher, A. I. Arwidsson, who started Finland's first political newspaper and soon found it prudent to cross over to Stockholm, albeit that the Russians at this stage regarded 'Fennomania' as a harmless project which weaned the people from any surviving loyalty to Sweden. Twelve years later the literary society at Helsinki university sponsored the publication of the first version of the collection of Finnish folk poetry known as *Kalevala*, which incorporated traditions from the unrecorded pre-Christian past; it had been made by a doctor, Elias Lönnrot, who practised in both Finnish and Russian Karelia and had even sought out materials in a peasant disguise. The epic form of the work was to a considerable extent his own invention; but what mattered was his gift to the Finnish people of the feeling that they had strong roots in the past, which did much to sustain them in a later period of conflict with the so-called Svecomans (see p. 276).

Still greater services were rendered to the Finnish cause by a third scholar of Swedish origins, J. V. Snellman, who based a long career in Finnish politics on the proposition: 'We are no longer Swedes; we cannot become Russians; we must be Finns.[14] His views cost him his place as a university teacher, but in 1844 be began to publish two periodicals, *The Farmer's Friend* in Finnish and *Saima* in Swedish. The latter, which took its name from the great lake Saimaa, preached the need for the natural leaders of the nation to learn to express themselves in its native language, and was soon suppressed by the Russian governor-general as a liberal organ. During the reaction after the revolutions of 1848 Snellman's doctrine was further combated by the restriction of Finnish-language publications to devotional and technical subjects, which would not present dangerous thoughts to the masses. Alexander II, however, was more concerned to turn their thoughts away from Sweden. In 1858 he allowed one of the first state-aided secondary schools in Europe to be set up to help Finns to reach the university, where he established a professorship in their language. Finally, his epoch-making revival of the Diet in 1863 was accompanied by the appointment of Snellman himself as the senator in charge of finance and of his leading supporter, Yrjö-Koskinen, to a university chair of history (see p. 276).

Although the Bernadotte kings of Norway had such insignificant powers of coercion at their disposal in comparison with the Romanovs in Finland, Norwegian national feeiings were from the outset very sensitive to the possibility of Swedish encroachments under cover of the common monarchy. The constitution, as we have already noted, was treated as sacrosanct, and Charles John from time to time incurred considerable odium among his Norwegian subjects by his demands for its amendment. The progressive amalgamation of Norwegian with Swedish institutions would have appealed to many Swedes, but the King's only formal step in that direction was taken in 1821, when the recalcitrance of the Storting regarding the debt to Denmark led him to advise the powers in a Circular Note that some unilateral modification of the constitution might become necessary. That he ever seriously contemplated resorting to naked force for this object is perhaps unlikely, but in 1821 and again in 1828 the former French marshal had Swedish troops in readiness on the Norwegian frontier,[15] whilst as late as 1836 – during a final quarrel which preceded his reconciliation for the last time with the Storting – he was advised by Löwenhielm that 15,000 men would suffice to enforce his wishes.[16]

When Oscar I succeeded his father in 1844, he sought to conciliate the Norwegian people systematically over minor grievances, as already noted; but this attitude was not rewarded by any show of enthusiasm on the part of his Norwegian ministers for the proposals of the first Union Committee, which reported later in the same year and would have given Norway a larger share in the management of a closer union. Nevertheless, the middle of the century proved to be the period of greatest harmony in the relations between the two kingdoms. The official classes at least were becoming better acquainted, and Norwegian public opinion was increasingly disposed to regard the Swedish connection as an asset in relation to the possibility of Russian encroachments in north Norway (see p. 241).

A closer parallel with Finland can be seen in the cultural sphere, where Norwegian nationalists set about the task of eradicating the effects of the four-century-long Danish ascendancy, as displayed in the language of the university, the Church, and the whole category of 'persons of condition'. The first steps in the creation of a wholly independent native literature were taken in the 1830s by Henrik Wergeland,* patriot, poet, and publicist, who made his appeal to the youth of the nation as a radical enemy of the Establishment. So far as the form of language was concerned, Wergeland aimed at a modification of Danish in accordance with current Norwegian usages, a process which was carried further during the 1840s by Asbjornsen and Moe (see p. 287), whose collection of folk tales introduced to the printed language many native elements of vocabulary and style. Their work harmonised with the romantic taste of the period, which sought in peasant life much of the inspiration for its music and painting, and with the researches of historians such as P. A. Munch. Almost to the day of his death in 1863, his voluminous correspondence testifies to the very large part which the tentative reshaping of their language played in the thoughts of a nation which felt itself to be at the same time old and young.

Whilst Danish was modified by slow degrees into a generally acceptable 'language of the realm' (*riksmål*), a minority of nearly one-third of the Norwegian people eventually rallied to the notion of deliberately creating the wholly national language which they would have liked to inherit from the past. This 'language of the land' (*landsmål*) provides such a striking illustration of the strength of separatist nationalism in twentieth-century Norway that its small beginnings must be mentioned here. In 1836 a cottar's son in a western fiord district, named Ivar Aasen, announced a plan for 'an independent and national language', to be based on a synthesis of rural dialects – which meant chiefly those of west Norway, with which he had familiarised himself – in the light of the Old Norse of the later middle ages, from which they were ultimately descended. In 1848–53 he published a grammar, a vocabulary, and specimens, which appeared in improved versions in the later years of a long but rather isolated life. Although Aasen himself had considerable literary gifts, it was not until 1858 that his new language attracted a second able exponent in the journalist and poet Aasmund Vinje, who employed it for his new periodical, *Dölen* ('The Dalesman').

In Iceland, which had once been in great measure an offshoot of Norway, the cultural impact of Danish rule had been much smaller, though the

* 1808–45. Son of a well-known cleric and 'Eidsvoll man', and educated for the Church; a student participant in the Battle of the Marketplace, he became a popular hero in a struggle over literary styles against the classical verse of Johan Welhaven, whom the authorities eventually rewarded with a professorship of philosophy (1846). Wergeland, whose prose works w... concerned with the enlightenment of the people as much as agitation, owed his only official post (as a state archivist) to King Charles John.

purification of the language was among the objects of the periodical *Fjölnir*, which in 1836–47 stimulated patriotic feeling by publishing the work of the chief lyric poets of the new Romantic era. The political and economic grievances of the islanders, however, were not abated either by the inclusion of two Icelandic representatives in the new Consultative Estates for the whole monarchy or by the institution in 1838 of a royal commission to visit the island biennially and report on its needs. But in 1843 the new king, Christian VIII, set in train a century of separatist nationalist activities by his revival of the ancient Althing, whose membership and powers were to conform with those of his other Estates. Dissatisfied with these limitations, the Icelanders found a formidable exponent of their grievances in Jón Sigurdsson,* a native scholar in great repute at Copenhagen, where his editing of sagas and other source materials brought the study of his country's history and literature into new prominence. In 1848 the renunciation of autocracy by the Danish monarchy furnished him with the argument that his country was thereby entitled to resume those historic rights which had been conceded to it in the original pact with Haakon IV of Norway, the *Gamli Sáttmáli* of 1262.

All that was regained, however, was economic liberty, the trade of Iceland being thrown open to all nations by a law of 1854. As regards their political future, the Icelanders were excluded at their own request from the new Danish Rigsdag. Instead, they were authorised to hold a constitutional convention of their own; but this was not allowed to meet until July 1851, by which time the position of the monarchy had been strengthened both by the general reaction in Europe and by its apparent triumph over the rebels in the Duchies. The majority in the convention demanded a separate constitution, leaving as the only links with Denmark a common monarchy, foreign policy, currency, and university. These demands were not to be reconciled with the Danish offer of the control of purely domestic legislation by the Althing, whilst the island would also be represented in proportion to its population in the Rigsdag: this would leave the Danish ministry with the executive power, and also involved acceptance of the validity for Icelanders of the constitution which the Danes had made without their participation in 1849. After a month the convention was dissolved by the Danish governor, who had troops on the spot in case his decision should be challenged. All protests were ignored, the Althing being relegated to the status of a Danish county council. It is significant that the Faeroese, who had met Danish wishes by electing members to the Rigsdag, fared no better: in 1856 their trade was freed, but their local council or

---

* 1811–1879. An unusual combination of scholar and statesman. He lived chiefly in Copenhagen, where he was secretary of the Armagnean Commission, but from 1849 onwards he visited Iceland in alternate summers to preside over the Althing. His objective of complete independence except for the common monarchy was kept in view from 1848 to 1907 by periodic meetings of representatives at Thingvellir, the ancient place of assembly, and in 1944 his birthday was chosen for the proclamation of the Icelandic Republic.

lagting was kept under the strict control of the Danish governor.

The political intransigence of the Danish government must be seen in relation to the more dangerous problem with which it was faced on the southern border, where since 1834 the meetings of the Consultative Estates had stimulated the growth of separatist nationalism in the Duchies. Even the little duchy of Lauenburg, acquired in 1815, had about as many inhabitants as Iceland; altogether, the lands between the Kongeå and the Elbe contained one-third of the area, three-eighths of the population, and possibly as much as one-half of the total economic resources of the monarchy. Holstein – as also Lauenburg – was wholly German in language and culture, rooted intellectually in its seventeenth-century university of Kiel and socially in its well organised aristocracy of big landowners or *Ritterschaft*, whose power stretched far across the River Eider, marking the boundary with Slesvig. The placename etymology and local building traditions of Slesvig suggest that the original cultivators of its soil were chiefly Danish; what is quite certain is that most of the land had come into the hands of the same class which dominated Holstein. By the 1830s, accordingly, German was the language of administration, the Church, and (for the most part) of the schools, so that only northern Slesvig could reasonably be classified as Danish, and even there the language was in a minority position in the towns.

As we have already seen, the cause of the Danes in Slesvig had already been taken up in the Consultative Estates by their compatriots in the Kingdom, who in July 1846 also induced Christian VIII to declare himself on another issue, which was entangled with the rival claims of nationality. He announced by Letters Patent that, in the event of his only son, the future King Frederick VII, leaving no male heir – which for physical reasons was virtually certain – the succession to Slesvig at least would be the same as for the Kingdom. This view was immediately challenged by the duke of Augustenborg,* who claimed that Slesvig no less than Holstein was subject to the Salic law and not to the Danish *lex regia*, which provided for inheritance through the female line. But it was the Year of Revolutions which first made it clear that the future of the Duchies was an issue on which men from both sides were prepared to stake their lives. In March, the month in which the first responsible government was formed in Copenhagen, the nationalist movement which had then set all Germany aflame kindled a rebellion in the Duchies. The consequence was a three-year war and a much longer period during which the so-called 'Eider Danes' strove to incorporate Slesvig into the Kingdom, whilst the Unified State party aimed at a constitutional link with Slesvig-Holstein, so as to foster conservative interests throughout the monarchy (see p. 242–3).

---

* Duke Christian Frederick of Augustenborg (1798–1869) claimed by descent in the male line from King Christian III. The Danes disallowed his claim to Slesvig on the very dubious basis that it had been incorporated in the Kingdom in 1721.

Delegates from the Duchies, who were sent to Copenhagen immediately before the outbreak of the rebellion in March 1848, proposed the division of Slesvig along the frontier of language, but the solution which has proved acceptable since 1920 was dismissed out of hand by the newly formed Danish Cabinet, from a National Liberal standpoint. Holstein might in the last resort be expendable, since it was a member of the German Confederation, but Danish patriots could not doubt their ability to triumph over rebel subjects in Slesvig. If the rebels were supported by the states of Germany, it was reasonable to suppose that non-German powers would be interested in restoring the *status quo* in a region which was important for the strategic control of the Baltic and the general balance of power in Europe. Last but not least, the ambitions of the 'Eider Danes' rested on the belief that they could rely on the help of Sweden-Norway in defending the line of the River Eider as the southern frontier of all Scandinavia.

SCANDINAVIANISM

The Scandinavianism of the mid-nineteenth century is often disparaged as a movement which flourished chiefly among the student population. But this was an age in which a small student body, recruited mainly from the upper levels of society, furnished each Scandinavian country with its ruling elite in political, cultural and economic life. Ideas which roused spontaneous enthusiasm among students were therefore assured of a widening influence if and when the turn of events made them in some degree practicable. Perhaps the moment for decisive action never came: at all events Scandinavian aspirations towards unity faded away, at the very time when Italians and Germans were learning to combine politically separated peoples into a larger national unity.

Scandinavianism originated in Denmark, where men's minds were most readily kindled by the notion of the common 'Nordic' past, to which the builders-up of the 'Germanic' past across the southern frontier looked back with obvious respect. Romanticism was brought to Copenhagen as early as 1802 in the lectures of the philosopher Henrich Steffens,* who although he spent most of his later life in Germany left a lasting impression on his student audiences; they had included both Grundtvig and Oehlenschläger, who was inspired to write his first Romantic verses by the recently lost archaeological treasure of the Gold Horns. The poets were helped by the rising interest in a history which antedated national divisions to call attention to a wider Scandinavian heritage, so that in 1829 Tegnér could delight the students of Lund by bringing Oehlenschläger across the

---

* 1773–1845. A Norwegian of Holstein descent and a mineralogist by training, he had imbibed the romantic spirit at Jena in 1798; one of his later visits to Norway prompted him to write a book on the Storting in German, which was also the language of his 10-volume autobiography, translated into Danish on publication in 1840–5.

Sound to be crowned as a Scandinavian poet laureate, acclaiming him with the words:

> The age of separation is past, nor should it ever have been
> In the boundless, free world of the Spirit.[17]

For nearly forty years periodic summer meetings provided Swedish and Danish students with the occasion for a popular steamboat excursion. The Finns who joined them at Uppsala in 1843 were afterwards suspended from their university, but from 1845 onwards Norwegians attended and took their turn as hosts. In 1839 Grundtvig employed the first number of a short-lived Scandinavian periodical, *Brage og Idun*, to argue for the replacement of existing institutions by a single Nordic university at Gothenburg. In the following year his plea for a common outlook in matters of culture was echoed by his fellow countryman, H. C. Örsted (see p. 293), in his address to one of a series of Scandinavian scientific congresses:

> A misconceived national pride has divided us and brought foreigners to consider our achievements of little significance . . . Let six million Scandinavians place their entire weight in one scale, and surely it shall not be found too light.[18]

But the growth of German nationalism to the south was soon to provide a sterner test, for which Orla Lehmann's eloquence sought to prepare his followers. In 1845, when 400 Swedish and nearly 150 Norwegian students were the guests of their Danish friends in Copenhagen, he secured a light-hearted assent to a 'sacred promise' that they would be 'faithful to the end, faithful in life and death' in their fraternal loyalty to 'our great common fatherland'.[19]

In March 1848 Lehmann was a member of the Danish government which was faced with rebellion in the Duchies; this had indeed broken out at Kiel even before their delegates returned from Copenhagen (as already mentioned) with the news that the Danes intended to include Slesvig in their forthcoming constitution. The rebels were defeated at the town of Slesvig on 23 April, but an overwhelming number of Prussian and other German troops under a veteran Prussian commander were then sent to the rescue, and quickly overran the two Duchies and Jutland as far as Århus. The Danes received the support of no more than 243 Swedish and 114 Norwegian volunteers,[20] but both legislatures voted the necessary expenditure when King Oscar offered a regular force of 15,000 Swedes and 3,000 Norwegians and a joint naval squadron to protect the Danish islands. One-third of the Swedes were shipped to Fünen and the rest held in readiness in Skåne, thus bringing considerable pressure to bear on the Germans, who had no naval resources. In early July the king acted as intermediary for an armistice between the Prussians and the Danes, and when the Prussian general refused to ratify the agreement (on the ground that he was answerable to the German Parliament then sitting at Frankfort) and threatened to reoccupy Jutland, the United Kingdoms were brought close to active involvement in the war. However, at the end of August Prussia signed on behalf of the Frankfort Parliament – whose authority dwindled as the reaction began to spread across Europe – and a seven-month suspension of hostilities followed, during which the Swedes withdrew from Fünen.

King Oscar deprecated the decision of the Danes to renew the conflict next year, when they hoped to secure an untrammelled sovereignty over Slesvig. Although the new conscription law had enabled them to increase their army to 41,000 men, they were still outnumbered three to two by their opponents, who again overran most of Jutland. But in early July command of the sea helped the Danes to win a substantial victory over the Slesvig-Holsteiners who were besieging Fredericia, and in the same month the economic pressure of the Danish naval blockade and the diplomatic pressure of the Tsar combined to induce the Prussians to negotiate a second armistice, which twelve months later was turned into peace without any settlement of the German claims in the Duchies. Fighting on alone, the Slesvig-Holsteiners were defeated again by the Danes at Isted, though the victors suffered the heavier casualties in 'the bloodiest battle that had ever been fought on Danish ground'.[21] The historic Danevirke was triumphantly regained, yet the disbandment of the rebel army in January 1851 was principally due to the abandonment of all plans for German unity after the Punctation of Olmütz, to which Prussia had submitted in the previous November. The rebels accordingly handed over the Duchies to a Prussian-Austrian commission, so that another year passed before they were formally restored to King Frederick.

The least impermanent result of a confused – and confusing – struggle was that the future of the Duchies had become a major European issue. In August 1850 the great powers (with the exception of Prussia and the addition of Sweden-Norway) had accepted the principle of the integrity of the lands of the Danish monarchy, and in May 1852 they all (including Prussia) agreed upon the Protocol of London, which recognised Prince Christian of Glücksburg as heir to the whole, subject to financial compensation for the Augustenborg claimant. This choice might appear satisfactory, since the 'protocol prince' was a loyal Danish subject, though with leanings towards Germany, and was married to a cousin of the reigning king. No consideration was given to the alternative solution of meeting national claims by a division of Slesvig, albeit during the second armistice period the Duchy had in fact been divided, with a Prussian garrison in the south and a Swedish in the north – an episode which added to the importance of King Oscar's mediatory role throughout the conflict. But the biggest part had been played behind the scenes by the Tsar, who inherited the Gottorp claims in Holstein* but was primarily interested in combating all revolutionary tendencies. He therefore supported the king of Denmark against his rebellious subjects in the Duchies, but deplored the Danish constitution of 1849 and opposed any suggestion of extending it to Slesvig.

Oscar I did not inherit his father's long-standing friendship with Russia, which had indeed been clouded to some extent during the last years of Charles John's reign by the Tsar's objecting to a Swedish project for establishing a free port to attract British trade to the island of Gotland. More serious disagreement developed over a claim which the Russians advanced on behalf of the nomadic Lapps of Finland, whose alleged need for hunting and fishing rights at some point on the Norwegian coast in the far north might conceal – as a vigilant British consul, J. R. Crowe, had suggested to Palmerston – a scheme for acquiring an ice-free harbour for the Russian navy. This dispute had already led to the closing of this remote frontier, which only the Lapps were accustomed to cross, when the Anglo-French attempt to check the aggrandisement of Russia at the other end of its long European border caused the great powers to drift into the Crimean War.

In December 1853 Denmark joined with Sweden-Norway in a declaration of neutrality which was designed to benefit the western allies: apart from seven specified naval bases, all Scandinavian ports would remain open to the warships of any belligerent. This meant that the British and French fleets gained full access to Baltic waters, where only the Russian navy had its own establishments. The Danes, who regarded Russian support as their best safeguard against the revival of German claims in the Duchies, afterwards adopted a more passive role, but the Swedish government promptly raised additional money for defence, and King Oscar himself is believed to have encouraged the flow of propaganda suggesting that the time had come to recover the ancient Scandinavian territories of Finland and the Åland Islands. On 24 July 1854 these were among his terms for an alliance, but he also stipulated the full participation of Austria in the war and a guarantee that its object was 'to reduce Russia to proportions which are less threatening to the future of Europe'.[22]

Until the allies made their landing in the Crimea in September, the Baltic was a prominent theatre of war, but as the Russian fleet kept close inshore its opponents at first confined themselves to blockading activities, varied by occasional raids on Finnish ports. Then in August a six-day bombardment of Bomarsund in Åland was followed by the landing of 10,000 French troops and a proposal that the Swedish army should take over the occupation of the islands, in which case the French would remain in Stockholm for the time being as a precautionary measure. King Oscar would not, however, run the risk of involvement at a juncture when the

---

* Through Peter III of Russia, who was descended from a son of Frederick I; this gave Tsar Nicholas a better claim to the Danish throne than Prince Christian's wife, a descendant of Frederick's grandson.

western allies were directing their attention mainly to the other end of Europe; and when the siege of Sebastopol – which he called 'the attack on the giant's little toe'[23] – was prolonged through the winter, he began to foresee the possibility of a post-war Russia equipping itself with a network of railways to threaten an increasingly disunited Europe. This cautious attitude was encouraged by the small scope of the Allied Baltic operations in the summer of 1855, which comprised largely ineffective bombardments of Kronstadt and Sveaborg.

The fall of Sebastopol after a twelve-month siege made the Swedish king more receptive to the plans presented to him by one of its more successful participants, General Canrobert, for joining the alliance and regaining Finland and Åland as his reward; a mobilisation scheme in his own hand-writing is dated 28 December 1855. He appears not to have suspected that the main object of the *démarche* was to use the prospect of Swedish intervention as an inducement to the new Tsar, Alexander II, to come to terms: when news of the armistice reached him in January, Prince Oscar observed that his father aged ten years in a day. Out of all that he had hoped to gain from the war situation, only two items were achieved. By the treaty of November 1855 he received an Anglo-French guarantee of his territories *vis-à-vis* Russia, undertaking in return to refuse any cession of land or rights to that power; and by the treaty of Paris which terminated the Crimean War, Sweden-Norway gained the modest advantage of a servitude imposed upon the Russians in the Åland Islands, which must henceforth be left unfortified.

Although the November Treaty had to some extent separated the interests of Sweden-Norway from those of Denmark, in the summer of 1856 a further gathering of students, this time under royal patronage, marked the re-establishment of a Scandinavian policy. At Uppsala the editor of *Fædrelandet* assured them that 'Russia looks as greedily towards the harbours of Finnmark as does Germany towards those of Slesvig', and on their return journey they were received by King Oscar at his summer residence, where he described himself with great emphasis as the King of Denmark's 'faithful ally'.[24] In the same year Denmark's negotiations with the United States and other powers, which resulted in the commutation of the Sound Dues (yielding an annual profit of 2 million dollars) for a single payment of 35 millions, were actively promoted by the Swedes, to whose coastwise traffic they had been a serious impediment. The Danes, however, had a less readily soluble problem on their hands in the new constitutional arrangements required for Slesvig-Holstein under the settlement imposed by the powers in 1852.

After the failure of the National Liberals to incorporate Slesvig with the Kingdom, they gave place to a Conservative government. Since the liberal constitution established in the Kingdom in 1849 made a return to the *status quo* impossible, two attempts were made to set up a Council of the Realm or *Rigsråd*, which would handle matters of common concern to the Kingdom and the Duchies. The first version enabled the representatives of the Rigsdag to be outvoted by those of the Duchies and the crown nominees, and was in any case almost purely advisory; this was promulgated as a royal decree by a strongly conservative ministry under A. S. Örsted (the most eminent of Danish jurists and a brother of the physicist), who at the close of 1854 was driven from office by the Rigsdag. The second version, which became law in the following year, gave the Council rather wider powers and an increased membership of 80 – 20 chosen by the Crown, 30 by the Rigsdag and the Estates of the Duchies, and 30 more elected by the wealthiest taxpayers according to the then novel method of proportional representation.

Biennial meetings were duly held, but nationalist resentment was inflamed on the German side because the constitution had not been submitted for the approval of the Estates of the Duchies. This hostility did not lack outside encouragement, for Holstein was a member of the restored German Confederation, whilst the settlement of 1852 entitled all the powers to insist that Denmark retained similar but separate relations with the two Duchies. Moreover, Danish post-war policy challenged the general sympathy with nationalist claims by unreasonably restricting the use of the German language in the parts of Slesvig with mixed population, from which a British vice-consul in 1861 reported 'almost universal dissatisfaction'.[25]

Such was the situation when Oscar I launched the last of his 'Scandinavian' ventures in February 1857. This took the form of the offer to Denmark of a defensive alliance, prompted in part by a visit paid to Scandinavia by Prince Napoleon, cousin of the French Emperor; he had welcomed the thought of a firm Scandinavian union – not 'something intangible like the union of Sweden and Norway'[26] – to be based on the substitution of King Oscar for Prince Christian as heir to Frederick's throne. The treaty project fell through, however, because Frederick's foreign minister* at this juncture was equally opposed to all German interests and to Scandinavianism, which he dismissed as 'such a poetical idea'.[27] Accordingly he induced his master to require that the 18,000 Swedes who were on offer to defend him against German aggression at the Eider frontier should also be available for the obviously impracticable and unjustifiable task of defending Holstein. In the course of the summer the Swedish king's health collapsed, and although he lingered until 1859 the leadership of the Scandinavian movement passed into the hands of his 32-year-old son, Prince Charles, who lacked both the ability and the experience to play any successful part in the hazardous game of power politics.

---

* L. N. von Scheele (1796–1874) was a Holsteiner by birth and a devoted supporter of the Unified State policy; as foreign minister from 1854 to 1857, his influence was enhanced by the support he gave to the king's morganatic wife and former mistress, Countess Danner, whose presence at court caused Frederick to be looked at askance by many other sovereigns.

'A BROTHER IN NEED'

In Denmark Scheele's high-handed action over the proposed alliance led to a reorganisation of the ministry under C. C. Hall, a lawyer of liberal leanings who tried to meet the opposition of the Holstein Estates by suspending the operation of the common constitution in Holstein and Lauenburg. Their reply to this gesture was not to suggest some realistic alternative but to make common cause with the German interests in Slesvig and rely on outside help. The details of the ensuing discussions are of little significance compared with the fact that intervention by the German powers would now have the sympathy of the Tsar, who regarded Denmark as endangering good order in Europe; his attitude in turn influenced Napoleon III, who was anxious to have the Russians on his side when he sought to modify the map of Europe in Italy or elsewhere on the principles of nationality. Some propaganda was, indeed, conducted in Paris and even in London for a solution on a genuinely national basis which had been suggested to Prince Napoleon by King Oscar: Slesvig to be partitioned and its German part joined with Holstein and Lauenburg to form a new independent state under Prince Christian.[28] This would have opened the way for a union of the Scandinavian crowns; but the Danish people, encouraged by the successes of their army in the Three Years War, were interested first and foremost in the Eider frontier, which Hall may all along have intended to claim at the most opportune moment.

In 1858 Hall revived the question of a Swedish alliance, but there was no immediate response from the newly established regent, Crown Prince Charles, or his newly chosen foreign minister, Ludwig Manderström, so Hall and his master returned to their futile negotiations with the hostile Estates. The prince, who succeeded his father on the throne in July 1859, had great personal charm and flamboyant ambitions in the style of his namesake, Charles XII, but the weakness of his character was well known to those who stood near him. More aware than King Oscar had been of deficiencies in the army, with which he had close relations, he tried to find ministers who would remedy them, in Norway as well as in Sweden – a reasonable project which might help to knit his realms together.

Whilst he was still regent, he had appointed as Norwegian minister of justice the son of a senior army officer, who had received his early schooling whilst his father was posted to Stockholm, and as Norwegian *statsminister* there a diplomat who had been in his service when he was for a time viceroy in Norway.* As king, he obtained the approval of the three leading members of his Swedish Cabinet to a plan for strengthening the hands of his ministers in Norway by a valuable 'accession gift' to his subjects there,

---

* C. H. Birch-Reichenwald (1814–91) resigned office as a result of the dispute over Charles XV's 'accession gift', but G. C. Sibbern (1816–1901) long retained the royal favour; apart from one very brief interlude, he held the post of Norwegian *statsminister* in Stockholm throughout the critical period until 1871, and in 1878–84 served as Swedish-Norwegian minister in Paris.

namely consent for the abolition of the obsolete office of Stattholder. However, when a bill to this effect had passed the Storting, all four Estates in the Riksdag demonstrated the feeling – which seems to have been widespread in Sweden by this time – that the Norwegians had proved disappointing partners; the proposed change was therefore unacceptable, except as part of a revision of the terms of union to make the partnership more effective. The result was a double defeat for the young king. By acquiescing in the Riksdag's decision, he gave the Norwegians a good reason for treating the monarchy henceforth as a Swedish institution. At the same time he was made to realise his dependence upon his Swedish Cabinet, of which only one member resigned because he had supported the king's original proposal. This was Charles's close friend, Count Henning Hamilton, whom he sent as his representative to Copenhagen, where he was often at variance with the policy of the minister of justice and foreign minister,* both of whom had originally agreed to the king's 'accession gift' for Norway.

King Charles continued to play an active part in both domestic and foreign affairs, offering his support to the Swedish Liberals in their agitation for a two-chamber parliament (see p. 259), visiting the French and English courts in the Scandinavian cause, and making rash promises of help at convivial meetings with King Frederick. But he found no Cavour to whom he could turn when his ministers thwarted him a second time. In 1859–60 the attention of all Europe, including the German powers, was concentrated upon the unfolding drama of Italian unification, but by the winter of 1862–3 the problem of the Duchies again loomed up. Whilst Hall moved slowly and cautiously to the view that the Eider frontier would have to be defended in arms, Lehmann and Monrad, both of whom were members of his government, made urgent though very secret representations to Hamilton that Denmark was now ready to cement a Scandinavian union by substituting the house of Bernadotte for the 'protocol prince'.

In the first months of 1863 Denmark's prospects appeared brighter, both because Prussia seemed to be crippled by the internal crisis which had just brought Bismarck to the post of minister-president and because the outbreak of rebellion in Russian Poland was expected to isolate the chief reactionary force in Europe. Napoleon III cherished new hopes of reshaping the map of Europe, and King Charles readily supposed that he might somehow regain Finland. As for Britain, the popular enthusiasm for the young Princess of Wales, Prince Christian's daughter Alexandra, might now be expected to counter the special regard for German interests which

* Baron Louis De Geer (1818–96) and C. R. L. Manderström (1806–73). De Geer led the government and in 1876 became the first titular prime minister of Sweden, but his energies were directed mainly to the solution of parliamentary reform, which had reached a critical stage. Manderström, on the other hand, sought to carry out the Scandinavian policy of Oscar I (whose confidant he had been) as far as his colleagues would permit. The course of events was also influenced by the finance minister, J. A. Gripenstedt (1813–74), who was opposed to Scandinavianism in any form and maintained the view that 'the Norwegians needed to be driven with firm reins (– and whip)'.[29]

Queen Victoria inculcated in her ministers. Hall therefore cut the Gordian knot by issuing the March Patent, which gave Holstein its own constitution and formally deprived it of any influence over the affairs of Denmark and Slesvig. When the German Confederation demanded the withdrawal of the Patent on pain of an occupation of Holstein, the two Scandinavian kings met in July, at Skodsborg on the Danish side of the Sound, to consider their common reaction.

Charles XV had only Hamilton in attendance at this momentous meeting, but he claimed that Manderström and the rest of the Cabinet had given advance approval for the alliance on which the Danes were certainly relying. He accordingly promised a force of 20,000 men to help if need be in the defence of the Eider frontier; the Scandinavian policy thereby reached its high-water mark, with Charles's younger brother, the future King Oscar II, giving a party of Danish officers the assurance, 'Denmark's enemies are also ours.'[30] Nevertheless, in early September the king's wishes were thwarted by his principal ministers (Sibbern included), who urged the need to sound the western powers before any further clarification of the aid to be rendered to the Danes. When the king rejoined that he was in any case bound in honour to defend the Eider frontier, Gripenstedt threatened to resign his post and did not scruple to remind his royal master of the fate of Gustavus IV. All that was formally agreed upon was to consult Britain and France, but these powers were at variance regarding Napoleon III's plans for a general European conference and the British foreign secretary, Lord Russell, was canvassing the idea of a new inquiry into the problem of the Duchies.* The prospects for the proposed consultation were therefore bleak in any case, and whereas Manderström would have been satisfied by the offer of support to Denmark by one of them, Gripenstedt was against a Danish alliance unless support was offered by both West European powers.

In mid-November two events in quick succession made Swedish help still more uncertain. A new constitution, which directly united Slesvig with Denmark through a bicameral legislature, offered a provocative challenge to the agreement in 1851–2, which forbade any closer Danish link with one Duchy alone. And before this 'November constitution' had been signed, King Frederick's sudden death resulted in the uncontested though passively received accession of Prince Christian,† which rendered it very unlikely that the reward for military help would be another throne. King Christian gave his signature to the new constitution, though with great reluctance, and before the year ended the troops of the German

---

* Palmerston's celebrated forecast in the House of Commons on 23 July that Denmark's aggressors 'would find in the result, that it would not be Denmark alone with which they would have to contend',[31] is supposed to have referred to action by France, such as is envisaged in a memorandum in Palmerston's handwriting, dated the 27th.

† According to a sixteen-year-old eyewitness, Edvard Brandes, not more than a couple of hundred persons attended the proclamation ceremony in Copenhagen, including a group of students who raised a counter-cry of 'Long live Charles the Fifteenth!'[32]

Confederation had entered Holstein in retaliation and the Augustenborg claimant was installed at Kiel as Duke Frederick VIII.* The only response from Sweden was a telegram to *Fædrelandet*, '22,000 men are coming with Himself',[33] founded upon a royal promise which the government repudiated. Its most warlike gesture was to ask the Riksdag for a war credit of 3 million dollars – about one-eighth of what would have been needed to mobilise and equip the force specified in the telegram. From Norway Birch-Reichenwald's successor, Fredrik Stang – who in 1873 became the first titular prime minister – had already advised the king against making any alliance in the changed circumstances of November.

Although Monrad formed a new Danish ministry, which was ready to repeal the November constitution as soon as public opinion permitted, the opportunity was not one which a Bismarck would let slip. Prussian and Austrian forces crossed the Eider on 1 February 1864, and Danish hopes suffered a severe blow when the Danevirke was abandoned in the first week without any serious fighting: Danish muzzle-loaders were ineffective against the breech-loading Prussian needle-gun, and no advance preparations had been made for a prolonged defence of the ancient earthworks. In mid-April the Danes were driven back from their second main position, at Dybböl, on to the island of Als, which opened Jutland to the enemy; but this time public opinion in Denmark was much encouraged by the stubbornness which had been shown in the defence. It also set great store by the workings of a naval blockade of the German states, which was successfully maintained against an Austrian squadron in an engagement off Heligoland on 10 May.

By then the Danes had reluctantly agreed to attend an international conference in London, which debated the situation under Russell's chairmanship during a suspension of hostilities. Since the French and British were most unlikely to intervene on behalf of what was now obviously a losing cause, Bismarck could afford to ignore the full diplomatic support which Sweden-Norway gave to the Danish claims. This belated display of 'Scandinavian' sympathies must, however, have encouraged Monrad in his refusal even at this late stage to countenance a partitioning of Slesvig at any point farther north than the line of the Schlei and the Danevirke, which left at least one-third of the German-speaking area in Danish hands. His attitude accorded with Danish pride, supposed future defence needs, and a special desire to retain the district of Angeln, which had only been Germanicised within the last two generations. But it also showed an obstinacy which alienated possible sympathisers and could only be based on an altogether unreal estimate of the military prospects.

When the conference broke up at the end of June, the Prussians attacked the island of Als. A plan drawn up by Moltke worked perfectly; the Danes

---

* Duke Christian August was still alive, but he disingenuously transferred the claim to his son, alleging that, as the latter was of age in 1852, he was not bound by his father's promise to allow no claim to be asserted by himself or his 'family'.

withdrew the ironclad which should have protected the crossing, because they were more concerned to defend Fünen; and the loss of Als, where the Danish casualties were ten times those of the invading Germans, created such panic in Copenhagen and such despondency in Jutland (where the occupying forces were already levying a war tax) that Moltke's further plan for crossing the Little Belt into Fünen was not needed. King Christian called to office a Conservative ministry in place of Monrad's, and peace negotiations began on 20 July. The king suggested the possibility that his kingdom should now be incorporated together with the Duchies as part of the German Confederation; alternatively, the Danish negotiators had belated proposals for dividing Slesvig along the more northerly line of Flensborg-Tönder or for redeeming the conquered territory by the offer of the Danish West Indies or even Iceland. But the Prussians and Austrians under Bismarck's guidance were quite inexorable: at Vienna in October all three Duchies were surrendered into their hands, subject to very minor frontier adjustments to allow for enclaves and a temporary provision for optants – Danes who retained their citizenship pending removal northwards across the new boundary.

The loss of population, territory and economic resources was a crushing blow to the Danish monarchy, which had already forfeited the sovereignty of Skåne and more recently of Norway. Since what had been lost included some land of which the population was Scandinavian in language and loyalty, Scandinavia had shrunk *pro tanto*, whilst tentative hopes of its political unification had ended in a complete fiasco. Sweden and Norway, which in the end provided no more than a handful of volunteers to help 'A Brother In Need',* had escaped lightly from a military involvement for which both psychological and practical preparedness were lacking. Next time the United Kingdoms of the House of Bernadotte became the object of international interest, their peoples were engaged in the converse operation of reducing one minor power to two yet smaller sovereign units on the European chessboard.

---

* Title of Ibsen's passionate appeal, published in *Illustreret Nyhedsblad* (Copenhagen) in December 1863 and widely distributed as an offprint in the Scandinavian countries.

Chapter 11

Small Powers in the Shadow of Great Empires, 1864-1914

AN UNOBTRUSIVE ROLE

For an entire generation after the war of 1864, the Scandinavian lands played virtually no part in international relations, a passivity which was encouraged by the fate of the Slesvig Danes after they passed from their control. The Prussian crown jurists in 1865 reached the convenient decision that the proper heir to the Duchies had not been Frederick of Augustenborg but Prince Christian; this prepared the way for the Seven Weeks War and the treaty of Prague, whereby Austria's claims in the matter were transferred to Prussia, subject to the retrocession of northern Slesvig to Christian, 'if the population give evidence in a free vote of their desire to be united with Denmark'.[1] No date was fixed for the fulfilment of a clause which had been inserted at the request of Napoleon III; but in the following year the elections to the parliament of the new North German Confederation recorded a 40 per cent vote for Danish candidates in Slesvig as a whole, which rose to 80 per cent in the rural districts of the north and a majority in Flensborg and three other towns.[2] However, the Franco-Prussian War soon removed Napoleon from the scene, and in 1878 Bismarck's policy no longer aimed at the conciliation of Tsar Alexander II, who favoured the holding of a plebiscite; an agreement was then published, in which Austria-Hungary released the Germans from their pledge. The wishes of the Scandinavian governments were at no point consulted, and the nationalist aspirations of the people of northern Slesvig were ignored for forty-one years – until their recognition was brought about by a war in which no Scandinavian state took part.

Whilst its political influence remained nugatory, Scandinavia underwent an economic transformation which by 1914 had removed all but its peripheral regions – such as the far north, Iceland, and most of Finland – from the category of underdeveloped countries to that of small-scale competitors of the most advanced industrial powers. At the same time, the Scandinavian states participated in the widespread advance towards the establishment of effective parliamentary institutions based on a wide franchise; their progress in this respect was by no means uniform, but by the outbreak of the First World War the individual Scandinavian citizen was among the most fortunate in the eyes of European liberals. This was partly due to the ease with which their small-scale societies were permeated by popular movements – such as co-operation, trade unionism, and social democracy – which originated elsewhere: the gap between the classes and the masses was relatively easy to bridge.

Yet among the features of Scandinavian history which demand attention in this period, the one which caught the contemporary eye most readily was still the workings of separatist nationalism. Iceland achieved self-government at the very time when European scholars were developing a fresh interest in its romantic past. Norway, which was now on the beaten path for tourists from both sides of the Atlantic, interested much larger numbers, and the disputes which ended in the severance of its dynastic link with Sweden were the subject of more or less well informed comment in the world press for a quarter of a century before the final crisis in 1905. Yet it was Finland's struggle against the rising tide of Russification which, from the late 1890s onwards, attracted the widest attention as a small people's dramatic fight for freedom. A brief survey of this conflict leads on naturally to the final topic of Scandinavia's reluctant re-involvement in international affairs through the growth of the rival power blocs in the opening years of the new century.

THE ECONOMIC TRANSITION

In 1865 the Scandinavian countries were still predominantly agricultural, which made their economic position extremely precarious when the cheap grain of America and Russia began to flood into the European market, so that between 1872 and the close of the century the price of corn fell by one-half. Nevertheless, they contrived to support a rising population at a generally rising standard of living. As to the former, the next half-century witnessed a growth in Sweden from a little over 4 to a little under 6 million inhabitants, in Denmark from $1\frac{3}{4}$ to $2\frac{3}{4}$ millions, in Norway from $1\frac{3}{4}$ to $2\frac{1}{2}$ millions, in Finland from $1\frac{3}{4}$ to $2\frac{3}{4}$ millions, and in Iceland from 67,000 to 89,000. As to the latter, a Swedish study points to an overall increase in real income of 310 per cent (1861–1914), falling to 270 for industrial workers and 230 for farm labourers.[3] No comparable studies are yet available for the other countries, and Finland and Iceland were certainly far behind Sweden because of a chronic shortage of both domestic and imported capital. But it is safe to say that in 1914 the typical Scandinavian citizen was better off than his father – and much better off than his grandfather – had ever been; and if the rich did not brook comparison with the millionaire class in the greater plutocracies neither was there any large mass of desperate misery to compare with the plight of the 'submerged tenth' in Charles Booth's London or Seebohm Rowntree's York.

The Danes showed a remarkable resilience in facing up to the economic consequences of the political catastrophe of 1864. Within two years a young road engineer in Jutland founded the Danish Heath Society to promote land reclamation, particularly in the sandy areas which the Jutland peasantry had neglected because it might take a whole generation's work to secure the full results. Draining and afforestation produced new farmland on which to settle a part of the landless rural proletariat; by 1914 the addition to the cultivated area in Jutland alone was equal to what had been lost to Danish enterprise in northern Slesvig. A still greater feat was the switch the Danes made in little more than a decade from corn to animal products, when their traditional export of the former suddenly became unprofitable. They continued to expand the area under cultivation, but devoted it increasingly to fodder crops and sugar-beet, so that they could take full advantage of the cheap imported bread-grain. Their own basic export was now dairy produce and pig meat, of which the farms contrived to send abroad standard types and qualities, carefully adapted to the British and continental markets. This was organised through a remarkable proliferation of agricultural co-operatives, for which the way was prepared by the broadening influence of the folk high schools, whose numbers were approximately quadrupled in the first decade after the war.*

Danish industry – especially handicraft products for the home market – derived some encouragement from the new frontier, which kept out competition from Holstein and helped Copenhagen to regain the central position which it had partly lost to Hamburg. The lack of native raw materials for manufactures was mitigated by Copenhagen's situation on the seaways, which facilitated the importation of coal and iron; and although half of the new industrial growth was in food products, such as beet sugar and beer, engineering and shipbuilding began to flourish. A single energetic entrepreneur, T. F. Tietgen, founded a telegraph company, a shipping company (DFDS), and the great engineering firm of Burmeister & Wain, which in the 1870s gave Denmark new world-wide connections. In 1897 these were consolidated by the foundation in Copenhagen of the East Asiatic Company, originally as a link between Scandinavia and Thailand: by 1914 it had a widespread network of 16,000 employees, providing trade outlets for the industries and shipping of the home country, and was the owner of the first oceangoing motor-ship in the world, built with diesel engines by Burmeister & Wain.

By the end of the century Norwegian agriculture had accommodated itself to world changes through a 15 per cent reduction of the arable area and an approximate doubling of the milk supply, whilst railway construction made it easier for dairy produce to find a market. The

---

* From 1872 onwards their courses attracted about 13 per cent of the relevant age-group, men being about twice as numerous as women; by the end of the century almost one-quarter of the pupils came from cottar homes.[4]

Norwegians had less need to reorganise their basic exports of fish, metals and timber, though from the 1880s onwards an increasing proportion of wood was sent abroad more profitably as pulp or paper. This was also the period when Svend Foyn (see p. 296) pioneered a more remunerative form of whaling along the coast of north Norway and farther afield, and refrigeration had not yet terminated the export of ice, which by 1898 totalled more than half a million tons. Nevertheless, the chief stimulus to economic growth came from the continued expansion of Norwegian shipping; this reduced freight costs for imports – such as coal in ballast – and exports, whilst its highly profitable carrying trade earned on distant voyages some of the capital needed for the growth of manufacturing industry, hitherto virtually confined to water-powered textile mills and small-scale engineering.

It was in 1868 that Björnson wrote his 'Song of the Norwegian Seaman', proclaiming:

> Our glory and our might
> Are borne on sail-wings white.[5]

Next year the opening of the Suez Canal marked a decisive stage in the long-drawn-out contest between sail and steam, but for two more decades the Norwegian mercantile marine continued in general to pursue the methods which had given it prosperity. Its ships were cheap, including the many which were bought second-hand when other fleets converted to steam; so were its crews, drawn from a countryside where the agricultural crisis reduced employment. As for its skippers, they were usually self-made men who combined their knowledge of the sea with a flair for striking bargains over the cargoes with which their vessels tramped from port to port. In 1880 Norway possessed the third largest of the world's merchant navies. By 1900 it employed steamers on all except the long, slow hauls, and even the sailing ships were now iron-built, so the little shipyards of southern Norway with their ready access to native timber supplies had had their day. But Norwegian shipowners turned instead to the building up of regular lines with fixed schedules, which enabled them to continue to deploy a larger tonnage than all except four or five of the great powers.

By the middle of the nineteenth century the progress of the enclosure movement had made Sweden a land of many medium-sized holdings, with high farming in the English sense flourishing particularly in Skåne. Although the agricultural crisis of the later 1870s brought about an ultimately successful agitation for a tariff (see p. 260), Swedish farmers suffered less than many others. Their export market was chiefly for oats, which did not cheapen as much as wheat; they resorted to selected strains of seed (some of which also proved applicable to Norwegian soils); and the cream separator (see p. 264) helped to make butter production a profitable alternative. As for industry, in the 1850s, when the steam-driven sawmill began to eat into the almost limitless forests of Norrland, Sweden developed a second export to match the traditional trade in bar-iron; this, too, had recently taken on a new lease of life through the introduction (from Monmouthshire) of the coal-economising 'Lancashire hearth'. In the years 1870–5, during which the GNP rose by 30 per cent, the export of timber was fast approaching its peak, whilst a start had been made in the manufacture of cheap steel by the Bessemer process, which a Swedish ironmaster (G. F. Göransson) was the first to exploit successfully.

Thus a third boom period at the turn of the century saw the highly industrialised Sweden of today beginning to take shape. The proportion of population engaged in agriculture fell rapidly; pulp and paper were proving to be even more profitable exports than timber; and the English invention of the basic process for the exploitation of phosphoric iron ores gave northern Sweden a new primary export, for which the demand has proved almost inexhaustible. Furthermore, the dawn of the age of electricity offered new scope for the engineering skills – an inheritance perhaps, from their long-established metal industries – which have made Swedish inventors and workmanship world-famous. A native survey of the years 1850–1914 therefore seems justified in concluding: 'Sweden's industrial development probably occurred more swiftly than any other European country's at that time.'[6]

Finland's development presents a rather bleak contrast to that of her western neighbour.* As late as 1910 two-thirds of a rapidly growing population depended on agriculture, which had at first concentrated on grain, much of it grown with meagre equipment in forest clearances; then, after the famine of 1867 (when the death rate for one year rose to approximately 8 per cent),[7] the larger properties were converted to dairy-farming, which produced an export of butter of less value than the imports of cheap Russian grain. Rural Finland therefore depended very much upon the timber trade, which provided one-half of the exports and employed much part-time labour at low wages in the forests. Industry made some important advances in 1859–85, when free trade with the Russian Empire stimulated the cotton factories of Tampere and the scattered ironworks, and after the reintroduction of tariffs in the latter year Finnish manufacturers contrived to find a new way into the Russian market with engineering products. Yet in 1914 Finland remained a land where industrial wages and conditions were depressed because of under-employment in the overpopulated countryside.

The pattern of events in the three Scandinavian kingdoms presents

---

* This is illustrated by the long-continued Finnish practice of migrating in times of dearth into certain areas of north Norway; these were too barren to attract Norwegian settlers, but a meagre livelihood might be eked out from the fisheries. As late as 1950 the county of Finnmark had a Finnish-speaking population of 1,400 – about one-fifth of the number that spoke Lappish.

many common features, including their dependence for economic growth upon periods of prosperity in the larger economies, especially those of western Europe. In spite of the collapse of political Scandinavianism in 1864, conferences of jurists, economists and various trade interests helped to keep them in step. In 1875, for example, the three states adopted the metric system together and also completed a more significant companion agreement, by which a new currency unit, the *krone*, was to have a gold value of £0·05625 and, though minted separately in each country, was to be legal tender in all. All three borrowed heavily abroad, through State loans, the connections of their commercial banks, and funds raised by particular industries. Sweden and Norway were also alike in that the great distances and difficulties of terrain and climate necessitated very heavy expenditure on road and rail communications. The railway did not enter the northern half of Sweden until 1886 and the network there took another thirty years to complete; in Norway, where the obstacles were still greater, even in the southern half, Oslo and Bergen (as mentioned earlier) had no rail link until 1909 and no uninterrupted road connection as late as 1976. Denmark's problems in these respects were much smaller, yet to travel overland between Copenhagen and the west Jutland port of Esbjerg, opened in 1868, involved two ferry crossings – and it was not until 1935 that even the $\frac{3}{4}$-mile-wide Little Belt was bridged.

So long as the coal-fired steam-engine was the basic factor in industrial development, the Scandinavian states all lay under a severe handicap. For Denmark, indeed, this continued into the twentieth century: in 1883 its industries had 30,000 steam hp at their disposal; in 1897, 73,000; and in 1909, 115,000.[8] But for Sweden and Norway the introduction of hydro-electricity marked a new era. It was used in a Swedish cotton-spinning mill as early as 1882, and in 1890 provided street lighting for Hammerfest in the far north of Norway. The main breakthrough came, however, after 1900: by that date both countries derived about two-thirds of their electricity from the waterfalls, whilst at Sarpsborg on Norway's largest river (Glomma) international enterprise had built a power station to supply both a carbide factory and the needs of a neighbouring town. In Sweden the total hp used in industry rose from 267,000 in 1897 to 518,000 in 1907 and 1,139,000 in 1913;[9] the proportion derived from the new source increased all the more rapidly because the Swedes were among the world's leading manufacturers of electrical equipment and their great commercial banks had relatively easy access to capital. Lacking these two advantages, Norwegian industry continued to be on a much smaller scale; yet by 1912 industrial hp per worker was twice what it had been two decades earlier and the huge falls at Rjukan operated the then largest generating station in the world.[10] The Swedes used the new power source to improve the performance of many existing industries, as for example the electric furnace and forge for steelmaking; the Norwegians took advantage of the proximity of many falls to the west-coast fiords to build up new manufactures, such as aluminium from Canadian bauxite, whilst at Rjukan and elsewhere the firm of Norsk Hydro exploited a native invention for its 'Norwegian saltpetre' (see p. 296). In both countries the state played an active part in the great changes. In 1906 the Swedish Riksdag decided to develop the Trollhättan falls on the Göta river as a government enter- prise, a pattern which was followed in other big power projects. From 1907 onwards Norway's hotly contested Concession Laws provided that foreign and other privately developed installations should eventually become state property, and in 1914 state help was made available for small installations built to meet local needs.

A general feature of the half-century was the fall in the proportion of population which derived its livelihood from agriculture. In Sweden it shrank from three-quarters to less than one-half (1870–1910), and even in Denmark efficient techniques reduced the amount of human labour required for dairy exports. Industrial employment was to some extent to be found in rural surroundings, especially when electric power became easily accessible, but the tendency was for persons in search of work to drift into the towns. In 1911 Copenhagen was still the largest town in Scandinavia; its 560,000 inhabitants represented almost a fourfold increase in half a century. The other capitals, industrial centres and ports followed suit in a process which affected both political and social developments, since an urban population was better able to claim political rights and what it regarded as social justice. But before turning to these subjects, some mention must be made of emigration as an economic factor which acted as a safety-valve.

In 1865–70, when the end of the American Civil War gave full weight to the Homestead Act's offer of free land to all comers, one in ten of all immigrants to the United States were Scandinavians. The proportion was never again so high, but in 1881–5 and 1901–5 the Scandinavian totals reached new heights and they remained important down to the First World War. The pull of America was strengthened by the growing ease of transport by passenger steamer and the transatlantic railroad; the cost of a ticket fell until in 1904 competition for a time reduced the fare from Copenhagen to Kr. 60.[11] The propaganda of the agents sent over by the various American interests was effectively supported by letters home, by visitors to the old country exuding their new prosperity, and by the growing practice of sending tickets purchased in America for bringing out one's family or friends. This was particularly important because family emigration gave place to an exodus of young adults: after 1900 two-thirds emigrated between the ages of fifteen and thirty.[12]

But for old and young alike 'the primary cause was without doubt the hope of improving one's economic condition', as a Swedish-American religious leader candidly acknowledged.[13] In the first place this meant the free land, which advances in transport and other technologies made it rewarding to cultivate for the export market. In the second place it meant the relatively high wages which could be earned on the far side of the Atlantic by miners, sailors and artisans, and even by unskilled labourers and domestic servants, because there the exploitation of abundant natural resources more than kept pace with a rapid growth of population. And by the turn of the century the wealth of America also attracted yet a third type of person to the emigrant ships, namely the many trained engineers and well qualified craftsmen who went out with every intention of returning with the quick fortune which was so hard to come by at home.

Generalisation as to the motives which drove the typical emigrant from the land he left is very difficult: there were special local emergencies, such as the famine in north Sweden and Finland in 1867; exoduses in search of the fuller religious liberty to be found where there was no state church; and a good many political radicals following in the wake of Thrane – including those whose radicalism expressed itself in a desire to escape compulsory military service. But in Sweden and Norway emigration was above all the safety-valve for the underprivileged elements in rural society – younger sons of farmers, cottar families, farm labourers – which had increased very rapidly in the first two-thirds of the century. As the gulf widened between their position in life and that of those who held a sufficiency of land, they tended to move first to the towns, where new-comers would find the competition for jobs and still more for living accommodation discouraging. The towns therefore in many cases served as staging-posts for the move to rural America, which offered what they lacked, namely land of their own. This remained true of the Norwegians right down to 1914, though the more rapid growth of industry in Sweden made it natural for an increasing proportion of Swedes to settle in the urban environment with which they were already to some extent familiar.

Emigration from Denmark was on a smaller scale; indeed, after 1900 it was sometimes below the European average.[14] Since a larger proportion of cottars had viable holdings, the movement was chiefly from the smaller, more stagnant towns; allowing for the early settlements in Utah, the Danes by 1900 were probably as urban in their preferences as the Swedes. In Iceland the Mormon missionaries played a part, as in Denmark, but large-scale emigration was confined to the years 1873–90, during which a population of little more than 70,000 sent out at least 12,000 to the United States and especially to newly opened-up areas in Canada, where 'New Iceland' was established on the west shore of Lake Winnipeg.[15] The up-swing of the fisheries and the down-swing of Danish political surveillance of the island then reduced the movement to a trickle of replenishments for existing settlements. As for Finland, the most striking feature is the belated commencement of emigration. When the famine of the late 1860s (already mentioned) sent 80,000 Swedes across the Atlantic in two years, they were accompanied by fewer than 1,000 Finns.[16] It was not until 1883, when a steamer route was established between Hanko and Hull, that they began to leave Ostrobothnia, where both tar distilling and wooden ship building had declined, and two more decades passed before there was any mass movement among the rural poor. Since they had for at least a generation constituted about three-fifths of the total agrarian population of a country where large-scale industry was of recent growth, it seems clear that it required the nationalist struggle against Russia to rouse a class which had been too desperately poor to assert itself.

The US Census of 1910, in which immigrants are reported under the two heads of 'foreign-born' and 'native of foreign parentage', counted 1,200,000 Swedes, 800,000 Norwegians, 330,000 Danes (including Icelanders), and 200,000 Finns.[17] These $2\frac{1}{2}$ millions were a not inconsiderable factor in a people of 92 millions, and although the moiety which was American-born passed rapidly into the melting-pot of American society, Scandinavian culture made some impact in the New World, to which reference will be made later. But the reaction on Old World politics was slight. As early as 1880 the Norwegian nationalist propaganda of Björnson (see p. 289) aroused only a tepid interest when he toured the Middle West, notwithstanding the considerable sums remitted to each of the Scandinavian countries to relieve the economic distress of which so many of the immigrants had bitter personal experience.

THE POLITICAL OUTLOOK

The internal politics of the Scandinavian peoples attracted little attention in the outside world. The issues were not dramatic, and the parliaments which discussed them occupied in general a middle position. They were more effectively democratic than the legislatures of the great empires of central (and, later, eastern) Europe, but were more class-ridden than those of France or, in some respects, Britain under the Reform Act of 1884. The principle that the ministers of the crown were responsible to popularly elected representatives was established in Norway in 1884, in Denmark in 1901, and in Sweden in 1917 – a 33-year spread which points to the fact that their political evolution was different and requires individual treatment.

The war had left Denmark with two sets of parliamentary institutions covering identically the same small area, namely the *Rigsdag* (dating from 1849) and the *Rigsråd* of November 1863, to which the first elections had been held in the spring. The lower house (*Folketing*) was based on the same franchise in both cases, but the November constitution had provided the *Rigsråd* with an upper house (*Landsting*) on a much narrower franchise, designed to make the intended union more acceptable in Slesvig. Since the National Liberals were discredited by the defeat, the lead was now taken by a group of conservative-minded large landowners, who induced all four existing Houses to approve the revised constitution of July 1866. The *Rigsråd* disappeared; the *Folketing* retained its existing democratic basis, with elections in single-member constituencies of which three-quarters were rural; and the *Landsting* was reshaped so as to represent large property. Twelve of its members were to be nominees of the Crown, two chosen in the Faeroes and Bornholm, and the other fifty-two by electoral colleges for the capital – which was allocated seven seats – and large provincial districts; one-half of each college was elected by all who had the Folketing franchise, the other half by the wealthiest taxpayers alone. No provision was made for resolving a deadlock between the two Houses.

The upshot was a long period of conservative ministries, which had the full support of King Christian IX and a majority in the Landsting, where many former National Liberals backed the big landowners in order to keep down the influence of the farmers, who by 1872 had a clear majority in the Folketing. In that year the latter established the first definite party, that of the Left (*Venstre*), which soon attracted a number of urban radicals such as Edvard Brandes, whose brother Georg was the champion of advanced views in the arts (see p. 288). The Right (*Höjre*) likewise formed an organised party under the able leadership of J. B. S. Estrup, and a bitter dispute developed over his determination to refortify Copenhagen – a project which advanced radicals denounced as useless and which many farmers also viewed with disfavour, as implying that rural Denmark was regarded as expendable in the event of another invasion. Estrup, however, raised the money he needed for this and other purposes by using provisional laws to collect the taxes which the Folketing refused to authorise. The conflict became so acute that in 1885 a special force of mounted gendarmes was set up to overawe the masses, especially in Copenhagen, where there was even an attempt on Estrup's life. Nine years later a compromise was reached, by which the Folketing accepted the obligation to maintain the forts already built in return for the acceptance of its right to approve the Budget. Estrup gave place to a more moderate Conservative, but Venstre was now more united than before under a resourceful leader, J. C. Christensen, and the Right so disunited that by 1901 it held only 8 seats in the Folketing – where the aged king could observe the ominous arrival of twelve Social Democrats.

The 'Change of System' began in that year with the appointment as premier of a legal expert acceptable to King Christian on account of his services to the new East Asiatic Company, the other ministers being Venstre nominees such as Christensen and – for the first time – a farmer. Significant reforms followed, such as the replacement of the ancient land tax on farms by property and income taxes which also tapped the wealth of the urban middle classes. In January 1905 Christensen succeeded to the premiership, but the execution of his policy of moderate reform was interrupted after less than four years in spite of the cordial support of King Frederick VIII, who succeeded his father in 1906. Venstre was challenged by a new party of Radicals (*Radikale Venstre*), in which urban intellectuals won the support of the underprivileged classes of the countryside for a programme of reduced defence expenditure and increased social services. In 1908 the challenge became serious, because Christensen

felt obliged to resign after his minister of justice received an eight-year
prison sentence for a long series of financial malpractices. A viable
administration was formed again in 1913, but its head was the Radical
leader, C. T. Zahle, and it was dependent upon Social Democratic support
in the Folketing. The Radical Cabinet included defence reductions in its
programme, and when war broke out in Europe next year Danish attention
was engrossed by the more congenial subject of constitutional reform.

Although the profound change which was made in Swedish institutions
in 1865 was not, like the Danish, due primarily to the crisis in foreign
relations, Charles XV's support for the Swedish liberals at this juncture
was connected with his dynastic ambitions, whilst some of the mass
support for their programme came from the volunteer movement in the
shape of petitions which denounced both 'the external and the internal
Russia'.[18] The replacement of the existing legislature by two chambers
had been mooted as early as 1810, and since then the composition of the
three lower Estates had been modified on no fewer than seven occasions.
In 1862 De Geer judged that the time was ripe for a larger step – the
reform of local government, including the introduction of county councils
and a new local government franchise, in which each taxpayer had a vote
weighted according to his wealth. This done, he presented the Estates
with his proposals for their own replacement by a bicameral system, of
which the United States offered a familiar example. The two lower
Estates being favourable and the Clergy having resolved to follow the
decision of the House of Nobles, the last-named was the scene of the
final debate in December 1865. Count Henning Hamilton headed the
opposition, but he was defeated by a vote of 361 to 294, and in 1867 the
new two-chamber Riksdag assembled for its first annual session.

The electors to the Second Chamber were to be the freeholders whose
property was valued at 1,000 dollars, tenants of agricultural property
valued at 6,000 dollars, and persons with an income of 800 dollars: this
enfranchised one adult male in five and many more farmers than townsmen. The electors to the First Chamber were to be the members of town
and county councils, who had themselves been chosen, as we have seen,
on a system biased on the side of wealth. The members of the Second
Chamber needed only the same qualification as their electors, but the
First Chamber was to be recruited from owners of freehold property
valued at 80,000 dollars or yielding a taxable income of 4,000 dollars,
qualifications possessed by about 6,000 persons in all. Legislation required
the assent of both houses, but financial disagreements were to be put to a
joint vote, which gave the advantage to the more numerous Second
Chamber. As for their relations with the Crown, they had no say in the
choice of ministers and although constituted for different periods – the
First Chamber by an annual renewal of one-ninth of its membership,
the Second by triennial general elections – were liable to be dissolved
jointly or separately at any time.

The result was a First Chamber of a more aristocratic or at least a more plutocratic complexion than the old House of Nobles (which had contained many impoverished heads of ancient families), and a Second Chamber where the farmers had most influence. The fact that for the first two decades only one-quarter of the electorate exerted its right to vote encouraged the retention of aristocratic Cabinets, as in Denmark; no commoner headed a ministry until 1883, no farmer held any Cabinet office until 1905. The course of events in Denmark was further paralleled by a bitter dispute between estate owners and farmers, the latter demanding the abolition of the *indelningsverk* and the land tax, both of which rested heavily on the farming population; in their place they wanted general conscription for a more economically managed army and taxation spread to other forms of wealth than land. But in Sweden a tentative compromise was fixed up as early as 1885, because protection loomed up as an issue which divided the agrarian party and closely interested the growing body of industrialists.

King Oscar II sided with the free traders, who included the dairy farmers and the fixed-income groups which benefited from cheap bread. In 1887 he employed his prerogative to dissolve the Second Chamber, so as to obtain a free-trade majority to match that which already existed in the First Chamber. The device succeeded, but before the end of the year the tables were turned on the king and the free-trade ministry when a technical irregularity was brought to light in an election return for Stockholm, which unseated all twenty-two representatives of the capital* and gave a majority to their protectionist opponents. In this rather roundabout way a moderate tariff was established for both agriculture and industry, the king accompanying his consent by a note in the Cabinet protocol that the extra revenue ought to be devoted primarily to the welfare of those classes of his subjects who suffered by the rise in prices. In the last nine years of the century the prevailing attitude of compromise inspired the highly successful ministry of E. G. B. Boström, who started the modern Swedish army on the basis of ninety days' recruit training for all and gradually replaced the ancient and inequitable land tax by taxes on income, property, and inheritance.

As we shall see later, military changes were necessitated by external dangers, which in 1901 caused the service period to be increased to a total of 8–12 months. But they automatically strengthened the case for enlarging the franchise. Boström was content to argue that rising prosperity would bring it within the reach of a larger proportion of citizens, but in 1900 a united Liberal Party was formed by Karl Staaff, who introduced a manhood suffrage bill during his first, short ministry in

---

* Before 1890 Stockholm was a single constituency returning twenty-two members; the free-traders had received enough votes to win all twenty-two seats, but their entire list was annulled because one of their candidates was found to be ineligible on account of a sum of Kr. 11·58 owing in municipal taxation.

1905-6, when the enfranchised population was still no more than 8 per cent. The reform was actually carried through both houses in 1909 in a compromise form adopted by the Conservatives; this gave every man a vote for the Second Chamber, provided he had reached the age of 24 (instead of 21, as previously) and had paid state and local taxes for the preceding three years. At the same time the elections to both houses were to be based on proportional representation, so as to safeguard minority interests, and the First Chamber was brought to some extent into harmony with the Second by reducing the predominance of wealth in the local councils which elected it: in future no person or institution could have more than forty votes in any local government area. The effect was to raise the enfranchised part of the population to 19 per cent, whilst the multiple constituencies required for P.R. added to the role of the political parties, which set up the lists of candidates; in 1911 the first election under the new system enabled Staaff to take office again with 102 supporters in the Second Chamber, where the Conservatives and the rising party of Social Democrats each mustered 64.

Norway in the meantime had moved more rapidly than the other two towards political democracy, which was linked with its separatist aspirations. These had been given more vigorous expression since 1869, when annual sessions were introduced into the Storting on the model of the Swedish Riksdag, so that the parliamentary talents of Johan Sverdrup* had freer play in building up an alliance between the urban radicals and a far more numerous body of nationally-minded farmers. He sought to bring the ministry, which was still composed of leading bureaucrats, under the control of the Storting by requiring its members to take part in parliamentary discussions (as in Sweden), but King Oscar protected their independent position by three times vetoing the bill which was passed for this purpose. On the third occasion Sverdrup's supporters, now organised as the Venstre Party, claimed that the veto was no longer valid, whilst the more loosely formed organisation of the officials or Right Party maintained that in constitutional issues the royal veto was not suspensive but absolute. In 1884 an impeachment of the ministers produced a partisan verdict, condemning them to loss of office and/or fines; after a tense interval, during which King Oscar found that neither the condemned Cabinet nor its colleagues in Sweden supported his vague proposals for a *coup d'état*, Sverdrup took office at the head of a Venstre ministry, which clearly derived its authority from the Storting instead of the Crown.

* 1816-92. The son of an estate manager who pioneered agricultural education in Norway, he was a lawyer with remarkable gifts of oratory and political manipulation; sometimes described as 'Norway's Gladstone', but inspired above all by the ideas of the French Revolution. In spite of his success in establishing the responsibility of the Cabinet to the Storting, his premiership lasted only from June 1884 to July 1889, as his personal followers dwindled to a small group of moderates (*Moderate Venstre*) after a bitter quarrel, in which they upheld Puritan ethics and Church principles against the Radical intelligentsia or *Rene Venstre*.

Since his support came principally from the wealthier element among the farmers, Sverdrup's franchise policy was very cautious, the income requirement for a vote being reduced in 1885 to an extent which added about one-half to the electorate in the towns but hardly more than one-quarter to the much larger rural electorate. Venstre, however, was very soon split between a dwindling group of Moderates under Sverdrup and a Radical element, both of which sought to achieve popularity by a confrontation with Sweden (see p. 269). It was only when this ended in temporary failure that the Radicals took seriously the demand for manhood suffrage which had long figured on their programme; this was made law in 1898, with an exception for persons in receipt of poor relief. Three years later the same democratic franchise was adopted in local elections, albeit that an increase of 125 per cent in those entitled to vote in national elections had added only 40 per cent to the numbers at the polls. But in the crisis of 1905 the democratic electorate (as we shall see) added greatly to the strength of the nationalist claims, since a turnout of 85·4 per cent voted almost unanimously in support of the separation from Sweden.

The desire to mobilise nationalist supporters also helps to explain a faster advance to votes for women in Norway than in the other two kingdoms. They had not lagged behind the Norwegians in the general feminist movement: the Danish Women's Association, founded in 1871 – two years after Georg Brandes had translated Mill *On the Subjugation of Women* – was the first of its kind in northern Europe, and both Swedish and Danish universities were opened to them in that decade, the Norwegian not until the 1880s. Yet in Norway the local franchise was thrown open in 1901, subject to a moderate income requirement from the voter or her husband, thus preparing the way for an address organised by the women's suffrage union in 1905, which added 75 per cent to the male vote recorded in the plebiscite. This in turn led to the opening of the franchise in national elections (subject to the existing income requirement) in 1907, followed by equal franchise laws for local and national elections in 1910 and 1913 respectively.

This legislation was completed by a Venstre Party government, which came into office with a strong majority in January 1913 and which also took a 'nationalist' line in confirming the Concession Laws (see p. 255). In both Sweden and Denmark, the aims of the Liberal parties regarding female suffrage were held in check by the conservative social attitude of the farming population, except that the Danish local franchise was opened to taxpayers of both sexes in 1909. The bitter nationalist conflict in Finland, on the other hand – where the high-handed measures of governor-general Bobrikov (see p. 277) included compulsory Russian-language instruction in girls' schools so as to infiltrate 'family life through the mediation of the women'[19] – produced even swifter advances than in Norway. The constitution of July 1906 was the first in Europe to establish universal suffrage, and in the following year nineteen women were elected to the Finnish Diet from an electorate where they were in the majority.

SOCIAL PROGRESS

In a period when the political, no less than the economic, life of the Scandinavian states was dominated by the middle class, the liberal tradition was nevertheless strong enough to allow free play to reform movements of every kind, even such as aimed at the eventual overthrow of the capitalist structure of society. Social progress in each country was stimulated in broadly similar ways, partly because they had the same human needs and partly because new impulses were derived from the experience of larger communities, both in America and western Europe.

The churches of Scandinavia, for example, were much influenced by German Lutheran theologians, since they had no single outstanding leader within their own ranks to compare with Grundtvig, who died in 1872. Religious life in each country centred upon two groups of clergy: High Churchmen, strongly entrenched in government circles and in the universities (except Uppsala); and Low Churchmen, often with an affinity for Pietism, who collaborated more readily with laymen's organisations for promoting higher moral standards at home and the conversion of the heathen abroad. In Sweden the death of Rosenius in 1866 was preceded by the establishment of an Evangelical Association, which after a century is still the main Low Church institution; in Denmark the Home Mission by 1900 had built about 400 centres, staffed by 150 evangelists; and in Norway the fundamentalist element in the Church was so strong that in 1908 it was able to set up its own Congregational Faculty (*Menighetsfakultetet*) on an equal footing with the theological studies of the University of Oslo. A parallel development was the growth of dissenting religious communities outside the State Church: these were strongest in Sweden – where part of the Evangelical Association seceded in 1878 to form a sect in which laymen might administer the Sacrament – but Baptists, Methodists, and the Salvation Army became active in all the larger Scandinavian towns. Whilst the Salvationists were probably the best organised to care for the body as well as the soul, the tendency was for each religious body, from the Home Mission to the smallest and most emotional of the sects, to engage in work for the aged poor, the sick, and other groups for whose needs the State as yet made little provision.

Church people, as we might expect, were prominent in the revival of the temperance movement, which met the challenge of the increased spending-power of many wage-earners by campaigning for total abstinence. This time the movement came to Norway through the Quaker contacts with England, to Sweden and Denmark through the Good Templar organisation from America, whilst the Finnish Friends of Temperance had a nationalist motive as well, because the Russians encouraged the importation of vodka. By 1914 its ramifications were wider than those of any other social welfare crusade, with 350,000 members in Sweden, 250,000 in Norway, and 175,000 in Denmark, whilst prohibition measures had been passed by the Finnish Diet (but subsequently vetoed) and actually brought into effect in Iceland, where all liquor was imported. The most important practical development, which attracted attention in the outside world, was the spread through much of Sweden, Norway and Finland of variations upon a licensing system which had been introduced at Gothenburg in 1865. Under its provisions a locality could transfer the trade in spirits to a company owned by the public, to whom its profits accrued; the social benefits of the system included a reduction in the alcoholic strength of the wares sold, a refusal to sell to persons under 18 (the legal limit then being 15 years), and the encouragement of the purchase of food in place of liquor.

The consumers' co-operative movement came to Scandinavia from England: the work of the Rochdale Pioneers had imitators in Sweden in 1850, by 1860 Eilert Sundt was lecturing on the subject to Oslo artisans, and in 1866 a fellow clergyman set up the first Danish store for workers in a small town in north Jutland. But growth was at first slow – in scattered rural districts it was difficult to collect customers, and at least in Denmark the Social Democratic movement opposed co-operative shops in the towns on the ground that, if the workers were enabled to live more cheaply, wages would fall. Co-operative wholesale societies, marking the achievement of full stability, were formed in Norway and Denmark in the 1890s, in Sweden and Finland in the first decade of the new century. Such societies became active manufacturers on their own account, yet the pioneer co-operator who launched Denmark's CWS* could still maintain as his creed: 'The co-operative cause has three distinct tasks, to be named in their order of importance: 1) improvement, 2) education, 3) economic support.'[20]

Although the first co-operative dairy in Scandinavia figured briefly in a Norwegian valley in 1856, producers' co-operation grew up chiefly in Denmark, where the small farmers saw the advantages enjoyed by the large estates in producing and marketing a standard export product. De Laval's cream separator – which had a Danish forerunner – made it attractively easy to systematise the production of butter, each farmer's milk being graded according to its fat content and the appropriate quantity of skimmed milk returned for the pigs. A similar improvement in bacon exports resulted from the introduction in 1887 of co-operative slaughter-houses, which paid the highest price for the precise type of streaky bacon then in favour for the British breakfast table; this in turn suggested the

---

* Severin Jörgensen (1842–1926) turned his own shop into a co-operative concern in 1868, and in later years combined the management of the Danish Wholesale Society with propaganda for the co-operative ideal, to which his original approach had been religious.

economy of combining for the purchase of fodder and farm equipment of all kinds. The rapid growth of the system was assured as soon as large and small farmers had learnt to trust each other on the democratic basis of one man, one vote, albeit that the wealthier members had a proportionately bigger financial stake in the efficient management of any producers' co-operative. These characteristically Danish institutions spread throughout rural Scandinavia, enhancing the farmer's income and making him more self-reliant in the field of politics.

In the towns, however, self-help depended on the twin forces of trade unionism and the Social Democratic movement, both of which entered Scandinavia across Denmark from Germany. Just as Thrane had brought to Norway the ideas which inspired the French Revolution of 1848, so Louis Pio, a former army captain who was roused by news of the Paris Commune of 1871 to study the teachings of Lassalle, had by September collected 700 members in Copenhagen alone for what proved to be a short-lived branch of the Marxist First International. Having called on the masses to support a bricklayers' strike, Pio was sent to prison and later paid by the police to emigrate to America, where he joined an emissary who had attempted to spread the work of the International to Oslo. In Sweden the socialist pioneer was August Palm, an eloquent tailor who had worked in Germany, but the agitation which he began in 1881 soon passed under the more effective management of the first Scandinavian socialist leader of European renown, namely Hjalmar Branting.

As in Britain, it was the growth of the trade unions which enabled Social Democracy eventually to make headway in politics. The decline of the gilds had been followed by the growth in both Norway and Sweden of Labour Associations, designed by such philanthropists as Sundt to stimulate a desire for self-improvement among the artisans. But in 1870 a meeting of Scandinavian workers in Stockholm marked the opening of a decade in which many small craft unions of a more modern type came into existence, town by town, often when an enterprising craftsman returned from a *Wanderjahr* in Germany. From privileged groups such as printers the idea of organisation spread to less skilled workers, who took advantage of the trade boom in the early 1870s. Their larger numbers created alarm among the possessing classes, who retaliated as soon as prices fell; in 1879 a strike by 5,000 sawmill workers at Sundsvall in Sweden was crushed with King Oscar's express approval by the use of soldiers, who installed strike-breakers in company houses from which the families of strikers were summarily evicted. Nevertheless, the last two decades of the century saw the growth of larger units. Trades councils were formed in the bigger Scandinavian towns, whose demands on the workers' behalf ranged from the ten-hour day to the manhood suffrage without which such measures might never reach the statute book. Nation-wide organisations began to make their appearance, such as that of the Swedish printers in 1887, the Norwegian iron and metal-workers in 1890, and the Danish Labourers (*Arbejdmandsforbund*) in 1897. Finally, a trade union federation was set up in each country in 1898-9, as had been advocated by a Scandinavian workers' congress.

In Denmark an immediate trial of strength with the corresponding organisation of employers, which the latter won, resulted in the September Compromise (1899), containing restrictive rules to govern both strikes and lockouts. The proportion of organised workers sank during the trade depression in the first years of the new century, but in 1910 it had risen to 51 per cent, twice as high as in the other Scandinavian states – or Great Britain. In Sweden a law of 1899 (*Åkarpslagen*), which provided two years' imprisonment for even verbal molestation of strike-breakers, aroused all the more class bitterness because it was sponsored by a Scanian farmer. The sequel was the general strike of 1909, in which 300,000 workers were called out to defeat a lockout in the engineering trade; but its effectiveness was impaired by the abstention of the railwaymen and after a month the workers had to give in for want of funds. In Norway the unions succeeded in obtaining nationally negotiated wage agreements in two industries, but frequent conflicts led the Liberal government to try to reduce friction by enacting compulsory arbitration – which displeased both sides.

By 1914, however, the most threatening problem in labour relations throughout Scandinavia was syndicalism, which also affected Finland, where the trade union federation (dating from 1907) was only about one-tenth as strong as in Sweden. The teachings of Georges Sorel in France, and still more the practices of the IWW in America, made direct action appear both quicker and more profitable than the pressure which could be exerted upon employers by lawful means. A 'trade union op-position' (*fagopposisjon*) therefore grew up, especially among the con-struction workers whom the hydro-electric and other large-scale industrial installations brought together in conditions of isolation and hardship, where they earned high but quickly spent wages.

Meanwhile the Social Democratic movement had grown from its very modest start in the 1870s, as a natural accompaniment to the rise of trade unionism and the trend towards manhood suffrage. The Erfurt Programme of 1891 was adopted in all three kingdoms, but the representation of the party in the respective legislatures increased without any achievement of office – exactly as in the German Reichstag. In Denmark two Social Democrats had been elected to the Folketing in 1884; when parliamentarism triumphed in 1901 they already numbered fourteen, and in 1913 they were the second largest party, through whose support a Radical ministry secured seven years in office. In Sweden Hjalmar Branting (see footnote, p. 311) in 1886 abandoned a distinguished scientific career to edit *Socialdemokraten*, and from 1897 onwards was making his mark in the Second Chamber, though his party did not reach double figures until

1906. In 1909 its representation in the Second Chamber was 34, which was almost doubled by the franchise reform of that year, but Branting was content in the main to support the Liberal policies of Staaff. In Norway the first four Social Democrats were sent to the Storting in 1904 by northern constituencies where the fishermen were campaigning against the whaling interests; ten years later the number had reached 23, but Social Democracy was still no challenge to the supremacy of Venstre.

One common feature of the Social Democratic parties was their hostility to conscription: was not the army the tool of the capitalist oppressor, and were not international conflicts readily soluble by peaceful means if the workers of all lands refused to be mobilised for war? Since military service was a burden resting chiefly on the young, the effect was to strengthen the youth sections, which often became the most vigorous element in the party and had international associations at which the elders looked with grave misgivings. In Sweden, for instance, a Young Socialist group was expelled from the Party in 1908 on account of its association with Finnish and Russian terrorists; in the same year some of its members were responsible for a bomb outrage on board the *Amalthea* at Gothenburg, when an English strike-breaker lost his life. All in all, the Social Democrats were feared and mistrusted as ruthless enemies of the established order, so that their immediate effect on social progress was less direct than the improvement of wages and conditions of labour achieved by the trade unions: but they nevertheless caused bourgeois governments to move in self-defence towards the welfare state.

The influence of the farmers had always been on the side of reductions in public expenditure, especially through keeping poor relief to a minimum. In Sweden at least, the auctioning of pauper families for maintenance by the lowest bidder survived into the new century; preventive measures such as the provision of money for additional smallholdings, obtained either by the subdivision of larger holdings or by subsidising new developments, were not in vogue until the Scandinavian countryside was in danger of being depopulated through emigration. Even then the pioneer Danish smallholdings legislation of 1899 restricted credit facilities from the State to such an extent that borrowers would still need to take part-time employment on larger farms.

The growth of industry, however, caused each country to make belated attempts to catch up with the best international practice in such matters as restriction of child labour, provision for accidents and sickness, and housing standards, which could usually be ignored in rural surroundings. Sweden led the way by the limitation of factory employment for children in 1881, which was followed in 1900 by a ban on the employment of women underground, and in 1901 by workmen's compensation for accidents. Denmark made rather similar piecemeal advances, but was first in the field with old-age pensions; these were granted in 1891 on the basis of need – a qualification which caused them to be opposed by the Social Democrats – and subject to the contradictory requirement that the recipient had not accepted poor relief in the preceding ten years. In Sweden and Denmark alike the State contributed increasingly large subsidies to voluntary sickness insurance schemes, but in 1913 Sweden moved ahead with a system of contributory old-age pensions at 67, offering additional sums to the needy. In Norway social reform was delayed by the concentration of political attention upon the long-drawn-out quarrel with Sweden; housing conditions, for example, though denounced by Sundt in 1860, remained so bad that the incidence of tuberculosis was at its peak in 1900. But in the last decade before the First World War Norway was a pioneer in the extension of accident insurance to fishermen and seamen, and conceded sickness insurance to the poorer wage-earners two years before a similar scheme was enacted by Lloyd George on the other side of the North Sea.

In 1914 the Scandinavian peoples had by no means reached their modern position as leading exponents of public welfare legislation. But national pride had combined with a feeling for equality – which perhaps spread more rapidly in Scandinavia because the scale of society was so much smaller than in the great empires – to give them the broadly based educational system on which their later achievements rested. In Sweden the percentage of twenty-year-olds matriculating at the universities doubled between 1896–1900 and 1916–20,[21] a result which was largely due to the marking out of a broad highway from the public elementary school through the intermediate school and *gymnasium*. In Denmark a similar system, established in 1903, satisfied the needs of more than half a century. In Norway, where the ardent nationalists had regarded the University of Oslo as the citadel of the conservative bureaucracy, their triumph found expression in democratic changes in the curriculum: in 1896 Norwegian educationists pioneered the removal of Latin from its traditional place as an essential requirement for university entrance, and in 1907 they introduced a unique stumbling-block for urban and upper-class opponents of *landsmål* by elevating the artificial language of a rural minority into a compulsory matriculation subject.

SEPARATION OF NORWAY FROM SWEDEN; HOME RULE FOR ICELAND

The fact that *landsmål* had continued to gain ground in Norway in face of the obvious disadvantages, economic as well as social, of bilingualism for a small people is indicative of the rapid growth of separatist nationalism in its rural communities: the Danish influence must be obliterated from their nation's past, the Swedish denied access to its future. In the year following the failure to support the Danes in their final struggle for Slesvig, King Charles XV and De Geer proposed the setting up of a second Union Committee, to which the Norwegian government agreed without difficulty. The result was a bill for a new Act of Union, under which all matters of mutual interest would be handled by a new 'union cabinet', where Norway would have half the seats, although its contribution to the common defence would be proportionate to its much smaller population. The bill was acceptable to both governments and to the Swedish Riksdag, but not to the Norwegian Storting, where the voice of Sverdrup was now predominant. In 1871, when the idea of reforming the union was buried by a vote of 92 to 17, he rhetorically denounced the Swedes as 'a nation which dares to offer the Norwegian Storting a proposition of barter and trade touching the nation's holy and supreme right of sovereignty'.[22]

The time for mending the common institutions having passed, the alternative of ending them was reached by slow but seemingly inevitable stages. The first of these was the victory of Venstre (as already noted) at the end of the long veto controversy in 1884, since the monarchy thereafter lacked the support of the solid phalanx of loyal bureaucrats which had for so long constituted the Norwegian Cabinet. Some reorganisation of the joint 'Ministerial Council' for foreign affairs became necessary at this juncture, because the Swedish Cabinet desired to have three representatives there. Venstre rejected with indignation an offer to increase the Norwegian representation to three in return for a formal agreement to the practice – which had existed since 1814 – of a Swedish subject being nominated as foreign minister; the Party even repudiated Sverdrup, when he proposed the common-sense solution of a minister nominated from either nationality but responsible to a delegation from both parliaments. Such an arrangement might have strengthened the union, so the Radical Left planned to achieve the opposite effect by demanding a separate foreign minister for Norway, which in 1891 gained them the first of their several electoral triumphs.

Yet, since the change in question involved too direct a confrontation with the interests of the monarchy, the Radical leaders turned their attention to the joint consular service, where the much larger size of the Norwegian mercantile marine and divergent commercial objectives gave them a strong case for a separate national organisation. However, Swedish opinion was outraged by the further demand that the change should be made by unilateral legislation without consulting the partner with whom the service had hitherto been shared, and the king – who sympathised with this view, as did many Norwegian Conservatives – vetoed the Norwegian bill on the subject. Accordingly, from 1893 to 1895 the country was governed by a minority Conservative ministry, whilst the Radical Left employed its majority in the Storting to block a joint review of the conduct of foreign relations by the two kingdoms, in which the consular question would have been included. The Storting also withheld a token part of the regular Norwegian contribution to the upkeep of the monarchy and diplomatic representation.

The attitude of the Swedes to their exigent partners had for a long time ranged between admiration for the Norwegians as pioneers of advanced self-government and indignation over their insistence upon the formal acknowledgement of their status of equality in a union which they had been in no position to reject; but a middle opinion, which regarded a disappointing connection with indifference, may well have been generally predominant. At this time, however, the Norwegian imbroglio aroused special interest among the Swedes because of their current concern with problems of defence and the tariff. Since 1891 an Uppsala history professor, Oscar Alin, had been demanding 'equal rights and equal duties'[23] – equality of status for Norway, if and when its people shouldered an equal share of military and financial responsibilities. This having proved an effective basis for electoral propaganda, in 1895 the Riksdag gave notice to terminate the Interstate treaty: this had been enlarged in 1874 to include free entry for shipborne goods, and exemption from the new Swedish tariff was proving highly beneficial to cheap Norwegian textiles. War credits were also voted, in case the Norwegians should continue obdurate, and in July a new foreign minister was appointed from the extreme Right in the person of Count Ludvig Douglas, who was a kinsman of Crown Prince Gustav's German consort.* The Swedish General Staff (as we now know) had detailed plans ready for action, a policy which the Crown Prince favoured and which was commended to his father by the German Emperor, who briefly visited Stockholm at this juncture. Since the Norwegian Radicals had taken no steps to reverse the policy of minimising all military expenditure, long maintained by Sverdrup, they could only climb down; in October a national coalition government was formed, which made amends financially and agreed to refer all matters in dispute to a new Union Committee.

This committee was even less successful than its two predecessors, for its report in 1898 offered four widely varying solutions, two from each side of the frontier. In the same year the Radical Left returned to office in Norway with the support of a record majority, so it kept the agitation alive by enacting a flag law, against which the king had twice used his suspensory veto; this rid the Norwegian mercantile marine of a badge of servitude consisting of the two national flags superimposed on each other in one corner of the standard. The patriotic emotions on which they had played throughout the decade also enabled the party to take the more serious step of strengthening Norway's defences by the purchase of the most up-to-date field artillery, the erection of a series of small forts or strongpoints along the Swedish frontier, and the doubling of an order for two modern ironclads which had been made belatedly in 1895.

* Married in 1881 at the age of nineteen, Princess Viktoria of Baden continued until her death in 1930 to exercise a strong pro-German and antiparliamentary influence upon her often hesitant husband. A granddaughter of the German Emperor William I and great-granddaughter of Gustavus IV, Viktoria never acknowledged Douglas as a second-cousin, though her husband eventually made him Marshal of the Realm.[24]

Nevertheless, at the turn of the century a *rapprochement* looked feasible. The leaders of the main political parties in Norway were disturbed by a decline in trade and a rise in socialism, whilst a new basis for agreement with the Swedes was made available in a report by Sigurd Ibsen,* showing that a separate Norwegian consular service could be harmonised with a common ministry of foreign affairs. Meanwhile, Boström had fostered a mutual economic interest by driving a measure through the Riksdag for building a rail link from the rapidly developing orefields of Swedish Lapland to the frontier, which gave the Norwegians the opportunity to open up a prosperous new port at Narvik. This step was followed by the construction of an extensive fortress at Boden on the new railway from the orefields to Luleå on the Bothnian Gulf (icebound for much of the winter), designed to strengthen the defence of the far north against Russian aggression, of which recent moves in Finland (see p. 277) might be a portent, and in 1901 the Swedish Riksdag decided after much discussion that the situation warranted the lengthening of the period of military training from 90 to 240 days. Although no such drastic measure was even contemplated by the Storting, many Norwegians were equally alarmed – and had no difficulty in identifying peregrinatory Russian saw-sharpeners as spies. The election of 1903 led to the formation of a second coalition government, based on the desire of the moderates in all parties to get rid of the union problem by implementing Sigurd Ibsen's plan; this required the enactment by both legislatures of identical consular laws, inalterable except by mutual agreement.

Since the Swedish First Chamber had pressed successive governments to take a stiff line in their negotiations with the Norwegians, for whom influential nobles of Douglas's type had no natural liking, Boström's proposals for the 'identical laws' could hardly do less than give the foreign minister of the Crown reserve powers of control over a recalcitrant consul. But since Norwegian popular opinion was chiefly interested in the projected separate consular service as a mark of independence, his proposals were no sooner made than they were rejected with contumely as 'clauses for a dependency' (*lydrikepunkter*)[25] and a breach of faith. The Boström administration was then replaced by a Cabinet of officials, authorised by the Riksdag to couple its offer of separate consular services with an explicit proviso that the foreign minister (whose rights of intervention were at issue) might in future be of either nationality. However, many Norwegians now desired to force the issue: 'Dependency clauses' made a good cry, and the long-continued dispute had generated a mood of impatience which called for action to relieve the tension. Furthermore, some far-sighted individuals thought that the weakening of Russia through

---

* 1859–1930. The only child of the dramatist, he had been educated in Germany and Italy and had served as a Swedish-Norwegian diplomat; in 1905 his attitude proved to be too balanced to suit Norwegian opinion, and his only later appointment was as a judge of The Hague Court.

its military failures against Japan gave a peculiarly favourable opportunity for settling the affairs of the Scandinavian peninsula. Accordingly, in March 1905 the coalition gave place to a ministry which included a Radical element and which had at its head a Bergen shipowner, Christian Michelsen, professionally accustomed to calculate odds and seize his chances.

Michelsen found a legal pretext for a sudden secession through the rapid enactment of a bill to establish a separate consular service for Norway without consulting Sweden in any way, which Oscar II as sovereign of both kingdoms was bound to veto. Thereupon the Norwegian ministry tendered its immediate resignation, which the king refused to accept on the constitutionally proper grounds that he 'could not now form a new government'. On 7 June Michelsen informed the Storting of the king's action, deliberately omitting the word 'now',[26] so that he could claim that the monarchy had ceased to exercise its constitutional functions and justify the reinstatement of himself and his colleagues to exercise the executive powers under the authority of the Storting. At the same time he sought to mollify Swedish and world opinion by offering the succession to the Norwegian throne to a cadet member of the House of Bernadotte.

With the important exception of the Social Democrats, all political parties in Sweden were outraged by the manner and regretted the practical effect of the Norwegian action. A special committee advised the Riksdag that no request for separation should be entertained until the Norwegians could justify it by the result of a general election or a plebiscite. A sum of £5 million was voted for emergency use, and the principal members of the committee formed the first fully parliamentary government in Swedish history under Christian Lundeberg, the Conservative leader in the First Chamber. Michelsen with characteristic adroitness had anticipated the demand for a plebiscite, which supported him with a nation-wide majority of 2,000:1 and duly paved the way to inter-governmental negotiations at Karlstad in September. Partial mobilisation on both sides of the frontier made the situation for a time look critical, but a secret session of the Storting showed that all except a foolhardy minority of Norwegian politicians paid regard to the disparity of resources, whilst most of the Swedes were disposed to compromise because in the last analysis the value of the Union to them was for purposes of defence – which could not be served by a military occupation of the sister kingdom.

The Swedish negotiators accordingly modified their demands on the crucial matter of the Norwegian frontier fortifications, the new ones being dismantled but those at Halden and Kongsvinger left conditionally intact on the plea of their historical significance. Minor frontier questions, such as the right of the Lapps to cross freely in search of reindeer pasture, were settled without difficulty, and the fortress agreement took on a much wider meaning through the establishment of a neutral zone from the coast to the 61st parallel, to be denuded of defences by both parties and given a permanently neutral status.* Lastly, it was agreed to submit future disputes to the recently formed international court of arbitration at The Hague; an exception was indeed made for matters affecting 'independence, integrity, or vital interests',[27] but this was almost the first instance in which arbitrators were empowered to decide whether 'vital interests' were in fact involved in any given dispute.

If the avoidance of war and the achievement of a settlement which has proved lasting are attributable primarily to the good sense and political maturity of the two peoples concerned, they were also fortunate in the fact that none of the great powers was interested in fomenting a conflict. When the Russian and German emperors discussed the Scandinavian situation at their meeting off Björkö in July, the former's throne was tottering as a result of the lost war against Japan and the latter was diplomatically in conflict with Britain and France in consequence of the claims Germany had advanced regarding Morocco. The Moroccan crisis, which continued into the following year, also helps to explain the British attitude. This was so well disposed towards Norway that Michelsen had no difficulty in raising a loan of £2 million in the City and the Polar explorer Nansen, who was sent over on an unofficial propaganda mission, found a universal welcome though Balfour as prime minister professed to regard war in Scandinavia as 'a "folly" so great as to make it outside the limits of practical politics'.[28] And when the negotiations at Karlstad nevertheless reached an impasse in which it seemed that 'folly' might after all prevail, the Russian and French ministers in Stockholm at Danish request likewise exerted a strong influence on the side of a peaceful settlement. Finally, Britain again played a special part in ensuring that Norway as a sovereign state should adopt the monarchical form of government which the pre-1914 world regarded as essential to stability.

Although Oscar II's wounded feelings prevented him from wishing any member of his family to accept the offer made by Michelsen on 7 June, he kept it open as a bargaining counter until he formally renounced the Norwegian throne on 26 October, more than a month after the signature of the Karlstad Conventions. Nevertheless, from June onwards King Edward VII had the British Cabinet's approval for his promotion of the candidature of his son-in-law, Prince Charles of Denmark, for which Fritz Wedel Jarlsberg, who had been Swedish-Norwegian minister in Spain, and Nansen worked at Michelsen's behest behind the scenes in Copenhagen. The prince, however, showed remarkable prudence by refusing to put himself forward until the rejection of the offer to the house of Bernadotte might enable his grandfather, King Christian IX, to give his approval without deeply offending Swedish opinion. The same prudence led him also to insist upon the holding of a plebiscite in Norway

* The Swedish Liberal leader, Karl Staaff, was from the outset the advocate of such an arrangement, which was seized upon by Michelsen as a safeguard for the smaller power and a means of placing the fortress demolitions in a wider (and less humiliating) context.

before he would accept the vacant throne, which was constitutionally in the gift of the Storting. The vote was 4:1 in his favour, but it is likely that the republican minority would have been larger if the average man had not felt an obligation to follow the lead given by Michelsen, who had carried the national cause to victory. In late November the Danish prince took office as King Haakon VII; his English wife became Queen Maud; and their only child, the two-year-old Olav, received the most heartfelt welcome of the three as potentially a 100-per-cent Norwegian.

This decisive nationalist success had a more slowly moving and less dramatic counterpart among the few and widely scattered Icelanders. Freedom of trade had given a new impetus to their commerce, of which the total value rose between the 1880s and the outbreak of the First World War from 10 to 35 million kroner. But the revision of the Danish constitution in 1866 was followed by a unilateral definition of the relationship with Iceland, an offer of very restricted constitutional powers, and the institution in 1872 of the post of Landshófdingi, which betokened some increase in the Governor's authority. All this gave great offence to the islanders. A leading newspaper (*Northanfari*) even canvassed the idea that they should either place their country under other sovereignty or emigrate *en masse* to America, whilst a popularly elected committee demanded that the approaching millennary celebrations of the traditional date of settlement should be marked by securing the same full powers for the Althing as were already possessed by the Storting in Norway. Jón Sigurdsson, however, managed to substitute a petition in more moderate terms, which might win the ear of a conservative king and ministry. The result was the promulgation on 5 June 1874 – the twenty-fifth anniversary of the Danish constitution – of the long-delayed constitution for Iceland, to which Christian IX later in the summer paid the first royal visit, when a poem by Bayard Taylor was among the votive offerings for the millennium.

The control of domestic legislation and finance by the Althing was now unfettered, except by the royal veto, and its membership comprised thirty persons elected by the taxpayers and only six Crown nominees – who, however, formed one-half of the tiny new Upper Chamber. But the executive power remained in the hands of the Governor, who was responsible to a member of the Danish Cabinet (the minister of justice), and appeals from the Icelandic courts were still heard in Copenhagen. Emigration from the island reached its peak in the 1880s, but the first consumers' co-operative and the first bank date from that decade and by the end of the century the fishing industry had taken on new dimensions through the general adoption of decked sailing vessels.* This was also an age in which the culture surmounted the handicap of poverty: Icelandic students who had sat at the feet of Brandes, for instance, introduced a

---

* As late as 1876 the Icelanders had only 38 of these, nearly all the fishing being done close inshore from their 3,208 rowing boats.[29]

new realist literature, and such scholars as Gúdbrandr Vígfússon, labouring single-handed in Oxford on his great *Icelandic-English Dictionary*, enhanced the prestige of this 'Saga Island'. Nevertheless, all proposals for amending their constitution were more or less brusquely rejected by the Danish authorities, pending the Change of System in 1901.

Two years later the island was given home rule within the framework of the Danish kingdom. The offices of governor and county governor were abolished and their powers transferred to a minister resident in Iceland, who would be directly responsible to the Althing. The legislature also acquired more weight through an increase in its membership, a reduction of the nominated element, and a lowering of the tax qualification for the franchise. But since the minister was required to submit bills and other major business to the King in Cabinet at Copenhagen, the more ardent nationalists continued to claim that Iceland ought not to be regarded as in any sense a part of the kingdom of Denmark – a claim which gathered additional strength when the Norwegians succeeded in abrogating their union with Sweden. The summer of 1907, in which their new king (Frederick VIII) was accompanied by a deputation from the Danish Rigsdag on a conciliatory visit to the island, was also marked by the formation of the Independence Party. The first native-born Minister for Iceland, Hannes Hafstein, and the moderate Home Rule Party supported the liberal constitutional proposals, which were drawn up by a Danish-Icelandic commission as a sequel to the royal visit. Both the party and the proposals were defeated at the elections of 1909, but Hafstein was restored to office by the voters three years later, when he warned the Althing that the failure to reach a settlement in their long-drawn-out dispute with Denmark was destroying their credit abroad and their unity at home.

Meanwhile, the laying of the first cable to the island, via the Faeroes, in 1906 stimulated the growth of trade, especially in fish, and fisheries protection was accepted in Denmark as an aspect of external relations in which the islanders ought to have special rights. In 1909 the introduction of prohibition in spite of opposition from Spain and other trade partners gave them a modest status as social pioneers, whilst the opening of a university at Reykjavik in 1911 was an impressive achievement for a people numbering less than 90,000. Yet in August 1914 the political situation was still deadlocked.

FINLAND AND RUSSIFICATION

The nationalist struggle in Finland differed in at least three important respects from the movements which have just been described. In the first place, as late as 1914 it seemed doomed to fail, and its eventual triumph required the endurance of civil war and foreign invasion. In the second place, the people of Finland were struggling against a sovereign power which threatened to absorb them into a civilisation which was wholly alien to their own. In the third place, their struggle was based increasingly upon the fuller development of the indigenous Finnish culture, which had for so many centuries been subordinated to the Swedish. The result has been the creation of a very formidable language barrier, making it difficult for this frontier people to maintain the close links with Scandinavian society which it cherishes in principle as a means of avoiding too close an involvement with its mighty eastern neighbour.

The convening of the Diet by Tsar Alexander II in 1863 was followed up by measures which allowed it to meet at intervals of five, and eventually three, years, whilst its membership was made slightly more representative. A few new nobles were created; teachers were added to the Estate of clergy; and by the close of the century 7·1 per cent of the urban population had been enfranchised – but only 4·3 per cent of the very much larger population of the countryside.[30] National pride was stimulated by the institution of an independent monetary system, the Finnish mark being placed on the gold standard almost twenty years ahead of the rouble, and the revival of the Finnish army for the defence of 'the throne and the fatherland'.[31] The Liberal Party succeeded in bringing local government, the elementary schools, and even the Church increasingly under popular control, though it is significant of the generally reactionary outlook of the clergy that toleration for nonconformist religious bodies was delayed until 1889. The Liberals also reduced the tariff, which stimulated the growth of the timber trade with western Europe and at the same time brought about a profitable commercial intercourse with the Russians.

Nevertheless, by the 1880s Liberalism lost its impetus, as the upper class became concerned first and foremost with the struggle of 'Svecomania' against 'Fennomania', the inherited position of the Swedish language being now seriously challenged both in administration and in polite society. The Fennomans based their position upon an ordinance which Snellman had secured in 1863, requiring that within twenty years public offices and the law courts must be able to use Finnish when requested in their dealings with the public; by 1889 Finnish was the language of half the secondary school pupils and university students; five years later it was heard for the first time in the House of Nobles; and by then it enjoyed majority support in each of the other three Houses. For the Svecoman cause was doubly handicapped. Its base among the rural population was limited to a south-western region (centred upon Åbo/Turku, which remained the seat of the archbishop) and the coast of Ostrobothnia farther north, whilst its position inside the governing class was weakened by the secession of those politicians who gave up the Swedish language as a hindrance to the national cause. Such, for example, was Yrjö-Koskinen,*

* 1830–1903. A devotee of the Finnish language, who therefore – as was the common practice – abandoned his Swedish name of Georg Forsman; in 1869–73 he published the first *History of Finland* which was Finnish in both language and feeling; Senator, 1882–99, and created a baron (1897). He was reviled by nationalists in the last years of his life for his leadership of the Old Finnish Party or 'Compliants' (see p. 278).

who eventually replaced Snellman in the Senate from which the latter was removed after a quarrel with the Russian governor-general in 1868.

The attitude of the Russian authorities to the language dispute in Finland was cautious: it took twenty-three years for Fennoman pressure to obtain a new ordinance, under which public offices were entitled to choose which language they used for internal purposes. But in the meantime their general approach to the affairs of the Grand Duchy underwent an ominous change, as the long-standing resentment of the Slavophils against the Finnish addiction to a western creed and culture developed into the imperialist viewpoint of the Panslavs, who from the time of the Congress of Berlin in 1878 saw in the Russification of Finland some possible compensation for disappointment in the Balkans. When Alexander III succeeded his murdered father in 1881, the Grand Duchy benefited indeed from the friendly interest of his consort, who was a daughter of Christian IX of Denmark. But by 1890 Panslav influences had persuaded him that its proper status was that of a conquered province, and the sequel was the first small but significant infringement of Finnish rights through inclusion in the Russian postal system. This was followed by far sterner measures in the reign of Nicholas II, under whom the autocracy ceased to exercise any firm control over the political passions of the day. In the case of Finland, however, it is only fair to bear in mind that its position as a frontier province became of increasing importance to the defence of Russia, as its Swedish neighbours were seen to favour the Triple Alliance rather than that which, from 1894 (the year of Nicholas's accession), linked the empire of the tsars to republican France.

The appointment of a reactionary general, Nicolai Bobrikov, to govern Finland prepared the way for the Manifesto of February 1899, by which the legislative power in matters affecting any Russian interest was arbitrarily reserved to the Grand Duke. Half a million Finns protested in vain, as did more than 1,000 European representatives of the arts and sciences, on whose petition the Tsar's minister commented regretfully, 'Scarcely a famous name is missing.'[32] Two years later the 'Finis Finlandiae' to which the Panslavs looked eagerly forward was brought nearer by a new conscription law, dissolving the Finnish army and making it possible for Finnish troops to be incorporated in Russian units. Resistance to the Russian call-up was organised by an underground movement, which borrowed its name of *Kagal* from the activities of the persecuted Russian Jews, whereupon military service was prudently commuted to a tax. But when Bobrikov was given dictatorial powers, which he used to deport his principal opponents, plans were made for a rebellion and in June 1904 the governor-general was shot dead by a young civil servant, who then committed suicide.

Nevertheless, the Finnish people remained dangerously divided between the policies of compliance and resistance. The party of the clergy and substantial farmers, who became known as the Old Finns, argued that it was wise to comply with the demands of their mighty neighbour whilst cherishing the hope of better days – when 'The sovereign and the nation can once more find each other'[33] – and that in the meantime it was right for them to take over administrative posts in which resisters would otherwise be replaced by Russians. In 1902 the loyalty of the Compliants was rewarded by a decree which gave the Finnish language equality of status. The resisters, on the other hand, claimed that a small nation must cling at all costs to its constitution; this view appealed to the Young Finns under the leadership of a lawyer, Per Svinhufvud, as well as to the remaining Svecomans and to the Social Democratic Party, which from 1898 onwards linked together the industrial workers and the landless rural labourers. The Old Finns secured every seat in the Senate, but were heavily defeated in elections to the Diet, and, when the Old Finn attorney-general fell as a further victim of 'propaganda by deed', Svinhufvud acted as defence counsel for his murderer.

In October 1905 the cleavage in Finnish opinion became less dangerous, because the Tsar's concession of civil liberties and a legislative Duma to the Russian people automatically relaxed the pressure upon Finland; indeed, the workers of Helsinki had joined in the last stages of the general strike which forced the surrender of an autocracy already discredited by military failure. The February Manifesto of 1899 was repealed in November (1905), and early in the following year a ministry formed from the resisters was authorised to present the Diet with a bill for a wholly new legislature. The result was the most democratic parliament in Europe – a single chamber of 200 members chosen by universal suffrage, the only conservative restraints being proportional representation at the polls, a minimum voting age of twenty-four, and the requirement of a qualified majority for the most important enactments. All four Estates agreed to their own extinction and a tenfold increase in the electorate, for the triumph of the national cause had engendered a tremendous feeling of patriotic solidarity. A brief episode in the summer of 1906, when 'Red Guards' rose in Helsinki in support of a mutiny of the Russian garrison at Sveaborg – and were suppressed by 'White Guards' with some loss of life – showed that recent events had indeed ended the submissiveness of the Finnish proletariat; but Conservative opinion was reassured by the fact that the ministry was not directly dependent upon the legislature and had in reserve the Grand Duke's right of veto.

In 1907 the first election gave 80 seats to the Social Democrats, 61 to the Old Finns (and their allies), 26 to the Young Finns, 24 to the Swedish People's Party, and 9 to a newly formed Agrarian Union directly representing the interests of the larger farmers. But Svinhufvud presided over a chamber in which the lines of division on national and social questions were so unrelated that, in spite of four dissolutions in three years, virtually no constructive legislation reached the statute book; even an attempt to alleviate the condition of the cottars, who together with labourers made up one-half of the rural population, was whittled away to insignificance by the farmers and larger landowners.

The opportunity to consolidate the national position quickly passed, for the Russification of Finland soon had the support of the representative organs set up under the new Russian constitution. In 1908 the Tsar required the reference of Finnish business to his Cabinet; next year the governor-generalship was given to Bobrikov's former chief assistant; and in 1910 the Duma and Council of State arrogated to themselves the power to enact all Finnish legislation 'if its effects are not limited to the internal affairs of that region'.[34] An offer of representation on these two Imperial bodies was inacceptable to Finnish opinion, and this time even the Old Finns refused to serve in a Russian-controlled Cabinet. By 1914 the country was under the direct rule of Russian officials. Its constitutional rights were championed in memorials from liberal parliamentarians in both France and Britain; but the prospect was in reality much darker than at the beginning of the century, since both the great democracies of western Europe were now forced to condone policies which they disliked in order to retain the support of the Russian Empire against their rivals of the Triple Alliance.

SCANDINAVIA AND THE GREAT POWERS

During the closing decades of the nineteenth century the vestiges of Scandinavianism in domestic affairs had no counterpart in foreign policy. The Norwegians were too concerned about their constitutional rights within the Union to desire any unnecessary co-operation with the Swedes in this sphere. The impossibility of recovering northern Slesvig in spite of its people's continued loyalty was now accepted in Denmark; noting this privately in 1898, Oscar II added a comment which was probably representative of opinion among his Swedish subjects: 'It may be said in this connection, as of Scandinavianism in general: the lovely dream belongs to the past.'[35] Moreover, Danish foreign policy as a whole was seriously hampered by the Compromise of 1894, when the Radical wing of the Venstre Party had agreed to the continuance of even a reduced annual call-up for military service only on the understanding that defence of neutrality was its sole object, and as late as 1904 – the year before they formed the separate Radical Party – they protested in the Folketing against the fortification of Saltholm in the Kattegat as a precautionary measure during the Russo-Japanese War. Accordingly, the Scandinavian states in principle stood aloof from the rivalry of the Triple and Dual Alliances as it developed in the 1890s, though a growing anxiety about the ultimate aims of Panslav imperialism won a good deal of popular support, in Sweden and to some extent in Norway, for King Oscar's cultivation of his personal friendship with the young German emperor, William II.

In 1905 Scandinavian co-operation suffered a further severe setback –

directly through the confrontation between Sweden and Norway, less directly through Swedish suspicion that Denmark had sided with Norway and helped to bring a Danish prince to the new throne. The Norwegian government, which had very little diplomatic expertise at its disposal, planned to replace the November treaty of 1855 (no longer valid for a wholly separate Norway) by negotiating a status of permanent neutrality, as proposed in a unanimous resolution of the Storting three years before. The four powers (Britain, France, Germany and Russia) would not concede this, and the guarantee of territorial integrity which they gave instead was rendered almost nugatory by a clause limiting the obligation of the guarantors to intervention 'by those means which might appear most suitable'.[36] In Sweden foreign policy passed in 1909 from the domain of the 'Ministerial Council' to that of the Cabinet at large, but from December 1907 its direction had to be shared with a new king, Gustav V, whose authoritarian and pro-German tendencies were not without significance in a reign which lasted for forty-three years. It began, indeed, with a proposal, favoured by Gustav and his foreign minister, for Swedish adherence to a secret Russo-German agreement for closing the Baltic Sea to the warships of all non-Baltic states, albeit that this involved allowing the Russians to refortify the Åland Islands. The proposal came to nothing, however, partly because of an outcry led by Branting and partly because of British assurances that the Åland servitude would not be modified without Swedish approval. The interests of the great powers in the Baltic were in fact changing as a result of the formation in August 1907 of the Anglo-Russian Entente, so the upshot was a treaty to maintain the *status quo* there, signed in the following April by the empires adjoining and their two small neighbours, Sweden and Denmark. A similar *status quo* treaty was signed at the same time by the powers bordering on the North Sea,* which meant that for the next six years the treaty of 1855 had a very ample replacement.

Meanwhile the Danes sought to restore the amity of Scandinavian relationships through the Inter-Parliamentary Union, where a special Scandinavian Section was set up in 1910 to bring the three states together again in the work for world peace (see p. 301). Two years later they issued a common declaration of neutrality on the outbreak of the Balkan Wars, and agreed that changes in neutrality rules should be mutually approved. In retrospect this seems to have been the most hopeful line of advance, as the division of Europe into two heavily armed camps made it increasingly hard for any of the three kingdoms acting in isolation to avoid being embroiled in an impending major conflict.

In the case of Norway, the concession of a permanent neutral status would have been acceptable to Britain only if it were extended to the

---

* Belgium and Norway excepted. The exclusion of Norway, which did not share the neutral status of Belgium, was due to a German initiative, which the Norwegians were not quick enough to challenge.

whole of Scandinavia. As it was, Nansen while serving as the first head of the Norwegian legation in London was made aware that a British naval base in southern Norway might be required to counter a German thrust towards the same region.[37] In the case of Denmark – where as late as 1909 an election was fought on defence issues, resulting in a further twelve-year reprieve for the existing fortifications of Copenhagen – the underlying situation was considerably more precarious. In 1906 an emissary approved by the king and the leading members of the government had established contact with the German General Staff, which resulted next year in a highly secret agreement with its Chief, the younger von Moltke, for 'benevolent neutrality'; if this could not be maintained in terms of a Danish defence system which was consistent with German interests, then the prime minister promised an alliance.

In the case of Sweden, the risk of embroilment was even greater, since the Conservative interest in a strong defence based on a close understanding with Germany was supported by continuing widespread fears of Russian machinations. In 1906 relations with Germany were fostered by a trade treaty, which secured favourable terms for the Swedish wood-working industries in return for the freer export of the high-grade Lapland iron ore, on which the German steel industry was increasingly dependent. Four years later, a Conservative foreign minister, who enjoyed the close support of the new king and his German consort, secured the acceptance of a German invitation for an exploratory meeting of the two chiefs of staff. This was the situation when the first elections under the enlarged franchise brought the Liberals into office under Staaff, whose followers – and still more their Social Democratic allies under Branting – attached primary importance to the financing of social reform.

On two occasions King Gustav V recorded his formal displeasure with Cabinet decisions limiting expenditure on defence; the explorer Sven Anders Hedin (see p. 299) joined in with *A Word of Warning*, an exposition of the Russian peril of which a million copies were soon in circulation; and when the premier ventured to postpone the construction of an improved armoured cruiser, known as 'the F-ship', the money for it was raised by private subscription. The conflict was further embittered by Staaff's refusal of an immediate lengthening in the period of military service, which he knew was anathema to the Social Democrats. In February 1914 matters were brought to a head by an address which the king gave in front of the palace (*Borggårdstalet*) to a demonstration by 31,000 farmers, whom the defence interests had brought to the capital for the purpose. His statement, 'The defence question ought to be settled at once . . . on the basis of expert professional opinion',[38] directly challenged the authority of the prime minister, and in spite of a counter-demonstration by 50,000 workers King Gustav persisted in claiming the right to address himself freely to the nation; Staaff therefore resigned office.

The ensuing election reduced the Liberal representation in the Second Chamber to 70 and increased the Conservatives (and other supporters of the defence policy) to 86, but the Social Democrats had risen to 74. When war broke out in Europe, Sweden was in the hands of a minority Conservative government, headed by Hjalmar Hammarskjöld – an expert in international law and the father of a more famous son; but its defence proposals seemed likely to be rejected by the Social Democrats, whose programme now included the establishment of a republic.

Chapter 12

Contributions to Civilisation:
I — The Nineteenth Century

INTRODUCTION: A BELATED RECOGNITION

The five small peoples of northern Europe had always been contributors to, as well as recipients of, the cultural influences which have moulded our Western civilisation. Yet it was only in the nineteenth century that their achievement came to be commonly appreciated. This was partly the result of general causes, such as the growth of transport and communications, the closer integration of world trade, and the wider interest taken in the advance of the arts and sciences, which linked together nations great and small. But in the case of Scandinavia there were three particular reasons why its contribution at long last became more readily identified.

One of these was an increasing awareness of the important role which the peoples of Scandinavia had played in the distant past. Appropriately enough, it was a Danish archaeologist, Christian Thomsen, who devised (in 1836) the division of prehistory into the stages of stone, bronze and iron: for the investigation of archaeological sites, from the incised rock-faces to the burial mounds of Viking ships, was to show that the cultural significance of Scandinavia long antedated its recorded history. Another Danish scholar, J. J. A. Worsaae,* pioneered the comprehensive study of the impact of the voyages which had carried the Vikings to the west, the south, and the east of their homelands. This in turn led on to a closer examination of their role as settlers and traders, based on the study of placenames and coin hoards, where again Scandinavian scholars have been to the fore. Thus their nineteenth-century expertise has helped to build up a far more vivid picture than had previously existed of the distinctive Scandinavian contribution to the early development of other European nations.

The growing interest in historical narratives based on records also served to some extent to identify the part played by Scandinavian states in later events. Study of the saga literature gave prominence not only to the

---

* According to G. P. Gooch (who was born in 1873) 'His works, translated into English and German, were for a generation the chief source of knowledge for the Vikings, and his richly illustrated writings created a taste for Scandinavian antiquities.'[1]

Icelandic Commonwealth but also to the early kings of Norway, on whom Carlyle published a volume in 1875, and to the mystery attaching to the first European settlement in Greenland, its extension to 'Vinland', and its eventual extinction. With some exceptions, however, the work of the native scholars who documented Scandinavian history and presented it in narrative form to their own public did not usually appear in other languages. E. G. Geijer's pioneer history of Sweden down to the abdication of Queen Christina was, indeed, translated into English in 1845, but a more typical experience was that of his distinguished Norwegian contemporary, P. A. Munch, who conducted extensive pioneer studies in the Vatican and other archives for his eight-volume history of his native land to the year 1397: less than one-quarter was reproduced in German and only a single chapter in English. For obvious reasons foreign publishers were even less readily attracted by the larger-scale national histories, embodying the work of numerous authors, which came into fashion in Scandinavia as elsewhere about the turn of the century. Nevertheless the fruits of national research became known abroad among scholars to whom an extra language or two was no grave obstacle, so that in the course of time the general public became more alive to specific Scandinavian contributions in the case of such major events as the Reformation, the Thirty Years War, and the eighteenth-century Enlightenment.

In the second place, the much reduced part which the Scandinavian countries played in the international relationships of the nineteenth century was balanced by other factors which drew attention to their way of life. English, German, and even Italian travellers published important accounts of visits paid to northern Europe at the time when most of the continent was closed to travel by the Napoleonic Wars. Later in the century, when Norway had become the mecca of the salmon fisher, rock climber, yachtsman and enthusiastic walker, it was the subject of an exceptionally large descriptive literature, especially in English. The popular press, too, from time to time found congenial themes in Scandinavia – a clustering of royalties in Copenhagen as the guests of Christian IX, 'the father-in-law of Europe'; Nansen's return to Norway from the voyage of the *Fram* (see p. 298); or the exhibition of art and industry at Stockholm to celebrate Oscar II's silver jubilee in 1897. But what was of the greatest continuing importance was the interest taken by outsiders in the struggles for internal political liberties – the Whig support for Norwegian aspirations in 1814; liberal concern for the movement towards full parliamentarism in each kingdom in turn; and the mobilisation of European opinion against the Russian infringements of the constitution of Finland.

In the third place, Scandinavian civilisation received a prompter and in some respects more generous recognition in the New World than in the Old. This is an important phenomenon of the later nineteenth century which has also had some lasting influence; a brief reference must therefore be made to a subject which American scholars have made their own.

The decision of so many individuals to cross the ocean was the result of fears as well as hopes, of disillusionment with the society they were leaving as well as a possibly illusory picture of that which they would be entering. Yet a body of immigrants drawn chiefly from the poorer classes and remoter districts of Scandinavia proved eminently adaptable. Besides their major contribution as agricultural pioneers – the Swedes, for example, ploughed up more virgin soil than the entire arable area in their homeland – they made some mark in commerce and more in industry, where John Ericsson, the expatriate Swede who designed the *Monitor,* had many well-known successors among engineers. A Norwegian journalist of long experience said of his own fellow countryman: 'Americanisation comes to him as a matter of course',[2] a generalisation of wider application, as is shown by the part which persons from every Scandinavian country came to play in public life. By 1921 six were serving in the US Senate and fifteen in the House of Representatives: the former group ranged from Knute Nelson, an illegitimate child from Voss in western Norway who had been the first immigrant of any nationality to become a state governor, to a direct descendant from the seventeenth-century Swedish colonists on the Delaware, whilst the latter group was made up of Norwegians, Swedes, Danes and a Finn. They had also provided America with such writers as Jacob Riis, Thorstein Veblen and Carl Sandburg, all of whom contributed powerfully to the critical discussion of the new industrial society.* Thus Scandinavia was identified in American eyes as ranking very high among the European sources from which the new nation had been recruited.

The respect which Scandinavia won in the New World in these various ways also helped the special culture which the immigrants brought with them from the Old World to maintain itself for a time; this was a prime objective of the Lutheran Churches which each nationality organised and of numerous educational and social institutions, all held together by a remarkably widespread language press. But, except in certain mid-western districts with an almost homogeneous Scandinavian population, the culture based on the use of several minority languages was already declining before the war of 1914 interrupted the flow of newcomers who were its natural supporters. There were, however, two lasting results. One was the survival of the Lutheran church organisations, whose services are normally conducted in English but whose basis is still national; these have important links with the homelands, especially for mission work (see p. 300). The other is the comparatively strong position which Scandinavian studies came to occupy in higher education. This originated with the colleges founded by early settlers, primarily for the training of the clergy, such as St Olaf College, Minnesota, where O. E. Rolvaag wrote *Giants in the Earth,* immortalising the life of the immigrant pioneer on the basis of his own youthful experience. In 1875 Wisconsin led the way by establishing a chair

* They were, for example, the authors respectively of *How The Other Half Lives* (1890), *The Theory of the Leisure Class* (1895), and *Chicago Poems* (1915).

of Scandinavian languages in its state university, whose first holder translated into English about 5,000 pages from various Scandinavian authors. By 1914 there were 25 universities and state colleges which made the study of Scandinavian literature old or new in some degree accessible to the rising generation of Americans.[3]

SOME MAJOR WRITERS

The flowering of their literatures was a feature of the national life in this period which stimulated the pride and sense of achievement in each of the Scandinavian peoples. Each literature therefore deserves to be studied in depth, as part of the total culture by which the nation identifies itself. But to a considerable extent they also constitute a common 'Scandinavian' heritage: the heroic legends of the past and the human condition in the present, sources on which the writers drew for inspiration and material, were broadly similar – at least in the three Kingdoms, where the languages too were no serious barrier to comprehension. The impact on the outside world, which is our concern here, was partly that of a 'Scandinavian' literature, which was reputed to be making a distinctive contribution to the great literary movements which swept across Europe and America. But an important direct influence could be exercised only by a few leading writers, whose works have surmounted the handicap of translation.*

As elsewhere in Europe, the first half of the century was an era of national poets. Adam Oehlenschläger has been named already in connection with the introduction of German Romanticism to Denmark in 1802, a link which he soon afterwards strengthened by a long visit to Goethe. The title of his great ballad-cycle, *Gods of the North* (1819), suggests the type of legendary theme which also predominated in his many tragic dramas. The Swede, Esaias Tegnér, owed something to his example, but more to the Gothic Society, whose exaltation of the misty past has already been mentioned. In 1811 a long patriotic poem, *Svea*, helped to gain him the professorship of Greek at Lund, where his name is still venerated, but his European fame came from *Frithiofs saga*, which was first published in 1825. This epic poem, based on a medieval Icelandic theme which was congenial to the Romantic taste of the age, has often been translated. Conversely, the 720-page epic about the Creation and much else, which came five years later from the pen of Henrik Wergeland at the age of twenty-two, has had few persistent readers, even among Norwegians. But this was only one of the many new impulses its author gave to the nation's literature, in prose as well as verse; and although he died young in 1845 – having composed some of his most memorable shorter lyrics in his long last illness – Wergeland

---

* An article on translation in the 1911 edition of the *Encyclopaedia Britannica* observes that, 'with the development of literature in countries whose languages are unfamiliar, the function of the translator increases in importance',[4] and cites Ibsen together with the Russian novelists as two instances in which it had been successfully performed.

left behind him the impress of genius which served to inspire a whole nation.

The people of Finland likewise received lasting inspiration from their great Swedish-language poet, J. L. Runeberg, author of *The Tales of Ensign Stål* and of various idylls of the Finnish countryside, such as *The Elk Hunters*, a pioneer description of everyday life in northern Europe. Side by side with this we must place the work done for the Finnish language by Elias Lönnrot, compiler of the folk epic *Kalevala* and collector of more than 600 other specimens of folk songs in *Kanteletar* ('the daughter of the lyre'). Published first in 1835 and at almost double length in 1849, *Kalevala* has been translated into more than twenty languages and is still widely known; this is all the more remarkable as the epic form was imposed by the compiler upon a mass of material which had been orally transmitted from different centuries and districts. But its appeal is not primarily that of a poetic masterpiece:* to Finns it is a precious re-creation of their prehistoric and largely unknown past, and to others a particularly fascinating glimpse into the eerie world of folklore.

The current interest in folklore inspired a Norwegian prose work, parts of which have found a permanent place in children's literature. P. C. Asbjörnsen and Jörgen Moe published their first collection of folk tales in 1841, and in less than two decades they had been launched successfully in Britain, by an influential translator (Sir George Dasent) who believed that the adventures of Askeladden and the antics of the trolls would lead to similar discoveries in the way of British folk tales. He was mistaken, but in Denmark the example of the two Norwegian researchers was partly responsible for a far more important development, since it was from the use of native folk tales that Hans Christian Andersen advanced to fictions which came from the unconscious. In his own words, 'They lay in his thoughts like a seed, which needed only a shower, a ray of sunshine, and a drop of wormwood to become a flower.'[5] Tales which appeal to the childish imagination the world over constitute at the same time a wholly adult commentary on the vicissitudes of human life, for he never forgot the deep poverty of his childhood in Odense and his rejection by each of the women he fell in love with – he was indeed the Ugly Duckling of his own story – throughout the long later period, when he was lionised by European society. Twenty years before his death in 1875, Hans Andersen's *Fairy Tale of My Life* told a story which is hardly less remarkable in its own way than those products of his genius which have spread to more than 100 languages.

If Hans Andersen was Denmark's counterpart of Dickens, in Grundtvig she possessed a seer of the type of Carlyle, albeit that his reverence for the Nordic past, shown in his historical works and numerous translations (including a version of *Beowulf*), did not prevent the Sage of Copenhagen from preaching a special Scandinavian form of liberalism, both in education

---

* Longfellow's *Hiawatha* borrowed both the style and the eight-syllabled trochaic metre from Schiefner's verse translation into German, which appeared in 1852.

and in religion. His prolific writings included five volumes of *Hymns and Spiritual Songs*, some of which are still treasured by all the Scandinavian Churches, but – like secular lyrics – they do not easily reach the outside world. Nevertheless, down to his death in his ninetieth year in 1872, Grundtvig was so clearly the central figure in Scandinavian religious life that no contemporary could have guessed that a wider fame awaited a fellow cleric who died young in 1855 without making any effective impact on Danish society. Sören Kierkegaard's life had been made miserable by an unhappy love affair, by his sensitiveness to criticism, and finally – in the year before his death – by a head-on collision with the Establishment, when he dared to criticise the conventional presentation of Christianity by the Primate-designate in a funeral oration on his predecessor. Yet from 1843 onwards he had written what are now recognised as a series of master-pieces, confronting the prevalent Hegelian philosophy with the view that 'subjectivity, what is in the heart [*inderligheden*] is the truth', and proclaiming a Christianity founded on something beyond reason: 'I am alone in a little boat in 70,000 fathoms of water, and yet I believe.'[6] Both Existentialist philosophers and modern theologians now acknowledge a deep indebtedness to the Dane.

In the early 1870s an important dividing-line, known as 'the breakthrough to modernity' (*Det moderne Gennembrud*), was provided for Scandinavian literature in general by the brilliant lectures delivered at Copenhagen University by Georg Brandes, a young radical newly returned from his literary studies on the continent. His critical biographies subsequently made him a European figure – his *Shakespeare*, for instance, was a best-seller in England, and he was equally appreciated in Germany as a devotee of Nietzsche – long before the ruling classes in Denmark learnt to tolerate the self-assured freethinker, who was kept waiting until 1902 for a professorship of aesthetics. Yet Brandes played his most vital role inside Scandinavia, where he popularised the idea that literature ought to concern itself with problems of the hour and stimulated the growth of Naturalism and other new schools of writing. Since this 'breakthrough' was effected chiefly in prose, presenting the translator with a much easier task than poetry, the return influence on the outside world was correspondingly enhanced.

At the time when Brandes appealed for problem plays, Björnstjerne Björnson was as yet better known than Henrik Ibsen at home and abroad. The former was the son of a country clergyman, the latter of a small town businessman who went bankrupt; and, although each made his name with a series of historical plays, Björnson was the more successful as a theatre manager and quickly went on to become an international favourite through his idealised tales of Norwegian peasant life, such as *A Happy Boy* (1860). In 1864 Ibsen was so discontented with his own position as well as the state of public affairs in Norway that he exiled himself to Italy and afterwards Germany; the two verse dramas in which he expressed his feelings at this juncture (*Brand* and *Peer Gynt*) at once enhanced his reputation, but he lived abroad until 1891 and never again played an active part in Scandinavian affairs. Björnson, on the other hand, was a publicist *par excellence*, whose first mild version of a problem play appeared as early as 1865 and had numerous successors to air his views on such themes as financial probity, sexual morals, republicanism, and religious doubt. They had a big box-office appeal in their day but are now forgotten, their author being remembered in Norway chiefly as a patriotic orator and elsewhere as a champion of humanitarian internationalism (see p. 301).

It was otherwise with Ibsen, whose so-called problem plays, such as *A Doll's House* and *Ghosts*, whilst rousing interest initially by their bearing upon the emancipation of women and other subjects of world-wide discussion, were designed to create, as their author said, 'human beings and human destinies',[7] whose fate makes an appeal which outlasts their problems. This profoundly poetic quality, though expressed through the medium of prose, is still more evident in the eight plays of Ibsen's final period (from *The Wild Duck*, 1884, to *When We Dead Awaken*, 1899) with their frequent use of symbolism. They are, indeed, so pregnant with meaning that James Joyce deprecates the habit of reading them: 'To prevent excessive pondering,' he declares, 'Ibsen requires to be acted.'[8]

The only other Scandinavian dramatist of the nineteenth century whose plays are still widely popular – not least on the television screen – is August Strindberg, who had no serious rival among contemporary Swedish men of letters. He first made his name as a novelist with *The Red Room* (1879), a satirical picture of Stockholm society, and the fifty-five volumes of his collected works include many other successful novels, short stories, essays and poems. Particular interest attaches to his autobiography, of which the first part, *Son of a Bondwoman*, has been compared with Rousseau's *Confessions*. Strindberg's youth was embittered by his humble origins, his adult life by the failure of his three marriages, and at times he came close to insanity. Apart from a cycle of twelve historical dramas, which were his response to the tense national feeling in Sweden at the turn of the century, the plays are mainly built round these inner experiences. In the 1880s *The Father* and *Lady Julia* were among the first Naturalist plays in Europe. In 1898 the first two parts of *To Damascus* employed symbolism to interpret the personal crisis which had ended in his conversion to Sweden-borgianism. Finally, in 1907 at the age of fifty-eight Strindberg launched an experimental theatre in Stockholm, for which during the last five years of his life he produced a whole series of chamber plays, including the *Ghost Sonata*, where he anticipates the ideas of the Surrealists.

The novel, however, was clearly a literary form which could reach a much wider public than even the greatest of dramas. As early as the 1840s, for example, tales by the Swedish feminist and traveller, Fredrika Bremer, were being translated for an English public, and Björnson followed up his initial success by a more realistic type of story, one of which (*Mary*) was

even tricked out with an American heroine. Two of his Norwegian contemporaries also for a time enjoyed a considerable vogue abroad. Jonas Lie
was at his best in tales of the far north and of the sea, though Norwegians
admired him above all as 'the writer of the home',[9] which meant especially
the milieu of the official class, in which he had himself grown up. Alexander
Kielland, a scion of one of the old merchant houses of Stavanger, described
its fortunes in two memorable volumes, *Garman and Worsè* and *Skipper
Worsè*, but the rest of his work, all of which was composed in 1880–91,
introduced so much heavy social satire that it soon dated. Arne Garborg,
the first Norwegian novelist to write with distinction in *landsmål*, became
known to some extent in Germany, but there a very much greater reputation awaited another son of the Norwegian peasantry, though one bred in
the north instead of the west and therefore lacking Garborg's predilection
for the new language-form.

In his youth Knut Hamsun led a wandering life, which brought him
twice to America and included a whole winter of semi-starvation in Oslo.
In 1890 his haunting picture of *Hunger* concentrated attention upon the
inner life of the individual; this brief masterpiece, which has been termed
'Hamsun's most characteristic work',[10] won him a name at once in
Germany, but was not translated into English until 1899, by which time
Pan and *Victoria* had likewise been well received on the continent. He
then turned his attention to the individual seen in contact with society,
often using the character of a wanderer, such as he himself had been, and
portraying the milieu of rapid urban growth which was to be observed in
some districts of early twentieth-century Norway.

Although they produced no rival to Hamsun, both Sweden and Denmark
to some extent gained the world's attention for their novels. Besides
Strindberg the Swedes had Selma Lagerlöf, known chiefly through the
first of her many works, *Gösta Berlings saga* (1891), a penetrating study
of the old aristocratic form of society in her own native province of Värm-
land. A Danish science student, J. P. Jacobsen, wrote two novels and a
number of short stories in immediate response to the new ideas proclaimed
by Brandes. In psychological depth he has been compared with Henry
James, but Jacobsen died in 1885 at the age of thirty-eight, and his work
was not put into English until a generation later. By then a bigger mark was
being made by Martin Andersen Nexö, a novelist born in the Copenhagen
slums; his proletarian epic, *Pelle the Conqueror*, gave two of its four volumes
to the exploitation he had himself experienced as a youthful farm-hand
in the island of Bornholm, the others to the socialist trade union movement,
of which he was then a staunch supporter.

The first novel in Finnish was *Seven Brothers*, a genial picture of the ways
of country people published in 1870 by a peasant, Alexis Kivi, who was also
the first Finnish playwright; but the story was not translated even into
Swedish for nearly half a century. Among his immediate successors only
Juhani Aho, a clergyman's son who had studied the novel in France,

attracted wider attention abroad. The Icelandic novel became known to a small extent through English, German and Czech translations of work by Gestur Pálsson, who settled as a journalist in Winnipeg shortly before his death in 1891. Another emigrant, Stephan Stephansson, is described as 'the greatest representative of all the Icelandic poets sprung from the common people in old or modern times'.[11] But his six volumes of poems entitled *Andvökur* ('Sleepless Nights') – composed in the scanty leisure of a pioneer who thrice broke new soil, the last time in Alberta – were read only by his fellow Icelanders.

INFLUENCE IN OTHER ARTS

In the universal arts, where language differences do not seriously impede communication, the principal Scandinavian contributors often merged into an international environment. Thus their painters, sculptors and musicians, having received their training in Düsseldorf or Munich, Vienna, Rome or Paris, became exponents of the prevailing school and were likely to find their wealthiest, most numerous, and perhaps their most appreciative patrons in foreign countries. J. C. Dahl, the 'father of Norwegian painting', had his atelier for more than forty years in Dresden; Ole Bull, the virtuoso violinist who claimed that his native Norwegian mountains had taught him his art, became an American citizen; and Jenny Lind, the 'Swedish nightingale', spent the last thirty years of her life in England. Movement in the opposite direction was less significant, except in the case of the Royal Danish Ballet, whose Italian founder was succeeded in 1816 by a Frenchman, Antoine Bournonville, and which reached its greatest heights under his son, Auguste. Nevertheless, Scandinavia produced at least four major creative artists to enrich the culture of the age.

The earliest of these is the sculptor, Bertel Thorvaldsen, the Copenhagen-born son of an Icelandic wood-carver. From 1797 onwards he worked in Rome, where a statue of Jason for an English art collector inaugurated a series of graceful neoclassical sculptures of mythical and allegorical subjects, including a 120-foot-long 'Alexander frieze' to welcome Napoleon to the second capital of his empire. On the coming of peace to Europe he adorned its cities with statues, from Copernicus and Poniatowski in Warsaw to Byron in Cambridge. After Canova's death in 1822 he had no rival in the interpretation of the classical ideals, and his return to Denmark in 1838 was that of a national hero, for whose work a museum was already planned in permanent commemoration. During the remaining seven years of his life Thorvaldsen completed his less happily conceived figures of Christ and twelve apostles as the sole ornament of the metropolitan church, rebuilt after the British bombardment of Copenhagen.

Edvard Grieg, who is now honoured by an annual music festival in Bergen, the city of his birth, found much of his inspiration in the contemporary interest in folk melodies. This was particularly strong in such countries as Norway at a time when the peasantry were waking to self-consciousness; and characteristic features of this type of melody coloured much of his work. Grieg's only symphony was not a success, but he wrote four sonatas, numerous 'lyrical pieces' for the piano, and settings for more than 100 songs. He was celebrated for his appearances on concert platforms all over Europe, where he figured as conductor or solo pianist, whilst many of his compositions – such as *Ich liebe dich*, for which Hans Andersen supplied the original Scandinavian text – were also well suited to the amateur performances of Victorian home life. Thus 'the Chopin of the North'[12] won a special place for Norway in the world of music; it is perhaps significant that the suites Grieg wrote for *Peer Gynt*, Ibsen's poetic study of the national temperament, still figure among his most widely appreciated works.

Jean Sibelius resembles Grieg in deriving inspiration from the folk melodies of his native Finland and in winning an international reputation for its music. His seven symphonies, of which four were composed before 1914, possessed, however, a much greater depth of meaning. Moreover, in comparison with the Norwegian, the symphonic poems and other parts of Sibelius's work had a closer relationship to the national history. Like the painter Akseli Gallén-Kallela,* he was captivated by the mysteries of *Kalevala*; he also chose such themes as 'Historic Scenes' and 'Karelia', and in 1899 his *Finlandia* (opus 27) was a contribution to the national struggle which the Russians attempted to suppress. In later days this work provided independent Finland with the music for its national anthem.

If Sibelius reached the foremost position among all his contemporaries as a symphonic composer, the same claim may be made for the Norwegian, Edvard Munch, as the pioneer of Expressionist painting. He was the son of a doctor practising in the poorer quarters of Oslo, and his early work was influenced by a group of amoral 'Bohemian' writers, to which Garborg for a time adhered. Although he was the nephew of the national historian, P. A. Munch, neither the subject nor the treatment of his first three significant paintings – 'The Sick Child', 'Puberty', and 'The Morning After' – appealed to the conventional taste of the day. But an exhibition in Berlin brought him fame in advanced circles there, and by 1902 the twenty-two items which he called 'The Frieze of Life' had served to launch the Expressionist movement. Munch also painted portraits, including a revealing series of self-portraits, and his lifelong interest in woodcuts and lithography caused his most characteristic works, such as 'The Cry', to be available in many versions. Like his intimate friend, August Strindberg, Munch suffered a complete nervous breakdown, and although he emerged from a Danish clinic in a stabler and happier frame of mind, his work was

---

* 1865–1931. Established the National Romantic movement in Finnish painting, as did Eliel Saarinen (1873–1950) in architecture; he also attracted foreign designers to Finland, and co-operated with Saarinen in asserting its position as a pioneer of the industrial arts at the World Exhibition in Paris, 1900.

still ill-received in orthodox circles in his own country. This was shown as late as 1914, when Oslo University hesitated to buy the huge murals he had designed for its Great Hall until their purchase for Jena already impended. Munch settled henceforth in Norway, winning wider appreciation and remaining productive almost to his death in 1943. Two decades later the English critic, Sir Herbert Read, summed him up as 'an exponent of the Zeitgeist, comparable to Ibsen or Dostoevsky in literature'.[13]

SCIENCE AND TECHNOLOGY

In the eighteenth century Swedes had contributed notably to the advance of pure science, and their iron industry had nurtured enterprising technologists; one of the latter, Mårten Triewald, even worked for a time with Newcomen on the erection of his pioneer steam engine. But for two generations after the Napoleonic Wars, when the steam engine in its final form was generating immense wealth for Britain and other rapidly industrialised regions in western Europe, Scandinavia as a whole remained poor and rural – conditions which favoured neither the science of the universities nor the inventiveness that is stimulated by commercial opportunity. Nevertheless, each Scandinavian country made at least sporadic contributions to the advance of science, whilst Sweden, besides excelling in this respect, was conspicuous in the later part of this period for its galaxy of inventors.

The University of Oslo had the misfortune to produce its most brilliant scholar at the very outset of its career, when poverty was deepest. The mathematical genius of Niels Henrik Abel was discovered whilst he was still a schoolboy, but after graduation the university could offer nothing better than a travel award. His masterpiece on algebraic functions was presented to the Paris Academy of Science in 1826, but was mislaid for fifteen years before it was published. Other papers, which revolutionised the algebra of the day, appeared in *Crelle's Journal* in Berlin, where Abel was eventually offered a professorship – news of which reached Norway a few days after he had died of tuberculosis in 1829 at the age of twenty-six. Half a century later, however, conditions were more propitious for the life work of G. H. Armauer Hansen, a physician stationed in Bergen, which was the centre for the treatment of leprosy, still rife in certain poorer districts in western and northern Norway. His identification of the leprosy bacillus in 1874, less than ten years after Pasteur's first demonstration of the link between bacteria and disease, was one of the great medical advances of the age. Isolation of the victims reduced the incidence of leprosy in his native land almost to vanishing-point, and the modern treatment of this world-wide scourge is still recognised as stemming from Armauer Hansen's discovery that it is a non-hereditary infection.

The most eminent Danish scientist of the nineteenth century, H. C. Örsted, was an apothecary's son with strong philosophic interests, whose work on *The Soul in Nature* was translated into German and other languages. As the elder brother of a prime minister, he also concerned himself with public education, acting for more than twenty years as director of the Copenhagen Polytechnic. His main achievement, however, was to clarify the relations between magnetism and electricity, which he established in 1820 in a Latin pamphlet. His observations on the behaviour of a magnetic needle, when placed near the conductor of an electric current, led directly to the further discoveries of Ampère, Faraday and others, which often involved consultation with Örsted. Another figure of scientific note connected with Copenhagen University was N. R. Finsen, who took up the study of the physiological effects of light after noticing the effect of its variations upon his own learning capacity, when sent from his Faeroese home to school in Iceland, with its constant alternations of sun and storm. His experiments led to the invention of a lamp for the treatment of skin diseases by ultra-violet rays, and the Light Institute which he founded in Copenhagen in 1896 (and which he subsequently endowed with half the proceeds of his Nobel prize) was the first great centre for the practice of phototherapy.

Sweden, unlike the other two kingdoms, was the home of at least one major scientist at both ends of the century. J. J. Berzelius, who was trained as a medical practitioner at Uppsala, was for a time professor of medicine at the Caroline Institute in Stockholm, though his primary interest was in chemistry. By 1818 he had fixed the atomic weights of 45 out of 49 elements then known, and he devised the system of notation which is still employed. After he extended his interest to organic substances, he published a textbook in six languages, which (though not free from error) dominated European chemistry; foreign countries honoured him with the membership of no fewer than eighty-one of their learned societies. S. A. Arrhenius, who had the seeming advantage that he was born in Uppsala, had a more chequered career. The theory of electrolytic dissociation, which was his prime contribution to physical chemistry, appeared in embryo in a thesis which was given so low a grade by the Swedish Academy of Science that he failed to obtain a post in any Swedish university. In 1886 – only three years later – the distinction of his work was reported to the British Association by Oliver Lodge, but a further nine years passed before Arrhenius was made a professor at the Stockholm High School. From 1905 until his death in 1927, however, he was director of the Nobel Institute for Physical Chemistry, where he had leisure to extend his interests to biochemistry and cosmic physics; in 1903 he was the first Swedish recipient of a Nobel Prize.

These prizes, which were first awarded in 1901, have a double interest in the present context. Looking forward, we can see that the three scientific prizes – to a greater extent than the Swedish Academy's necessarily more subjective selections in the field of literature – have become an institution of generally recognised importance. This adds considerably to the international standing of the Academy of Science, which makes the annual choice of the outstanding work done in physics and chemistry, and of the Caroline Institute, which chooses for physiology with medicine. Looking back, we may also reflect that the will of Alfred Nobel, which he formulated after much consideration in the year before his death in 1896, is a striking indication of the closer relationship which had been gradually established between science and technology.

Nobel was, indeed, the first of a long line of Swedish inventors who gained for their country a special (and highly profitable) position in the new phase of industrial development which began in the 1870s. He was the son of an entrepreneur with an inventive turn of mind, who prospered greatly for a time through moving with his family from Stockholm to St Petersburg, and some part of his own vast fortune was made from oil developments in Baku under the control of his brothers. His first successful invention was a detonator for blasting with nitro-glycerine. Then in 1867 Nobel patented 'dynamite', a form in which the nitro-glycerine was safe for use, thus substituting a new 'force' for gunpowder in the rapidly expanding mining and construction industries of the world. Two further developments were blasting gelatine, which under various patent names became 'the cause of many changed features in the face of Mother Earth',[14] and ballistite, which was one of the first smokeless powders for the battlefield. Although the last two years of his life were devoted mainly to the expansion of the Swedish arms industry through his purchase of the Bofors steelworks, Nobel's business activities were widely international; he organised companies in France, Germany, and Great Britain – where the firm he founded later became one of the three constituents of Imperial Chemical Industries – and challenged du Pont de Nemours for possession of the transatlantic market in explosives.

Gustaf De Laval, descended from an immigrant French soldier of fortune, is perhaps the best known of Nobel's younger Swedish contemporaries. His cream separator, which found a big domestic market in the 1880s when butter was a major Swedish export, spread to dairy farms in all parts of the world. This machine was worked by a small turbine, which led its inventor to perfect (in 1890) the first high-speed steam-turbine, which twenty years later was made reversible. Meanwhile he had produced other new devices with a versatility which rivalled that of Thomas Edison, and at one time he had 100 engineers in his employment. Advanced engineering of all kinds was, indeed, becoming a Swedish speciality, of which it must suffice to name examples. In 1878 L. M. Ericsson devised the table apparatus for Graham Bell's telephone, of which the Swedes in consequence became prominent European manufacturers. In 1880 Jonas Wenström invented the slotted armature for the newly established electric dynamo; in 1907 Sven Wingquist introduced the ball-bearings for which 'Skefco' (Svenska Kullagerfabriken) became world-famous; and by 1914 a compound reaction turbine independent of the English version had been produced by the brothers B. and F. Ljungström.

The wood-working industries were a natural interest for Sweden, to which its chemists made numerous contributions, one of the earliest being a safety-head for matches, invented at the Stockholm Technical Institute in 1846, and one of the most valuable C. D. Ekman's pioneer sulphite process for cellulose, which spread abroad from Sweden in the late 1870s. But even the match manufacture engaged the attention of the engineers, one of the earliest European examples of full automation being the machine completed by Alexander Lagerman in 1892 for a daily output of 2,400,000 matches. A Swedish engineer was also responsible for another form of automation, which spread quickly to every sea, namely the adaptation for the functioning of unmanned lighthouses and light-buoys of the automatic sun-valve. This was invented in 1912 by Gustaf Dalén, who in that year received the Nobel Prize for physics.

Although both Norway and Denmark shared to some extent in the growth which transformed the Swedish economy, their technology was still derived almost entirely from abroad. One of the two main exceptions in the case of Norway was the harpoon-gun, which was introduced in 1868 by an experienced whale hunter, Svend Foyn. This made the large finback whales for the first time an easy prey, the missile exploding with deadly effect inside the body. Whaling in Antarctic waters then became a speciality of the Norwegians, who in 1912–13 also conducted the first experiment with a factory-ship for processing the catch at sea. In 1905 they found the means of exploiting a quite different opportunity, thanks to the close co-operation between an entrepreneur who had been trained as a civil engineer (Sam Eyde) and a physics professor (Kristian Birkeland) whose interest in the aurora borealis had led on to the discovery of an electric arc. By adapting this to the fixation of nitrogen from the atmosphere, they were able to employ Norway's cheap hydro-electric power for the 'Norway saltpetre' which helped to meet a rising demand for fertilisers.

Having pioneered the large motor-ship (see p. 251), the Danes achieved a worldwide reputation for their marine engines. Otherwise their inventiveness was directed mainly to the processing of agricultural exports and to handicraft work, since raw materials to stimulate large-scale industry were generally lacking. Two exceptions were limestone and clay; possession of the former led to the development of cement-machinery, of the latter to important contributions in the field of pottery and ceramics. Thus the coal-saving tunnel-kiln was a Danish invention of 1839 and the insulating properties of moler – which became one of the few raw-material exports from Denmark – were discovered there in 1890, whilst a long period of trial and error has perfected the coloured crystal glazes with which Royal Copenhagen ware is still embellished.

EXPLORATION

In the nineteenth century the exploration of the land and water surfaces of the globe had the glamour which now attaches to voyages into space. The task was not prohibitively expensive for small nations hoping to enhance their prestige, and in the case of the polar regions, which Man had hitherto failed to penetrate, the Scandinavian peoples had strong natural reasons for participation. Three of them were familiarised with problems of survival in ice and snow by conditions in the north of their homelands; the fourth, namely the Danes, were the accepted owners of the huge Arctic *terra incognita* of Greenland; and the Norwegians in particular had hunted sea mammals and fished in Arctic waters from time immemorial.

The Spitsbergen archipelago, a no-man's-land whose southern extremity was only 355 miles north of Norway, made an obvious starting-point for investigation. In 1827 the islands were visited by a geologist from Oslo university; ten years later, a Swede was the first to dredge in the surrounding waters; and in 1863 a Norwegian hunting-vessel completed the circumnavigation. An even larger part was played by the Danish settlements on the west coast of Greenland, from which control was exercised over the primitive Eskimo tribes of native Greenlanders; in 1829 and 1884 Danish naval officers also sailed up the ice-bound east coast, eventually discovering an isolated group of Greenlanders under Stone Age conditions at Angmagssalik, whilst expeditions from several nations tried in vain to cross the ice-cap in between. In 1888 this problem was solved by the young Norwegian scientist and ski expert Fridtjof Nansen, who crossed from east to west, reaching a height of almost 9,000 feet and ignoring the fact that, if his route had proved impracticable, he and his five companions (including two Lapps) had no possible line of retreat. The dramatic story told in his *First Crossing of Greenland* has perhaps tended to distract the attention of the world from the later achievements of Knud Rasmussen, the son of a Danish clergyman and his half-Greenlander wife; in 1910 he established Thule as a trading post for the rediscovered Polar Eskimos of the extreme north-west, and two years later made it his base for the first of his seven expeditions, journeying across the vast northern spaces of the island in both directions.

The north polar regions were also explored in three famous voyages, each of them under Scandinavian auspices. A. E. Nordenskiöld was a Finnish citizen, but his political outlook was too liberal for the Russian governor-general, so he made his way in Sweden as a mineralogist. He played a considerable part in the exploration of both Spitsbergen and Greenland, but was particularly attracted by the quest for a north-east passage; this seemed more hopeful when the circumnavigation of Novaya Zemlya by Norwegian seal hunters in 1870 suggested that it might be feasible to pass through the Kara Sea to the mouths of the great Siberian rivers. After twice reaching the mouth of the Yenisei, Nordenskiöld set out from Tromsö on 4 July 1878, hoping to get right through to the Bering Strait before the ice was impassable. He failed by a margin of 120 miles, which imposed a delay of nine months before he could complete the passage. His achievement, which was rewarded in Sweden with a barony, was not repeated until 1914–15, when two Russian ships made the voyage in the opposite direction.

Nansen's scientific mind was attracted to the same expanse of frozen waters by the theory of a transpolar current, which arose from the discovery near the southern extremity of Greenland of wreckage originating in the New Siberian Islands. Hence the voyage of the *Fram*, specially shaped so as to lift under the enormous pressure of the drift-ice in the Arctic Ocean, to which it was consigned at a position north of the Islands in September 1893. Its line of drift went farther south than Nansen had anticipated, but after two years the vessel emerged safely near Spitsbergen under Nansen's second-in-command, H. O. Sverdrup. He himself with one companion had left the ship on a heroic but unsuccessful attempt to reach the Pole with sledges drawn by dogs; they returned to civilisation on almost the same day as their ship, having survived a winter in Franz Josef land in an ice hut of their own building, on the scanty animal life which came within range of their rifles. In an age when the outside world had had to wait two whole years for any news of the ship or its crew, Nansen's *Farthest North* became a popular classic, whilst the six volumes of scientific results (completed in 1906) helped to establish the new science of oceanography, to which Nansen now devoted his attention.

In the last years of the century the Swedes made the first attempt to reach the North Pole by air – a balloon flight which cost all three participants their lives – and Sverdrup employed the *Fram* on an attempted circumnavigation of Greenland; this resulted in the exploration of the Canadian islands farther west which bear his name. But the third historic voyage was that which penetrated the North-West Passage, vainly sought by so many famous navigators, from Frobisher to Franklin. Roald Amundsen, a Norwegian medical student for whom polar exploration early became an all-absorbing interest, gained experience as mate in a Belgian expedition to Antarctica before he set off for Arctic waters in the 47-ton seal-hunter *Gjöa*, which he had equipped with a small petrol engine. He was held up for nearly two years off King William Island, where he studied the Eskimo inhabitants and made a precise determination of the north magnetic pole. Eventually, however, after yet a third winter in the ice, a passage of only eight days carried him through to open water in the Beaufort Sea, from which Amundsen reached the Bering Strait in August 1906.

Distance was a serious deterrent to Scandinavian exploration of the Antarctic, but from 1892 onwards the Norwegians went there in search of new whaling-grounds, and three years later the support of Svend Foyn enabled them to be the first to set foot on the mainland at Cape Adare. In 1901–4 a Swedish expedition also went south under a nephew of Baron Nordenskiöld. Amundsen, however, planned to follow up his first great success by an improved version of the drift of the *Fram*, leaving the South Pole to be the objective of a large-scale British venture under Captain

Scott, which was also to carry out an elaborate scientific programme. But eventually the news of Peary's arrival at the North Pole in 1909 caused Amundsen to head south instead, waiting until the *Fram* touched at Madeira before informing his companions, his supporters at home, and Captain Scott.

Both expeditions spent the Antarctic winter of 1911 on the edge of the ice shelf, where Amundsen's position offered the shorter but rougher route to the common objective; his intention was to dispense with any form of scientific observations on the way, whilst he made a rapid dash for the goal with his dog-teams. Scott and his four companions, on the other hand, finding too late that their Siberian ponies were useless in Antarctic snow conditions, had to pull their own sledges. The Norwegian party were a month ahead of them at the Pole, and the Englishmen all perished on the return journey in an agonising contest with deteriorating weather, compounded by disappointment and some maldistribution in their supply depots. The pathos of Scott's diary, written up to the day of his death, struck home to the British people in a way which for a long time prevented them from doing justice to Amundsen's feat, completed in ninety-nine days with eleven dogs and some other food in hand. But his is now acknowledged to have been 'the most successful polar journey on record'.[15]

The Scandinavian nations had less direct interest than the great imperial powers in the opening up of the inhabited regions of the world. They even preferred to divest themselves of their existing tropical possessions: the Danes sold Tranquebar to the British in 1845, followed five years later by the forts on the Gold Coast; the Swedes sold Saint Barthélemy to the French in 1878, thirty years after the abolition of slavery had made the ownership of the West Indian islands finally unprofitable. Nevertheless, in the person of Sven Hedin Sweden produced one of the most eminent in the long succession of modern travellers who have sought out the mysteries of inner Asia. A Kiplingesque figure of partly Jewish ancestry, he was devoted to the service of God, King and country – both as an adventurer prepared to endure any physical hardship and as a scholar whose many books showed a solid scientific basis. He visited Persia when he was twenty, and before he was thirty had begun the exploration of East Turkestan, Tibet, and the Trans-Himalayas which he was the first to record and name. After the fourth of his many journeys he was ennobled by Oscar II, and became politically prominent, both as an opponent of the dissolution of the union with Norway and as a champion of the pro-German politics of Gustav V. In the decade preceding the First World War, Hedin published on an average two volumes a year, with translated versions which reached a world-wide public.

SERVICES TO THE WORLD AT LARGE

In the then commonly accepted use of the word 'mission', the peoples of Scandinavia were certainly among the most enthusiastic participants in a movement which was characteristic of the nineteenth century, when it seemed almost certain that the white man's religion was destined to conquer the world as surely as his military and industrial technologies. Moreover, the record of the Scandinavian Churches in this respect has a continuing importance, because native populations do not forget the fact that their work, unlike that of many of the missionaries sent out by the empire-building powers, had no undercurrent of imperialism. The Norwegians, who have never held territory in Asia or Africa, record a higher proportion of missionaries to population than any other country in Europe.

Although periodic Nordic missionary conferences date from 1863 and a common missionary periodical from 1891, the basis of organisation was national or even local, funds being raised and interest sustained by committees in which the laity (including women) were often more active than the regular Church authorities. In spite of the pioneer achievements of Hans Egede in Greenland, the first Norwegian missions in the 19th century sprang up in Stavanger in 1826–36 under English and German influences, whilst the first Swedish missionary college was established in Lund in 1846 by Peter Fjellstadt, who had worked in South India under the English Church Missionary Society. But by the 1860s the Swedes had their own mission in Ethiopia, the Norwegians in Zululand, the Danes in Madras, and the Finns in South-West Africa, where Marti Rauttanen toiled for sixty years. By the end of the century Swedish missions had penetrated the Dark Continent in three other areas; the Norwegians had become the chief Protestant influence in the development of Madagascar; and Norwegians were co-operating with Danes in a special mission to the depressed Santals in what is now Bangladesh, where a Norwegian crofter's son, Lars Skrefsrud, pioneered self-support through agricultural and tea-planting projects. The Danes had been active since 1819 in China, and the first Finnish missionaries were about to enter Japan.

As preachers of the Gospel, the Scandinavians were as zealous for Lutheranism as other religious propagandists for other creeds. Their social approach, however, made its special mark through the interest shown in the Malagasy, Hindu, and other indigenous cultures; the work done in the fields of health and education; and a noteworthy reluctance to rely on the white man's prestige as a safeguard for their missionaries. It was a Norwegian who gave the World Missionary Conference at Edinburgh in 1910 the forward-looking advice, 'Let the Bible be our Consul.'[16]

The widespread voluntary financial support for foreign missions is all the more striking because Scandinavia as a whole did not as yet occupy a position of economic strength in comparison with more fully industrialised regions in Europe and North America. One consequence was the time-lag already noted in the growth of the modern social services. Yet there were at least three spheres in which Scandinavian society was often held up for admiration. One was the position of women, whose advance towards legal equality of status and political emancipation had been accompanied by the growth of a liberal attitude regarding 'suitable' types of employment and social activity. It is significant that the segregation of the sexes in school life was not a common Scandinavian practice. Secondly, Scandinavia enjoyed a flying start in all that comprises protection of the environment, with its wealth of natural beauty and abundant space in relation to any conceivable growth of population. An industrial revolution based on hydro-electricity reduced pollution of the atmosphere to the minimum, and the ease with which the new power could be brought to any location encouraged an enviable growth of small urban units in harmony with their rural surroundings.

Thirdly, the Scandinavians had some special reputation at this time in the sphere of physical culture. The schools of many other lands were taught 'Swedish drill', which derived from the system established in 1813 by P. H. Ling of the Gothic Society in Sweden, who doubled the roles of fencing master and poet. Skiing as a sport was popularised through the Norwegian Holmenkollen competitions, which date from 1890; its practical usefulness had, indeed, been advertised many years earlier in America, when a Norwegian immigrant, 'Snowshoe Thomson', conveyed the mail across the snowbound Sierra Nevada. And when the Olympic Games were held in Stockholm in 1912, the host nation occupied the first place and the Finns came fourth.

More enduring laurels were won by Scandinavia in the very different field of the work for international peace, where the work done did not always evoke immediate recognition. Peace associations having been established in each of the three Kingdoms in 1882–5 with obligatory international arbitration as a central aim, the Norwegian Storting expressed unanimous support for such a policy as early as 1890, whilst the Danes had already been prompt to make three unrestricted treaties of this kind under the Hague Convention of 1899. Ten years later a Norwegian, Christian Lange, became secretary of the Inter-parliamentary Union of self-governing states, which had been at work for two decades to promote peaceful co-operation. But it seems likely that the publicity which attended the numerous pronouncements of Björnson on the ethics of international relations – these were of course particularly well known in the other Scandinavian countries – played a part in Nobel's decision that the fifth of his prizes should be entrusted to the judgement of a small committee of Norwegians appointed by the Storting.

In the early years the Peace Prize was awarded mainly to specialised peace-workers. In 1908, for instance, it was divided between a Swedish writer, K. P. Arnoldson, who had presented the peace movement to the world in *Hope of the Centuries*, and the Danish founder-president of the Peace Bureau at Berne, F. Bajer, who was also a veteran of the war of 1864 and a devotee of Scandinavianism. But the debatable awards, which have often made Oslo the focus of international discussion as to what constitutes work for peace, also began in this period with the honour done in 1906 to

President Theodore Roosevelt, who had recently mediated the peace treaty between Russia and Japan – but who also vaunted his reliance on 'carrying a big stick'. However, when he came to Oslo in 1910 to receive the prize, Roosevelt justified the Norwegians in their choice by his advocacy of something very like the League of Nations which was set up ten years later – after the war which better peace-keeping institutions might have postponed or even prevented.

Chapter 13

Aspirations of the Northern Neutrals, 1914-1939

INTRODUCTION

During the quarter-century between the outbreak of the First World War in August 1914 and that of its successor, which was to affect northern Europe much more closely, the sovereign states of Scandinavia gained in prestige, acquiring some degree of recognition as a significantly homogeneous group at the same time as their number grew to five. The Finns proclaimed their independence on 6 December 1917, though they seemed at that time likely to pass almost at once from Russian to German control; and on 1 December 1918 the Icelanders, too, became independent, on the basis of an agreement with Denmark for the retention of a common monarchy. The increase of prestige resulted chiefly from the ability which these countries – with the partial exception of Finland – showed to achieve satisfactory solutions of their pressing internal problems by strictly democratic methods. In international affairs, on the other hand, the Scandinavian standpoint was often inacceptable to the greater powers, yet its distinctiveness emphasised their position as a like-minded group which championed peace and the rule of law: even Iceland was a signatory of the Kellogg Pact, albeit that its people rejected a proposal that the millennium of the Althing in 1930 might fittingly be marked by adhesion to the League of Nations.

THE WAR YEARS

In the autumn of 1914 each of the Scandinavian peoples sought above all to preserve its neutrality, but their situation differed considerably. The Norwegians felt safe so long as Britain controlled the seas, and expected that a decisive naval battle would be fought not far from their shores. In Sweden the upper classes hoped that Germany would win the war, still more that Russia would lose it; the only activists were a few groups which aspired to rescue Finland from the Russian clutches. The Finns were fortunate in having no army and therefore no call-up for the service of the Tsar-Grand Duke; but a big increase in the Russian garrison and, early in

1915, the refortification of the Åland Islands boded ill for their future, especially as the control of finance and education were now transferred into Russian hands. The risk of immediate involvement was most serious, however, for the Danes, who were required by the Germans on 5 August 1914 to mine the Great Belt – international waters through which the British navy might enter the Baltic. The government complied, mining the Little Belt and the Danish side of the Sound as well, so that their action might seem to be related to the defence of Danish territory, and to their great relief a personal appeal from King Christian to George V was favourably received by the latter's ministers. Britain had no means of protecting Denmark from a German invasion, such as would have followed a Danish refusal, and British plans for forcing an entry into Baltic waters were at that time in abeyance.*

The positions of the Swedish and Norwegian governments were similar enough for them to achieve an immediate *rapprochement*; on 8 August they jointly announced their firm intention 'to maintain the neutrality of the respective kingdoms in relation to all the belligerent powers'.[2] This was followed in December by a well publicised meeting of the three Scandinavian kings and their foreign ministers at Malmö, and when they met again at Oslo three years later the King of Sweden (who took the lead on both occasions) called for 'a new union, not of the old sort, but a union of heartfelt understanding'.[3] One practical result was the vigorous assertion of common claims against belligerents on both sides by Hjalmar Hammarskjöld: the Swedish prime minister consequently became better known in the outside world than his two colleagues, though their ministries lasted longer.†

In spite of friction over neutral rights, each kingdom derived large profits from neutrality. The warring powers outbid each other to secure their goods and services, such as shipping, and the Germans paid liberally for clandestine purchases of goods from America and other overseas sources which had been allowed through the Allied blockade for use inside Scandinavia. This traffic was eventually reduced to a mere trickle by refusing supplies to firms which were black-listed as 'trading with the enemy', but Scandinavian business had many other openings. The Swedes shipped across the

---

* Such plans were seen to presuppose a close blockade of the Heligoland Bight, for which Churchill as First Lord of the Admiralty had ordered preliminary studies in January 1913; on 31 July 1914 he asked the Prime Minister for inter-service examination of the prospects for seizing any of eight named bases for this purpose, including Egersund in Norway, Kungsbacka in Sweden, and Laesö or Esbjerg in Denmark.[1] But expert naval opinion was hostile to every aspect of the Baltic project, not least because it had originated in the fertile imagination of Admiral of the Fleet Lord Fisher, whose surviving records contain no evidence that he had ever studied the problem in depth or in detail.

† Hammarskjöld's minority government – which depended for survival upon an emergency truce in party politics – had to resign when food became scarce in the spring of 1917. In Norway Gunnar Knudsen enjoyed the support of a Venstre majority, 1913–20, and in Denmark Theodor Zahle's Radical government was kept in office for the same period by Social Democratic votes.

Baltic the iron ore for German armaments and their own advanced engineering products. The Danes sold their agricultural exports across the land
frontier to Germany and over the North Sea to Britain, which supplied
coal in return. The Norwegians at first obtained top prices for fish from
Germany, but were later obliged to let all but 15 per cent go to British
purchasers or else forfeit supplies essential for the fisheries. Their sulphur
pyrites and copper were even more valuable in time of war, so in the winter
of 1916–17 a coal embargo was imposed in order to secure the entire output
for the British market.

In sum, 1914–16 were boom years, in which the workers had full employment, though a general policy of *laissez-faire* allowed war profiteers to
flourish whilst wage rates lagged behind the rise in the cost of living. Then
came a period of increasing hardship for the Scandinavian neutrals. In
February 1917 they protested jointly but vainly against the German
unrestricted submarine campaign. By the end of the war the Norwegians,
who were induced to charter to Britain most of their 2½ million tons of
shipping, lost one-half* of it, together with the lives of 2,000 crew members.
The Swedes and Danes, whose fleets in 1914 were respectively a little
more and a little less than 1 million tons, lost a quarter and a third, in each
case with a roughly proportionate loss of life. Moreover, the entry of the
United States into the war at this juncture worsened the position of all the
remaining European neutrals, as all transatlantic supplies were withheld,
pending the negotiation of much stricter trade agreements than the Allies
had hitherto ventured to exact. The Norwegians – although they sent
Nansen to press their case in Washington – had to wait until April 1918 for
supplies, the Swedes until May, and the Danes until September. The
Norwegian flour ration fell to half a pound a day, whilst in Sweden,
where the harvest of 1917 was the worst since the 1860s, even potatoes were
rationed. The Danes never lacked food, though the shortage of foodstuffs
caused the pig population to be reduced by 80 per cent, and they sent much
dairy produce to both their Scandinavian neighbours, receiving fertiliser
from Norway and industrial raw materials from Sweden in exchange.

Although wages rose faster in the later war years as a result of popular
unrest, they did not compensate fully for the rise in the cost of living, which
in the course of four years amounted to 280 per cent in Norway, 250 in
Sweden, and 200 in Denmark. In addition to the quick fortunes made by
speculation, shipowners, industrialists and self-employed farmers and
fishermen in general prospered, whilst the existence of a black market in
foodstuffs added to the sense of social injustice felt by the wage-earners.
In all three Kingdoms the news of the two revolutions in Russia in March
and November 1917 made the situation more tense. In May 1917 a Left
Socialist Party was founded in Sweden, which won eleven seats in the

---

* The loss was 49·3 per cent of the 1914 tonnage, as compared with the British loss of
37·6 from a much larger total. In absolute figures Britain alone sustained a heavier loss than
Norway, whose place among the mercantile marines of the world fell from fourth to sixth.[4]

following year's elections to the Second Chamber; in Copenhagen the syndicalist trade-union opposition in February 1918 staged an attack by unemployed upon the Stock Exchange, which did some damage to 'the symbol of the capitalist society';[5] and in the following month the Norwegian Labour Party Conference passed a motion in favour of 'revolutionary mass action'.[6] Sporadic attempts were also made to set up local Soviets as in Russia, but Finland alone became the scene of a serious effort to establish a proletarian government on Scandinavian soil, the upshot being a civil war which was at the same time a war of independence.

The split between classes in Finland had hitherto been prevented from widening – except for the brief clash over the Sveaborg mutiny in 1906 – by the pressure for unity in the nationalist struggle against Russia. Since the outbreak of war in Europe the nation had pinned its hopes on the victory of the Germans, who promised their support for Finnish autonomy at an eventual peace conference and offered training facilities for volunteers from Finland; about 2,000 students and other youthful patriots were smuggled into Germany via Sweden and sent to fight on the eastern front as a battalion of Prussian Light Infantry. Factory workers, on the other hand, found their wages depressed by an influx of Russian labour at a time when industrialists were making record profits. Moreover, in 1916 the cleavage of classes was further emphasised by a split in the rapidly growing co-operative movement, so that the urban wage-earners (many of whom looked to co-operation to promote social change) became organised separately from the farmers and other bourgeois, for whom it was merely a device for saving money. In the same year elections were held in advance for a post-war Diet. A low poll gave the Social Democrats an overall majority of three seats (in 200), a result which has been attributed to middle-class neglect of an election which would have no practical consequence in the immediate future.

Be that as it may, the Russian Revolution of March 1917 led to the summoning of the Diet and the appointment of a preponderantly Social Democratic Senate, under whose auspices a law was enacted in July to transfer to the Diet the powers formerly held by the Grand Duke-Tsar, foreign policy and defence alone excepted. This 'power law' went too far to be tolerated by Kerensky and his colleagues in Russia, who instructed the governor-general to hold a new election. The poll in early October, which was much heavier than before, returned only 92 socialists to the Diet – a result which both surprised and aggrieved the more radical among their supporters, who turned to direct action. Widespread unemployment and the mutinous condition of the Russian garrison made it easy for them to find both men and arms for a Red Guard, whilst by the end of October the first shipment of arms from abroad had reached Vaasa for a White Guard, whose avowed aim was the expulsion of the Russians from Finnish soil.

The accession of Lenin and the Bolsheviks to power in Russia on 7 November affected both the national and the social issues in Finland.

Only eight days later the new Diet assumed rights of sovereignty on a provisional basis, and on 6 December an independent republic was formally proclaimed by Svinhufvud, whom the bourgeois majority in the Diet placed at the head of the ministry. His accession to office (26 November) had been delayed by a general strike, in which the strikers perpetrated at least 100 murders but failed to secure more than a part of their sweeping demands for immediate social reforms. The more extreme of the socialists in the Diet were therefore disinclined to sever the last links with Russia. Nevertheless, the independence of Finland was formally recognised by Lenin, whose theories left him in no doubt that it would gravitate in due course into the Soviet sphere; indeed, in the troubled months which followed, Stalin as commissar for nationalities counted it among the Soviet republics. Recognition of independence by Sweden, Germany and France quickly followed.

Thus the social and national issues were already closely intermingled before Svinhufvud entrusted the command of the armed forces of the infant republic to Gustaf Mannerheim,* a Finnish baron who spoke no Finnish and who had returned from long service in the Russian army as recently as 18 December 1917. Within a month he had left Helsinki again for the north-western province of Ostrobothnia; Svinhufvud and other ministers followed him, whilst all the main towns of southern Finland and about one-half of the entire country passed under the control of a commission of left-wing socialists, headed by a former president of the Diet and supported by the native Red Guards and mutinous Russian soldiers and sailors from the garrisons. The Finnish Reds, as we may call them, disfigured their rule by paying off old scores against class enemies, of whom about 1,500 perished, and failed to gain the support of the more moderate Social Democrats of the type of Väinö Tanner.† They were also stigmatised as traitors because of their dependence upon Russian help, which consisted mainly of demoralised private soldiers without their officers; a colonel who acted as military adviser to the Red Guards was one of the few exceptions.

Since Finns on both sides displayed the same capacity for desperate valour, experienced leadership was almost bound to be the deciding factor. Mannerheim's first move was to disarm and send home the isolated Russian garrisons on the Bothnian coast, and then to build up his own forces from the yeoman farmers of that conservative region, who knew that their privi-

* 1867–1951. A member of a Dutch family which became ennobled in Sweden in the seventeenth century and which first entered Finland in the service of Gustavus III; he had married the daughter of a Russian general, was well regarded by Tsar Nicholas II, and fought with distinction in the Russo-Japanese War and the First World War. In 1917 he had commanded an army corps in Transylvania, so for bewildered bourgeois politicians his arrival on the scene in Finland was that of a veritable *deus ex machina*.

† 1881–1964. He had been a member of the Diet since 1907 and director of the Helsinki consumers' co-operative society (Elanto) since 1915; prime minister of a Social Democratic minority government in 1926, and in 1927–40 chairman of the International Co-operative Alliance. From the Winter War onwards the best known of Finnish Social Democrats.

leged position was threatened by the landless rural proletariat. He had brought with him a credit of 15 million marks from a Helsinki bank, and was able to draw munitions and supplies from Sweden, which also sent about 1,000 volunteers. Moreover, he was able to officer his partly conscript army from the men of the light infantry battalion, who began to arrive in Vaasa at the end of February. At about the same time a small Swedish force took over the maintenance of order in the Åland Islands, but it was withdrawn in the middle of March on the arrival of German troops, whose intervention in Finnish affairs Mannerheim had at first strongly deprecated.

In anticipation of a fuller German intervention, Mannerheim laid siege to Tampere, 'the Manchester of Finland' and the principal Red base in the west; it was surrendered in the first week in April after a defence which prompted a foreign eyewitness to write: 'Les Rouges font, ma foi, une très jolie résistance . . . Cette frénésie a quelquechose de profondément émouvant.'[7] In the same week German forces under Major-General R. von der Goltz landed at two points on the south coast, from which they advanced successfully on Helsinki. Mannerheim had already initiated operations in the Karelian Isthmus, where a Russian advance across the frontier was repelled, so the Reds were caught between two fires. Viipuri fell at the end of the month, and in mid-May the most sanguinary internal conflict in Scandinavian history ended with the White army's victory march through the streets of the capital. A rump Diet, from which the Social Democratic members were excluded, made Svinhufvud regent, with J. K. Paasikivi (see p. 330) as prime minister. The security of the propertied classes was further assured by 8,000 executions after trial by court martial and by the deaths from hunger or disease of about 12,000 more of the 70,000 prisoners held in Sveaborg and other detention camps as proven enemies to the national cause.[8]

Independence, however, had not been finally assured by these social convulsions, since Imperial Germany was unlikely to relinquish control over any of the border lands whose freedom from Russia had been exacted by German arms at the Peace of Brest-Litovsk in March. In the case of Finland, as we have seen, German troops were already on the spot under a commander described by Mannerheim as 'a general with an interest in politics and intrigue';[9] for a time it seemed likely that they would advance into Eastern Karelia to dislodge small British forces which had been sent to establish positions at Murmansk and later at Archangel. Both Svinhufvud and Paasikivi saw salvation in the election of a German king, who might even add Karelia to the kingdom, and were not deterred by the resignation of Mannerheim from his military command; he was sceptical about both the abilities and the intentions of the Germans, and would have preferred the throne to go to a Scandinavian or even a Russian royalty. Various Germans came under consideration, with the result that the surrender of November 1918 lay only a month ahead when the election of Prince Charles Frederick of Hesse, a brother-in-law of the Emperor William II, was carried out by

the Diet in due accordance with the Swedish Form of Government of 1772.*
The king-elect began to study the language but never set foot in his kingdom, from which all von der Goltz's men were shipped home by the end of
the year. The victory of the Western Allies had given the Finns a new start,
which they marked by transferring the office of regent to Mannerheim and
dissolving the rump parliament.

POST-WAR SCANDINAVIA

Although they had not been among the combatant powers in the First
World War, the Scandinavian states all underwent important territorial
and/or political changes as a direct consequence of its outcome. In a brief
description of these changes, it may be convenient to complete the story of
events in Finland first.

In March 1919 elections were held under Mannerheim's regency, in
which the Social Democrats, a number of whose leaders were in prison or
in exile, nevertheless won 80 seats. Since the two monarchist parties,
namely the conservative National Coalition of Old and Young Finns and
the Swedish People's Party, held only 50, the balance of power rested with
the 70 representatives of the middle-class republican parties (Agrarians
and liberal National Progressives). A new constitution was accordingly
drawn up, which combined the existing democratic parliamentary structure
with a presidential executive strong enough to withstand any renewed
attempt at subversion by left-wing forces aided and abetted from outside.
The result has stood the test of time, for in all Europe it is the sole creation
of that era of liberal hopefulness which has not been swept away or at the
very least – as in the case of Austria – forcibly suspended. The parliament
or *Elskunta* continued to be unicameral, with its 200 members elected by
universal suffrage on a basis of proportional representation which has only
once – in 1916 – given any single party a majority. The Elskunta has sole
power over the budget, can in theory override the presidential veto on the
bills it passes, and is constitutionally entitled to require that the Cabinet
shall enjoy its confidence. But the President's position is at least equally
powerful. Except when an *ad hoc* law determines otherwise, he is chosen by
the electorate, through an electoral college of 300; his term of office is six
years, as compared with the three – later, four – years of the legislature;
and he may in any case dissolve the legislature at his discretion. As head
of the executive, he is supreme commander of the armed forces and has
specific responsibility for the conduct of foreign policy; moreover, he
not infrequently nominates caretaker Cabinets which have no parliamentary basis – an illustration of what a political science expert describes as 'a tendency to see in the President an official who is under

---

* The 'also-rans' included the Emperor's younger sons, for whom he declined 'the
crown of thorns';[10] Duke Adolph Frederick of Mecklenburg, who was the Finns' first
choice; and Prince Wilhelm of Wied, who had been puppet-king of Albania before the war.

an obligation to keep the machinery of State running smoothly'.[11]

In July 1919 the first President was elected exceptionally by the Elskunta, where the moderates joined with the Social Democrats to reject Mannerheim in favour of K. J. Ståhlberg, a law professor of liberal convictions who had drafted the constitution. But the seven months of Mannerheim's regency bequeathed a further problem to his republican successor: his distinguished social connections had indeed helped to secure prompt recognition of the new Finland from the victorious powers, yet its frontiers remained uncertain in two areas. His ties with Sweden were always very close, but, when he visited King Gustav as part of a programme of strengthening Finland's Scandinavian relationships, a proposal to meet Swedish claims on Åland by allowing a share in the refortification of the islands proved wholly unacceptable. Mannerheim likewise had strong ties with the White generals who were trying to overthrow the Bolshevik regime in Russia, and to some extent with Churchill and their other non-Russian backers. Since Finland too was nominally at war with the Bolsheviks, the Regent entertained hopes of big territorial gains in Karelia if a Finnish army enabled Yudenich to capture Petrograd. But it was inherent in the reactionary outlook of the White Russian commanders that they would not unreservedly acknowledge the independence of the Finns, much less their claims to expansion.

Mannerheim's successor being less inclined to any military adventure, the Finns were content to remain in occupation of two frontier districts in Karelia until the civil war in Russia ebbed out, when the success of the Polish armies in its concluding phase gave them a favourable opportunity for negotiating peace with the Russians at Dorpat (October 1920). In the south-east they held on to the frontier of 1812, which had been granted at a time when its nearness to St Petersburg involved no possible military risk to Russia, and in the far north gained a modest outlet to the Barents Sea at Petsamo, which had nickel mines in its vicinity. But the Finns had to withdraw their irredentist claim to Eastern Karelia, and they appealed in vain to the Hague Court when the Soviet government later broke their promise to grant the Karelian population full autonomy.

The fate of the Åland Islands took even longer to settle. In 1919 the Russian fortifications were removed under a Swedish-Finnish agreement (to which Germany was also a party), but when the islanders recorded a 96 per cent vote for reunion with their fellow Swedes the Finnish government established military control and placed the separatist leaders under arrest. In June 1920 the British foreign secretary referred the dispute to the League of Nations as constituting a threat to world peace, and although an impartial observer found that 'both the Finns and the Swedes were very obstructive',[12] in the end they accepted the judgement of the League Council's commission of inquiry. This confirmed the Finnish sovereignty over the islands, both on historical grounds reaching back to 1643 and on the contemporary ground that the right of self-determination could not reasonably be invoked by a fraction of a fraction, that is to say, by the Åland element in a Swedish-speaking population of only 11 per cent in the whole of Finland. But the islanders were awarded the protection of a local legislature and a system of privileges in matters of culture, trade, and military service, infringements of which could be referred directly to the League; this made them the best protected minority population in Europe. The demilitarisation of the archipelago was also re-established in a treaty signed by the three European great powers and all states bordering on the Baltic, with the significant exception of Soviet Russia – a step which reduced but did not remove a standing threat to the safety of Sweden.

Though disappointed over a frontier rectification, the Swedish people profited by the impetus which the result of the war gave to the spread of democracy within their existing frontiers. In October 1917 a more progressive group of Conservatives which had replaced the Hammarskjöld ministry yielded office to a Liberal-Social Democratic coalition (including Hjalmar Branting,)* whose supporters held a majority of seats in a newly elected Second Chamber of the Riksdag. Thus Gustav V had already been brought to at least a tacit acceptance of parliamentarism before the war ended; three days after the armistice, his ministers announced that the local government franchise would be conceded on an equal footing to every taxpayer and that constitutional amendments to render the national elections more democratic would quickly follow. Although eligibility to the First Chamber continued to require a substantial income qualification and both electors and elected were limited by special age requirements, its members henceforth were in some degree representative of every party. As for the Second Chamber, the vote was conceded in 1922 to all men and women over twenty-three without respect to payment of taxes or fulfilment of military service obligations, the only important exception being persons in permanent receipt of poor relief.

In Denmark the outbreak of the war had engendered a general desire to complete the constitutional discussions already in progress as quickly as possible. Accordingly, in June 1915 a new constitution was adopted, of which the most important provisions were the introduction of universal suffrage at twenty-five for elections to the Folketing and a big change in the composition of the Landsting; three-quarters of its members were to be elected indirectly by Folketing voters above the age of thirty-five, the other quarter by the Landsting itself on the basis of its existing party membership. The Folketing was to sit for three years, unless dissolved by the Crown,

* 1860–1925. He was the son of a titular professor, who had suceeded Ling as head of the Gymnastics Institute, and distinguished himself in mathematics and astronomy at Uppsala, where he became attracted to radical politics. On the present occasion he held office (as finance minister) for only three months, but he later headed three Social Democratic Cabinets (1920, 1921–3, 1924–5). Thirty years after his death he was described by a Norwegian socialist historian as 'indubitably the most outstanding personality which the Scandinavian Labour movement has so far produced'.[13] It was no disadvantage to his governmental career that he had been a schoolfellow of King Gustav.

whilst one-half of the members of the Landsting were to be replaced at four-year intervals. The first elections under the new system, held six months before the end of the war, resulted in the continuance of the Radical government under Zahle, whose virtual dismissal by the king two years later was to provide a more serious test of Denmark's entry into a more democratic post-war era.

The 'Easter Crisis' of 1920 was occasioned partly by the supposed short-comings of Zahle's policy over the return of North Slesvig to Denmark (see p. 313), but mainly by his refusal to agree to the dissolution of the Folketing until a bill had been passed for extending to rural constituencies the system of proportional representation which already applied to Copen-hagen and to a number of seats distributed on a national basis. Venstre, which would be handicapped by the change, was in agreement with Conservative interests in demanding an immediate election in order to sweep away wartime controls of economic life, as required by the indus-trialists; and at this juncture the latter indicated their intention of counter-ing wage demands by a large-scale lockout. When Christian X used his prerogative to summon a new ministry to hold the election, for which Zahle would not take responsibility, the Social Democrats arranged for the trade unions to call a general strike, whilst crowds outside the palace shouted for a republic. At 4 a.m. on Easter Day the king decided to give way by appoint-ing a caretaker ministry with the approval of the political parties for the purpose of passing the electoral law in advance of the election. Venstre was successful at the polls, but the trade unions had shown a strength which caused the employers to abandon the intended lockout, whilst the monarchy had learnt the desirability of limiting its role to that of an impartial umpire in the game of democratic party politics.

The Icelandic constitution had been made more democratic in June 1915 in company with the Danish; thirty-four members were now returned to the Althing by universal suffrage in single constituencies, and the six former nominees of the Crown were added by a system of proportional representation. But the prosperity of the war period, during which the Icelandic fish trade was directed to Britain and America rather than Den-mark, stimulated further demands. In the summer of 1918, when President Wilson had made self-determination one of the main issues of the war, all Danish parties except the Conservatives joined in sending delegates to Iceland who negotiated far-reaching terms of agreement, which the islan-ders accepted by a vote of 12,040 to 897. Iceland was to become a sovereign state, linked with Denmark by a common monarchy; also by the right to acquire citizenship through residence in each other's territory and by unrestricted access to each other's fisheries, which was particularly im-portant for the Faeroese. Foreign relations were to be conducted by the Danes in accordance with Icelandic wishes, but no provision was made for common defence, as Iceland announced its perpetual neutrality. The rather tenuous nature of the union was further indicated by arrangements for its termination at any time after 1943, given the failure of a three-year period of negotiation and the approval of two-thirds of the legislature and three-quarters of the electorate in the seceding country.

Having enacted these terms at the behest of the Icelanders in the month of the armistice in Europe, the Danes were well placed for backing the claim to self-determination of their compatriots under German rule in North Slesvig.* Close contact had always been maintained across the border, but as Denmark had been neutral in the war it was for the Slesvigers themselves to petition the peace conference for the fulfilment of the promise of a plebiscite, dating from the treaty of Prague in 1866. The Allies agreed to incorporate into the peace treaty with Germany a border revision to be made in accordance with the votes recorded in two zones, of which the northernmost would vote *en bloc* and the other, where the population was more intermingled, by separate polling in each local government area. In February 1920 the first zone produced a three-quarters majority for re-union, but a month later the second zone disappointed the Danes by an even stronger vote in the opposite sense, not one area producing a Danish majority. What made this a particularly grievous blow was the fact that it included the important town of Flensburg, which had only recently become germanised, so Zahle's failure to challenge the result in any way helped to bring about the Easter Crisis. But the next government could do no more than suggest unofficially that the second zone might be internationalised. No further change was made, and on 10 July Christian X rode ceremoniously across the frontier which Christian IX's subjects had been forced to accept by the politics of 'blood and iron'. A striking contrast to the school system with which the Prussians had reinforced their conquest was provided by the Danish treatment of their new German minority, which was allowed separate village schools wherever one-fifth of the voters could present a minimum of ten German-speaking children.

In Norway the suffrage was more widely distributed before the war than in Sweden or even Denmark, but it was afterwards further extended by reducing the age of enfranchisement from 25 to 23 and by abolishing disfranchisement for the acceptance of poor relief. The system of voting was also made in principle more democratic by reverting in 1919 to large constituencies, where proportional representation gave a much better chance to the Labour Party, which had been unable to win single seats outside the larger towns because its supporters were too widely scattered. At the next election the number of Labour members was almost doubled. The most striking direct result of the war, however, was the addition of new territory to a realm which for five centuries had experienced only a long series of deprivations.

* In 1917 the Danish government had sacrificed a possible bargaining counter in future dealings with the Germans over North Slesvig by the sale of their West Indian possessions to the USA for $20 million; but they had at the same time secured American recognition that their sovereign rights in Greenland extended to every part.

In view of the part which Norwegian ships and sailors had played in the defeat of the German submarine blockade, the peacemakers at Paris briefly considered the possibility of conceding territory or trading privileges in tropical Africa, where Belgium for example was rewarded at Germany's expense. A more natural alternative presented itself in the Arctic archipelago of Spitsbergen, which may have been the Svalbard of medieval Icelandic annals and which had certainly had the Danish-Norwegian monarchy among its early claimants. Besides sporadic hunting activities, the Norwegians had a coal company there, which had recently taken over the interests of an American minerals prospector, J. M. Longyear, at Longyearby, and they shared with Sweden and Russia in a three-man administration which had been set up before the war. As in the case of Åland, the Allies saw fit to ignore Bolshevik Russia in the matter; and, after a Swedish proposal that Norway should be fobbed off with a League Mandate had been rejected, a treaty of 1920 granted Norway the sovereignty over the group, including Bear Island. Norwegian administration, which began five years later, was made subject to two limitations: the islands must remain unfortified and their economic exploitation was to be open to all powers acceding to the treaty, as did Soviet Russia in 1935.

FOREIGN POLICY UNDER LEAGUE OF NATIONS AUSPICES

The three Scandinavian kingdoms welcomed the establishment of the League, in which they saw both an agency for the maintenance of world peace and an organisation based on democratic principles, where they might be able to exert an influence which the world of great powers had hitherto denied them. In 1917 they had set up commissions of their own, which produced a common scheme for such a league; in March 1919 their representatives were accorded a brief hearing in Paris before the victors drew up their League Covenant for insertion in the peace treaties; and although little regard had been paid to their views, all three countries figured among the thirteen neutrals who adhered to the Covenant at its coming into force in January 1920. Finland was admitted in the following December, but played at first a less active part, for it was not until 1922 that the legislature rejected the idea of basing security against hypothetical Russian aggression upon a defence alliance with Estonia, Latvia and Poland. The three kingdoms, on the other hand, strove from the outset to shape the League into a foolproof system for the observance of law among the nations. Although the failure of their efforts to promote agreement on such matters as arbitration and disarmament forms only a very small part of the general record of frustration, in which the world's hopes quickly faded, it is important for the history of Scandinavia to observe that its spokesmen were heard with some respect at Geneva, where they usually worked together, and that the attitudes they adopted there were strongly reflected in their countries' mutual relations.

A special role was played by Fridtjof Nansen, the Norwegian explorer, scientist and statesman, described by an English politician, with whom he often collaborated in the business of the League, as 'perhaps the only man alive who could venture to say whatever he thought right to any prince, prime minister, or president'.[14] Up to his death in 1930 he was the leading champion of the humanitarian aspirations of the Covenant, demanding (for example) with partial success that the Assembly should control the operation of the Mandates system, under which the victors of the war administered the former German and Turkish empires as 'a sacred trust of civilisation'.[15] But his outstanding achievements were as League High Commissioner, first for the repatriation of nearly half a million widely scattered prisoners of war; then for the resettlement of the refugees from the Russian Revolution, reduced to utter destitution; and finally for the interchange of populations between Thrace and Asia Minor, a novel experiment in pacification after the Greco-Turkish war in 1922. Nansen performed other rescue work, which for political reasons was not directly supported by the League (see p. 396); but after his death it set up an office in Geneva to continue the help he had provided for refugees from many nations, and the 'Nansen passport' to carry stateless persons across frontiers was still in use after the Second World War.

From 1923 onwards the Scandinavian states were treated as a homogeneous group to which one of the non-permanent seats on the Council of the League should be allotted in rotation. Sweden was represented first, by Hjalmar Branting, whose influence in the Council was strengthened by his fellow countrymen's loyal acceptance of the League's recent disallowance of their claim to the Åland Islands. When Mussolini reintroduced the rule of force by bombarding the Greek island of Corfu and then refusing to accept the arbitrament of any more disinterested body than Italy's wartime allies, Branting strove hard to assert the League's authority. Undaunted by failure, he also stood up for the rights of the German population in the Saar, where French exploitation of the mines did not easily harmonise with political control by the League; and he pleaded for the immediate admission of the defeated powers to League membership. After his death in February 1925 the Swedish foreign minister, Östen Undén, helped to obtain a permanent Council seat for Germany, and as an expert in international law he was an influential figure in the League Assembly down to its demise and in the United Nations Assembly which replaced it. The most prominent Danish representative in the Council and the Assembly was the leader of the Radical Party. Peter Munch, who as foreign minister in 1930 caused his country to be the first to adopt in full the League's long-projected General (i.e. universally applicable) Act for the Peaceful Settlement of International Disputes. The Danish example was followed promptly by Norway and Finland, but not by any of the major powers, which still found diplomatic bargaining more advantageous.

The Scandinavians maintained from the outset that a prime function of the League was to organise disarmament. The earliest proposal for an objective study of the problem by a committee of civilians came from the Norwegians, whose experienced spokesman in such matters, Christian Lange (see p. 399), challenged the British view that causes of conflict must be eliminated before disarmament could be contemplated, pointing out that 'States which still possess great armaments produce distrust by their neighbours and cause international crises.'[16] In 1927 Munch's *Projet danois de Désarmement* argued cogently for a general reduction by 80 per cent, such as was being canvassed in Denmark, where defence expenditure had been reduced initially by one-quarter in 1922; this was followed by further big cuts, especially in the navy, and only the opposition of the Landsting prevented the conversion of the entire land and sea forces into a mere neutrality watch, as demanded by the Social Democrats. The Swedes made sweeping reductions in 1925 in their defence budget, the duration of compulsory service, and the number of their historic regiments. As one far-sighted editor wrote uneasily: 'The Småland cavalry ride off; phantoms of the past flit by; the Sandler Cabinet* remains, basking in the sunshine.'[17] Next year the Norwegians followed suit, reducing the standard period of training to 108 days (compared with 140 in Sweden) and making drastic cuts in military expenditure, which was further diminished by one-eighth in 1933.

The advocacy and practice of disarmament measures by the Scandinavian nations was closely related, however, to their belief that League membership involved them in only a qualified abandonment of their traditional neutrality. At the initial discussion in Paris they had demurred to the proposition that the League should be entitled to exact participation in military sanctions against an aggressor, and the wording of the Covenant was modified accordingly. But they remained uneasy about the economic sanctions which the League could order them to apply – and which might so easily lead on to war. Here the position of the Finns was different: their fear of Russia caused them to maintain their defences at full strength, with the former White Guard as an additional safeguard against external and internal dangers, and they favoured a scheme for collective financial assistance to any member of the League who might be threatened by aggression – to which the other three were significantly opposed. Unlike the Finns, the governments of the three Scandinavian kingdoms believed that their own frontiers were no longer at risk, so that economic sanctions were a liability which they incurred solely for the sake of other people.

Co-operation in League of Nations activities stimulated the growth of Scandinavian ties, which the war years had fostered. In 1919 a 'Scandinavian Association' (*Foreningen Norden*) was set up, so that cultural and

---

* Rikard Sandler (1884–1964), Folk High School teacher and translator of *Das Kapital*, followed Branting as Social Democratic prime minister in 1925–6; as foreign minister in 1939, his Nordic sympathies caused him to favour co-operation with Finland in the defence of the Åland Islands, so in December he was dropped from the government.

social co-operation might be fostered by methods of voluntary organisation; branches were soon to be found in Iceland as well as in the four
main countries, and a Danish manor house was taken over as a centre for
educational activities. At the governmental level the four states established
permanent conciliation commissions – a peace-keeping device which they
had already urged upon the attention of the League of Nations. In 1925–6
they went further, when (together with Iceland) they signed a series of
unlimited arbitration treaties, so that inter-Scandinavian disputes of any
kind, even those concerning questions alleged to be domestic or affecting
vital interests or the national independence, should be determined – in
any case whatever where existing jurisdictions, such as that of the Hague
Court, did not apply – by reference to a specially appointed arbitral
tribunal.

Two further events must be mentioned to round off the picture of inter-
Scandinavian activities in the League of Nations era. On the one hand,
they received a modest extension through the enterprise of the Norwegian
prime minister, J. L. Mowinckel, a Venstre politician and shipowner of
liberal principles, when the League Assembly of September 1930 proved
unable to combat the growing trade depression by an agreement to reduce
tariffs. He then proposed a more modest obligation to give thirty days'
notice for objections to any intended increase, which was accepted initially
by the three Scandinavian kingdoms and the Netherlands, and later by
Belgium, Luxembourg, and Finland, thus creating an 'Oslo Group' which
might be used for larger purposes. On the other hand, harmony was
temporarily reduced by a bitter quarrel between Norway and Denmark,
whose sovereignty over all Greenland, as accepted by the Americans in
1917, had been left unchallenged by the Norwegian government, until the
Danes interfered seriously with the exclusive use by Norwegian hunters of
the desolated east coast, remote from the region of Danish colonial enterprise. In June 1931 the hunters raised the Norwegian flag over 'Eric the
Red's Land' from 71°30' to 75°40'N; a weak Agrarian Cabinet supported
their action and even added a second area further south. Denmark appealed
to the Hague Court, which held that Danish sovereignty had been
fully established since the treaty of Kiel in 1814, whereupon a new
Norwegian government – of which Mowinckel was once more the head –
submitted to the judgement with exemplary promptness. This was in
April 1933, when the coming into power of Hitler in Germany was
beginning to create a world situation in which small powers could ill afford
to quarrel.

THE PATTERN OF DOMESTIC EVENTS, 1919–1933

The advance towards full political democracy, which had been achieved at
the end of the war, was followed by a wearisome period of political
frustration. Between 1920 and 1933 no single party ever commanded a

majority in the popular chamber of any Scandinavian legislature: hence a procession of coalition, minority, and caretaker Cabinets under leaders whose sway lasted on average about two years in Denmark and Finland, in Sweden and Norway for only one. The Conservative Party now had a rather narrow basis in its devotion to the interests of private capital and the defence services, the latter being regarded by many opponents as a safeguard for the former. The Liberals were a force to be reckoned with in Sweden and Finland; in Denmark the Radicals, though never very numerous, usually provided weighty intellectual support for Labour; and in Norway Liberalism constituted one element in the historic, but now declining, Venstre Party. The big agricultural interest continued to be represented in Denmark by Venstre and in Finland by the well established Agrarian Party, whilst in both Sweden and Norway a new party grew up under that name, later changed to Centre.

Since none of these parties had any close natural affinity with the Social Democrats, for whom the war had been in general a period of rapid growth, they first took office on sufferance – in Sweden under Branting in 1920, in Denmark under Thorvald Stauning* in 1924, in Finland under Tanner in 1926, and in Norway under Christopher Hornsrud in 1928. Although in both Sweden and Denmark these first Labour governments were quickly followed by others, in no case did they command enough support to carry out any far-reaching programme of social reform. Their position was made more difficult by the course of events in Russia. In 1921–3 this led to the formation of native Communist parties, which formed a separate group in each legislature except the Danish, where they did not win their first seat until 1932. What was much more serious, the survival of the Communist regime in a country so close to Scandinavia lent greater reality than, for example, in England to the belief that Labour's ultimate aim was the seizure of complete power by unparliamentary means.

As an argument against the Labour Party this had most justification in Norway, where at first the entire party and then, until 1923, the majority of its membership did actually operate under the auspices of the Third International and was represented on its executive committee in Moscow. It is therefore hardly surprising that, although the first Norwegian Labour Cabinet was headed by a moderate who had been a small-scale farmer, it was manoeuvred out of office in less than three weeks by Mowinckel and other scared capitalists. More generally, however, the fear of Communism militated against any agreed national solution to the eco-

---

* 1873–1942. A cigar sorter of humble origins, who made his way through trade union activities to the Folketing (1906) and entered the Zahle Cabinet in September 1916 as 'the first worker-minister in Scandinavia'.[18] In 1924–6 he headed a minority administration, but in 1929 Radical support gave him a majority, and he remained in office until his death. His popularity with the masses as a kind of father-figure seems to have been little affected by the German invasion, although since 1933 he had been directly responsible for the Defence Ministry.

nomic difficulties which confronted successive governments of various party complexions.

There were two main crises. The first depression followed immediately after a short post-war trade boom – during which the eight-hour day became generally established – and was complicated by fluctuations in the currency and serious bank failures, especially in Norway. The cost of living fell almost continuously, but this did little to mitigate the situation of the unemployed industrial worker: hence serious labour disputes, such as that which helped to produce the Easter Crisis in Denmark. Sweden's mounting industrial and commercial strength enabled it to recover first, as indicated by a return to the pre-war gold standard in 1924 – a year ahead of Britain. Denmark and Norway waited until 1927 and 1928 respectively before they followed suit; but by the end of the decade Danish agricultural production was 50 per cent above that of the best pre-war years, and the Norwegians were again deriving large profits from their mercantile marine, from Antarctic whaling, and from the flourishing condition of the metal industries (see p. 391). The Finns, on the other hand, had to reduce the burden of the debt incurred during the civil war by revaluing the mark at one-sixth of its former gold equivalent. But theirs was a country where two-thirds of the population still depended upon the farms and the forests, so the economy was stabilised by the agrarian reforms of 1918–22, under which 117,000 leaseholders became freeholders and 27,000 viable smallholdings were made available to the rural proletariat.[19]

But the collapse of world trade which began in the autumn of 1929 created a graver crisis. At its culmination in the winter of 1932–3, the percentage of unemployment rose to 31·5 in Sweden, 42·4 in Norway, and 42·8 in Denmark;[20] in the two latter countries the industrial labour force was very much smaller than in Sweden, but they had a further problem of the many farmers who were sold up under bitter protest because they could no longer meet their mortgage payments. No full returns are available for Finland, since only one local government area in three possessed an employment board, but the mention of a category of 7,900 'unemployed landowners'[21] points to the doubtless very large number of smallholders who could no longer eke out a living by seasonal work in the lumber camps. The Icelanders too, whose fisheries had been on the upgrade ever since the war, now experienced a six-year fall in export values, as a result of which 'the depression had more enduring influence than on most of Iceland's trading partners'.[22]

In Scandinavia as in other parts of Europe, the situation exacerbated the conflict of classes. Swedish trade unionists were greatly incensed by an episode in which five lives were lost, when troops were used to protect strike-breakers employed by a big timber concern in Ådalen. Although the Liberal government in the following year (1932) instituted a body of state police, so that soldiers should no longer be called in during industrial conflicts, its moral position was weakened by the discovery that its head had been secretly in the pay of the financier, Ivar Kreuger.* In Norway, where state police had been introduced a little earlier, their deployment in defence of alleged strike-breakers under Norsk Hydro's auspices at Menstad resulted in their being routed by the workers, whom troops were then sent to overawe. Although the industrial situation soon quietened down, reactionary forces gave covert support to vague proposals for imposing discipline upon the wage-earners corrupted by Marxism, which were advocated by the then minister of defence, Vidkun Quisling.† In 1933, and again in 1936, he went unsuccessfully to the polls at the head of 'National Unification' (NS), a party modelled upon the ideas of the Italian and German dictatorships.

Quisling's supporters averaged only 2 per cent of the electorate, in- cluding the fruits of an alliance with a short-lived rural movement (*Bygdefolkets Krisehjelp*), which employed methods of intimidation to prevent the selling up of farm property on behalf of creditors. In Denmark, on the other hand, similar forced sales helped to give rise to a much more formidable 'Agriculturists' Alliance' (*Landbrugernes Sammenslutning*, LS), which in 1935 brought 40,000 farmers to Copenhagen to petition the Crown for preferential treatment. LS had spread over the countryside, especially in Jutland, from the former German area in North Slesvig, calling loudly for direct action against urban capitalists and trade unionists alike as exploiters of the farming population. The German element in the movement soon became separated from the Danish members because of the control exercised by the German Nazi Party south of the border, but another result of the proximity of Hitler's Reich was the growth of the native Danish Nazi Party (DNSAP), which dated from 1930. In 1933 it obtained a new leader, Fritz Clausen, a Dane born south of the old frontier, who had therefore done German war service before taking up medicine; his capacity for leadership must be judged inferior to Quisling's, but by 1939 he was one of three representatives of his party in the Folketing.

Nevertheless it was only in Finland, with its recent memories of civil war, that antiparliamentary activities seriously threatened the stability of the nation. In November 1929 a Communist youth demonstration in Lapua/Lappo – a historic centre in the ultra-conservative province of

---

* 1880–1932. The son of a match manufacturer, who by 1928 had gained control of more than half the match production of the world, in many cases by offering a loan to the state in return for a monopoly. After he had shot himself in Paris (12 March 1932) the Stockholm stock exchange was closed for a week, and the unpleasant discoveries included the falsification by Kreuger personally of Italian government securities to a value of £21 million. One school of thought maintains, however, that he was murdered, and that he was in general more sinned against than sinning.

† 1887–1945. A highly qualified army officer, he had been Nansen's assistant in Russia and Armenia and received an honorary CBE for services in Moscow when Anglo-Russian relations were broken off. As defence minister in the Agrarian government of 1931–3, he was erroneously believed to have been the 'strong man' of the Menstad episode; his hostility to Communism had already been announced in much cloudy rhetoric, including that of his book *Russia and Ourselves* (English translation, 1931).

Ostrobothnia – gave rise to a 'Lapua movement', whose members were not content with securing the total exclusion of the Communist Party from political activity. With the encouragement of the reactionary rural clergy, a large part of the Civic Guard (the former White Guards), and certain banking interests, the 'Lapua-men' indulged in beatings and deportations across the Russian frontier; they even kidnapped Ståhlberg, ex-president and author of the constitution. They were not suppressed until February 1932, when they attempted a military *coup* at Mäntsälä close to the capital, which constrained Svinhufvud to take action, albeit that they had helped to elect him to the presidency. Yet the sentences passed on the participants were only nominal, and next year a smaller but still dangerous Patriotic People's Movement (IKL) came into existence, modelled on the party which had just risen to power in Germany.

Before we examine the more hopeful turn which the domestic politics of Scandinavia as a whole took in the same climacteric year 1933, brief mention must be made of a non-political issue which added greatly to the confusion of the political scene in the 1920s. The combination of strong voluntary organisations with an influential Puritan element in the Lutheran Churches had long made prohibition a major social question. In Iceland, as we have seen, it had been enacted before the war, and in 1917 a move in the same direction was made in Sweden, when a doctor named Ivan Bratt obtained the introduction of a system of pass-books; these entitled each holder in principle to buy – eventually from a government monopoly – such quantity of liquor as he could be trusted not to misuse. This was followed in 1922 by a referendum, in which the Swedes rejected total prohibition by a small margin, whilst a Danish measure passed three years later amounted to no more than restrictive licensing.

The Norwegians, however, having experienced a near approach to prohibition as a wartime expedient, adopted it on a full permanent basis in 1919 by a popular vote of 5:3, which was reversed seven years later by a similar majority. In the meantime complications arising out of trade reprisals from France, Spain and Portugal had helped to overthrow three Cabinets, whilst the moneyed classes set a dangerous example of lawlessness by resorting to bogus medical prescriptions, illicit distilling, and the employment of smugglers prepared for violent resistance. In Finland, where the Social Democratic Party had favoured prohibition since 1906, a similar measure was among the first fruits of independence. The short sea crossings made the coastline even more open to smugglers' activities than were the Norwegian fiords, and by 1929 convictions for drunkenness were eight times as many as in 1910; after thirteen years' experience the majority for repeal in 1932 was 70 per cent. Both the Norwegians and the Finns substituted a government sales monopoly of wines and spirits, which still exists, and in 1933 prohibition, which had enjoyed its chief European successes in Scandinavia, vanished from the scene when the Icelanders capitulated to the exigencies of their fish trade with Spain.

SOCIAL DEMOCRACY IN THE ASCENDANT

In the last six years before the Second World War the domestic politics of the Scandinavian countries became more stable, and the Social Democratic parties obtained their first real chance to carry out substantial reforms. These engrossed the attention of the peoples concerned and even attracted favourable notice in the outside world, where it was widely supposed that 'the quiet corner of Europe' might remain sheltered from the gathering storms.

The turning-point came first in Denmark, where the veteran Social Democrat Stauning had been in office since 1929, but found his actions circumscribed by the existence of a hostile majority in the upper chamber or Landsting. In January 1933, however, he negotiated an agreement with Venstre leaders at his residence in Kanslergade (hence the name of *Kanslergade-Forliget*); this gained him the support of the farmers, who dominated the Landsting, by promising a 10 per cent devaluation to stimulate their exports, a buying-up of surplus cattle for destruction, and lower taxes on farm property. Venstre in return approved a one-year ban on strikes and lockouts, so as to avert an impending labour conflict; a large programme of public works for the relief of unemployment; and a series of major reforms proposed by K. K. Steincke, the minister for social affairs. The compromise was so successful that by 1936 the Social Democrats and their Radical allies had control of the Landsting as well as the Folketing. Later in the same year 1933 a rather similar bargain was struck by the Swedish Social Democratic leader, Per Albin Hansson,* who had come into office after the collapse of the Liberals in the preceding year. Confronted with the largest unemployment figures in his country's history, he secured a majority in the Second Chamber by the help of the Agrarians, whom he rewarded with a devaluation and fixed minimum prices for farm produce; they in return agreed to support relief works and other measures designed to make Sweden 'a home for all its people'.[23]

In Norway the election of 1933 gave the Labour Party more seats than ever before, but not enough to prevent Mowinckel from lingering on for two more years at the head of his third minority Venstre ministry. Then came a development similar to the Danish and Swedish but even more remarkable, for Labour obtained power in 1935 by an alliance with the Agrarian Party, which had been the bitterest opponent of rural trade unionism and of every concession to the needs of the unemployed. The Labour leader, Johan Nygaardsvold, was a former sawmill worker who cared

---

* 1885–1946. Left school at twelve, and at eighteen helped to found the Social Democratic youth movement, where he made a name as a bitter opponent of military service. As defence minister under Branting and as premier (1932–46), he showed himself ready to compromise over this and other questions; a brilliant parliamentary tactician, he triumphed decisively at the election of 1936, when he had been temporarily ousted from office by an alliance between the Agrarians and other non-socialist parties, and became during the war years a symbol of national unity.

little for ideologies; he paid the required price of heavy financial support for the hard-pressed farmers; but when the next election returned fewer Agrarians to the Storting, he was quite willing to 'shop around for votes'[24] to pass his later measures.

In Finland the Social Democrats had to wait until 1937 for even a share of power: as long as Svinhufvud remained President, the largest party was forbidden access to the Cabinet. Under the Presidency of K. Kallio, who had been the main author of the land reforms, they formed part of a majority coalition under a Liberal professor, A. K. Cajander, but its Agrarian and other Finnish-nationalist members gave prime attention to the language question. The constitution having recognised the existence of two 'national languages', the Finnish-speakers had nevertheless restricted bilingual rights to districts where the minority was at least 10 per cent. The speakers of Swedish in return made the most of their entrenched position in traditional institutions such as the faculties of Helsinki University, where the natural inclination of the students to oppose authority was encouraged by an ultra-nationalist (and originally irredentist) organisation called the Academic Karelia Society (AKS). Cajander placated the students by making Finnish the principal language of instruction – an important symbolic victory.* The Finnish people as a whole could then address itself to the long-delayed programme of social reform planned by the Social Democratic finance minister, Tanner. A significant attempt was also made by the young Agrarian Minister of the Interior, Urho Kekkonen, to ban the new 'Patriotic' Party, IKL, which held fourteen seats in the Riksdag.

The achievement of a considerable degree of social harmony in the Scandinavia of the mid-1930s was partly the cumulative result of influences which had been long at work. Foreign observers often called attention to the wide ramifications of the co-operative movement – its virtual monopoly of the marketing of Danish agricultural produce; its manufacture of electric light bulbs in Sweden, which grew into a North European Society cutting the price by one-third; the spread to Iceland, which was eventually to become on a per head basis the most co-operatively-minded country in the world; and the fact that in Finland – the only part of Scandinavia where (as we have seen) the movement was affected by class cleavages – two co-operative societies grew in rivalry and by 1939 embraced about one-half of all Finnish families. Another well-known influence is that of the Folk High School, which had prepared the way for a genuinely democratic system of education. This in turn meant that, as compared with many larger nations, these peoples already had cultural interests and leisure activities which bridged the gap between classes: significantly few Scandinavian

---

* The Swedish-language percentage of the population declined from 12·89 in 1900 to 10·14 in 1930 and 8·64 in 1950. The change may be illustrated from the situation in Turku/Åbo, the historic centre of Swedish interests, where the endowment of a Swedish university in 1918 prompted a Finnish foundation only four years later. At the present day the visitor who knows no Finnish is better received if he addresses the man in the Turku street in English than if he tries out his Swedish.

newspapers or magazines were aimed specifically at an educated or an uneducated readership. Nevertheless, the new social policies clearly had far-reaching effects.

The most comprehensive legislation was the work of a Danish reformer and jurist, K. K. Steincke, who reduced fifty-five existing laws or parts of laws to four, comprising a full system of insurance and a Public Care Act. This measure was to be administered by local authorities on the liberal principle that public assistance should henceforth involve no stigma of pauperism unless the recipient was directly to blame for his condition of need. Whereas these Danish measures were financed by a 30 per cent increase in taxes over a seven-year period, Swedish prosperity permitted a rise of 50 per cent in five years, which made it possible to finance both family and maternity allowances on a generous scale. Moreover, in Sweden the repeal of the law for the protection of strike-breakers – already modified in 1914 – and the enactment of holidays for all employees at the employer's expense fostered a conciliatory atmosphere for a big breakthrough in industrial relations. In 1938 prolonged negotiations at Saltsjöbaden resulted in the first General Agreement regarding wages and conditions of employment, to which the trade union organisation (LO) adhered henceforth as readily as the industrialists. Norway followed in the wake of Sweden with extensions of the insurance system, a modest commencement of old-age pensions, and public works to help the unemployed, whilst farmers and fishermen were kept in step with Labour by statutory provision for producers' associations to fix remunerative prices for everything they sold. In Finland the position of the trade unions was still weak, but a start was made with family allowances and with urgently needed health measures, especially against tuberculosis, of which the incidence was twice that in Sweden; Tanner's proposals for old-age and disablement pensions were due to take effect in 1940.

These social advances occurred during a period of reviving world trade, in which the Scandinavian states as a whole were among the more flourishing. The Swedish economy recovered faster than the British: in 1932-9 the GNP increased by 50 per cent. In Norway the annual growth rate at this time was 4 per cent, with the result that by 1938 industrial production was 75 per cent larger than before the war. The Finns – whose low rate of imports had encouraged them to earn the distinction of being the only debtor country which kept up its payments to America throughout the crisis – were exporting as much, both in volume and value, by 1937 as they had done in 1928. The Danish position was less fortunate, the restriction of the British market for Danish dairy produce being largely responsible for the fact that unemployment in Denmark fell by only one-half, in spite of the government's efforts to stimulate industrial activity.

Sweden's exceptional prosperity made it the prime object of interest to the American journalist, Marquis W. Childs. But in 1936 his widely read *Sweden: The Middle Way* also invited his fellow countrymen – then eagerly canvassing the merits and demerits of President Roosevelt's New Deal – in more general terms to admire 'progress in these northern countries that the world-wide collapse has hindered but not destroyed'.[25] The Manchester expert on social services, later Lord Simon of Wythenshawe, who toured Scandinavia in 1938, grouped the three kingdoms together as 'the most encouraging thing in the world today', whilst the government of Finland also seemed to him 'to display the typical Scandinavian qualities of practical common sense and moderation'. Simon's book ends, however, with the sombre reflection: 'A European war might well shatter all these splendid attempts to build a better social order.'[26]

The four prime ministers whose governments achieved such promising domestic results were still in office when the Second World War came to test their foreign and defence policies, which were almost inevitably much less effective. Scandinavian loyalty to the League of Nations had already been shaken in 1931–2, when the great powers inside and outside the League declined to take any steps against Japanese aggression in China; but the failure of the League either to prevent or to defeat Mussolini's war of conquest in Ethiopia had a bigger effect, partly because it was much nearer home. In August 1935 all four Scandinavian states had pledged their support for action by the League, and they were among the fifty members which undertook to join in economic sanctions. But when the great powers shrank from enforcing them at the risk of war with Italy, of which Britain and France would have had to bear the brunt, the Norwegian foreign minister, Halvdan Koht,* took the lead in claiming for the seven European neutrals of the 1914–18 war that economic sanctions could no longer be regarded as obligatory. His Swedish colleague, Sandler, later carried the matter further by advising a League committee that 'for the time being, the system of sanctions is in fact suspended'.[27]

In these circumstances the attempt to return to unqualified neutrality, which had in general served their interests before the League of Nations came into existence, obliged each of the Scandinavian governments to reconsider its defence arrangements. The Swedes took steps in 1936 to build up their air force and to a much smaller extent their navy; the military training period was extended from 140 to 175 days; and some further expenditure in 1938–9 stimulated technical progress in a small-scale but efficient armaments industry. The Finnish government was still more active: the conscript forces and their Civic Guard reserve had been reorganised as recently as 1932, and by May 1938 the proportion of the Budget allocated to defence had risen from 12 to 24 per cent.

In Norway and Denmark, however, the Social Democratic Parties re-

---

* 1873–1965. An eminent historian, which helped to give him an ascendancy over his Cabinet colleagues, though his brilliant achievements in the world of books did not necessarily qualify him to handle the practical problems of international relations. He was still active as a writer at the age of ninety, when his publications totalled 184 in five languages, including both forms of Norwegian.

tained their traditional dread of any move which might build up a 'reactionary force' or a veritable 'White Army'.[28] Furthermore, disarmament had
the backing in Norway of the ex-premier, Mowinckel, and in Denmark
of the Radicals, headed by Stauning's experienced yet doctrinaire foreign
minister, Peter Munch. It was not until 1938 that the Norwegian Cabinet
under Nygaardsvold agreed to extend the training period from 72 to 84 days
although this extension had been designed to form part of a minimum
defence system approved in 1933. In May 1939, indeed, the last of a series
of small extra appropriations for defence, which had aroused angry controversy in the three previous years, was passed almost unanimously by the
Storting. But it was too late: before twelve months had passed, the Germans descending upon Oslo found much-needed American aircraft still
in their crates. In Denmark the Social Democratic Party programme of
1934 had sadly acknowledged, 'There is no sufficient basis for isolated
disarmament at the moment.'[29] Three years later this was considered to
justify increased expenditure on the modernisation of military equipment,
so as to produce more efficient results – from a smaller call-up. The
Danes were in any case powerless to keep the Germans out, but a concession to democratic opinion, which meant that many military installations
were left unmanned for seven months of the year, might be judged tantamount to inviting them in.

Whilst seeking to adopt a neutral posture, which none of them could be
certain of maintaining against ruthless pressure, each of the Scandinavian
states inevitably canvassed the possibility that there might be safety in
numbers. Sweden would have been the natural leader in any defence
alliance, but the idea made little appeal to either Norwegian or Danish
opinion, though for contrasting reasons. Most Norwegians still believed
that they were automatically protected from invasion by the British fleet,
nearly all Danes that they could not be protected from a German invasion
by any outside support. The Norwegian foreign minister, Koht, was thereby encouraged to trust to his own ability to steer a neutral course for
Norway by a quiet avoidance of all commitments. Stauning went further.
Speaking at Lund in March 1937, he rejected the notion that Denmark
should be 'a dog on a chain' (*lænkehund*) for guarding the southern frontier
of Scandinavia, and reminded his Swedish audience that no help had been
forthcoming from their side of the Sound in 1864.[30] Exactly two years later,
Denmark separated itself from the other Scandinavian states as the only one
which accepted Hitler's offer of a non-aggression pact.

Finland, on the other hand, had passed in 1937 under the control of a
government whose generally liberal outlook predisposed it to welcome
closer relations with Scandinavia: might not a link with Sweden free their
country from dependence upon Germany for a counterpoise to Soviet
predominance in the Baltic region? The upshot was the Stockholm Plan
for the remilitarisation of the Åland Islands, to be undertaken by the Finns
with the assurance that Swedish troops would be earmarked to come to their

assistance in the event of Russian aggression. The Swedish foreign minister, Sandler, envisaged this arrangement as leading on to a more general military co-operation, but it was never put to the test. The termination of the servitude which had been reimposed on the islands in 1921, though approved by Germany as well as the Western powers, was blocked by Soviet opposition in the League Council, and in June 1939 the proposal was therefore allowed to lapse. Only two months later, the Russo-German pact placed all the states bordering the Baltic – and, indirectly, Norway as well – in a more hazardous situation than any they had experienced since Napoleon and Alexander divided the Continent between them at Tilsit.

Chapter 14

The Impact of World War, 1939-1947

THE NORTH DIVIDED

When war broke out in Europe in September 1939, the Scandinavian states were wholeheartedly bent on preserving their neutrality, as in 1914. But their chances of doing so this time were much smaller. The development of mechanised ground forces and still more that of air power meant that their defences were less of a deterrent than before to any prospective invader, especially as they had carried disarmament much further than their great-power neighbours. In the very first phase of the war, whilst the full contents of the Russo-German 'non-aggression' pact could only be surmised, the partitioning of Poland and the Soviet acquisition of bases in the three Baltic states already suggested that Finland too might be in peril from a 'Soviet Monroe Doctrine'.[1] For Sweden and Norway, on the other hand, there was a serious risk of British and French action to stop the iron-ore trade to Germany through Narvik and Luleå, both because the Allied economic blockade was weakened this time by the changed position of Russia and because Churchill as an ambitious and experienced First Lord of the Admiralty was likely to regard the German use of the passage through the Norwegian Leads as calling for drastic naval action. In actual fact, the mining of the approach to Narvik was first proposed by Churchill to the British Cabinet on 19 September, and even before this the French prime minister Daladier had voiced to the Supreme War Council the desirability of 'successful naval action in the Baltic',[2] where Churchill's plans ranged from a foray by specially equipped battleships down to the mining of Luleå harbour by seaplanes.

As for the Germans, Hitler wished initially to preserve the neutrality of Scandinavia, which worked to his advantage, but on 14 December – the day of his first interview with Quisling – he gave orders for an attack on Norway to be studied. His true motivation is largely unknown. He had some reason to fear that the Western allies might get in ahead of him. He was not altogether unsympathetic to the naval arguments that a breakthrough to the Norwegian coastline was the bold stroke which the Kaiser's

High Seas Fleet ought to have undertaken and that the rewards of boldness would be great. It may even be that his enthusiasm for uniting the 'Nordic race' was kindled by Quisling's notions of a federation of germanic peoples. Whatever the relative weight of the different motives, by 1 March Hitler had in readiness his plans for occupying both Norway and Denmark, which brought them into the area of conflict between the great powers less than a month after Finland had for the time being ceased to be directly involved. Henceforth all three were at the mercy of events in an ever-widening war, from which Norway emerged as a full member of a victorious alliance, Denmark as the equivalent of an ally (see p. 349), and Finland as a last-minute seceder from the ranks of the defeated.

The fortunes of the two remaining states present a contrast. Sweden retained its neutral status, internal political cohesion and social well-being throughout the war. Its prestige was, however, lowered considerably though temporarily by the many unneutral concessions made to the Germans whilst they were in the ascendant; these were more spectacular than what was conceded (chiefly in the economic field) to the Allies later on. Iceland alone lost nothing by the war, emerging from one year of British and four years of American protection as a fully sovereign power with five years of uninterrupted prosperity as a base on which to build. Nevertheless, in 1945–7 it seemed likely that all five Scandinavian peoples would return by degrees to the common policies and world outlook which had marked the 1930s – as soon as the troubled aftermath of war gave place to the expected harmonies of peace.

THE INVOLVEMENT OF FINLAND

In April 1938, and again a year later, the Russians had negotiated in secret with the Finnish government, with a view to closing the Gulf of Finland to an attack on Leningrad by Germany or the Western powers. Both the first request, for the large island of Hogland (Suursaari), 110 miles west of Leningrad, and the second, for the group of smaller islands nearer in, were rejected by the Finns, although approval for a Finnish remilitarisation of Åland and territorial compensation in Karelia were offered in return. Mannerheim, who had returned to public life in 1931 as chairman of the defence council, vainly opposed the outright rejection of proposals from so powerful a neighbour, for the political leaders clung to absolute neutrality as the policy which linked them with Scandinavia at large. They were also influenced by the fear that any concession would be followed up by heavier demands, to which the nation might offer a less united resistance, and by the hope or even the belief – then widespread in the Western world – that Stalin's ruthless purges had reduced Russia to a condition in which she would not venture to take drastic action against a resolute adversary, however small. Finally, memories of 1918 made it appear unlikely that an anti-Communist Finland would be left to fight alone.

On 12 October 1939 a Finnish delegation, led by Juho Paasikivi,* went at Russian request to the Kremlin; although the subjects for discussion had not been specified, its departure was preceded by a precautionary mobilisation. Stalin in person put forward his demands: a thirty-year lease of the Hanko Peninsula for a naval base to close the mouth of the Finnish Gulf; the cession of Hogland and the group of islands farther in; the frontier on the Karelian Isthmus to be moved back, so that its nearest point would be 50 instead of 20 miles distant from Leningrad; and a small section of the Barents Sea coastline transferred to Russia to protect the approaches to Murmansk. In return Stalin offered twice as much territory from Soviet Karelia and an agreement over Åland, provided Sweden had no share in its remilitarisation. Paasikivi, Tanner (who joined in the later stages of the negotiations), and Mannerheim all favoured major concessions; but the government persisted in its belief that Russian wishes could safely be disregarded. Its intransigence received no encouragement from the Germans, who were bound by their pact with Russia, nor – at this stage – from the British government, which hoped that Russian gains might cause Germany to regret the pact. Even the Swedes were discouraging: the Scandinavian heads of state met in Stockholm on 18 October to demonstrate their general solidarity, but the Swedish prime minister would give no assurance whatever regarding military assistance.

In the absence of any access to the Kremlin records, the view that Stalin was concerned only with Russia's strategic needs (as he saw them) and had no designs on the integrity of Finland is supported chiefly by his prolongation of the negotiations and his final offer to accept three small islands in lieu of the much more convenient Hanko Peninsula. The Finnish government, however, took this as a sign of weakness. Military precautions and the general sense of tension were relaxed, and although Mannerheim continued his preparations for meeting an attack on the Karelian Isthmus, even a border incident there was regarded for four days as part of a mere war of nerves – until the first bombs fell on Helsinki on the morning of 30 November.

On crossing the border the Russians set up a Finnish People's Government under a Communist exile, Otto Kuusinen, which agreed to the concessions already demanded and was promised all districts with a mainly Karelian population in return. Nearly 6,000 Finnish exiles were duly brought across the frontier to support this regime, but the Communists in Finland failed to rise, partly because of the arrest of known party members but chiefly because of widespread disillusionment over

* 1870–1956. An ex-premier and the negotiator of the treaty of Dorpat, he nevertheless played his most important role in politics after he had entered his seventieth year. The basis had been laid by his early historical studies, which made him – at least until 1909 – a Compliant, gave him a deep knowledge of Russia (including its language), and convinced him that in all secondary matters national sentiment must yield to realism. Presumably the only banker who has received the Order of Lenin.

the development of the Russian Communist state under Stalin.* Nevertheless, for almost two months the Russian authorities refused to have any dealings with the government in Helsinki, which had become a national coalition under Risto Ryti, the governor of the Bank of Finland, with Tanner as foreign minister. The bitter internal struggles of the past were forgotten, as men of the right and left and devotees of rival languages fought side by side against what they regarded as an alien and inferior civilisation, sustained by world applause for David facing up to Goliath.

The odds were heavily against them. Besides blocking the 88-mile-wide Karelian Isthmus, the Finns had to protect the flank north of Lake Ladoga and deal with half a dozen other incursions along the remaining 625 miles of frontier as far as the Barents Sea. They were outnumbered by about four to one in men, were deficient in artillery of all kinds, and had virtually no aircraft or tanks. But most of this frontier area was a wilderness of snowbound forest and frozen lakes with few roads and no railway, which offered many advantages to small detachments of hardy and determined infantrymen, to whom their skis gave great mobility. They fell back from Petsamo, their port on the Barents Sea, but stayed close enough to block the way south for any outflanking movement. Then at Tolvajärvi, north of Lake Ladoga, they destroyed rather more than a division of Russians, and in the last days of December they annihilated two more divisions at Suomussalmi in the narrow waist of Finland, where the land connection with Sweden might otherwise have been cut. Consequently, when the cold at the turn of the year became more intense than at any time in the past quarter-century, their enemies ceased to attempt any further advances on the whole of this long front, though the Finns could not eject them from the larger of their hedgehog positions or *motti*, which were supplied from the air.

On the Karelian Isthmus, too, the first month witnessed a successful defence. The 'Mannerheim Line' was protected by fortress artillery at both ends and included forty-four modern concrete bunkers, but consisted mainly of a trench system with tank barriers. Seven Finnish divisions were able to hold out in these not very imposing defences against twice as many Russians, because the latter consisted mainly of unseasoned troops from the Leningrad garrison, carelessly deployed in the expectation of little more than nominal resistance. But in the first week of January Stalin appointed General Timoshenko, who had been in charge in Poland, to overall command on the Finnish front, where he made thorough preparations for a breakthrough on the Isthmus. The disparity of resources was so great that the approaching dénouement had all along been

---

* Kuusinen himself was a second choice. The first leader of crypto-Communist activities in Finland after the civil war, Arvo Tuominen, had declined to return to Russia from Stockholm (where he was a Comintern agent) in preparation for the new post in Finland, the nature of which was explained to him nine days before the invasion.

inevitable – unless the justice of their cause and the valour of their resistance produced the massive foreign intervention to which many Finns pinned their hopes.

In Western Europe this was the period of the featureless 'Phoney War', which made it possible for the fighting in Finland to receive enormous press coverage, and sympathy for the anti-Communist cause was in any case widespread. The League of Nations, which had procrastinated on so many other occasions, took only a fortnight to endorse the case of the Finns by formally expelling the USSR from membership, so it was natural for them to suppose that moral would be followed by practical support. Individual volunteers, humanitarian aid of all kinds, and some munitions came to Finland from many countries, but not the fully trained formations and heavy equipment which would result from an alliance. Their fellow Scandinavians were generous in the provision of supplies (including arms from Sweden) and volunteers: 8,000 Swedes and 725 Norwegians saw action in the last weeks of the war, 33 of whom were killed, and 800 Danes were among the many other national groups which arrived too late. But all three governments refused at the League Assembly to commit themselves in advance to apply any League sanctions against the Russian aggressors. In Sweden a national coalition government was formed during the emergency, which called 100,000 men to the colours; no proclamation of neutrality was issued, but direct intervention was judged to be too hazardous, in spite of repeated secret assurances from the Germans that they would allow any degree of intervention which did not implicate the Western powers.

In public the Germans remained strictly loyal to their pact with the Russians, which made it all the more likely in Finnish eyes that help might be forthcoming from Germany's enemies, Britain and France. In appearance, the Allied plans for helping were thwarted by the unwillingness of the Swedish and Norwegian governments to allow an expedition under nominal League of Nations auspices to cross their territory in order to operate in Finland. In reality, as the Swedes and Norwegians suspected, intervention in Finland was the third and least important purpose of those plans. For the first object was to stop the flow of Swedish iron ore to Germany both from Norwegian Narvik and from Swedish Luleå (which lies conveniently close to the Finnish frontier), and the second to engage the Germans at a disadvantage, if they should be provoked into invading neutral Scandinavian territory, to which their enemies had obtained access by strategem. In the end (as we shall see) the Finns sued for peace without making the formal appeal for Allied help which would have launched the proposed expedition. Its ability to have saved the Finns is highly doubtful, and few critics believe that its build-up could have matched the speed of the prospective German advance across Scandinavia to counter it; the French government in particular seems to have been hypnotised by its hopes of defeating Communism at home and abroad into taking a very unrealistic view of the strategic possibilities.* There remains the larger question: would Stalin have accepted the pretence that such Allied troops as reached the Finnish front were 'volunteers'? Or would he have made good his recent words to Hitler about a 'lasting and firm friendship of peoples, cemented by blood',[4] and by entering the general war as Germany's ally have changed, it may be, the history of the world?

However, by 5 February 1940, the day on which the Allied Supreme Council decided to set up this equivocal rescue operation, Tanner had been able to make secret contacts with the Russians through Stockholm, which showed that their terms no longer included acceptance of the satellite Kuusinen government. At the same time an assault had been mounted on the Karelian Isthmus, employing heavy artillery, bombing aircraft, and massed tanks, against which the Finns had no chance. On the 14th the Russians breached the Mannerheim Line, from which the Finns withdrew to a weaker line in front of Viipuri. When the inlet on which the city stands froze so hard that even tanks could cross the ice to outflank the new position from the west, Mannerheim as commander-in-chief and all but two members of the government agreed that large cessions of territory were inescapable. Negotiations began on 7 March, when the alternative of appealing for Allied help was still open: but the prospect of 12,000 men coming to the rescue in mid-April with about three times as many to follow later,[5] was not enough to prevent the signature of the treaty of Moscow (12 March).

A campaign in which nearly 25,000 Finnish soldiers had been killed and 45,000 wounded – about one in three of all who served – resulted in harder terms than had been available before it began. The south-eastern frontier of Finland was withdrawn to where it had stood in 1721, which meant the sacrifice of its fourth largest city, Viipuri, along with the entire Karelian Isthmus, and of a second area of about the same extent north of Lake Ladoga. The islands inside the Gulf were lost and the Hanko Peninsula leased to the Russians. A further belt of territory was lost in the waist of Finland – where the Finns were also required to construct a rail link, so that the Murmansk railway should have a through route to Sweden – as well as a small strip of land east of Petsamo. About 12 per cent of the entire population of Finland moved out of the lost territory, most of them farming families which had to be resettled at very short notice – the Russians allowed only twelve days for evacuation – on land expropriated from existing holdings. The industrial losses, which were almost equally serious, included about 10 per cent of the textile, chemical and metal

---

* Clearly shown by the alternative French proposal for an attack on Petsamo, where the Allies were to dislodge the Russians and join hands with the Finns; this was firmly rejected by the British at the Supreme War Council meeting of 5 February. In the same month, however, the underlying thought is tersely expressed in the private correspondence of General Weygand, then in command of French forces in the Middle East, where other moves against the Russians were eagerly canvassed: 'I consider it of paramount importance to break the back of the USSR in Finland and elsewhere.'[3]

industries; nearly 100 power stations; the Karelian forests and sawmills and other related plants; and the lower half of the Saimaa Canal, by which the timber of the great lake district had hitherto been brought down to Viipuri Bay for export.

Failing any fundamental change in Russo-German relations, the only hope of strengthening the Finnish position now was an arrangement with Sweden and Norway. This possibility had been pressed upon the Swedish prime minister by Tanner in February, when Hansson had conceded that, if a Scandinavian defence alliance had existed before the start of the Winter War, the Russians might well have been induced to leave Finland alone. He therefore held out hopes that a defence agreement might be coupled with Swedish economic aid for reconstruction, so that a diminished Finland might face the future with confidence. But when the Finnish President renewed the idea of a defence alliance after the end of the campaign, it was immediately disallowed by the Russians under a clause in the treaty of Moscow which forbade hostile agreements with a third party; its anti-Russian character, as was pointed out, was implicit in the welcome given to the proposal by a Norwegian Conservative politician, C. J. Hambro – who was shortly to become better known by a more opportune intervention.

THE INVOLVEMENT OF NORWAY AND DENMARK

Hitler's belief that the neutrality of Scandinavia worked to his advantage was strictly conditional upon the continued acceptance of that advantage by his opponents. The outbreak of the war in Finland made this appear problematic, which helps to explain his readiness to pay some attention to Quisling when he urged the need for – and feasibility of – a *coup* against the existing Norwegian government, which was allegedly in league with Britain. Although their two meetings in mid-December brought about the initial studies for an operation against Norway, which might also require the seizure of bases in Jutland, Hitler's positive desire for an aggressive move seems to date clearly from the British incursion into the Jössingfiord on 16 February; this was when a boarding party from a destroyer rescued nearly 300 British seamen who were being clandestinely conveyed through the Norwegian Leads as prisoners of war on the *Altmark*. A fortnight later Hitler defined the objectives:

> This operation should prevent British encroachment in Scandinavia and the Baltic; further, it should guarantee our ore base in Sweden and give our Navy and Air Force a wider start-line against Britain.[6]

Weserübung in its final form allocated 38,000 men for the overrunning of all Denmark, whilst the allocation to Norway was six divisions, including one of mountain troops. But success there depended upon a doubly hazardous thrust by 11,000 men conveyed northwards in warships: they had to pass through waters controlled by the British fleet and their objective was the seizure of a long line of ports, whose defences though weak were capable of causing a fatal delay. Once seized, however, these positions would be consolidated by the help of 1,200 aircraft, based on north Germany and the airfields to be captured in Denmark and Norway. Prepared with German thoroughness and in almost complete secrecy, *Weserübung* was ready for action on 20 March, but ice in the southern Baltic caused it to be postponed until the night of 8–9 April.

After the treaty of Moscow the Western allies had returned to Churchill's proposal, repeated at intervals since September, for sowing mines in the Leads off Narvik as a first step in settling the still wholly unsettled problem of the Swedish iron ore. A much smaller force than had been projected for the Finnish expedition was therefore made ready, to act as soon as there might be 'clear evidence'[7] of some German countermove against Norwegian territory: it would then take control of Narvik and the railway to the Swedish frontier, establish itself at Trondheim and Bergen, and immobilise the only big Norwegian airfield at Sola, near Stavanger. The expedition was lightly equipped, on the supposition that it would forestall the Germans and co-operate with the Norwegians: if the latter misunderstood their intentions, their orders entitled them to do no more than brush aside perfunctory local opposition. As compared with the German plan that of the Allies was lacking in boldness, thoroughness and clarity, but it was also free from the inhumanity of the instructions given to the Germans: 'Resistance is to be broken ruthlessly in accordance with the directions in the operational orders.'[8]

The German expedition was already on its way to seize the whole of Norway when the British minelaying took place in the early morning of 8 April; its objectives were so audacious that the British strategists failed to grasp what the movements meant. Instead, they held back their own troops, who were already on board ship, whilst the Home Fleet tried to bring about a major naval encounter, which heavy weather in the North Sea, a quick turn-round, and the help of the *Luftwaffe* enabled the Germans to evade, even on the return journey. Meanwhile, on the 9th at 4.15 a.m. (Central European Time), which had been designated as *Weserzeit*, German mechanised forces crossed the Danish frontier on their way to seize the Jutland airfields, whilst their troop transports sailed along the Sound to Copenhagen, and small groups of warships completed the more hazardous approach to the main Norwegian ports through the fiords, from the Oslofiord right along the coast as far north as Narvik. The Danish and Norwegian governments were not taken wholly by surprise, as the most recent reports from Berlin, sightings of warships, and even the sinking of a fully loaded transport by a Polish submarine in British service off south Norway had shown only too clearly that trouble was brewing. The British minelaying was a distraction, especially for Koht, who found plenty to do in castigating the Chamberlain administration for its breach of international law. But in any case only close and purposeful co-operation between the civil and military authorities, established in advance of the emergency, could have enabled Norway to bar the way to its ports during the first critical hours of an attempted invasion, whilst the overland route into Denmark lay inevitably open to a strong aggressor from the south.

The Danish king and government surrendered to the threat that Copenhagen would be bombed, when two and a half hours' hesitation had already cost fourteen Danish lives. In Norway a respite for considering the situation, which the geographical factor made in any case less hopeless, was gained by the action of a single resolute fortress commander, who sank the heavy cruiser *Blücher* in the inner reaches of the Oslofiord, so that the capital did not fall into German hands until airborne forces arrived about midday. This gave time for the resourceful President of the Storting, C. J. Hambro, to organise the escape of king, Cabinet, and parliament into the interior.

Since the Germans were in possession of all the main mobilisation centres, the Norwegian authorities knew that they would have no properly organised forces of their own except in the far north, where one brigade had been stationed during the Finnish war and a second could be mobilised without German interference. They received immediate promises of assistance from Britain and France; but the determining factor was almost certainly the indignation of the king and Cabinet when they found that the Germans had allowed Quisling to proclaim himself the head of a new government, which Hitler required them to acknowledge. Sooner than submit to foreign interference with the independence of Norway in its internal affairs, they decided to rely on help from the powers whose recent illicit minelaying in their territorial waters, however reprehensible in Norwegian eyes, suggested that they were not unready for military action.

The two-month campaign which followed was a military fiasco for the Allies and a triumph of all arms for the Germans, who (with the reinforcement of a seventh division) secured possession of all except the three counties of the far north before the planned date for the opening of their main campaign on the western front on 10 May. Out of the eight British battalions sent to central Norway, five were Territorials, whose training had not been completed for any form of warfare; but even the French Chasseurs Alpins proved unable to cope with the snowbound terrain of north Norway, where the two Norwegian brigades bore the brunt of the fighting. The weaknesses in personnel were made worse by the material shortages: tanks and artillery were almost entirely lacking, and much other equipment was lost or delayed through wrong loading. The Germans, on the other hand, did not run short of supplies or reinforcements, except in the Narvik area, because the use of airfields in Denmark and southern

Norway enabled them both to use air transport and to maintain sea communications across the Skagerrak. At the very outset of the campaign the intervention of the British Home Fleet was restricted because of the belated discovery of the unacceptable risk to big ships if they attempted to patrol in the vicinity of a coast from which enemy bombers could operate. In its later stages the campaign also proved a corollary, namely that bases could not be improvised on a foreign shore in face of enemy air superiority.

The blocking of the iron-ore route having been for so long under consideration, the first échelon of an expedition to that area was sent off in all haste on 12 April: the ten destroyers which had put ashore the 2,000 men of the German mountain division to secure Narvik had already been attacked by light forces on the 10th, and their destruction was completed on the 13th by HMS *Warspite*. A landing at that juncture might have met with little resistance, but the British general's orders sent him to establish his base at Harstad, an island roadstead 70 miles distant from Narvik through the Leads. Confident that the iron-ore port would nevertheless fall readily into his hands, the government diverted reinforcements already at sea to the Trondheim area in central Norway; the northern expedition found, however, that a frontal landing under the guns of the navy was impracticable in the deep snow, once the enemy had recovered their nerve and doubled their numbers from the destroyer crews. For the rest of April the Norwegians continued their containing operations in the high mountains, whilst their allies awaited the arrival of reinforcements sufficient for an indirect approach to Narvik.

Meanwhile the attempt to retake Trondheim, which would have given the Norwegian king and his ministers a much-needed temporary capital, had begun with landings at Namsos and Åndalsnes, small ports to the north and south of the town, on which an advance by road and rail might be made in co-operation with Norwegian forces. The main thrust, however, was assigned to eight battalions (two of them Canadian) which were to be conveyed up the long fiord in warships after a battleship bombardment. But the last-minute cancellation of this operation because of the danger from the air then left a pincer movement against the city as the only alternative. The advance from Namsos got within 70 miles, when the way was blocked by two German destroyers, which made skilful use of the continuation of the fiord northwards beyond the port. The two Territorial battalions from Åndalsnes were routed by the Germans, after the Norwegian commander-in-chief had insisted that they should be thrown piecemeal into the fight at the foot of the Gudsbrandsdal, on the route by which the enemy was pressing forward from Oslo for the relief of Trondheim. A Regular brigade fought several stubborn engagements higher up the same long valley, but could do no more than delay the Germans, who prevented them from coming within 130 miles of their original objective. In both cases air superiority helped the enemy to drive them back – along with the disorganised Norwegians; but the planned arrival of reinforcements and especially of heavy equipment might still have enabled them to achieve results in the field, if the persistent bombing of both bases had not made evacuation in the first days of May inevitable. The small and scattered bodies of Norwegian troops in the southern half of the country had then no option but to surrender.

There remained the operations in the Narvik sector, where French and Polish troops began to arrive at the end of April, and where the military command was soon afterwards transferred to a future field-marshal, Claude Auchinleck, who had under him a French general, M.-E. Béthouart, whose aggressive spirit won him the full confidence of the Norwegians. The Germans, however, derived a double profit from the collapse in central Norway: a small relief expedition began to advance overland from the Namsos area, and the German air force likewise began to range farther into the north. Accordingly, the British Guards brigade, which had hitherto been based on Harstad, was sent south to hold up the advance. Although they had the support of five Independent Companies (improvised forerunners of the Commandos) and a Norwegian battalion, the enemy outmanoeuvred them by land and water – not to mention the *Luftwaffe*'s control of the air. However, whilst they fell back rapidly on Bodö, British fighter aircraft were brought over by carrier to cover a concerted attack on Narvik. The Norwegians having driven back the German outposts in the mountains, French and Polish troops closed in upon the town itself; and on 26 May, with British naval and air support, the final assault across the narrow fiord was made by two battalions of the Foreign Legion and one of Norwegians.

Little loss was incurred in the first land victory of the Second World War, but it yielded little profit, since the decision had already been taken for an immediate evacuation. Hurried demolitions put the iron-ore route out of action for no more than a year, and the Norwegians were not even given time to round up the Germans, who were retreating before them to the Swedish frontier. Men, ships and aircraft must all be recalled because of the rapidly deteriorating situation in northern France, and a delayed evacuation would be increasingly perilous. As it was, the sinking of one overcrowded aircraft-carrier (HMS *Glorious*) on the long passage home cost 1,515 lives. This was nearly as much as the total British casualties on land, three times those of the French and Poles, and rather more than those of the Norwegian forces – in what was after all a very small two-month campaign.

Norway, no less than Denmark, had now passed under German control, but the prolonged resistance of the Norwegians had as its natural consequence the transfer of the King, government, and a nucleus of the armed forces to continue the struggle from the territory of their allies. Their biggest remaining asset was the mercantile marine, of which $2\frac{1}{2}$ million tons had already been chartered to Britain in November 1939; the total was nearly twice as great, including a tanker fleet of such value that the Norwegian contribution to the Battle of the Atlantic was said to be worth an army of a million men. The freight earnings also financed the provision in Britain of new warships, squadrons of fighter planes, and an infantry brigade which was trained in Scotland and included some ski troops. King Haakon and his Cabinet, too, acquired more weight than most of the governments in exile, the King's personality being widely appreciated in wartime Britain, whilst his Labour ministers – to whom representatives of the other parties had been added on 9 April – adapted themselves by degrees to an unfamiliar environment, especially perhaps after the dogmatic Koht had surrendered the control of foreign affairs to a pragmatic trade-union lawyer, Trygve Lie. Their position was strengthened by increasingly close liaison with the population at home, facilitated by the long land frontier with Sweden, movement across which was never completely suspended.

The Swedes, were, indeed, left without direct contact with the West, except by air or through the remote Finnish port of Petsamo. Fear that they were next on the list for invasion had caused them to alert 400,000 men[9] under arms, but they also sought ways and means of placating Hitler. In the first weeks of the Norway campaign they allowed certain 'humanitarian' traffic to pass over the Swedish railways from Germany to beleaguered Narvik, and at its close they extended this to a wider transit agreement, especially for leave trains. Britain retaliated by refusing to allow any ships to pass in or out of Gothenburg, but in general had to accept the loss of direct influence even on the neutral half of the Scandinavian Peninsula.

Naval power provided a modest compensation in the Faeroe Islands and Iceland. The former were taken under British protection on 12 April, and although the county governor and council made a formal protest, the garrison was welcomed by the population at large, which conveyed both its own and a part of the Icelandic fish catch to the British market. By the time Iceland was similarly brought under protection on 10 May, its people had already resolved to take upon themselves the functions of the monarchy they shared with Denmark. Having made no provision for self-defence, they would have been at the mercy of any German raider. Yet the fourteen months' occupation by forces which could with difficulty be spared from their own hard-pressed island were marked by 'problems' and 'clashes', which Icelandic historians seem to notice more readily than the services they rendered.[10]

SCANDINAVIA AND THE GERMAN HEGEMONY IN EUROPE

Later in the summer during which the fall of France and the entry of Italy into the war destroyed what was left of the balance of power in Western Europe, Churchill set up the SOE (Special Operations Executive) with orders to 'set Europe aflame'.[11] But sporadic raids on enemy-occupied territory, attempts to contact and co-ordinate native resistance movements, and the widely heard voice of the BBC could at this stage do little but help to keep alive the hopes of deeply discouraged peoples. Pending the entry of other great powers into the conflict – a development which was not easily foreseeable – the military, political and economic situation in Europe remained overwhelmingly in Hitler's favour, even when the year ended without Britain itself having been invaded from the sea or bombed into submission from the air.

Viewed as a whole, the democratic political institutions of the Scandinavian democracies stood up well to the strain. In Denmark Stauning, who had brought representatives of the other parties into his Cabinet on 9 April, stayed at the head of affairs. Much authority passed, indeed, to a non-party foreign minister of long experience, Erik Scavenius,* but even in the summer of 1940 public opinion compelled him to abandon his interest in negotiations for a customs and currency union with the Reich, which would allegedly have given Danes and Germans equal rights in both countries. It was then made clear that, when the war in Europe was over, the Danes would be given cause to regret their failure to accept this offer of a privileged position in the 'New Order' (see p. 343). For the time being the Germans went no further than to give financial backing to the native Nazi leader, Fritz Clausen, who had been elected to the Folketing in 1939 (as already mentioned) after nine years of agitation among the German minority in North Slesvig and discontented agriculturists in other parts of the country. In October the German minister, who was still the main controlling agent in Denmark, also required the removal from the government of the Conservative leader, J. Christmas Möller, and other determined adversaries, whilst the Nazi agitation grew to such dimensions that a group of leading citizens tried to convince the King that a non-party Cabinet under his cousin, Prince Axel, would be the only means of avoiding the intrusion of a Nazi ministry, as in Norway. However, Danish parliamentarism weathered the storm; Stauning remained in office until his death in May 1942, when he was followed by another Social Democratic premier, Vilhelm Buhl.

In Norway the unpopularity of the government under his own leadership, which Quisling had announced on 9 April, had been so extreme that the Germans preferred to deal with an Administrative Council of officials. But when the campaign was over, the *Reichskommissar*, Josef Terboven, negotiated with the party groups of the Storting for the setting up of a new government, whose co-operation with Germany might make

---

* 1877–1962. A professional diplomat, who had been foreign minister in 1909–10 and 1913–20. When he replaced Munch in July 1940 he had the strong support of the King, which he appears to have retained to the end of the war as the man who helped his sovereign to ensure that 'Copenhagen was not bombarded or the country devastated'.[12] John Christmas Möller (1894–1948) was his bitter opponent.

his presence superfluous. The first stumbling-block was the demand for the suspension of the royal house, which after much heart-searching and hesitation was accepted by a majority of nearly 2:1; the second, the intention of the Germans to give office to the supporters of Quisling, whose failure had not lost him the ear of Hitler. When this became clear, compliance ceased, so at the end of September Terboven appointed executive ministers (*kommissariske statsråder*) as heads of departments, acting under the supervision of his own highly organised German bureaucracy. A much more bitter opposition was henceforth directed against the Quisling ministers than against the Germans themselves. Their party (*Nasjonal Samling* or NS) was now the only legal party and local government fell entirely into their hands; but resistance to their decrees was based upon other major institutions such as the Supreme Court, the Church, the teachers' organisations, and (later) the trade unions. In February 1942 the reinstatement of Quisling as Minister-President at the head of what was formally his Cabinet only intensified the feeling against NS, whose membership never rose above five per cent of the electorate.

The Swedish government and people were united by the desire at all costs to escape their neighbours' fate. The equivalent of a press censorship was maintained for four years,* and in 1941 the period of military service was extended to 450 days. The German transit traffic with Norway was allowed to grow, so that it included war materials and carried altogether two million military passengers. Whilst the public never lacked sympathy for Norwegian refugees making the hazardous journey across the frontier, the official attitude to occupied Norway was initially at best correct. But although Stockholm had two pro-German newspapers (owned by a brother of Ivar Kreuger), the elections in the autumn of 1940 not only brought record support to Hansson and the Social Democratic Party but also deprived the native Nazis of their handful of secret supporters in the Second Chamber.

Finnish politics pursued a tortuous course, influenced by fears of Russia and hopes of Germany. The Russians followed up the treaty of Moscow by exacting the use of the Finnish railway to supply their leased base at Hanko, by encouraging the revival of Communism in Finland, and by direct intervention in internal politics. Thus Tanner was eventually excluded from the Cabinet, and he was one of four potential candidates whom they blackballed for the Presidency, which passed on Kallio's death to Ryti. But the most striking event of what was to prove a very brief inter-war period was a Swedish proposal for a confederation under the Swedish crown, as of old. This would allay Swedish fears that a Russian occupation of Finland would be counterbalanced by a German occupation

---

* Control was exercised mainly by refusing transport facilities but sometimes by outright confiscation, as in the case of eight issues of *Göteborgs Handels- och Sjöfarts-Tidning* containing anti-Nazi articles by its editor, Torgny Segerstedt, to whom Goering had telegraphed his menaces as early as 1933.

of Sweden, whilst in Finnish eyes the prospective advantages outweighed the condition that they should expressly renounce any right to reclaim by force of arms the territory lost to Russia. Since Finland's prospective partner was a proven neutral, the Russians might have gained a high degree of security on their northern flank. Instead, Molotov went to Berlin in November with vague remonstrances against German intervention in 'the still unsolved Finnish question',[13] and approval for any Finnish agreement with Sweden was withheld until May 1941 – when it was too late.

In the previous September President Ryti, Mannerheim, and a minority of the Finnish Cabinet had approved a transit agreement on the Swedish model, for German troops on leave and supplies to pass between the head of the Gulf of Bothnia and Kirkenes in north Norway via Rovaniemi and the Finnish Arctic Highway. This was soon extended to cover a line of supply bases on Finnish soil, the Finns in return receiving both armaments and food which were denied them by the Russians. Before the end of May 1941 at latest, both President Ryti and Mannerheim and other military commanders were aware of the use to be made of Finnish territory in the event of a Russo-German war; a week before the invasion of Russia began, they mobilised their own army and placed two divisions under German command.

Hitler's last great venture, in whose success and failure the Finns participated, affected in a different way all the rest of Scandinavia. But it may be convenient to consider first the economic impact of the German hegemony, as it had begun to develop in the twelve months since the fall of France. Even Finland, which had lost so much at the treaty of Moscow, was made to feel the pressure, one of the Russian grievances being the German insistence on a three-fifths share in the nickel mines near Petsamo. Sweden was almost completely within the German trade sphere, for Petsamo offered only a very small outlet for Finland and Sweden combined, and it was not until December 1940 that Britain allowed four ships a month to pass between Gothenburg and American ports. Swedish dependence upon Germany for coal and other essentials caused the iron-ore supply, which the Allies had struggled to check, to flow very smoothly. The Germans never took the entire 10 million tons scheduled in the annual trade agreements, but Swedish miners were released from call-up and loading arrangements at Luleå improved so that there should be no hitch, and in 1941 the proportion of ore conveyed in Swedish shipping was doubled. In that year the export of ore with a low phosphoric content, essential for certain high-grade steels, reached its highest total of 2·8 million tons.[14]

German trade reports from time to time treated 'the three Nordic states' as a unit.[15] This had the twofold justification that the two German-occupied countries were at least as dependent as the neutral upon German supplies to avert a complete economic breakdown, and that they were the natural trading partners still available to Sweden, which traded with them to the extent that Germany allowed. But both Norway and Denmark were exploited by the occupying power in ways from which Sweden was still sheltered. They were compelled to finance the costs of occupation, including airfields and defence works constructed mainly by their own labour force. Norwegian fish and Danish dairy produce went into German rations, and industrial raw materials and manufactures were diverted to the service of the *Wehrmacht*. Since the Germans in appearance paid at satisfactory rates for both goods and services, it was all too easy for the ordinary man and woman to practise without demur what was later condemned as 'collaboration with the enemy'; post-war calculations show that the actual occupation payments for the first two years amounted to 1,842 kroner (£100) for every Norwegian and about one-third as much for every Dane.

In early July, 1940, one of the earliest references to 'the New Order in Europe' figured in an article by Scavenius for the *Berliner Börsenzeitung*.[16] The previously mentioned proposal for a German-Danish customs and currency union, which followed later in the same month, is an example of the many far-reaching German plans for an integrated European economy, in which the disappearance of unemployment might be expected to compensate for the basis of exploitation in the interest of the *Herrenvolk*. Both Danes and Norwegians were to function as food producers; the former would provide corn and fodder for themselves as well as dairy produce for export; the latter, whilst increasing the cultivated area so as to become self-sufficient, would make a special contribution to the European protein supply through their fish, for which freezing plants were to be installed on an ample scale. The Danes, whose soil was made to yield 78 per cent larger crops than during the First World War,[17] contributed substantially to the German food supply. The Norwegian fisheries were prevented by Allied action from making up more than one-half of the wartime shortfall in the German catch, and the yield of their land harvest had each year to be eked out by considerable imports, even to provide rations averaging about 10 per cent below the German level. Nevertheless, it is easy to understand that, in Norway as well as Denmark, the food producers were the category of the population which was most inclined to acquiesce in the occupation regime.

Albeit that the industries of the New Order were to be concentrated in Germany, so that its entrepreneurs and workers would form the new European elite, the hydro-electric resources of Norway were supposed to give its fiord-side plants a special role in producing the aluminium for German manufactures. Indeed, the pressing needs of the aircraft makers caused the first planners to arrive in Oslo in the first week of the invasion, and the plan grew until it envisaged an eventual annual output of more than 240,000 tons of aluminium, using bauxite and alumina from every part of German-controlled Europe. In cold fact, however, the modest amount of 18,000 tons which reached Germany in 1940 was not equalled in any later year,[18] as the grandiose schemes of the New Order gave place to the improvisations of a war economy, in which Germany was thrown increasingly on the defensive.

Hitler's invasion of Russia at midsummer 1941, the climacteric event to which we now return, did not at first destroy the image of his New Order, for the German armies overran nearly all the territory (except the oilfields of the Caucasus) which he needed to supplement his existing command of economic resources. How successful those armies were may be illustrated by the fortunes of the Continuation War waged by the Finns. Three days after the Germans had commenced operations across the Finnish-Soviet frontier, which brought Russian bombers over Finnish territory, the parliament in Helsinki announced a state of 'defensive war';[19] but Mannerheim now had command of an army strengthened by a longer training period and equipped from German sources with heavy artillery, anti-tank guns, and much else in which it had previously been deficient. In early July his Order of the Day pointed to 'the freedom of Karelia and the Greater Finland' as 'the goal that beckons us in a holy war at the side of mighty Germany'.[20] The old frontiers were quickly regained, and the evacuated population returned home. The Finnish forces then went on to take Soviet Karelia right up to the River Svir, which joins the southern ends of Lakes Ladoga and Onega. Mannerheim refused indeed to commit his troops to the siege of Leningrad or even to help the Germans to cut the Murmansk Railway; yet 1,400 volunteers served under German command (though against the government's wishes) in the Ukraine, and in June 1942 relations were so cordial that Hitler visited the Marshal's headquarters to offer his congratulations on his seventy-fifth birthday.

Although the Finns alone saw a direct national interest in promoting the so-called anti-Communist crusade, its ideology had some effect in other parts of Scandinavia. Sweden this time sent only about 1,000 volunteers to the Finnish front, but committed a signal breach of neutrality by allowing an entire German division to reach the same front by transit from Norway. The part played by anti-Soviet as distinct from pro-German feeling on this occasion is not clear, but Hansson overrode the objections of his fellow Social Democrats by indicating that a refusal would have been followed by the King's abdication. Other minor concessions followed, such as the convoying of German troops and munitions through Swedish territorial waters and an embargo imposed on Norwegian merchant vessels in Gothenburg harbour, six of which were sunk by the Germans in March 1942 during a delayed break-out.

In Denmark Scavenius was the only member of the government who readily accepted the German demand, when they were required to join the Finns as signatories of the Anti-Comintern Pact on the occasion of its renewal in November 1941. Of the 3,000 volunteers who went to the eastern front, one-half were drawn from the German minority in north Slesvig;

but they also included 77 officers of the Danish army released from their regular duties. In Norway Quisling had taken an anti-Communist position consistently since 1931, so the powers which the Germans conceded to him and his party were used to the full in propaganda concerning the eastern front, for which he enlisted about 7,000 volunteers. In both countries, however, these enlistments were much more than offset by the stimulus which Hitler's breach with Russia gave to the resistance movement among workers, whose political opinions had held them back as long as Hitler had the world's chief anti-capitalist regime for an ally.

The Danish government was required by the Germans to intern known Communists, but on 29 June 1941 they nevertheless managed to start Denmark's first illegal newspaper; in the first half of the following year twenty-one acts of sabotage took place, and twenty in the third quarter. Not all of these were attributable to Communists or other working-class activists, but the co-operation of these two groups was indispensable to the task of building up a national will to resist, undertaken by the Conservative political leader, Christmas Möller. Having escaped to London in April 1942, he became chairman of the Danish Council there and an unwearied propagandist on the BBC. In the case of Norway, the exiled government in London was able to give a clear lead by its immediate acknowledgement of Soviet Russia as an ally. Moreoever, in September 1941 the workers were made to feel what German rule meant, when minor industrial unrest in Oslo was used as a pretext for executing two of their leaders within a few hours of their arrest.

In the same month a representative of the expanding Home Front organisation was added to the Cabinet in London, and 1942 became 'the great year'[21] for the resistance movement. Quisling's authority as 'Minister-President' was successfully defied by the Church and the teachers' organisations, and his plan for a Chamber of Corporations (*Riksting*) on the Italian model thwarted by mass resignations from the trade unions. The entry of Russia into the war had given immediate importance to the supply route to Murmansk round the North Cape, where British convoys suffered such heavy losses that Churchill himself would have liked to turn feigned Allied landings on the Norwegian coast into a permanent lodgement. Thus it came about that the most active elements in the resistance, including some Communists, shared with SOE in the landing of arms and agents and attempts at sabotage. These resulted in many executions and reprisals against innocent persons, but served the strategic object of confirming Hitler in his belief, 'Norway is the zone of destiny in this war';[22] this caused him to spread a third of a million men along the entire coastline, from where they could not easily be transferred to other fronts.

However, from December 1941 onwards the entry of America into the war made it certain that preference would be given to operations of a larger scope. So far as Scandinavia was concerned, President Roosevelt had already secured what mattered most for his purposes. In April 1941 the

Danish minister in Washington, who had acted independently since the invasion of his country, signed an agreement which transferred the defence of Greenland to American hands for the duration of the emergency. The Danes retained the internal administration of the colony, which was facilitated by the high wartime price for cryolite, whilst the Americans established two big air bases ('Bluie One' and 'Bluie Two') in the south and weather stations in remoter areas, where they even encountered German meteorologists already in possession. In July 1941 American forces arrived for similar purposes in Iceland. German submarines and aircraft were increasingly active in the vicinity of the island, which had recently been included in the German war zone, so the Icelandic government gave its formal consent to protection by what was still nominally a neutral power.

For Norwegian and Danish peoples under the German yoke the news of America's direct involvement through the Japanese attack on Pearl Harbor spelt new hope. Moreover, the intimate knowledge of its strength imparted by generations of immigrants served to offset the news of the Far Eastern triumphs of Germany's Japanese allies, which helped to make 1942 a third year of disaster. The Swedes, too, were similarly encouraged to doubt the inevitability of a final victory for German arms, and the Finns derived what consolation they could from the fact that the United States, unlike Britain, refrained from declaring war on them as co-belligerent with the Germans.

SCANDINAVIA AND THE COUNTER-OFFENSIVES AGAINST GERMANY

In the winter of 1942–3 Allied propaganda to the Continent was for the first time reinforced by news of great victories, over Rommel's tanks in the Western Desert and over the German armies massed for the capture of Stalingrad. Spread far and wide by the illegal press, this was most opportune for the Norwegian people, who were to some extent discouraged by the apparent failure of their efforts in the preceding year. However, the military branch of the resistance ('Milorg') continued its secret preparations to co-operate with an eventual Allied landing, and in the same month as the relief of Stalingrad (February 1943) a small group of saboteurs made the first of two immensely bold and successful attacks against the heavy-water supply which the Germans obtained from Rjukan, thus delaying the manufacture of a German atomic bomb, which was then believed to be imminent. Other feats of sabotage against important installations in Norway were undertaken likewise with men and material dropped by the Allied air forces, as an alternative to bombing, which often wrought havoc among persons and property not working for the enemy.

Among the Danes, on the other hand, the autumn of 1942, when the King apologised profusely for an unintended slight to Hitler and Scavenius became prime minister at the German behest, was a time in which Christmas Möller's first direct appeals for sabotage were widely disapproved, and as late as March 1943 a general election testified to the peaceful conditions obtaining in Hitler's 'Model Protectorate'.[23] The inter-party coalition of 9 April 1940 received 95 per cent of the votes in what is still a record poll. Three seats went to a nationalist party, *Dansk Samling*, which had not previously been represented in the Folketing and was now clearly associated with resistance to the Germans, and only the same number to the Danish Nazis, whose percentage of the votes had increased by an insignificant 0·3 per cent.

The change came suddenly, with a rapid growth of strikes and sabotage; the latter was stimulated by SOE and the Allied air forces, as in Norway, but an underlying factor was the growth of a public opinion which thought risks were worth taking because the democracies now seemed to be the winning side. The result was that on 29 August 1943 the Danes were placed under what they called 'Norwegian conditions'. A state of emergency was proclaimed by the German military authorities, who disarmed the Danish army and seized the fleet: but a number of vessels were either scuttled or taken across to Sweden, an operation costing twenty-four Danish lives – which was more than the losses on 9 April 1940. The Cabinet was at the same time replaced by an administration of civil servants* under the permanent head of the Danish Foreign Office; this body also exercised legislative powers when necessary, in order to avoid direct German rule.

Moral authority rested henceforth with the Freedom Council, which was established secretly in Copenhagen in September; it had links with all political parties, including the Communists, and with the active forces of the resistance. One striking success was the smuggling over to Sweden of all but a few hundred of the 7,000 Danish Jews, a humanitarian action which had a precedent on a smaller scale in Norway, where the order for their deportation to Germany had been issued a year earlier. In Denmark, as in Norway, many saboteurs lost their lives in the service of the Allied cause, especially as the Germans received much help from the native Nazis, who practised both counter-sabotage and systematic delation against the property and persons of patriots; in retaliation 343 informers (*stikkere*) were liquidated in less than two years.

In the case of neutral Sweden the change in the Allied fortunes was clearly marked by two events. One was the distribution to the public in June 1943 of an invasion pamphlet, requiring that 'Resistance shall be made under all circumstances';[24] the other a new trade agreement with the Allies, signed in September. Although still dependent on German coal, for which

---

* The Scavenius government having been suspended by the action of the Germans, the King (whom they had omitted to suspend) refused to accept its resignation, and declared that he was constitutionally unable to appoint any new government without the approval of the Rigsdag. The political party leaders sought to avoid implication in any further compromise with German wishes, so the Rigsdag remained in abeyance until after the Liberation, whilst the Supreme Court authorised the twenty-four principal civil servants to issue ordinances and collect taxes in relation to their several departments.

neither wood not peat had proved a satisfactory substitute, and knowing from experience that the Germans could at any time block the trickle of neutral trade passing in and out of Gothenburg, the Swedes agreed to a 30 per cent drop in exports to the Germans, measured by value. The maximum quantity of iron ore was reduced to $7\frac{1}{2}$ million tons, and in the first half of 1944 the amount sent was below this figure. The agreement also provided for a reduction of 50 per cent (by value) in ball-bearings, and in this case the pressure on the Swedes was renewed after the German manufacture of ball-bearings had been systematically bombed in the following autumn and winter. But the basis of their economic compliance was plainly shown by the refusal of a second big cut, in spite of American threats of reprisals against SKF, until 8 June 1944 – when the Swedes had news of the Allied landings in Normandy.

However, 1943 witnessed a definite change in the political attitude of the Swedish government to the fellow Scandinavian peoples, when it terminated the transit arrangement for the German garrison in Norway and allowed the Norwegian government in London to appoint a new minister to the Stockholm legation, which had been kept vacant since October 1940. A sum equivalent to £1,250,000 was collected by a Relief Organisation for Norway (set up in August 1942), and official protests were made against such German measures as the deportation of Norwegian university students and the pogrom against the Danish Jews. But the most important step was the agreement in the summer of 1943 which allowed 8,700 Norwegian exiles to assemble in 'health camps' on Swedish soil, where by the end of the year they were receiving military training as 'police troops' in readiness for the day of liberation. In the autumn the same facility was allowed to the Danes; they were only about half as numerous, but had the advantage of a fleet of small transports, smuggled across from Denmark to facilitate a quick return whenever the moment to fight in support of an Allied landing should arrive.

No such happy dénouement could be expected by the Finns, although the news of the German defeat at Stalingrad was followed immediately by a conference between Mannerheim and the political leaders, who agreed that they must get out of the war as quickly as possible. Both Sweden and the United States were willing to act as intermediaries, but the first sign of faltering produced a month's cessation of German food supplies – five-sixths of all imports now came from Germany – and it was clear that the German army would always be prompt to revenge itself upon a small brother-in-arms. Although the Social Democrats and the Swedish People's Party agitated behind the scenes for peace, and economic support for a return to neutrality was available from Sweden, a new Finnish Cabinet failed to face up to a rapidly deteriorating military situation. A year passed before Paasikivi was sent to Moscow to learn the precise Russian demands in terms of territory, indemnification, and the expulsion of German troops. These terms were then rejected, not because prospects might brighten but because 'acceptance would imperil independence'[25] – and the prime minister's view received the unanimous approval of the Elskunta.

Consequently, the great Russian offensive which was synchronised with the landing of the Western allies in Normandy included a devastating onslaught on the Karelian Isthmus by Soviet artillery, bomber aircraft, and tank forces. Mannerheim tried to concentrate his troops from positions farther north, but before midsummer the Russians were in Viipuri. In this desperate situation the Finns obtained a respite by inducing the Germans to send anti-tank weapons, a division of tired soldiers, and some much-needed grain in return for a pledge not to make a separate peace. This was given in a personal letter to Hitler from President Ryti; but the promise was declared in August to have no further binding force, because Mannerheim then took over the Presidency and appointed a new Cabinet. In the meantime the Finnish front had become stabilised, as the Russians diverted their main pressure to the south shore of the Baltic; so Mannerheim had slightly more favourable circumstances in which to sue for an armistice, which came into effect on 5 September.

The news of the Normandy landings created an atmosphere of joyful expectancy in Norway and Denmark, as in other occupied territories, but from June to December 1944 their orders from Supreme Headquarters were: 'No steps must be taken to encourage . . . overt action, since no outside support can be forthcoming.'[26] How easily a grave predicament might arise was shown almost immediately in Copenhagen, where the imposition of a curfew provoked a more or less spontaneous general strike, in which barricades were erected and more than 100 Danish lives lost; whole quarters were due for bombardment by German artillery, when the civil service administration fortunately effected a compromise. The only activities approved by SHAEF were the continuance of sabotage against enemy communications and supplies and the secret training of Home Forces; both Norway and Denmark eventually held between 40,000 and 50,000 men in readiness, partially equipped by their allies and trained for guerrilla warfare.*

However, the only part of Scandinavia from which the Germans were destined to be ousted by force of arms was the far north, where the armistice terms of September required the Finns to expel their former comrades in arms, numbering about 200,000, from their territory. It was not until April 1945 that they succeeded in clearing the tongue which projects northwest towards Tromsö in north Norway: their casualties were, indeed, much smaller in this campaign than in either of its predecessors, but the retreating Germans were ruthless in exacting retribution for the desertion of their cause. Rovaniemi, the capital of the Lapland province, was system-

---

* A SHAEF mission to Denmark was set up in October and a Danish military mission to SHAEF in the following month, the formal basis being that, though not an ally, Denmark would be 'treated in the same way as an ally, as the Danish people has shown a strong determination to resist the Germans'.[27]

atically destroyed in the retreat, as were roads and bridges and more than one-third of all buildings. Meanwhile, the Russian advance along the Arctic coast went fast, securing possession of the Petsamo area (which the Finns were now required to cede), and pursuing the Germans across north Norway as far as the River Tana, about 100 miles west by road from Kirkenes, where the Russians settled down in November for the winter.

The Germans continued to fall back southwards to the vicinity of Tromsö, leaving behind them a protective belt of totally devastated territory. The local population, many of whom went into hiding rather than evacuate under enemy orders, suffered extreme hardship, and although the Allies sent supplies for their benefit to Kirkenes they would not countenance any serious military effort on their behalf. A token Norwegian force was allowed in by the Russians from Murmansk; two companies of the police troops were brought by air from Sweden; and local recruitment raised the total Norwegian force in north Norway by degrees to 3,200 men. But the brigade which had been training for so long in Scotland was not allowed to sail, partly for fear of complicating relations between the Western allies and the Soviet Union, but more particularly because of the need to husband all resources in men and ships for the western front.

In the last phase of the war in Europe, which may be said to have begun with the German counter-offensive in the Ardennes in December 1944, the main function of the Norwegian and Danish resistance movements was railway sabotage, though the Norwegians also stepped up the measures they had organised for the destruction of enemy shipping. The Danish rail saboteurs claimed a total of 1,301 actions in just over four months, whilst the Norwegians concerted 750 breaks in the line in a single night, during which they also blew up the main railway administration building in Oslo. Altogether, it is believed that three-quarters of the movement of enemy troops southwards was held up. But in the uncertain situation created by the final advance into the heart of Germany from east and west, it seemed for a time possible that the huge enemy garrisons, still held back in powerful fortifications along the entire Norwegian coastline, might be used for a final stand. In that event, the Norwegian and Danish Home Armies would presumably have seen service in an operation for which Scandinavia was regarded as a single whole. 'Norway', reported General Eisenhower less than a month before the German surrender, 'can be approached in strength only via Sweden. This, in turn, will necessitate the liberation of Denmark . . . as early and as quickly as possible.'[28]

The neutrality of Sweden was not in the end infringed, but the Allies required the export of ball-bearings to be cut off in October, the export of the long-disputed iron ore reduced to a trickle, and the last remnants of any trade with Germany discontinued on 1 January 1945. In February Count Folke Bernadotte, a nephew of King Gustav V and head of the Swedish Red Cross, negotiated successfully with Hitler's police minister, Heinrich Himmler, for the transfer to Sweden of certain categories of interned persons, including 7,000 Danes and Norwegians. The Swedish government also hoped to facilitate a peaceful surrender of the Germans in Norway by arranging for their internment in Sweden, and had alternative plans for direct military intervention in both Norway and Denmark if their peoples were exposed to further severe suffering by a wilful German prolongation of the struggle. The Western allies, however, did not wish their demand for unconditional surrender to be obfuscated in any degree, and the Russians would have regarded a Swedish action with particular suspicion. As it was, Denmark was liberated by the capitulation made to Montgomery in north-west Germany on the evening of 4 May, and Norway by the comprehensive surrender to Eisenhower on the early morning of the 6th.

Although the German units in Norway mustered 365,000 men, neither there nor in Denmark did they offer any opposition to the small Allied force flown in to control them or to the members of the Resistance movement and the police troops returning home from Sweden, who took the main responsibility for preserving order. The Russian garrison in the far north of Norway, said to have been 40,000 strong, departed in September, and before the end of the year the British closed down their headquarters in Oslo. In Denmark, where the Germans were far fewer and could easily be sent across the frontier, the Allied presence came more quickly to an end, except for the island of Bornholm, which was not relinquished by the Russians until April 1946.

THE AFTERMATH

When the war in Europe came to an end, the five Scandinavian peoples shared an almost ecstatic sense of relief because their national and individual liberties were no longer in danger of extinction. At a time when so many other European states were in the melting-pot, they desired no more than the preservation of their pre-war boundaries and pre-war systems of government. In Norway the ministers who returned with King Haakon from exile gave place at first to a Cabinet composed mainly of Resistance leaders under Einar Gerhardsen (see p. 362), but in October an election provided Labour with its first overall majority. Denmark, too, had what was mainly a Resistance Cabinet pending an election in October; this brought in a Venstre ministry, which fell after two years on an issue of external policy (see p. 353), when a new election transferred office to the Social Democrats. In Sweden the wartime coalition came to an end in July 1945, Hansson continuing as premier with a Social Democratic Cabinet based on the election results of the previous October.

For twice-defeated Finland its pre-war boundaries could only be the subject of nostalgic longing, but its stubborn resistance had preserved it – alone among all the continental belligerents – from enemy occupation. The Finnish constitution therefore continued to function, although retro-active legislation was necessary in order to carry out the armistice undertaking to penalise the political leaders responsible for the Continuation War, seven of whom served terms of imprisonment. After the trials of his former colleagues were completed, Mannerheim was duly succeeded as President by Paasikivi, who had been prime minister in 1944–6, when the Communist Party was for the first time included in the government. Here also there was a parallel trend in other parts of Scandinavia. Iceland included the first Communists in its Cabinet in 1944–7, and in each of the other three states the election at the end of the war carried what was still in 1976 a record number of Communists into the legislature. The fact that Russia was now a world power made it easier to acknowledge the role of native Communists in the Resistance movements.

In many respects, however, the war had driven these small peoples farther apart. Although most Swedes had been well aware that their own liberties would not long survive a German victory, their King and government had done nothing to prevent such a victory as long as they judged the Germans to be the winning side. Although they made generous gifts to assist post-war recovery in Norway as well as Finland, it was natural for their neighbours to look askance at their prosperity: during the six years of world-wide suffering, the Swedish GNP had risen by 20 per cent; in 1946–9 the US dollar was valued at only 3·60 Kroner. Part of their wealth had been devoted to a large expansion in armaments, yet as early as January 1946 the Swedish government found itself powerless to resist a demand from Stalin for the repatriation of refugees from the former Baltic states, who had entered into German service after the reconquest in 1941. Many Scandinavians would have echoed the sentiment attributed to King Haakon, 'There must be no more talk of Sweden as the big brother.'

Both Norway and Denmark bore the scars of five years of occupation by a ruthless and in many respects resourceful enemy, plus those imposed by sabotage and bombing. To estimate the total economic cost is difficult, but for Norway it has been calculated at the equivalent of $1\frac{1}{2}$ years GNP in the prosperous later 1950s, and for Denmark as having set back the economy to the same depressed condition as in 1930.[29] The amount soon ceased to matter, since – contrary to all expert forecasts – it took only three years for the Norwegian GNP to return to its pre-war level, whilst by 1949–50 Danish industry was producing more than before the war and Danish agriculture was held back by difficulties not of production but of marketing. Both countries also bore the scars of political conflict, since legislation which was partly retroactive brought to book the many citizens who had in varying degrees collaborated with the enemy. The twenty-five Norwegians and forty-six Danes who paid the supreme penalty had themselves been directly or indirectly guilty of murder, but the prison sentences – about 20,000 in Norway and about half as many in Denmark – and the much larger numbers of heavy fines or reductions to poverty by deprivation of civil rights caused a bitterness which outlasted a general amnesty accorded in the mid-1950s.

Norway, however, emerged from the war with an increase of prestige which was commensurate with her greater sufferings – the two-month campaign in 1940, the loss of almost half the mercantile marine with one-tenth of its crews, and the laying waste of north Norway in the last war winter. King Haakon's government in exile had been recognised as a full ally by Britain, Russia and the United States, and its forces had played a small but highly creditable part in the Battle of the Atlantic, the air defence of Britain and the Normandy landings. The Danes, on the other hand, had difficulty in escaping the consequences of their forced signature of the Anti-Comintern Pact; as we have seen, Denmark was never formally part of the alliance against Hitler, but on 5 June 1945 the withdrawal of Russian objections enabled Norway to secure its admission to the San Francisco Conference as the fiftieth member of the United Nations. In the autumn of 1946 Sweden and Iceland were among the first states to be admitted from the wartime neutrals.

Norway's stronger position in relation to the larger allies did not exempt her from anxiety about the future of her overseas possessions in the Arctic. In the last month of the war in Europe the government in exile approved a secret declaration with the USSR, contemplating a joint militarisation of Svalbard. No action followed, but when the Americans were informed of the agreement later in the year, their first reaction was to hold on to Jan Mayen island farther west, which was not returned to the Norwegians until February 1946.

Denmark was faced with much graver territorial problems. The situation in South Slesvig, where the miseries of the defeated Germans were in-creased by an influx of refugees from the Soviet zone of occupation, prompted a resuscitation of the century-old 'Eider Dane' movement. So many of the resident Germans would have welcomed incorporation in Denmark in order to escape from the ranks of the defeated and the en-cumbrance of the refugees that the British authorities, who controlled this part of Germany, offered to hold a plebiscite or even to hand over South Slesvig to Denmark forthwith. Most Danes preferred to wait and see – and were proved right by the rapid collapse of the agitation as soon as West Germany began to recover. But the prime minister persisted in an activist attitude which had ceased to commend itself to the Conservatives or to any elements in his own party (Venstre); hence the fall of his adminis-tration in November 1947. The Americans waited only until the Russians had left Bornholm before making it clear that they would retain their air bases on Greenland. Nearer home Danish sovereignty became an issue in the Faeroes, where the British had allowed the islanders their own flag, currency, and full powers of self-government, though on a strictly pro-visional basis. King Christian's ministers expressed their willingness to concede independence to a decisive majority among the islanders, but the first election to their legislature (*Lagting*) after the war returned 12 to 11 members against independence, which became 11 to 12 after a plebiscite had supported independence by a majority of 1 per cent. The upshot was a law which gave full legislative and executive powers to the Lagting, except as regards foreign relations, and continued a token Faeroese representation in the parliament of the Danish Kingdom.

Whilst a tenuous link with the 30,000 Faeroese was thus with difficulty re-established, Denmark had no alternative but to accept in 1950 the dissolution of the common monarchy which the 130,000 Icelanders had carried out unilaterally after an almost unanimous plebiscite in the summer of 1944. Although King Christian acknowledged the *fait accompli* in a congratulatory telegram to the new republic – whose first president had been for fifteen years a minister accredited to his court – the Danes have not been alone in thinking that it seemed ungenerous to take such action at a time when Denmark's fate contrasted so unhappily with their own. The war years had brought undreamed-of prosperity to the Icelanders – from high-priced fish exports, from construction work on airfields for the Americans, and from services of all kinds for American forces which at times amounted to as much as one-third of the native population. The real national income grew by 60 per cent and, as fish sent to Britain was paid for in Lend-Lease dollars, a plentiful supply of goods flowed in from the United States.

Although their neutrality had not saved the Icelanders from the loss of 352 lives by German action at sea, they refused an invitation to join the Allies in the final months of the war and immediately on its termination demanded the withdrawal of the American forces. In October 1946 this was qualified to the extent that 600 civilian specialists were allowed to remain at Keflavik, the huge American air base which was urgently needed for communication with their forces stationed in Germany. But the secession of the Communists from the government on this issue and the defeat of the opposition in the Althing by no more than 32 to 19 marked the start of a continuing conflict.

The Finns during these years were working desperately hard to bring a much sterner conflict to an end by punctilious fulfilment of the armistice terms of September 1944. The expulsion of German troops and the trials of 'war criminals' have already been mentioned. The forfeiture for the second time of territory regained in the Continuation War was accompanied by the loss of Petsamo, which shut Finland off from the Barents Sea and deprived it of the valuable nickel mines, and the leasing of the Porkkala Peninsula to the USSR for fifty years; situated only a dozen miles west of Helsinki, a base here was a much graver threat than when it had been placed Hanko. A small nation, whose manpower was reduced by 85,000 deaths in action and 50,000 permanent disablements, was further pressed by the problem of resettlement, involving about 12 per cent of population; the majority, who could not be absorbed in industry, were accommodated with the help of a draconian measure for partitioning all farm properties in excess of 62 acres. But on top of all this the Finns undertook to pay the Russians reparations in kind to the value of 300 million American dollars, the prices to be in principle those obtaining in 1938 and a percentage to be added for any delay in the delivery of the six annual quotas. Since two-thirds had to be provided from metallurgy and shipbuilding and only one-third from Finland's established forestry industries, exactions in the first year amounted to 78 per cent of all exports, and a complete economic collapse was only staved off by Swedish and American loans. Yet the determination with which the Finns erected and manned new workshops and shipyards led the Russians to extend the period for deliveries to eight years, to remit fines for delay, and to reduce the total quantities by one-quarter; the successful discharge of their debt also left the Finns with a much expanded manufacturing potential. Meanwhile, in February 1947 Finland was among the lesser enemy states with which the Allies made peace at Paris.

The official meetings of Nordic foreign ministers had been resumed immediately after the war, and they looked forward to a gradual approximation of their policies within the framework of the new UN Organisation. As early as May 1945 the Swedish prime minister at a meeting of Scandinavian Labour Party delegates proposed a regional defence league under UN auspices; but both the Norwegians and the Danes had a modest share in the occupation of the British zone in Germany, which made it natural for them to base their post-war armaments upon close relations with the British services. As regards foreign policy, the Norwegians had the support of the Finns in their attempts to act as bridge-builders between east and west.

These dated back to the war period, when Lie as foreign minister in exile had learnt the need to couple his advocacy of a special Norwegian link to other North Atlantic powers with 'a development of our good relations with the Soviet Union'.[30] His success in this role was one reason for his acceptability as the first secretary-general of the United Nations, where the new Norwegian foreign minister, Halvard Lange (see footnote, p. 358), likewise tried to avoid taking sides between east and west. In January 1947, however, the negotiations over Svalbard came to light, whereupon the agreement of 1945 was disowned on the score that it had not been formally signed; but the Russians were assured that it was now contrary to Norwegian policy to negotiate with any single power regarding 'the defence of an area under Norwegian sovereignty'.[31] Given a world at peace, Norwegian bridge-building was not altogether unlike Sweden's continued concern for the adoption of neutral attitudes, so the four Scandinavian members of UN – to which Finland was not admitted until 1956 – could pursue a common policy on many international issues. Outside the field of politics, too, new ventures opened up vistas of Scandinavian co-operation: in 1946 SAS organised its first flights to the western hemisphere, and in the following year all five ministries of education were busy with the inaugural meeting of a Nordic Cultural Commission.

Chapter 15

Survey of the Latest Age

INTRODUCTION

The nearer an historical narrative approaches to the present day, the more easily it can lose perspective. With December 1976 as a terminal date, a purely chronological survey of almost thirty crowded years might prove not merely confusing but misleading. The impact of world events in 1948-9 necessarily provides our starting-point, because Scandinavia became divided between the three adherents to NATO, neutralist Sweden, and a would-be neutral Finland. The further course of Scandinavia's relations with the outside world will, however, be left to the end of the chapter, for to a much greater extent than could have been foreseen in 1949 each of these countries has been free to concentrate upon its own internal development.

That internal development is generally treated as the separate histories of five small nations – praiseworthy but not significant. The present survey will concentrate instead upon four subjects in which it is possible to see a common achievement. The first is the continued growth and vigour of democratic political institutions. The second is the mounting prosperity of the Scandinavian economies from the late-1940s up to the early 1970s. The third subject is the accompanying record of social achievement, a field in which these peoples not infrequently acted as pacemakers for their larger neighbours. Finally, attention must be given to the remarkable experiment of the Nordic Council, which has brought about much new co-operation in cultural relations, the institution of a common Labour Market and the removal of all kinds of barriers to communication. In the economic sphere, however, the Council was less successful than EFTA in binding together the northern nations, and in 1972 their unity in this respect was impaired because Denmark, and Denmark alone, chose to join the enlarged European Community – which will bring us back to the course of relations with the outside world.

THE COLD WAR'S NORTHERN FLANK

In 1947 – the year in which peace was formally restored between the

Allies and the German satellites, including Finland – the so-called 'cold war' between the former allies had already reached such a pitch that the Americans offered the vast subsidies known as Marshall Aid to stave off a Communist take-over of Western Europe; they also encouraged Bevin as British foreign secretary to form a military alliance with France, which later became the six-power treaty of Brussels. But for Scandinavia the first alarm did not come until February 1948, when Czechoslovakia, whose government had practised much the same 'bridge-building' policy as the Norwegian, was suddenly pulled behind the Iron Curtain. This was followed almost immediately by a demand that the Finns should accept a treaty of mutual assistance, such as already linked Hungary and Romania with the Soviet Union. President Paasikivi was able in the end to modify the terms of agreement, but Finland's prospective fate directly alarmed the Norwegians, whose fears were further fed by reports from American and other sources that they might expect a similar demand at any moment. The common frontier with Soviet Russia made Norway especially vulnerable, and almost 12 per cent of votes at the election after the war had been cast for the Communists, whose representatives in the Storting it was judged necessary to exclude from the special committee which handled the situation.

When the Scandinavian states, with the significant exception of Finland, met with the other twelve in Paris in March 1948 to arrange the distribution of the American economic aid, Lange learnt from Bevin of the possibility that American military aid might likewise be made available through the system later to be called the Atlantic Pact. Lange was soon in direct contact with the Americans, whose interest was not only in the fate of north Norway but also in the possibility that Norwegian influence might help them to keep control of Iceland and Greenland, which were even more important to their own defence. Conversely, the Americans were not particularly interested in furthering a Nordic defence union, which Sweden would direct towards neutralism.

In early May the Swedish foreign minister visited Oslo to propose a union such as had been adumbrated in 1945, and the proposal was carried a little further at a party congress in Stockholm, when the Danish representative Hedtoft (see p. 374) urged in the presence of his fellow premiers that whatever endangered one Scandinavian country was a threat to all.[1] It was not made public until September, when a civilian and military committee was appointed for the three kingdoms, and the Swedish initiative then had the clear support of all parties except the Communist, in Denmark as well as Sweden; in Norway too, a Gallup poll[2] showed more support for a defence link with a Scandinavian than with any other group of powers. The dénouement came in January 1949, when ministers and representatives of all non-Communist parties in the three legislatures met in Copenhagen at the most comprehensive Scandinavian assembly since the days of the Union of Kalmar. But on this occasion the leadership, which had long ago passed from Danish into Swedish hands, was in effect challenged by the Norwegians, whose wartime achievements had given them close relations with America and Britain in the diplomatic field which counterbalanced Sweden's far greater capacity for defence. The negotiations broke down completely on two related issues. The Swedes insisted that no step should be taken which might compromise the neutral policy which had brought them alone unscathed through six years of war in Europe. The Norwegians were equally insistent that no alliance should be formed on terms which might make American military supplies unavailable in an emergency; Lange had himself been instrumental in clarifying the American attitude, which signified that the Swedish ban on any link-up with America and Britain would in fact debar them from immediate help.

The die was cast. After a second fruitless meeting in Oslo, for which ambassadors were called home from Washington, Moscow, London and Paris, Lange went to Washington in early February to secure Norway's admission to the forthcoming Atlantic Treaty. The Danes, who had inclined to the side of the Swedes in the discussions, found that they were regarded as too much of a defence liability for a bilateral pact to be offered them; they therefore followed Norway's example. Both countries, however, declared before signing that no foreign power would be allowed to establish bases on their territory, 'so long as it was not attacked or threatened with attack'.* The Icelanders, who had dismissed the idea of a Nordic defence treaty as offering no benefits to them, signed with the other two but made larger reservations: Iceland alone would decide when a condition of war justified the concession of bases and facilities for foreign troops as in 1941–5, and would herself be liable for no contribution in men or money. Even so, the treaty was opposed by one-quarter of the legislature (as compared with one-fifth in Denmark and one-tenth in Norway), stones being hurled through the windows at the assembled Althing.

The Swedes were seriously disappointed at the rejection of their Nordic defence plans, which they believed to be realistic on the score that the Americans, though refusing to endorse in advance an alliance which aimed at strict neutrality, would be obliged by self-interest to supply their military needs if they were attacked. But few Swedish voices were now raised in favour of signing the Atlantic Treaty at the cost of abandoning the neutralism which might keep them safe. Moreover, some compensation for the failure to hold the rest of the north together under their leadership was available to them in their relations with the Finns, who were well aware that the interposition of Sweden between their territory and that of the Atlantic Treaty powers tended to reduce Russian pressure; their

---

* Norwegian foreign minister's reply of 1 February to an inquiry from the Russian ambassador;[3] a similar assurance was given by the Danish foreign minister in the Folketing on 22 March. The North Atlantic Treaty was signed in Washington on 4 April.

gratitude for this increased their readiness to regard Sweden as their principal link with the West.

The terms of the Soviet-Finnish treaty of mutual assistance had proved to be much less alarming than had been anticipated at the outset. President Paasikivi included Communist ministers in the delegation which went to Moscow in early April, but he insisted that they must negotiate a result which the Finnish parliament would accept. Why the Russians proved co-operative is uncertain: perhaps they never intended to exact more than the precautions proposed ten years before (see p. 329), since when their experience of *sisu** in two wars had disinclined them for overmuch direct intervention in Finnish affairs. Paasikivi was able to insert a preamble stating Finland's intention to remain outside conflicts of interest between great powers, and reduced the initial duration of the treaty from twenty to ten years. The direct military obligation was narrowly defined to cover only the case in which Finnish territory was 'the object of an armed attack by Germany or any state allied with the latter', such aggression being aimed against Finland or the Soviet Union. A separate, less clearly worded article provided for mutual consultation 'if it is established that the threat of an armed attack is present'.[4] When it was ratified on 28 April 1948, the Agreement of Friendship, Co-operation and Mutual Assistance compared very favourably with the obligations imposed at the same period on Romania and Hungary, and seven years later Finland escaped involvement in the much more precise defence arrangements of the Warsaw Pact.

The Finnish institutions of self-government stood the strain of the crisis successfully. The ratification of the treaty was, indeed, expected to provide the occasion for an attempted Communist *coup*, based on control of the Ministry of the Interior, the state police, and the broadcasting network. Paasikivi placed troops and a gunboat in position to protect the capital, but no plot came to light, allegedly because the Minister of the Interior (though subsequently dismissed) supported the President. In any case the elections in the same summer showed that the Communists were losing ground, whereupon the President called into office a Social Democratic Cabinet, which included no near-Communist, and abolished the state police which had been their favourite means of exerting pressure. In that year the Communists organised a number of semi-political strikes and in 1956 a general strike of three weeks' duration; but although they continued to command 20–25 per cent of the votes cast at elections, it was not until 1967 that the President deemed it safe to

---

* A superhuman capacity for physical endurance, exemplified by the long-distance runners such as Nurmi, was believed at the time to be the main explanation of the achievements of Finnish soldiers in the Winter War. Certainly its history has developed a stubbornness of character in the people as a whole, without which it could not have survived as a political and cultural entity.

readmit them to the Cabinet. Thus Finland, too, remained firmly attached to Western forms of parliamentary government.

DOMESTIC POLITICS

In both Denmark and Sweden the general trend towards full democracy was clearly marked in the new constitutions which came into force after long deliberation in 1953 and 1969–75. The abolition of the Danish Landsting and the Swedish First Chamber meant that in all five countries a general election gave full authority to a single body of legislators, albeit that in Norway and Iceland they still operated mainly in two divisions of their own making. The Danes extended the use of the referendum, which had been required since 1915 for constitutional changes, so that a one-third minority in the Folketing could henceforth require almost any bill to be submitted to the decision of the electorate. In Sweden and Norway the referendum was also in use, but only in the form of an advisory plebiscite. The Danes also adopted the Swedish institution of the *ombudsman* to protect the rights of the individual against the usurpations of officialdom; this had been introduced in Norway for military service the previous year, and was extended to civil life in 1962. The Swedish constitution brought the age of enfranchisement down to eighteen, a democratic development which the other nations also approached by stages.

The powers of the three Scandinavian monarchies were already confined within narrow limits by law and precedent, but their recent history deserves mention here, not least because the sovereigns of minor states are often better known than their ministers in the outside world. Haakon VII had returned to Norway with his authority greatly enhanced by the five years of exile, and down to his death was regarded by all classes as a veritable 'father of his country'. His son, Olav V, whose Swedish consort had died while he was still crown prince, had strong contacts with Britain and America, but confined himself strictly to representational duties, including state visits which marked Norway's growing international prestige. Christian X of Denmark – an elder brother of King Haakon – had recovered much of the popularity forfeited through the Easter Crisis in 1920 by serving as a dignified if impotent symbol of national unity and independence for his subjects under the German yoke. The long reign of his son, Frederick IX (1947–72), gave a less formal and more democratic tone to the court, the continuance of which was assured by a constitutional modification allowing his eldest daughter to succeed him in due course. Margaret II, married to a French diplomat, may be said to emulate her fourteenth-century namesake only in the regal skill with which she performs a strictly limited range of official duties.

In Sweden the death of Gustaf V in 1950 brought to the throne his 68-year-old son (Gustaf VI Adolf), who had cultivated an almost professional interest in archaeology and had counterbalanced the influence of his German mother, who deplored his liberal tendencies, by his two English marriages. Nevertheless, the Social Democratic Party did not forget the anti-democratic and pro-German policies pursued by his father, with the result that the new constitution included a series of provisions depriving future occupants of the throne of any remaining semblance of influence or formal control over the Cabinet, the Riksdag, or the armed forces. In addition, the constitution-makers refused to modify the law of succession, so that in default of a male heir to Carl XVI Gustaf, who succeeded his grandfather in 1973 and three years later married a wife from the West German bourgeoisie, the Swedish monarchy would die a natural death.

Paradoxical as it may appear, the elective Finnish presidency has proved much more likely to restrict the popular will than any of the three monarchies. For the wide powers, which were originally given to this office as a safeguard against left-wing subversion, have proved well adapted to a kind of discretionary intervention on the political scene whenever Russian wishes might be inadvertently or otherwise flouted. The Finns have been fortunate in their two post-war choices. That of Paasikivi in 1946, which was made exceptionally by the Elskunta for the last four years of Mannerheim's term, was clearly based on his success as prime minister under the armistice, and his re-election by the normal procedure in 1950 reflected his successful management of the crisis of 1948. On Paasikivi's retirement in 1956, the electoral college – nominated by 50 per cent more voters than had bothered to go to the polls for this purpose before the war – chose Kekkonen* by the margin of a single vote. The fact that his term of office has twice been renewed by the ordinary procedure and finally extended by special legislation to 1978 is clearly related to the proven unwisdom of any deviation from the 'Paasikivi-Kekkonen line' in foreign policy; but it also means that the President has achieved a strong position in relation to the political parties, which in the rest of Scandinavia are accepted without qualification as the sovereign instrument of democratic government.

The Social Democratic or non-revolutionary Labour Party has maintained its general ascendancy throughout the post-war era. In Sweden it was continuously in office, either alone or as the dominant party in a coalition, from 1936 to the autumn of 1976. The Norwegian Labour Party has had an almost comparable predominance: apart from the years 1965–71 its tenure of office has only been interrupted in 1963 for a single month, and in 1972–3 by a caretaker ministry to cover the gap between

---

* Urho Kaleva Kekkonen (b. 1900) became Agrarian leader in 1936, worked with Paasikivi in opposition to the Continuation War, and was five times prime minister during the latter's presidency. In the 1960s his power as President, derived in large measure from his close personal relations, first with Khruschchev and later with Kosygin, was already so great that a limitation of tenure to two terms in future was widely canvassed.

the Common Market plebiscite (p. 378) and the next election. Tage Erlander* held the premiership of Sweden for the record period of twenty-three years; his Norwegian counterpart, Einar Gerhardsen,† had a shorter run, but the part he had played in the Resistance gave him a special authority with members of all parties. In Denmark (where no single party has commanded a majority in the Folketing since the eve of the First World War) the Social Democrats have likewise been in office for about three-quarters of the time, including the two crucial periods of Denmark's admission to NATO and to the European Community, where a Danish Social Democratic leader came to play an active part (see p. 364).

In Finland, where the only party majority had been held by the Social Democrats in 1916, their influence on policy has been enhanced through the post-war growth of industry and consequently of trade unions. In addition to their key administration of 1948–50 (already mentioned), the Social Democrats headed a number of coalition governments and in 1958 they were permitted by the Russians to make the veteran Väinö Tanner their party chairman. From 1966 onwards they were more strongly represented in the legislature than either of their two main rivals – the Agrarians, who are the party of President Kekkonen, and the Communist 'People's Democrats' (SKDL), who are from time to time of tactical importance to the Russians. In Iceland alone did the sympathisers with Communism poll more votes than the Social Democrats – 15–19·5 as compared with 12·5–18 per cent[5] – but there too, the latter figured more frequently in the government coalitions.

Every Scandinavian state bases its elections upon proportional representation, which enables small splinter parties to appear and even in some cases to survive; it also has the more important effect of encouraging the division of the non-socialists into as many as three main parties of roughly equal strength. Among the younger generation the Conservative championship of traditional values attracts fewer voters than its support for industrial capitalism repels, but the Conservative Party has remained important in each state except Denmark (where Venstre shares many of its principles); in Finland, however, size has not meant direct influence, since its past links with Germany caused its exclusion from the great majority of coalition Cabinets. Liberalism has continued to be a strong

* 1901–76. The son of a Liberal with Free Church interests, he became a Social Democrat at Lund University and entered the Riksdag in 1933. After only two years in the Cabinet, his youth helped him to secure the premiership – by a very narrow majority in the Party – after Hansson's unexpected death in 1946. Erlander proved to be adroit as well as earnest, with a reputation for negotiating compromises behind the scenes at Harpsund, the Swedish counterpart to Chequers.

† Born 1897. A road-worker's son, he had been active in left-wing politics until he was removed from the chairmanship of the Oslo City Council and imprisoned by the Germans (1941–5) for his role in the resistance movement. This brought him into touch with men of all parties, which greatly mitigated the opposition to his post-war socialist programme, which was in any case more moderate. He retired temporarily from the premiership in 1951–5 (when he was succeeded by his own nominee) and definitively in 1965.

force in Sweden; in Denmark its followers are found chiefly in the ranks of the Radical Party, which functions generally as a small ally of the Social Democrats; in Norway the decline of the old, partly liberal Venstre Party has been accompanied by the growth, especially after the war, of a religiously based Christian People's Party; and in Finland too, liberalism is on the decline. In Denmark the agricultural interest is still represented by Venstre, whereas the other three countries each have a highly organised agrarian or Centre Party; this is especially strong in Finland, where the post-war settlement greatly increased the number of smallholders in desperate need of subsidies, and for most of the time this party has provided the political base for the prime minister as well as the President.

Whilst the programmes of the non-socialist parties, formulated by conferences at national and local level and publicised by a very extensive party press, have generated much sound and fury in the respective legis-latures, this has not usually prevented government by consensus. Pros-perity within a mixed economy, full employment achieved in co-operation with the trade unions, and a steady approximation to full social equality are aims to which these opposition parties have in principle subscribed, whilst challenging in detail the methods which Social Democratic ministries have used to carry them out. Instead, the main challenge to social democracy in Scandinavia has come from parties lying further to the left.

The fears of Russian intervention which led to the foundation of NATO in 1949 brought about the total eclipse of the Communist Party in Norway and Denmark; in Sweden its representation in the Second Chamber declined by more than one-half; and its exclusion from any place in Finnish governments has already been noticed. However, in 1959 the former long-time leader of the Danish Communists, Axel Larsen, founded a Socialist People's Party (SF), which was uncompromisingly Marxist in internal policy but independent of Moscow in its external policy. 'Out of NATO' was a cry which appealed strongly to neutralist sentiment, especially among the young, whilst the advocacy of disarmament had the special advantage of capturing votes from the Radical Party, which had recently abandoned this line as the price of office in a coalition ministry. By 1966 SF held twenty seats in the Folketing, and although it later lost some ground through the formation of smaller rival groups, its basis in a kind of grass-roots nationalism, much in vogue among people to whom the Establishment is anathema, made it a formidable pressure-group towards the left in many issues, great and small.

In 1961 the movement spread to Norway, where the two members it secured in the Storting held the balance, so that it was able to overthrow the Labour government – on a charge of mismanaging the state coal mine on Spitsbergen – and one month later restore it to office (August–September 1963). In both countries SF played a leading part in the propa-ganda against the Common Market, and when the plebiscite in 1972 (see p. 378) had shown that in Norway majority opinion sided with the party on this issue, its representation in the Storting rose to fifteen. An alliance was then formed with splinter groups on the radical side under the name of 'Socialist Left' (SV), though the Communists, whose votes have long been too few to obtain any representation in the Storting, preferred to remain a separate party. In Sweden the Communist Party itself adopted a more nationalist standpoint in 1967 under the name of 'Left Party Communists'. They won 19 seats in the first single-chamber Riksdag (1973–6), when their help enabled the Social Democratic ministry to survive in a legislature divided 175–175, and in the latter year they retained 17 seats in the new total of 349. In the Iceland of the 1970s, where every party was strongly nationalist, the third largest was the People's Alliance, whose domestic policy was broadly Communist; in 1971–4 it formed part of the government coalition, and thereafter led the opposition. In Finland the position was more complex: Communism had a strong following among the hard-pressed smallholders as well as in the industrial trade unions, and the support which the Stalinist element among the People's Democrats might receive from Moscow was always an uncertain factor. But in 1966–76 the majority of the party joined in coalitions with the Social Democrats and Agrarians which were tantamount to a Popular Front.

By 1976, however, the trade depression spreading outwards from the continent was producing a kind of polarisation in Scandinavian politics. In Norway it seemed increasingly important to obtain control of the prospective oil earnings, so the three main non-socialist parties tried to sink their differences in preparation for the next election. In Sweden, where this was election year, the non-socialists obtained a majority of 180 to 169, but their first victory for more than a generation was clouded by the commitment of the new prime minister, a farmer from north Sweden (Mr Thorbjörn Fälldin), to an eventual ban on nuclear power development; this was approved only by his own Centre Party and by the Communist Left. In Finland the Communists and 'fellow travellers' were so strongly opposed to the government's crisis measures that it had to be reconstructed as a minority ministry resting upon the middle parties alone, and passed its budget with the help of the Conservatives. Denmark, however, where the economic difficulties came first and were perhaps hardest to solve, was the only Scandinavian country in which parliamentary institutions seemed to weaken under the strain. Between February 1975 and December 1976 a minority administration of Social Democrats under Mr Anker Jörgensen* came near to collapse on four occasions through

---

* Born 1922 and formerly a warehouse worker. As chairman of the General and Semi-skilled Workers, he opposed the anti-Common Market policy of his union and became premier for the first time in October 1972, immediately after the decision in favour of Danish membership; in December 1973 he presided over the summit meeting which drew up the Declaration of European Identity. From December 1973 to February 1975 the Social Democrats gave place to a Venstre Ministry, but neither party had adequate support in the electorate.

the difficulty of securing support in a ten-party legislature for crisis measures which were as urgent as they were inevitably unpopular. The prime minister himself pointed to the ominous fact that antiparliamentary parties of the left now had a counterpart on the right, since the third largest party in the Folketing was that of the 'Progressives', whose demagogic leader* proposed to revive a sick economy by dismantling the whole edifice of taxation and bureaucracy which constitutes the welfare state.

ECONOMIC DEVELOPMENT

Until the general economic crisis of the 1970s spread eventually into the north, the Scandinavian countries as a whole enjoyed about a quarter of a century of almost uninterrupted advances. The last vestiges of the rationing of consumer goods disappeared soon after 1950, and the government controls which had been built up partly in anticipation of a post-war trade depression could be adapted entirely to planning for prosperity. Norway became well known for its introduction in 1947 of a National Budget, based on the principle that the public and private sectors of the economy were to serve common purposes. Nine years later the director of the Statistical Office reported on the results as follows:

> Unemployment was practically non-existent . . . The rate of investment was extraordinarily high . . . Direct taxation and subsidies had the effect of equalising disposable personal incomes . . . The two remaining goals – prevention of inflation and long-term balance in external transactions – were not achieved.[6]

Sweden, too, had been prepared for economic planning by a commission representing the political parties and other interests, which worked in 1944–5 under the chairmanship of Gunnar Myrdal.† With the help of Sweden's inherently advantageous position in the post-war era, planning had such momentum that in 1970 a five-year forecast even 'directed attention towards 1990'.[7] Although Denmark and Iceland (as we shall see) experienced special difficulties in their foreign trade relations, whilst the Finnish economy was so much under Russian control that the stimulus of Marshall Aid had to be forgone, the five states may be regarded as having had broadly speaking similar economic policies and achievements.

As in other parts of Western Europe, the primary aim has been the maintenance of full employment, but Scandinavian governments proved

---

* Mr Mogens Glistrup, a lawyer; he retained his popularity in spite of some 3,000 charges of tax evasion and fraud, which had engaged the attention of the courts for several years without result, as the defendant could seldom spare time to stand trial except on Saturday mornings.

† Born 1898. Author of *An American Dilemma* (1944) and many economic works; minister of trade in Sweden, 1945–7, and general secretary of ECE (the UN economic commission for Europe), 1947–57.

particularly zealous in pursuing egalitarian policies as well – less concerned about the ingredients of the cake than about its slicing. Taxation of higher incomes and all accumulations of capital was therefore intensified, and other financial controls ranged from the fixing of interest rates and limitation of dividends to the extensive use of subsidies. State ownership, however, was increased more cautiously. If we take the forests as an example of a basic industrial resource, in Finland the state's share was 35 per cent, in Sweden and Norway 20 per cent. Some leading mines are state-owned, including Europe's richest source of iron ore at Kiruna in north Sweden (of which the second half was taken over in 1957) and its largest copper mine at Outokumpu in central Finland. New hydro-electric projects and large steelworks have been built by the state to stimulate employment in particular districts, chiefly in the north of the peninsula, and in Norway the state has developed a major aluminium plant which had been planned by the Germans. But the position in Norsk Hydro, where the government now has one-half of the shares, is more typical of the trend in Scandinavian industry.

If we view the semicapitalist systems of the Scandinavian countries as a single whole, the contribution of their 22 million citizens to the West European economy is impressive, witness some returns for 1973 – the year of the enlargement of the Common Market.[8] Grain crops totalled 17·9 million tons, a little less than the UK harvest and consisting of barley and oats rather than wheat; the milk supply of 12·8 million tons was 2 millions below that of the UK; and the livestock (preponderantly pigs) only half as numerous. In fisheries, however, the Scandinavian catch of 5·6 million tons was not merely five times the British but twice that of the United States. As for industrial materials, the Scandinavian supply was particularly important in two fields: the output of 25·2 million tons of iron ore was considerably larger than that of Britain, France, and West Germany combined, and was almost half that of the USA; and the output of 49 million tons of sawn wood, pulp, newsprint and other paper not only dwarfed that of the three named European states (as we might expect) but was more than a quarter of what the USA produced from its continent-wide resources. The total Scandinavian production of electric energy (196 million kWh) was more than the French and two-thirds the West German or the British, an achievement which points to highly developed engineering techniques as well as to a plentiful supply of fast running water. Engineering skill and organisation show still more clearly in shipbuilding, where Scandinavia's 4·7 million tons exceeded the combined output of British, French, West German and American yards. Even more remarkable was the size of the Scandinavian merchant fleet – 37 million tons, which was 6 millions larger than the British and well over twice as large as the American. The population of Scandinavia being under 22 million, which is hardly more than two-fifths that of any of the three European countries named in the above comparisons and one-tenth that of the USA, the figures per head are the most noteworthy. On that basis the Gross Domestic Product of the Scandinavians (measured in purchasers' values) was four-fifths of the American, a little below the West German, a little above the French, and 75 per cent higher than the British.

Although most Scandinavians will readily agree that together they constitute a group of peoples which is identifiable in the modern world by its high standard of living, they prefer to look at the economies which have produced such gratifying results as entirely separate national structures. But before looking at them *seriatim*, it may be helpful to point out that each country depends upon exports (including invisible exports such as shipping services or profits from tourists) to maintain and improve its standard of living. For none of them is self-sufficient in foodstuffs or in the raw materials of industry, nor are their internal markets big enough to justify the making of many highly desirable consumer goods and much equipment essential for their manufactures. In 1973, for instance, Scandinavian import requirements amounted to 1,029 US dollars per head, whereas export amounts averaged 931. They therefore followed the pattern of many industrialised countries in reducing the workforce employed in agriculture and preferring those manufactures where a large input of highly skilled labour enhances the export value. In one respect at least the Scandinavians have husbanded their resources with particular success, namely in the elimination of labour conflicts. In the ten years 1965–74 only Finland had two years in which the number of working days lost exceeded half a million; Sweden and Denmark had one such year each; and when allowance is made for the smaller number of employed persons, Norway too had one year of roughly equivalent stoppages. The Swedish record is quite outstanding: with a total labour force approaching four millions, it experienced five years in which the average loss of working days was no more than 5,000, and in one of these years the figure fell to 400.[9]

The Swedish worker had indeed good reason to be satisfied with his lot: he lived in a country where the GNP doubled in the first two decades after the war, so that the average subject of Gustav VI disposed of ten times the material resources which had been available to the subjects of his grandfather's grandfather in 1840. Whilst the share of population engaged in agriculture, forestry, and fishing has fallen since 1940 from 30 to 8 per cent, the major increase has been in service activities, which now amount to 25 per cent as compared with the immensely productive 30 per cent employed in industry.[10] Technical leadership has been extended to new fields such as shipbuilding, where Sweden's share of the world market has grown in half a century from 0·5 to 10 per cent. The financial position has become so strong that virtually the whole of the national debt is held by Swedish citizens. Giant firms such as SKF, with its 50 ball-bearing factories scattered about the world, and L. M. Ericsson, whose telephones are represented in 90 countries, have expanded so fast that, out of a total of 384 Swedish establishments overseas in 1965, two-thirds were less than fifteen years old.[11] When the merchant banker dynasty of the Wallenbergs organised an international mining consortium in 1961 for operations in Liberia, the *New York Times* commented significantly upon 'the emergence of Swedish industrial management skill to a position of prominence in areas of the world often associated with so-called "colonial powers" '.[12]

The Norwegian economy had been run down during the German occupation, which left behind few additional assets except some railway and airfield construction and had had the effect of stimulating agriculture and the fisheries at the expense of industry. The numbers engaged in farming, forest work, and part-time fishing declined rapidly after the war, but technical progress maintained the Norwegian output – except for the Antarctic whale fishery, which unrestricted Japanese and Russian competition had rendered unprofitable. The full-time regular fishermen, on the other hand, kept up Norway's position as Europe's principal exporter; they were encouraged by subsidies, by new labour-saving devices on board ship and quick-freezing plants on land, and (last but not least) by the exclusion of British and other foreign trawlers from the waters nearest home. Lakes and rivers were dammed and power stations constructed at such a rate that consumption of electricity per head was almost twice as high as in any other country; more than 60 per cent went to industry. Norway became the fourth largest producer of aluminium in the world and supplied much of Europe with ferro-alloys, whilst retaining its place in the chemical and wood- and metal-working industries. Meanwhile the mercantile marine secured an even stronger position than it had had in 1939, based particularly upon special-purpose ships which included 11 per cent of the world's tanker tonnage.

Norway may therefore be deemed peculiarly fortunate in that the world economic crisis of the 1970s, which affected tankers even more severely than the rest of the carrying trade, coincided with the early stages of the exploitation of North Sea gas and oil. According to a 1970 estimate Western Europe contains not much more than 1 per cent of the world reserve of oil, but more than half of this lies under Norwegian control – as compared with a British share of less than one-sixth. The government's policy, endorsed fully by the Storting, was to develop this new and easily exhaustible source of wealth with great caution and meticulous attention to planning, so that hazards to workers, damage to fisheries, and dislocation of the labour supply in particular coastal districts might be kept to the minimum. A state oil directorate was established in Stavanger, and the activities of the international companies were further restricted through the setting up of a large, wholly state-owned company, *Statoil*, which received preferential treatment in the allocation of areas of operation. By 1976 gas had been piped to West

Germany and Scotland and a modest quantity of oil was being shipped to Norway, where the building of rigs and ancillary equipment employed much labour. The future rate of advance was uncertain, especially as the government had not yet allowed trial borings to be made anywhere north of 62°. But in 1976 the Norwegian Labour Cabinet appeared confident that within four or five years a vast revenue would begin to accrue from *Statoil* and the heavy taxation imposed on the private companies, whilst the other NATO powers were suggesting that Norway would soon be their richest member and might well bear an increased proportion of the common burden of armaments.

For Denmark the first decade after the war was marked only inter-mittently by recovery: both Britain and the continent imposed high tariff barriers against its agricultural exports, which were then three-quarters of the whole, and the necessity of following the British devaluation of 1949 made fodder and other imports from the dollar area very dear. The second decade, however, was a period of rapid progress: by 1970 mechanisation enabled one farm worker to supply food for 85 persons, as compared with 35 in 1950, and the workforce released from agriculture found profitable employment in industry. This was now the major source of exports; Burmeister & Wain in Copenhagen remained the largest single enterprise, but specialised workshops spread into semi-rural areas as far afield as the island of Als near the German border. In 1957–65 the total industrial product grew by more than 50 per cent, and at the latter date one-fifth consisted of machinery and instruments for export markets, such as West Germany and Sweden. The improvement of communications through the development of Kastrup, Copenhagen, as a major inter-national airport and of fast new road and rail routes to the continent helped to make Denmark and its wares better known abroad, as did the established excellence of 'Danish design' (see p. 392).

The settlement imposed on the Finnish people after the war had left them, as we have seen, with an increased industrial capacity and an agriculture which was more dependent than ever before upon small-holdings. Employing much less machinery and working much more marginal land than other Scandinavian farmers, they grew crops of which the average yield as late as 1974 was about one-half as large; in spite of subsidies, a well qualified foreign observer found that slums, which had disappeared from the towns, still existed in the countryside. But the growth of industry was impressive. Productive woodland, which still covers more than half the total area, has been the source of new exports, ranging from plywood (of which Finland is the principal European supplier) to prefabricated bath-houses or *saunas*, in addition to the traditional staples of timber, pulp, and paper. Metallurgy and engineering, however, now have most employees; besides satisfying domestic needs, the Finns supply foreign markets, especially in Eastern Europe, with products – such as icebreakers, woodworking plants, and copper smelters –

which are backed by practical experience. Since the interior of Finland with its multitudinous lakes is mainly too flat for the easy generation of hydro-electricity, important complementary imports from Russia include oil and natural gas, which are brought overland from the Black Sea area, and the reactors for the first nuclear power station.

The Icelandic economy has had a chequered history, with peaks of prosperity and troughs of depression brought about by variations in the annual catch and the prices obtainable in foreign markets, including the market for frozen fish in Eastern Europe. Memories of the halcyon days of the war may help to account for the effectiveness of wage demands; in 1945–72 cost of living rose by 986 per cent and wages by 1,429 per cent. Attempts have been made to diversify the sources of income. A loan from the World Bank made it possible to provide hydro-electricity on a sufficient scale for a Swiss firm to produce aluminium, and an American company put up nearly half the capital to process diatomite (for filters) by geothermal heat available near the site. But all such schemes meet with the objection that 'the influence of foreign capital will gradually endanger Iceland's independence and distinctive culture'.[13] No such objection applies to measures for establishing a monopoly of the fisheries in surrounding waters, frequented since the later middle ages by foreign vessels whose presence became additionally unwelcome as the stock of fish showed signs of exhaustion. Hence the successive unilateral extensions of the reserved coastal zone to 12, 50, and 200 miles, which were contested by the United Kingdom in the three so-called 'Cod Wars' (see p. 382). These ended in 1976 with the complete acceptance of the Icelandic claims; but the livelihood of their 5,000 full-time fishermen and of the much larger numbers employed in the fish-processing industries was still to a considerable extent dependent on the islanders' ability to develop harmonious relations with the European Community, which in 1974 was their principal trading partner for both exports and imports.

SOCIAL AIMS AND ACHIEVEMENTS

In 1952–3 'Social patterns in the northern countries of Europe' were the subject of an inquiry sponsored by the five ministries of social affairs. One interesting feature of the resulting volume was the basic assumption that the Scandinavian states constituted 'a more or less distinct family group . . . where differences in the social field are less essential than in several other domains'; another, the pride in their achievement when judged by international standards. Thus the reader is told that these countries 'have frequently been likened to a social laboratory, a place of experiment and research'; that 'they enjoy standards of hospital and medical care probably unequalled anywhere else'; and that their social expenditure ranks them with 'the socially most advanced countries such as the United Kingdom and New Zealand'.[14] Broadly speaking, these claims are borne out by statistics. Whilst Attlee's Britain spent about 10 per cent of net national income on these purposes, the Danish social expenditure in 1950 was 9·9, the Swedish and Finnish (the latter including the heavy cost of war injuries) 8·9, the Icelandic 8·0, and the Norwegian 7·8 per cent. The age of affluence which was then dawning brought substantial increases in this expenditure almost everywhere, but the growth in Scandinavia remains impressive. In 1973 the percentage allocation was 25·5 in Denmark, 23·1 in Sweden, 22·1 in Norway, 20·2 in Finland, and 16·0 in Iceland.*[15]

Although a number of other nations may now spend more on these purposes, the Scandinavians as a whole have several advantages which tend to make their social expenditure particularly effective. Firstly, the population of each country is remarkably homogeneous: apart from the Lapps in the far north, the Swedish-language Finns are the only long-established citizen minority, whilst the recent influx of Finnish and other foreign workers into Sweden does not exceed the proportion with which so wealthy a society can readily cope. Secondly, the level of education among the masses has long been good; even in higher education, class barriers were lowered much earlier than, for example, in England. Thirdly, the late industrialisation of Scandinavia means that its social services are saved from wrestling with the intractable problems of vast conurbations: the four capitals are still the only cities with populations exceeding half a million and the Sound region, where Sweden and Denmark are narrowly separated, the only considerable urban agglomeration. Finally, the increasing emphasis laid upon the collective provision of amenities and opportunities for recreation and the open-air life likewise discloses a special advantage for Scandinavians, since it requires so little public organisation and expenditure to bring an unspoilt countryside and the opportunity for open-air pastimes within the general reach.

The larger economic resources of Sweden, which since the 1930s had been administered by the party whose ambition was to create 'a home for the people', made it the natural leader in social policies. Contributory old age allowances for all were started in 1946, children's allowances in 1947; eight years later the Swedes introduced compulsory sickness insurance and substituted 'social help' for poor relief with its traditional stigma. But the most far-reaching development was the proposal for a 'general supplementary pension' (*allmän tilläggspension*, ATP), which the Social Democrats raised in 1957 during their coalition with the Agrarians. Compulsory contributions were objected to by all the non-socialist parties because, though levied nominally on the employee, they would in

* The *Yearbook of Nordic Statistics*, from which the Scandinavian figures are taken, points out that 'The extent of what is here presented as social security expenditure is not unambiguous, which is of particular significance when comparisons between countries are made.' This is of course still more true of comparisons with countries outside Scandinavia; but the size of the total income from which Sweden makes its allocation means that its services are in many cases the most lavish in the world.

fact lay a heavy burden on the small employer. A big new central fund would also be a dangerous instrument at government disposal; and it was also claimed that the farming population had its own methods of providing for old age through local investments. After an unsuccessful attempt to settle the dispute by a referendum, in which the Social Democratic proposal failed to get a clear majority over two alternative schemes put forward by the opposition, the coalition broke up and the bill was consequently defeated in the Second Chamber. A special dissolution – the first since 1914 – resulted in a tie, but the abstention of one Liberal carried the day for the system which has since been copied in Denmark and Norway. Thirty years' work secures a pension amounting to two-thirds of average earnings in the best fifteen of those years; a minority are disadvantaged because there is a ceiling to the amount which qualifies for contributions and pension, but all are gainers by the fact that the pension is protected against inflation.

In Norway the strong sense of national unity which followed the liberation encouraged the government as early as 1948 to envisage a comprehensive system of social security, which has been called 'the Norwegian Beveridge Plan'.[16] Using 1948 prices as a basis, expenditure for this purpose per head of population doubled in the 1950s and again in the 1960s, special emphasis being laid on 'help to self-help' for such categories as the handicapped and disabled, widows and unmarried mothers in need of employment, and persons living in remote areas.

Denmark had been relatively well equipped by the reforms of 1933, which provided the framework of its social legislation until the 1960s, when expenditure increased more rapidly than in Norway under seven new laws on the Swedish pattern. The Danes also made great efforts to raise the standard of living in Greenland, which under the constitution of 1953 became an integral part of the kingdom, with two representatives elected to the Folketing and a democratic provincial council in Godthaab. In twenty years the population of what was formerly a closed colony rose from 24,000 to 48,000, supported by the free development of the cod and shrimp fisheries (to which oil and other minerals may make big additions possible) and by extensive Danish backing for the 'Greenland experiment'.[17] Capital investment, material supplies, and professional and technical personnel from Denmark have engineered the resettlement of the widely scattered and primitive Greenlanders in modern urban communities. In spite of the problems of alcoholism and psychological maladjustment, there is clearly a general raising of the social level which would have gladdened the heart of Hans Egede.

Although most of the traces of Finland's ancient poverty have disappeared since 1945, the pressure for extending the social services at large was held up for a time by the burden of reparations and the overriding claims of the war-disabled and the war-displaced. In the 1970s conditions were still such that Finnish industrial workers flocked for shorter or longer periods to Sweden. By then the social service network included health insurance as elsewhere, and it was intended that the contributory pension should likewise reach the general Scandinavian level by 1980. But the Finns still had a higher death rate, a much heavier mortality from tuberculosis, once the scourge of all Scandinavia, and a smaller provision of medical practitioners.

Whereas the general use of social services is to level up the community by reducing the effects of indigence, ill health, old age, and other causes of incapacity, two of the most important ones may also level down. Housing became a major concern of the Scandinavian governments after the war – even in Sweden, where the six years interruption of normal building was not made worse by the havoc of bombing or other military operations. The scarcity continued, however, into the 1970s, partly as the result of the movement of population into industrial centres old and new, but still more because of the mass demand for more room-space and better domestic equipment. The result has been a very strict control of housing developments through district planning, the pre-emption of available land by local authorities, and the financing of construction to specified requirements (and often for approved categories of occupants) through state-owned Housing Banks or their equivalent. The general standard of housing accommodation has risen accordingly, especially as regards the heating and plumbing which the cold climate renders so costly. Yet the system operates to the direct disadvantage of the middle class, who are now seldom able to buy additional space, privacy, and other similar amenities of the traditional bourgeois home. Iceland constitutes an exception: a rise in two generations from a condition in which the majority of the people lived in squat cottages with roofs of turf to one in which 'apartments are generally larger than in Scandinavia . . . with an average area of about 120 square metres',[18] represents a vast increase of amenities for all classes in the wet and windswept island.

The Scandinavians continue to spend heavily on public provision of education. OECD statistics from the later 1960s, showing the percentage of GNP so allocated by its twenty-three member states, place Sweden first and Finland, Denmark and Norway respectively fourth, fifth, and sixth. In 1962 the Swedes led the way with a compulsory nine-year school for all their children, whilst subsequent legislation broadened the path to the *gymnasium* and gave the same official status to other types of training which do not prepare for the university. The other Scandinavian states followed suit, and there has been a corresponding growth of universities and equivalent institutions, with some faculties open at virtually no cost to applicants with very slender aptitudes, who nevertheless are eligible for interest-free state loans. But for the intellectual elite such a system offers a reduced stimulus throughout, the effect being most obvious in the last two years of compulsory schooling, when instruction has to be adapted to the pace of the least competent and least willing element in a difficult age-group.

The pressure towards full social equality is seen at its most deliberate and most effective in economic measures which have already received passing mention. As between different levels of earnings, a steeply progressive income tax has made a high salary or even the rewards of overtime or subsidiary employment less attractive than in societies like the American, where a competitive spirit and intensive application to a job are regarded as a national asset. As between capitalist rentier and proletarian, the former is deprived of a large part of his savings, not merely by the effects of inflation as elsewhere, but also by a stringently assessed annual tax on all forms of wealth. As between industry and agriculture, subsidies and price controls have been widely applied for the purpose of securing for land workers and fishermen the same standard of living as the average in urban surroundings. As between different types of employment, statutory limitations of working hours, a four weeks' paid annual holiday, and rules to insure the healthiness and general amenities of the workplace make for equal desirability. Finally, as between master and man, new laws requiring formal consultation at all levels between the leadership in firms and workshops and the elected representatives of those who serve under them have done much to destroy the old hierarchic relationship. On the factory floor, no less than in the home, the classroom, and the platoon of recent conscripts, it is no longer a matter of course that he who pays the piper calls the tune.

THE NORDIC COUNCIL; RELATIONS WITH EFTA AND APPROACHES TO THE EEC

Although the defence union project of 1948–9 came to nothing, the years after the war had been marked by other Nordic activities – the revival of the Foreningen Norden with a membership of 120,000, intergovernmental commissions on social and legal as well as cultural questions, and the highly successful development of the Scandinavian Airlines System. Based on public and private capital from all three kingdoms and a general monopoly of external and internal traffic, SAS was soon prospecting for the transpolar air routes which gave it a world reputation. In these circumstances it took less than two years for an initiative taken by the Scandinavian section of the Interparliamentary Union to lead to the inaugural session of the consultative Nordic Council, opened by King Frederick in Copenhagen in the summer of 1953. The Danish prime minister, Hans Hedtoft,* was the most active promoter of the new venture, which also received unqualified support in Sweden – apart from the Communist contention

---

* 1903–55. Hans Hedtoft-Hansen (later Hedtoft), a typographer by trade and Stauning's intended successor in the Social Democratic leadership, had been active in the resistance movement; prime minister, 1947–50 and 1953–5. He did not decide to take Denmark into NATO until both a Nordic defence union and a Swedish-Danish alliance proved impracticable, and was therefore a natural promoter of the Nordic Council. Also important as the sponsor of the new Danish policy for Greenland, which he was the first prime minister to visit.

that the country was being inveigled into NATO. In Norway and Iceland, however, legislative approval was given by votes of 74 to 39 and 28 to 17, figures which suggest that their past history had left these nations chary of taking any step which might somehow compromise their absolute independence. The Finns, on the other hand, joined with alacrity when the Russians withdrew their objections in 1955, though making it clear that they would be no party to any discussion of defence policy or to the adoption of a united standpoint towards any conflict of interest among the great powers.

An equal number of delegates for each state (except Iceland, which has about one-third as many) is chosen by the respective parliaments on a basis of proportional representation, so that all main parties are included; they are nevertheless seated alphabetically at meetings, in the hope of encouraging Scandinavian rather than national or party affinities. The annual session of the Council, held in rotation among the capitals and lasting for about a week, is usually attended by prime, foreign, and other ministers, but only the actual delegates are entitled to vote in the Assembly itself or its various committees. Apart from a general debate on Scandinavian problems, the main business of the session is to examine in committee and then vote upon a score or more of specific proposals affecting two or more of the five states. After being duly recommended, such proposals are entrusted to ministers in the governments concerned, their further progress being reported back to subsequent sessions of the Council. Statistics for the first ten years showed that one-half of the 269 recommendations had resulted in positive action and 78 others remained under consideration at governmental level.[19] Allowing for the purely local scope of many proposals, the impact on governments compares not unfavourably with that of the advisory assembly of the Council of Europe at Strasbourg, where the Scandinavian states with the exception of Finland had been zealous participants since its initiation in 1949.

The Nordic Council began its second decade by adopting the Convention of Helsinki, whose 40 articles pledged the member states to closer cooperation in various fields and urged governments to seek the Council's views on such matters of principle as affected them jointly. The Danish and Finnish delegations have been increased, so as to include representatives of the Faeroes and Åland. A 'Ministerial Council' has been introduced, which is attended by a member of each Cabinet, so that Nordic Council business can be transacted throughout the year and reported subsequently to the annual session, when ministers are also subjected to parliamentary questions. To complete the picture, we may note the establishment of three small secretariats – in Stockholm to serve the Council itself, in Oslo for the business done by ministers, and in Copenhagen for cultural matters – and of regular publications under Council auspices. These range from a bilingual *Yearbook of Nordic Statistics* to *Nordisk Kontakt*, a periodical which covers current Nordic activities alongside the main political trends in the separate countries, using four languages.

The Council has done much to improve communications among the five countries by land, sea and air, though no practical result has yet been achieved in the biggest such project, namely the linking together of Sweden and Denmark by tunnelling under and/or bridging the Sound. Common services have been provided in many border districts, and attention given to the development of the long-neglected *Nordkalott*. This is partly a problem of communications in a vast tract of thinly populated territory, which the chances of history have divided among three sovereign powers; partly too, it concerns the rights of about 40,000 Lapps, whose reindeer-herding and other means of support are encroached upon by new developments. Although the Nordic Council has not so far admitted the Lapps to membership, it has encouraged the formation of a consultative organ (*Nordisk Sameråd*) for their benefit and has initiated various measures to safeguard the Lapp language and culture.

Many tasks in the cultural field lie ready to hand. Schools could be stimulated in their Nordic language studies, and the universities induced to allow free circulation of students by giving full credit to each other's examinations. Some progress has been made with the co-ordination of scientific and technical research, as in the case of the atomic physics institute at Copenhagen (see p. 390), thereby reducing the handicap imposed on small nations by their limited individual resources both of money and manpower. Grants are made to all kinds of projects designed to enrich the cultural life of two or more of the Scandinavian peoples; Nordic Prizes are awarded annually for the most distinguished work in literature, music, and other arts; encouragement is given to the traditional folk high schools, which have always supported Scandinavian solidarity; and at the other end of the cultural spectrum *Nordvision* has been set up to bring common TV programmes into Scandinavian homes.

In the field of jurisprudence, as in that of culture, the Nordic Council has been able to build upon many earlier efforts.* But its attempts to bring about uniformity of civil rights and similarity in the legal systems have a further motive. Passport control for Scandinavian citizens travelling inside the confines of Scandinavia had been abolished in July 1952 – it was later waived for foreigners as well – and this prepared the way for the Council to establish a common labour market among the Scandinavian peoples. In 1954 working permits for wage-earners from other Scandinavian countries were abolished (except in Iceland); two years later full entitlement to all social services was accorded in the country of residence; and the same freedoms were gradually extended to nearly every profession and to self-employed workers. By 1976 the Council had secured agreement that the local government franchise should be conceded to all such immigrants; they totalled about 300,000 (including dependants), much the largest

* An American expert on Scandinavian affairs has pointed out that 'by the 1970s the independent countries of Scandinavia had more legislation in common than did the states of the United States'.[20]

element being the Finnish employees of the big Swedish industrial concerns.

The course of events in the economic field has been more chequered. In the first years of its existence the Council worked out various projects for a Nordic Common Market of limited dimensions; but the Finns excluded themselves for political reasons, neither Swedish nor Norwegian farmers would accept free competition from Danish agriculture, and Norwegian industrialists also required time if they were to avoid being crushed by Sweden's large-scale manufactures. Negotiations were still proceeding slowly when the six members of the Coal and Steel Community established their Common Market in 1958, as a result of which Scandinavian interests became linked with those of the United Kingdom through the European Free Trade Association. This was set up by the Convention of Stockholm (1959), which the Swedes helped to negotiate, and the position of the Scandinavian element among the seven EFTA powers was further strengthened in 1961 and 1970 by the addition of Finland as an associate and Iceland as a full member. Inter-Scandinavian trade stood up particularly well to the removal of industrial tariffs: in 1966–72, when this was virtually complete, the trade of the Scandinavian countries with one another grew by more than 25 per cent, compared with a growth of less than 20 per cent for their trade as a whole.

Nevertheless, the British government's intention that EFTA should serve as a halfway house to the European Common Market was fairly widely shared in the Scandinavian states during the decade of the first two British applications, rejected at the behest of General de Gaulle in 1963 and 1969. The Danes were the most eager to join, in the hope that it would secure access for their farm products to both the West German and the British market. The Norwegians, though highly sensitive to any encroachment upon their national independence, passed a law to permit transfer of powers to international authorities by a three-quarters majority of the Storting, the constitution-making power excepted. The Swedes wanted to preserve their neutral status, but on the second occasion were induced by the industrial interests to apply for membership without any express reservation. This left only the Finns, who held back for political reasons, and the Icelanders, who desired no more than an extension of the free-trade agreement available to them from EFTA.

But when the second British application was seen to be failing, the Danes turned the attention of all five peoples to the advantages of an economic treaty among themselves, known for convenience as *Nordök*, to be negotiated under the auspices of the Nordic Council. Such a customs union might provide 'a dynamic framework'[21] for the growth of all their economies, irrespective of the final outcome of attempts to come to terms with the Common Market; it would also provide their mutual relationship with the firm basis which they had been unable to establish over defence. For a time hopes ran high, and in the early months of 1970 a definitive treaty lay ready for signature by prime ministers and ratification by parliaments. However, at the last moment the Finnish premier, who had previously expressed doubts, announced his country's withdrawal for a reason which another Finnish representative made clear when the Danes tried to renew the project in the following year: 'The formation of economic blocs leads on to political bloc-making.'[22] Since the Swedes shrank from participating in any measure which might isolate the Finns, the Nordic Council had no means of harmonising the attitudes of its component states when the European Community made ready to increase its membership beyond the original six.

Although the fear that national identity might be lost in a surge of foreign influences backed by mammoth capital was clearly widespread, both Denmark and Norway were expected to follow the United Kingdom into the Community on the terms negotiated by their Social Democratic governments, which had the general approval of the politicians. In both cases, however, an advisory referendum was held in the autumn of 1972, when the Danes voted 'Yes' by a majority of nearly two to one, the solid agricultural interest outweighing the opposition of the industrial workers of Copenhagen, where the vote was 52·5 per cent negative. But the Norwegians, who went to the polls a week earlier, were 53·5 per cent opposed to membership, which had majority support only in Oslo and the adjoining counties. Rural Norway was overwhelmingly hostile, its farmers and fishermen fearing to lose their economic safeguards. Moreover, the younger generation as a whole responded readily to a well organised agitation which claimed to champion the nation against the Establishment – that is to say, the Cabinet, the majority in the Storting, and the official trade union leaders – and which stooped to the employment of such cries as 'Norway is not for sale'. Thus Denmark became one of the Nine, whilst the Norwegian negotiation of a trade agreement in the following May was accompanied by a tacit understanding among the politicians that a debate which had generated so much bitter feeling would not lightly be reopened.

In the meantime the Swedish government in November 1972 had signed a rather less restrictive treaty than the Norwegian, being fully confident that Swedish industry could stand open competition in the Common Market, though all parties except the Conservative had come to the conclusion that full membership was incompatible with political neutrality. Another twelve months passed before the Finns made their treaty, which was on a narrower basis than the other two; President Kekkonen also took the precaution of making a parallel treaty with Comecon. As for the Icelanders, they were able to negotiate the same privileges for their trade with the enlarged EEC as they already had with EFTA.

Since the Danes have always been the warmest supporters of the Nordic Council, they act as willing intermediaries between their fellow members and the larger Community to which they alone belong. Conflicting pressures, however, make their ability to achieve positive results so uncertain that it may be wise to accept the regretful conclusion of one of the Danish champions of Nordök: 'Nordic co-operation will continue to be shaped in the future in a field of tension between the solidarity of the peoples and the actual necessities of politics.'[23] Suggestions have been made for giving the Council a party basis, which might be strengthened by direct election of members; in 1976 those of the extreme left already acted together in demanding a direct condemnation of the United Kingdom in the Icelandic fisheries dispute, which the Presidential Body had difficulty in evading. But the obstacles to a common policy in foreign affairs, let alone defence, are so great that the Council turned with some alacrity to the organisation of a Nordic Investment Bank, which in the last months of 1976 set to work to attract capital for economic projects of common interest. Another hopeful line of development was the recent coming into force of a Convention on the Environment, which made Scandinavia (except Iceland) a zone within which rights of protection against noxious activities were in no way restricted by frontiers.

WORLD RELATIONSHIPS SINCE 1949

The cleavage of the north by the Atlantic Treaty was to some extent made good by close co-operation in the United Nations, to which Finland was admitted in 1956. A delay of ten years (which affected numerous other applicants) was due to the acute rivalry between the super powers in the affairs of the General Assembly, and this led Kekkonen to adopt the wary standpoint, 'Rather than as judges we see ourselves here as physicians.'[24] The Finns accordingly abstained from any condemnation of Russian aggression, even in the case of their Hungarian kindred; but in general the five small states of Scandinavia have acted as a bloc, whose influence in UN enterprises has often been disproportionately great because of their disinterestedness and realistic humanitarianism. The achievements of the first two secretaries-general, a Norwegian and a Swede (see p. 397), attracted world-wide attention, as did more briefly the work of the Swedish Count Folke Bernadotte, who was murdered by Jewish terrorists in 1948 whilst acting as UN mediator between Jews and Arabs. Since the Suez crisis of 1956 Swedish, Norwegian and Finnish contingents have been prominent in UN peace-keeping operations, for which a part of their armed forces is always held in readiness. Less spectacular but no less remarkable has been the Scandinavian contribution to the needs of the underdeveloped countries, including three East African projects initiated by the Nordic Council. Sweden and Norway were the first UN members to reach the agreed target of 1 per cent of GNP for public and private aid, and by 1974 the total of official assistance by the four Scandinavian states, with Iceland as a small-scale participant, amounted to 737 million US dollars – about three-quarters of the amount allocated by the United Kingdom.

Whilst the loyalty to UN ideals is common to all five, their membership of NATO has given three Scandinavian states specific rights and duties. At the outset they enjoyed a sudden access of security from the financial and technological resources of their American allies, in return for which the Norwegians and Danes extended the period of military service for their nationals and prepared to place them at the full disposal of the alliance in the event of war. The reservation against allowing the use of bases in peacetime was made by the Icelanders as well as the other two, but the outbreak of the Korean War occasioned the admission of an American Defence Force of about 5,000 men for the protection of the Keflavik airfield. In the previous month (April 1951) the Danes had agreed to a new arrangement for the defence of Greenland, which was entrusted to the Americans for the duration of the Atlantic Treaty with full liberty to develop a great air and radar base at Thule. North Norway was also important for the radar screen, and Allied forces were brought there from time to time for winter and other manoeuvres. But the defence of western Scandinavia (less south-west Sweden) – the whole area from the Russo-Norwegian frontier to Slesvig-Holstein and the entrance to the Russian-dominated Baltic Sea – remained a contingent responsibility, for which a British general and inter-allied staff were posted to NATO North Head-quarters in the outskirts of Oslo. In the event of aggression, all would depend on the speed and strength of the reaction from across the Atlantic, involving factors which were partly unknown but clearly variable.

Since all three Scandinavian states continued their NATO membership when the original term ran out in 1969, the situation can be described as static, but the very fact that the kind of aggression which was widely feared in 1949 has not taken place serves to render the neutralism of Sweden and even Finland more attractive. In 1961, for example, there was widespread indignation in Norway when it was discovered that American U-2 reconnaissance planes had used Bodö airfields in connection with illicit high-level flights over Russian territory, and in the same year both Norway and Denmark explicitly forbade any stationing of atomic weapons on their territory in peacetime to make its defence more practicable in the event of war. In Iceland the removal of the American Defence Force figured in the programme of the government formed in 1974, as it has done in previous periods of *détente* in East-West relations. Next year President Kekkonen's view, that those relations would now permit of the conversion of the north into a zone from which both alliances and atomic weapons were excluded, was brought to the attention of the Nordic Council by his prime minister, a Social Democrat. Only some Norwegian representatives of the far left expressed approval on that occasion, but in all parties except the Conservative the events of 1940 and the anxieties of 1949 mean much less to the younger generation of voters than the limitation of political indepen-dence and association with allegedly 'reactionary powers' which are the price of NATO membership. The supposed risk to the national culture is also brought into the argument at times, as when the Icelandic authorities took formal steps to repel the invasion of Icelandic homes by television programmes from the American base.

Both Norway and Denmark have increased their expenditure of money and manpower in order to meet NATO defence standards, but a much greater effort has been necessary for Sweden in its isolated position. In 1952 the period of compulsory military training rose to 394 days; twenty years later Swedish defence expenditure per head was the fourth highest in the world, and, although its share of GNP was subsequently reduced, in 1976 a special Report examined the problems of total defence, including 'guerrilla warfare if need be'.[25] The navy, which concentrates upon the smaller types of vessel, has been provided with a complete underground base, hewn out of granite on Muskö in the Stockholm archipelago, and the big Swedish aircraft manufacturer, SAAB, has equipped the arm on which the nation mainly relies with a supersonic fighter, the *Viggen*, matching up to the most advanced American and Russian types. The result has been to achieve credibility for a consistently pursued policy of peacetime non-alignment as a basis for neutrality in time of war.

On some occasions, such as the outbreak of the Korean War, the repression of the Hungarian revolt by Russia in 1956, and Khrushchev's revival of the ancient Russian ambition to convert the Baltic into a *mare clausum*, the Swedish viewpoint has coincided with the American. On others, such as the long-contested admission of Communist China to UN membership, the American intervention in Vietnam, and the triumph of the left-wing MPLA with Cuban assistance in Angola, Sweden has been on the other side. These latter occasions have attracted most attention in the United States – which from December 1972 to March 1974 withdrew its ambassador from Stockholm – because there is felt to be a deliberate challenge when Communist policies are endorsed by the most successful capitalist society in Europe or perhaps the world. But it is probably more correct to see Swedish policy as genuinely – and perhaps a little self-righteously – independent: until 1962 it was formulated chiefly by Undén, whose experience went back to the heyday of the League of Nations, and in more recent years by a young prime minister, Olof Palme,* whose hatred of colonialism can be traced back to his encounter with Asiatic poverty in the seminal year 1953. A total blindness to other forms of oppression is not, however, to be attributed to a prime minister whose mother had experienced the hardships of the Bolshevik revolution in her native Riga and whose first wife was a refugee from Czechoslovakia, nor to a people for whom the great lesson of their history is the need for defence against the east.

* The son of the director of an insurance company, he spent one year as a student in America and several in a post on the Swedish defence staff before entering Erlander's official secretariat. While Minister of Education, he occasioned some unfavourable comment by taking part in a public demonstration on behalf of North Vietnam, but in the following year (1969) he became prime minister at forty-two – the youngest in Europe.

Whilst the Finns had the same aspirations towards an independent and neutralist standpoint, their means of realising it were much more restricted. As regards defence, The Treaty of Paris had limited the army to 34,400 men (though conscription was allowed to continue) and severely restricted the navy and air force both in manpower and equipment. In 1956, indeed, the Russians returned the Porkkala base, and a few years later the peace-treaty ban on guided missiles was lifted by agreement, so that the Finns should be able to defend their airspace. But foreign policy has continued to be governed by the Agreement of Mutual Assistance, which at the time of the return of Porkkala was extended until 1976 and later until 1990. For although the military situation against which it offers protection to both parties has never in fact arisen, the Agreement serves as a constant reminder of the broad limits within which the Finns are free to interpret their preferred policy of neutralism in accordance with their own political traditions.

The realism of Paasikivi, who taught his fellow countrymen that 'The Kremlin is no local police court',[26] caused his eight-year presidency to be crowned indeed by Finland's membership of both the Nordic Council and the United Nations. Nevertheless, it required a highly skilled interpretation of his predecessor's policy by President Kekkonen to carry him successfully through two early crises. In the autumn of 1958 the Russians recalled their ambassador and withdrew their credits and orders to Finnish industry – a silent menace which was aptly nicknamed 'the night frost'. But relations returned to normal when the President appointed a new Cabinet, from which he excluded the presumably pro-German Conservatives together with a definitely anti-Communist follower of Tanner. Three years later the great-power crisis over Berlin occasioned a Russian note, claiming that the situation required consultations under the 'threat' clause of the Agreement; the effort to implicate the Finns was dropped, however, after the abandonment of an attempt by Conservative and other interests to challenge the re-election of Kekkonen to the presidency. The subsequent leasing to Finland of the part of the Saimaa Canal which runs through territory ceded to Russia was a signal mark of the confidence which Kekkonen has continued to enjoy among successive masters of the Kremlin. Indeed, the choice of Helsinki as the venue for far-ranging security discussions between East and West indicates that a carefully balanced neutralism has to some extent gained the sympathy of both sides.

The position which the Baltic Sea once held, as the area in which the interests of the great powers impinged most readily on the affairs of the Scandinavian states, has now been transferred northwards. The exploitation of North Sea oil is a subject of international interest, which will increase as the prospecting advances farther into the north. The North Atlantic fisheries have also attracted widespread attention because of the 'cod wars' of 1959–61, 1972, and 1975–6. These had an *opéra bouffe* character, since the British navy employed only pacific methods for checking the depredations of Icelandic patrol boats, and the dragging out of the conflict enabled the islanders to achieve complete success, as mentioned earlier. World opinion from the outset tended to support a very small people, who could claim that their principal economic resource risked exhaustion from being overexploited, and towards the end was influenced also by the spread of a 200-mile limit to other coasts. These considerations overshadowed the fact that in July 1974 the Hague Court ruled unequivocally in Britain's favour – a jurisdiction which Iceland had pledged itself to accept in an agreement of 1961. The longest shadow, however, was cast by the fear that a further exacerbation of the dispute might play into the hands of those elements among the Icelanders which resent the American presence at Keflavik as an impairment of their national integrity and, in the case of the Communists, would like to break off the whole NATO connection.

A survey which terminates in 1976 must point in conclusion to the potential importance for all Scandinavia of recent developments in the huge Russian naval and air base at Murmansk, linked with the Baltic by the White Sea canal. Some of the significance which Tsarist governments attached to the egress from the Black and Baltic Seas now attaches to the passage of the Barents Sea between the Norwegian coast and the limits of the drift ice. An existing disagreement as to the line of division between the respective rights of control over offshore fisheries and the continental shelf – where the sector principle adopted in the Antarctic would bring the Russians farther into the west – therefore became more serious at the end of 1976, when the Norwegians after much deliberation established a 200-mile fishing limit along their coasts. If north Norway has indeed become a highly sensitive area, one result is that the position of Sweden and Finland is increasingly precarious – not to mention that of Denmark as Norway's partner in NATO. Iceland, and Greenland, too, are in addition rendered more essential than ever for control of the sea and air routes upon which the reinforcement of northern Europe in emergency must depend.

And beyond the Barents Sea lies Svalbard, where the exploitation of the islands themselves or of the adjoining sea area may at any time acquire new significance. The exercise of Norwegian sovereignty there is complicated, not only by the treaty obligation to set up no defences and allow all signatories to share equally in the economic development, but also by the presence on West Spitsbergen of a Russian coal-mining population twice as large as the Norwegian. Minor friction over the use of Norway's newly constructed Svalbard airfield emphasised the fact that by 1976 even the outermost periphery of Scandinavia – if we may so describe it – was no longer remote enough to escape the interplay of great-power interests.

Chapter 16

Contributions to Civilisation: II – The Twentieth Century

Two world wars and the political and technological revolutions which they stimulated have brought mankind into an age of superpowers, but this does not necessarily reduce the impact of a smaller state or group of states. In Western Europe the loss of colonial empires has had a levelling influence. The newly established or re-established states of Asia and Africa in many cases form their most fruitful contacts with small peoples who in their view are not tainted by imperialism. International organisations such as hardly existed before 1914 offer considerable scope to talented representatives of small nations, who have something to add to the common stock of political wisdom and experience. And the shrinking of the globe by new methods of transport and communication enables ideas and cultural modes from even the smallest centres to circle it as never before.

In the case of Scandinavia three additional factors have caused its contribution to civilisation to be more widely appreciated than in the nineteenth century. In the first place, its role on the world stage has been more striking: Finland's 'Winter War', the Norwegian and Danish resistance movements, Sweden as 'the America of Europe', and Norway as the oil-sheikhdom of the north have all made an impression on the public mind. In the second place, there is the double effect of the enormous growth in the international tourist industry. Climatic conditions encourage the Scandinavians to spend much of their new wealth on holidays abroad, where they become better known than before, whilst Scandinavian scenery and lonely spaces attract visitors – including about half a million a year from the United States and Canada – who likewise learn something of its people in their native haunts. In the third place, these developments have stimulated Scandinavian studies, as is shown by the rapidly increasing literature of the subject and by its place in the universities. Since 1945 such courses have spread more widely through the United Kingdom from their original bases in Cambridge and University College, London. In the United States the number of students attracted by them has doubled, whilst Faculties of

Politics reported in 1972 that 48 per cent of their staff had travelled in Scandinavia and, more surprisingly, that 9 per cent could read at least one of the languages.[1]

This final chapter will try to review more recent achievements in the same general categories as were adopted for the nineteenth century. In conclusion it will attempt the still more difficult task of defining a Scandinavian 'image' which the author believes to have made some special impact upon our world.

LITERATURE AND OTHER ARTS

Although the Academy has on two occasions awarded the Nobel Prize for literature to Swedish poets,* the impact of Scandinavian writers upon the outside world has continued to be made chiefly through the novel, with Knut Hamsun as an increasingly dominant figure. The translation of *Growth of the Soil* in 1920 created a vogue for his work in English-speaking countries, such as it had long enjoyed among the Germans. Hamsun now lived the life of a gentleman farmer on the south coast of Norway, and his intense love of Nature as well as his psychological insight were features of his writing which came through more easily to the average reader than his contemptuous impatience with modern society as he saw it. The sequel was the total eclipse of his reputation, when he lent his support to the German invaders of Norway and was later heavily fined; but in 1949, the year of his ninetieth birthday, he published his apologia, *On Overgrown Paths* – a stylistic *tour de force* which still arouses interest, whilst its author's political aberrations are otherwise readily forgotten.

Another Norwegian novelist, whose fame for a time rivalled Hamsun's, was Sigrid Undset, a burning patriot whose wartime propaganda attracted attention in America, where she took refuge from the Germans. Her earliest writings were concerned with the problems of a woman's life in the modern urban milieu, which in her case meant pre-1914 Oslo, and those of her last phase likewise dealt with the contemporary scene, now viewed from the standpoint of a Catholic convert. Her principal achievement, however, was made in 1920–7, through the historical trilogies. *Kristin Lavransdatter* and *The Master of Hestviken*, set respectively in the Norway of the fourteenth and thirteenth centuries. As the daughter of an archaeologist and herself a keen student of medieval records, she was well qualified to weave an elaborate backcloth of minutely convincing detail for her presentation of intensely felt characters, whose story carries the reader along and creates an unusually effective illusion of recapturing a vanished past. Two other

* Verner von Heidenstam, whose widely acclaimed classical poems, *Nya dikter*, were published in 1915, the year before the award, and E. A. Karlfeldt, 'the voice of Dalecarlia', in 1931. In addition, the German-Jewish poet, Nelly Sachs, who received the prize in 1966, had become a Swedish subject after her escape from Berlin in Hitler's day with the help of Selma Lagerlöf, whose work she translated.

distinguished Norwegian novelists, Olav Duun and Johan Falkberget, had similar historical leanings, but the milieu – Namdal, north of the Trondheimsfiord, and the copper mines of Röros – was in both cases less interesting to the world at large; and even within the confines of Scandinavia Duun limited his direct appeal by the use of *nynorsk*.*

The other Scandinavian literatures at present have a smaller following among foreigners than the Norwegian. Pär Lagerkvist, for example, is honoured by his fellow Swedes for his poems and plays as much as his novels, but is known to the English-reading public only through symbolic stories with a restricted popular appeal, such as *The Dwarf*, set in the court of a Renaissance prince, and *Barabbas*, in a New Testament setting. To find a Swedish writer whose reputation is completely world-wide one must resort to the sphere of children's books, where Astrid Lindgren's creation of 'Pippi' has captured some part of the imaginative realm which Hans Andersen once made his own. Perhaps it is significant that exceptional interest was aroused by Vilhelm Moberg's epic of the emigration to the New World, the English version of which was published as a trilogy in 1956–61, for he is one of the relatively few Swedish writers of note whose background is not academic; he was born in a crofter's home in stony Småland, where the fortunes of thirteen aunts and uncles across the Atlantic were a subject of lively concern.

The Danish proletarian author, Martin Andersen Nexö, published a second trilogy, *Ditte Menneskebarn*, describing a poor girl's unsuccessful struggle against fate. Although it achieved the distinction of three English translations in four years (1920–23), each under a different title, it was less successful than his earlier work. In 1922 Nexö became a Communist – which led to his internment during the German occupation of Denmark – and his *Memoirs*, translated in part in 1938, are said to rank with those of Maxim Gorky. A social contrast is provided by Karen Blixen, the Danish wife of a Swedish baron, whose first book, *Seven Gothic Tales*, was written in English, whilst the later ones, such as *Out of Africa* (evoking her experience of life on a Kenya coffee plantation), were published in Danish and English simultaneously. The Danish public, indeed, attaches a deeper significance to Johannes V. Jensen, whose stories embrace the modern interest in myth, but his six-volume cycle of novels, entitled *The Long Journey*, appears at best paradoxical to foreigners: evolution is found to culminate in Nordic man, the prime source of every European achievement, down to and including Columbus's discovery of the New World.†

---

* Another *nynorsk* writer of novels, plays and lyrics, Tarjei Vesaas (1897–1970), has been described as 'the most considerable Norwegian writer of the mid-twentieth century';[2] but none of his work was translated into English before 1964, the year in which he received the Nordic Literature Prize.

† The Nobel Prize for 1917 was shared between Karl Gjellerup, who was a disciple of Brandes, and Henrik Pontoppidan, neither of whom is well known outside his native country, where two of Pontoppidan's profoundly pessimistic works, in eight and five volumes respectively, are acclaimed as 'perhaps the greatest novels in the Danish language'.[3]

The novelists of Finland and Iceland may have benefited by harnessing the imagination to themes which lay nearer home. The most representative Finn, F. E. Sillanpää, who was much influenced by Hamsun, wrote first about the impact of the civil war of 1918 upon the class of small tenant-farmers to which he himself belonged. His masterpiece too, *The Maid Silja or Fallen Asleep While Young*, was founded upon the deep poverty of the Finland he had himself experienced, where tuberculosis was too common a scourge for an early death from its ravages to attract much attention. Although the Icelanders found in lyric poetry the art-form that appealed to them most, an exception is provided by Gunnar Gunnarsson, who left the island in 1906 to spend the first thirty-three years of his adult life in Denmark, wrote mainly in Danish, and was a spokesman for Nordic unity; translations of his novels did something to familiarise the world with the little-known Icelandic scene. A later and more important figure is Halldor Laxness, a poet and essayist who is nevertheless best known by his novels depicting Icelandic life from the eighteenth century to the so-called 'American era', which he satirises in *The Atom Station*. A Catholic turned Communist, Laxness received the Stalin Prize in 1953, three years before he became the first Icelander to win a Nobel award.

No younger Scandinavian painter bears comparison with the towering genius of Edvard Munch, whose influence has continued to grow since his death, still active at the easel, in 1944. Sweden had one important sculptor in Carl Milles, who assembled many of his works on his estate in the environs of Stockholm, alongside classical pieces from which he derived much of his inspiration. In 1929 he obtained wider scope by removing to the United States, many of whose cities he adorned with the superb fountains which were his *chefs d'œuvre*. Finland, too, produced a sculptor of genius in W. V. Aaltonen, who carved in the native granite as well as the more conventional marble and bronze. His famous bronze figure of Paavo Nurmi seems to run with the same effortlessness as did its famous subject; but Aaltonen also practised a more monumental style, as in his tercentenary memorial of the first Swedish landing in Delaware. The most widely known of modern Scandinavian sculptors, however, is Gustav Vigeland, the excellence of whose portrait statues and other early work induced the Oslo municipality to set him up for life with a salary, a fully equipped atelier, and a public park in which to display whatever he might choose to create. Vigeland's art proliferated germanic figures, which variously adorn a bridge, support and surround a gigantic fountain, or struggle upwards on a 56-foot monolith. The aesthetic value and the meaning of the work have been much debated, but its sheer mass leaves a lasting impression upon the mind of even the most casual of the innumerable visitors to a centrally situated tourist attraction.

Although each of the three kingdoms emphasised the concurrent growth of democracy and wealth by adorning its capital with a sumptuously decorated town hall – Copenhagen in 1905, Stockholm in 1932, and Oslo in

1950 – Finland made the first and by far the largest impact in the field of modern architecture. The first great name is that of Eliel Saarinen, whose design for the Helsinki railway station (completed in 1914) marked a transition from national romanticism to rationalism, notwithstanding the enormous caryatids which flank the entrance. After winning the second prize in a famous architectural competition in Chicago, he moved in 1922 to America, where his style became increasingly functional and had a marked influence on city development. Milles was among his collaborators, and after his death in 1950 his work was continued in Detroit and elsewhere – as far afield as Oslo – by his son, Eero Saarinen.

Meanwhile, his disciples in Finland, who found the new functionalism congenial to the austere national spirit, produced one of its leading exponents in Alvar Aalto. In 1942–7 he was visiting professor of experimental architecture at the Massachusetts Institute of Technology, but the reconstruction of war-devastated towns such as Rovaniemi and the rapid growth of industry and new urban communities gave him ample scope in his native land as architect, as town planner, and as the designer of fitments and furniture to harmonise with his buildings. Whilst Aalto's name stands alone among Scandinavian architects as that of a world leader, at least three other functionalists have made a name abroad; Aalto's pupil, V. Rewell, who won first prize for Toronto City Hall; Arne Jacobsen, a sober Danish counterpart to Aalto, with the same interest in furnishings, who successfully placed a new college (St Catherine's) in the tradition-ridden milieu of Oxford; and a younger Dane, Jörn Utzon, who designed the sail-like vaults and podium for the Opera House in Sydney.

Sibelius composed three more symphonies in 1914–24 and some minor works in the following five years; he then kept silence, though he did not die until 1957. No contemporary musician of the north has attracted anything like the same attention abroad, though mention must be made of the atonal experiments of the Norwegian, Fartein Valen, which were widely appreciated in London by the time of his death in 1952. Denmark had two prolific composers in Carl Nielsen and Vagn Holmboe, and the symphonies of Hilding Rosenberg, at one time conductor of the Royal Theatre in Stockholm, were performed under his own direction in Paris and Chicago. As regards the newer types of music, Karl-Birger Blomdahl (a pupil of Rosenberg) was the leading figure among several Swedish composers who sought to 'escape from a paling nationalism through Central European techniques',[4] but the Scandinavians have not been prominent innovators. On the other hand, modern methods of recording have enabled Scandinavian music old and new – like that of many hitherto unfamiliar regions – to reach a wider public. For special distinction, however, one might single out the singers of the Stockholm Opera and still more the dancers of the Royal Danish Ballet, albeit that in 1951 their most eminent choreograph, Harald Lander, transferred his talents to the Opera in Paris.

Both Danish and Swedish producers won international acclaim in the forgotten art of the silent film, where language interposed no barrier and the Danes acquired a special reputation for the less decorous forms of humour. One of the leading producers in Sweden, the Finnish-born Mauritz Stiller, after employing a little-known Swedish actress in a film version of *Gösta Berlings saga*, brought her to work for him in 1925 in Hollywood. This was the beginning of the long career of Greta Garbo, who had an unrivalled, world-wide success in the long-feature talking-film of historical or romantic content. And insofar as the film still keeps its place as an influential art-form, especially among the young, this is to a considerable extent the single-handed work of Ingmar Bergman. His special concern is the problems and fantasies of modern youth, but no Swede since Strindberg has appealed so widely to the student of human nature, with the result that a large foreign public sees Sweden for better or worse through his eyes. Since he wrote his first film script in 1944, Bergman has produced on an average a film a year, whilst also working for the theatre, radio and television; almost a third of a century later, his dramatic departure into exile from his native land was of international interest, not solely because it was occasioned by the alleged rapacity of the tax authorities.

SCIENCE, TECHNOLOGY, AND INDUSTRIAL DESIGN

Each Scandinavian people has made a distinctive contribution to the international commonwealth of scientific studies. It was a Finnish bio-chemist, A. I. Virtanen, who developed the AIV-method for the conservation of fodder, silage having a special value for a dairy-farming land with the shortest of summers. In the inter-war period, when Norway with its big maritime connections still possessed only one university, it had half a dozen institutions to further different branches of oceanography, which Nansen had pioneered as a major national interest. Another such interest had been stimulated by a leading Norwegian physicist, V. F. K. Bjerknes, who returned from a professorship in Leipzig to a post in Bergen in 1917, when war had interrupted the international weather reports essential to the fisheries. He then developed the theory of the 'polar front' to such effect that he became the founder of the generally accepted 'Bergen school' of weather forecasters; his son, J. A. B. Bjerknes, trained American meteorologists for their military responsibilities in the Second World War.

Nevertheless, if the Nobel awards can be taken as a rough and ready standard of comparison, neither Finland nor Norway cuts a big figure. Apart from Virtanen, there has been one Finnish prize-winner – and he worked mainly in Sweden; the first quasi-Norwegian success was as late as 1969.* The record of Swedish science, on the other hand, is impressive by

* Lars Onsager was awarded the Chemistry Prize then for work in thermodynamics which was published in 1931 – only three years after he left Norway to settle in the United States. It was also in 1969 that Dr Ragnar Frisch shared in the first award of the Nobel Memorial Prize for Economics; he was a Norwegian pioneer in econometrics, the science which provides the planners with mathematically based predictions.

any standard: when every allowance is made for the stimulus of the long tradition embodied in their universities and scientific institutions, and for the wealth which enables their research projects to be equipped on an American rather than a European scale, the ratio of leading scientists to population is enviable. The nuclear physicist, Manne Siegbahn; a succession of important biochemists, including Arne Tiselius, Hugo Theorell, and the two von Eulers, father and son; and the several pioneers of new, life-saving methods in medicine and surgery – all these can receive no more than a mention here.

Denmark, however, which has nurtured only about half as many Nobel prize-winners as Sweden, presents one scientific genius of world-wide importance. Niels Bohr, the son of a professor of physiology at Copenhagen University and a Jewish banker's daughter, took part in 1914–16 in Rutherford's epoch-making atomic researches in Manchester; but he then elected to return home to set up the Copenhagen Institute for Theoretical Physics. Under his direction this became, in the words of an English authority, 'one of the great intellectual centres of Europe . . . visited by students from all over the world'.[5] Bohr was the first to apply the quantum theory to problems of atomic structure, and his theory of Complementarity (though never accepted by Einstein) was fundamental to the advance of atomic studies. In 1943 he fled to Sweden to escape arrest by the Germans, whereupon he was brought to England and thence to America, in order that he might 'review all phases of the work'[6] conducted by British and American scientists, including many of his former pupils, for the production of the first atomic bomb. Bohr's attention became to some extent diverted to the political implications, as we shall see in another connection (p. 397); but after the war the scientific activities of his old age ranged from a search for uranium ores in Greenland to the establishment of a Scandinavian Institute for Theoretical Atomic Physics (Nordita) in Copenhagen – a step towards the unrestricted international co-operation among scientists which had been his constant aim.

In technology the Swedes extended the lead which they had already established: the later 1920s have indeed been termed a second 'Age of Greatness'[7] for Sweden, and their privileged position during the Second World War gave their industries a further advantage over the rest of Europe. In some cases Swedish enterprise improved upon inventions purchased from abroad, such as the Austrian Kaplen turbine, to which Olaf Englesson in 1926 added hydraulic rotation of the blades so as to accommodate different pressures, with a huge resulting increase in the horsepower developed from turbines of record dimensions. Twelve years later this led on to a new type of ship's propeller, productive of great economies because it could be stopped or driven in reverse without changing the action of the engine. The 1920s also witnessed Carl Montelius's patenting of the IMO screw, consisting of several screws which rotate against each other and against an outside cover; the effect being that of a piston moving always in the same direction, by the 1960s it was in common use for high-pressure transmission of gases and liquids. In 1951 the Swedish electrical company ASEA solved another transmission problem, when it found the means of conveying a record strength of 400 kV from the Norrland power stations to the main consumer areas in southern Sweden; this was followed by a new method for transmitting power by submarine cable, which has likewise found a world market.

In the traditional forest industries Swedish ingenuity developed the defibrator, which breaks up the wood under high-temperature steam pressure, so that mechanical pulp and fibre board can be obtained by a continuous process. A professor of metallurgy at the Stockholm Technical High School, Count B. Kalling, gave his name to the Kaldo method of refining iron by blowing oxygen directly into the molten metal; a process which could produce 100 tons of steel in 20 minutes was eagerly adopted on the other side of the Atlantic. Mining, together with tunnelling in general, yields a final illustration of efficient enterprise in the so-called 'Swedish method',[8] for which one firm devised a more easily manoeuvred type of boring machine, a second developed an exceptionally hard alloy for the drill-heads, and a third tried out the combination in practice.

Norwegian technology suffered a serious reverse in 1927, when Norsk Hydro found it economically essential to abandon its own nitrates process for the newer German method; but the firm was able to exploit new processes in light metals and plastics as well as fertilisers, and later planned to base a Norwegian petrochemical industry on North Sea oil. The Soderberg continuous self-baking electrode and the Tysland-Hole electric furnace were the work of three Norwegian inventors; their importance for electric steelmaking was matched by that of the Pedersen process in the production of aluminium oxide, and that of the 'Simrad' electronic fishing equipment, designed by W. C. Simonsen. As regards shipping, in the inter-war period Norway led the way in the introduction of floating factories, with a special slip to haul the carcase of the Antarctic whale on board for processing at sea; its yards later pioneered the gas tanker and other specialised cargo-carriers; and in the 1970s, when giant tankers became a drug on the market, Norwegian inventiveness was applied to rigs and ancillary equipment for the North Sea and other submarine oilfields.

Whereas the technological achievements of the Swedes were rooted in their traditional metal industries and those of the Norwegians in their more recently exploited hydro-electric resources, the Danes and Finns made the best of a generally less favourable situation. Lacking the raw materials of modern industry, the Danes learnt to specialise in advanced engineering equipment and in the building abroad of giant structures comparable to the great bridges which link Fünen with Jutland and Zealand with Falster; in 1976 the latter was still the longest in Europe. As for the Finns, they turned the handicap of the long winter to good account by pioneering ice-breakers with 35,000 hp engines for sale in other hard climates, whilst their long-established woodworking industries put on the world market new types of plywood, veneers and laminates.

These two countries have also been the leaders in the projection of Scandinavian design. Danish design in porcelain and silver had a high reputation abroad in the first years of the twentieth century, whilst the Copenhagen gild of cabinetmakers sedulously maintained the standard of its members' wares. Moreover, the Danish architect Arne Jacobsen was second only to Aalto in the influence which he exerted through furniture and other paraphernalia designed to harmonise with his buildings. Yet from the 1920s onwards, it was the renown of Finnish architecture which specially stimulated the appreciation of Scandinavian aesthetic accomplishments in general. Finally, in the 1950s the Finns had a remarkable run of success at the triennial Milan Exhibitions, where only the Italians themselves won more prizes, so that by 1965 a British expert could maintain, 'The standard of design is probably higher in Finland than anywhere else in the world.'[9]

Viewing Scandinavian design as a whole, we can see that the period after the First World War offered opportunities for a breakthrough, as functionalism spread from architecture to the handicrafts and the growth of democracy made it natural also to think in terms of 'More beautiful things for everyday use.'[10] At this juncture the Scandinavian countries already possessed the advantage of long-established traditions of peasant handicraft; these had been preserved for the modern world by Nordic, national, and regional museums, and also through societies of industrial design, such as had been instituted in both Sweden and Finland in the mid-nineteenth century. In addition, the relatively late arrival of large-scale industrialisation made it easier than elsewhere for the small studio or workshop, producing items for the connoisseur, to survive alongside modern manufacture, for which it set aesthetic standards. At the Paris Exhibition of 1925 Scandinavian glass already made an impression, both through highly engraved specimens and as ware for everyday use; five years later, the 'Sweden of Today' Exhibition at Stockholm presented all types of domestic equipment as redesigned along functional lines. Scandinavia attracted further attention at the two big American Exhibitions of the 1930s, and after the Second World War its design standards achieved new prominence. The Finns, as we have seen, came eventually into the lead, but the last two decades have been marked by travelling exhibitions on a common Nordic basis, which have been taken across the Atlantic, and by exhibitions for tourists, set up on a common plan in each of the Scandinavian capitals.

Rya rugs are now woven for export in both Norway and Sweden, though the colours are less striking than in the original *ryijy*, which has relieved the bareness of Finnish homes since the fifteenth century. The techniques of Danish silverwork, Norwegian enamelling, and Swedish glass-blowing have all been shared to some extent with their neighbours. In furniture-making the reputation of Danish craftsmen has been challenged by the other three countries, which benefit from their larger resources of native timber. In the case of ceramics – where design has always travelled fast – it might be legitimate to speak rather of a harmonious specialisation. Danes meet an artistic demand from small potteries, with Royal Copenhagen china as the crowning achievement; the Norwegians also work on a small scale, specialising in stoneware; and the Swedish factories supply mainly the mass market. Finland, too, has the mass-produced technical wares of Wärtsilä-Arabia, which is the largest porcelain manufacturer in Europe; but these finance a whole team of artists, whose brilliant creations reflect their country's position on the edge of the Orient. In every case Scandinavian design seems to combine an instinct for elegance with a strict attention to purpose.

EXPLORATION AND DISCOVERY

Whether they acted separately or collectively, the Scandinavian states obviously lacked the economic resources to launch men into space, so their services to exploration have inevitably become less spectacular in recent years. But the Polar regions long retained their fascination. Thus Roald Amundsen left Oslo at midsummer 1918 to improve upon the voyage of the *Fram* by setting another specially designed vessel, the *Maud*, to drift right over the North Pole. He followed Nordenskiold's course through the North-East Passage, but otherwise the only results of six years' efforts were the scientific observations made by H. U. Sverdrup.* Instead, Amundsen reached the second Pole by airship with Lincoln Ellsworth in May 1926, a few days after Byrd had likewise flown over it from Spitsbergen in a heavier-than-air machine. But no new land was sighted in the ice-bound Arctic Ocean, where Amundsen perished in 1928 in the air search for the crew of a wrecked Italian dirigible.

In 1929 the Norwegians annexed the remote Arctic island of Jan Mayen, where they already maintained a weather station; but it was significant that their Polar Institute, set up in Oslo in the previous-year, envisaged scientific exploration in both the Arctic and Antarctic regions. For the boom in the whale fisheries was diverting their attention to the far south, where one of the factory-ship owners organised a series of expeditions and air reconnaissances. As a result Norway annexed two small islands (Bouvet and Peter I) and laid claim in 1939 to a sector of the mainland of the Antarctic continent and the adjoining sea area between 20°W and 45°E, of which Norwegians had been the sole explorers, naming it Queen Maud Land. This was the scene of operations for the Norwegian-Swedish-British expedition of 1949–52, of which H. U. Sverdrup was the organiser, whilst Swedish members played a leading part in aerial cartography and glacio-

---

* 1888–1957. Meteorologist and oceanographer, and a distant connection of Otto Sverdrup; in the 1930s he was Director of the Scripps Institution and Professor of Oceanography at the University of California, and since 1960 the American Meteorological Society has administered a Memorial Foundation in his honour.

logical and medical investigations. Norway was the only Scandinavian signatory to the twelve-power Antarctic Treaty of 1959, which restricted exploration to purposes of peace and provided for full international scientific co-operation, but avoided any final adjudication on unsettled rights of sovereignty.

The Swedish explorer, Sven Hedin, set out from Peking in 1927 on his last great journey, which he completed eight years later at the age of seventy. He had settled the long-disputed question, important for climatology as much as geography, of the shifting location of the Lopnor salt lakes in the Gobi desert, and had brought to light a major Stone Age culture in the little-known region between Manchuria and Sinkiang. The latter achievement points forward to the post-war era, in which – apart from the conquest of Mount Everest – the most significant ventures in terrestrial exploration have been designed to extend our knowledge of Man's past.

The Danes, as we might expect, shed light on the prehistory of Greenland, particularly through their expedition in 1948–50 to the so-called 'arctic oasis' of the Pearyland plateau, where the island directly faces the North Pole. Within 470 miles of the Pole itself they found traces of a Stone Age culture, including semi-permanent dwellings, pointing to a very early occupation by Eskimo hunters, who are believed to have made their first entry into Greenland from the far north of the American continent about a thousand years ago. The Danes also found the remains of an iron-riveted boat, showing that another group among the widely scattered Eskimos travelled the long sea-route to this area somewhere about the time when the south-west coast of the island re-emerged into the light of history through the enterprise of Hans Egede.

Spectacular results were achieved in two very different parts of the world by a Norwegian ethnographer, Thor Heyerdahl, who had interested himself in the origins of the people and culture of Polynesia. In April 1947, he set sail from Peru with four Norwegians and one Swede, on a balsa-wood raft of a native type, to see whether an unrecorded movement could have been made by this means and in this direction. Their safe arrival at the Tuamotu archipelago after a journey of a little over four months, in which the *Kon-Tiki* sailed and drifted some 5,000 miles, was a brilliant vindication of a hypothesis and the dramatic conclusion of an adventure which has since been recounted in thirty-six or more languages. In the 1960s Heyerdahl carried out a further maritime exploit, when he proved (at the second attempt) that a raft of a pattern still constructed in west Africa provides a means by which African voyagers may have made their landfall in the West Indies long before Columbus. His two rafts, *Kon-Tiki* and *Ra*, now occupy an honoured place in a national museum area at Oslo, alongside the *Fram*, the *Gjöa* – and the Viking ships.

Although these surviving relics happen to be Norwegian, Danes and Swedes shared equally in those voyages of the distant past, to which new interest has been imparted in the last half-century by the discoveries of the archaeologists. Scandinavian scholars have naturally been prominent in these activities, as excavators of trading sites at home and abroad; as experts in the interpretation of coins, weapons, and treasure hoards; and as students of the ancestral journeyings which had so big an impact in East and West. Some part of their work is available in English; its principal findings in any case leave their mark upon every up-to-date presentation of the Viking Age. One recent discovery must, however, be mentioned here as having involved the particularly arduous pursuit of a bold hypothesis. Helge Ingstad, who in his youth had been a Norwegian official in East Greenland and Svalbard, took up the quest for 'Vinland', in connection with which he minutely examined the ancient Greenland settlements, in order to determine the most probable route of approach to the American shoreline. This brought him to the northern tip of Newfoundland, where his close study of the saga account led him to a likely area of search. At L'anse aux Meadows he succeeded in identifying a site on which six buildings had stood: carbon-dating proved that they were medieval and careful examination of the archaeological remains that the occupants were Norsemen. *Westward to Vinland*, which Ingstad published in four languages in 1972, strengthens his case to some extent by arguing that 'Vinland' means 'land of meadows', not of wine, and that its grapes were a kind of wild berry, such as *Viburnum pauciflorum*.* But time alone can show whether his work has brought to a final conclusion a controversy which engaged the attention of the American Association for the Advancement of Science as long ago as 1856.

THE INTERNATIONAL PEACE MOVEMENT

'The impression of human suffering and annihilating conflicts forces itself upon us and cannot fail to engage our thoughts and feelings, fears and hopes.'[11] The sombre comments of the future Swedish prime minister, Olof Palme, on the first American bomber-strikes in North Vietnam in 1965 roused indignant controversy in Scandinavia and elsewhere. Looking back, however, over the preceding half-century, it is possible to see that an impartial humanitarianism, leading to an ardent championship of the world peace cause as they understand it, is strongly characteristic of the Scandinavian peoples as a whole. Before 1914 they preached arbitration, and the Nobel Peace Prize awards began to exert an influence. Since then they have preserved their pacific ideals, in spite of numerous disappointments over the turn of events and their own disillusioning experiences of the 1940s, whilst at least five individual Scandinavians have been conspicuous in different ways among the leading promoters of world peace.

Nathan Söderblom, who had been appointed archbishop of Uppsala in the spring of 1914 at the early age of forty-eight, first made his mark in the

---

* The derivation was proposed by a Swedish philologist, S. Söderberg, in 1910; the 'red and very tasty berries', sampled by Ingstad, are said to grow prolifically along the coast.

following November, when he published an eloquent appeal in seven languages for the restoration of peace in Europe; this bore the signatures of Protestant Church leaders in the neutral European states (plus Finland and the Hungarian province of Transylvania) and of two American Churchmen. It fell on deaf ears, but three years later Söderblom organised a Neutral Church Conference at Uppsala, which proclaimed the duty of Christians to work for peace through the development of international law and was described by an English observer as 'laying the foundation of a Christian International'.[12] In the more hopeful atmosphere of the post-war years the man whom the Danish primate hailed as a veritable 'archbishop of the North'[13] – and who consecrated the first national bishops in newly independent Estonia and Latvia – laboured to conciliate the German Lutherans, embittered by the war guilt clauses of the Treaty of Versailles, and also established close relations with the Eastern Orthodox Churches. Finally in 1925 he brought together more than 600 delegates from 37 countries, representing all the main Christian denominations except the Roman Catholic, at an ecumenical conference in Stockholm. This great gathering has been called 'the Nicaea of ethics', because Söderblom had chosen to direct attention to questions concerning life and work, where it was easier for Christians to unite than over faith and order. Thus on the eve of the signature of the Locarno treaties, when great hopes were based on Germany's impending entry into the League, Söderblom was urging with prophetic insight: 'The League of Nations needs a soul, a spirit, an attitude in the nations – or else it becomes a dead mechanism.'[14]

The Swedish cleric, with his vision of what an informed public opinion among churchmen might do to render the League effective in the cause of world peace, died in 1931 – the year when Japanese aggression in Manchuria was allowed to pass unchecked. But the Norwegian scientist and humanist, Fridtjof Nansen, who left the scene the year before, had already been rebuffed in his efforts to give a firm moral basis to the League's activities. For the successes which he achieved under its auspices would have been still greater if the bitter political prejudices of some member states had not twice caused the refusal of official financial backing for his efforts. In the case of the great famine in the Volga region of Russia in 1921–3, Nansen acted as the delegate of the Red Cross organisations and raised big sums by eloquent private appeals – but he had failed to persuade the League to take the official lead in a humanitarian task which might have made international relations more harmonious. In the smaller but even more pitiful case of the remnant of the Armenian people who had survived the Turkish attempts at genocide, Nansen planned a National Home in Erivan, designed to 'forge another link in the fabric of peace';[15] but Churchill and other representatives of the great powers refused to allow a modicum of the League's resources to be used for a development inside the boundaries of Soviet Russia.

During the critical later years of the Second World War an even bigger role in the service of world peace was attempted by the Danish scientist, Niels Bohr. He was among the very first to realise that, once the atomic bomb came into existence, it would face mankind with problems of pacification stretching far beyond the imposition of surrender upon the Germans or – as it turned out – the Japanese. He therefore urged that the closely guarded secret of the American-British project should be shared with the Russians before it became operational, in the hope of enlisting their support for full international control of nuclear developments in the post-war era. Bohr's pre-eminent position in the scientific world gained him access to both the masters of the Western alliance. Churchill, preoccupied with the final preparations for the Normandy landing, brushed his views angrily aside; in Bohr's restrained account of their half-hour interview, 'They did not even speak the same language.'[16] President Roosevelt gave him more time and consideration; but by September (1944) he was no less sure than Churchill that 'the matter should continue to be regarded as of the utmost secrecy', and the man who had voiced the internationalist view, shared by Einstein and other responsible scientists, was for a time regarded as a threat to the security of the Western allies.[17]

Bohr nevertheless took up the cause of world pacification a second time in 1950, when the Cold War had become a source of greatly increased anxiety because of the unexpected speed with which the Russians achieved their first nuclear explosion. His Open Letter to the United Nations called for full co-operation in establishing 'an open world' as the only safe course for its inhabitants, now that 'The progress of science and technology has tied the fate of all nations inseparably together.'[18] So far as Europe was concerned, he was able to further his aims to some extent as chairman of the fourteen-nation committee which eventually set up CERN, the European Centre for Nuclear Research, at Meyrin near Geneva. In the wider field Bohr failed, albeit that President Eisenhower in conferring the first 'Atoms for Peace' Award in 1957 pronounced him 'a scientist and a great human being who exemplifies principles the world sorely needs'.[19]

The work which Trygve Lie and Dag Hammarskjöld accomplished for world peace derived in part from the office they held as the first two secretaries-general of the new United Nations, but much more from the principles and methods which they brought with them to its execution. Lie's account of his stewardship, published in 1954, is entitled *Seven Years for Peace*. He had been accepted as a compromise candidate because he had co-operated well with the Russians in the later years of the world war. But this co-operation came to an abrupt end at the outbreak of the Korean War in 1950, when the Russian boycotting of the Security Council made it possible for the intervention of American and other forces to receive immediate endorsement as a UN enterprise. The Russians retaliated by refusing any further recognition of Lie, after his tenure of office was extended by a 51 to 5 vote of the Assembly. He nevertheless rendered enduring service to the cause of peace by the energy with which he built up the Secretariat to a total of 5,700 persons of 67 nationalities, thus providing the indispensable basis for the promotion of the global food supply, public health work, and cultural development by such agencies as FAO, WHO and UNESCO, which were then in their infancy. It seems likely, too, that UN activities as a whole have benefited by the location of their headquarters as planned by him in the gigantic building on East River, New York, where for better or worse they cannot easily be ignored. Lie was, however, much harassed by the intrusion of American anti-Communist investigators, prompted by Senator McCarthy to check the loyalty of their fellow countrymen upon his staff; in April 1953, almost a year before his mandate expired, he welcomed with evident relief the arrival of a successor in what he had come to regard as 'the most impossible job on this earth'.[20]

In the following eight years Dag Hammarskjöld exercised an influence in world affairs such as no citizen of a minor European state had wielded before him. The neutralism of his native land commended him to the Russians at the outset, and he was fortunate in the fact that the international disputes which he was called upon to handle arose in regions where neither the Russians nor the Americans were then aiming at complete dominance. But it must be acknowledged that his qualifications for the tasks he undertook were quite exceptional. He was the son of a prime minister; he had studied economics under Keynes and had represented his country in OEEC; and he had been both the civil-service head of the Swedish foreign office and a non-party Cabinet minister before his arrival in New York at the age of forty-eight. In addition, he arrived with an exceptionally strong sense of a personal mission, which the posthumous publication of his *Markings* shows to have been based on a deeply felt Christian belief.*

Hammarskjöld insisted on a UN presence – whether in the form of a peace-keeping force, a corps of observers, or a commission of inquiry – wherever a crisis developed, alike in the Middle East, the Far East, and the new danger zone of post-colonial Africa. His efficiency was clearly demonstrated in his handling of the Suez imbroglio in 1956, when he himself accompanied the rapidly formed UN Expeditionary Force to the Canal Zone, where they rectified the breach of the peace by Britain and France. In the following year the Assembly confirmed him in office for a further five years by a unanimous vote, whereupon he formally asserted the right and duty of the Secretary-General to take independent action 'in order to help in filling any vacuum that may appear in the systems which the Charter and traditional diplomacy provide for the safeguarding of peace and security'.[22] Hammarskjöld's second major intervention came in 1960, when the newly independent Belgian Congo seemed fated to disintegrate

---

* Some critics found the unexpected revelation that this greatest of international officials regarded his work as a call to take up his Cross daily and follow a Divine Master forced and theatrical. Its authenticity as genuinely felt religious experience was, however, attested by the most venerable of Swedish theologians, Bishop Gustaf Aulén.[21]

in tribal conflicts fomented by the mining interests. He mustered 20,000 men from 18 countries for a UN peace-keeping enterprise which was eventually successful, although in September 1961 he himself was killed in a mysterious air accident in Zambia (the former Northern Rhodesia) whilst negotiating to hold in check the warring factions. The ambitions which he had cherished for the secretary-generalship as an independent pacificatory influence in world affairs perished with him.

The Nobel Peace Prize was awarded to Hammarskjöld in the December after his death; other recipients since the end of the First World War have included not only Nansen and Söderblom but also the Swedish socialist, Branting, who had been mainly responsible for the peace conference attempted under Socialist auspices at Stockholm in 1917, and the indefatigable Norwegian peace-worker, Christian Lange.* Some of the other names on the list have aroused controversy, yet the Scandinavian record is such that it still seems fitting for a committee appointed by one of their parliaments to make the invidious annual decision. The interest which the nominations arouse at the present day suggests an increasing awareness of the supreme value to humanity at large of a task to which some of the best Scandinavian minds have long been devoted.

IMPACT OF THE SCANDINAVIAN 'IMAGE'

The contribution which a group of small peoples makes to civilisation is most readily assessed by recounting what has been achieved by a few outstanding representatives. But some attempt must also be made to judge the value of their general outlook as an influence upon the world at large. In this instance the task is all the more difficult because the Scandinavians themselves prefer to be looked upon as five different nations, which enrich our common civilisation by idiosyncrasies growing out of their separate geographical backgrounds and contrasting historical experiences. Yet from outside the common features seem to have a prior claim to attention: they are more plainly visible to us, just as the stranger detects a family likeness which escapes its members.

A decade ago two exceptionally valuable and reflective travel books, covering all five Scandinavian lands, were published almost simultaneously by American and Australian writers of considerable experience. Though each took as his starting-point the then widespread allegation that the salient features of Scandinavian society were 'sex, suicide, and socialism',[23] both concluded that neither uninhibited sex nor recourse to suicide was central to the way of life of these peoples and that the results of their socialist leanings were good as well as bad. Indeed, they went much further;

* 1869–1938. As general secretary of the Interparliamentary Union from 1909 to 1933, he built up its membership, prevented its dissolution during the First World War, and afterwards moved its headquarters to Geneva. His son, Halvard M. Lange (1902–70), provided Norway with an unusually well qualified foreign minister in the period 1946–65.

for the American reported 'the creation of a humane society of luminous integrity', whilst the Australian held that 'The Scandinavians are closer to having Civilization that deserves to be spelled with a capital C than any other countries in the world.'[24] Perhaps these writers go too far, but what they write encourages the supposition that a general Scandinavian image is worth looking for, notwithstanding the exceptions by which each generalisation might properly be qualified.*

We may start with the fact that Scandinavia is a part of the world in which democratic politics still command general respect. Indeed, the ability of the politicians to solve their problems unsensationally in accordance with 'the rules of the parliamentary game' is one reason why news published abroad so often calls attention to the vagaries of private rather than public life. If one engages in political discussion with Scandinavians or, better still, visits one of the countries during an election campaign, the image is certainly that of people who take their individual participation in the policy-making process very seriously. If they nevertheless approve of the activities of long-term planners, that is because the planning is done in a pragmatic spirit which matches the attitude of the electorate.

The struggles over franchise reform, the long experience of voluntary organisations, such as the ubiquitous co-operatives, and the care which has been devoted to popular education have all contributed to this sober attitude. It is further inculcated by state-owned systems of broadcasting and television and by a newspaper press which is both assiduously read and seriously political. As to the former, in 1963 Sweden came first, Iceland fourth, and the other three Nordic states seventh, ninth, and tenth in a world list of newspaper purchases in proportion to population. As to the latter, a system of subventions is expressly designed to prevent the newspapers of any locality from being monopolised by a single party standpoint. From *Dagens Nyheter*, with a circulation of almost half a million centred on Stockholm, to the five daily organs of opinion published in Reykjavik (which has a total population of 83,000) each of the Scandinavian capitals provides an impressive forum for democratic discussion, whilst in remote provincial communities one may still find a party viewpoint sustained by crudely printed news-sheets with only a few hundred regular subscribers.

Although the press is necessarily based upon the towns, the dominant outlook is in many respects rural. Except in Copenhagen, Stockholm and one or two other urban areas of relatively early growth, the Scandinavian image is still broadly speaking that of a countryman; few families are more than a couple of generations removed from the farm or its equivalent. This shows itself, for example, in wholehearted support for the protection of the

---

* Recent statistics[25] show, for example, that the much-discussed Scandinavian proclivity to suicide is not shared in any degree by the Norwegians, and that the Finns continue to provide a startling exception to the low homicide rate which might be expected to accompany the humane Scandinavian outlook on life. Moreover, in 1973–6 the splintering of political parties in Denmark rendered the Folketing – for the time being at least – a clear exception to the image of smoothly functioning Scandinavian democracy.

environment, not merely against pollution but often against any form of development, on the score that an unspoilt Nature has aesthetic and even moral values which transcend mere practical considerations. To own a holiday 'hut' out of eyesight and earshot of any neighbour is the *summum bonum* of the typical Scandinavian family, and in the world of sport team games tend to be overshadowed by those forms of contest, such as skiing, skating, sailing, shooting and orienteering, in which the individual pits himself primarily against the forces of Nature. In an age when expertise in advanced industrial technologies provides the essential prop for his high standard of living, the Scandinavian is still prone to treat the farmer, the fisherman and the forest-worker as the main pillars of society.

This closeness to Nature perhaps helps to explain one aspect of Scandinavian humanitarianism, namely an indulgent attitude towards whatever conduct may be defended as natural. The unmarried mother and her child received full legal protection from an early date; divorce became respectable much sooner than, for example, in Britain; and from the inter-war period onwards these were pioneer countries in the provision under official auspices of explicit sexual instruction to meet the needs of ever-younger age-groups. Again, the prohibition experiments of the 1920s have given place to a public opinion which often regards alcoholic excesses as a natural foible in a cold climate. The visitor to the larger Scandinavian towns is made painfully aware of laws which tolerate open drunkenness in public places and even reward the habitual drunkard with a full invalidity pension. As regards public order in general, Scandinavian society is very reluctant to meet a serious increase of juvenile crime by any measures which would deprive the young of their natural liberty. For adults too, their prison system involves a minimum of physical restraint, and a Swedish penologist has forecast a situation in which a population of eight millions will eventually retain not more than 500 hard-case criminals in regular confinement.

Their generally humanitarian outlook is a feature of their image in which many Scandinavians take a conscious pride. This shows itself, as we have seen, in some adulation of their own version of the welfare state; but it is also a driving-force in their work for world peace and in the generous help they give to underdeveloped nations from both public and private sources. In addition to the forms of peace-work already examined, their membership of the Council of Europe has been used by the three Kingdoms – sometimes to the displeasure of larger states – to bring to book offenders against its Covenant of Human Rights. Nearer home, too, recent Swedish legislation has set a high ethical standard before its citizens for the treatment of immigrants, who now constitute 8 per cent of population. As for the readiness to give, an example is provided by the Churches. In a generation when traditional Lutheranism has lost much of its hold on men's minds and disestablishment is in the air, Lutheran missions have nevertheless found the means to expand into new fields, such as Equatorial Africa and South America, where the work which they finance is as much social as religious.

Last but by no means least, the image is egalitarian in matters great and small – from the enormous inroads which the tax collector makes on any above-average capital or income to the omission of the Scandinavian equivalent for 'Mr' from the envelope which encloses his demand. But here it may suffice to point to two recent illustrations from Sweden, since that is the land where, according to tradition, only the King and the eighteen members of the Academy were entitled to *tutoyer* their compatriots; where 18,000 names still figure in the calendar of nobility; and, what is much more important, fifteen families are reputed to control one-fifth of all private industry. For this is also the land where the constitution of 1975 has deprived the monarchy of the last remnants of formal authority – even the harmless power of creating more nobles – and where the 'Consultation law' (*Medbestämmandelagen*, MBL), passed in the following year, has cut down the rights of ownership, in public and private concerns alike, to an extent which gives the Swedish worker fuller control than any other in the Western world over 'the general management of the undertaking'.[26] To sum up, it may be conceded that exceptional accumulations of private wealth still make their mark in Sweden – and more infrequently in the other countries as well. Yet the foreigner who studies the upbringing, the home life, and the leisure interests of the present generation of Scandinavians is tempted to conclude that full social equality is no longer a programme but an established and possibly enviable condition.

The author of a recent scintillating monograph *On Being Swedish* warns us that 'The character of a whole people can only be spoken of in the past . . . The nearer one comes to the moment of observation, the more diffuse and diffident becomes its description.'[27] History has, however, given the Scandinavian peoples a bent which will not easily be changed. Their particular location on the Earth's surface has kept them always close to Nature, and (as this book has tried to show) it is through many stages of development that what was once 'the unknown north' has come to represent in some special degree the ideas and ideals of democracy, humanitarianism, and social equality. The world has only lately learnt to see Scandinavia in this light: but was there not something prophetic in the tale of the Frankish messenger, sent to inquire who was the master of the Viking ships which had been rowed up-river beyond Rouen? 'None', came the answer: 'We are all equals.'[28]

APPENDICES

Parallel Table of Events

Denmark	Norway	Sweden	Finland	Iceland	Scandinavian Culture
c. 800-10 K. Godfred, originator of Danevirke	793 Raid on Lindisfarne recorded	839 Khaganate of Rus recorded by Frankish chronicler		825 Dicuil records displacement of Irish monks by Vikings	c. 850 First skaldic poems*
					c. 850-900 Oseberg and Gokstad ship burials
c. 965 Baptism of K. Harald Bluetooth	c. 900 B. of Hafrsfjord (Harald Fairhair)	c. 900 Occupation of Danish trade centre of Hedeby		c. 874 Settlement begun	c. 950-1000 Hávamál,* Rígsthula,* Völuspá*
	995-1000 Olaf Tryggvesson			930 Althing instituted	
				c. 986 Colonisation of south-west Greenland begun	*Date very uncertain
		c. 1008 Conversion of Olof Skötkonung		1000 Acceptance of Christianity by the Althing	
1018-35 Cnut the Great	1015-28 Olaf, later the Saint			– Leif Ericsson sighted 'Vinland'	
1027 Cnut's pilgrimage to Rome	1030 B. of Stiklestad				
	1043 B. of Lyrskog Heath (Magnus of Norway and Denmark)				
	1093-1103 Magnus (III) Bareleg				
1103 Archbishopric of Lund	1130-1228 Intermittent civil war			1117-18 Laws placed on record	c. 1130 Íslendingabók; Landnámabók
1131-57 Civil Wars		c. 1135-1249 Rival dynasties of Sverker and Eric	c. 1158 Bishop Henry martyred after 'first crusade'		
1134 B. of Fotevig	1152 Archbishopric of Trondheim (Nidaros)	c. 1160 Death of Eric, later the Saint	1171-2 Papal Bull urging subjugation	1160-1260 Feuds of the Sturlung and other clans	
1157-82 Valdemar (I) the Great		1164 Archbishopric of (Old) Uppsala	1191, 1202 Danish invasions		
1177 Absalon archbishop of Lund	1184-1202 Sverri		1216 Bishopric placed under Uppsala		
	1198 Interdict of Pope Innocent III		c. 1229 Conversion of Tavastia		
1202-41 Valdemar (II) the Victorious	1217-63 Haakon IV				c. 1220 Saxo: Gesta Danorum
1219 Conquest of Estonia					1220-35 Snorri: Heimskringla
1227 B. of Bornhöved					

Denmark	Norway	Sweden	Finland	Iceland	Scandinavian Culture
1241 Jutland law code	1247 Coronation by William of Sabina	1250–75 **Valdemar**, first 'Folkung' king	1240 Swedes and Finnish supporters defeated by Alexander (Nevski)	1262–4 Acceptance of Norwegian sovereignty	
		1266 Death of Earl Birger	1249 Earl Birger's 'second crusade'		
	1263 B. of Largs	1275–90 **Magnus Barnlock**			
	1263–80 **Magnus (VI) Lawmender**				
	1276 Law code				c. 1280 *Njáls Saga*
1282 Charter granted to Barons		c. 1280 Statute of Alsnö			
	1299–1319 **Haakon V**	1290–1318 **Birger Magnusson**	1293 Viipuri fortified by Torgils Knutsson		c. 1300 Balladry spreading from Denmark
		1306 Execution of Marshal Torgils Knutsson			
	1312 Marriage of Ingebjorg to Duke Eric				c. 1320 *Chronicle of Eric*
		1319–64 **Magnus Ericsson**	1323 T. of Nöteborg		
	c. 1330 Hanseatic Counter in Bergen				c. 1340–70 Birgitta's 'Revelations'
1332–40 Interregnum under Counts of Holstein	1349 Black Death enters Norway at Bergen	c. 1350 Law code			
1340–75 **Valdemar (III) Atterdag**		1364–89 **Albrecht of Mecklenburg**	1362 Right of participation in elections to the Crown granted		
1370 T. of Stralsund		1386 Death of Bo Jonsson Grip	1374–86 Bo Jonsson Grip holds all Finnish fiefs		
1387 **Margaret** regent of Denmark and Norway	1387 Death of Olaf IV, last Norwegian king	1389 B. of Falköping	1399 'Victualling Brothers' expelled		
1397 **Eric** crowned at Kalmar					
				1402–4 Visitation of plague	
1412 Death of Queen Margaret				1412 Establishment of English fisheries, followed by trade	
1429 Sound Tolls first exacted				1434 First recorded Hanseatic trade	
		1434–6 Engelbrektsson's revolt and alliance with Council			
		1438 Karl Knutsson Guardian of the Realm			
1440–8 **Christopher of Bavaria**					

Denmark

1448–81 **Christian I**
1460 Christian Duke of Slesvig and Count of Holstein
1481–1513 **Hans**
1501 Knut Alvsson's Rising
1506–11 Prince Christian Viceroy
1513–23 **Christian II**
1522 Rebellion in Jutland
1523–33 **Frederick I**
1526 Papal consecration of bishops abolished
1534–59 **Christian III**
1534–6 The Count's War
1526 Lutheranism preached to Germans in Bergen
1531 Ex-king Christian in Oslo
1537 Flight of Archbishop Engelbrektsson
– Merging of the realm in Denmark
1537 Lutheran Church Ordinance
1544 P. of Speyer
1550 Danish Bible

Sweden

1448–70 **Karl** intermittently King
1471 Sten Sture victorious at B. of Brunkeberg
1503 Svante Nilsson Regent on death of Sten Sture
1512–20 Regency of 'Sten Sture the Younger'
1517 First important meeting of Estates
1520 Bloodbath of Stockholm
1521 Rising in Dalecarlia
1523 Gustav Vasa elected king at Strängnäs
1523–60 **Gustavus (I)**
1527 Riksdag of Västerås
1541 Gustav Vasa's Bible
1542 Final rebellion, in Småland

Finland

1475 Olofsborg built by Eric Axelsson Tott
1495–7 Russian invasion
1539 Lutheran mañuals in Finnish
1548 Agricola's New Testament

Iceland

1541 Lutheranism established in Skálholt bishopric
1550 Execution of last Catholic bishop of Hólar

Other

1477 University of Uppsala founded
1478 University of Copenhagen founded
1490–7 Anglo-Danish free-trade treaty
1539 Olaus Magnus: *Carta marina*

Denmark	Norway	Sweden	Finland	Iceland	Scandinavian Culture
			1554–7 Agricola Bishop of Turku		1554 Johannes Magnus's 'gothic' History
					1555 Olaus Magnus: *Historia de gentibus septentrionalibus*
			1556 John made Duke of Finland		
1559–88 **Frederick II**	1559 Action against German artisans in Bergen				
		1560–68 **Eric XIV**			
1563–70 Seven Years War of the North			1563 Surrender of John at Turku		
	1564 Swedish occupation of Trondheim				
		1565–6 First naval victories			
		1568–92 **John III**			
			1570–95 'The Long Wrath'		
					1573 Tycho Brahe: *De nova stella*
		1577 The Red Book			
		1587 Sigismund elected King of Poland		1584 Icelandic Bible printed at Hólar	
1588–1648 **Christian IV**					
		1592–9 **Sigismund**			
		1593 Church Assembly at Uppsala			
			1595 T. of Teusina		
1596 End of Regency			1597–8 The Club War		
	1599 Christian IV at Vardöhus	1599 Duke Charles becomes Administrator			
				1602 Full Danish trade monopoly	
		1603–11 **Charles IX**			1604–42 Embellishment of Copenhagen by Christian IV
		1607 Foundation of Gothenburg			
1611–13 Kalmar War		1611–32 **Gustavus (II) Adolphus**			
1616 East India Co. acquires Tranquebar	1612 Scots ambushed in Gudbrandsdal				
		1617, 1626 Regulation of Riksdag and House of Nobles	1617 Kexholm and Ingria annexed by T. of Stolbova		
	1623 Silver mined at Kongsberg				
	1624 Oslo refounded at Christiania				1624 Gustavus Adolphus's endowment of Uppsala
1626 B. of Lutter					
1627–9 Wallenstein occupies Duchies and Jutland				1627 Algerian pirates carry away captives	
		1631 B. of Breitenfeld			
		1632 B. of Lützen			
		1632–54 **Christina**			
		1634 Form of Government			
		1638 Fort Christina on the Delaware			1640 Åbo Academy founded
	1641 Foundation of Christiansand				
1643–5 Torstensson occupies Duchies and Jutland	1642–51 Sehested Stattholder				
1645 P. of Brömsebro	1642 Army organised	1644 End of Regency			

1648–70 **Frederick III**
1649 Ulfeldt's defence treaty with Netherlands
1658 T. of Roskilde
1658–9 Defence of Copenhagen
1661 Hereditary Autocracy Act
1665 *Lex Regia*
1670–99 **Christian V**
1683 Code of Christian V

1661 Autocracy accepted by Estates
1664–99 U. F. Gyldenløve Stattholder
1665 Anglo-Dutch battle in Bergen harbour
1687 Norwegian Code of Christian V
1688 Quantum saws established

1699–1730 **Frederick IV**
1700 T. of Travendal
1702 Abolition of *vornedskab* begun
1709–10 Last attempt to recover Skåne
1716 Tordenskiold's victory in the Leads (Dynekilen)
1718 Charles XII killed at Fredriksten

1648 Recognition as a German power (P. of Westphalia)
1654–60 **Charles X Gustavus**
1655 Invasion of Poland
1658 Crossing of the Belts on the ice
1660–97 **Charles XI**
1660–61 Peace made at Copenhagen, Oliva, and Kardis
1672 End of Regency
1676 B. of Lund
1682 *Indelningsverk* elaborated
1693 Declaration of Sovereignty
1697–1718 **Charles XII**
1700 B. of Narva
1706 T. of Altranstädt
1709 B. of Poltava
1714 Charles's return from Turkey
1718–20 **Ulrika Eleonora**

1656 Russian invasion of Ingria and Karelia
1696–7 Great Famine
1710 Fall of Viipuri
1714 B. of Storkyro (Napue)
1714–21 'The Great Wrath'

1662 Autocracy accepted
– Trade monopoly extended to fisheries and Crown estates
1683 Resident *amtmand* and finance officer
1707–9 Smallpox epidemic, killing one-third of population

1653 Rudbeck's study of the lymphatics
1658 Sternhielm: *Hercules*
1666 Pétursson: *Passion Hymns*
1668 Lund University founded
1678 Dass began *Nordland's Trumpet*
1699 Polhem's advanced metal-working (Dalecarlia)
1711 Torfaeus: *Historia Rerum Norvegicarum*

Denmark	Norway	Sweden	Finland	Iceland	Scandinavian Culture
1720 P. of Frederiksborg securing Slesvig		1719 Age of Freedom begins			
		1720–51 **Frederick I**			
		1721 T. of Nystad			1722–7 Holberg's principal comedies
	1721 Hans Egede's mission to Greenland				
1730–46 **Christian VI**	1730 Monopoly for Norwegian iron in Denmark				
1733 *Stavnsbånd* instituted					1735 Linnaeus: *Systema Naturae*
	1735 Monopoly for Danish corn in south Norway				
1736 Confirmation Ordinance					
		1738 End of Horn's Chancellorship			1739 Swedish Academy of Science
		1739–64 Hat Party in office			
1741 Conventicle Ordinance		1741–3 Unsuccessful war against Russia	1741 B. of Villmanstrand		1741 Holberg: *Nils Klim*
			1741–3 'The Lesser Wrath'		
			1743 T. of Åbo		1745 Juslenius's Finnish Dictionary
1746–66 **Frederick V**					1755 Lappish New Testament printed in Sweden
1751–70 J.H.E. Bernstorff Foreign Minister	1751 Swedish–Norwegian frontier delimited in north	1751–71 **Adolphus Frederick**		1752 Economic improvements of Skúli Magnússon	1757 *Economic Magazine for Denmark and Norway*
		1756 Royalist *coup* planned			1760 Trondheim Scientific Society
		1757–62 Pomeranian or 'Potato' War			
1762 Gottorp claims revived by Tsar Peter III	1765 Poll-tax riot in Bergen	1765–72 Cap Party predominant in lower Estates			1765 Chydenius: *The Nation's Profit*
1766–1808 **Christian VII**		1771–92 **Gustavus III**			1766–78 Porthan: *De poesi fennica*
1770–72 Struensee in power		1772 Age of Freedom ended by royal intervention	1772 Sveaborg completed		1772 Ólafsson: *Reise igiennem Island* published
					Wessel: *Love Without Stockings*

1780 1st Armed Neutrality of the North
1784 Guldberg regime overthrown by Crown Prince Frederick
1786 Great Land Commission appointed

1787 Lofthus arrested
1788 Expedition against Gothenburg

1792 Abolition of slave trade (effective in 1802)
1800 2nd Armed Neutrality of the North
1801 B. of Copenhagen
1807 Capture of fleet at Copenhagen
1808–39 **Frederick VI**

1813 National bankruptcy
1814 T. of Kiel
– Compulsory primary education

1786 G. M. Sprengtporten fled to Russia
1788 League of Anjala

1788–90 Attack on Russia during Russo–Turkish war
1789 Act of Union and Security
1792–1809 **Gustavus IV**
1796 End of Regency

1805 Involvement in War of Third Coalition
1808 War against Russia, France, and Denmark–Norway
1809 King deposed and new constitution enacted
1809–18 **Charles XIII**
1810 Bernadotte elected Crown Prince
1812 Alliance with Russia

1796 Conversion of Hauge

1807 Christian August heads Commission of Government

1809 Norway Welfare Society founded
1814 (May) Constitution formulated at Eidsvoll
– (Nov.) Union with Sweden accepted by Storting

1783–4 Eruption and earthquake leading to resettlement proposal

1787 Trade thrown open to all Crown subjects

1801 Althing replaced by High Court at Reykjavik

1809 Usurpation by Jürgensen

1808 (Feb.) Russian invasion
– (May) Surrender of Sveaborg
1809 (March) Diet of Borgå/Porvoo

1812 Reunion of 'Old' and 'New' Finland
– Capital transferred to Helsinki

1782/6/8 Gustavus III's Opera, Academy, and Theatre

1790 Bellman's songs published (*Fredman's Epistles*)

1802 Steffens' lectures in Copenhagen

1813 University opened in Norway

Denmark	Norway	Sweden	Finland	Iceland	Scandinavian Culture
		1818–44 **Charles XIV John**			1819 Oehlenschläger: *Gods of the North*
	1821 Charles John's Circular Note				1825 Tegnér: *Frithiofs saga*
	1825 First emigrants from Stavanger		1827 University removed to Helsinki		
	1829 'Battle of the Marketplace'				1831–5 Cultural conflict of Welhaven and Wergeland
1834 Consultative Estates established	1835 Representation on Ministerial Council				1835– Hans Andersen's fairy tales
	1837 Local self-government law				1838 Thorvaldsen's return to Denmark
		1840 Liberal influences in reformed Cabinet			1841 Asbjörnsen and Moe: *Norwegian Folk Tales*
1839–48 **Christian VIII**				1843 Consultative Althing established	1843–55 Philosophy of Kierkegaard
1844 First Folk High School		1844–59 **Oscar I**	1844 Snellman's periodicals		
1845 Scandinavian students addressed by Lehmann					
1848–63 **Frederick VII**	1848–51 Thrane's reform movement	1848 Mediation in Slesvig-Holstein War			1848 Runeberg: *Tales of Ensign Stål*
1848–51 Three Years War					– Aasen: *Grammar of Norwegian Popular Speech*
1849 (June) Constitution established					1849 Lönnrot: *Kalevala* (expanded version)
1850 Slesvig-Holsteiners defeated at Isted			1850 Finnish publications repressed	1851 Constitutional convention dissolved by Governor	
1852 Protocol of London				1854 Trade freed	
		1855 November Treaty	1854 Anglo-French Åland expedition		
1857 Sound Tolls abolished		1859–72 **Charles XV**	1856 Saimaa Canal opened		
	1859 Bill for abolishing Stattholder vetoed				

1863 March Patent for Holstein
1863–1906 **Christian IX**
November constitution adopted
1864 2nd Slesvig-Holstein War
1866 Constitution modified

1872 Venstre majority in Folketing

1879 Slesvig plebiscite undertaking abandoned

1880–84 Venstre attacks use of veto
1884–9 Responsible government introduced under Sverdrup

1895 Radical Left's surrender over separate consuls
1898 Manhood suffrage

1863 (July) Negotiations with Danish King at Skodsborg

1867 First bicameral Riksdag

1872–1907 **Oscar II**

1888 Return to protective tariffs

1891–1900 Boström modernises fiscal and military systems

1863 (Aug.) First Finnish-language Edict
– (Sep.) Diet opened by Alexander II

1867 Famine

1878 Army revived under Conscription Act

1890 Alexander III's Postal Manifesto

1899 Legislative independence abolished

1869 Storting meets annually

1874 Constitution granted under *Landshöfdingi*

1866/7 Ibsen's *Brand* and *Peer Gynt*

1870 Kivi: *Seven Brothers*
1871 Brandes' lectures on modern literature
1874 Vigfússon: *Icelandic-English Dictionary*
1879 Strindberg: *The Red Room*
1879, 1881 Ibsen: *A Doll's House* and *Ghosts*

1888 Grieg's piano concerto performed in London
– Strindberg: *Lady Julia*
1890 Hamsun: *Hunger*
1891 Lagerlöf: *Gösta Berlings saga*
1897 Nansen's *Farthest North*

1899 Sibelius: *Finlandia*

Denmark	Norway	Sweden	Finland	Iceland	Scandinavian Culture
1901 'Change of System'		1900 United Liberal Party			1901 First Nobel Prize awards
					1902 Munch's 'Frieze of Life' exhibited in Berlin
					1903 Björnson awarded Nobel Literature Prize
	1904 Outcry against 'dependency clauses'		1904 Assassination of Bobrikov	1904 Home Rule in force	
	1905 Union with Sweden terminated		1905 General Strike spread from Russia to Finland		
1906–12 **Frederick VIII**	1905–57 **Haakon VII**		1906 Diet based on universal suffrage	1906 First cable laid, via Faeroes	1906–10 Nexö: *Pelle the Conqueror*
	1906–9 Concession laws	1907–50 **Gustaf V**	1908 Russification resumed	1907 Independence Party formed	
	1907–13 Female suffrage	1908 Baltic and North Sea Treaties	1909 Old Finns (Compliants) resign from Senate		
1909 First Radical minority ministry		1909 Franchise extended			1911 University of Iceland founded
1912–47 **Christian X**	1913–20 Venstre majority government	1911–14 Liberal Ministry under Staaff			
		1914 (March) King intervenes in defence dispute			
1915 New constitution enacted		1914 (Dec.) Meeting of Scandinavian Kings at Malmö	1916 Social Democratic election majority	1915 Universal suffrage under new Danish constitution	
		1917–21 Democratic political system introduced	1917 (Dec.) Independence declared		
	1919–23 Labour Party adheres to Third International		1918 (Jan–May) Civil War	1918 Independence under Common Monarchy	
	1920 Svalbard Treaty		1919 Republican constitution adopted		1920 Bohr's Physics Institute
1920 'Easter Crisis'	1920–30 League of Nations activities of Nansen		1920 T. of Dorpat	1920 Supreme Court established	– Hamsun's *Growth of the Soil* in English translation
– Recovery of North Slesvig			1921 Åland award by League of Nations		

				1920–22 Undset: *Kristin Lavransdatter*
1924 First Social Democratic Government	1924 Return to Gold Standard			1925 Söderblom's Ecumenical Conference, Stockholm
				1925– Greta Garbo's film performances
	1930 'Oslo Group' formed	1929–32 Lapua Movement		1930 'Sweden of Today' Exhibition
	1931 East Greenland claim disallowed by Hague Court			1931 Sillanpää: *The Maid Silja*
			1932–9 Trade depressed	1932 Aalto's first functional building
1933, Steincke's social reforms	1933, Quisling founds NS Party			
	1935 Labour Government under Nygaardsvold and Koht	1936–76 Social Democrats in power (including coalitions)		
		1937 Coalition government including Social Democrats		
		– Language law for university		
1939 Non-aggression pact with Germany		1939–40 Winter War		
1940 (April 9) German invasion	1940 Two months campaign against German invasion	1941–4 Continuation War	1940 (May) British garrison accepted under protest	
1941 American defence of Greenland set up		1941 (Dec.) British declaration of war	1941 (July) American forces land after agreement	
	1942 The 'great year' of the Resistance	1941 German Division transported to Russian front		
1943 Parliamentary government suspended	1943, 1944 Heavy water supply sabotaged at Rjukan	1943 Training camps for refugees from Norway and Denmark	1944 Republic formally established	1944 Lagerkvist: *The Dwarf*
	1944–5 Germans lay waste north Norway in retreat before Russians			– Ingmar Bergman's first film
	1945 First majority Labour Government			

Denmark	Norway	Sweden	Finland	Iceland	Scandinavian Culture
1947–72 **Frederick IX**			1946–56 Paasikivi President		1948 Heyerdahl: *The Kon-Tiki Expedition*
1948 Faeroese Home Rule Act		1948 Nordic Defence Alliance proposed	1947 P. of Paris		1950– Finnish successes at Milan Exhibition
1949 NATO membership	1949 NATO membership		1948 Mutual Assistance Pact with USSR	1949 NATO membership	
1953 New constitution in force		1950–73 **Gustaf VI Adolf**		1951 American Defence Force at Keflavik	1956 Nobel Prize to Laxness
– Nordic Council's first meeting in Copenhagen			1956 (Jan.) Porkkala returned (Feb.) Kekkonen elected President		1957 Nordita founded by Bohr
– Greenland incorporated in Kingdom			1958 'Night Frost'	1958 Outbreak of 'Cod Wars' against UK	
1959 SF Party founded	1959– **Olav V**	1959 EFTA treaty signed in Stockholm			
	1961 Protest against American U-2 flights		1961 Crisis about consultation under Pact		1962 Nordic Literary Prize established
	1961–5 SF hold balance of power in Storting		1962 Saimaa Canal reopened		
	1965–71 Coalition cabinet of non-socialist Parties		1966 Communists readmitted to coalition governments		
			1970 Withdrawal from 'Nordök' proposals	1970 EFTA membership	
	1972 Common Market rejected in plebiscite	1971 First single-chamber Riksdag			
1972– **Margaret II**					
– Common Market plebiscite		1973– **Carl XVI Gustaf**		1974 Hague Court judgement for UK disregarded	
1973 Ten Parties in Folketing	1974 'Statoil' established	1975 New constitution in force		1976 'Cod Wars' end in UK's acceptance of 200-mile limit	
		1976 Bourgeois coalition under Centre Party premier			

Reference Notes

Where a page reference gives only the name of an author or editor, details will be found under the name in the Selected Bibliography of Works in English; the place of publication of other English language books is London or New York unless otherwise stated. Full particulars of books in Scandinavian languages are given when first mentioned except for the following collective works, which are referred to by initials:

DH   Danstrup, J., and Koch, H. (editors): *Danmarks Historie*, (14 vols, Copenhagen, 1963–6).

HDH   Hvidfeldt, J. *et al.* (editors): *Danmarks Historie*, (2 vols, Copenhagen, 1950–1).

NFLH   Bull, E., Keilhau, W., Shetelig, H., and Steen, S.: *Det norske folks liv og historie gjennom tidene*, 11 vols (Oslo, 1930–8).

SDH   Friis, A., Linvald, A., and Mackeprang, M.: *Schultz Danmarkshistorie* (rev. ed.) (6 vols, Copenhagen, 1941–3).

SH   Carlsson, S., and Rosén, J. (editors): *Den Svenska Historien*, (10 vols, Stockholm, 1966–8).

SUPH   Ahnlund, N. (editor): *Den Svenska Utrikespolitikens Historia*, (5 vols, Stockholm, 1951–61).

VFH   Dahl, T., Coldevin, A., and Schreiner, J. (editors): *Vårt Folks Historie*, (9 vols, Oslo, 1961–4).

CHAPTER 1

1 Sömme, Table 7.4.
2 *Vårt avlånga land* (Mead *Economic Geography of Scandinavia*, p. 32).
3 Table derived from the Swedish Tourist Association's Annual for 1955 (Mead ibid., p. 67).
4 *Germania*, c. 44.
5 *Ecclesiastical History of the English Nation*, Book I, chapter xv.
6 *quasi officina gentium aut certe velut vagina nationum* (*De origine actibusque Getarum*, c. iv; C. C. Mierow's translation, reprinted in *Speculum Historiale*, Cambridge, 1966).
7 Shetelig, p. 231.
8 G. N. Garmonsway and J. Simpson: *Beowulf and its Analogues*, London, 1968, p. 3. The quotations in the following paragraph are from the same masterly translation, pp. 4–5, 33, and 82.
9 R. L. S. Bruce-Mitford: *The Sutton Hoo Ship-Burial*, new ed. 1968, p. 69.
10 J. L. N. O'Loughlin in *Medieval Archaeology*, VIII (1964), pp. 15–16.

CHAPTER 2

1 Number 6 in his communications included in *Littérature latine et histoire du moyen âge* (Paris, 1890).
2 James Ingram's translation (Everyman Library), pp. 55 and 54.
3 S. H. Cross and O. P. Sherbowitz-Wetzov: *The Russian Primary Chronicle Laurentian Text* (Cambridge, Mass., 1953), p. 146.
4 *Rígsthula*, translated by H. E. Bellows: *The Poetic Edda* (1923), I, 206.
5 Constantine VII: *De administrando imperio* (*DH* II 388).
6 Foote and Wilson, p. 286.

7 *History of the Archbishops of Hamburg-Bremen*, translated by F. J. Tschan (1959), pp. 207-8.
8 *Eyrbyggja Saga* (Turville-Petre, *Myth*, p. 87).
9 *Orkneyinga Saga* 12 (ibid., p. 254).
10 *Hávamál* 78 (Foote and Wilson, p. 432).
11 Musset, *Le second assaut*, p. 217.
12 ibid., p. 129.
13 E. Gunnes: *Norges Historie* II, (Oslo, 1976), p. 141. This is one of the first volumes of an up-to-date popular history, to be completed in 18 volumes.
14 *Vellekla* (Turville-Petre, *Myth*, p. 193). A fuller translation in the same author's *Scaldic Poetry* (Oxford 1976, pp. 60-63) ends: 'I say that the most mighty gods strengthen the authority of Håkon.'

CHAPTER 3

1 F. M. Stenton: *Anglo-Saxon England* (3rd edition, Oxford, 1971), p. 397.
2 *SH* I 322.
3 *Sagas of Bishops* I 26-7 (Johannesson, p. 144).
4 The Church Law of St Olaf and Grimkell (A. Bugge: *Norges Historie* I Pt 2, 1910, p. 380).
5 *Knytlinga Saga* (Garmonsway, p. 18).
6 Tigernach's *Annals*, cited by Stenton, *Anglo-Saxon England*, p. 567.
7 Ingram's translation (Everyman), p. 142.
8 A. L. Poole: *From Domesday Book to Magna Carta* (Oxford, 1951), p. 286.
9 This *storhetstid* was restricted by E. Bull to the years 1240-63 (*NFLH* II 311), but C. Joys implies a longer period (*VFH* III 61; cf. sub-title of volume).
10 *Håkonssaga* (*NFLH* II 356).
11 Johannesson, p. 282; the agreement is also translated in Gjerset, pp. 206-7.
12 A. Schück: *Befolkning under Medeltiden* (Stockholm, 1938), p. 161.
13 Musset, *Les peuples*, p. 175.
14 According to 'Greygoose', the surviving ms collection of Commonwealth laws (Johannesson, p. 90).
15 *The Early Kings of Norway* (People's Edition, London 1875), p. 1. Carlyle used Samuel Laing's translation of 1844, republished in a revised edition by P. Foote (Everyman Library, 1961).
16 Prologue to *Grýla*, the first part (J. Sephton: *The Saga of King Sverri of Norway*, 1899, p. 1).
17 *Njal's Saga*, c. 128 in G. W. Dasent's translation of 1841 (now in Everyman Library).

CHAPTER 4

1 P. Ziegler: *The Black Death* (1969) pp. 18-19.
2 L. A. Norborg and L. Sjöstedt: *Grannländernas Historia* (Lund, 1970), p. 39.
3 Heckscher, p. 42.
4 E. F. Jacob: *The Fifteenth Century* (Oxford, 1961), pp. 363-4; *NFLH* III 184.
5 T. Knudsen and P. Sveaas Andersen (editors: *Lærde brev fra og til P. A. Munch* (Vol. III, Oslo, 1971), p. 263.
6 Narrative of Quirini's travels, first printed at Venice in 1559 (*Norges land og folk*, 1908, XVIII Part 2, p. 905).
7 Andersson, p. 52.
8 Lübeck Chronicle (*DH* IV 413).
9 *SH* II 82; the Norwegian title is in *VFH* IV 14.
10 J. Rosén: *Svensk Historia*, I (3rd ed. 1969), p. 198.
11 Holstein Chronicle (*HDH* I 188).
12 Nordal, p. 43.
13 *VFH* IV 104.
14 Krabbe, p. 98.
15 *HDH* I 238.
16 Draft of *Landlov*, Article III (E. Arup: *Danmarks Historie* II 367).

CHAPTER 5

1 Heckscher, p. 67.
2 Geijer (Heckscher, p. 68).
3 Section 3 (*VFH* IV 212).
4 E. Arup: *Danmarks Historie*, II 534.
5 *SDH* II 551.
6 *renliga predikas* (*SH* II, pp. 313, 316).
7 Jutikkala, p. 66.
8 Hallgrimur Pétursson; the 50 hymns were first printed in 1666, seven years after their completion and only eight before their author's death. An English verse translation by A. C. Gook was published in Reykjavik in 1966.
9 *DH* VI 402.
10 Professor Nicolaus Olai Bothniensis, 5 March 1593, 'according to a doubtful source' (*SH* III 302).
11 Andersson, p. 157; see also Jutikkala, p. 84.
12 Jutikkala, p. 75.
13 *SH* IV 33.
14 'He is the man to do it.' (Hallendorff and Schück, p. 216).
15 *New Cambridge Modern History*, III, 33, 425.
16 S. Steen: *Bergen byen mellom fjellene* (Bergen, 1969), p. 95.
17 *HDH* I 292; M. Roberts, *The Early Vasas* (Cambridge, 1968), p. 35.
18 Roberts, I 16.

CHAPTER 6

1 C. V. Wedgwood: *The Thirty Years War* (1938), p. 270; Roberts, II 615; Andersson, p. 175.
2 *SH* IV 37.
3 Address to the Örebro Riksdag (Andersson, p. 165).
4 Roberts, II 234.
5 *DH* VII 207.
6 *DH* VII 271.
7 Roberts, II 418.
8 J. Rosén: *Svensk Historia I* (3rd ed. 1969), p. 412.
9 Roberts, II 676.
10 Roberts, II 789.
11 Preamble to the Form of Government (Rosén: *Svensk Historia I*, 447).
12 E. Arup: *Danmarks Historie*, III 274.
13 Andersson, p. 195.
14 B. Whitelocke: *Journal of the Swedish Embassy* (2 vols, 1855), I 307.
15 Heckscher, pp. 85, 87.
16 *SH* IV 243.
17 Interview with Whitelocke, 14 March 1654 (Whitelocke, II 34).
18 Roberts, II 606.
19 *SUPH* I Part iii, p. 111. (Såvida Möjligt är).
20 John Selden's *Mare Clausum*, published in 1635, had been brought to the attention of the Swedes by Whitelocke.
21 Job xxix. 18 (*DH* VII 492).
22 A. Johnson: *The Swedes on the Delaware* (Philadelphia 1914), p. 356.

CHAPTER 7

1 *SDH* III 392.
2 A pun on the Danish *herrer* ('masters'). cf. *DH* VIII 18.
3 *DH* VIII 129.
4 R. Molesworth: *An Account of Denmark as it was in the year 1692* (1694), p. 232.
5 *SDH* III 398.
6 *DH* VIII 330.
7 *DH* VIII 338.

8 Gjerset, p. 339.
9 *DH* VIII 172.
10 W. King: *Animadversions on a Pretended Account of Denmark* (1694), p. 74.
11 Lorenzo Magalotti (*SH* V 92).
12 M. Roberts: *Sweden as a Great Power, 1611–1697* (documents), p. 87.
13 *SH* V 155.
14 M. Roberts (editor): *Sweden's Age of Greatness 1632–1718* (1973), pp. 246–7.
15 ibid., p. 168.
16 ibid., pp. 23, 44.
17 Molesworth, *Account of Denmark* (1694), pp. 266, 269.
18 *SH* V 185.
19 Hatton, p. 305.
20 'An expression that in traditional Finnish historical writing has become a symbol of all the terrifying things that can befall a nation' (Jutikkala, p. 135).
21 Conversation with a Swedish general, Baron F. B. von Schwerin, at Fredriksten, as recalled by him ten years later (Hatton, p. 475).
22 R. N. Bain: *Encyclopædia Britannica*, 11th ed., XXVII 51.

CHAPTER 8

1 Andersson, p. 254.
2 Andersson, p. 275.
3 *DH* IX 30.
4 C. Nordmann: *Grandeur et Liberté de la Suède* (1660–1792) (Paris, 1971), p. 297.
5 *DH* IX 210.
6 Bosi, p. 151.
7 P. J. Charliat: *Histoire universelle des explorations*, 1955, p. 130 (*Grandeur et Liberté*, p. 317).
8 Jutikkala, p. 149.
9 *Grandeur et Liberté*, p. 267; Hatton, p. 416.
10 H. Nielsen: *Nordens Enhed Gennem Tiderne* (3 vols, Copenhagen, 1938), I 320.
11 *DH* IX 382.
12 *DH* X 9.
13 Jens Vibæk (*DH* X 35).
14 Esaias Tegnér, poem for the 50th anniversary of the Swedish Academy, 5 April 1836 (Andersson, p. 286).
15 *SH* VII 22.
16 *Grandeur et Liberté*, pp. 424–5.
17 S. Carlsson: *Svensk Historia II* (3rd ed, 1970), p. 195.
18 Carlyle's *French Revolution*, Pt II, Book iv, c. 3.
19 *SH* VII 125.
20 Reier Giellebol, who was of peasant ancestry; earlier in the year he had published a description of his parish, dedicated to Struensee.
21 Bjarni Pálsson, with whom he travelled about the island in 1752–7 at government expense; their book was translated into French and German as well as English (Nordal, pp. 47, 91).

CHAPTER 9

1 Jacob Aall: *Erindringer*, 3 vols 1844–5 (*VFH* V 422).
2 According to Magnus Stephensen (Gjerset, p. 347).
3 Frederik Sneedorff, in a lecture to the Nordisk Selskab in London in the spring of 1792, which was printed in *Skandinavisk Museum*, Copenhagen 1798 (*Nordens Enhed*, I 370).
4 His *Recollections* were published in 1850–1 (*DH* X 231).
5 B. Tunstall: *Nelson* (1933), p. 96.
6 Jörgen Jürgensen, who was present, believed that 'upwards of 1,500 perished' (J. F. Hogan: *The Convict King*, 1891, p. 62). The only statistical information is that the projectiles destroyed or damaged 1,071 properties.
7 Edvard Holm: *Danmark-Norges Historie 1720–1814*, Vol. III, Pt I (1907), p. 3.

8 Hogan: *Convict King*, pp. 15, 24.
9 *vådlig för allmän säkerhet* (*SH* VIII 56).
10 Letter of April 1812, advocating the establishment of an independent Norwegian monarchy (*NFLH*, VII 339).
11 S. Steen: *Det frie Norge* (Vols I–VI, Oslo 1951–72), I 135.
12 ibid., I 267. The deputation was headed by Wedel Jarlsberg.
13 *SH* VIII 18.

CHAPTER 10

1 G. M. Gathorne-Hardy: *Bodö-saken* (Oslo, 1926) gives an authoritative account in English.
2 P. G. Bang, the jurist who had drafted the reform (*DH* XI 228).
3 Figures for the three kingdoms are available in Hovde, II 587, for Finland in Stenius, p. 75, and for Iceland in Nordal, p. 74. The census returns for Norway are studied in depth by M. Drake: *Population and Society in Norway 1735–1865* (Cambridge, 1969).
4 Carlsson: *Svensk Historia II*, p. 66.
5 S. Skappel: *Om husmands væsenet i Norge* (1922), p. 170.
6 *DH* X 92, XI 94.
7 Carlsson: *Svensk Historia II*, pp. 56, 57.
8 Steen: *Det frie Norge*, IV 37.
9 S. Laing: *A Tour in Sweden in 1838* (London, 1839), p. 183.
10 Carlsson: *Svensk Historia II*, p. 60.
11 ibid., p. 73.
12 Part of the definition made by Philippe Buchez in 1866 (*New Cambridge Modern History*, X 213).
13 Gjerset, p. 368. As a National Anthem, however, Bjarni Thorarensen's work has been displaced by that of Matthias Jochumsson.
14 Jutikkala, p. 203.
15 Steen: *Det frie Norge*, III 225, V 119 and 128.
16 ibid., V 421.
17 *Vid magister-promotionen i Lund 1829*.
18 Presidential address of welcome, Copenhagen, 3 July 1840 (Jorgenson, p. 103).
19 C. C. J. Reinhardt: *Orla Lehmann og hans Samtid* (Copenhagen, 1871), pp. 110–11.
20 *SH* VIII 219.
21 *DH* XI 299.
22 *SUPH* III Pt iii, p. 95. The author (A. Jansson) interprets this as an assertion that the war must have northern Europe instead of the Balkans as its main theatre; Swedish historians vary, however, in their assessment of Oscar I's policy at this juncture (Carlsson: *Svensk Historia II*, pp. 325–6).
23 *SH* VIII 270.
24 Jorgenson, pp. 224, 225.
25 F.O. Report (F. D. Steefel: *The Schleswig-Holstein Question*, Cambridge, Mass., 1932, p. 32).
26 *SUPH* III Pt iii, p. 132.
27 ibid., p. 135.
28 *SUPH* III Pt iii, p. 132; Jorgenson, pp. 234–6. 'Charles Edmond', a Polish refugee who had accompanied Prince Napoleon, presented this project in his *Voyage dans les mers du Nord* (Paris, 1857).
29 *SH* IX 299.
30 *SUPH* III Pt iii, p. 197.
31 L. Woodward: *The Age of Reform 1815–1870* (Oxford 1962), p. 320. cf. A. J. P. Taylor: *The Struggle for Mastery in Europe 1848–1918* (Oxford 1954), p. 146.
32 *DH* XI 462.
33 *SH* VIII 302-3.

CHAPTER 11

1 Article V (Steefel: *Schleswig-Holstein Question*, p. 32).
2 *DH* XI 518.

3 Heckscher, p. 260.
4 *DH* XII 52.
5 *Norsk Sjömandssang*, stanza 6.
6 Jörberg, p. 6.
7 Jörberg, pp. 33, 11; E. Jutikkala: *Bonden i Finland genom tiderna* (Helsinki, 1963), p. 341.
8 *DH* XII 233.
9 S.O.S. (Stockholm): *Fabriker och Handtverk för 1897*, p. xv; . . . *för 1907*, p. xxii; *Industri för 1913*, p. 62.
10 Derry, p. 194.
11 Article by I. Semmingsen (*Scandinavian Economic History Review*, XX 58).
12 *Emigrationen fra Norden indtil 1. Verdenskrig*, Report presented to Conference of Nordic Historians, Copenhagen 1971, p. 42).
13 Report, p. 32 (Eric Novelius).
14 Report, p. 13.
15 Report, pp. 160, 163-5.
16 *SH* IX 37; Report, p. 37.
17 *Thirteenth Census of the United States*, Vol. V.
18 *SH* VIII 314.
19 Jutikkala, p. 229.
20 Speech at Co-operative Congress, 1903 (*DH* XII 106).
21 *SH* IX 241.
22 Jorgenson, p. 361.
23 *SH* IX 169.
24 *SH* IX 269, 209.
25 Introduced into the discussion as a pejorative expression by Sigurd Ibsen.
26. J. V. Heiberg (editor): *Unionens Oplösning 1905* (Oslo, 1906), pp. 195, 205-6.
27 Article 2 of First Convention (*Oplösning*, p. 651).
28 F. Nansen: *Dagbok fra 1905* (Oslo, 1955) (Introduction by J. S. Worm-Müller, p. xxxi).
29 W. C. Chamberlin: *Economic Development of Iceland Through World War II* (1947), p. 27.
30 L. A. Norborg and L. Sjöstedt: *Grannländernas Historia* (Lund, 1970), p. 220.
31 Jutikkala, p. 223.
32 Jutikkala, p. 232.
33 The aspiration of an historian, J. R. Danielson-Kalmari (Jutikkala, p. 234).
34 M. T. Florinsky: *Russia* (1953), II 1202.
35 *Memoarer*, III 113 (*DH* XII 13).
36 Treaty of 2 November 1907 (*NFLH* X 498); for the treaties of April 1908, see Lindberg, pp. 285, 322-3, and *NFLH* X 498-9.
37 R. Omang: *Norsk Utenrikstjeneste*, II (1959), p. 27.
38 *SH* IX 295.

CHAPTER 12

1 *History and Historians in the Nineteenth Century* (2nd ed. 1952), p. 413.
2 N. A. Grevstad, in H. Sundby-Hansen (editor): *Norwegian Immigrant Contributions* (New York, 1921), p. 122.
3 Professor G. Bothne, in J. B. Wist (editor): *Norsk Amerikanernes Festskrift 1914* (Decorah, 1914), pp. 330-8.
4 *Encyclopædia Britannica*, 11th ed., XXVII 186.
5 *DH* XI 107.
6 *DH* XI 218.
7 H. Koht: *Life of Ibsen* (rev. ed., New York, 1971), p. 322.
8 *Fortnightly Review*, April 1900 (McFarlane, p. 72).
9 *hjemmenes dikter* (cf. H. Beyer in *Aschehougs Konversasjons Leksikon*, 4th ed. (18 vols, Oslo, 1954-61), XII 477).
10 Gabriel Scott, a Norwegian novelist of the same generation (McFarlane, p. 128).
11 Professor Sigurdur Nordal (Nordal, p. 96).
12 Phrase used by H. G. von Bülow (*Encyclopædia Britannica*, 11th ed., XII 593).

13 *Edvard Munch 100 år* (published by Oslo Kommunes Kunstsamlinger, Oslo, 1963), p. 129.
14 E. Bergengren: *Alfred Nobel* (English translation, 1962), p. 75.
15 L. P. Kirwan: *The Great White Road* (1959), p. 190. The author was Director and Secretary of the Royal Geographical Society.
16 Lars Dahle: *Norsk Misjons Leksikon*, 3 vols, (Stavanger, 1965–7, I 354). cf. W. H. T. Gairdner: '*Edinburgh 1910*' (1910), p. 168.

CHAPTER 13

1 A. J. Marder: *From the Dreadnought to Scapa Flow II* (1965), p. 180; cf. 192.
2 Norwegian Foreign Ministry Papers (Riste, p. 37).
3 *SH* IX 301.
4 Westergaard, p. 360.
5 The term used by the syndicalist leader in diverting the mob from the more practical objective of the bacon market (*DH* XIII 143).
6 E. Bull: *Arbeiderklassen i norsk historie* (Oslo, 1947), p. 260; cf. 258.
7 H. Laporte: *Le Premier Échec des Rouges* (Paris, 1929), pp. 161–2. The author was a war veteran, returning from an official mission to Russia, whose experiences in Tampere were published at the time in *Le Correspondant*.
8 Jutikkala, p. 259.
9 S. Jägerskiöld: *Gustaf Mannerheim*, III (Helsinki, 1967), p. 191.
10 ibid., p. 347.
11 Professor T. Tarkiainen of Tampere (Toivola, p. 87).
12 Letter of H. A. L. Fisher to Gilbert Murray, 27 June 1921 (J. Barros: *The Åland Islands Question*, New Haven 1968, p. 333).
13 Edvard Bull (the younger): *Aschehougs Konversasjons Leksikon*, III, p. 362.
14 P. Noel-Baker (P. G. Vigness: *The Neutrality of Norway in the World War* (1932), p. 129.
15 Article 22, Para. 1, of the League Covenant.
16 S. S. Jones, p. 223.
17 The editor of *Göteborgs Handelstidning*, Torgny Segerstedt (*SH* X 47).
18 Caption to a contemporary photograph (*DH* XIII 121).
19 Wuorinen, p. 259; E. Jutikkala: *Bonden i Finland genom tiderna* (1963), p. 466.
20 *League of Nations Statistical Year-Book 1933–4* (Geneva, 1934), Table 10. Trade union returns, of which the bases are not strictly comparable.
21 Jackson, p. 156.
22 Gíslason, p. 48.
23 Hansson's slogan since 1928 (*SH* X 102).
24 (*Norsk*) *Historisk Tidsskrift*, XXXIX (1959–60), p. 139: *å ta stemmene i det frie marked*.
25 Childs, p. 18.
26 E. D. Simon: *The Smaller Democracies* (1939), pp. 175, 158, and 191.
27 Jones, p. 263.
28 Phrases used in 1935–6 by Halvard Lange, later Norwegian foreign minister, and Olav Scheflo, editor of a Norwegian Labour paper (N. Örvik: *Sikkerhets Politiken 1920–1939*, Vol. II (Oslo, 1961), p. 106; cf. p. 27).
29 *DH* XIII 464.
30 *DH* XIII 467.

CHAPTER 14

1 Jakobson, *Winter War*, p. 98; cf. p. 70.
2 PRO/CAB 99/3 (cited by F. Bédarida, *Scandinavian Journal of History*, vol. 2 (1977), p. 10).
3 French Parliamentary Commission of Enquiry: *Les événements survenus en France de 1933 à 1945*, Annexes, Vol. II, p. 417 (cited by Bédarida, *loc. cit.*, p. 13).
4 Reply to Hitler's 60th-birthday message, 21 December 1939 (I. Deutscher: *Stalin*, 1961 ed., p. 445).
5 Upton, p. 132; these figures are about one-half of the numbers projected a month before (see J. R. M. Butler: *Grand Strategy*, II (1957), p. 10).

424   *A History of Scandinavia*

6 *Fuehrer Conferences on Naval Affairs 1939–45* (*Brassey's Naval Annual*, 1948, p. 83).
7 PRO/COS (40) 269 (S) (T. K. Derry: *The Campaign in Norway*, 1952, p. 15).
8 *Brassey*, as above, p. 91.
9 *SH* X 133.
10 See Nordal, p. 55, and Gíslason, p. 74.
11 H. Dalton: *Memoirs*, II (1957), p. 366. (Reference kindly supplied by Professor David Dilks).
12 *DH* XIV 316; V. Sjöqvist: *Scavenius* (Copenhagen, 1970), II 272.
13 C. L. Lundin: *Finland in the Second World War* (Bloomington, Ind., 1957), p. 93.
14 M. Fritz: *German Steel and Swedish Iron Ore 1939–1945* (Gothenburg, 1974), p. 99.
15 ibid., p. 119.
16 *DH* XIV 92.
17 *DH* XIV 233.
18 A. S. Milward: *The Fascist Economy in Norway* (Oxford, 1972), p. 253.
19 Mazour, p. 144.
20 Lundin: *Finland in the Second World War*, p. 127.
21 *Det store året* (*VFH* IX 300, 344).
22 Fuehrer Conference of 22 January 1942 (*Brassey*, as above, p. 260).
23 *Muster-Beschützung* (S. Gudme: *Denmark: Hitler's 'Model Protectorate'*, London, 1942, p. 31).
24 *Directions for Citizens in Time of War* (summarised by Scott, p. 236).
25 Statement on 12 April 1944 by Edwin Linkomies, the second of four Conservative premiers in 1941–4 (summarised by Lundin, as above, p. 201).
26 Section 1 of Directive of 1 June, which remained in force until 5 December (S. Kjelstadli: *Hjemmestyrkene I*, Oslo 1959, pp. 324–5, 443).
27 *DH* XIV 283. This declaration by SHAEF, in anticipation of an Allied entry, followed the line taken by the American Secretary of State and British Foreign Minister after the Russians had refused in July to agree to a common declaration.
28 Eisenhower to Combined Chiefs of Staff, 14 April 1945 (John Ehrman: *Grand Strategy VI*, 1956, p. 148).
29 *VFH* IX 478; W. G. Jones, p. 181.
30 Speech in London, 19 January 1944 (N. M. Udgaard: *Great Power Politics and Norwegian Foreign Policy*, Oslo, 1973, p. 94).
31 Recommendation of the Storting, 15 February 1947, approved in secret session by a vote of 101 to 11 with 38 abstentions (ibid., p. 200).

CHAPTER 15

1 Meeting on 9 May 1948 (M. Skodvin: *Norden eller NATO?* Oslo, 1971, p. 137).
2 Published in *Aftenposten*, Oslo, 25 September 1948 (Udgaard: *Great Power Politics*, p. 230).
3 Skodvin: *Norden*, p. 335.
4 Articles 1 and 2 (full translation in Wuorinen, pp. 519–21).
5 Gröndal, p. 97.
6 P. J. Bjerve: *Planning in Norway 1947–1956* (Amsterdam, 1959), p. 356.
7 Scott, p. 190, citing *Svensk ekonomi, 1971–1975, med utblick mot 1990* (S.O.U., Stockholm, 1970, no. 71).
8 Comparative figures in Nordic Council's *Yearbook for 1975* (Stockholm, 1976), Table 1.
9 ibid., Table 41; cf. Table 13.
10 S. Carlsson: *Svensk Historia II*, p. 362; *Yearbook*, as above, Table 15.
11 *SH* X 152.
12 Connery, p. 359.
13 Gíslason, p. 61.
14 Nelson, Foreword, p. i, and pp. 501, 504, and 60.
15 Percentages in *Yearbook*, as above, Table 184; the *caveat* is on p. 238.
16 *The Norway Year Book 1967* (7th – and last – edition, Oslo, 1966), p. 222.
17 Kjersgaard, p. 91; the section under this title occupies one-eighth of the space allotted to 1945–72.
18 Gíslason, p. 44.

19 F. Wendt: *Nordisk Råd*, 2nd edn (Oslo, 1967), p. 22.
20 Scott, p. 267.
21 According to J. O. Krag, leader of the Social Democratic Party in Denmark (*Nordisk Kontakt*, Stockholm, 28 November 1969).
22 The Foreign Minister, V. Leskinen (ibid., 26 February 1971, p. 119).
23 P. N. Andersen, the economic expert of the Venstre Party (ibid., 7 February 1973, p. 80).
24 Address to the General Assembly, October 1961 (Stenius, p. 68).
25 *Säkerhetspolitik och totalförsvar* (*S.O.U.*, Stockholm, 1976, no. 5), p. 31.
26 'An oft-quoted saying of Paasikivi's' (Norborg and Sjöstedt: *Grannländernas Historia*, p. 272).

CHAPTER 16

 1 *Scandinavian Studies*, XLIII (1971), p. 270; XLV (1973), pp. 149–51.
 2 Popperwell, p. 265.
 3 E. L. Bredsdorff (*Penguin Companion to Literature: Europe*, rev. ed. 1971), p. 621.
 4 *The New Oxford History of Music*, Vol. X (1974), p. 494.
 5 E. N. da C. Andrade (*Encyclopædia Britannica*, 1947 ed., III 788).
 6 R. Moore: *Niels Bohr* (1966), p. 323, summarising conferences with Groves and Oppenheimer at Los Alamos.
 7 *SH* X 197.
 8 Article by a civil engineer (*SH* X 279).
 9 The director of the London Building Centre (Simpson, p. 227).
10 Slogan of the Deutsche Werkbund, founded in 1907 (U. Hard af Segersted: *Scandinavian Design*, Oslo, 1961, p. 11).
11 Address to Congress of Christian Social Democrats, 30 July 1965, as deputy for the foreign minister (H. Hederberg: *Detta fantastiska land*, Stockholm, 1973, p. 128).
12 Canon J. H. B. Masterman (B. Sundkler: *Nathan Söderblom*, Lund, 1968, p. 205).
13 Hans Ostenfeld, Bishop of Copenhagen (R. Rouse and S. C. Neill, editors: *A History of the Ecumenical Movement 1517–1948*, 1954, p. 521).
14 Sundkler: *Söderblom*, p. 376.
15 Speech in 6th Assembly, 1925 (E. E. Reynolds: *Nansen*, p. 263).
16 R. Moore: *Niels Bohr* (1966), p. 343.
17 ibid., p. 353.
18 ibid., p. 405.
19 ibid., p. 426.
20 B. Urquhart: *Hammarskjold* (1973), p. 15.
21 H. E. Fey (editor): *Dag Hammarskjold's White Book* (Philadelphia, 1959).
22 Urquhart: *Hammarskjold*, p. 253.
23 Connery, p. xv; Simpson p. 48.
24 Connery, p. 547; Simpson, p. 57.
25 *UN Demographic Yearbook 1974*, Table 27.
26 *Medbestämmendelagen*, Section 23 (*Aftenposten*, Oslo, 17 January 1977, p. 21). See also *The Encyclopædia Britannica Book of the Year 1975* (1976), p. 408.
27 P. B. Austin: *On Being Swedish* (London, 1968), p. 175.
28 Bröndsted, p. 241.

Select Bibliography of Works in English

All books have been published in London or New York unless otherwise stated. Translations are marked by an asterisk.

A. PERIODICALS (literary and historical journals which include articles on Scandinavian as well as national subjects).

Cooperation and Conflict (Stockholm, 1965–). A Nordic journal of international politics.

Excerpta Historica Nordica (Copenhagen, 1955–). Summaries of monographs; published 5–6 years in arrears.

Mediæval Scandinavia (Odense, 1968–).

Norseman, The (London, 1943–58). An index to the 16 volumes, published in Oslo in 1959, facilitates reference to the more general articles.

Saga-Book of the Viking Society for Northern Research (London, 1892–). Concerned mainly with the early period.

Scandinavian Economic History Review (Copenhagen, 1953–).

Scandinavian Journal of History (Stockholm, 1976–). Established by co-operation among the four national historical journals.

Scandinavian Political Studies (Helsinki, 1966–).

Scandinavian Review (New York, 1913–). The first 62 volumes were published under the name of *The American-Scandinavian Review*.

Scandinavian Studies (Lawrence, Kansas, and formerly Urbana, Illinois, 1911–). Concerned mainly with literature.

Scandinavica (London, 1962–). Concerned mainly with literature.

B. GENERAL HISTORIES OF SCANDINAVIA (A French and a German manual are included as having no counterpart in English).

Bukdahl, J. *et al.* (editors): *Scandinavia Past and Present** (3 vols, Odense, 1959). A sumptuously illustrated work, written largely in national sections.

Butter, E.: *The Horizon Concise History of Scandinavia* (1973). A 'swift sketch' with numerous attractive illustrations.

Imhof, A. E.: *Grundzeuge der Nordischen Geschichte* (Darmstadt, 1970).

Jeannin, P.: *Histoire des pays scandinaves* (Paris, 1956). In the 'Que sais-je?' series.

Kenney, R.: *The Northern Tangle* (1946). A history written originally in 1944, and based on the author's intimate knowledge of wartime events in Scandinavia.

Scott, F. D.: *Scandinavia* (Cambridge, Mass., 1975). A new and much enlarged version of an earlier work in the 'American Foreign Policy Library'.

Toyne, S. M.: *The Scandinavians in History* (1949; reissued 1970). An enthusiastic introduction concentrating on Sweden and Denmark.

Wuorinen, J. H.: *Scandinavia* (1965). A contribution to a series on 'modern nations in historical perspective'.

C. EARLY AND MEDIEVAL HISTORY (The list includes only a few representative samples of the many recent works on the Vikings).

Anker, P., and Andersson, A.: *The Art of Scandinavia** (2 vols, 1970).
Arbman, H.: *The Vikings** (1961).
Bröndsted, J.: *The Vikings** (Harmondsworth, 1965).
Foote, P., and Wilson, D. M.: *The Viking Achievement* (1970). Paints a broad and very interesting picture of society.
Garmonsway, G. N.: *Canute and His Empire* (1964). An illuminating lecture.
Jones, Gwyn: *The Vikings* (1968).
Larson, L. M.: *Canute the Great* (1912). In the 'Heroes of the Nations' series.
Musset, L.: *Les peuples scandinaves au moyen âge* (Paris 1951). After a quarter-century this French work is still an unrivalled study of medieval Scandinavia as a single entity.
Musset, L.: *Les invasions: le second assaut contre l'Europe chrétienne* (Paris, 1965). Includes a full bibliography for the Viking activities.
Sawyer, P. H.: *The Age of the Vikings* (2nd ed. 1971).
Shetelig, H., and Falk, H.: *Scandinavian Archaeology** (Oxford, 1937).
Simpson, J.: *Everyday Life in the Viking Age* (1967). Draws material from the dependencies and from the sagas.
Turville-Petre, G.: *The Heroic Age of Scandinavia* (1951). Based on the legends and poetry.
Turville-Petre, G.: *Myth and Religion of the North* (1964).
Wilson, D. M.: *The Vikings and their Origins* (1970).
Wilson, D. M. and Klindt-Jensen, O.: *Viking Art* (1966).

D. MODERN HISTORY (From the early sixteenth century to the 1950s).

Bain, R. N.: *Scandinavia: A Political History from 1513 to 1900* (Cambridge, 1905). Denmark and Sweden treated alternately – and very dramatically.
Friis, H. (editor): *Scandinavia between East and West* (Ithaca, N.Y., 1950).
Garstein, O.: *Rome and the Counter-Reformation in Scandinavia*, Vol. I, 1539–1583 (Oslo, 1963). A learned work, which so far deals mainly with Sweden.
Hovde, B. J.: *The Scandinavian Countries, 1720–1865* (2 vols, reissue, Ithaca, N.Y., 1948). A mine of information on economic, social, and cultural topics, supported by detailed references to Scandinavian sources.
Jones, S. S.: *The Scandinavian States and the League of Nations* (1939).
Jörberg, L.: *The Industrial Revolution in Scandinavia 1850–1914** (1970). Vol. IV, Section 8 in the 'Fontana Economic History of Europe'.
Jorgenson, T.: *Norway's Relations to Scandinavian Unionism 1815–1871* (Northfield, Minn., 1935). A pioneer study which has not been followed up by later scholars.
Lindberg, F.: *Scandinavia in Great Power Politics, 1905–1908* (Stockholm, 1958).
Lindgren, R. E.: *Norway-Sweden, union, disunion, and Scandinavian integration* (Princeton, 1959). A study of the United Kingdoms.
Nevakivi, J.: *The Appeal That Was Never Made** (1976). A Finnish study of the links between the Winter War and the Allied operations in Norway, using British and French archives.
Tennant, P. F. D.: *The Scandinavian Book* (1951). Descriptive excerpts from Scandinavian literature of the earlier nineteenth and previous centuries.
Upton, A. F.: *The Communist Parties of Scandinavia and Finland* (1973). A full account of Finnish Communism, and three short essays from other pens.
Wendt, F.: *The Nordic Council and Co-operation in Scandinavia* (Copenhagen, 1959). Includes a survey of earlier ventures in collaboration.

Westergaard, H. and Heckscher, E. (editors): *Sweden, Norway, Denmark, and Iceland in the World War** (New Haven, Conn., 1930). An abridgement of the Scandinavian Series, published by the Carnegie Endowment for International Peace.

E. CONTEMPORARY SCANDINAVIA (Works published *c.* 1950, describing political, economic, social, and cultural aspects).

Ahlmann, H. W. (editor): *Norden i Kart og Tekst* (Stockholm, 1976). Pending an English translation, the maps by themselves are of great value for the economic pattern and for outlying areas such as *Nordkalotten*.

Anderson, S. V.: *The Nordic Council* (Stockholm, 1967). Organisation and procedure.

Andrén, N.: *Government and Politics in the Nordic Countries* (Stockholm, 1964).

Arneson, B. A.: *The Democratic Monarchies of Scandinavia* (2nd ed. 1949). A description of institutions.

Bredsdorff, E., Mortensen, B., and Popperwell, R.: *An Introduction to Scandinavian Literature* (reprint, Westport, Conn., 1970). Includes the twentieth century.

Cerny, K. H. (ed.): *Scandinavia at the Polls* (Washington, 1977). Elections of 1973 analysed in the light of each country's social and economic background.

Connery, D. S.: *The Scandinavians* (1966). The fullest and most fascinating of recent studies, apart from the virtual omission of Iceland.

Gathorne-Hardy, G. M., *et al.*: *The Scandinavian States and Finland: A Political and Economic Survey* (1951). A study made for the RIIA.

Haskel, B. G.: *The Scandinavian Option* (Oslo, 1976). The proposals for a Scandinavian defence pact and Common Market, etc., examined from a transatlantic standpoint.

Hunter, L. S. (editor): *The Scandinavian Churches* (1965).

Lund, R. (editor): *Scandinavian Adult Education* (2nd ed., Stockholm 1952).

Mead, W. R.: *An Economic Geography of the Scandinavian States and Finland* (1958). Illuminates the present from a detailed knowledge of the past.

Mead, W. R.: *The Scandinavian Northlands* (1974). A study of *Nordkalotten*.

Mead, W. R., and Hall, W.: *Scandinavia* (1972). Two-thirds on the region as a whole.

Miljan, T.: *The Reluctant Europeans* (1977). Scandinavian attitudes towards European integration.

Nelson, G. R. (editor): *Freedom and Welfare* (Copenhagen, 1953).

Nordic Council and Statistical Secretariat: *Yearbook of Nordic Statistics* (Stockholm 1966–). The first of *c.* 250 Tables compares the Nordic countries as a whole with France, West Germany, UK, and USA.

Paulsson, T.: *Scandinavian Architecture* (1958).

Ruge, H.: *Educational Systems in Scandinavia* (Oslo, 1962).

Sansom, W.: *The Icicle and the Sun* (1958). A travel book which concludes that 'politically and socially these four countries are slowly merging'.

Shirer, W. L.: *The Challenge of Scandinavia* (Boston, 1955). Expert journalism.

Simpson, C.: *The Viking Circle* (1966). The tour includes both Iceland and Greenland.

Sömme, A. (editor): *A Geography of Norden* (new ed., Oslo, 1968).

Zahle, E. (editor): *Scandinavian Domestic Design* (1963).

F. HISTORIES OF SCANDINAVIAN COUNTRIES (A few introductory works).

(1) *Denmark*
Birch, J. H. S.: *Denmark in History* (1938). A detailed work, useful for reference.

Bredsdorff, E.: *Hans Christian Andersen* (1975). An illustrated account of his life and tales by a Danish writer long resident in England.
Danstrup, J.: *A History of Denmark** (2nd ed., Copenhagen, 1949).
Jones, W. Glyn: *Denmark* (1970). Two-thirds on the twentieth century.
Klindt-Jensen, O.: *Denmark Before the Vikings** (1957).
Kjersgaard, E.: *A History of Denmark** (Copenhagen, 1974). A brief ,well illustrated popular account, issued by the Foreign Ministry.
Krabbe, L.: *Histoire de Danemark* (Paris, 1950). A clear, well-rounded narrative.
Oakley, S.: *The Story of Denmark* (1972). Gives considerable space to the arts, and has a very helpful survey of books and articles on all periods of Danish history.
Miller, K. E.: *Government and Politics in Denmark* (Boston, 1968).
Skovgaard, J. A.: *A King's Architecture. Christian IV and his Buildings* (London, 1973). An illustrated account with wide ramifications, based on a Manchester University thesis.
Thomas, J. O.: *The Giant-Killers* (1975). The Resistance movement of 1940–5.

(2) *Norway*
Andenæs, J., Riste, O., and Skodvin, M.: *Norway and the Second World War* (Oslo, 1966).
Derry, T. K.: *A History of Modern Norway 1814–1972* (Oxford, 1973). The bibliographical essay offers further guidance.
Ekeland, S.: *Norway in the Modern World* (2nd ed., revised by T. Raa, Oslo, 1976). Economic study with Statistical Tables, issued by the Foreign Ministry.
Gathorne-Hardy, G. M.: *Norway* (1925). Based on intimate knowledge of the people and their literature.
Larsen, K.: *A History of Norway* (Princeton, 1948). The fullest single-volume account in any language.
McFarlane, J. W.: *Ibsen and the Temper of Norwegian Literature* (London, 1960). Discusses more than a dozen leading writers, listing English translations.
Midgaard, J.: *A Brief History of Norway** (Oslo, 1969).
Moulton, J. L.: *The Norwegian Campaign of 1940* (1966). A critical study by a military expert.
Popperwell, R. G.: *Norway* (1972). The language, literature, and contemporary culture are examined in detail.
Riste, O.: *The Neutral Ally* (1965). Events of the First World War.
Riste, O., and Nökleby, B.: *Norway 1940–1945. The Resistance Movement.* (Oslo, 1970).
Sveaas Andersen, P.: *Vikings of the West* (Oslo, 1971).

(3) *Sweden*
Andersson, I.: *History of Sweden** (2nd ed. 1970). By a leading Swedish historian.
Childs, M. W.: *Sweden The Middle Way* (1936).
Hallendorff, C. and Schück, A.: *History of Sweden** (Stockholm, 1929).
Hatton, R.: *Charles XII of Sweden* (1968). A big book, which comprehends the man as well as the wars and diplomacy of his reign.
Heckscher, E. F.: *An Economic History of Sweden** (Cambridge, Mass., 1954).
Mortensen, B., and Downs, B. W.: *Strindberg* (Cambridge, 1949).
Oakley, S.: *The Story of Sweden* (1966). Gives four chapters specifically to the economic life and culture, and has a very helpful survey of books and articles on all periods of Swedish history.
Roberts, M.: *Gustavus Adolphus, A History of Sweden, 1611–1632* (2 vols, 1953, 1958). A full and authoritative account of the reign, for which the same author

provides an easier introduction in *Gustavus Adolphus and the Rise of Sweden* (1973).

Samuelsson, K.: *From Great Power to Welfare State* (1968). Reviews social development through three centuries.

Scobbie, I.: *Sweden* (1972).

Scott, Franklin D.: *Sweden: The Nation's History* (Minneapolis, MN., 1977).

Steinberger, M.: *Sweden* (1963). Prehistory.

(4) *Finland*

Jackson, J. H.: *Finland* (1938). A vivid account, concentrating on 1917–37.

Jakobson, M.: *The Diplomacy of the Winter War, 1939–40* (Cambridge, Mass., 1961). A classic study.

Jakobson, M.: *Finnish Neutrality* (1968). An introductory chapter covers 1917–44.

Jutikkala, E.: *A History of Finland** (rev. ed., 1974). A political history by a leading Finnish professor.

Mazour, A. G.: *Finland Between East and West* (1956).

Mead, W. R.: *Finland* (1968). A commentary on Finnish history which has a geographical and economic basis; the full survey of sources includes a note of fiction available in English translation.

Stenius, G. (editor): *Introduction to Finland 1963** (Helsinki, 1963).

Toivola, U. (editor): *Introduction to Finland 1960** (Helsinki, 1960) Two complementary volumes covering all aspects of Finnish life, with the help of statistics, a series of biographical notes, and a full bibliography.

Upton, A. F.: *Finland 1939–40* (1974). A campaign study.

Warner, O.: *Marshal Mannerheim and the Finns* (1967).

Wuorinen, J. H.: *A History of Finland* (1967). Political and economic history, mainly confined to the nineteenth and twentieth centuries, with appendices of treaties, etc.

Wuorinen, J. H.: *Nationalism in Modern Finland* (1931).

(5) *Iceland*

Gjerset, K.: *History of Iceland* (1923). The work of a Norwegian-American historian, which has not been superseded as a survey for all periods.

Gíslason, G. T.: *The Problem Of Being An Icelander** (Reykjavik, 1973). A historical survey with colour plates, by a former Minister of Education.

Griffiths, J. C.: *Modern Iceland* (1969). An enthusiastic account by an Englishman resident there in 1967.

Gröndal, B.: *Iceland From Neutrality to NATO Membership* (Oslo, 1971).

Jones, Gwyn: *The Norse Atlantic Saga* (1964). Includes sources in translation.

Nordal, J., and Kristinsson, V. (editors): *Iceland 874–1974** (Reykjavik, 1975). A comprehensive survey of the national life by experts, with a bibliography of about 500 books in foreign languages.

Nuechterlein, D. E.: *Iceland, Reluctant Ally* (Ithaca, N.Y., 1961).

Johannesson, J.: *A History of the Old Icelandic Commonwealth** (Winnipeg, 1974). The work of a major Icelandic historian, terminating at 1262.

Stefansson, V.: *Iceland. The First American Republic* (1939). By the Arctic explorer, whose parents were Icelandic immigrants to Canada.

(6) *Peripheral Regions*
The Faeroes/Faroes

West, J. F.: *Faroe, the emergence of a nation* (1972). History from the ninth to the twentieth century; full English bibliography.

Williamson, K.: *The Atlantic Islands* (2nd ed., with post-war chapter by E. Kallsberg, 1970). A descriptive account based on war service in the archipelago.

Greenland
 Ingstad, H.: *Land under the Pole Star** (1966).
 Williamson, G.: *Changing Greenland* (1953). Useful bibliography.

Lapland
 Bosi, R.: *The Lapps** (1960). Bibliography.
 Collinder, B.: *The Lapps* (Princeton, 1949).
 Nesheim, H.: *Introducing the Lapps* (2nd ed., Oslo, 1966).

Spitsbergen/Svalbard
 Greve, T.: *Svalbard* (Oslo, 1975). A short, illustrated account.
 Mathisen, T.: *Svalbard in International Politics 1871–1925* (Oslo 1954).

'Vinland'
 Ingstad, H.: *Westward to Vinland** (1969).

Index

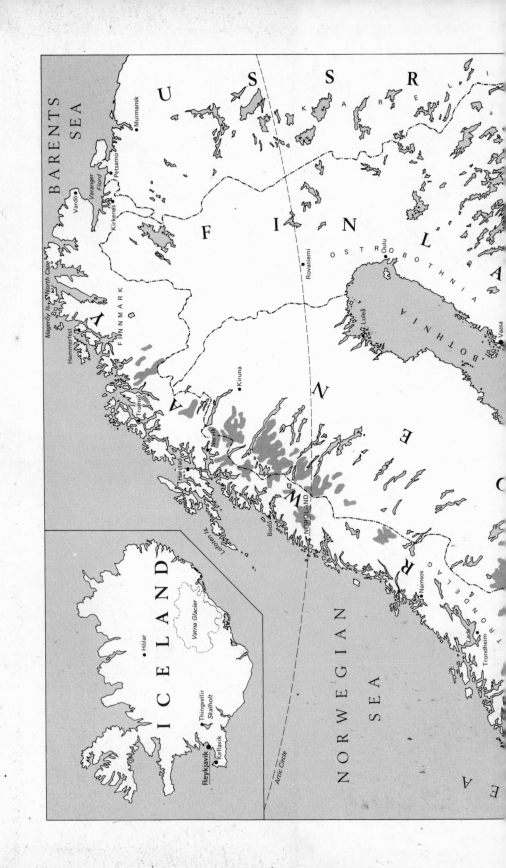